D0009354

CROSSFIRE
THE PLOT THAT KILLED KENNEDY
JIM MARRS

The great masses of the people will more easily fall
victims to a great lie than to a small one . . .

—Adolf Hitler
Mein Kampf

Carroll & Graf Publishers, Inc.
New York

First Carroll & Graf hardcover published in 1989
First Carroll & Graf paperback edition 1990

Carroll & Graf Publishers, Inc.
260 Fifth Avenue
New York, NY 10001

Library of Congress Cataloging-in-Publication Data

Marrs, Jim.
    Crossfire: the plot that killed Kennedy / Jim Marrs.
      p.   cm.
    Bibliography: p.
    ISBN 0-88184-648-1 : $12.95
    I. Kennedy, John F. (John Fitzgerald). 1917–1963—Assassination.
  I. Title.
  E842.9.M36   1989
973.922′092—dc20   89-30468
                                                             CIP

Manufactured in the United States of America

Second Hardcover Edition 1992

Eighth Paperback Edition 1992

TABLE OF CONTENTS

Acknowledgments

Preface

Part I: "The Kill Zone"   1
  A. DALLAS—The Stage is Set
      The Thirty-fifth President   1
  B. DEALEY PLAZA—November 22, 1963
      The Motorcade   9
      The Crowd   17
         Two Suspicious Men   29
         The Babushka Lady   36
      The Texas School Book Depository   40
         The Distracting Seizure   42
         The Man in the Doorway   45
         The Oswald Encounter   50
      The Triple Underpass   55
         Smoke on the Grassy Knoll   56
         The Third Wounded Man   60
      The Grassy Knoll   64
         The Zapruder Film   64
         The Black Dog Man   72
         The Badge Man   78
         A Grassy Knoll Witness   81
      Summary   86

PART II: "Means, Motives, and Opportunities"   90
  A. LEE HARVEY OSWALD (Assassin or Patsy?)   91
         A Mother in History   91
         Ferrie and Oswald's Library Card   99
         Oswaldskovich the Marine   101
      Summary   111
  B. RUSSIANS (Soviets and Solidarists)   113
         Oswald and the U-2   114
         Robert E. Webster—Another Oswald?   116
         Comrade Oswald   121
         A Whirlwind Romance   124
         A Soviet Defector's Story   130
      Summary   134
  C. CUBANS (Pro and Anti-Castro Cubans)   135
         Fidel Castro   136
         Disaster at the Bay of Pigs   138
         544 Camp Street   147
         Oswald and the Exiles   149
      Summary   154
  D. MOBSTERS (Organized Crime)   156
         Bootleggers and Boozers   157

CONTENTS

Lucky Goes to War   161
Carlos Marcello   164
Santos Trafficante and Cuba   168
The War on Hoffa   171
Momo and His Girlfriends   175
Summary   179
E. AGENTS (The CIA and Other Intelligence Agencies)   181
The Manchurian Candidates   184
CIA-Mafia Death Plots   187
New Orleans   188
Was Oswald a Spy?   189
A Message from Oswald   196
DeMohrenschildt and the Agency   199
The French Connection to the Assassination   202
Summary   210
F. G-MEN (J. Edgar Hoover's FBI and the Secret Service)   211
The Top G-man   213
Did Oswald Work for the FBI?   226
544 Camp Street   235
The Secret Service   240
A Few Drinks at the Cellar   246
Summary   251
G. REDNECKS AND OILMEN (Right-wing extremists and
Texas Millionaires)   253
A Bullet for the General   255
The Miami Prophet   265
Nixon and the JFK Assassination   267
A Killing on Wall Street   274
Kennedy and Oilmen   276
Oswald's Friends   278
All the Way with LBJ   289
Summary   299
H. SOLDIERS (The Military)   301
The Military-Industrial Complex   301
Kennedy and Vietnam   306
The Man Who Was to Kill Oswald   309
Summary   311

PART III: "Aftermath"   313
A. DALLAS   313
Mysterious Secret Service Men   319
The Black Car Chase   325
The Strange Saga of Roger Craig   328
The Role of Hitman Harrelson   333
The Mafia Man in Dealey Plaza   337
The Shooting of J.D. Tippit   340
The Arrest of Oswald   350
Summary   358
B. TWO HOSPITALS   361

CONTENTS

Jack Ruby at Parkland 366
The David Lifton Investigation 373
Summary 378
C. JACK RUBY 380
Jack Ruby—Gangster 387
Jack Ruby—Gun Runner and Agent 391
The Woman Who Foresaw the Assassination 401
Did Ruby and Oswald Know Each Other? 402
The Shooting of Lee Harvey Oswald 414
The Mysterious Death of Jack Ruby 429
Summary 433
D. THE EVIDENCE 435
An Incriminating Palm Print 443
Questionable Backyard Photos 450
Reenactment Problems 454
Summary 457
E. THE WARREN COMMISSION 459
The Reluctant Chairman 461
Oswald and the FBI 472
Conflicts in the Testimony 477
The Single-Bullet Theory 485
Summary 492
F. THE GARRISON INVESTIGATION 494
The Clay Shaw and Permindex 498
Summary 515
G. THE HOUSE SELECT COMMITTEE ON ASSASSINATIONS 518
Blakey at the Helm 524
The Dallas Police Radio Recording 530
Summary 537
H. WAS OSWALD REALLY OSWALD? (The Oswald exhumation) 539
New Questions on Oswald 550
Summary 553
I. CONVENIENT DEATHS 555

PART IV: "Conclusions" 567
Assassination Coverage 574
A Likely Scenario 580

Sources and Notes 591
Selected Bibliography 615
Index 620

Acknowledgments

When a final "truth" concerning the assassination of President John F. Kennedy is accepted by the general population of the United States, it will have to be acknowledged that this truth came not from the government, the legal profession, or the news media—rather that truth will have come from the legion of individual citizens who have refused to accept superficial explanations.

No one person will be credited with such a final "truth" because the names of the people who have fought to learn what really happened to President Kennedy—often at the risk of public ridicule and worse—have grown too numerous to enumerate.

However, most researchers would include the names of Penn Jones, Jr., Mark Lane, Vincent Salandria, and Harold Weisberg as leaders of that first generation of critics who raised serious questions about the government's official lone-assassin theory.

Special recognition will go to the two leading researchers, the late Sylvia Meagher, whose incisive dissection of the Warren Commission Report set the standard for assassination research and Dallas's Mary Ferrell, that indefatigable collector of assassination lore.

Acknowledgment also will have to be given to Judge Jim Garrison—regardless of history's final judgment on his performance as district attorney—for the abundance of assassination information gleaned through his ill-fated investigations in New Orleans.

Others who have contributed greatly to the advancement of assassination knowledge—in no particular order—include Josiah Thompson, Col. Fletcher Prouty, George O'Toole, Gary Shaw, Larry Harris, Richard E. Sprague, Carl Oglesby, Mort Sahl, Seth Kantor, Edgar Tatro, Fred Newcomb, Greg Lowrey, Jack White, Gary Mack, Earl Golz, Anthony Summers, David Lifton, Bernard Fensterwald, William Turner, Gaeton Fonzi, Mark Allen, Jeff Goldberg, Dick Russell, Alan Weberman, Paul Hoch, Peter Dale Scott, Robert Sam Anson, Jerry Rose, Robert Groden, and Harry Livingston.

Other names eventually will be added to this distinguished list.

Every citizen who gave of his time, effort, and resources to study, assimilate, and disseminate assassination information will someday come to be regarded as part of an object lesson on how the individual citizen can indeed make an impact on a system that has proven either unable or unwilling to police itself.

And on that day, all of the assassination researchers will receive the public acknowledgment they so richly deserve.

Preface

Do not trust this book.

In fact, when it comes to the assassination of President John F. Kennedy, don't trust any one source or even the basic evidence and testimony.

In the case of the JFK assassination, belief and trust have long been part of the problem.

One's view of the events in Dallas in 1963 has depended upon whom one chooses to believe.

Do you believe government experts who state that a man reputed to be a bad shot could take a bolt-action rifle that wholesaled for three dollars and twice hit a man in a moving car at more than two hundred yards with three shots in less than six seconds?

Do you believe a commission handpicked by Kennedy's successor, which concluded that Kennedy was killed by a lone assassin firing from a building behind him and who was, in turn, killed by yet another lone assassin?

Or do you believe witnesses who saw a rifle fired at Kennedy's right front and films that show the rearward fall of the wounded president indicating just such a shot?

For far too many years a majority of the American public chose to believe their federal government, which assured them that Kennedy's death was the result of a tragic meeting between a powerful national leader and a warped solitary young man wanting to be somebody.

Today many people believe differently. A poll taken by the *Washington Post* in 1983 showed more than 80 percent of the respondents expressed the belief that Kennedy died as the result of a high-level conspiracy.

However, beliefs are neither facts nor knowledge.

This book is an effort to break through the massive amounts of obfuscation regarding this topic and bring to the public a basic overview of this tragic event.

It is a distillation of the numerous books, articles, and documentaries that have been produced over the years.

Already the assassination of President John F. Kennedy is recognized as a turning point in American history.

Beginning on November 22, 1963, American attitudes slowly changed from post–World War II optimism and idealism to cynicism and mistrust of government. This loss of faith in government accelerated in the wake of the Vietnam War, the Watergate and Iran-Contra scandals. A significant portion of this cynicism has been prompted by the wide difference between the official government version of the Kennedy assassination and the beliefs of a majority of Americans.

Beginning only a week after the Dallas tragedy, national polls showed a majority of Americans disbelieved the official "lone assassin" theory of the assassination. By the late 1980s, that number has risen to nearly 90 percent of the population.

Like the attack on Pearl Harbor, November 22, 1963, has been etched into the memory of every American who was of age on that day. In this Information Age, more than half the population alive today followed the events of that sad day through both broadcast and print media.

Who could forget the shock of the early announcements from Dallas, the horror of the slaying of the chief suspect or the tears as "John John" Kennedy saluted his father's casket?

To those today who were not yet born or of age in 1963, their knowledge of the assassination comes from history books—which for the most part are strangely silent about the details of the tragedy—stories from older people, and other public sources.

No event in American history has caused such an abiding interest on the part of the general public.

The assassination has spawned a legion of independent researchers—of all ages and classes—who study the bits of information seeking to determine what really happened to our thirty-fifth president.

Crossfire: The Plot That Killed Kennedy for the first time pulls together the massive amount of available facts and information concerning that tragic day in 1963. Until now, this material has been available only by carefully studying a wide range of books—many now out of print—and by researching periodicals on a continuing basis.

Crossfire has been designed to provide an abundance of material in a concise and readable manner, so that both the mildly interested and serious researcher alike may get the overview necessary to detect and understand the broad outlines of the conspiracy behind the assassination.

Long-standing sources of controversy—such as mysterious men photographed in Dealey Plaza and the Oswald look-alike standing in the doorway of the Texas School Book Depository at the time of the shooting—are examined as well as new issues—such as the acoustical evidence indicating the existence of a second gunman and some brand-new questions concerning the 1981 exhumation of Lee Harvey Oswald.

This book takes a close look at the events in Dealey Plaza through the eyes of the witnesses—including many overlooked by the government investigations and some new witnesses whose stories have never before been made public.

As in any good homicide investigation, a list of suspects has been drawn up with information detailing their means, motives, and opportunities. *Crossfire* provides detailed background information on the men and organizations considered most likely to have been involved in a plot against the president.

Also covered in *Crossfire* are the various attempts by governmental bodies to investigate and resolve what happened in Dallas. Attention is paid to the people behind these investigations, how they arrived at their conclusions, the reliability of the information made available to them, and the possibility of misdirection and deceit.

As an award-winning Texas journalist with more than twenty-five years of news-gathering experience in the Dallas-Fort Worth Metroplex, I have been in a unique situation to learn the true story of the assassination.

I have talked with many people closely connected to the assassination, including Dallas area government and law-enforcement officials and newsmen. I spent many hours with Marguerite Oswald (mother of the accused assassin) and with Jeanne DeMohrenschildt (she and her husband, George DeMohrenschildt, were close friends of Oswald). I have interviewed assassination witnesses such as James Tague, Jean Hill, Bill Newman, and many others. I have talked with witnesses never questioned by the official investigations, such as Ed Hoffman, Gordon Arnold, Ester Mash, and Madeleine Brown.

And I have kept in contact with serious researchers of the assassination, collecting and correlating their work.

Most important, I lived through the assassination time in the Dallas area.

As a college student, I met Jack Ruby while visiting his Carousel Club in September 1963. In the fall of 1964, I conducted an in-depth interview with Maj. Gen. Edwin A. Walker. Within five years of the assassination, I was working as a professional reporter in the Dallas-Fort Worth Metroplex.

As a native Texan who grew up in this area, I understand its people, history, and politics. Yet, as a journalist, I have maintained a professional objectivity. I have had time to study the JFK assassination both as a working newspaperman and a researcher.

Since 1976 I have taught a course on the JFK assassination at the University of Texas at Arlington. I have been told that I was the first person in the United States to offer a university-level course on the assassination. Through this course, many new leads have been developed— such as a witness to gunmen on the Grassy Knoll and the intimidation of Dallas witnesses by Warren Commission staff members and FBI agents.

My public presentations of assassination material—including talks to Texas police and medical-examiner organizations—have always been well received.

To truly understand what happened in Dallas in 1963, one must get an overview of the event. Any one particular issue can be rationalized away as coincidence or happenstance. Only by gaining a broad view of the assassination can one begin to detect the outlines of the conspiracy that resulted in the deaths of Kennedy, policeman J. D. Tippit, and the accused assassin, Lee Harvey Oswald.

Always keep in mind that the United States in 1963 was an entirely different place and time from today. The public had a blind faith in government, which seems hard to believe in light of today's cynical standards. The news media uncritically accepted official pronouncements—a far cry from today's adversary relationship with officialdom. And police work was done in an unsophisticated manner that would shock the highly trained and educated officers of today.

Also know that many people were untruthful in their testimony to investigators while the statements of others were misrepresented by investigating officials—for reasons both benign and otherwise.

Many people tried to distance themselves from the accused assassin. Some—either due to ignorance, a desire to be helpful, or on orders—lied about critical evidence in the case. Even government agencies were deathly afraid of rumors linking Oswald to their organizations.

Not one single matter of fact in this case can be accepted uncritically. Evidence of deceit, misrepresentation, and manipulation is too plain to be ignored.

What then is the truth?

One truth has become painfully obvious in recent years—the federal government has not told the truth about the assassination to the American people.

It has been left up to students, historians, and private researchers to continue to dig out critical information. This book means to provide this information to a wider audience.

While mistakes undoubtedly have slipped by, every effort has been made to present the best account of assassination issues in this book. Statements have been checked and double-checked; facts reviewed and reviewed again.

Whether it is read from start to finish or simply kept as a reference source, *Crossfire: The Plot That Killed Kennedy* is intended to be a thorough source book for the library of anyone with the slightest interest in learning what actually happened in Dallas in 1963.

So, who is to be believed when it comes to the JFK assassination? No one—not this author, not the various assassination researchers, and certainly not the government officials who have already been proven in error about so many aspects of this case.

Think for yourself. Review *all* the information available in this book and trust in your own judgment. Believe that cerebral computer designed by God, which allows each of us to comprehend the truth around us each day.

Only by studying *all* of the relevant information about the assassination and then applying common sense can one come to an understanding of the truth of the JFK assassination.

PREFACE

Why seek the truth of Kennedy's death? The answer is simple. Unless we, as a nation, come to a truthful understanding of what happened to our chief elected official in 1963, we obviously cannot begin to correctly understand the events that are affecting us today.

I seek not only the killers of President Kennedy, I seek the persons who killed Camelot—who killed the confidence and faith of the American people in their government and institutions. I seek elementary justice—for both the accused assassin and for the United States of America.

J.M.

Don't let it be forgot
That once there was a spot
For one brief shining moment
That was known as Camelot
                    —Alan Jay Lerner

Part I
The Kill Zone

Dallas—The Stage Is Set

Although one of the youngest cities in Texas, Dallas has recorded a meteoric rise to greatness and prosperity. Beginning in the days before Texas became a state, Dallas has grown from a small way station for pioneers to a center of corporate business, insurance, banking, and oil and gas. By 1963, Dallas already was the most influential city in the Lone Star State, next to oil-rich Houston.

However, Dallas also had a reputation for being the stronghold of archconservatives, if not outright right-wing extremists. It is well known in Texas police circles that during the 1940s and 1950s—and stretching into the early 1960s—if a man wanted a job as a Dallas policeman, it helped if he was a member of the Ku Klux Klan or, at least, the John Birch Society. The city police and other governmental offices were filled with members of the Klan, the John Birch Society, and other conservative groups.

But Dallas was instrumental in carrying Texas in a national election. So in 1963, it was included on a quick political trip by President John F. Kennedy.

The Thirty-fifth President

John Fitzgerald Kennedy was the first U.S. president born in the twentieth century. At age forty-three, Kennedy became one of the youngest presidents and, at the time of his death at age forty-six, he had lived a shorter life than any other president.

1

His brief presidency—1,026 days—stirred the emotions of nearly every American. Hardly anyone was neutral about Kennedy. They either loved him or hated him.

Yet Kennedy seemed oblivious to the controversies surrounding him. Perhaps due to his wealthy background, he appeared more concerned with great historical issues such as civil rights, war and peace rather than the parochial matters of business and politics.

Kennedy was born on May 29, 1917, in Brookline, Massachusetts, an unpretentious middle-class suburb of Boston. He was the second oldest son of a family that began their American life with the immigration of Patrick Kennedy from Ireland in 1848. Both grandfathers were prominent Democratic Party ward bosses during the time when a group of Irish leaders ruled the local party.

While he grew to manhood, his father, Joseph P. Kennedy, amassed a considerable fortune. By age twenty-five, Joe Kennedy had gained control of a bank in East Boston. By adroit investments in real estate, the stock market, and the film industry—and perhaps some bootlegging money— Kennedy built an empire worth an estimated $250 million.

Jack, as the future president was called, attended only the best schools, beginning with the Choate School in Connecticut, where he won an award for best combining sports and scholastics. While he graduated near the bottom of his class, he nevertheless was selected as the man "most likely to succeed."

A bout with jaundice forced him to drop out of college, but upon recovery, he joined his older brother, Joseph Kennedy, Jr., at Harvard. Maintaining only a C average, Kennedy concentrated on sports, particularly football.

A somewhat sickly child, Kennedy had continuing bouts with illness compounded by a football injury that aggravated an already-weakened spinal column. For the rest of his life, he suffered recurring back problems. In an effort to recuperate, Kennedy left school during his junior year to travel in Europe, where his father had been appointed U.S. ambassador to Great Britain after generous contributions to Franklin Roosevelt's election campaign. After war broke out, Ambassador Kennedy was forced to resign because of his undisguised admiration for Germany's Nazi regime.

As a result of this trip and the contact he made with major British political figures, young Kennedy returned to write a senior thesis about England's complacent attitudes just before World War II. This thesis was well received at Harvard and later was rewritten to become the best-selling book, *Why England Slept*.

He began to show interest in a writing career, but was interrupted by joining the U.S. Navy two months before the December 7, 1941, attack on Pearl Harbor by Japan. Early in the war, Kennedy served as an intelligence officer in Washington, but was transferred to the South Pacific after J. Edgar Hoover told his father about young Kennedy's love affair with a suspected Nazi agent.

In the summer of 1943, Kennedy was in command of a Navy patrol boat, the PT-109. During a patrol in the Solomon Islands, the boat was struck and broken in half by a Japanese destroyer, the only such incident during the war. Although some negligence appeared to be involved, Kennedy went on to become a hero after saving the life of one of his men and helping to arrange his crewmen's rescue. He pulled his wounded chief engineer, Patrick McMahon, to a nearby island by swimming for four hours with the man on his back held in place by gripping a strap of the man's life jacket between his teeth. Later, Kennedy arranged for local natives to alert Navy officials to the groups' location in enemy-held territory. Soon they were all rescued.

The story hit the front page of the *New York Times* and Kennedy's name became well known in Boston. While recovering from his ordeal, Kennedy learned that his older brother had been killed while flying a secret mission over Europe. The political aspirations of his father now fell on Jack Kennedy. After the war, a reluctant Kennedy ran for and won a House seat from Massachusetts.

In later years, Joe Kennedy was quoted as saying: "I told him Joe was dead and it was his responsibility to run for Congress. He didn't want to. But I told him he had to."

With the Kennedy name and Kennedy money behind him, Kennedy easily won two more elections to Congress. Then, in 1952, he defeated Henry Cabot Lodge to become junior senator from Massachusetts.

In 1954, his back condition forced him to use crutches and Kennedy underwent dangerous and painful back surgery. While recuperating, he wrote *Profiles in Courage,* a book detailing how past senators had defied public opionion. This book, actually written by associates such as Theodore Sorensen, helped identify Kennedy with political courage in the minds of voters.

It was during this bedridden convalescence that Kennedy was conveniently absent during the stormy Senate debates on Joseph McCarthy's censure. In fact, Kennedy refused to take sides on the issue.

Despite an uninspiring senatorial career, by 1956 Kennedy's name was brought up as a possible running mate for Democratic presidential hopeful Adlai Stevenson. Although edged out as vice presidential candidate by Estes Kefauver, a graceful concession speech caused Kennedy's political stock to rise to new heights.

With an eye toward the 1960 election, Kennedy and his supporters went all out to ensure an impressive victory in his 1958 Senate reelection campaign in Massachusetts. Indeed, he won by the largest margin in the state's history. By 1960, Kennedy was ready for the Democratic presidential nomination, but there were hurdles to overcome. One of these was the fact he was a Catholic and no Catholic had ever been elected president. He overcame this problem by entering—and winning—a series of state primary elections. In West Virginia, with 95 percent Prostestant voters, Kennedy beat Senator Hubert Humphrey handily, thanks, according to FBI reports, to large organized crime donations made through Frank Sinatra.

At the Democratic National Convention in Los Angeles, Kennedy was challenged only by conservative Texas Senator Lyndon B. Johnson. Despite a late "draft Adlai Stevenson" movement, Kennedy won on the first ballot by 806 votes to Johnson's 409. The pragmatic Kennedy immediately knew that conservative Democrats were needed to win against Republican Richard Nixon, so he forged a temporary coalition by selecting the defeated Johnson as his vice presidential running mate, despite objections from labor and liberals. There was no thought of Johnson's qualifications as president should anything happen to Kennedy. It was sheer spur-of-the-moment political tactics.

In his acceptance speech, Kennedy set the tone for his campaign and his presidency:

> . . . we stand today on the edge of a new frontier—the frontier of the 1960s . . . Beyond that frontier are uncharted areas of science and space, unsolved problems of peace and war, unconquered pockets of ignorance and prejudice, unanswered questions of poverty and surplus. It would be easier to shrink back from that frontier, to look to the safe mediocrity of the past . . . But I believe the times demand invention, innovation, imagination, decision. I am asking each of you to be new pioneers on that new frontier.

Nixon, and his running mate Henry Cabot Lodge (whom Kennedy had defeated in the 1952 Massachusetts Senate race), tried to raise the issue of experience during the ensuing 1960 election campaign. "Experience Counts" was their slogan, despite the fact that both Nixon and Kennedy had been elected to Congress in 1946 and that Nixon was only four years older than JFK. The slogan mostly was to call attention to Nixon's role as vice president to the popular Ike Eisenhower.

Again the issue of Kennedy's Catholicism came up. Fundamentalist preachers regaled their congregations with the spectre of a Vatican-dominated White House. The issue prompted Kennedy to tell a meeting of Protestant ministers in Houston:

> Because I am a Catholic and no Catholic has never been elected president, it is apparently necessary for me to state once again—not what kind of church I believe in, for that should be important only to me, but what kind of America I believe in. I believe in an America where separation of church and state is absolute—where no Catholic prelate would tell the president (should he be a Catholic) how to act and no Protestant minister would tell his parishioners for whom to vote.

Perhaps the real turning point in the 1960 election came in September when Kennedy and Nixon met in the first televised debates in American history. The four debates were viewed by nearly half the population of the nation and no one denies that Kennedy emerged the victor—although radio listeners judged Nixon the winner.

The debates were TV show business, prefiguring the slick marketing of candidates of today. It was all image—Kennedy with a good makeup job appeared robust and self-confident while Nixon, suffering from little makeup and five-o'clock shadow, appeared uneasy and unsure of himself. Their images aside, there was very little difference in the positions of the two candidates on most issues.

Ironically, when Kennedy called for support of the Cuban exiles in their attempts to regain Cuba from Castro, he was propounding the very program that Nixon had been pushing for many months. However, Nixon felt compelled to attack Kennedy's suggestions as irresponsible since "the covert operation [the Bay of Pigs Invasion] had to be protected at all costs" and, thus, Nixon came out opposing his own plan.

On Election Day, Kennedy won, but by one of the slimmest margins in American history. He polled 34,227,096 votes to Nixon's 34,108,546—a margin of 49.9 percent to 49.6 percent. Affluent whites, college graduates, women, Protestants, farmers, senior citizens, business and professional people mostly voted against this eastern liberal.

On January 20, 1961, standing coatless in bristling twenty-degree temperature in Washington, Kennedy took the oath of office from Chief Justice Earl Warren (who would later head the commission looking into his death) and announced: "The torch has been passed to a new generation of Americans . . ." Later in his speech, he issued his famous challenge: "Ask not what your country can do for you, but what you can do for your country." (His original text carried the word "will" but Kennedy had marked it out and substituted "can.")

Oddly enough, Kennedy's highest ratings in the polls came just after the disastrous Bay of Pigs Invasion as Americans rallied to their president. About 82 percent of those polled expressed approval of his handling of the situation, which prompted Kennedy to remark: "My God, it's as bad as Eisenhower. The worse I do, the more popular I get."

By the fall of 1963, polls showed Kennedy's popularity had dropped to 59 percent, largely due to his stand on civil rights. However, his desire to negotiate with the communist world, his attack on the tax havens of the wealthy corporations, and his attempts to regain civilian control over the Pentagon and its intelligence agencies also engendered hatred and fear among the most powerful cliques of this country.

Newsweek magazine reported that no Democrat in the White House had ever been so disliked in the South. A theater marquee in Georgia advertised the movie *PT-109* with these words on its marquee: "See how the Japs almost got Kennedy."

Kennedy supporters were looking toward the 1964 election, hoping for a mandate that would give Kennedy's ambitious programs much needed popular support. It never happened.

In the fall of 1963, he went to Texas.

*   *   *

Kennedy had carried Texas by the slimmest of margins in 1960, largely through the efforts of Lyndon Johnson. He needed the state badly in 1964, particularly if his hopes of achieving a large mandate were to be realized. According to Texas governor John Connally, Kennedy first talked of coming to Texas in the summer of 1962. He again mentioned it in the summer of 1963.

According to former Senator Ralph Yarborough, he was contacted by Kennedy aides in mid-1963 and was asked what could be done to help the president's image in Texas. Yarborough told this author: "I told them the best thing he could do was to bring Jackie to Texas and let all those women see her. And that's what he did, although I thought it was premature. I didn't think he was going to do that until 1964."

So, in an effort to enhance his image and to raise money, Kennedy, along with his wife, made the fateful journey to Texas in November 1963. On November 21, they visited Houston and San Antonio, both cities with heavy defense and space industries. There Kennedy came out strong for defense and NASA expenditures. The crowds loved it. That evening, he flew to Fort Worth, landing at Carswell Air Force Base and driving to the historic Hotel Texas for the night.

In his hotel suite, original paintings by Van Gogh and Monet had been hung on the walls in an effort to impress the Kennedys with Texas sophistication.

The morning of November 22, Kennedy spoke at a breakfast in the hotel sponsored by the Fort Worth Chamber of Commerce. Beforehand, more than a thousand persons crowded in front of the hotel stood in light drizzling rain to hear the President make brief remarks. As the presidential party prepared to leave the hotel, Vice President Lyndon Johnson arrived to introduce his sister, Lucia Alexander, to Kennedy. Reflecting on the surprisingly warm welcome he had received in Texas, Johnson later was to recall Kennedy as saying: "We're going to carry two states next year if we don't carry any others: Massachusetts and Texas." Johnson wrote in *The Vantage Point* that these were the last words spoken to him by Kennedy.

As the rainclouds were breaking up, Kennedy drove back to Carswell for the fifteen-minute flight to Dallas. Fort Worth and Dallas are so close that even before reaching its full climb, *Air Force One* began its descent to Dallas. Looking out the plane window, Kennedy commented to Governor Connally: "Our luck is holding. It looks as if we'll get sunshine."

When *Air Force One* landed at Love Field the sky had cleared and a bright sun brought Indian summer weather to North Central Texas. By the noon hour, many people were in their shirtsleeves. The occasional cool breeze from the north was welcomed by Texans weary of the interminable summer heat, which often lasts well into the fall. It was the sort of day that stirs the blood, causing people to seek action outdoors, whether it is working in the yard or attending the local football game.

This day there was another reason for wanting to get outside. The President was coming to town. The local media had been full of the news for days. *The Dallas Morning News* carried headlines that morning reading, LOVE FIELD BRACES FOR THOUSANDS and DETAILED SECURITY NET SPREAD FOR KENNEDY. That morning's edition had even run a small map of the President's motorcade route, which would take him from Love Field to the new modern Trade Mart. However this map only indicated the motorcade would travel west on Main Street through the downtown area, through the well-known Triple Underpass, and on to Stemmons Freeway and the Trade Mart, where President John F. Kennedy was scheduled to attend a 12:30 P.M. luncheon.

The city's other daily paper, the *Dallas Times Herald,* had given a more detailed description of the route. In a story published the previous Tuesday headlined YARBOROUGH GETS JFK TABLE SPOT, it told how liberal senator Ralph Yarborough had been invited to sit with Kennedy at the head table during Friday's luncheon. It also mentioned that the motorcade would "pass through downtown on Harwood then west on Main, turning back to Elm at Houston and then out Stemmons Freeway to the Trade Mart."

This was one of the only newspaper mentions of the zigzag in the motorcade route, which would violate Secret Service procedures and place the President in a small park area surrounded by tall buildings on one side and shrubs and trees on the other.

The motorcade had been scheduled to pass through the downtown business section during the noon hour so office workers could watch the parade during lunch. This strategy worked well. Literally thousands of Dallasites turned out in the balmy sixty-eight-degree weather for a view of Kennedy, already acknowledged as one of this nation's most controversial presidents.

For his part, Kennedy really had had no choice but to visit the Lone Star State. With the 1964 election year coming up, everyone—even his enemies—agreed he seemed unbeatable. However, Kennedy still needed to win over a few states in order to acquire the broad mandate he was seeking. Texas was one of them.

Texas politics were in disarray. The Democrats had been aghast the previous year when a Republican, former schoolteacher and radio disk jockey John Tower, had been elected to fill Johnson's Senate seat. Tower was the first Republican to win a Texas Senate seat since the Civil War. The Democratic Party, dominant in the state since Reconstruction, was split between conservatives, headed by Vice President Lyndon B. Johnson and Governor John B. Connally, and a small but noisy group of liberals, led by Senator Ralph Yarborough. The party rift was serious. Yarborough and Connally were hardly speaking to each other. And Texas conservatives were highly vocal against Kennedy's policies toward Cuba, civil rights, and a nuclear test ban with Russia, not to mention his plan to rescind the 27.5 percent oil depletion allowance, a mainstay of Texas oil wealth.

Democratic unity was needed badly as the 1964 election year approached. And a presidential visit to Texas seemed just the remedy.

Houston was the oil capital of the state while Fort Worth and San Antonio were big defense industry centers. It would be easy to tell those folks what they wanted to hear. Dallas was a problem. No visit to Texas could ignore Dallas, yet the city had earned a reputation for being both politically bedrock conservative and intolerant of any deviation from that position.

A month earlier, U.S. ambassador to the United Nations Adlai Stevenson had been pushed, spat upon, and hit in the head with a picket sign while visiting in Dallas. Just the previous Tuesday, cashiered Army major general Edwin A. Walker had made the news by shoving a TV cameraman during a Dallas speech by Governor George Wallace of Alabama.

Stevenson, along with others close to Kennedy, warned the young president not to journey to Dallas. But in early June plans for a trip to Texas were finalized during a meeting between Kennedy, Connally, and Johnson in El Paso. In October, a motorcade was added to the plans.

On November 22, the apprehension of the Kennedy entourage about the trip was still evident, especially in light of a full-page newspaper ad that ran that morning in the *Dallas Morning News* suggesting the President was soft on communism and guilty of traitorous activities.

A leaflet handed out to some of the people lining the motorcade route was not as subtle as the newspaper ad. It pictured Kennedy under a headline reading WANTED FOR TREASON.

Yet after landing at Love Field about 11:45 A.M., the Kennedy entourage found the Dallas crowds large, enthusiastic, and friendly. With horns honking, radios blaring, and the shouts and cheers of the crowd ringing off the sides of the office buildings, the scene was chaotic despite what had been hailed as one of the tightest security efforts in recent memory.

As the motorcade swept toward the central business district, it reached speeds of almost thirty miles per hour. But once downtown, the crowds became larger, often spilling out into the street, and the pace slowed considerably.

The motorcade was the center of attention.

Dealey Plaza—November 22, 1963

The Motorcade

Leading the presidential motorcade on November 22, 1963, was an enclosed sedan driven by Dallas police chief Jesse Curry. Sitting to Curry's right was Secret Service advance man Winston G. Lawson. In the back seat, behind Curry, sat Dallas county sheriff J. E. "Bill" Decker and, to his right was Secret Service special agent-in-charge Forrest Sorrels.

More than two car lengths behind this car was the presidential limousine, a specially-made long blue Lincoln Continental convertible sedan designated Secret Service Car No. 100-X.

Driving the limousine was Secret Service agent William Greer, the oldest man in the White House detail. Next to Greer sat Roy Kellerman, assistant special agent-in-charge of the Secret Service White House detail.

In the center of the car in fold-down jump seats were Governor Connally, on the right, and Mrs. Connally. In the rear, on a padded seat that could be raised or lowered mechanically sat Kennedy with Mrs. Kennedy on his left.

Behind the limousine about a full car length was a follow-up car for Kennedy security guards, a 1956 Cadillac convertible touring sedan specially equipped for the Secret Service and designated SS Car No. 679-X.

Following this security car was a 1964 Lincoln four-door convertible carrying Vice President Lyndon Johnson, Mrs. Johnson, and Senator Ralph Yarborough. The driver was Texas state trooper Hurchel Jacks and Secret Service agent Rufus W. Youngblood rode to the right of him. Their car was trailed by Johnson's Secret Service guards and the rest of the motorcade, consisting of five cars for local dignitaries, three cars for press photographers, one bus for White House staff, and two press buses.

A pilot car, which preceded the motorcade by a quarter of a mile checking for "motor vehicle accidents, fires and obstructions along the route," contained Dallas deputy police chief G. L. Lumpkin, two Dallas homicide detectives, and Lt. Col. George Whitmayer, commander of the local Army Intelligence reserve unit.

Oddly, while a press pool station wagon had been designated to follow Kennedy's Secret Service follow-up car (it had the number 5 taped on its

9

side), for some unexplained reason it was shoved farther back in the
motorcade. This prevented the media photographers from witnessing the
assassination or capturing it on film.

Everyone in the presidential limousine appeared to be enjoying the
open-air ride and the cheering admiration of the crowd, although Mrs.
Kennedy was beginning to feel warm in her pink wool suit and pillbox hat.
As the motorcade cruised into the downtown area, apprehensions of the
Dallas visit seemed to dissipate as quickly as the morning's overcast.

Bob Hollingsworth, veteran Washington correspondent for the *Times
Herald*, had accompanied the Washington press corps to Dallas. He noted:

On into Harwood and then into Main the motorcade traveled and the
amazement over the size of the crowd turned to awe. For those of us
who had been with the President since he left the White House for
Texas Thursday morning, this was the largest, the most enthusiastic and
the best reception he had received in Texas.

The awe of the news reporters was reflected in the silence that prevailed
within the long, dark-blue Lincoln Continental limousine of the President.
Few words were spoken by the car's occupants as they basked in the
tumultuous shouts and cheers of the dense crowd packed along Main
Street.

Up ahead clear blue sky could be seen as the presidential car began
entering a small triangular-shaped plaza at the end of the long, dark corridor
of tall buildings.

The motorcade broke into the open space of Dealey Plaza, named after
George Bannerman Dealey, a pioneer Dallas civic leader and founder of
the *Dallas Morning News*. The 3.07-acre plaza, the site of the first home in
Dallas as well as the first courthouse, post office, store, fraternal lodge and
hotel, has been called the "birthplace of Dallas." It was acquired by the
city for the construction of the Triple Underpass, which allows railroad
traffic to pass over Commerce, Main, and Elm streets. The property was
christened "Dealey Plaza" in 1935 and placed under the authority of the
city's Park Board in 1936 with the official opening of the underpass.

Both incoming and outgoing traffic between downtown Dallas and the
major freeway systems to the west is channeled through Dealey Plaza. It is
bounded on the east by Houston Street. Facing onto Houston are the new
County Court House (still under construction that day), the historic old
County Court House, the Criminal Courts Building containing the county
jail and the Sheriff's Office, the Dallas County Records Building, and the
Dal-Tex office building. Just west of the Dal-Tex building, across Houston, is the red-brick building that in 1963 contained the Texas School
Book Depository and publishers' offices.

Bisecting Dealey Plaza is Main Street, with Commerce Street branch-
ing off to the south and Elm Street curving in on the north. These three

main arteries converge on the west side of the plaza at the railroad bridge known as the Triple Underpass. Facing Houston Street on the west are fountains and monuments to Dealey. On the north and south sides of the plaza are two small arbors or pergolas, flanked on the east by a line of trees and shrubs and on the west by a wooden stockade fence about five feet high.

With a phalanx of Dallas police motorcycle officers clearing the way ahead, the big limousine carrying the Kennedys made a 90-degree turn from Main onto Houston in front of the Dallas County Sheriff's Office. Almost two dozen deputies and other lawmen stood on the sidewalk watching. All had been ordered not to take part in motorcade security.

The bright sun began warming the car's occupants as they approached the Texas School Book Depository. Atop the building was a large Hertz Rent-A-Car sign containing a digital time and temperature display. In front of the Depository, the limousine slowed to a crawl to make a 120-degree turn onto Elm Street, although turns of more than 90 degrees were prohibited by the Secret Service. The turn was so tight that Greer almost ran the limousine up onto the north curb near the Depository's front door, according to Depository superintendent Roy Truly.

The car continued a slow glide down the incline of Elm into Dealey Plaza, maintaining its position in the center lane of the three-lane street. The crowds thinned out as the Triple Underpass approached and security men began to relax. About three car lengths ahead of the presidential limousine in the lead car, Agent Lawson, a former Army counterintelligence man now with the Secret Service White House detail, was sitting in the right front seat. He looked at his watch. It was 12:30 P.M. Picking up the car's microphone, he radioed the Trade Mart saying: "We'll be there in about five minutes."

In the presidential limousine, Kennedy was waving to his right at a group of people standing near a sign reading STEMMONS FREEWAY. His right arm and hand were slightly over the side of the car. Mrs. Kennedy had been waving to her left, but her thoughts were on the Texas heat. Mrs. Kennedy later told the Warren Commission: "And in the motorcade, you know, I usually would be waving mostly to the left side and he was waving mostly to the right, which is one reason you are not looking at each other very much. And it was terribly hot. Just blinding all of us." Sensing her discomfort, Mrs. Connally turned and said: "We'll soon be there."

Mrs. Kennedy recalled seeing the Triple Underpass ahead: "We could see a tunnel in front of us. Everything was really slow then. And I remember thinking it would be so cool under that tunnel."

Mrs. Connally had been wanting to mention the warm and enthusiastic welcome for some time, but she had held back. Now she could contain herself no longer. Turning to Kennedy, she said: "Mr. President, you can't say that Dallas doesn't love you." According to Mrs. Kennedy, the President smiled and replied: "No, you certainly can't."

Soon after his remark, Mrs. Connally heard a frightening noise off to her right. She looked in that direction and caught a peripheral glimpse of Kennedy raising both hands to his neck. She heard no sound from the President, but noticed a blank, "nothing" expression on his face.

Kellerman, sitting directly in front of Connally and Kennedy, noticed they had just passed a highway sign when he heard a "pop" to his right and immediately looked in that direction, surveying the easternmost slope of the Grassy Knoll. Kellerman told the Warren Commission:

. . . as I turned my head to the right to view whatever it was . . . I heard a voice from the back seat and I firmly believe it was the President's [saying] "My God, I am hit," and I turned around and he has got his hands up here like this [indicating both hands up near the head] . . . [It] was enough for me to verify that the man was hit. So, in the same motion I come right back and grabbed the speaker and said to the driver, "Let's get out of here; we're hit," and grabbed the mike and I said, "Lawson, this is Kellerman . . . we are hit; get us to the hospital immediately." Now in the seconds that I talked just now, a flurry of shells come into the car . . .

Mrs. Connally testified she heard Kellerman say: "Pull out of the motorcade. Take us to the nearest hospital." The limousine indeed pulled out of the motorcade and raced to Parkland Hospital.

Driver Greer said he was busy looking ahead to the railroad overpass when he heard a noise he thought was a motorcycle backfire. Then he heard the noise again and caught a glimpse of Connally starting to slump over. He then heard two more noises that seemed to come one on top of the other. Greer said after the second noise and a glance over his right shoulder at Connally, he stepped on the accelerator. However, a film taken that day shows the limousine brake lights remained on until after the fatal head shot to Kennedy.

Mrs. Connally recalled that after the first sound "very soon there was the second shot which hit John [Connally]."

Connally, in testimony consistent both with that of Mrs. Connally and with films made that day, confirmed he was not hit by the first shot. The governor said just after making the turn onto Elm he heard a noise he took to be a shot from a high-powered rifle. He turned to his right because the sound appeared to come from over his right shoulder, but he couldn't see anything. He began to turn to his left when he felt something strike him in the back.

Although critically wounded, Connally was conscious of shots being fired other than the one that struck him. Realizing that he had been hit a second or so after hearing a shot, Connally told the Warren Commission: ". . . there were either two or three people involved or more in this or someone was shooting with an automatic rifle." Connally then heard a final boom and heard the bullet hit home. He later recalled: ". . . it never entered my mind that it ever hit anyone but the President . . . He never uttered a sound that I heard."

Connally noticed blue brain tissue covering his suit and knew Kennedy was dead. He also noticed blood on the front of his shirt and realized he was hurt badly, perhaps fatally. Crumpling into the arms of his wife, Connally screamed out: "My God, they're going to kill us all!" Connally heard his wife saying over and over, "Be still, you're going to be all right," and he felt the car accelerate. He then lost consciousness.

During the initial phase of the shooting, Mrs. Kennedy did not realize what was happening. She was accustomed to the sounds of motorcycle escorts backfiring and the motorcade had been a cacophony of sirens, racing motors, cheering, and shouting. She did hear Connally shout, "Oh, no, no, no!" She heard "terrible noises" to her right and turned to see Kennedy with his hand at his throat and a "quizzical look on his face." Then, the chief executive was struck in the head and fell into her lap. All she could do was cradle him and say: "Oh, my God, they've shot my husband . . . I love you, Jack."

Over the years a great deal of misinformation has been presented about her next actions. Many persons have stated she tried to climb out of the car in panic or to help Agent Hill. Actually, she crawled onto the trunk of the limousine and, reaching out, picked up a piece of her husband's head.

Mrs. Kennedy, when talking to the Warren Commission on June 5, 1964, did not even recall this activity. But her action was captured in the films taken that day and later, sitting in Parkland Hospital, she still had the piece of skull clutched in her hand, according to a nurse who relieved her of the gruesome fragment.

Also, there is the testimony of Clint Hill, who told the Warren Commission:

Between the time I originally grabbed the handhold and until I was up on the car, Mrs. Kennedy—the second noise that I heard had removed a portion of the President's head, and he slumped noticeably to his left. Mrs. Kennedy had jumped up from the seat and was, it appeared to me, reaching for something coming off the right rear bumper of the car, the right rear tail, when she noticed that I was trying to climb on the car.

In the lead car, which was just about to enter the Triple Underpass when the firing began, Agent Lawson was trying to signal a policeman standing with a group of people on top of the underpass. He didn't like the idea of the President's car passing directly below these people, so he was trying to get the officer to move them to one side. The policeman never noticed him.

Just then, Lawson heard a loud report to his rear. It sounded more like a bang instead of a crack and Lawson didn't think it was a rifle shot. His first impression was that it was a firecracker. This description was to be repeated by nearly everyone in Dealey Plaza, with some notable exceptions.

Forrest V. Sorrels, head of the Dallas office of the Secret Service, like Connally was certain the first sound was a gunshot. After a brief pause, Sorrels heard two more shots coming close together. He shouted to Curry: "Let's get out of here!"

On hearing the first burst of firing, Sheriff Decker glanced back and thought he saw a bullet bouncing off the street pavement.

Another Dallas motorcycle officer, Starvis Ellis, in 1978 told the House Select Committee on Assassinations that as he rode alongside the car in which Decker was riding he, too, saw a bullet hit the pavement. Neither Decker nor Ellis were ever questioned about this by the Warren Commission.

Motorcycle officer James Chaney told newsmen the next day that the first shot missed.

Curry saw a "commotion" in the presidential limousine. Then a motor-cycle officer drew up alongside. "Anybody hurt?" asked Curry. "Yes," replied the officer. Stepping on the accelerator, Curry shouted: "Lead us to the hospital." Both Decker and Curry took the car's radio and ordered their men to rush to the top of the underpass and the railroad yards where they thought the shots had come from.

Like the crowd of witnesses in the Dealey Plaza, those persons deep into the plaza believed shots were fired from the Grassy Knoll, while those farther back in the motorcade—still on Houston and Main streets—believed shots came from the direction of the Depository.

Motorcycle policeman Marrion L. Baker was riding near one of the press cars. He had just turned on to Houston and his cycle was about to tip over because of a gust of wind and the slow speed. He had just returned from a deer-hunting trip and recognized the first sound as a high-powered rifle shot. He thought the sound came from either the Depository or the Dal-Tex building. Seeing pigeons fluttering off the Depository's roof, he gunned his motor and roared up to the entrance of the building. Within seconds, he and Depository superintendent Roy Truly would encounter Lee Harvey Oswald calmly standing in the second-floor lunchroom of the Depository.

Secret Service agent Paul Landis was riding in the right rear of the Secret Service follow-up car when he heard the report of a high-powered rifle. He saw Kennedy turn to look in the direction of the shot, which Landis believed came from ". . . somewhere towards the front, right-hand side of the road."

With Landis was Secret Service agent Glen Bennett, who thought the sound was a firecracker. But then he looked at the President. In notes he said were made later that day, Bennett wrote: "[I] saw a shot that hit the Boss about four inches down from the right shoulder; a second shoot [sic] followed immediately and hit the right rear high [side?] of the Boss's head."

The Secret Service agents assigned to Kennedy all acted with remarkable sluggishness when the firing began. Perhaps it was due to the visit
they had paid to a "beatnik" nightspot in Fort Worth, where they stayed
until early that morning. (The club, The Cellar, was owned by an acquaintance of Jack Ruby who had connections with both big-time gamblers
and police officials.)

The only agent to react with speed was Clint Hill. Hill had not been
scheduled to make the Dallas trip, but came only after Mrs. Kennedy made
a personal request. Hill also thought the initial sound was a firecracker and
began looking to his right for the source of the sound when he saw
Kennedy grab at himself and lurch forward slightly. He then realized
something was wrong and jumped off the follow-up car. He was racing the
few feet to the limousine when he heard more shots. Hill had just secured
a grip on a handhold when the car began accelerating. Looking into the
back seat of the limousine, Hill saw that the right rear portion of the
President's head was missing.

Nearly everyone present recalled a pause of several seconds between the
first burst of fire and the final two shots, these coming rapidly one after
another. It was the third and final shot, or volley of shots, that killed
President John F. Kennedy. Until then, he had been immobile and quiet,
only sagging slightly to his left. Then his head pitched forward violently
for a split second only to be pushed hard to the left and rear. A halo of
crimson liquid and tissue surrounded his head momentarily and then fell to
the rear. The head shot lifted him slightly then threw him against the car's
back seat. He bounced forward and over into his wife's lap.

The two Dallas motorcycle officers riding to the left rear of the limousine, Bobby W. Hargis and B. J. Martin, were splattered by blood and
brain matter. Martin, who had looked to his right after the first shots, later
found bloodstains on the left side of his helmet. Hargis, who was riding
nearest the limousine about six to eight feet from the left rear fender, saw
Kennedy's head explode and was hit by bits of flesh and bone with such
impact that he told reporters he thought he had been shot.

Presidential assistant David Powers was riding with Secret Service
agents in the car directly behind the President. From this vantage point, he
described the entire assassination:

> . . . I commented to Ken O'Donnell that it was 12:30 and we would
> only be about five minutes late when we arrived at the Trade Mart.
> Shortly thereafter the first shot went off and it sounded to me as if it
> were a firecracker. I noticed then that the President moved quite far to
> his left after the shot from the extreme right hand side where he had
> been sitting. There was a second shot and Governor Connally disap-
> peared from sight and then there was a third shot which took off the top
> of the President's head and had the sickening sound of a grapefruit
> splattering against the side of a wall. The total time between the first

and third shots was about five or six seconds. My first impression was that the shots came from the right and overhead but I also had a fleeting impression that the noise appeared to come from the front in the area of the Triple Underpass. This may have resulted from my feeling, when I looked forward toward the overpass, that we might have ridden into an ambush.

Several persons in the motorcade smelled gunpowder as the cars swept through the lower end of Dealey Plaza.

Mrs. Earle Cabell, wife of the Dallas mayor, was riding in an open convertible six cars back from the motorcade's lead car. At the opening shots, the car in which she was riding was passing the Depository building. She told the Warren Commission she jerked her head up on hearing the first shot because "I heard the direction from which the shot came . . ." Looking up, she saw an object projecting from one of the top windows of the Depository building. She said:

> . . . I jerked my head up and I saw something in that window and I turned around to say to Earle, "Earle, it is a shot," and before I got the words out . . . the second two shots rang out. . . . I was acutely aware of the odor of gunpowder. I was aware that the motorcade stopped dead still. There was no question about that.

Mrs. Cabell was riding beside Congressman Ray Roberts. She said he acknowledged smelling gunpowder too.

Former senator Ralph Yarborough also smelled gunpowder as the car carrying him and Lyndon Johnson drove through the plaza. Yarborough, a former Army infantry officer and an avid hunter, also failed to recognize the sound of the first shot. He told this author:

> I thought, "Was that a bomb thrown?" and then the other shots were fired. And the motorcade, which had slowed to a stop, took off. A second or two later, I smelled gunpowder. I always thought that was strange because, being familiar with firearms, I never could see how I could smell the powder from a rifle high in that building.

It does seem strange that people would smell powder from a shot fired more than sixty feet in the air and behind them. However, it's not so strange, if a shot were fired on top of the Grassy Knoll less than twelve feet in elevation with a breeze from the north to carry smoke to street level.

One of the strangest omissions in the subsequent investigation by federal authorities concerns a Navy commander who was assigned to film major events involving President Kennedy. In early 1963, Thomas Atkins was assigned as an official photographer for the Kennedy White House. As such, he traveled to Texas with Kennedy and was photographing the motorcade with a quality camera, a 16 mm Arriflex S.

He was riding six cars behind Kennedy and filming as the motorcade moved through Dealey Plaza.

In a 1977 article, Atkins said the car he was in had just turned onto Houston Street and was facing the Texas School Book Depository, and

> . . . Kennedy's car had just made the left turn heading toward the freeway entrance. Although I did not look up at the building, I could hear everything quite clearly. . . . The shots came from below and off to the right side from where I was [the location of the Grassy Knoll]. . . . I never thought the shots came from above. They did not sound like shots coming from anything higher than street level.

After returning to Washington on *Air Force Two,* Atkins assembled his film into a movie he entitled *The Last Two Days.* That film was described as "terribly damaging to the Warren Commission finding that Lee Harvey Oswald was the lone assassin." Perhaps this explains why neither Atkins's testimony nor his film were studied by either of the federal panels investigating the assassination. Atkins said in 1977: "It's something I've always wondered about. Why didn't they ask me what I knew? I not only was on the White House staff, I was then, and still am, a photographer with a pretty keen visual sense."

Obviously, the federal authorities didn't want to hear from a man with a "keen visual sense" and strong credentials who might have told them things they did not want to hear.

But if the stories of the motorcade witnesses differed from the later official version of the assassination, that was nothing compared to the stories to come from the crowd of bystanders.

> I saw a man fire from behind the wooden fence.
> —Assassination witness Jean Hill

The Crowd

The crowd of witnesses along the motorcade route through Dealey Plaza saw many things that differed from the later official version.

Even before the motorcade arrived, men with rifles were seen by people in downtown Dallas.

Shortly before noon, Phillip B. Hathaway and coworker John Lawrence were walking on Akard Street toward Main to get an observation spot for the motorcade when Hathaway saw a man carrying a rifle in a gun case. He described the man as very tall, six-foot-five or more, weighing about

250 pounds and thick in the chest. The man was in his early thirties with "dirty blond hair worn in a crewcut" and was wearing a gray business suit. Hathaway said the case was made of leather and cloth and was not limp, but obviously contained a rifle.

He remarked to Lawrence that it must be a Secret Service man.

Lawrence also saw the big blond man, but did not see the rifle due to the growing crowd around them. Lawrence said the man gave him the impression of being "a professional football player."

This same man may have been seen later that day by Ernest Jay Owens, who told sheriff's officers the afternoon of the assassination that he was driving on Wood Street near Good-Lattimer Expressway when he saw a white male of "heavy build" carrying a "foreign-made rifle" out of a parking lot. Owens said the man was bare headed and wearing a dark colored suit.

Once Oswald was captured and proclaimed the assassination suspect, there was no effort to investigate these stories further.

A similar—and more ominous—incident involved Julia Ann Mercer. Mercer, then twenty-three years old, later told authorities that shortly before 11 A.M. the day of the assassination she was driving a rented white Valiant west on Elm Street just past the point where Kennedy was killed about two hours later. Just after passing through the Triple Underpass, she found her traffic lane blocked by a green Ford pickup truck.

While waiting for the truck to move, she saw a young man get out of the truck, walk to a long tool compartment along the side, and remove a long paper bag. She could see the outlines of a rifle in the bag. The man then walked up on the Grassy Knoll carrying the package and was lost to her sight. She described this man as in his late twenties or early thirties, wearing a gray jacket, brown pants, a plaid shirt, and some sort of wool stocking cap with a tassel on it. Mercer said as she pulled alongside the truck, she locked eyes with the driver, whom she described as heavily built with a round face and light brown hair.

She said during this time, she saw three Dallas policemen standing by a motorcycle on the underpass talking. In Warren Commission Document 205, a policeman did tell of seeing the truck, but believed that it had broken down.

When she was finally able to change lanes, Mercer drove on toward Fort Worth, stopping at the halfway point of the Dallas-Fort Worth Toll Road (now Interstate 30) to have breakfast. While eating, she told her experience to some policemen, commenting, "The Secret Service is not very secret."

Later, as she drove on to Fort Worth, she was stopped by the policemen, who informed her of the assassination and took her back to Dallas for questioning. She was held for several hours and questioned by both local and federal authorities, although no one showed her a badge or identified himself.

Early the next morning, FBI men came to her home and took her back to the Dallas Sheriff's Office where she was shown some photographs of various men. She picked out two as the men she had seen in the truck the day before. Turning one photo over, she read the name, "Jack Ruby." During the TV coverage of the Oswald shooting the next day, Mercer claims she again recognized Ruby as the man driving the truck and that Oswald resembled the man carrying the rifle.

Oswald's mother also claimed to have been shown a picture of Ruby prior to the Sunday shooting of her son.

Mercer later claimed that her story concerning the truck and its occupants was twisted and changed by both the FBI and the Dallas Sheriff's Office.

Mercer's experience may have been partly corroborated by another Dallasite, Julius Hardie, who told *The Dallas Morning News* years later that on the morning of November 22, he saw three men on top of the Triple Underpass carrying longarms, although he could not tell if they were rifles or shotguns. Hardie said he reported the incident to the FBI, but no such report has been made public.

As the motorcade arrived in Dealey Plaza, it passed almost twenty sheriff's deputies standing at the intersection of Main and Houston in front of the Sheriff's Office.

The deputies almost unanimously agreed they thought the shots came from the railroad yards located just behind the Grassy Knoll.

They all began running in that direction even before Decker's radio order to ". . . saturate the area of the park, railroad and all buildings . . ." arrived.

Deputy L. C. Smith, in a report made that day, told a story that was typical of the deputies' experiences:

> . . . I was standing in front of the Sheriff's Office on Main Street and watched the President and his party drive by. Just a few seconds later, I heard the first shot, which I thought was a backfire, then the second shot and third shot rang out. I knew that this was gun shots and everyone else did also. I ran as fast as I could to Elm Street just west of Houston and I heard a woman unknown to me say the President was shot in the head and the shots came from the fence on the north side of Elm. I went at [once] behind the fence and searched also in the parking area. Then came . . . word the shot was thought to have come from the Texas School Book Depository . . .

Supporting the deputies stories was W. W. Mabra, then a county bailiff. Mabra, too, was on the corner of Main and Houston:

> . . . so close to the President that I could almost have reached out and touched him. Then I heard the first shot. I thought it was a backfire.

People ran toward the knoll. Some said they saw smoke there. I thought at first the shot may have come from there.

Across Main Street from the deputies and Mabra stood Dallas County surveyor Robert H. West, who watched the presidential limousine move slowly toward the Triple Underpass. He heard one small report "similar to a motorcycle backfire" then three like "rifle fire." He said the shots came from the "northwest quadrant of Dealey Plaza (the area of the picket fence on the Grassy Knoll." West later participated in reconstructions of the assassination for both *Life* magazine and the FBI, which convinced him the crime could not have been the work of one man.

Mr. and Mrs. Arnold Rowland were both high-school students who had come to town to see the President. They were standing on Houston Street near Decker's office, the west side of which faces Dealey Plaza. Both of the Rowlands believed the shots came from down near the Triple Underpass despite the fact that fifteen minutes before the motorcade arrived they had remarked about seeing two men, one with a rifle and telescopic sight, on the sixth floor of the Texas School Book Depository. Arnold Rowland had assumed the men were part of the Secret Service protection.

He said the man with the rifle was in the far west window of the Depository's sixth floor while the other man, described as an elderly Negro with thin hair wearing a plaid shirt, was seen in the easternmost window (the so-called "sniper's nest" window). Rowland said he lost sight of the man with the rifle as the motorcade approached, but again saw the black man just before Kennedy arrived.

During the excitement of the moment, Rowland said he neglected to mention the black man when he talked to authorities in the Sheriff's Office. However, he said the next day FBI agents came to his home and got him to sign a statement. He recalled: "At that time I told them I did see the Negro man there and they told me it didn't have any bearing or such on the case right then. In fact, they just the same as told me to forget it now."

Although the agents "didn't seem interested" in Rowland's story of the two men on the sixth floor, they did attempt to get an identification of the man with the gun by showing Rowland photos of Oswald. However, Rowland said: "I just couldn't identify him . . . because I just didn't have a good enough look at his face."

Rowland's story of seeing two men was corroborated to the Warren Commission by Deputy Sheriff Roger D. Craig. Craig said Rowland told him about seeing two men pacing the Depository approximately ten minutes after the assassination as Craig interviewed Rowland in Dealey Plaza.

The two men also were seen by Mrs. Carolyn Walther, who worked in a dress factory in the Dal-Tex Building.

About noon, she and another employee joined the crowd on the east side of Houston just south of Elm to watch the motorcade. Years later she recalled:

I had gone out on the street at about twenty after twelve to get a look at the President when he came by. While I waited, I glanced up at the Depository building. There were two men in the corner window on the fourth or fifth floor. One man was wearing a white shirt and had blond or light brown hair. This man had the window open. His hands were extended outside the window. He held a rifle with the barrel pointed downward. I thought he was some kind of guard. In the same window, right near him, was a man in a brown suit coat. Then the President's car came by. I heard a gunshot. People ran. Like a fool I just stood there. I saw people down. I walked toward them, with the thought they maybe were hurt and I could help them. People were running toward the Grassy Knoll. A woman cried out, "They shot him!" In all, I heard four shots.

Steelworker Richard Randolph Carr, who was working on the seventh floor of the new Dallas Courthouse (then under construction at the intersection of Commerce and Houston), also reported seeing a man wearing a brown coat. Carr said minutes before the motorcade arrived he saw a heavyset man wearing a hat, horn-rimmed glasses, and tan sportcoat standing in a sixth-floor window of the Depository. After the shooting, Carr saw the man walking on Commerce Street.

Ruby Henderson, standing across the street from the Depository, also saw two men on an upper floor of the building. While she was uncertain if it was the sixth floor, she saw no one above the pair. She described the shorter of the men as having a dark complexion, possibly even a Negro, and wearing a white shirt. The shorter man was wearing a dark shirt.

The story of two men on the sixth floor of the Depository moments before the shooting has since been bolstered by two films made that day. One, an 8 mm home movie made by Robert Hughes, who was standing at the intersection of Main and Houston, shows the front of the Depository just as Kennedy's limousine passes the building turning onto Elm. The film shows movement in both the corner window of the sixth floor and the window next to it. Deep within the Warren Commission exhibits is an FBI report acknowledging receipt of Hughes's film. In another FBI document, it is claimed that the figure in the second window from the corner was simply a stack of boxes. No reference is made to movement.

In 1975, CBS television asked Itek Corporation to look again at the Hughes film. The company concluded that there were no moving images in the double window next to the sixth-floor corner window, a conclusion that is still disputed by various photographic experts.

And in late 1978, a second movie surfaced that supports the two-men allegation. This film, taken by Charles L. Bronson, who was standing only a few feet west of Hughes, also shows the sixth-floor corner windows of the Depository just moments before the Kennedy motorcade passed.

Bronson's film was viewed in 1963 by an FBI agent who reported that it "failed to show the building from which the shots were fired," thus relegating the film to obscurity. It was rediscovered in 1978 when the film was mentioned in declassified FBI documents and was obtained by *The Dallas Morning News*.

The newspaper commissioned Robert Groden, who served as staff consultant on photographic evidence for the House Select Committee on Assassinations, to study the film. Groden told the newspaper:

> There is no question that there is movement. And, I'm sure, given time and money, a computer could probably clarify the images a bit more . . . You can actually see one figure walking back and forth hurriedly. I think what was happening there is the sniper's nest was actually being completed just prior to the shots being fired.

The House Assassinations Committee studied the Bronson film further and, while acknowledging movement in the second window, stated it was "more likely . . . a random photographic artifact than human movement." However, the committee did recommend that the film be analyzed further. There is no evidence such further study has been done.

Another witness to the pair of men in the Depository was an inmate of the Dallas County Jail, located just across the street to the east of the Depository. Several prisoners were in a sixth-floor cell on a level with the sixth-floor Depository window.

Oddly, none of the jail inmates were ever identified or sought by federal investigators despite their excellent vantage point. However, one of the inmates told the *Dallas Morning News* in 1978 that the prisoners saw two men, one with a rifle, in the Depository at the time of the assassination.

Confirmation of the presence of two men on the sixth floor might have come from Canadian journalist Norman Similas, who was in Dallas for a convention of carbonated-beverage bottlers. It was a trip he would not soon forget. On November 21, Similas photographed and spoke with Vice President Lyndon Johnson, who had addressed the convention. Later that evening, Similas visited the Carousel Club and spent more than an hour talking with its owner, Jack Ruby. The next day, Similas strolled over to Dealey Plaza to photograph President Kennedy's motorcade. He stood on the south side of Elm not ten feet from Kennedy's car at the time of the first shots. In a report published in the Canadian magazine *Liberty*, Similas said:

> The Presidential limousine had passed me and slowed down slightly. My camera was directly angled toward the Texas School Book Depository in the background. The picture I took on the curb of Elm Street was trained momentarily on an open, sixth-floor window. The camera lens recorded what I could not possibly have seen at that moment—a rifle

barrel extended over the windowsill. When the film was developed later, it showed two figures hovering over it.

Were there two people in Similas's photo? No one will ever know for sure. In that same article, he added:

Upon my return to Toronto, I submitted my developed negatives to a daily newspaper. When they were not used on Monday, November 25, I phoned and asked that they be returned. Later I received a fat cheque in the mail, but the one negative which clearly showed what I believe to be two figures in the window of the assassin's nest was missing. When I pressed for it, I was told that this negative had somehow become lost. It has never been returned to me.

An advertising salesman for the *Dallas Morning News,* Jim Willmon, was standing with the crowd along Houston Street. He recalled:

The car turned down Elm Street. A car backfired, or so I thought. I said to my buddy, "The Secret Service is going to have a heart attack!" But it wasn't a backfire. It was shots. People ran toward the Grassy Knoll. No one seemed to look up at the Book Depository.

Ronald B. Fischer, an auditor for Dallas County, and another county worker, Robert E. Edwards, were standing on the southwest corner of Elm and Houston, directly across the street from the Depository. Less than ten minutes before the motorcade arrived, Edwards commented: "Look at that guy there in the window." Looking up, Fischer saw the head and shoulders of a man wearing a white T-shirt or possibly a light sportshirt. The man was surrounded by boxes and was staring "transfixed," not toward the approaching motorcade, but in the direction of the Triple Underpass. Less than a minute later the motorcade passed their position and both Fischer and Edwards forgot the man in the window. Then Fischer heard what he thought was a firecracker followed by sounds he knew to be shots. They seemed to be coming from ". . . just west of the School Book Depository building [the location of the Grassy Knoll]."

Hugh W. Betzner, Jr., was twenty-two years old on November 22, 1963, and was taking pictures with an old camera near the intersection of Houston and Elm. After taking Kennedy's picture as he turned in front of the Depository, Betzner ran west into Dealey Plaza following the presidential limousine. In a sheriff's report that day, Betzner stated:

I started to wind my film again and I heard a loud noise. I thought this noise was either a firecracker or a car had backfired. I looked up and it seemed like there was another loud noise in a matter of a few seconds. I looked down the street and I could see the President's car and another one and they looked like the cars were stopped.

Betzner said he then heard at least two more shots fired and saw the impact in the limousine. The motorcade then sped up and Betzner joined spectators running up the Grassy Knoll toward the wooden picket fence where he assumed the shots came from. Minutes later, he looked across Elm Street and saw ". . . police officers and some men in plain clothes . . . digging around in the dirt as if they were looking for a bullet."

Near Betzner was another photographer, Phillip Willis, who took a series of pictures considered by many as the most important photos taken of the assassination other than the Zapruder film.

Willis, along with his wife and two young daughters, was in Dealey Plaza to get pictures of the President and Lyndon Johnson, whom Willis said was a personal friend. As the presidential limousine turned onto Elm in front of the Depository, Willis snapped a photo, then ran farther west on Elm. He told the Warren Commission: ". . . Then my next shot . . . in fact, the shot caused me to squeeze the camera shutter, and I got a picture of the President as he was hit with the first shot. So instantaneous, in fact, that the crowd hadn't had time to react." Willis said he did not see the effects of the next shots because his two daughters, Linda and Rosemary, were running along Elm and he became concerned for their safety.

As a retired Air Force major and World War II veteran, Willis said he had absolutely no doubt that the shots were from a high-powered rifle and were coming from the direction of the Texas School Book Depository. (An interesting note: Willis was in Hawaii during the attack on Pearl Harbor and captured the sole surviving member of a Japanese midget submarine, thus becoming the first American to take a Japanese prisoner during World War II.)

Willis's youngest daughter, Rosemary, ran back to her father, saying: "Oh, Daddy, they have shot our President. His whole head blew up and it looked like a red halo."

Willis said he took more photographs "knowing that the party had come to a temporary halt before proceeding on to the underpass . . .''

In later years, this author interviewed Willis, who refuted two of the theories to come from federal investigations of the assassination. One, the single-bullet theory of the Warren Commission, states that one shot (identified by the commission as the first shot) struck both Kennedy and Connally. Willis said: "There is no damn way that one bullet hit both men. That is the most stupid thing they ever stuck to—that one-bullet theory."

The House Select Committee on Assassinations, also attempting to deal with the wounds in Kennedy's back and throat which do not support a conclusion of one shot from the high rear, theorized that Kennedy may have bent over momentarily while out of the Zapruder camera view and thus received a back wound lower than the throat wound. Willis retorted: "That is not right. I got the nearest, best shot while JFK was behind the

[Stemmons Freeway] sign. He was upright and waving to the crowd. A split second later, he was grabbing at his throat.''

Willis also had a comment after telling of Kennedy falling to the left rear after the fatal head shot: "As many deer as I have shot, I've never known one to fall towards me."

Although the Warren Commission quoted Willis as saying that he heard three shots, all from the Depository, Willis said:

I always thought there had to be another shot from somewhere. I have always gone against the one-gunman theory. I always thought there had to have been some help. I saw blood going to the rear and left [of Kennedy]. That doesn't happen if that bullet came from the Depository.

Willis further claimed:

I also got a photo, taken immediately after [the shooting stopped] that shows Ruby standing in front of the Depository building. He was the only person there wearing dark glasses. He was identified by people who knew him and no one else has been able to say it was someone else. Ruby made a big effort to show he was in the *Dallas Morning News* at the time, but it wouldn't take five minutes to walk from the *News* [to Dealey Plaza].

Interestingly, the Warren Commission cropped Willis's photograph right through the face of the man Willis claimed was Jack Ruby.

Linda Willis, who was running along Elm Street with Rosemary, told this author in 1978: "I very much agree that shots came from somewhere other than the Depository. And where we were standing, we had a good view. So many of the people who have decided they know what happened there weren't even there. I was, and that's what makes the difference."

Neither Willis nor his daughters believed the Warren Commission or the House committee were serious in finding out the truth of the assassination.

Behind Willis, sitting on a concrete retaining wall across the street from the Depository was forty-five-year-old Howard Leslie Brennan, who was to become the star witness for the Warren Commission. Brennan, who had been working as a pipe fitter on a construction project behind the Depository, had eaten lunch and then taken this position to view the motorcade. It was determined that Brennan was 120 feet from the sixth-floor window. He said he saw a man in an upper floor of the Depository shortly before the motorcade arrived. He described the man as a slender white male in his early thirties wearing "light-colored clothing." Brennan stated:

. . . I heard what I thought was a backfire. It ran in my mind that it might be someone throwing firecrackers out of the window of the red brick building [the Depository] and I looked up at the building. I then

saw this man I have described in the window and he was taking aim
with a high-powered rifle. I could see all of the barrel of the gun. I do
not know if it had a scope on it or not. I was looking at the man in this
window at the time of the last explosion. Then this man let the gun
down to his side and stepped out of sight. He did not seem to be in any
hurry . . . I believe I could identify this man if I ever saw him again.

Brennan, who immediately rushed into the Depository to tell a policeman what he saw, apparently was one of the only witnesses to have
actually seen a gunman fire from the Depository. However, later that
evening Brennan was unable to pick Lee Harvey Oswald out of a police
lineup.

Much later, it was determined that Brennan had poor eyesight and, in
fact, a close examination of the Zapruder film shows that Brennan was not
looking up at the time of the shooting.

Furthermore, Brennan's job foreman, Sandy Speaker, told this author:

They took [Brennan] off for about three weeks. I don't know if they
were Secret Service or FBI, but they were federal people. He came back
a nervous wreck and within a year his hair had turned snow white. He
wouldn't talk about [the assassination] after that. He was scared to
death. They made him say what they wanted him to say.

Brennan's story of a man firing from the sixth-floor window was
supported by a statement to sheriff's deputies that day by fifteen-year-old
Amos Lee Euins. Euins, a schoolboy, was standing near Brennan south of
the Depository across Elm when he heard a shot. He stated:

I started looking around and then I looked up in the red brick building. I
saw a man in a window with a gun and I saw him shoot twice. He then
stepped back behind some boxes. I could tell the gun was a rifle and it
sounded like an automatic rifle the way he was shooting.

Another witness who saw a gunman in the Depository was L. R. Terry,
who was standing across Elm Street near Brennan and Euins. Terry told
this author:

I was right across from that book store when Kennedy was shot. I saw a
gun come out of there just after I saw Kennedy and Connally go by. I
could only see a hand, but I couldn't tell if [the man] was right-handed
or left-handed. He did not have on a white shirt. The parade stopped
right in front of the building. There was a man with him. They
[investigators] could find out that the man who killed Kennedy had
somebody with him. But I don't know who it is. . . . I just saw the gun
barrel and the hand.

Across the street from Brennan, Euins, and Terry were Texas School Book Depository superintendent Roy Truly and Depository vice president O. V. Campbell.

They had started to go to lunch about 12:15 P.M. when they saw the crowds and decided to wait and see the presidential motorcade. As the motorcade approached, they were having difficulty seeing over the heads of the crowd, so the two men moved closer to Elm Street and a bit farther west into the plaza. Here they were joined by Mrs. Robert A. Reid, the Depository's clerical supervisor.

Just after the presidential limousine had turned onto Elm and started into the plaza, both men heard an "explosion . . . from west of the building [depository]." Truly thought it was a firecracker or toy cannon.

When Mrs. Reid turned to Campbell and said, "Oh my goodness, I'm afraid those came from our building," he replied: "Oh, Mrs. Reid, no, it came from the grassy area down this way."

Danny G. Arce, who had been working in the Depository, also was standing near Truly and Campbell. He told the Warren Commission shots "came from the railroad tracks to the west of the Texas School Book Depository."

Truly said after the initial explosion, everything seemed frozen. Then there were two more explosions, and he realized that shots were being fired. He saw the President's car come to a stop.

Another Depository employee saw a bullet hit the street at the time of the first shot. Virgie Rachley (by the time of her Warren Commission testimony she had married and was Mrs. Donald Baker) was a bookkeeper at the Depository. She and other workers were standing near Truly and Campbell in front of the Depository facing Elm Street. She told the Warren Commission:

> . . . after he passed us, then we heard a noise and I thought it was firecrackers because I saw a shot or something hit the pavement. . . . It looked just like you could see the sparks from it and I just thought it was a firecracker and I was thinking that . . . somebody was fixing to get in a lot of trouble and we thought the kids or whoever threw it were down below or standing near the underpass or back up here by the sign.

Mrs. Baker told Commission attorney Wesley Liebeler that the stray bullet struck the middle of the southmost lane on Elm Street just behind the presidential limousine.

Truly said the crowd around him began to surge backward in panic. He became separated from Campbell and quickly found himself back on the steps of the Depository. Moments later a motorcycle policeman pushed past him and ran into the Depository. Truly caught up with him in the lobby and they went toward their encounter with a Depository employee— Lee Harvey Oswald.

Campbell ran with many others to where he believed the shots had come from, ". . . near the railroad tracks located over the viaduct on Elm Street."

Mary E. Woodward, a staff writer for the *Dallas Morning News,* had gone to Dealey Plaza with four co-workers to get a look at the President while they ate lunch. As the limousine passed, she and another writer who had seen Kennedy during the final weeks of the 1960 campaign, commented on how relaxed and robust he appeared. Standing near the Stemmons Freeway sign located down the slope to the west of the Depository, Woodward heard a "horrible, ear-shattering noise" coming from behind them and to their right. She thought it was some sort of joke, a car backfiring perhaps.

She saw both the President and Mrs. Kennedy look around as if they, too, had heard the sound. The presidential limousine came to a halt. Then Woodward heard two more shots, coming close together, and the President slumped down in the car. A woman nearby began weeping and cried, "They've shot him!"

Mrs. Gloria Calvery and Karen Westbrook, both employees of a publishing firm with offices in the Texas School Book Depository, had gone out during lunch to see the President. They were standing almost halfway between the corner of Elm and Houston and the Triple Underpass. Both heard the first blast and saw Kennedy struck by a bullet just as the presidential limousine got directly in front of their position. Neither were questioned later as to the direction of the shots.

A. J. Millican, a co-worker of Howard Brennan, had no difficulty in determining where the shots came from. Millican told authorities that day he was standing on the north side of Elm Street about halfway between Houston and the Triple Underpass. He said he noticed "a truck from Honest Joe's Pawn Shop" park near the Depository, then drive off about five or ten minutes before the President arrived. He told sheriff's deputies:

Just after the President's car passed, I heard three shots from up toward Elm right by the Book Depository Building, and then immediately I heard two more shots come from the arcade between the Book Store and the Underpass, then three more shots came from the same direction only sounded further back. It sounded approximately like a .45 automatic, or a high-powered rifle.

Millican, who provided perhaps one of the clearest descriptions of the firing sequence and the location of the shots, was never interviewed by nor called to testify to the Warren Commission or the House Select Committee on Assassinations. He died in 1986, apparently having never been questioned by anyone.

However, his supervisor, Sandy Speaker, said his entire work crew

was there and they all corroborated Millican's story. In an interview with
this author, Speaker said:

> I was the superintendent of construction for the Republic Bank project at
> the time. Millican and also Howard Brennan were working for me. We
> were fabricating plumbing piping for the Republic Bank Building under
> construction at the west end of Pacific Street [north of the Texas School
> Book Depository]. Millican and the whole crew had knocked off for
> lunch and were by the Depository building to watch the parade. I hadn't
> gotten there when [the motorcade] passed. I was less than a half-block
> away and heard the shots. I heard at least five shots and they came from
> different locations. I was a combat Marine with the First Marine Divi-
> sion in World War II, hand-to-hand combat, missions behind enemy
> lines, and I know what I am talking about. I've said for years there were
> more than three shots fired.

John A. Chism, along with his wife and three-year-old son, were near
Millican, standing directly in front of the Stemmons Freeway sign. They
said the first shots were fired just as the President got in front of them.
They saw Kennedy slump to the left and into his wife's arms. Mrs. Chism
told Dallas authorities that day: "And then there was a second shot that I
heard, after the President's wife had pulled him down in the seat. It came
from what I thought was behind us [the Grassy Knoll] and I looked but I
couldn't see anything."
Chism also looked behind him at the sound of the shots, then, as he
again looked forward and saw "the motorcade beginning to speed up."
Jean Newman was a twenty-one-year-old manufacturing company employee who came to view the motorcade in Dealey Plaza. She told sheriff's
deputies she was standing between the Stemmons Freeway sign and the
Book Depository when the shots were fired. She stated: "The first impression I had was that the shots came from my right." To her right was the
Grassy Knoll.
Also near the Stemmons Freeway sign were two of the most suspicious
characters in Dealey Plaza that day. Despite their activities and the fact
that both were captured in several photographs made at the time, this pair
was never mentioned publicly until the House Select Committee on Assassinations investigation in the late 1970s.

Two Suspicious Men

About the time that Kennedy was first hit by a bullet, two men standing
near each other on the north sidewalk of Elm Street acted most strangely—
one began pumping a black umbrella while the other waved his right arm
high in the air. These and subsequent actions by this pair aroused the

suspicions of researchers over the years, yet the initial federal investigation ignored both men. Their activities are known only through analysis of assassination photographs.

As Kennedy's limousine began the gentle descent into Dealey Plaza, a man can be seen standing near the street-side edge of the Stemmons Freeway sign holding an open umbrella. He holds the umbrella in a normal fashion and the top of the umbrella almost reaches the bottom of the sign.

In photos taken minutes before Kennedy's arrival, the umbrella is closed and, immediately after the shooting, pictures show the umbrella was closed again. The man's umbrella was only open during the shooting sequence. Furthermore, as seen in the Zapruder film, once Kennedy is exactly opposite the man with the umbrella, it was pumped almost two feet into the air and then lowered.

At the same time, the second man—in photos he appears to be dark complected, perhaps a black man or Hispanic—raised his right hand into the air possibly making a fist. This man was located on the outer edge of the Elm Street sidewalk opposite the umbrella man, who was on the inner edge.

The man with the open umbrella was the only person in Dealey Plaza with an open umbrella. Under the warm Texas sun, there was no reason to carry an open umbrella at that time.

Two main theories have emerged concerning the "umbrella man" and his activities that day. Assassination researcher Robert Cutler has long maintained that the umbrella may have been a sophisticated weapon that fired a dart or "flechette" filled with a paralyzing agent. Cutler's theory is supported by the 1975 testimony of a CIA weapons developer who told the Senate Intelligence Committee that just such an umbrella weapon was in the hands of the spy agency in 1963.

Charles Senseney, who developed weaponry for the CIA at Fort Detrick, Maryland, described a dart-firing weapon he developed as looking like an umbrella. He said the dart gun was silent in operation and fired through the webbing when the umbrella was open. Senseney said the CIA had ordered about fifty such dart weapons and that they were operational in 1963.

Cutler theorized that the umbrella was used to fire a paralyzing dart into Kennedy immobilizing him for marksmen with rifles. He claims this theory accounts for the small puncture wound in Kennedy's throat described by Dallas doctors, but which was altered by the time of the Bethesda autopsy. According to Cutler, this dart explains Kennedy's lack of motion during the shooting sequence. Since such a weapon existed and since both the actions of Kennedy and the "umbrella man" were consistent with the operation of such a weapon, Cutler's theory cannot be completely dismissed.

However, most assassination researchers prefer the alternative theory that both of these suspicious men may have been providing visual signals to hidden gunmen. This theory suggests that Kennedy was killed by a crossfire coordinated by radiomen. The two men, who were among the closest bystanders to the President when he was first struck, gave signals indicating that he was not fatally hit and therefore more shots were needed.

A fascinating twist on this latter theory came from researcher Gary Shaw, who said the two men may have been providing Kennedy with a last-second sign of who was responsible for his death. Shaw recalled that throughout the planning of the Bay of Pigs invasion, CIA officers had promised an "umbrella" of air protection of the Cuban invaders. This "umbrella" failed to materialize because Kennedy refused to authorize U.S. military support for the invasion. According to Shaw's theory, the man with the open umbrella symbolized the promise of an air-support "umbrella" while the dark-complected man may have been one of the anti-Castro Cuban leaders known to Kennedy. Thus, in the last seconds of his life, Kennedy may have seen the open umbrella and the face of a Cuban he knew was involved in the Bay of Pigs and realized who was participating in his death.

But this is all speculation. The existence of the "umbrella man" and the dark-complected man is fact. Even their activities after the assassination bear study. While virtually everyone in Dealey Plaza was moved to action by the assassination—either falling to the ground for cover or moving toward The Grassy Knoll—these two men sat down beside each other on the north sidewalk of Elm Street.

Here the dark-complected man appears to put a walkie-talkie to his mouth. In a photograph taken by Jim Towner, what seems to be an antenna can be seen jutting out from behind the man's head while his right hand holds some object to his face.

Several photos taken in the seconds following the assassination show both of these men sitting together on the Elm Street sidewalk. Moments later, the man with the umbrella gets up, takes one last look toward the motorcade still passing under the Triple Underpass, and begins walking east in the direction of the Depository. The dark-complected man saunters toward the Triple Underpass passing people rushing up The Grassy Knoll. He can been seen stuffing some object—the walkie-talkie?—into the back of his pants.

Despite the suspicious actions of these two men, there is no evidence that the FBI or the Warren Commission made any effort to identify or locate them. Offically they did not exist. Yet over the years, this pair became the focal point of criticism by private researchers. Researchers claimed the lack of investigation of these men was indicative of the shallowness of the government's handling of the assassination.

Once the House Select Committee on Assassinations was formed, researchers urged an investigation of both men. The Committee finally released a photograph of the "umbrella man" to the news media and urged anyone with knowledge of the man to come forward.

Coincidentally—if it was a coincidence—the "umbrella man" suddenly was identified in Dallas a few weeks after this national appeal. In August

1978, a telephone caller told researcher Penn Jones, Jr., that the man with the umbrella was a former Dallas insurance salesman named Louis Steven Witt. Jones contacted some local newsmen and together they confronted Witt, who then was working as a warehouse manager. Witt refused to talk with newsmen but acknowledged that he was in Dealey Plaza on the day Kennedy was killed.

Jones later wrote: "I felt the man had been coached. He would answer no questions and pointedly invited us to leave. His only positive statement, which seemed to come very quickly, was that he was willing to appear before the House Select Committee on Assassinations in Washington."

Witt indeed appeared before the Committee during its public testimony. His story was comic relief compared to the intense scrutiny of witnesses like Marina Oswald and Warren Commission critics. His story was facile and improbable and when the umbrella that Witt claimed was the same one he had had in Dealey Plaza in 1963 was displayed, it suddenly turned wrong-side out, prompting one Committee member to quip: "I hope that's not a weapon."

Witt told the Committee that on the spur of the moment, he grabbed a large black umbrella and went to Dealey Plaza to heckle Kennedy. He claimed that someone had told him that an open umbrella would rile Kennedy. While Witt offered no further explanation of how his umbrella could heckle the president, Committee members theorized that the umbrella in some way referred to the pro-German sympathies of Kennedy's father while serving as U.S. ambassador to Britain just prior to World War II. They said the umbrella may have symbolized the appeasement policies of Britain's prime minister Neville Chamberlain, who always carried an umbrella.

According to Witt:

I think I went sort of maybe halfway up the grassy area [on the north side of Elm Street], somewhere in that vicinity. I am pretty sure I sat down. . . . [when the motorcade approached] I think I got up and started fiddling with that umbrella trying to get it open, and at the same time I was walking forward, walking toward the street. . . . Whereas other people I understand saw the President shot and his movements; I did not see this because of this thing [the umbrella] in front of me. . . . My view of the car during that length of time was blocked by the umbrella's being open.

Based on the available photographs made that day, none of Witt's statements were an accurate account of the actions of the "umbrella man" who stood waiting for the motorcade with his umbrella in the normal over-the-head position and then pumped it in the air as Kennedy passed.

Witt's bizarre story—unsubstantiated and totally at variance with the actions of the man in the photographs—resulted in few, if any, researchers accepting Louis Steven Witt as the "umbrella man."

And there continues to be no official accounting for the dark-complected man who appears to have been talking on a radio moments after the assassination. The House Committee failed to identify or locate this man and Witt claimed he had no recollection of such a person, despite photographs that seem to show the "umbrella man" talking with the dark man.

Witt claimed only to recall that a "Negro man" sat down near him and kept repeating: "They done shot them folks."

Interestingly, one of the Committee attorneys asked Witt specifically if he recalled seeing the man with a walkie-talkie, although officially no one has ever admitted the possibility of radios in use in Dealey Plaza.

These two men are still among the mystery people of Dealey Plaza.

*   *   *

Dolores Kounas was a clerk-typist with McGraw-Hill Publishing Company, which had offices on the third floor of the Depository building. She, along with two other McGraw-Hill employees, were standing just west of the Depository across Elm Street from Millican and the Chisms. She, too, thought the first shot was a firecracker, but after hearing a second shot and seeing people fall to the ground, she realized they were shots. She later told the FBI:

Although I was across the street from the Despository building and was looking in the direction of the building as the motorcade passed and following the shots, I did not look up at the building as I had thought the shots came from a westernly direction in the vicinity of the viaduct.

James Altgens, forty-four, a photographer for the Associated Press in Dallas, arrived in Dealey Plaza early. He had been assigned to get a picture of Kennedy as he passed through downtown Dallas and decided the west end of Dealey Plaza would provide an excellent opportunity to catch the President with the downtown buildings in the background. However, when Altgens tried to station himself on the Triple Underpass, he was shooed away by a Dallas policeman, who told him it was railroad property and only railroad employees were allowed there.

So Altgens walked around by the Depository, then on to the intersection of Main and Houston, where he took a photo as the President passed. He then ran farther into the plaza, where he made several photographs as the motorcade approached from the south curb of Elm. Altgens told the Warren Commission:

I made one picture at the time I heard a noise that sounded like a firecracker. . . . I figured it was nothing more than a firecracker because from my position down here the sound was not of such volume that it would indicate to me it was a high-velocity rifle. . . . It sounded like it was coming up from behind the car . . . who counts fireworks explosions? I wasn't keeping track of the number of pops that took place, but I could vouch for No. 1 and I can vouch for the last shot, but I cannot tell you how many shots were in between. There was not another shot fired after the President was struck in the head. That was the last shot—that much I will say with a great degree of certainty.

One of Altgens's photos was taken just seconds after the first shots were fired and showed a slender man standing in the doorway of the Depository. Many people have claimed the man was Lee Harvey Oswald.

In the May 24, 1964, issue of the *New York Herald Tribune* magazine section, there was an article regarding Altgens's photograph. This article raised the question:

> Isn't it odd that J. W. Altgens, a veteran Associated Press photographer in Dallas, who took a picture of the Kennedy assassination—one of the witnesses close enough to see the President shot and able to describe second-by-second what happened—has been questioned neither by the FBI nor the Warren Commission?

On June 2, 1964, Altgens was interviewed by FBI agents. The agents reported: "He recalled that at about the instant he snapped the picture, he heard a burst of noise which he thought was firecrackers . . . he then turned the film in his camera . . . when he heard another report which he recognized as a gunshot."

Near Altgens on the grassy triangle in the lower part of Dealey Plaza were a handful of people, all the closest witnesses to the actual assassination. Only a couple of these witnesses testified to the Warren Commission and one of the closest was never identified until years later when she was interviewed by an assassination researcher.

Charles Brehm, along with his five-year-old son, had watched the presidential motorcade turn onto Houston from near the Depository building. Then, holding his son, Brehm ran across Elm and stationed himself halfway between Houston and the Triple Underpass on the grassy triangle south of Elm. In a 1966 film documentary, Brehm stated:

> I very definitely saw the effect of the second bullet that struck the President. That which appeared to be a portion of the President's skull went flying slightly to the rear of the President's car and directly to its left. It did fly over toward the curb to the left and to the rear.

Brehm said the piece of skull landed in the grass not far from his location. He told the FBI some days later that "it seemed quite apparent to him that the shots came from one of two buildings back at the corner of Elm and Houston Streets. Brehm also said "it seemed to him that the automobile almost came to a halt after the first shot," but he was not certain.

Brehm, an ex-serviceman with experience in bolt-action rifles, was probably the closest witness to the fatal head shot. He was not called to testify to the Warren Commission.

Two significant home movies were made of the assassination other than the famous Zapruder film. One was made by Mrs. Maria Muchmore, who had moved from a position near Main and Houston to the center of the grassy triangle behind Brehm. She caught the final and fatal head shot to Kennedy and the disappearance of the limousine into the Triple Underpass on the frames of her film.

Further behind Muchmore, across Main Street, Orville Nix captured the entire assassination sequence. It is the Nix's film that most clearly shows the presidential limousine coming to a brief halt with its brake lights on prior to the fatal head shot. Also in the Nix film are suspicious flashes of light on the Grassy Knoll, which is in the background of the movie. Are these muzzle flashes from rifles? To date, no sophisticated analysis has been conducted.

Nix was interviewed by an assassination researcher some years later and asked about the direction of the shots. He stated: "I thought it [shots] came from a fence between the Book Depository and the railroad tracks."

Nix also said that he later talked about the assassination with a friend, Forrest V. Sorrels, then head of the Dallas Secret Service office. He said at the time of the assassination, Sorrels, too, believed shots had come from the picket fence on the Grassy Knoll.

The Warren Commission never called Nix to testify, although he indicated he was willing to do so to the FBI, nor did the Commission have his film adequately analyzed. Only after some researchers claimed that photographs of a gunman on the Grassy Knoll were visible in the Nix film was it closely studied. In late 1966, Itek Corporation, which handles government contacts and is closely tied to the CIA, studied the film on the request of United Press International. Itek scientists concluded that the gunman figure was actually shadows from a tree branch.

It might be noted that even this conclusion is not totally accepted by suspicious researchers since, moments later, Nix panned back over the same area and the "shadow" figure is no longer visible. If the figure was merely shadows, it would seem that they should still be there in the later frames.

Also taking films on the south side of Elm Street was Beverly Oliver, who stood filming right behind Brehm and his son. From her vantage point, Oliver's movie would show not only the Grassy Knoll in the background, but also the Texas School Book Depository at the time of the shooting.

Despite the most intensive FBI investigation in history, federal authorities officially were unable to locate Oliver and, for years, she was known to researchers only as the "babushka lady" because of a triangular kerchief she wore on her head that day.

The Babushka Lady

Perhaps the reason that the federal authorities were unable to identify or locate the "babushka lady" is the explosive story she has to tell. Located only in recent years by assassination researchers, Beverly Oliver is now married to an evangelist, is a "re-born" Christian, and claims:

—Her film was taken and never returned by FBI agents.
—She was a friend of Jack Ruby and many of his employees.
—Ruby once introduced her to "Lee Oswald of the CIA."
—She knows that Ruby, Oswald, and David Ferrie were closely associated.
—She married a Dallas underworld character closely connected to Ruby and his associates who, in 1968, met briefly with Richard Nixon.

Oliver was nineteen years old at the time of the assassination and worked for the Colony Club, a strip-show club located next door to Jack Ruby's Carousel Club.

On November 22, she took a new Super-8 Yashica movie camera to Dealey Plaza and ended up just behind Charles Brehm on the grassy triangle just south of Elm Street.

Photos taken that day show that Oliver filmed the entire assassination as the motorcade moved down Elm. Undoubtedly her film would have included the windows of the Texas School Book Depository as shots were fired, clear pictures of the "umbrella man" and the "dark-complexioned man" on the north side of Elm, and the Grassy Knoll area at the time of the fatal head shot.

Oliver said on Monday following the assassination, she was approached by two men near the Colony Club. She believed they were either FBI or Secret Service agents. They said they knew she had taken film in Dealey Plaza and wanted to develop it for use as evidence. Oliver was told her film would be returned to her within ten days. She complied.

She never saw her film again. There was no mention of either her or her film in the Warren Report.

(Years later, when shown photographs of FBI agents involved in the assassination, Oliver identified Regis Kennedy as one of the men who took her film. Kennedy played a key role in the New Orleans aspect of the assassination investigation and came under suspicion in later years because of his insistence that reputed New Orleans Mafia Boss Carlos Marcello was merely a "tomato salesman.")

Not long after the assassination, Oliver married George McGann, a Dallas underworld character whose best man was R. D. Matthews. Matthews, a close friend of Jack Ruby, was described by the House Select Committee on Assassinations as "actively engaged in criminal activity since the 1940s."

The committee also developed evidence connecting Matthews with associates of Florida Mafia chieftain Santos Trafficante. Further, Matthews was a father figure to another Dallas thug, convicted murderer-for-hire Charles V. Harrelson.

Oliver told researcher Gary Shaw that during the presidential campaign of 1968, she and McGann had a two-hour conversation with candidate Richard Nixon in a Miami hotel. Why former President Nixon would meet with a well-known criminal is unclear, but in light of information that has been made public since the Watergate affair linking Nixon to organized crime figures, this story no longer seems so far-fetched.

In 1970, McGann was killed in a West Texas gangland-style slaying.

Oliver also said that two weeks prior to the Kennedy assassination, she was visiting in Ruby's club. There she met a man whom Ruby introduced as "Lee Oswald of the CIA." She later recognized Oswald when his picture was broadcast following the assassination.

She also said David Ferrie was in Ruby's club in late 1963, in fact, he was there so often, Oliver mistook Ferrie as an assistant manager of the Carousel Club.

A friend of Oliver's also knew of Oswald being in Ruby's club and spoke openly about it. According to Oliver, her friend disappeared and she "decided it would be in her best interests not to say anything." She remained quiet until the mid-1970s when she was located and interviewed by Shaw and, later, by Texas newsmen.

Although Beverly Oliver was the object of a secret briefing by HSCA attorney Robert Tannenbaum on March 17, 1977 (a transcript of this briefing was accidentally leaked to the newsmedia), there is no mention of her or her film in the Committee's report.

Obviously it is highly suspicious to researchers that one of the closest witnesses to the assassination and a witness who claimed to have been with both Ruby and Oswald prior to November 22, 1963, was never located or identified by federal authorities.

*   *   *

A few feet to the west of Oliver were two women—Mary Moorman, who took a photograph at the moment of the fatal head shot that may have pictured the gunman on the Grassy Knoll, and her friend, Jean Hill, who, like Willis, claims to have seen Jack Ruby in front of the Texas School Book Depository at the time of the shooting.

Ironically, neither Moorman nor Hill, probably the closest witnesses to the fatal head shot other than Brehm, were there to see Kennedy. Both women had come to Dealey Plaza to take pictures of a Dallas police motorcycle officer. Hill had just moved to Dallas from Oklahoma and Moorman was showing her the city, as well as trying to get her a date with the policeman, who was escorting the motorcade.

The women were stopped by a policeman at the corner of Elm and Houston and prevented from entering the grassy triangle in the plaza.

However, after some flirting, the officer allowed them through and they took up a position on the south side of Elm midway between Houston and the Triple Underpass.

Hill, who said she was getting in a "cops and robbers frame of mind" hoping to date the policeman, noticed a van with writing on it saying UNCLE JOE'S PAWN SHOP was allowed through the police lines and drove in front of the Depository and behind the concrete pergola on top of the Grassy Knoll. She thought this was suspicious since no one else had been allowed into that short street in front of the Depository. She jokingly said to Moorman: "Do you supposed there are murderers in that van?"

As the presidential motorcade turned onto Elm, Moorman began taking snapshots with a Polaroid camera and handing the photos to Hill, who applied fixative and put them in the pocket of her red-cloth raincoat.

Hill said Kennedy was smiling and waving to a crowd of people on the north side of Elm. She told this author:

I knew he'd never look our way because all the people were on the other side of the street, so I jumped out into the street and yelled, "Hey, Mr. President, look this way. We want to take your picture." As he began turning toward us, he was hit. Then a bullet hit his head and took the top off. Mary fell to the ground and shouted, "Get down, they're shooting!" But being young and dumb, I kept standing for a minute trying to see where the shots came from. It was eerie. Everything seemed frozen. I saw a man fire from behind the wooden fence. I saw a puff of smoke and some sort of movement on the Grassy Knoll where he was. [She later pinpointed this location as about fifteen feet north of the eastern corner of the wooden picket fence—the exact location of the figure discovered in Moorman's photograph.] Then I saw a man walking briskly in front of the Texas School Book Depository. He was the only person moving. Everybody else seemed to be frozen with shock. Because of my earlier thoughts, I became suspicious of this man and thought he might be connected with that truck I saw.

Hill said she heard between four and six shots altogether and then ran across the street in an effort to locate the men she had seen. She didn't find them, but she claimed that on the following Sunday morning she recognized TV photos of Jack Ruby as the man she had seen in front of the Depository. Minutes after the shooting, Hill said she was standing just west of the Depository when she was taken into custody by two men who identified themselves as Secret Service agents.

Meanwhile, a Dallas reporter had talked with Moorman and taken her to the sheriff's office. Here she was later joined by Hill who said their photographs had been taken by federal authorities.

Directly across Elm from Hill and Moorman was the Newman family. Bill Newman, his wife Gayle, and their two small children were standing west of the Stemmons Freeway sign directly below the Grassy Knoll. Newman told sheriff's officers:

> We were standing at the edge of the curb looking at the [president's] car as it was coming toward us and all of a sudden there was a noise, apparently a gunshot. . . . By [the] time he was directly in front of us . . . he was hit in the side of the head . . . Then we fell down on the grass as it seemed that we were in direct path of fire. . . . I thought the shot had come from the garden directly behind me, that was an elevation from where I was as I was right on the curb. I do not recall looking toward the Texas School Book Depository. I looked back in the vicinity of the garden.

A bit later, during a television interview, Newman was apparently the first person to speak of the Grassy Knoll. When asked where the shots had come from, Newman responded: ". . . back up on the, uh, knoll . . . what you call it."

Another witness was far above the crowd in Dealey Plaza. He had a bird's-eye view of the assassination. Jesse C. Price was the building engineer for the Union Terminal Annex, which is the southern counterpart of the Texas School Book Depository. The building stands at the corner of Houston and Commerce. Price said he went up on the roof to get "a better view of the caravan." While sitting on the edge of the building's roof overlooking the plaza, Price heard shots ". . . from by the . . . Triple Underpass."

In an affidavit signed that day, Price stated: "There was a volley of shots, I think five and then much later . . . another one." He said the shots seemed to come from "just behind the picket fence where it joins the underpass."

Price also said he saw a man, described as young, wearing a white dress shirt, no tie, and khaki-colored pants, running behind the wooden picket fence "towards the passenger cars on the railroad siding . . ." with something in his hand "which could have been a gun."

Price was never called to testify to the Warren Commission.

Despite the contradictions of evidence and testimony of those in Dealey Plaza, one fact seems inescapable—most of the witnesses in the crowd believed shots came from the Grassy Knoll.

However, it is certain that at least one or more shots were fired from the red-brick building at the northwest corner of Elm and Houston—the Texas School Book Depository.

> I thought at the time the shots . . . came from a point
> to the west of the building
> —Depository employee Dorothy Ann Garner

The Texas School Book Depository

Overlooking Dealey Plaza at its northeast corner is the seven-story red-brick building which in 1963 housed the Texas School Book Depository—which had almost nothing to do with Texas public schools.

The Depository was a private company that acted as an agent for a number of book publishers, furnishing office space and providing warehousing, inventorying, and shipping.

School systems would place orders with the publishers for textbooks and the publishers would send the orders along to the Depository, where about a half dozen young men acted as order fillers—locating and collecting the books as per each order.

On November 22, 1963, one of these order fillers was Lee Harvey Oswald.

Oswald and his wife, Marina, had separated at the time he left for New Orleans in the spring of 1963. They reunited in that Louisiana city, but in September, it was decided that since Marina was about to have a baby, she would return to Texas with a friend, Ruth Paine, while Oswald continued his activities—reportedly a trip to Mexico City.

When Oswald arrived back in Dallas on October 3, Marina was living in Irving, a suburban city west of Dallas. She was staying in the home of Michael and Ruth Paine—they, too, were separated at the time—and over the weekend of October 12–13, Oswald had arrived there to visit. During this weekend, Mrs. Paine said she gave Oswald, who had no driver's license, a driving lesson in her car.

About a week before, Oswald allegedly had returned from his trip to Mexico City. However, there continues to be much controversy concerning this journey.

On Monday, October 14, Mrs. Paine drove Oswald to Dallas, where he rented a room at 1026 N. Beckley Avenue from Mrs. A. C. Johnson for eight dollars a week. Oswald had filled out applications at the Texas Employment Commission and reportedly was looking for work.

That same day, Mrs. Paine mentioned Oswald—and the fact that he needed work because his wife was about to have another baby—to neighbors, including Mrs. Linnie Mae Randle. Mrs. Randle mentioned that Wesley Frazier, a younger brother who lived with her, worked at the Texas School Book Depository and that a job might be a available there. Marina Oswald, who was present at this gathering, reportedly urged Mrs.

Paine to check into the job possibility. Mrs. Paine agreed and called Depository superintendent Roy Truly that very day.

Before the Warren Commission, Truly recalled getting a call from a woman in Irving who said she knew a man whose wife was going to have a baby and needed a job. Truly agreed to talk with the man.

Mrs. Paine mentioned her call to Oswald later that evening and the next day, October 15, Oswald interviewed with Truly for the job. Oswald began working as temporary help the next day. Truly said the fall was their busiest time of year. Truly told the commission:

> Actually, [it was] the end of our fall rush—if it hadn't existed a week or two longer [than usual], or if we had not been using some of our regular boys putting down this plywood, we would not have had any need for Lee Oswald at that time, which is a tragic thing for me to think about.

Oswald was paid $1.25 an hour to fill book orders. Once he had been shown the procedures, he worked on his own. Truly described Oswald as "a bit above average" as an employee. Co-workers said Oswald was pleasant enough, but kept mostly to himself.

During his first week at work, Oswald got acquainted with Frazier and soon asked Frazier to drive him to Irving to visit his family. Frazier, who had only started working at the Depository the month before, said he was eager to make friends in Dallas. So Frazier agreed and, in fact, gave Oswald a ride to Irving every weekend prior to the assassination—except one when Oswald told Frazier he was staying in Dallas to take a driving test.

On Sunday, November 17, Marina Oswald had Mrs. Paine call a Dallas telephone number Oswald have given her. When she asked for Lee Oswald, Mrs. Paine was told there was nobody there by that name.

The next day, Oswald called the Paine home and angrily told Marina he was using a ficticious name at the Beckley Avenue address and not to call him there.

On Thursday morning, November 21, Oswald reportedly asked Frazier to drive him to Irving after work because he wanted to get some curtain rods to put in his Beckley Avenue apartment. According to this curtain rod story—only Frazier and his sister claimed to have seen Oswald with a package and their descriptions were inconsistent and vague—Frazier's sister saw Oswald the next morning place a paper-wrapped package in Frazier's car and Frazier noticed the packet as the pair drove to work. Frazier later said Oswald told him it was the curtain rods. He also said he would not be riding to Irving as usual, but he gave no explanation, according to Frazier. Frazier said once at the Depository, Oswald got out of the car and walked ahead into the building carrying his package with one end gripped in his right hand and the other tucked under his right arm, parallel to his body.

Most researchers who have studied the Mannlicher-Carcano rifle claim that, even disassembled, the barrel is too long to carry in this position.

When Frazier entered the building, he could not see Oswald and never knew what became of the "curtain rods."

When questioned by the authorities about what he had taken into the Depository, Oswald denied the curtain rod story, saying he only carried his lunch to work.

Jack Dougherty, another Depository employee whose Warren Commission testimony appears somewhat incoherent, nevertheless said: "Yes, I saw [Oswald] when he first came in the door . . . [Commission attorney Joseph Ball asked, "Did he have anything in his hands or arms?"] Well, not that I could see of."

Many Depository employees saw Oswald that morning. He appeared to be carrying on normal work duties, particularly on the sixth floor where he was assigned that day.

Frazier said he didn't notice Oswald after noon. He told the Warren Commission that as the presidential motorcade approached, he joined other Depository employees who were standing on the steps of the building facing Elm.

Minutes before the presidential motorcade arrived an odd incident occurred that has puzzled researchers for years.

The Distracting Seizure

About 12:15 P.M., a young man described as wearing green Army fatigues collapsed at 100 N. Houston, near the front door of the Texas School Book Depository. He apparently suffered some sort of seizure. Dallas policeman D. V. Harkness radioed the police dispatcher to send an ambulance to that location at 12:18 P.M. Radio logs showed that the ambulance, after picking up the victim, radioed, "We are enroute to Parkland." However, Parkland never recorded a patient registering at this time, and the entire incident seemed forgotten.

Despite the timing and proximity to the assassination, there is no mention of this incident in the Warren Commission Report and the FBI didn't get around to investigating until May 1964.

And this investigation took place only after a former employee of O'Neal Funeral Home called the Bureau's Dallas office to report the incident, adding the patient "disappeared" after arriving at Parkland. Apparently more curious about the incident than the FBI, this caller stated he "felt it possible that this incident may have been planned to distract attention from the shooting that was to follow."

The FBI detailed their investigation of the matter in Commission Document 1245, which was not included in the Warren Report or its twenty-six volumes.

Agents contacted the ambulance driver, Aubrey Rike, who said he had picked up a man "who was conscious and only slightly injured with a facial laceration." Rike added that in the confusion at Parkland, this man had simply walked off. Rike also said a Secret Service agent at Parkland told him to remain there "because they might need [his ambulance] to move the President to another location."

On May 26, Bureau agents located the "victim" after finding his name in O'Neal records. Jerry B. Belknap had paid his $12.50 ambulance charge back on December 2, 1963. Based on a later FBI report and an interview with Belknap by assassination researcher Jerry D. Rose, the following story came to light.

Belknap said he had suffered from seizures since being struck by a car while getting off a school bus as a child. He was standing near the Depository when he stepped back from the crowd and lost consciousness. He said the next thing he knew a policeman was standing over him.

Once at Parkland, he was sitting on a small table and, after asking for attention, was told to lie down. He said that a short time later there was a great rush of people who went into a different section of the emergency room.

He said a male attendant finally brought him some water and an aspirin, but that, after realizing that he was not going to get immediate treatment, he walked out without registering.

Outside, Belknap caught a bus back downtown, where he first learned of the assassination.

Intriguingly, Belknap told Rose that he had been interviewed by both Dallas police and the FBI within days of the assassination, months before the FBI's reported investigation in May 1964. He commented that the two police agencies apparently distrusted each other and both asked him the same questions. Asked about the June 1964 FBI report concerning him, Belknap offered the explanation that perhaps an agent had called him on the phone and simply confirmed the results of the earlier interview. Belknap also stated in 1983 that an investigator from "some committee in Washington" had contacted him within the past few years. However, if this investigator was with the House Select Committee on Assassinations, there is no reference to him in its report or attendant volumes.

Belknap died in 1986.

The entire "seizure" episode is strange and full of contradictions and coincidence—Belknap even reported seeing Jack Ruby once "acting like a bigshot" and he said he lost consciousness while the FBI report said he didn't.

Researchers view the incident as either a strangely convenient coincidence or as some as-yet-undiscovered plot to distract police and bystanders while assassins moved into position just prior to Kennedy's arrival in Dealey Plaza.

All agree that the incident deserves further investigation, particularly in light of the fact that the ambulance drivers who reportedly took Belknap to Parkland—Rike and Dennis McGuire—were the same ones who, while at

Parkland Hospital, loaded Kennedy's body into their ambulance for the return trip to Love Field that fateful afternoon.

*   *   *

At the time of the shooting, even persons within the Depository believed the shots came from elsewhere.

Steven F. Wilson was vice president of a school textbook-publishing company and had an office on the third floor of the Depository. Wilson told the FBI he watched the motorcade go by from a closed third-floor window but lost sight of the President when he "became obscured by some trees which are on Elm Street." He further stated:

> In a matter of ten seconds or less . . . I heard three shots . . . there was a greater space of time between the second and third shots than between the first and second. The three shots were fired within a matter of less than five seconds. The shots sounded to me like rifle shots. At that time, it seemed like the shots came from the west end of the building or from the colonnade located on Elm Street across from the west end of our building [the pergola on the Grassy Knoll]. The shots really did not sound like they came from above me.

Mrs. Elsie Dorman, who worked for Scott-Foresman Co. in the Depository, was in her fourth-floor office filming the presidential motorcade as it passed below. With her were fellow workers Dorothy Ann Garner, Victoria Adams, and Sandra Styles. Garner told the FBI: "I thought at the time the shots or reports came from a point to the west of the building."

Adams told the Warren Commission:

> . . . we heard a shot, and it was a pause, and then a second shot, and then a third shot. It sounded like a firecracker or a cannon at a football game, it seems as if it came from the right below [the area of the Grassy Knoll] rather than from the left above [the sixth-floor window].

Styles told Bureau agents she could not tell where the shots came from, but that she and Adams "left the office at this time, went down the back stairs, and left the building at the back door." Neither she nor Adams remarked about hearing anyone on the stairs moments after the shooting, although it was these same stairs that Oswald would have had to descend in time for his meeting with a Dallas policeman.

Wesley Frazier, who had driven Oswald to work that morning, was on the front steps of the Depository. He told the Warren Commission of his experience:

> . . . right after he [Kennedy] went by . . . I heard a sound and if you have ever been around motorcycles you know how they backfire, and so I thought one of them motorcycles backfired because right before his car

came down, now there were several of these motorcycle policemen, and they took off down toward the underpass down there . . . I heard two more of the same type, you know, sounds, and by that time people were running everywhere and falling down and screaming . . . I figured it was somebody shooting at President Kennedy . . . and from where I was standing it sounded like it was coming from down [at the] railroad tracks there. . . . So, we started back into the building and it wasn't but just a few minutes that there were a lot of police officers and so forth all over the building there.

Frazier said one of the Depository employees standing by him on the steps of the building as Kennedy passed by was Billy Lovelady, who was to become well-known to researchers as "the man in the doorway."

The Man In the Doorway

Associated Press photographer James Altgens snapped a picture seconds after Kennedy was first struck by a bullet. In the background of this photo a man can be seen standing in the west corner of the Texas School Book Depository's front doorway.

Soon after the assassination, many people—including his mother— suggested the man in the doorway looked amazingly like Lee Harvey Oswald. Obviously, if the man in the photo was Oswald, he could not have been firing a rifle on the sixth floor.

The Warren Commission, based primarily on testimony from Depository employees, concluded the man in the doorway was Billy Lovelady. After being interviewed at length by the FBI, Lovelady identified the man in the photo as himself.

Lovelady, who had worked at the Depository since 1961, was one of the men assigned to lay plywood flooring on the sixth floor that day. He said about 11:50 A.M. he and other employees stopped work so they could clean up before taking their lunch break. Lovelady said the workers took both of the Depository's two elevators and were racing each other down to ground level. He recalled hearing Oswald shout to them from the fifth floor to wait or to send an elevator back for him.

After buying a soft drink, Lovelady told the Warren Commission, he went out the main door and sat on the steps of the Depository to eat his lunch with some co-workers. Lovelady said he remained there as the motorcade passed by, then heard some noises: "I thought it was firecrackers or somebody celebrating the arrival of the President. It didn't occur to me at first what had happened until this Gloria [Calvary] came running up to us and told us the President had been shot."

Asked where he thought the shots came from, Lovelady replied: "Right there around that concrete little deal on that knoll."

In fact, Lovelady, along with his supervisor, joined the throng of people rushing toward the Grassy Knoll, but a short time later returned to the Depository, entering though a back door unchallenged.

William Shelley, Depository manager and Oswald's immediate supervisor, acknowledged that Lovelady was on the steps of the building when Kennedy passed by. He told the Warren Commission he heard "something sounded like it was a firecracker and a slight pause and then two more a little bit closer together." He said the shots sounded like they came from west of the Depository.

Shelley said Gloria Calvary ran up after about a minute and told them the President had been shot. Shelley and Lovelady both ran across a small street in front of the Depository to the north curb of Elm, then trotted down toward the railroad yards where police were converging. However, after seeing nothing remarkable, Shelley returned to the Depository.

Additionally, Wesley Frazier and a Depository clerk, Sarah Stanton, both signed statements averring they were with Shelley and Lovelady on the Depository steps at the time of the shooting.

That should have been the end of questions concerning the identity of the man in the doorway. However, on February 29, 1964, the FBI interviewed Lovelady and photographed him wearing a short-sleeved shirt with vertical stripes, totally unlike the dark, mottled long-sleeved shirt in the Altgens picture.

Later Lovelady explained the discrepancies in the shirts by telling CBS News: "Well, when the FBI took [my picture] in the shirt, I told them it wasn't the same shirt."

The shirt Lovelady was wearing that day—and subsequently tried to sell for a large sum of money—was a broad plaid, which he said was buttoned at the neck. The man in the doorway photo appears to be wearing a dark shirt open to the naval with a white T-shirt underneath, exactly what Oswald had on when arrested less than an hour and a half later.

And even Dallas police chief Jesse Curry seemed to continue to question the identity of the man in the doorway. In his 1969 book, Curry compared photos of the doorway man with Oswald and wrote: "The Warren Commission attempted to prove that the man was Billy N. Lovelady who worked at the depository."

The House Select Committee on Assassinations considered this issue in depth. They had anthropologists study the features of the man in the photograph and were given photographic analyses of the man's shirt. The Committee concluded: ". . . that it is highly improbable that the man in the doorway was Oswald and highly probable that he was Lovelady."

However, since Lovelady said he was sitting on the steps and the man in the photo is standing, peering around the edge of the front door alcove— and since the FBI did such a dismal job of proving it was Lovelady, some suspicion still lingers about the identity of the man in the doorway. Most researchers today are ready to concede that the man may have been Lovelady.

*   *   *

But if the man in the doorway was not Oswald, then where was he? Was he on the sixth floor firing the Mannlicher-Carcano just as two federal panels have concluded?

Despite the years of confident statements by federal authorities, no one has unquestionably placed Oswald on the sixth floor at the time of the shooting.

Dallas police chief Jesse Curry in later years admitted to newsmen: "We don't have any proof that Oswald fired the rifle, and never did. Nobody's yet been able to put him in that building with a gun in his hand."

Oswald told Dallas police he was eating lunch on the first floor of the Depository in what was called the "domino room" at the time of the assassination, and there is some evidence to back up his statement.

Bonnie Ray Williams was one of the Depository workers who were laying plywood flooring on the sixth floor that day. During the elevator race to the first floor a few minutes before noon, Williams said he heard Oswald call, "Guys, how about an elevator?" from either the fifth or sixth floor. Oswald also apparently asked them to send an elevator back up to him.

Williams told the Warren Commission he thought the others planned to gather on the sixth floor to watch the motorcade, so he returned there with his lunch, consisting of chicken, bread, and a bag of chips in a brown paper sack along with a soft drink. Williams said he sat on some boxes near a window facing out onto Elm street and ate his lunch. He said he saw no one else on the sixth floor, which was one large open area. However he noted stacks of book cartons here and there. Becoming impatient because no other workers had joined him, Williams threw down the remains of his lunch and left the sixth floor at "approximately 12:20." In a January 14, 1964, FBI report, agents quoted Williams as saying he left the sixth floor after about three minutes. However, Williams denied ever saying that and it is reasonable that he couldn't have eaten his lunch in only three minutes.

At the time, the news media made a great deal of comment about the chicken bones and lunch sack found on the sixth floor. Many people thought this proved that a cold and calculating assassin had patiently eaten his lunch while waiting for Kennedy to arrive.

Going down one of the elevators, Williams saw two other workers, Harold Norman and James Jarman, on the fifth floor and joined them to watch the motorcade. Two of these men were captured in a photograph taken that day as they leaned out of the fifth-floor window directly below the famous sixth-floor "sniper's" window to view the President.

Williams told the Warren Commission:

After the President's car had passed my window . . . [there] was a loud shot—first I thought they were saluting the President, somebody—even maybe a motorcycle backfire. The first shot—[then] there was two shots rather close together. The second and the third shot was closer together then the first shot . . . well, the first shot—I really did not pay any attention to it, because I did not know what was happening. The second shot, it sounded like it was right in the building . . . it even shook the building, the side we were on. Cement fell on my head. . . . Harold was sitting next to me and he said it came from right over our head. . . . My exact words were, "No bullshit?" And we jumped up. . . . I think Jarman, he—I think he moved before any of us. He moved towards us, and he said, "Man, someone is shooting at the President." And I think I said again, "No bullshit?" . . . Then we all kind of got excited. . . . But, we all decided we would run down to the west side of the building. . . . We saw policemen and people running, scared, running— there are some tracks on the west side of the building, railroad tracks. They were running towards that way. And we thought . . . we know the shots came from practically over our head. But . . . we assumed maybe somebody was down there.

Norman said he and Jarman had eaten lunch in the domino room on the first floor, then walked out the front door where they saw other Depository employees, including Lovelady, sitting on the steps.

As the motorcade approached, they took an elevator to the fifth floor and got seated in a southeast corner window, where they were joined by Williams moments later. Norman said he heard three loud shots and "I could also hear something sounded like shell hulls hitting the floor . . ." Later, he said he also had heard the sound of the bolt working on a rifle above them.

After the three men ran to the west window and saw police combing the railroad yards, Norman said he and Jarman tried to leave the Depository, but were turned back by police officers.

Jarman told the same story but said he didn't hear the shells hit the floor or hear the sound of the rifle bolt. He did say that when the three men ran to the Depository's west window: ". . . I saw policemen and the secret agents, the FBI men, searching the boxcar yard and the passenger train and things like that."

One thing that has always puzzled assassination researchers is Williams's statement of being on the sixth floor until "approximately 12:20" then Norman's claim of hearing ejecting shell casings and the working of the rifle bolt.

It has been established that the plywood floor in the Depository was thin and full of cracks, which accounts for the plaster dust that fell on Williams's head. It could also account for Norman hearing shell casings hit the floor and even the working of the rifle bolt—except that apparently none of the three men on the floor below heard anyone moving above them.

How could they have heard shells dropping and a rifle bolt operating and not heard movement above them in the minutes before the shooting? As confirmed by photographs taken at the time and the testimony of witnesses below, someone constructed a "sniper's nest" of book cartons in the minutes preceding the shooting.

Yet Williams, Norman, and Jarman heard nothing?

Obviously, there was someone on the sixth floor, but was it Oswald?

Oswald told police he had followed the workers down to the first floor and had eaten lunch in the domino room on the Depository's first floor.

Oswald told interrogators he recalled two black employees walking through the room while he was there. He said he thought one was named "Junior" and the other was short.

Jarman's nickname was "Junior" and Norman was indeed short. Norman, in commission testimony, said he ate his lunch in the domino room, adding: "I can't remember who ate in the . . . domino room with me . . . I think there was somebody else in there . . ."

Jarman tells of helping Oswald correct a book order earlier that morning, then talking with him again on the first floor. Then at lunch time, Jarman said he bought a soft drink and returned to where he had been sitting by a first-floor window "where Oswald and I was talking." His testimony is confusing and appears incomplete. It was not helped by any clarifying questions from the Warren Commission attorney.

But if Oswald was not in the first-floor domino room as he said, how could he have noted the presence of two men and described Norman and Jarman?

Bill Shelley, Oswald's supervisor, told the commission he saw Oswald near a telephone on the first floor about ten minutes till noon.

Carolyn Arnold, secretary to the Depository's vice president, was quoted in an FBI report saying "she thought she caught a fleeting glimpse of Lee Harvey Oswald standing in the [first floor] hallway" as she left the building to watch the motorcade. In 1978, Arnold told the *Dallas Morning News* she had been misquoted by the FBI. After reading over her statements of 1963, she stated:

> That is completely foreign to me. [The FBI account] would have forced me to have been turning back around to the building when, in fact, I was trying to watch the parade. Why would I be looking back inside the building? That doesn't make any sense to me.

After telling how Oswald had come to her office often for change, she gave this account of the incident:

> About a quarter of an hour before the assassination . . . about 12:15, it may have been later . . . I went to the lunchroom on the second floor for a moment . . . Oswald was sitting in one of the booth seats on the right-hand side of the room as you go in. He was alone as usual and

appeared to be having lunch. I did not speak to him but I recognized him clearly.

While it is still possible that Oswald could have raced upstairs in time to be in the "sniper's" window by 12:30 P.M., recall that the Arnold Rowlands saw two men in the sixth-floor window, one with a rifle, at 12:15. This time can be fixed with confidence because Rowland reported seeing the man with the gun just as a nearby police radio announced that the presidential motorcade was approaching Cedar Springs Road. Police dispatcher's records showed the motorcade passed Cedar Springs between 12:15 and 12:16 P.M.

The Warren Commission concluded that Oswald stayed on the sixth floor after he was seen by the elevator racers about 11:55 A.M. and remained there to commit the assassination.

As can be seen, there is quite credible evidence that he was exactly where he said he was—in the first-floor break or domino room—at the time of the shooting.

Oswald then apparently walked to the Depository's second-floor lunchroom to buy a soft drink. It was here that a Dallas policeman encountered Oswald less than ninety seconds after the final shot was fired in the assassination.

The Oswald Encounter

Since at 12:30 P.M. November 22, 1963, the presidential motorcade was running approximately five minutes behind schedule—probably due to the two unscheduled stops along the way ordered by Kennedy—it is unbelievable that an assassin would leisurely wait in the Depository domino room until 12:15 to make his move to the sixth floor.

It is equally unbelievable that, having committed the "crime of the century" an assassin could make his way down five flights of stairs and be standing calmly when a policeman rushed into the lunchroom.

Understand that the first floor of the Texas School Book Depository is slightly above ground level. One entered the building by walking up a flight of outside steps, then an additional flight of stairs led to the second floor. It was here that an employees' lunchroom was located to the rear of the building away from Elm Street.

Dallas motorcycle patrolman Marrion Baker rushed to the Depository after seeing pigeons fly off the building's roof at the sound of the first shots. In a later reenactment for the Warren Commission, it took Baker only fifteen seconds to park his cycle and race up the front steps of the Depository.

Baker told the Warren Commission: "I had it in mind that the shots came from the top of this building . . ." He continued:

As I entered this lobby there were people going in as I entered. And I asked . . . where the stairs or elevator was, and this man, Mr. Truly, spoke up and says to me . . . "I'm the building manager. Follow me, officer, and I will show you." So we immediately went out through the second set of doors, and we ran into the swinging door.

Depository superintendent Roy Truly had followed Baker into the building. He quickly went to the building's elevators, but could not bring them down since someone had left them locked in position on an upper floor. Truly told the commission:

. . . those elevators . . . were both on the fifth floor, they were both even. And I tried to get one of them . . . it would have been impossible for [Oswald] to have come down either one of those elevators after the assassination. He had to use the stairway as his only way of getting down—since we did see the elevators in those positions.

Truly yelled, "Bring that elevator down here!" to no avail and Baker said, "Let's take the stairs." Moving up the stairs trailing Truly, Baker said he noticed a man walking away from him through a glass window in a door near the rear second-floor landing. With drawn pistol, Baker confronted the man and ordered him to come to him. In a handwritten report to the FBI on November 23, Baker stated: "On the second floor where the lunchroom is located, I saw a man standing in the lunchroom drinking a Coke." However, the words "drinking a Coke" were scratched out in this report and there was no reference to the Coke in his Warren Commission testimony.

Truly said the man, whom he recognized as Oswald, "didn't seem to be excited or overly afraid." He told the Warren Commission he noticed nothing in Oswald's hands, but this was months later, after many discussions with federal authorities.

Baker turned to Truly and asked if the man was an employee and Truly replied he was. Baker then turned and continued his race for the roof.

Oswald apparently simply sauntered down the steps and out the front door of the Depository.

Mrs. Robert Reid, clerical supervisor at the Depository, was standing with Depository officials in front of the building at the time shots were fired. She then turned and ran into the building to her second-floor office. She told the Warren Commission:

. . . I looked up and Oswald was coming in the back door to the office. I met him by the time I passed my desk several feet and I told him, "Oh, the President's been shot, but maybe they didn't hit him." He mumbled something to me, I kept walking, he did too. I didn't pay any attention to what he said because I had no thoughts of anything of him having any connection with it at all because he was very calm. He had gotten a Coke and was holding it in his hands . . . The only time I had seen him in the office was to come and get change and he already had a Coke in his hand so he didn't come for change . . .

Like Baker, Mrs. Reid reenacted her movements for the Warren Commission on March 20, 1964. She said it took approximately two minutes to move the distance from where she heard the final shot to the point she met Oswald.

As can be seen, the issue of the Coke becomes critical here.

It strains one's imagination to believe that anyone could fire on the president of the United States, then run to the opposite corner of the sixth floor—where the rifle was discovered a short time later—stash the weapon, race down five flights of stairs, and show no sign of exertion or anxiety when confronted by a policeman with a drawn pistol.

This scenario becomes absurd if the purchase of a Coke from a vending machine with its attendant fumbling for pocket change is thrown into the time frame.

Baker told the FBI the next day that Oswald was "drinking a Coke" when he saw him, but then deleted any reference to the drink in his Warren Commission testimony. Truly, months later, said he did not notice anything in Oswald's hands. But Reid said Oswald was holding a Coke when she saw him seconds after his encounter with Baker.

Even the accused assassin had something to say about the soft drink. In Appendix XI of the Warren Report, an FBI report tells of Oswald statements to police while in custody. According to this report:

Oswald stated that on November 22, 1963, at the time of the search of the Texas School Book Depository building by Dallas police officers, he was on the second floor of said building, having just purchased a Coca-Cola from the soft drink machine, at which time a police officer came into the room with pistol drawn and asked him if he worked there.

This Coke issue is a small one, but one that is indicative of the loopholes riddling the official story of the assassination.

The issue of Oswald's documented presence in the Depository's lunchroom, with or without Coke, is further complicated by the statements of a Dallas deputy district court clerk. Lillian Mooneyham, clerk of the 95th District Court, told the FBI that she watched the motorcade move west on Main from windows in the Dallas Criminal Courts Building, then ran with two others to the west side of the building. She heard an initial shot, which she took to be a firecracker, followed by a "slight pause and then two more shots were discharged, the second and third shots sounding closer

together." According to an FBI report of January 10, 1964, Mrs.
Mooneyham said:

"I left Judge [Henry] King's courtroom and went to the office of Judge
Julian C. Hyer . . . where I continued to observe the happenings from
Judge Hyer's window. . . ."

Mrs. Mooneyham estimated that it was about four and a half to five
minutes following the shots fired by the assassin, that she looked up
towards the sixth floor of the TSBD and observed the figure of a man
standing in the sixth floor window behind some cardboard boxes. This
man appeared to Mrs. Mooneyham to be looking out of the window, however, the man was not close up to the window but was standing slightly
back from it, so that Mrs. Mooneyham could not make out his features. . . .

Adding support to Mrs. Mooneyham's account of a man standing in the
"sniper's nest" window minutes after the shooting are photographs taken
about that time by military intelligence agent James Powell and news
photographer Tom Dillard.

Dillard, who was riding in the motorcade, said he took a picture of the
Depository façade seconds after the last shot was fired. Powell estimated
his picture was made about thirty seconds after the final shot.

A comparison with photos taken just prior to the shooting led photographic experts of the House Select Committee on Assassinations to
conclude: "There is an apparent rearranging of boxes within two minutes
after the last shot was fired at President Kennedy." Obviously, Oswald
could not have been in the Depository lunchroom meeting Baker and Truly
while arranging boxes on the sixth floor at the same time.

Needless to say, Mrs. Mooneyham was never called as a witness before
the Warren Commission. Her credible testimony remains buried in the
Commission's twenty-six volumes.

A further point here is that several Depository employees, including
Billy Lovelady and William Shelley, were on or about the back stairway of
the building just after the assassination. No one heard footsteps or saw
Oswald racing down the five flights of stairs for his encounter with Baker
and Truly.

Recall that Victoria Adams and Sandra Styles, who worked for Scott-
Foresman and Company in the Depository, told the FBI they both ran from
the building down the back stairway after viewing the assassination from
their fourth-floor office window. Neither encountered Oswald on the stairway or remarked of hearing footsteps.

Did Oswald indeed fire the fatal shots, then stop to arrange his box
supports, then race to the opposite end of the Depository's sixth floor
where he reportedly stashed his rifle, then race silently down five flights of
stairs to be discovered calmly standing by a soft drink machine by Baker
and Truly less than two minutes later?

Or was it someone else who fired, then arranged a "sniper's nest" before quietly slipping out the rear of the Depository about the time Oswald was encountering Baker and Truly?

*   *   *

Also on the steps of the Depository was Joe R. Molina, the company's credit manager. Like most everyone else, Molina thought the shots came from west of the building.

In 1964, Molina specifically asked to testify to the Warren Commission because of what happened to him after the assassination. Molina said about 1:30 A.M. on the Saturday following the assassination, he and his family were awakened by Dallas police, who began searching his home. Molina told the commission: ". . . they were looking for something . . . they sort of wanted to tie me up with this case in some way or another and they thought that I was implicated."

He said he was questioned about his membership in G.I. Forum, a predominately Hispanic group actively working to help veterans, and was told to report to Dallas Police Headquarters later that day. Molina was kept waiting at the police station most of the day, then learned that his name had been given to the news media by Chief Curry, who described Molina as someone associated with "persons of subversive background."

Unable to get a retraction from the Dallas police, Molina asked to testify to the Warren Commission in an attempt to clear his name. But the damage had already been done.

On December 13, twenty-one days after the assassination, Molina was told that the Depository's credit system was to be automated and that he was to be replaced. He said the action came as no real surprise because the company had been receiving hate mail and phone calls accusing it of hiring communists.

Despite assurances from Depository officials that Molina's firing was not connected to the events of the assassination, it appears obvious that Joe Molina, too, became one of its victims.

Many Depository employees went outside to view the motorcade. Most of them signed reports to the FBI during March 1964. Oddly, the reports all begin to sound alike in that the agents apparently never asked critical questions such as "Where did shots come from?" "How many shots?" or "Did you see the effect of any shot?"

As the evidence quickly piled up against Oswald and the Depository became the center of the investigation, the authorities, news media, and public soon forgot the initial focus of attention in Dealey Plaza—the Triple Underpass.

I saw something hit the pavement to the left rear of the car.
—Assassination witness Royce G. Skelton

The Triple Underpass

On the west side of Dealey Plaza is a large railroad bridge that spans the three main downtown Dallas traffic arteries of Commerce, Main, and Elm Streets.

Since all three streets converge under this concrete bridge, it quickly became known as the Triple Underpass. To the east of the underpass is Dealey Plaza and downtown Dallas, while on the west are several roads leading to freeway systems and an industrial area.

Atop the east side of the Triple Underpass, one has a panoramic view of Dealey Plaza from a position about fifteen feet in the air.

This was the position of about a dozen men on November 22, 1963, as they stood along the eastern edge of the underpass to watch the presidential motorcade approach and pass beneath them.

Dallas policeman J. W. Foster was one of two police officers assigned as security guards atop the Triple Underpass. His orders were to prevent any "unauthorized" personnel from standing on the railroad bridge when Kennedy passed.

Foster had allowed some railroad workers, who had been repairing rails, to remain on the underpass after checking their identity. Since the bridge actually was railroad property and it was railway workers who walked over to the eastern banister to view the motorocade, he did not believe they fell into the "unauthorized" category.

He told the Warren Commission he had earlier prevented some people from standing on the bridge—one of these was AP photographer James Altgens.

Foster said as the motorcade approached he was standing just behind the line of railway workers, about ten or eleven of them, when he heard what sounded like a large firecracker. He moved up to the concrete railing to get a better view. He said he saw: ". . . the President slump over in the car, and his head looked just like it blew up."

From his vantage point—above and directly in front of the car—this trained and experienced police officer may have been one of the best witnesses to what actually happened at the time of the shooting. However, neither in his report of December 4, 1963, nor in his April 9, 1964, testimony to the Warren Commission was he asked to describe in detail what he saw.

Warren Commission lawyer Joseph Ball did ask Foster his opinion as to the source of the shots and Foster replied: "It came from back in toward the corner of Elm and Houston Streets [the location of the Texas School Book Depository]."

Foster said he ran from the underpass toward the Depository building, where he watched the rear exits until a sergeant came and told him to check out railroad cars in the nearby switching yard. However, Foster said he went instead to the front of the Depository and told a supervisor where he was when shots were fired, then "moved to—down the roadway there, down to see if I could find where any of the shots hit."

He was successful. Foster told the Commission he "found where one shot had hit the turf . . .''

Foster said he found where a bullet had struck the earth just beside a manhole cover on the south side of Elm Street. Foster remained at this location for a time until the evidence was taken away by an unidentified man.

The spot where Foster found a tear in the grass was near where witness Jean Hill was standing at the time of the assassination. Shortly after the shooting, she was questioned by Secret Service agents, one of whom asked her if she saw a bullet land near her feet.

Foster's counterpart on the west side of the Triple Underpass was Officer J. C. White. White said he was approximately in the middle of the underpass when the motorcade passed below, but that he didn't see or hear anything because a "big long freight train" was moving north between him and Dealey Plaza. Oddly, close scrutiny of films and photographs taken that day show no such freight train moving at that time.

But if the stories of the two Dallas policemen on top of the underpass seem strangely incomplete and sketchy, this was not the case of the railroad workers standing over the motorcade. These workers not only heard shots from their left, the direction of the infamous Grassy Knoll, but also saw smoke drift out from under the trees lining the knoll.

Smoke on the Grassy Knoll

Sam M. Holland, a track and signal supervisor for the Union Terminal Railroad Company, told the Warren Commission he went to the top of the Triple Underpass about 11:45 A.M. that day. He said there were two Dallas policemen and ". . . a plainclothes detective, or FBI agent or something like that . . ." there and that he assisted in indentifying the railroad employees. He said by the time the motorcade arrived, other people were lining the Triple Underpass, but that the police were checking identification and sending them away.

By the time the presidential limousine was approaching the underpass, Holland was standing just in front of Officer Foster. He told the commission:

And the motorcade was coming down in this fashion, and the President was waving to the people on this [north] side [of Elm]. . . . the first report that I heard . . . was pretty loud . . . and the car traveled a few yards and Governor Connally turned in this fashion, like that, with his hand out and . . . another report rang out and he slumped down in his seat . . . [then Kennedy] was hit again along . . . in here. . . . I observed it. It knocked him completely down on the floor . . . just slumped completely over . . . I heard a third report and I counted four shots . . . There was a shot, a report. I don't know whether it was a shot. I can't say that. And a puff of smoke came out about six or eight feet above the ground right out from under those trees.

Holland said the first two or three shots seemed to come from "the upper part of the street," followed by others of "different sounds, different reports."
In a 1966 filmed interview, Holland was even more specific:

I looked over to where I thought the shot came from and I saw a puff of smoke still lingering under the trees in front of the wooden fence. The report sounded like it came from behind the wooden fence. . . . I know where the third shot came from—behind the picket fence. There's no doubt whatsoever in my mind.

Due to Holland's credibility and clear description of what he saw, the Warren Commission Report accurately stated:

According to S. M. Holland, there were four shots which sounded as though they came from the trees on the north side of Elm Street where he saw a puff of smoke.

Having mentioned the smoke in the trees, the report went on to conclude:

In contrast to the testimony of the witnesses who heard and observed shots fired from the Depository, the Commission's investigation has disclosed no credible evidence that any shots were fired from anywhere else.

The clear implication by the Warren Report is that Holland was mistaken in believing shots came from behind the wooden picket fence. However, the testimony of the other railroad workers on the Triple Underpass—none of whom were asked to give testimony to the Warren Commission—corroborated Holland's version of the assassination. The only account of what they saw is in FBI reports made during March 1964. These reports are sketchy and seem very incomplete in view of the questions that these men should obviously have been asked.

James L. Simmons, a Union Terminal car inspector, was in the group on the Triple Underpass. In his FBI report, it merely states:

. . . when the President's car started down Elm Street he heard three shots ring out. President Kennedy slumped down in his seat and appeared to have been hit by a bullet. . . . Simmons said he thought he saw exhaust fumes of smoke near the embankment in front of the Texas School Book Depository building.

During a 1966 filmed interview, Simmons's account is much clearer:

As the President's limousine rounded the curve on Elm Street, there was a loud explosion . . . It sounded like it came from the left and in front of us, towards the wooden fence. And there was a puff of smoke that came from underneath the trees on the embankment directly in front of the wooden fence. . . . I was talking to Patrolman Foster at the time and as soon as we heard the shots, we ran around to [behind] the picket fence . . . There was no one there but there were footprints in the mud around the fence and footprints on the two-by-four railing on the fence . . .

Railroad workers who also saw smoke off to their left included Nolan H. Potter, Richard C. Dodd, and Clemon E. Johnson.

Simmons was quoted in his FBI report as seeing smoke near the Depository, yet he plainly stated later that it was in front of the Grassy Knoll fence. There is no mention of smoke in Dodd's FBI report, yet in a later filmed interview, he plainly stated: "Smoke came from behind the hedge on the north side of the plaza."

In 1966 interviews in Dallas, both Walter L. Winborn and Thomas J. Murphy—who were among the railroad workers on the Triple Underpass—confirmed seeing smoke in the trees on the Grassy Knoll.

It would be most interesting to talk to the other people who stood on the Triple Underpass that day. Perhaps they, too, saw the smoke, but this sighting was left out of their reports—if any report was made.

Further corroboration of the smoke came well into the 1980s, when a frame from TV news film was analyzed by assassination researchers. NBC photographer Dave Weigman was riding in the seventh car in the motorcade. Hearing shots, Weigman started filming even before the firing stopped. He then jumped out of the convertible and ran up the Grassy Knoll with his camera still operating. Because of all this motion, his blurred and jerky film was overlooked as assassination evidence until recently. However, in one clear frame, which depicts the presidential limousine just entering the Triple Underpass, a puff of smoke is clearly visible hanging in front of trees on the knoll—exactly where Holland and the other railroad workers claimed to have seen it.

It has been well established that there was no other natural source of smoke in that area that day. FBI reports attempted to show that it may have come from police motorcycles but none were on the knoll at the time.

Warren Commission apologists for years have tried to argue that modern rifles do not smoke. This is an error, since a recently oiled rifle or deficient ammunition certainly can cause white smoke during firing. This was made clear to this author in the summer of 1978 when the House Select Committee on Assassinations fired rifles in Dealey Plaza in connection with their acoustical studies. Visible puffs of smoke were common.

And considering the slightly gusting breeze from the north that day, the idea that smoke drifted over Elm Street from the knoll is most plausible. It is now obvious that many people that day saw this puff of smoke drifting down from the knoll—also recall those witnesses who said they smelled gunpowder in the lower end of Dealey Plaza. However, it is equally obvious that the authorities, particularly the FBI and the Warren Commission, did not want to hear about it.

Sam Holland also was supported in his testimony that shots came from the knoll by fellow railroad workers Richard Dodd, James Simmons, and Thomas J. Murphy.

Another railroad worker, Royce G. Skelton, supported the statements of Sheriff Decker and others who saw one of the first bullets strike the pavement near Kennedy's car.

In an affidavit signed the day of the assassination, Skelton stated:

I was standing on top of the train trestle where it crosses Elm Street with Austin Miller. We saw the motorcade come around the corner and I heard something which I thought was fireworks. I saw something hit the pavement at the left rear of the [President's] car, then the car got in the right-hand lane and I heard two more shots. I heard a woman [say] "Oh no" or something and grab a man inside the car. I then heard another shot and saw the bullet hit the pavement. The concrete was knocked to the south away from the car. It hit the pavement in the left or center lane . . .

Austin Miller, standing next to Skelton on the Triple Underpass, also mentioned this errant bullet in his affidavit that day. Miller stated:

. . . I saw a convertible automobile turn west on Elm off Houston Street. It had [proceeded] about halfway from Houston Street to the Underpass when I heard what sounded like a shot [then in] a short second two more sharp reports . . . One shot apparently hit the street past the car. I saw something which I thought was smoke or steam coming from a group of trees north of Elm off the railroad tracks.

Dallas policeman Earle Brown was standing on the catwalk of a railroad bridge crossing over Stemmons Freeway located just north of the Triple

Underpass. Because of his location, Brown said he was unable to get a clear view of the motorcade. He told the Warren Commission: ". . . actually, the first I noticed the car was when it stopped . . . after it made the turn [onto Elm Street] and when the shots were fired, it stopped."

Commission attorney Joseph Ball asked, "Did it come to a complete stop?" Brown replied: "That I couldn't swear to." "It appeared to be slowed down some," offered Ball, encouraging a subtle change in Brown's testimony. Brown responded: "Yes, it slowed down."

Brown said the first indication to him that something was wrong was when a large flock of pigeons suddenly flew up from a grassy low area between him and the Underpass. He said: ". . . they heard the shots before we did because I saw them flying up . . . then I heard these shots and then I smelled this gunpowder . . . It come on . . . maybe a couple of minutes later."

Brown said the gunpowder smell seemed to come from the direction of the Depository. However, the Grassy Knoll was almost in a direct line between the officer and the Depository.

*   *   *

But the one assassination witness who singlehandedly caused more concern within the 1963–64 federal investigation than anyone else was Jim Tague, who was the third man wounded in Dealey Plaza on November 22, 1963.

The Third Wounded Man

James Thomas Tague, like Jean Hill and Mary Moorman, was not planning to see Kennedy. Shortly after noon that day, he had driven downtown to take a girlfriend (later his wife) to lunch.

As Tague drove his car east on Commerce Street, he found himself stopped in the traffic that was halted at Houston Street due to the arrival of the presidential motorcade. The hood of his car was just poking out the east side of the Triple Underpass. Tague got out of his car and stood by the underpass on a small concrete median separating Commerce and Main to watch the motorcade.

In an interview with this author, Tague said when the shots were fired, he immediately thought, "Who's the nut throwing firecrackers?" However, after hearing more shots, he realized what was happening and ducked behind the corner of the underpass. He said the shots were coming from the area of the Grassy Knoll "behind the concrete monument."

Tague was watching a policeman run up the Grassy Knoll with a drawn pistol when another policeman came up to him asking, "What happened?" "I don't know," mumbled the shocked Tague.

Dallas motorcycle patrolman Clyde A. Haygood had been riding back in the motorcade on Main Street approaching Main when he heard a shot, then a pause followed by two shots close together. He gunned his three-wheeled motorcycle up on Houston and turned on Elm in time to see people pointing toward the Grassy Knoll and the railroad yards.

Haygood said he got off his cycle on Elm Street just below the Grassy Knoll and went up into the railroad yards but saw nothing suspicious despite quite a number of people in the area. He said he returned to his motorcycle after speaking to a man he believed to be a railroad detective.

Haygood told the Warren Commission:

At that time some people came up and started talking to me as to the shooting . . . one came up . . . and said he had gotten hit by a piece of concrete or something, and he did have a slight cut on his right cheek, upper portion of his cheek just to the right of his nose.

Haygood said just then another witness came up and told him the first shot had come from the Texas School Book Depository. Using the call number 142, Haygood radioed the police dispatcher and asked that the Depository be sealed off. He also mentioned a man who had been wounded by flying concrete.

Tague and the policeman walked into the plaza a bit and encountered a man, who was sobbing, "His head exploded!" This man apparently was Charles Brehm.

Moments later Deputy Sheriff Eddy Walthers arrived and, pointing to Tague, said, "You've got blood on your face."

In his report that day, Walthers, who was standing with the other deputies in front of the Sheriff's Office, stated:

. . . I immediately went to the Triple Underpass on Elm Street in an effort to locate possible marks left by stray bullets. While I was looking for possible marks, some unknown person stated to me that something had hit his face while he was parked on Main Street . . . Upon examining the curb and pavement in this vicinity I found where a bullet had splattered on the top edge of the curb on Main Street . . . Due to the fact that the projectile struck so near the underpass, it was, in my opinion, probably the last shot that was fired and had apparently went high and above the President's car.

Tague said he called the Dallas FBI office later that afternoon, to tell them about the bullet striking the curb, but "they didn't want my testimony about the stray bullet." Apparently no one else wanted to hear about the extraneous bullet either. There was no mention of the incident in the news accounts at the time nor was there any investigation of the bullet mark on the curb until the summer of 1964.

During late 1963 and early 1964, it was widely reported that the first shot struck Kennedy in the back, the second bullet hit Connally, and the third was the fatal head shot. This was a consistent theory of three bullets.

Tague's story of yet another bullet was totally inconsistent with the lone-assassin/three-shot theory being formulated by the Warren Commission, which initially appears to have been prepared to ignore both Tague and the bullet mark on the curb.

In fact, there may have been an effort to eliminate the evidence. In late May 1964, about a month before the Warren Commission finally talked to Tague, the car salesman took a camera to Dealey Plaza to photograph the mark on the curb. He was surprised to find that it was not there. Only faint traces of the bullet mark were found. Tague said it looked as if someone had tried to repair the curb.

Apparently it was a letter from an assistant U.S. attorney in Dallas that finally prompted the Warren Commission to confront the Tague wounding. Martha Jo Stroud mailed a letter to Commission general counsel J. Lee Rankin on June 9, 1964. In the letter was the comment:

I am enclosing a photograph made by Tom Dillard of the *Dallas Morning News*. It is a shot of the curb which was taken shortly after the assassination on November 22, 1963. When I talked to Mr. Dillard yesterday he indicated he did not know whether the photograph was material. He did say, however, that he examined the curb when the photo was taken and that it looked like a piece of lead had struck it.

Faced with this official notification of the curb shot, the Commission was stirred to action. On July 7, 1964, the Warren Commission asked the FBI to look into the matter. In an FBI document dated July 17, the FBI stated: "The area on the curb [where the bullet or fragment hit] was carefully checked and it was ascertained there was no nick in the curb in the checked area, nor was any mark observed."

The disappearance of a mark that had been plainly seen eight months earlier was explained in this document:

It should be noted that, since this mark was observed on November 22, 1963, there have been numerous rains, which could have possibly washed away such a mark and also that the area is cleaned by a street cleaning machine about once a week, which could also wash away any such mark.

But if the FBI could ignore the mark, the Commission could not. Since both a Dallas policeman and a sheriff's deputy had mentioned Tague in their reports, although not by name, and after the arrival of Stroud's letter, his story could no longer be ignored.

On July 23, 1964, Tague finally was deposed in Dallas by Commission attorney Wesley Liebeler.

Following Tague's testimony, the Commission again asked the Bureau to investigate the matter. This time the FBI removed the piece of curb in question and took it to Washington for analysis. In an August 12, 1964, report signed by J. Edgar Hoover, it was stated:

> Small foreign metal smears were found adhering to the curbing section within the area of the mark. These metal smears were spectrographically determined to be essentially lead with a trace of antimony. No copper was found. The lead could have originated from the lead core of a mutilated metal-jacketed bullet such as the type of bullet loaded into 6.5 millimeter Mannlicher-Carcano cartridges or from some other source having the same composition . . . The absence of copper precludes the possibility that the mark on the curbing section was made by an unmutilated military-type full metal-jacketed bullet . . . Further, the damage to the curbing would have been much more extensive if a rifle bullet had struck the curbing without first having struck some other object. Therefore, this mark could not have been made by the first impact of a high-velocity bullet.

So the FBI, which at first had stated no bullet hit the curb now said the mark had to have been made by a rifle bullet. If the FBI is correct—and keep in mind the many instances of misinformation and omission by the Bureau regarding assassination evidence—the mark on the curb could only have been made by the lead fragment of a bullet.

Yet the only one that could have lost such an amount of lead is the final head shot and that was at a location more than 200 feet away, a considerable distance for a small fragment to travel and still impact the curb as described.

If the bullet mark on the curb was a miss, it was an incredible miss. If the shot that struck the Main Street curb came from the Texas School Book Depository's sixth floor, it must have missed Kennedy by thirty-three feet in the air and twenty-one feet to the right. Such a miss is hardly compatible with the claim that Oswald was able to hit home with two out of three shots from his inefficient rifle aiming at a target moving laterally and away from him at about two hundred yards.

Another possibility, never considered by the Warren Commission, was that the mark was made by a lead bullet without copper jacketing. But of course, this would indicate different ammunition and perhaps a different rifle from the one allegedly used by Oswald. Or perhaps the curb was hit by a large fragment of bullet that had already struck the street (recall the witnesses who saw one do just that) and had separated from the copper jacket.

Whatever the truth of the curb bullet, and despite the attempt to ignore this evidence, the matter of the wounding of Tague was finally acknowledged and the Warren Commission was compelled to construct a scenario of the assassination that included the "single-bullet theory," a theory that has not been accepted by a majority of Americans.

*   *   *

Despite immediate attempts to establish the Texas School Book Depository as the sole location from which shots were fired, public attention, both in 1963 and even today, continued to be drawn to the wooded area to the west of the Depository that has become known as the Grassy Knoll.

[Policemen were] running right behind me . . . in the line of the shooting.
—Assassination witness Abraham Zapruder

The Grassy Knoll

Probably no small section of land in the United States has been the object of more controversy than that small portion of Dealey Plaza known as the Grassy Knoll.

While Elm Street and two large grassy areas of Dealey Plaza dip down approximately 24 feet as one travels the 495 feet from Houston Street on the east, the Grassy Knoll remains at ground level.

There actually are two grassy knolls on both the north and south sides of the west end of the plaza, but during the assassination of President John F. Kennedy, it was the north knoll that drew public attention.

Located between the Texas School Book Depository and the Triple Underpass, the Grassy Knoll provided an ideal ambush site. Running along the top of the knoll was a wooden picket fence about five feet high. In front of this fence were shrubs and evergreen trees which, even in late November, provided a leafy canopy over the fence. The fence ran east approximately seventy-five feet from the north edge of the Triple Underpass, then turned north for about fifty feet, ending in a parking area behind a concrete pergola located to the west of the Depository.

It was from a vantage point atop a low concrete wall on the south end of this pergola that the most famous home movie of all time was made—the Abraham Zapruder film.

The Zapruder Film

A twenty-two-second, 8mm film made on November 22, 1963, became the cornerstone of investigations, both public and private, in the years after the Kennedy assassination. It has been regarded as the most objective, and thus most important, piece of evidence in the attempts to unravel what actually happened to President Kennedy. And it almost didn't happen.

Abraham Zapruder, a ladies' dress manufacturer with offices at 501 Elm Street in downtown Dallas near Jack Ruby's nightclub, had not intended to film that day. What with his work and the morning rains, Zapruder thought "I wouldn't have a chance even to see the President." But his secretary, Lillian Rogers, urged him to make use of his new camera—a Bell & Howell 8mm camera with a telephoto lens. So Zapruder made a fourteen-mile round-trip drive to his home to pick up his camera. By the time he returned, crowds were already gathering to watch the motorcade.

After trying several different locations—none of which proved suitable for viewing the President without obstructions—Zapruder finally climbed onto a four-foot-high concrete block at the end of two steps leading to the pergola on the Grassy Knoll. He almost lost his balance while testing his camera on some nearby office workers, so he asked one of the group, his receptionist Marilyn Sitzman, to join him and provide steady support. From this excellent vantage point, Zapruder and Sitzman watched the motorcade approach Elm Street. Having set the camera's speed control on "run" and his lens on "telephoto," Zapruder proceeded to film the entire assassination sequence.

The film must be seen run in its entirety for a viewer to actually receive its maximum impact. But, in synopsis, the film shows:

> The motorcade curves onto Elm and begins moving slowly toward the camera. President Kennedy and his wife are smiling and waving to opposite sides of the street. Then the presidential limousine disappears for a brief second behind a freeway sign and when it emerges, Kennedy is already reacting to a shot. He clenches his fists and brings both up to his throat. He does not appear to say anything, but only remains stiff and upright, sagging slightly to his left. Connally turns to his right, apparently trying to see behind him, then begins to turn back to his left when he freezes. His hair flies up and his mouth opens. He is obviously struck by a bullet. Mrs. Kennedy meanwhile has placed her hand on her husband's arm and is looking at him horrified as he continues to sag toward her. Seconds go by and, by now, Kennedy is bent slightly forward. Suddenly, after an almost imperceptible forward motion of his head, the entire right side of his skull explodes in a halo of blood and brain matter. Kennedy is slammed violently backward to the left rear where he rebounds off the back of the seat and falls toward the car's floor. Mrs. Kennedy climbs onto the trunk of the limousine in an effort to grab something while a Secret Service agent leaps onto the rear of the car, which finally begins to accelerate.

On July 22, 1964, Zapruder told the Warren Commission: "I heard the first shot and I saw the President lean over and grab himself like this [holding his left chest area]."

His testimony is very pertinent because the Warren Commission, in its attempt to prove a lone assassin fired from the sixth floor of the Depository, stated:

. . . the evidence indicated that the President was not hit until at least frame 210 and that he was probably hit by frame 225. The possibility of variations in reaction time in addition to the obstruction of Zapruder's view by the sign precluded a more specific determination than that the President was probably shot through the neck between frames 210 and 225.

By placing the moment of the first shot at the point where Kennedy was out of Zapruder's sight behind the sign, the commission moved the shot closer to the visual effect of a strike on Connally, buttressing the "single bullet" theory. By moving the time of the shot forward, the Commission also abolished the worrisome problem of how an assassin in the sixth-floor window could have accurately fired through obscuring tree branches.

The problem with the Commission's scenario of a hit between frame 210 and 225, of course, is that Zapruder claims he saw Kennedy react to the first shot, which had to have happened before he disappeared from camera view.

Zapruder went on to tell the Commission that following the shooting, he saw some motorcycle policemen "running right behind me . . . in the line of the shooting." He said: "I guess they thought it came from right behind me." When asked where he thought the shots came from, Zapruder replied: ". . . I also thought it came from back of me."

In fact, during his testimony, Zapruder indicates on four separate occasions that he thought shots came from behind him in the direction of the picket fence on the Grassy Knoll.

But then Commission Attorney Wesley J. Liebeler asked Zapruder, "But you didn't form any opinion at that time as to what direction the shots did come from actually?" Zapruder—who by this time was fully familiar with the public position that Oswald had fired three shots from the Depository—replied, "No."

Zapruder, who was very shaken by the assassination, noted that there was considerable reverberation in Dealey Plaza at the time. He said he did not remember jumping down from the cement block and crouching for cover inside the white pergola with Sitzman (as determined by photographs taken at the time) nor going back to his office. He only recalled walking back up Elm Street in a daze, yelling: "They shot him, they shot him, they shot him."

His secretary called authorities and soon men came to take his film for processing.

By Monday, November 25, Zapruder's film had been sold to *Life* magazine. In charge of the sale was *Life*'s publisher C. D. Jackson, who later claimed he was so horrified by the film that he wanted to lock it away. However, in later years, Jackson was shown to have been closely associated with CIA officials. In one instance, when former CIA director Walter Bedell Smith wanted prominent Americans as members of the shadowy and elitist Bilderberger organization, he said he "turned the matter over to C. D. Jackson and things really got going."

Asked about this sale by Liebeler, Zapruder said:

Well, I just wonder whether I should answer it or not because it involves a lot of things and it's not one price—it's a question of how they are going to use it, are they going to use it or are they not going to use it . . .

He finally said:

I received $25,000, as you know, and I have given that to the Firemen's and Policemen's Benevolence with a suggestion, [to use the money] for Mrs. Tippit [wife of the Dallas policeman slain the afternoon of the assassination]

Later in his testimony, Zapruder told of giving his camera to Bell & Howell for its archives. He said, in return, he asked the company to donate a sound projector to the "Golden Age Group." He told Liebeler: "I didn't want anything for myself. . . . I don't like to talk about it too much."

Like so much of the Warren Commission testimony, Zapruder's statement was less than truthful. A copy of his contract with *Life* reveals that his eighteen-second film brought him more than $150,000. Why so much for one film? Perhaps it has something to do with the fact that no member of the American public saw the Zapruder film run as a movie while it was in the sole possession of Time-Life Corp.

While few, if any, of the Warren Commission members viewed the film, single frames from this important piece of evidence were printed in Volume XVIII. But an odd thing happened. No one who has viewed the Zapruder film has been unaffected by the final, gory head shot followed instantaneously by Kennedy's violent fall rearward. Most researchers consider this moment in the film as obvious evidence of a shot from Kennedy's right front (the area of the Grassy Knoll).

Yet when published by the Warren Commission, the critical frames that depict the rearward motion of Kennedy's head were transposed to indicate a forward motion. In 1965 FBI director J. Edgar Hoover explained this reversing of the Zapruder frames as a "printing error."

Further twisting of what was depicted in the film came soon after the assassination. In its December 6, 1963, issue, *Life* magazine reported the fact that the Dallas doctors regarded a small wound in Kennedy's throat as an entrance wound, a real problem considering that the Texas School Book Depository was to his rear at all times. So a *Life* writer simply threw out the explanation:

But [Zapruder's] 8mm film shows the President turning his body far around to the right as he waves to someone in the crowd. His throat is exposed—toward the sniper's nest—just before he clutches it.

This account is patently wrong, as anyone who has seen the film can verify. The reason for such wrongful information at such a critical time will probably never be known, as the author of this statement, Paul Mandel, died shortly afterward.

Then there is the story of Dan Rather, which has been known to assassination researchers for years. Rather, then a CBS newsman, was the only newsman present at a private screening of the Zapruder film the day after the assassination. He described what was in the film over nationwide radio and was fairly accurate until he described the fatal head shot.

Rather stated Kennedy's head "went forward with considerable violence," the exact opposite of what is in the film. Several months later, Rather was promoted to White House correspondent for CBS and by the 1980s, he was chief news anchorman.

Another questionable statement by Rather involves his location at the time of the assassination. In his book, *The Camera Never Blinks,* Rather wrote how he was waiting to pick up news film from CBS cameraman in the presidential motorcade. He wrote he was standing on the west side of the Triple Underpass and missed witnessing the assassination by only a few yards.

However, recently discovered film footage of the west side of the underpass has now become public. This film plus some still photographs show the Kennedy limousine speeding through the underpass and on to Stemmons Freeway—but no sign of Dan Rather.

The American public finally got the opportunity to view the Zapruder film only because of the Clay Shaw trial in New Orleans during 1967–69. During that turbulent trial, New Orleans district attorney Jim Garrison attempted to prove there was a conspiracy to kill President Kennedy and that New Orleans Trade Mart director Clay Shaw was a member of that conspiracy.

As part of Garrison's attempt to prove the existence of a conspiracy, he subpoenaed the Zapruder film from Time-Life Corp. Time-Life fought this subpoena all the way to the Supreme Court, which finally ruled that the corporation had to comply with the legal subpoena.

Time-Life grudgingly turned over to Garrison a somewhat blurry copy of the film—but that was enough. Soon, thanks to the copying efforts of Garrison's staff, bootleg Zapruder films were in the hands of several assassination researchers.

Finally in March 1975, a copy of the film was aired nationally about midnight on ABC's "Goodnight America." At long last, the American public was able to see for themselves the assassination of their thirty-fifth president.

Within a few years clearer copies of the Zapruder film became available to the public.

From the beginning, researchers have used the Zapruder film as the cornerstone of assassination evidence—a virtual time clock of the events in Dealey Plaza, based on the known average camera speed of 18.3 frames per second.

Today the Zapruder film itself has been called into question. In 1971, author David Lifton was permitted to view an exceptionally good-quality copy of the Zapruder film in Time-Life's Los Angeles office. He said the rear of Kennedy's head in the critical moments following the head shot appeared to have been "blacked out" and he discovered "splices on the film which had never been mentioned by Time-Life."

His suspicion that the film may have been tampered with by persons with access to sophisticated photographic equipment was heightened in 1976 with the release of CIA Item 450. This group of documents, pried from the agency by a Freedom of Information suit, indicated the Zapruder film was at the CIA's National Photo Interpretation Center (NPIC) possibly on the night of the assassination and "certainly within days of the assassination." One of the documents tells of the existence of either a negative or a master positive of the film and calls for the production of four prints—one "test print" and three duplicates.

Interestingly, that number of prints is exactly what existed in Dallas the day after the assassination—one original and three copies.

Lifton wrote:

In my view, previously unreported CIA possession of the Zapruder film compromised the film's value as evidence: (1) the forward motion of Kennedy's head, for one frame preceding frame 313, might be the result of an altered film, and if that was so, it made the theory of a foreward high-angle shot . . . completely unnecessary; (2) an altered film might also explain why the occipital area [of Kennedy's head], where the Dallas doctors saw a wound, appears suspiciously dark, whereas a large wound appears on the forward, right-hand side of the head, where the Dallas doctors saw no wound at all.

Photographic analyst and researcher Jack White concurs with Lifton, stating he detected evidence of photographic retouching in some Zapruder frames.

If the CIA indeed tampered with the Zapruder film after the assassination, this piece of evidence—long considered one of the best pieces of evidence—becomes problematical in understanding what really happened in Dealey Plaza.

And like so much else in the assassination case, the suppression and deception surrounding the Zapruder film may eventually reveal more than the film itself.

*   *   *

Just down the slope of the Grassy Knoll from Zapruder was the Bill Newman family. They not only noticed Zapruder with his camera, but in later years, Newman told this author: "At first I thought he shot the President."

Bill and Gayle Newman, along with their two young sons, had gone to Love Field to see Kennedy. But when they didn't get a good view, they rushed downtown and situated themselves on Elm Street just below the concrete cupola.

Newman recalled for this author:

We hadn't been there five minutes when the President turned onto Elm Street. As he was coming straight toward us there was a boom, boom, real close together. I thought someone was throwing firecrackers. He got this bewildered look on his face and was sort of slowing moving back and forth. Then he got nearer to us and, bam, a shot took the right side of his head off. His ear flew off. I heard Mrs. Kennedy say, "Oh, my God, no, they shot Jack!" He was knocked violently back against the seat, almost as if he had been hit by a baseball bat. At that time I was looking right at the President and I thought the shots were coming from directly behind us. I said, "That's it! Get on the ground!" The car momentarily stopped and the driver seemed to have a radio or phone up to his ear and he seemed to be waiting on some word. Some Secret Service men reached into their car and came out with some sort of machine gun. Then the cars roared off. Very soon after this a man asked us what happened and we told him and he took us to Channel 8 [WFAA-TV] studios.

Newman said some sheriff's deputies were waiting for them after the TV interview and took them to the Sheriff's Office, where they joined other Dealey Plaza witnesses who were held for about six hours.

He said that on Sunday, November 24, some FBI agents came to their home and "took down what we said." That was the last contact the Newsmans had with federal authorities. He said:

I was a little disappointed that I didn't get called to testify to the Warren Commission. Someone told me that the reason I wasn't asked to testify was that I was talking about shots from someplace other than the Depository building. . . . I've already been corrected several times that I was wrong about several things and that there are experts who know more about it than I do. But it's real hard for me to believe that it was the act of one lone individual. I've gotten the feeling over the years that people in Washington know what really happened but it's never been divulged. But then I have no evidence to that.

Near the Newmans was Cheryl McKinnon, who later became a reporter for the *San Diego Star News*. In 1983, she wrote of her experience:

On Nov. 22, 1963, I stood, along with hundreds of others, on the Grassy Knoll in Dealey Plaza, waiting for just one thing—a chance to see, even just for a moment, that magical person, the President, John F. Kennedy. . . . As a journalism major in school, my plans were to write about my experiences as a class project. . . . As we stood watching the motorcade turn onto Elm Street, I tried to grasp every tiny detail of both President Kennedy and Mrs. Kennedy. "How happy they look," I thought. Suddenly three shots in rapid succession rang out. Myself and dozens of others standing nearby turned in horror toward the back of the Grassy Knoll where it seemed the sounds had originated. Puffs of white smoke still hung in the air in small patches. But no one was visible. . . . I tried to maintain the faith with my government. I have read the Warren Commission Report in its entirety and dozens of other books as well. I am sorry to say that the only thing I am absolutely sure of today is that at least two of the shots fired that day in Dealey Plaza came from behind where I stood on the Knoll, not from the book Depository. . . . I have never quite had the same faith and trust in those that lead us as I did before.

Sitting on the steps leading to the top of the Grassy Knoll at the time of the assassination was Emmett J. Hudson, one of the groundskeepers of Dealey Plaza. With Hudson were two other men, neither apparently were ever identified by the federal investigations. In his Warren Commission testimony, Hudson recalled:

Well, there was a young fellow, oh, I would judge his age about in his late twenties. He said he had been looking for a place to park . . . he finally [had] just taken a place over there in one of them parking lots, and he came on down there and said he worked over there on Industrial and me and him both just sat down there on those steps. When the motorcade turned off of Houston onto Elm, we got up and stood up, me and him both . . . and so the first shot rung out and, of course, I didn't realize it was a shot . . . the motorcade had done got further on down Elm . . . I happened to be looking right at him when that bullet hit him—the second shot. . . . it looked like it hit him somewhere along about a little bit behind the ear and a little above the ear [on the right-hand side of his head] . . . this young fellow that was . . . standing there with me . . . he says, "Lay down, mister, somebody is shooting the President." . . . he kept on repeating, "Lay down," so he was already laying down one way on the sidewalk, so I just laid down over on the ground and resting my arm on the ground . . . when that third shot rung out . . . you could tell the shot was coming from above and kind of behind.

In his testimony, Hudson plainly tried to tell Commission attorney Liebeler that the shots came "from above and kind of behind" him, the location of the picket fence on the Grassy Knoll. Liebeler led Hudson, saying: "And that would fit in with the Texas School Book Depository, wouldn't it?"

"Yes," replied an agreeable Hudson. Liebeler then asked Hudson if he saw anyone standing in the area with a rifle ". . . on a grassy spot up there near where you were standing or on the overpass or any place else?"

Hudson replied: "I never seen anyone with a gun up there except the patrols."

Asked Liebeler, "The policemen?" "Yes, sir," said Hudson.

In an affidavit signed the day of the assassination, Hudson was even more specific as to where shots came from. He stated: "The shots that I heard definitely came from behind and above me."

Sitting near the midway point of the steps leading to the top of the Grassy Knoll, a location "behind and above" would be the exact position of the easternmost leg of the wooden picket fence.

Hudson said he did not know the young man who sat with him and, apparently, the federal authorities were never able to locate him.

The third man appears behind Hudson in photographs taken in the seconds during which the head shot occurs. He, too, has been unidentified but, perhaps, is the explanation for one of the enduring assassination mysteries.

The Black Dog Man

In at least two photographs taken during the assassination by separate photographers, a human figure is visible behind a low retaining wall to the south of the Grassy Knoll pergola behind Zapruder's position. In photos made seconds later, this figure has disappeared, leading many assassination researchers to suspect that this figure may have been an assassin. This suspicion was heightened when the House Select Committee on Assassinations had photographs of the figure computer enhanced and concluded that it indeed was the figure of a person, who appeared to be holding a long object.

With no known identity, this person was dubbed the "black dog man" by researchers and committee staffers because in a photo taken by Phil Willis the figure resembles a black dog sitting on its haunches atop the wall. Closer examination of the photos, however, indicates the figure is most likely farther back from the retaining wall. And this may provide a partial answer to the figure's identity.

In photos of the assassination, a third man can be seen joining Hudson and his companion on the steps of the Grassy Knoll just as the presidential limousine arrives opposite them on Elm Street. Within scant seconds of the fatal head shot, the third man lifts his left foot and within seconds has disappeared back up the steps.

Life magazine, in its November 24, 1967, issue, displays the photographs of Hugh Betzner and Phil Willis and comments:

A dark shape is seen in both pictures on the slope—which has become famous as the "grassy knoll"—to the left of the Stemmons Freeway sign and half hidden by a concrete wall. By photogammetry Itek has verified it as the figure of a man. Previously published photographs, taken at the moment of the fatal head shot, show that by then he had joined two men seen in Willis' picture standing behind a lamppost at left. There is no evidence to indicate he was anything more than an onlooker.

So the riddle of the "black dog man" appeared solved. It was the figure of a man seen from waist up as he stood or walked on the sidewalk behind the retaining wall approaching the top of the steps. Yet today many assassination researchers still deny it was the man who joined Hudson.

Seconds later—as determined in photographs—the unidentified man joined Hudson and companion, who were apparently unaware of the man behind them, then turned and ran back up the steps immediately after the head shot.

However, this explanation does not exonerate the third man as simply an "onlooker." Who was he? Where did he come from? What did he see both before and after he joined the two men on the steps? And why did he turn and race back up the steps (he was gone within seconds) at a time when everyone else in Dealey Plaza was stationary with shock?

The federal investigations could provide no answers to these questions, so in the minds of some researchers, the "black dog man" joins the "umbrella man" and the "dark-complected man" as one of the more suspicious persons in Dealey Plaza.

* * *

Almost immediately after the final shot was fired, many people— including policemen, sheriff's deputies, and spectators—began rushing toward the Grassy Knoll.

Dallas motorcycle officer Bobby Hargis thought the shots had come from the Triple Underpass because ". . . I had got splattered, with blood [and] I was just a little back and left of Mrs. Kennedy, but I didn't know."

Hargis stopped his motorcycle on the south side of Elm and ran up the Grassy Knoll to where the concrete wall of the Triple Underpass connected with the wooden picket fence on the Knoll. Peering over the wall, Hargis looked at the crowd standing on the Underpass.

Asked if he saw anything out of the ordinary, Hargis told the Warren Commission: "No, I didn't. That is what got me."

Hargis returned to his still-running motorcycle and rode through the Triple Underpass. He told the commission: ". . . I couldn't see anything that was of a suspicious nature, so I came back to the Texas School Book Depository. At that time it seemed like the activity was centered around the . . . Depository."

Seymour Weitzman was a college graduate serving as a deputy constable of Dallas County. He had been standing with Deputy Constable Bill Hutton at the corner of Main and Houston when the motorcade passed. The pair had turned to walk to a nearby courthouse when Weitzman heard three shots, "first one, then . . . a little period in between . . . [then] the second two seemed to be simultaneously," Weitzman told the Warren Commission:

> I immediately ran toward the President's car. Of course, it was speeding away and somebody said the shots or firecrackers . . . we still didn't know the President was shot . . . came from the wall. I immediately scaled the wall. . . . apparently, my hands grabbed steampipes. I burned them. [In the railroad yards behind the picket fence.] We noticed numerous kinds of footprints that did not make sense because they were going different directions . . . [with Weitzman at the time were] other officers, Secret Service as well . . .

Behind Weitzman came Dallas policeman Joe M. Smith, who had been handling traffic at the intersection of Elm and Houston in front of the Depository. Smith had helped at the scene of the strange seizure incident minutes before the motorcade arrived and had returned to his position in the middle of Elm where barricades had been placed to halt traffic.

Moments after the President's car passed him, Smith heard shots, but he couldn't tell from which direction they came. He told the Warren Commission an hysterical woman ran up to him, crying: "They are shooting the President from the bushes!"

Smith said he immediately went up the short street that branches off of Elm in front of the Depository and entered the parking lot behind the wooden picket fence. He told the Commission:

> I looked into all the cars and checked around the bushes. Of course, I wasn't alone. There was some deputy sheriff [Weitzman] with me, and I believe one Secret Service man when I got there. I got to make this statement, too. I felt awfully silly, but after the shot and this woman, [I] pulled my pistol from my holster, and I thought, this is silly, I don't know who I am looking for, and put it back. Just as I did, he showed me that he was a Secret Service agent. . . . he saw me coming with my pistol and right away he showed me who he was.

In 1978, Smith told author Anthony Summers that "around the hedges [lining the parking lot], there was the smell, the lingering smell of gunpowder."

Smith then moved toward the Triple Underpass because "it sounded to me like they [shots] may have come from this vicinity here." In his testimony, Smith said he saw "two other officers there," but it is unclear if he was speaking about behind the fence or the Triple Underpass. After fifteen or twenty minutes, Smith said he returned to the front of the Depository, where he helped other officers seal the building.

(For some unexplained reason, at the end of his testimony Commission attorney Wesley Liebeler suddenly asked Smith if there was any reason why the presidential motorcade could not have gone straight down Main Street and turned onto Stemmons Freeway on its way to the Trade Mart. "As far as I know, there is no reason," replied Smith.)

One witness who was in a position to observe the area behind the picket fence was Lee Bowers, a railroad supervisor who was stationed in a tower located just north of the Grassy Knoll. Bowers told a fascinating story of suspicious cars moving in the sealed-off railroad yards minutes before the motorcade arrived and of seeing strange men behind the picket fence. Incredibly, his testimony takes less than six pages of the Warren Commission volumes.

Bowers, an ex-Navy man who had studied religion at Southern Methodist University in Dallas, was working for the Union Terminal Company, controlling the movement of trains in the railroad yards from a tower about fourteen feet off the ground. The tower is located about fifty yards northwest of the back of the Texas School Book Depository. A block-long street breaks off from Elm and passes in front of the Depository, ending in a parking lot bordered on the south by the wooden picket fence atop the Grassy Knoll. It was the only paved artery in or out of the parking area.

Bowers told the Warren Commission:

. . . the area had been covered by police for some two hours. Since approximately 10 o'clock in the morning [of the assassination], traffic had been cut off into the area so that anyone moving around could actually be observed. Since I had worked there for a number of years, I was familiar with most of the people who came in and out of the area. . . . there were three cars that came in during the time from around noon until the time of the shooting. They came into the vicinity of the tower, which was at the extension of Elm Street . . . which there is no way out. It is not a through street to anywhere.

Bowers said he noticed the first car about 12:10 P.M. It was a blue-and-white 1959 Oldsmobile station wagon with out-of-state license plates and some bumper stickers, "one of which was a Goldwater sticker." The station wagon circled in front of the railroad tower "as if he was searching for a way out, or was checking the area, and then proceeded back through the only way he could, the same outlet he came into."

About 12:20 P.M., a black 1957 Ford with Texas license plates came into the area. Inside was "one male . . . that seemed to have a mike or telephone or something . . . He was holding something up to his mouth with one hand and he was driving with the other . . ." Bowers said this car left after three or four minutes driving back in front of the Depository. "He did probe a little further into the area than the first car," Bowers added.

Minutes before the assassination, Bowers said a third car—this one a white 1961 or 1962 Chevrolet four-door Impala—entered the area. Bowers said:

> [It] showed signs of being on the road . . . It was muddy up to the windows, bore a similar out-of-state license to the first car I observed [and was] also occupied by one white male. He spent a little more time in the area. . . . he circled the area and probed one spot right at the tower . . . and was forced to back out some considerable distance, and slowly cruised down back towards the front of the School Depository Building. . . . The last I saw of him, he was pausing just about in—just above the assassination site. . . . Whether it continued on . . . or whether it pulled up only a short distance, I couldn't tell. I was busy.

Bowers said about eight minutes later, he caught sight of the presidential limousine as it turned onto Elm Street. He stated:

> I heard three shots. One, then a slight pause, then two very close together. Also, reverberation from the shots. . . . The sounds came either from up against the School Depository Building or near the mouth of the Triple Underpass.

Standing directly between Bowers's vantage point and the Triple Underpass, the tower operator said he saw two men, but they "gave no appearance of being together" although they were only ten or fifteen feet from each other.

Bowers described this pair:

> One man, middle-aged, or slightly older, fairly heavyset, in a white shirt, fairly dark trousers. Another younger man, about mid-twenties, in either a plaid shirt or plaid coat or jacket. . . . They were facing and looking up toward Main and Houston and following the caravan as it came down.

Bowers also saw the railroad employees and the two Dallas policemen standing on the Triple Underpass.

Toward the eastern end of the parking lot, Bowers saw two other men. He said: "Each had uniforms similar to those custodians at the courthouse." And speaking of the white Impala again, Bowers said:

. . . at the moment of the first shot . . . the car was out of sight behind this decorative masonry wall in the area. . . . at the moment of the shots . . . I do not think that it was in sight. It came in sight immediately following the last shot.

Bowers then described what he saw following the shots:

At the time of the shooting there seemed to be some commotion, and immediately following there was a motorcycle policeman who shot nearly all of the way to the top of the incline. . . . He was part of the motorcade and had left it for some reason, which I did not know. . . . He came up into the area where there are some trees and where I had described the two men were in the general vicinity of this . . . one of them was [still there]. The other one, I could not say. The darker-dressed man was too hard to distinguish from the trees. The one in the white shirt, yes, I think he was.

Asked by Commission attorney Joseph Ball to describe the "commotion" that attracted his attention, Bowers said:

I just am unable to describe rather than it was something out of the ordinary . . . but something occurred in this particular spot which was out of the ordinary, which attracted my eye for some reason, which I could not identify. . . . Nothing that I could pinpoint as having happened that—

Ball interrupted. "Afterwards did a good many people come up there on this high ground at the tower?" he asked, before Bowers could tell what caught his attention on the knoll.

In a later filmed interview, Bowers did describe what caught his eye. He stated:

At the time of the shooting, in the vicinity of where the two men I have described were, there was a flash of light or . . . something I could not identify . . . some unusual occurrence—a flash of light or smoke or something which caused me to feel that something out of the ordinary had occurred there.

Bowers said after the shooting, "a large number of people" converged on the parking lot behind the picket fence, including "between fifty and a hundred policemen within a maximum of five minutes." He added: "[Police] sealed off the area and I held off the trains until they could be examined, and there were some transients taken [off] at least one train.''

One witness who may have encountered one or more of the men Bowers saw behind the picket fence was Gordon Arnold, who never testified to either of the federal panels investigating the assassination. On the day of the assassination, Arnold was a twenty-two-year-old soldier who had just arrived back in Dallas after Army training. He went downtown to have lunch when he decided to take movies of the President. Parking his car near Bowers's railroad tower, Arnold took his movie camera and walked toward the Triple Underpass. He told this author:

I was walking along behind this picket fence when a man in a light-colored suit came up to me and said I shouldn't be up there. I was young and cocky and I said, ''Why not?'' And he showed me a badge and said he was with the Secret Service and that he didn't want anyone up there. I said all right and started walking back along the fence. I could feel that he was following me and we had a few more words. I walked around to the front of the fence and found a little mound of dirt to stand on to see the motorcade. . . . Just after the car turned onto Elm and started toward me, a shot went off from over my left shoulder. I felt the bullet, rather than heard it, and it went right past my left ear. . . . I had just gotten out of basic training. In my mind live ammunition was being fired. It was being fired over my head. And I hit the dirt. I buried my head in the ground and I heard several other shots, but I couldn't see anything because I had my face in the dirt. [His prone position under the trees on the knoll may explain why Arnold did not appear in photographs taken of the knoll at that time.] I heard two shots and then there was a blend. For a single bolt action [rifle], he had to have been firing darn good because I don't think anybody could fire that rapid a bolt action. . . . The next thing I knew, someone was kicking my butt and telling me to get up. It was a policeman. And I told him to go jump in the river. And then this other guy—a policeman—comes up with a gun. I don't recall if it was a shotgun or what. And he was crying and that thing was waving back and forth. I felt threatened. One of them asked me if I had taken any film and I said yes. He told me to give him my film, so I tossed him my camera. I said you can have everything, just point that gun somewhere else. He opened it, pulled out the film, and then threw the camera back to me. All I wanted to do was get out of there. The gun and the guy crying was enough to unnerve me.

Arnold ran straight back to his car and drove out of the parking area unchallenged. Two days later, Arnold reported to duty at Fort Wainwright in Alaska and he did not return for several years.

Arnold's presence on the Grassy Knoll has been questioned by some researchers because he doesn't appear in photographs taken that day. His position well under the overhanging trees on the Knoll left him in deep shadow. He was seen, however, by at least one person in the presidential motorcade. Former senator Ralph Yarborough, who was riding in the same car as Vice President Johnson, confirmed Arnold's position in 1978 when he told *The Dallas Morning News:*

> Immediately on the firing of the first shot I saw the man you inter-
> viewed [Arnold] throw himself on the ground. He was down within a
> second of the time the shot was fired and I thought to myself, "There's
> a combat veteran who knows how to act when weapons start firing."

Arnold, later an investigator for the Dallas Department of Consumer Affairs, did not give his name to authorities and was never questioned by either the Warren Commission or the House Select Committee on Assassinations, although his account of the assassination appeared in the July 27, 1978, edition of *The Dallas Morning News.*

Corroboration of Arnold's story may have come in 1982 with discovery of a figure in the background of a snapshot made at the instant of the fatal head shot to Kennedy by a woman standing on the south curb on Elm Street.

The Badge Man

Mary Moorman took a now well-known Polaroid picture just as Kennedy was struck in the head. She sold her rights to the photo that day to United Press International for six hundred dollars. The photo was never examined nor printed by the Warren Commission, but it was published widely in newspapers and magazines after the assassination.

For years, researchers pored over the Moorman picture looking for evidence of a Grassy Knoll gunman. Despite some tantalizingly blurry objects discovered along the top of the west leg of the picket fence, no credible photo of a gunman was found.

The House Select Committee on Assassinations did study the picture, but found it had badly faded and "was of quite poor quality." However, because of acoustical evidence (see "The House Select Committee on Assassinations"), the committee recommended ". . . this particular photograph should be reexamined . . ."

Then, in 1982, Texas researchers Gary Mack and Jack White began studying the Moorman photo in light of the experience of Gordon Arnold. After obtaining a clear slide made from an original, quality copy of Moorman's photo, Mack and White began studying the bushy area east from the corner of the fence. It was here they discovered what appeared to be two figures. Interestingly, the figures appear in the same general area that the House Committee's acoustical tests indicated shots were fired from, though the sound experts located a shot west of the corner of the fence, while the figures are north of the corner.

When blown up, the figures are detectable by untrained observers. One police official even commented that one man seemed to be wearing "shooter's glasses." The main figure has been dubbed the "badge man" because he appears to be wearing a dark shirt with a semicircular patch on the left shoulder and a bright shiny object on his left chest—the exact configuration of a Dallas police uniform.

Although the "badge man's" hairline, eyes, left ear, and jaw are visible, his mouth and neck are obscured by a bright flash—apparently the muzzle blast of a rifle he is holding in the classic rifle-firing position.

After analyzing the photographic blowup as well as making reenactment photos in Dealey Plaza, Mack and White feel the "badge man" and perhaps even a companion are standing behind the wooden picket fence about fifteen feet north from the corner. This places the figure just to the left of Gordon Arnold's position and to the right and rear of Abraham Zapruder.

Mack and White tried unsuccessfully to interest a major news organization in financing a scientific analysis of the "badge man" photo. Finally in 1980, a national tabloid agreed to have the blowup studied. White and a representative from the news magazine flew to the Massachusetts Institute of Technology, where the photo was subjected to sophisticated computer enhancement. They were told that, without question, the photo showed a man firing a rifle.

The next day, however, the chairman of the MIT department involved suddenly gave all materials back to them and, with no explanation, told them the school would no longer participate in any study of the photo.

Today, efforts continue to have the photo enlargement further enhanced by sophisticated means.

The "badge man" blowup was included in "The Men Who Killed Kennedy," a British television documentary produced in 1988. In this program, the "badge man" was identified as a professional Corsican assassin named Lucien Sarti. This documentary, which was nominated for awards in Britain and shown to millions of people around the world, has yet to be aired in the United States.

Whatever the end result of a scientific study of the blowup may be, the collection of supporting evidence indicates that the "badge man" may indeed have been the Grassy Knoll gunman whom many witnesses in Dealey Plaza reported sighting on November 22, 1963. The "badge man" fits the following accounts:

—Gordon Arnold's story of hearing a shot come from his left rear.
—Zapruder's testimony that shots came from his right rear.

—Bowers's testimony that he saw a flash of light and smoke near two men wearing uniforms near the east end of the fence. He also saw a man in a white shirt behind the fence moments before Kennedy was shot.

—The House Select Committee on Assassinations, which placed at least one shot within ten feet of the fence corner (although on the west leg).

—Jean Hill, who said she saw smoke and movement north of the fence corner at the moment of the head shot.

—Sam Holland and others who told of finding muddy footprints, cigarette butts, and mud on a car bumper behind the picket fence minutes after the shots were fired.

—Numerous witnesses who ran behind the fence but said they only saw railroad workers and policemen there.

—The testimony of Emmett Hudson, Constable Weitzman, and Officer Smith, all of whom saw policemen on the knoll when there were none officially accounted for in that area.

All in all, the photographic blowup of these figures on the knoll may be the most important evidence yet confirming the existence of assassins on the Grassy Knoll.

Amazingly, however, no official government agency or major news organization seems willing to either make a serious study of the Moorman photo or present it to the general public.

* * *

Further evidence of what went on behind the picket fence at the moment of the assassination can be found in the heretofore untold story of a crucial witness.

A Grassy Knoll Witness

It is strange irony that the one person who apparently witnessed men with guns behind the wooden picket fence on the Grassy Knoll at the time of the Kennedy assassination was unable to tell anyone what he saw. Ed Hoffman of Dallas has been deaf since birth and, as is common with that disability, he cannot speak. However, this did not prevent him from attempting to alert authorities to what he saw behind that fence.

Although Hoffman told his family and friends what he saw at the time and later reported it to the FBI, his story has remained unpublicized over the years. Finally, in the summer of 1985, he told his story to this author. It was later substantially confirmed by FBI documents.

Hoffman was twenty-six years old on November 22, 1963, and at noontime was driving toward downtown Dallas on the Stemmons Expressway when he noticed numerous people lining the freeway. He suddenly realized that President Kennedy was to motorcade through the city that day, so he stopped his car just north of a railroad bridge across Stemmons and joined the spectators.

(Only someone who was there that day could have known that many people were lining Stemmons to get a glimpse of the President since all news coverage of the motorcade stopped after the shooting in Dealey Plaza.)

After waiting for a time, Hoffman decided to walk along the shoulder of the freeway to a point where it crossed over Elm Street in hopes of getting a view into Dealey Plaza. From this vantage point, Hoffman was approximately two hundred yards west of the parking lot behind the picket fence at an elevation of about the height of the first floor of the Texas School Book Depository.

Being unable to hear, he was not aware that Kennedy's motorcade was passing through the plaza. However, he was aware of movement on the north side of the picket fence. He became aware of a man running west along the back side of the fence wearing a dark suit, tie, and an overcoat. The man was carrying a rifle in his hands. As the man reached a metal pipe railing at the west end of the fence, he tossed the rifle to a second man standing on the west side of the pipe near the railroad tracks that went south over the Triple Underpass. The second man was wearing light coveralls and a railroad worker's hat.

The second man caught the rifle, ducked behind a large railroad switch box—one of two at that site—and knelt down. The man disassembled the rifle, placed it in a soft brown bag (Hoffman's description matches that of the traditional railroad brakeman's tool bag), then walked north into the rail yards in the general direction of the railroad tower containing Lee Bowers.

The man in the overcoat, meanwhile, had turned and run back along the picket fence until midway, when he stopped and began walking calmly toward the corner of the fence. Hoffman could not see the corner of the fence due to cars and overhanging tree branches.

Unable to hear, Hoffman was at a loss to understand what was happening as he watched these men.

However, moments later Kennedy's car came into sight out of the west side of the Triple Underpass. Hoffman saw the President lying on the seat of the blood-splattered car and realized something terrible had occurred.

As the presidential limousine turned onto the Stemmons access ramp just below his position, Hoffman decided to try to alert the Secret Service agents to what he had witnessed. He ran down the grassy incline waving his arms and trying to make them understand that he had seen something, when one of the agents in the President's follow-up car reached down and produced a machine gun, which he leveled at him. Hoffman stopped and threw up his hands and could only watch helplessly as the motorcade rushed past him onto Stemmons in the mad rush to Parkland Hospital.

There was no mention at the time of any Secret Service man with a machine gun, yet Hoffman was emphatic that it was an automatic weapon with a pistol grip and clip. It is now known that Secret Service agent George W. Hickey, Jr., in the follow-up car did display an AR-15, the civilian model of the M-16 machine gun, further corroborating Hoffman's story.

Upset over what he had seen, Hoffman looked around for help. He saw a Dallas policeman standing on the railroad bridge crossing Stemmons and he walked toward him waving his arms in an attempt to communicate what he had seen. However, the policeman, unable to understand, simply waved him off. (This part of Hoffman's story also is corroborated, since policeman Earle Brown filed a report stating that he was on the Stemmons railroad bridge at the time of the assassination. However, questioned recently about these events, Brown said he has no recollection of seeing Hoffman.)

Unable to get help, Hoffman walked back to his car, then drove behind the Texas School Book Depository for several minutes trying to locate the man with the rifle in the brown bag. He was unsuccessful. However, this is indicative of the total lack of security around the Depository in the chaotic minutes following the assassination. Hoffman was able to drive around in the rail yards behind the Depository for some time and then leave without being stopped or questioned by authorities.

He then drove to the Dallas FBI office but found no one there except a receptionist. He left his name and address with the FBI. The FBI never responded.

At the time, Hoffman had a relative at the Dallas police station, and he drove there next, hoping to find some help. However, the station was sealed off and the officer on the door refused to allow him to enter.

Thwarted in his attempts to tell authorities what he had seen, Hoffman finally went home, where his parents, also deaf-mutes, urged him not to become involved.

Hoffman remained silent until Thanksgiving 1963, when he met his policeman relative at a family function. Despite his parents' warnings, he told his story to the policeman, who assured him that the federal authorities were investigating the case and that, in fact, the assassin had already been caught. Confident that the case was closed, Hoffman said he didn't consider telling his story to anyone else.

However, as the years went by, Hoffman became more and more aware of the official version of the assassination and knew that the theory that one man had fired from the sixth floor of the Depository did not agree with what he had seen.

Finally on June 28, 1967, at the urging of co-workers, Hoffman visited the Dallas FBI once again. Apparently Hoffman had difficulty in communicating with the agents or they purposely distorted his story, because the FBI report of that day states:

Hoffman said he observed two white males, clutching something dark to their chests with both hands, running from the rear of the Texas School Book Depository building. The men were running north on the railroad, then turned east, and Hoffman lost sight of both of the men.

The report added:

Approximately two hours after the above interview with Hoffman, he returned to the Dallas office of the FBI and advised he had just returned from the spot on Stemmons Freeway where he had parked his automobile and had decided he could not have seen the men running because of a fence west of the Texas School Book Depository building. He said it was possible that he saw these two men on the fence or something else *[sic]*.

Whether or not the FBI agents were able to understand Hoffman correctly, they did talk to his father and brother on July 5, 1967. Both said Hoffman loved President Kennedy and had told his story to them just after the assassination. However they also said Hoffman "has in the past distorted facts of events observed by him." (Of course, it was his father who had urged him not to become involved in the case at all, so there was motivation to downplay his son's story.)

Officially, this was the end of any investigation into Hoffman's story at that time. Unofficially, Hoffman said one FBI agent told him to keep quiet about what he had seen or "you might get killed."

Hoffman kept quiet until October 3, 1975, when his interest was rekindled by talk of reopening the investigation into Kennedy's death. This provoked him to write of his experiences to Senator Edward Kennedy. Experts in deafness who have seen the letter say it is typical of the writing of a deaf person, many of whom try to write as they sign. Although somewhat disjointed, the letter briefly mentioned what Hoffman had seen and added that his relatives said he could be in danger from the CIA or other persons if he told what he saw.

In a letter dated November 19, 1975, Kennedy responded:

My family has been aware of various theories concerning the death of President Kennedy, just as it has been aware of many speculative accounts which have arisen from the death of Robert Kennedy. I am sure that it is understood that the continual speculation is painful for members of my family. We have always accepted the findings of the Warren Commission report and have no reason to question the quality and the effort of those who investigated the fatal shooting of Robert Kennedy.

Kennedy concluded that sufficient evidence to reexamine the two Kennedy deaths would have to come from "legal authorities responsible for such further investigation [and] I do not believe that their judgment should be influenced by any feelings or discomfort by any member of my family.''

Despite this further, if more gentle, attempt to tell Hoffman to be quiet, he continued to tell his story to fellow workers at the Dallas electronics firm where he has been employed since before the assassination.

On March 25, 1977, one of Hoffman's supervisors who understood sign language contacted the Dallas FBI office. He said he felt that the FBI did not fully understand what Hoffman was trying to tell them during the 1967 interview and that Hoffman deserved to be heard.

At this urging, FBI agents again talked with Hoffman on March 28, 1977, and even accompanied him to the site on Stemmons Expressway. This time, with his supervisor acting as translator, Hoffman was able to give more details. He said he thought he saw a puff of smoke near where the men were standing, and essentially his story was the same as the one he told in 1985 except he said he saw both men run north into the rail yards.

Although this time the FBI took photographs of the area based on Hoffman's testimony, they again showed little interest in pursuing his story.

On the cover sheet of their report to the FBI director, the Dallas agents wrote:

On Pages 71–76 of the 'Report of the President's Commission on the Assassination of President John F. Kennedy,' the witnesses at the Triple Underpass are discussed, but the Warren Commission's investigation has disclosed no credible evidence that any shots were fired from anywhere other than the Texas School Book Depository building. In view of the above, the Dallas Office is conducting no additional investigation . . .

In other words, since the federal government concluded Oswald was the lone assassin, Hoffman must have been mistaken.

In fact, there was no mention of Hoffman or his testimony by the U.S. government until researchers obtained reports on him through the Freedom of Information Act in 1985.

Since Hoffman, despite his hearing disability, appears to be a most credible witness and since his story only reinforces others who told of gunmen on the knoll, it deserves serious consideration.

There are several interesting aspects of Hoffman's story. First, since many of the details have been independently corroborated—the crowds on Stemmons, the machine gun, the cop on the railroad bridge—his story may be the best version of what happened behind the picket fence to date. Hoffman's story also may have pinpointed the role of convicted Texas hitman Charles V. Harrelson, who has admitted participating in the JFK assassination. His story also serves as a vivid commentary on the FBI's failure to follow serious leads and its attempts to intimidate witnesses into silence.

Summary

In reviewing the experiences of the people in Dealey Plaza the day Kennedy died, it is apparent that not one single person saw the assassination as it was described by the Warren Commission.

In the motorcade, Governor Connally's testimony—totally corroborated by the Zapruder film—indicated that both he and Kennedy could not have been struck by the same bullet.

Many people, including Sheriff Decker, Royce Skelton, and Austin Miller, saw one bullet strike Elm Street. Others, like Policeman Foster, saw a bullet hit the grass on the south side of Elm.

Many people heard shots coming from at least two separate locations, while those on the Triple Underpass even saw smoke drift out from under the trees on the Grassy Knoll.

The motorcade had difficulty negotiating the sharp turn onto Elm that the Secret Service advance men had failed to properly scrutinize. The Secret Service also refused additional security offered by Dallas police.

An unexplained change in the motorcade lineup moved press photographers far back in line, preventing them from photographing the assassination.

Motorcade riders heard shots from separate locations, but the majority believed shots came from the direction of the Triple Underpass. Both Sheriff Decker and Police Chief Curry ordered their men to rush to the railroad yards behind the Grassy Knoll.

The only Secret Service agent to react quickly to the assassination was Clint Hill, who was not originally scheduled for the Dallas trip and was assigned to Mrs. Kennedy.

Mrs. Cabell and former senator Yarborough, among others, reported smelling gunpowder while passing through Dealey Plaza.

Some members of the crowd, such as Phillip Hathaway, Julia Ann Mercer, Julius Hardie, and the Arnold Rowlands, saw men with rifles in the area of Dealey Plaza long before the Kennedy motorcade arrived.

Several bystanders, their testimony supported by at least two films made that day, claimed to have seen more than one man on the sixth floor of the Texas School Book Depository moments before the assassination.

Some witnesses—Phil Willis, Jean Hill, Julia Mercer, and Dallas policeman Tom Tilson—even claim they saw Jack Ruby in Dealey Plaza at the time of the assassination.

People standing in front of the Depository thought shots came from down near the Triple Underpass.

Others, such as A. J. Millican, the John Chisms, and Jean Newman, who were standing between the Depository and the Underpass, believed the shots came from the Grassy Knoll.

Two of the most suspicious men in Dealey Plaza—subsequently nicknamed the "umbrella man" and the "dark-complected man"—were never identified or even mentioned by the Warren Commission. Yet both men made visual signals just as Kennedy drew opposite them. Moments later the dark man appeared to be talking into a radio.

The House Select Committee on Assassinations claimed to have located the "umbrella man," but the man they found told a story totally inconsistent with the activities of the "umbrella man" as recorded on film that day. And the Committee never bothered to mention the man with what appeared to be a walkie-talkie.

Neither could the Warren Commission seem to locate a woman filming the assassination who came to be known to researchers as the "babushka lady." The House Committee took testimony from this woman after she was identified by researchers as Beverly Oliver, but never mentioned her in its report.

Oliver, an acquaintance of Jack Ruby, has told researchers she was introduced by Ruby to "Lee Oswald of the CIA" prior to the assassination.

Jean Hill, who was standing beside Mary Moorman on the south side of Elm Street at the moment of the assassination, said she saw a man fire from behind the wooden picket fence on the Grassy Knoll and saw smoke drift from his location.

Hill's story is supported by the testimony of railroad supervisor S. M. Holland, who told government investigators he, too, saw smoke drifting from the Knoll. Holland's account is corroborated by other men on the Triple Underpass, such as Richard Dodd, James Simmons, Austin Miller, Frank Reilly, and Thomas Murphy—none of whom were asked to testify before the Warren Commission.

Even employees of the Depository, both inside and outside that building, stated shots came from the direction of the Grassy Knoll.

Three employees—Bonnie Ray Williams, Harold Norman, and James Jarman—were sitting just below the sixth-floor window later identified as the sniper's window. Despite their later testimony that they heard shots right above their heads, they all said they ran to the west side of the building because they believed that shots had come from west of the Depository.

Less than sixty seconds after shots were fired, Dallas policeman Marrion Baker and Depository superintendent Roy Truly encountered another Depository employee—Lee Harvey Oswald—in the building's second-floor lunchroom holding a Coke in his hand and appearing calm and unperturbed.

At least one Depository employee, Joe Molina, was intimidated by authorities and lost his job soon after the assassination.

One man, James Tague, was the third man wounded in Dealey Plaza when his cheek was bloodied by cement sent flying by a bullet striking the curb just east of the Triple Underpass.

Apparently it was reports of Tague's wounding that forced the Warren Commission to revise their account of the assassination. Where they had originally concluded that one shot hit Kennedy in the upper back, another struck Governor Connally, and a third struck Kennedy's head, they finally settled on the "single-bullet theory," which states that one bullet passed through both Kennedy and Connally, another missed altogether, striking the curb near Tague, and a third shot struck Kennedy fatally in the head.

Despite great efforts on the part of authorities to establish the Depository as the source of all shots, public attention—both in 1963 and today—kept returning to the infamous Grassy Knoll.

Photographer Abraham Zapruder clearly stated that the shots came from the Knoll behind him. His testimony is corroborated by Dealey Plaza groundskeeper Emmett Hudson, who reported that shots came from the Knoll above and behind him.

Lee Bowers, a railroad employee who was in a railroad tower overlooking the back of the Knoll, told of seeing men with radios in strange cars cruising the area just prior to the assassination. He also reported seeing a flash of light and smoke from behind the fence on the Knoll at the time of the shooting.

Gordon Arnold, a young soldier, said he was chased from behind the wooden picket fences shortly before Kennedy arrived by a man showing Secret Service indentification. He said he was in front of the fence on the Knoll filming the motorcade when a shot was fired from over his left shoulder from behind the fence. He said moments later two policemen took his film and he fled.

A gunman behind the picket fence may have been captured in a photograph taken by Mary Moorman. A recent enlargement of the Knoll area in her photo seems to reveal a man firing a rifle. The man is dressed in what appears to be a police uniform. The existence of this gunman is further confirmed by the acoustical studies commissioned by the House Select Committee on Assassinations in 1979. The results of these tests forced the Committee to reluctantly conclude that a second gunman fired on Kennedy from behind the Knoll fence.

The deaf-mute Ed Hoffman tried to inform the FBI after the assassination that he had witnessed a man with a rifle behind the picket fence on the Grassy Knoll. However, Hoffman was warned to keep quiet or "you might get killed" by an FBI agent, and reports of his sighting were hidden from the public for twenty-two years.

Conclusions to be drawn from the wide range of testimony by people in Dealey Plaza on November 22, 1963, include:

—There was much confusion and panic among the people watching the presidential motorcade.
—The majority of witnesses originally believed the shots came from the area of the Grassy Knoll.
—The preponderance of evidence indicates shots came from two different directions—the Grassy Knoll and the direction of the Depository.

—There is nothing in the available evidence that rules out the possibility that more shots from other directions were fired.

—The activities of the federal authorities, especially the Secret Service and FBI, before, during, and after the assassination, have raised serious suspicions in the minds of researchers.

I knew then what I know now: Oswald was on an assignment in Russia for American intelligence.

—Oswald's Marine roommate James Botelho

Part II
Means, Motives, and Opportunities

The assassination of President John F. Kennedy was not an isolated event. It occurred within a complex matrix of national and international events and issues. Therefore, this event must be placed within a context of the times.

As President, John F. Kennedy daily was juggling a wide variety of responsibilities on many different fronts—foreign policy, civil rights, agriculture, finance, politics, crime-busting, and defense considerations.

Likewise, Lee Harvey Oswald—the man identified by two government panels as Kennedy's assassin—did not live isolated from the world of his time. During his brief twenty-four years of life, Oswald came into contact with an incredible array of groups and individuals, all of whom had reason to wish for the elimination of Kennedy. Beginning with an uncle connected to organized crime, young Oswald moved through a shadowy world of soldiers, intelligence agents, Russian communists and anticommunists, pro- and anti-Castro Cubans, FBI men and right-wing anticommunists. To place the events of November 22, 1963 in proper perspective, it is necessary to become familiar with these groups and with their relationships to Oswald and each other.

After all, every good detective begins his murder investigation by determining who had the means, motive, and opportunity to commit the act. The obvious starting place is with the one man universally acknowledged as being the person most closely connected with the assassination—Lee Harvey Oswald.

Lee Harvey Oswald—Assassin or Patsy?

Prior to his enlistment in the Marines and with the exception of the death of his father, Lee Harvey Oswald's boyhood was little different from that of millions of other Americans.

Oswald was born in New Orleans, Louisiana, on October 18, 1939, two months after the death of his father, Robert E. Lee Oswald, a collector of insurance premiums. While this unfortunate event must have had some effect on young Oswald, it was a fate endured by thousands of other young Americans, none of whom have felt compelled to murder national leaders.

In 1945, Oswald's mother married for a third time, but three years later the marriage ended in divorce. From that point on, Oswald and his brother, Robert, were brought up by their mother, Marguerite.

A Mother in History

The House Select Committee on Assassinations in 1979 concluded that President Kennedy was "probably assassinated as the result of a conspiracy." However they maintained that Lee Harvey Oswald was the actual killer and that another gunman—whose presence was established by two separate scientific tests based on a Dallas police recording of the gunfire in Dealey Plaza—escaped and remains unidentified.

This finding was a milestone to the many Americans who had come to disbelieve the lone-assassin theory of the Warren Commission.

Typically, however, this reversal of official American history was still not enough for the mother of the accused assassin, Marguerite Oswald. She told newsmen:

> The committee members have made a first step in the right direction. It's up to us to do the rest . . . I hope and know the future will vindicate my son entirely. It took us 15 years to come this far. It may take another 15 years or longer. I probably won't be around, but the world will know that Lee Harvey Oswald was innocent of the charges against him.

This was the statement of a woman who was much more than just a supportive mother. It came from a woman who faced more public hostility

91

than most murderers . . . a woman who faced the autumn of her years alone and in poverty. And all because of a child she bore.

Marguerite Claverie was born in New Orleans in 1907. Her family was of French and German extraction. Her mother died a few years after her birth, leaving young Marguerite and her five siblings in the care of her father, a streetcar conductor. According to relatives, the Claverie family was poor but happy.

Marguerite, at the age of seventeen, completed one year of high school. She then dropped out to become a law-firm receptionist. In August 1929, she married Edward John Pic, Jr., a clerk. However, the marriage was not successful and the couple divorced in 1931, several months after the birth of her first son, John Edward Pic.

In 1933, she married Robert Edward Lee Oswald, himself recently divorced. She described her marriage to Oswald as the "only happy part" of her life. Out of this union came a second son, Robert. Then her happiness came to an end. Two months before the birth of Lee Harvey Oswald in October 1939, her husband died of a sudden heart attack. Making her way alone, she saw an opportunity of establishing a family once again by remarrying in 1945. Sending the two elder sons off to boarding school, she and her new husband, Edwin A. Ekdahl, took six-year-old Lee and moved to Benbrook, Texas, a small town south of Fort Worth.

However, there were soon arguments over money and charges of infidelity against Ekdahl. A divorce was granted in 1948 and she was allowed to use her former name of Oswald. It is interesting to note that Ekdahl's divorce attorney was Fred Korth, who in the fall of 1963 was fired as secretary of the Navy by President Kennedy amid charges that Korth may have been involved in a scandal over the General Dynamics TFX airplane.

John Pic and Robert Oswald rejoined their mother, but both soon left home to join the military. Marguerite was left with only young Lee. Some accounts say Lee was overly mothered by her, while others claim she neglected the boy. However, the former seems to be closer to the truth in light of the fact that she became a practical nurse charged with keeping the children of prominent Texans such as the late Amon Carter, Jr., and former congressman Tom Vandergriff. Despite much conjecture, there is little evidence that Lee's childhood was any better or any worse than others.

In 1959, after serving three years in the Marines, Lee received a sudden discharge and came back to Fort Worth for a two-day visit with his mother. Lee said he was off to New Orleans to work for an import-export firm, but several weeks later, Mrs. Oswald read that her twenty-year-old son had turned up in Russia, where he told U.S. officials he wanted to defect.

Mrs. Oswald's statements to the press at that time were unpopular. Instead of branding her son a traitor, she said:

I feel very strongly that as an individual, he has the right to make his own decision. Lee has definite ideas. I believe God gives us a conscience and the ability to know right and I feel he has the right to make his own decision.

Despite this motherly support, Lee seemed to make every effort to avoid Marguerite after his return from the Soviet Union in 1962. At one point he moved his family from Fort Worth to Dallas without leaving his mother a forwarding address.

Her family was reunited only briefly during those dark days of November, 1963.

Mrs. Oswald was on her way to work on November 22, when she heard over the car radio that Kennedy had been shot while riding in a motorcade in downtown Dallas. She also learned that a young ex-Marine named Lee Harvey Oswald was being held by police as the suspected assassin.

Concerned by the broadcasts and apparently with no friends to turn to, she contacted the local newspaper, *The Fort Worth Star-Telegram*, and asked if someone would take her to Dallas. She told the newspapermen who drove her to the Dallas police station: "I want to hear him tell me that he did it."

Mrs. Oswald also told them that she had been persecuted since her son's journey to Russia and knew the meaning of suffering. She also told of being fired by her last employer, *Star-Telegram* publisher Amon Carter, Jr. She said she had been acting as a day nurse for the Carters' children until about two weeks prior to the Kennedy assassination. After a weekend trip to Las Vegas, the Carters suddenly let her go.

She once told this author: "You don't know what it's like to have someone look at you and say, 'You've done a good job, but we no longer need your services.' "

In Dallas Mrs. Oswald was disappointed in her desire to hear a confession from her son. She was not allowed to talk with him. And Oswald steadfastly maintained his innocence. He shouted to newsmen gathered in the police station hallway: "No, sir, I didn't kill anybody. I'm just a patsy!"

After the murder of Oswald by Jack Ruby two days later, his mother's tone changed to one of suspicion and accusation, blaming the Dallas police and federal authorities for her son's death. She asked bitterly: "Why would [Jack Ruby] be allowed within a few feet of a prisoner—any prisoner—when I could not even see my own son?"

To compound her suspicions, she maintained until her death that the FBI had shown her a photo of Ruby the night before her son was slain. She said about 6:30 P.M. on November 23, the night after the assassination, an FBI agent and another man knocked on the door of the hotel where she and Lee's wife were staying. After being told that her daughter-in-law was tired and couldn't talk with the men, the FBI agent said he wanted to ask her a question. She recalled the incident to newsmen a week later:

> He had a picture coupled [sic] inside his hand and asked me if I had ever seen that man before. I told him, "No sir, believe me, I never have." Then he left. A few days later, I walked into the room where I was staying and, in front of my son Robert and lot of witnesses, I picked up a paper and when I turned it over I said, "This is the picture of the man that FBI agent showed me." I did not even know at the time he was the man who shot my son. I was told that the picture was [of] Mr. Jack Ruby.

FBI officials, when informed of her statement, speculated that she must have been confused as to the date she was shown the photograph.

On July 10, 1964, FBI agent Bardwell D. Odum signed an affidavit with the Warren Commission stating that he had shown the picture to Mrs. Oswald. He said the photo was furnished by FBI superiors, who obtained it from the CIA. The FBI said they included the photo as a Warren Commission exhibit. It was reportedly supplied by the CIA, which was secretly photographing visitors to the Soviet embassy in Mexico City.

This incident was the beginning of a lifelong suspicion of federal authorities by Mrs. Oswald. To the end of her life, she maintained that Lee had been working as some sort of agent for the U.S. government and that unnamed "high officials" were part of the plot to kill Kennedy and blame her son. After Watergate, she told a local newspaper: "If you called in all the FBI men involved in Lee Harvey Oswald's life and questioned them, one thing would lead to another and it would probably break the assassination case."

Just after the assassination, Mrs. Oswald said: "They [the public] all turned their backs on me before [when Oswald appeared in Russia] and they will turn their backs on me again, but my faith will see me through." And faith was truly about the only thing left for Mrs. Oswald.

With the exception of a couple of mysterious "benefactors" who kept her supplied with publications concerning the assassination, Marguerite Oswald was forced to live through the next two decades on less than five hundred dollars a month in Social Security payments. In the Bicentennial summer of 1976, she was without a refrigerator for almost two months because she could not afford to repair hers. The loneliness and poverty of her life, however, failed to crush her fighting spirit. She continued to assail the official version of the assassination and to strike out at media presentations of the event.

In 1978, after viewing a CBS "docudrama" entitled "Ruby and Oswald," she told the local newspaper:

I have every right to be upset over that program as well as many other things because they are talking about my son and my family. They sit there and tell the gullible American public that their program is the truth and based on documentation. Well, I'm sitting here with things you've never heard of. I can tear that CBS program apart like I did the Warren Commission.

Her thoughts on the Warren Commission, whose conclusions were taken as gospel at the time but gradually lost the confidence of the majority of Americans, are summed up in a letter Mrs. Oswald wrote to several congressmen in 1973 at the height of the Watergate crisis:

On Nov. 29, 1963, the then President of the United States, Lyndon B. Johnson, created a commission to evaluate all the facts and circumstances surrounding the assassination of President John F. Kennedy and the subsequent killing of the alleged assassin and to report its findings and conclusions to him. . . . President Johnson selected Earl Warren, Chief Justice of the United States, as its chairman. Because I was critical of the commission, I was asked, "Mrs. Oswald, are you implying that the Chief Justice would whitewash evidence or hide information so that the American people, as well as the whole world, would never learn the truth?" I answered, yes, in the name of security, men of integrity and who are the most esteemed, most respected and honored, who have the welfare of the country at heart, would be most likely to do what the White House wanted and thought necessary. The Watergate affair has followed this pattern. Those we believe are above reproach, those who have reached the pinnacle or are near it, those who are guiding our nation's destiny are found to have manipulated events to accomplish certain things they think were for the good of the country. Those who have a deep sense of patriotism and loyalty are most likely to twist events to accomplish their purposes. . . . The Watergate affair only strengthens my convictions and proves my theory. [In 1963] The suspect was my son and seven such respected men branded a dead man who was neither tried nor convicted, assassin.

Through the years, Mrs. Oswald, who always claimed to be a "mother in history," was quick to point out that her defense of her son went beyond simple motherly love. She once told this author: "If he was truly guilty, I can accept that. But whether it's my son or someone else's son, I want the proof and the proof is just not there."

In her last years, Mrs. Oswald was virtually a recluse in her modest but well-kept brick home on the west side of Fort Worth. An occasional visitor—usually a journalist—and her small dog, Fritz, were her only company.

Neither her other sons nor Lee's wife, Marina, ever spoke to her again after those days in November 1963. When money problems pressed too hard, she would sell a book or a letter from her mammoth collection of assassination materials. It was such money problems that helped create the belief that Mrs. Oswald would only talk for profit.

However, as several Fort Worth newsmen can confirm, she never hesitated to pick up her telephone and call the media when a particular news item rankled her. She once explained the charge of talk-for-cash this way:

> Well, here I am without money, wondering where my next meal is coming from and these writers come to my house wanting an interview. Then they go out and write some piece—some of them don't even talk to me more than fifteen minutes or so—and they get all this money for their work. That's not fair!

Over the years, Mrs. Oswald made repeated attempts to publish a book based on her knowledge, memories, and research of the assassination. Oddly enough, in light of the hundreds of books on the subject by authors ranging from the famous to crackpots, no one would publish a book by the mother of the accused assassin.

In January 1981, Mrs. Oswald quietly entered a Fort Worth hospital. Rumors circulated that she had cancer. By the end of that month, Marguerite Claverie Oswald was dead. Her memorial service was private. But her cause lives on. In one of her last letters to this author she wrote but one simple sentence: "Again—The charges against my late son Lee Harvey Oswald are false."

*   *   *

Oswald's early life is shrouded in innuendo and misinformation, much of it stemming from the passionate attitudes following the assassination.

Anyone who had had any contact with Oswald was hunted down and interviewed by newsmen and many were deposed by the Warren Commission.

And no one, including some family members, had anything good to say about the man accused of killing one of this nation's most popular presidents.

Some examples of misinformation include the statement that his two older brothers, and eventually Lee himself, were placed in an orphanage by their mother. While true in one respect, a closer look shows that Mrs. Oswald had to work to earn a living for their fatherless family. Keep in mind there were no daycare centers in 1942.

Mrs. Oswald explained to newsmen years later that she placed the boys in the Bethlehem Children's Home, operated by the Lutheran Church. Admittedly it was also an orphanage, but more precisely, it was the forerunner of a daycare center. She saw the boys on weekends and holidays. It was quite a different situation from that described in the Warren Commission Report: "Reminding her sons that they were orphans and that the family's financial condition was poor, she placed [them] in an orphans' home."

Lee's oldest brother, John Pic, told the Warren Commission that Lee slept with his mother until almost eleven years old, thus supplying much fodder for later psychological speculation. Mrs. Oswald's version sounds more mundane:

> . . . [while] I was married . . . Lee had his own bed, of course, all the while. After I divorced this man [Ekdahl], all I got from this divorce was $1,500 and I paid a $1,000 down on a home. Well, I had to buy furniture. I bought used furniture, and one of the boys slept on an army cot, and the other on a twin bed, and, because of the circumstances, Lee slept with me; which was a short time because then his brother joined the service and when he did, Lee took his bed. But it just implies that all through his life he slept with his mother, which isn't the case, you see. It's quite a difference.

Robert Oswald supported his mother's version of this issue by writing: "If this [sleeping arrangement] had a bad effect on Lee, I'm sure mother didn't realize it. She was simply making use of all the space she had."

Much was made of Oswald's truancy in New York during 1953–54, as well as the psychological testing resulting from this infraction.

In the summer of 1952, shortly before Lee's thirteenth birthday, he and his mother had gone to live with his half-brother John Pic and his wife in New York City, where Pic was stationed with the Coast Guard. There were reports of fights and divisions within the group and by the start of the school year, Lee and his mother had moved into their own apartment in the Bronx.

Teased at junior high school because he wore jeans and spoke with a Texas accent, Lee began staying away. However, unlike most truants who ended up in pools halls or street gangs, Lee continued his education on his own, frequenting the local library and the zoo. Finally caught, the young-ster was handed over for psychiatric observation to an institution called Youth House. Here he stayed from April 16 until May 7, 1953. Mrs. Oswald said it was only after having both her gifts and her person searched for cigarettes and narcotics, that she realized Youth House was one step short of jail. She said her son implored her: "Mother, I want to get out of here. There are children in here who have killed people and smoke. I want to get out."

While under the care of the state, Oswald was given psychiatric tests. The results were essentially inconclusive. They showed him to be a bright and inquisitive young man who was somewhat tense, withdrawn, and hesitant to talk about himself or his feelings.

Even the Warren Report, which generally tried to depict Oswald in the worst possible light, conceded:

Contrary to reports that appeared after the assassination, the psychiatric examination did not indicate that Lee Oswald was a potential assassin, potentially dangerous, that "his outlook on life had strongly paranoid overtones," or that he should be institutionalized.

After his experience in Youth House, there were no further truancy problems with young Lee. In January 1954, Lee and his mother returned to New Orleans, where he finished the ninth grade and began the tenth. Upon arriving in New Orleans, the Oswalds lived initially with Mrs. Oswald's sister and her husband, Lillian and Charles "Dutz" Murret, before finding an apartment of their own.

Everyone who knew Oswald as a youth agrees that he was somewhat introverted and was what could be best described as a "bookworm." His interests were widely varied, including animals, astronomy, classic literature . . . and, eventually, politics. Reading comic books and listening to radio and TV were also among his favorite pastimes.

Robert Oswald later recalled:

One of his favorite [TV] programs was "I Led Three Lives," the story of Herbert Philbrick, the FBI informant who posed as a communist spy. In the early 1950's Lee watched that show every week without fail. When I left home to join the Marines, he was still watching the reruns.

There can be little doubt that the well-read but lonely young Oswald spent much of his time daydreaming, fantasizing about being an important person some day.

Oswald appears to have been drawn at an early age to the epic and intense ideological struggle between communism and democratic capitalism. He claimed his first contact with communist ideology came with a pamphlet handed to him on a New York street corner. In a Moscow interview shortly after arriving in Russia, Oswald told newspaper reporter Aline Mosby:

I'm a Marxist . . . I became interested about the age of 15. From an ideological viewpoint. An old lady handed me a pamphlet about saving the Rosenbergs . . . I looked at that paper and I still remember it for some reason, I don't know why.

Julius and Ethel Rosenberg had been convicted of passing atomic bomb secrets to the Russians in a celebrated—and still controversial—case beginning in 1950. They were executed on June 19, 1953.

However, this story of early interest in communism must be taken with a grain of salt. After all, this is simply what Oswald told a reporter at a time he was trying hard to prove he was a devout communist supporter.

His brother Robert also expressed puzzlement over this story, writing:

If Lee was deeply interested in Marxism in the summer of 1955, he said nothing about it to me. During my brief visit with him in New Orleans, I never saw any books on the subject in the apartment on Exchange Place. Never, in my presence, did he read anything that I recognized as Communist literature. I was totally surprised when the information about his interest in Marxism came out, at the time of his defection to Russia. I was amazed that he had kept to himself ideas and opinions that were evidently so important to him.

In New Orleans, Oswald's study of communism allegedly intensified. Strangely enough, at the same time he was making a patriotic move— joining the Civil Air Patrol (CAP).

It was at this point that Oswald made one of the most intriguing connections of his life. And it may have been in the Civil Air Patrol that Oswald the "communist" was truly born.

It has been established that Oswald's CAP leader was a mysterious character named David W. Ferrie. Ferrie, an airline pilot, private investigator, and outspoken right-winger, went on to have connections with reputed Mafia boss Carlos Marcello, anti-Castro Cuban groups, former FBI agent Guy Banister and his anti-Castro activities, and the CIA. Ferrie will be discussed at length in other sections of this book.

Could Ferrie, who reportedly used his CAP position to establish homosexual contacts with young boys, have influenced Oswald to begin making a procommunist "cover" for himself with an eye toward becoming a U.S. agent?

Did Ferrie seek to take advantage of the impressionable young Oswald with stories of using his intelligence contacts to help Oswald enter the exciting world of espionage? Considering Ferrie's known homosexuality and intelligence connections, this speculation is not as farfetched as it sounds.

We may never know, however, since in 1967 Ferrie was found dead in his New Orleans apartment the day after being released from protective custody by District Attorney Jim Garrison, who named Ferrie as his chief suspect in a plot to assassinate President Kennedy and described him as "one of history's most important individuals."

Ferrie and Oswald's Library Card

A puzzling incident occurred involving David Ferrie and Oswald's library card which, while not proving ongoing links between the two men, provides tantalizing evidence that such a connection may have existed.

Within hours of Kennedy's assassination, an employee of former FBI agent Guy Banister contacted New Orleans authorities and said both

Banister and Ferrie had been in touch with Oswald. (Oswald used the same address—554 Camp Street—as Banister's office on some of his Fair Play For Cuba material, which will be discussed later in more detail.)

Banister, a supporter of right-wing causes, had been assisting anti-Castro Cubans through his New Orleans private detective agency.

Authorities could not immediately locate Ferrie. Some time later, Ferrie told New Orleans police he had driven to Texas the night of the assassination to go goose hunting. However, subsequent investigation of Ferrie's companions revealed that they had decided not to hunt geese but, instead, had gone to a Houston skating rink where Ferrie spent two hours at a pay telephone making and receiving calls.

One of Ferrie's friends told New Orleans police that shortly after Kennedy's assassination, an attorney named C. Wray Gill had come to Ferrie's home and mentioned that when Oswald was arrested in Dallas, he was carrying a library card with Ferrie's name on it.

Gill, an attorney for Carlos Marcello, promised to act on Ferrie's behalf upon his return to New Orleans. On the evening of the Sunday that Jack Ruby killed Oswald, Ferrie contacted Gill, who then accompanied Ferrie to the authorities the next day. Ferrie denied knowing anything about Oswald or the assassination and was released.

However, one of Oswald's former neighbors in New Orleans later recalled that Ferrie visited her after the assassination asking about a library card. And Oswald's former landlady said Ferrie came to her asking about the library card just hours after the assassination and *before* the bizarre Texas trip. After all this furor over the library card, there is nothing in the official record indicating such a card was ever found in Oswald's possession. Yet the Secret Service, when they questioned Ferrie, reportedly asked if he had loaned his library card to Oswald.

Could such a library card have disappeared from Oswald's belongings while in Dallas police custody? It certainly would not be the only such incident—an incriminating photograph of Oswald was discovered after nearly fifteen years among the possessions of a retired Dallas policeman. And if such a card existed, it would have been strong evidence that a relationship between Oswald and Ferrie continued long after young Oswald moved away.

*   *   *

In the fall of 1955, Oswald began the tenth grade at Warren Easton High School in New Orleans but dropped out soon after his birthday in October.

Oswald himself wrote to school authorities, stating:

To who it may concern,
Because we are moving to San Diego in the middle of this month Lee must quit school now. Also, please send him any papers such as his birth certificate that you may have. Thank you.
Sincerely,
Mrs. M. Oswald

This note gave evidence of what young Oswald had in mind. He had his mother sign a false affidavit stating he was seventeen and he tried to join the Marine Corps. Undoubtedly he was looking forward to Marine training in San Diego. His brother Robert, who had joined the Marines three years earlier, had given Lee his training manual. His mother later recalled: "He knew it by heart."

His desire to join the Marines was decidedly odd if we are supposed to believe, as the Warren Commission did, that he was a full-blown Marxist by this time. It makes more sense to believe that Oswald eagerly looked forward to serving in the military because he already knew that plans were being made for his service in intelligence. But his hopes were dashed when the recruiting authorities failed to believe the affidavit. Oswald had to wait another year for his chance at the Marines. His mother noted: "Lee lived for the time that he would become seventeen years old to join the Marines— that whole year." During that time, he continued to build an identity as a communist sympathizer.

During a meeting of the New Orleans Amateur Astronomy Association, he began expounding on the virtures of communism, saying communism was the only way of life for the workers and that he was looking for a Communist cell to join but couldn't find one. Another time, he was kicked out of the home of a friend after the friend's father overheard him praising the communist system.

Some have interpreted this penchant for communism as sincere and as evidence of how deeply disturbed Oswald had become. However, when viewed from another side, there is the real possibility that—believing the promises of Captain Ferrie that the adventuresome world of spies lay ahead of him—Oswald was already concocting a procommunist cover.

After all, up until his meeting with Ferrie his interest in politics and ideology had been no different from that of any other bright kid. And his family had a tradition of honorable military service.

It is clear that Oswald couldn't wait to join the military, yet at the same time was going out of his way to offend nearly everyone with his procommunist posturing.

The question of the genuineness of his regard for communism only intensified after he entered the Marine Corps.

Oswaldskovich the Marine

Six days after his seventeenth birthday, Oswald was sworn in as a U.S. Marine.

On October 26, 1956, Oswald arrived at the Marine Corps Recruit Depot in San Diego, California. Here he completed basic training with no apparent problems, although his marksmanship on the rifle range was less than what was desired by his fellow Marines.

Former Marine Sherman Cooley recalled that Oswald was given the name "Shitbird" because initially he couldn't qualify on the M-1 rifle. Cooley said: "It was a disgrace not to qualify and we gave him holy hell."

Another Marine buddy, Nelson Delgado, also has publicly told of Oswald's ineptness with a rifle. However, when Delgado tried to tell this to the FBI after the assassination, he claimed: "They attacked my competence to judge his character and shooting ability and criticized my efforts to teach him Spanish." A hounded and fearful Delgado finally moved his family to England because ". . . the conspirators may think I know more than I do."

Oswald went on to qualify as a "sharpshooter" by only two points in December, "sharpshooter" being the second of three grades of marksmanship. He did not do nearly so well when he again fired for the record shortly before leaving the Marines.

On January 20, 1957, he completed basic and went on to Camp Pendleton, California, where he completed advanced combat training. While learning combat skills, Oswald reportedly continued to speak favorably of communism—an odd circumstance for the Marines in the 1950s unless he was still trying to establish a procommunist "cover." Odder still is the fact that at no time did any of Oswald's Marine superiors note for the record his displays of procommunist sentiment.

During this time, Oswald apparently was liked well enough by his fellow Marines, who called him "Ozzie Rabbit" after a TV cartoon character "Oswald the Rabbit."

In March, Oswald reported to the Naval Air Technical Training Center in Jacksonville, Florida. Here he studied to be a radar air controller, a job given only to men with higher-than-average intelligence. This job also required a security clearance of "Confidential," which Oswald obtained the time he was promoted to private first class.

Daniel Patrick Powers, who was with Oswald in Jacksonville, recalled that Oswald used almost all his weekend passes to go to New Orleans, presumably to visit his mother. However, Mrs. Oswald was in Texas at the time and relatives in New Orleans could only recall one phone call from Oswald.

Could he have been gaining more advice on how to concoct a procommunist "cover" in preparation for becoming a spy from Captain Ferrie or someone else?

He graduated May 3 and was sent to Kessler Air Force Base in Mississippi, where he completed an Aircraft Control and Warning Operator Course.

After finishing seventh in a class of fifty, Oswald was given a Military Occupational Specialty (MOS) of Aviation Electronics Operator and, after a brief leave, was sent to the Marine Corps Air Station at El Toro, California. He stayed there until shipped to Japan aboard the U.S.S. *Bexar* on August 22. Shipmates noticed that Oswald read *Leaves of Grass* by Walt Whitman, and other "good type of literature."

Upon arriving in Japan, the young Marine was sent about twenty-five miles southwest of Tokyo to the air base at Atsugi, home of the First Marine Aircraft Wing—and one of two bases where the then top-secret U-2 spy plane flights were originating. Also at Atsugi was an innocuous group of buildings housing what was known only as the "Joint Technical Advisory Group." In reality, this was the CIA main operational base in the Far East and it was here that speculation has arisen that the young Oswald got into the real spy business.

During his duty hours, Oswald sat in a hot, crowded, semicircular radar control room known as the bubble and intently watched his radarscope for signs of Russian or Chinese aircraft crossing into allied airspace. The job was mostly monotony, broken only by an occasional unidentified aircraft and the strange utility plane code-named "Race Car."

The radar operators would overhear Race Car asking for wind information at ninety thousand feet. They at first thought this was some sort of joke, since the world altitude record at that time was only slightly more than sixty-five thousand and the radar height-finding antenna read only up to forty-five thousand.

However, slowly the men of Oswald's unit, Marine Air Control Squadron No. 1 (MACS-1), realized that they were overhearing conversations from the strange-looking aircraft that they would soon see wheeled out of a large nearby hangar and scream into the air. When asked about the craft, the officers would only say it was a "utility plane." The men didn't know this utility plane, or U-2, was being used to penetrate Soviet and Chinese airspace for the purpose of photographing military and industrial targets.

Oswald seemed to show particular interest in the "secrets" of Atsugi. One Marine recalled seeing Oswald taking photographs of the base and he showed special interest during unit briefings on classified material.

Just as he had gone off alone to New Orleans, Oswald began making two-day visits to Tokyo. Years later, Oswald is reported to have confided that he made contact with a small group of Japanese Communists in Tokyo while in the Marines. Even Warren Commission lawyers, W. David Slawson, and William T. Coleman, Jr., stated in a report that was classified for a time: ". . . there is the possibility that Oswald came into contact with Communist agents at that time . . ."

Oswald told a friend at the time that he was having an affair with a Japanese girl who worked as a hostess in a Tokyo nightclub called the Queen Bee.

This was an intriguing connection indeed, for the Queen Bee at that time was one of the three most expensive nightspots in Tokyo. An evening at the Queen Bee could cost up to a hundred dollars. It catered especially to officers and pilots (including U-2 pilots, according to author Edward Jay Epstein). It was believed that the hostesses of the Queen Bee, one hundred of the most beautiful women in Tokyo, were using their charms to gain information from American servicemen.

It was a decidedly odd meeting place for Oswald, who was making less than eighty-five dollars a month with much of that being sent back to help support his mother.

Was the poor Marine, Private Oswald, being used to gather intelligence or was Oswald testing his intelligence abilities to infiltrate Communist agents in the Queen Bee? The answer to this question may have come when author/researcher Mark Lane interviewed one of Oswald's former Marine pals from Atsugi.

David Bucknell, who was never interviewed by the Warren Commission, told of an incident in which he and Oswald went for beers at a bar near Santa Ana, California, where they were both stationed in 1959. While sitting there, the two Marines were approached by two women who engaged them in conversation. Bucknell said later that day Oswald said this incident reminded him of a similar experience at Atsugi. According to Oswald's story, he was sitting alone in a Japanese bar when an attractive woman joined him and began asking questions regarding his work at Atsugi. Since his work involved the highly-secret U-2 plane, Oswald reported this meeting to his superior officer. Soon this officer arranged a meeting between Oswald and a man in civilian clothes. Oswald told Bucknell the man explained that Oswald could do his country a great service by giving false information to the woman, a known KGB agent. Oswald agreed and thus became an intelligence operative. Oswald said he had been encouraged to continue meeting the woman and was given money to spend at the Queen Bee.

While no U.S. intelligence agency has admitted it, there is further evidence to suggest that he was indeed used as an agent. Sgt. Gerry Patrick Hemming, who served in Japan with Oswald and later went on to join anti-Castro Cubans, said he was recruited into the CIA while in the service and, while Oswald never said so, he believed the same thing happened to Oswald—based on conversations between the two.

A former CIA finance officer, James Wilcott, testified to the House Select Committee on Assassinations that colleagues told him that Oswald was a secret operative for the spy agency in Japan. Wilcott, who served in the CIA from 1957 through 1966, said after Kennedy's assassination he had several conversations with CIA personnel involved in covert operations. He said, based on these conversations and his experience of paying CIA funds to secret operations through the use of code names, or "cryptos," he became convinced that Oswald was brought into the CIA while serving as a radar operator in Japan and later was sent to infiltrate Russia as a spy.

When CIA officials denied these charges—one went so far as to suggest that Oswald was actually recruited by the Soviet KGB while in Japan—the Committee decided not to believe Wilcott.

Another tantalizing piece of evidence that Oswald was involved in intelligence work while stationed in Japan comes from his Marine Corps medical records. Those records show that on September 16, 1958, Oswald was treated for "Urethritis, acute, due to gonococcus . . ." Gonorrhea is a venereal disease preached against loudly by the military. For servicemen, a case of gonorrhea often results in disciplinary measures. However, Oswald's medical record goes on to state: "Origin: In line of duty, not due to own misconduct." The fact that Oswald was absolved of any responsibility in contracting gonorrhea astounds service veterans and is strong evidence that his extracurricular activities had the blessings of the military, if not of the CIA.

Another small but eye-opening revelation came from secret meetings of the Warren Commission. General counsel J. Lee Rankin—armed with initial reports from the military—told Commission members two months after the assassination: ". . . we are trying to run that down, to find out what he studied at the Monterey School of the Army in the way of languages . . ." The Monterey School, now called the Defense Language Institute, is one of the government schools for giving sophisticated and rapid language courses. Rankin's remark, made public only after a Freedom of Information suit, seems to imply that the Commission had knowledge of Oswald attending courses at Monterey.

And it is certainly easier to believe that Oswald got a crash course in the Russian language in the military than to believe that this high-school dropout learned one of the world's hardest languages by reading books and listening to records, as implied by the Warren Commission. (Incidentally, fellow Marines testified they could not recall Oswald listening to any language records.)

It is possible that undercover work was behind a strange shooting incident that took place just as his unit was scheduled to be transferred to the Philippines in late 1957. On October 27, Oswald was gathering gear from his locker when reportedly a .22-caliber derringer fell onto the floor and discharged, grazing his left elbow. As nearby Marines rushed into his room, all Oswald would say was: "I believe I shot myself."

Before the incident, Oswald had told a friend, George Wilkins, that he had ordered the derringer from a mail-order firm in the United States. At least two of the Marines present, Thomas Bagshaw and Pete Connor, now claim the bullet missed Oswald altogether. Others at the time had the impression that Oswald shot himself in an attempt to prevent being transferred to the Philippines. If that was the case, it failed. Although absent almost three weeks for medical treatment, he was returned to duty just in time to ship out with his unit on November 20.

The maneuvers of Oswald's unit in the Philippines and South China Sea were largely uneventful, although one companion recalled: "He did a little growing up in that time . . . he started acting like a man."

Interestingly, while the unit was on Corregidor, actor John Wayne stopped in briefly and a photograph was taken of him. In a background doorway stands Marine Oswald, who was serving his third straight month on mess duty.

His hospital stay following the derringer incident and the amount of time he spent pulling KP (Kitchen Police) may be indicative of time away from his regular unit spent in intelligence training. According to witnesses, his elbow wound was very minor, yet Oswald spent nearly three weeks in a hospital. More time gaps in his military career were to come.

Back at Atsugi, Oswald was court-martialed for possessing an unregistered weapon—the derringer. On April 11, 1958, he was found guilty and sentenced to twenty days at hard labor, forfeiture of fifty dollars in pay, and reduced back to the rank of private. His confinement was suspended for six months on the condition that he stay out of trouble.

It was about this time that Oswald put in for a hardship discharge. As this application was being processed there apparently was a need for more time away from his unit for additional intelligence training. This may have been accomplished by an incident that began in the Enlisted Men's Club at Atsugi. Oswald, who heretofore had not been known as violent, tried to pick a fight with Technical Sgt. Miguel Rodriguez, allegedly the man who had assigned him to so much KP duty. Rodriguez failed to rise to the bait.

On June 20, Oswald sought out Rodriguez at the Bluebird Club in Yamato and again tried to fight with the sergeant. After Oswald poured a drink on Rodriguez, military police intervened, and the next day, Rodriguez signed a complaint against Oswald. At the court martial, Oswald acted as his own defense, claiming he was drunk and spilled the drink on Rodriguez accidentally. Rodriguez said then—and after the assassination—that Oswald had not been drunk and had poured the drink on him deliberately.

The judge ruled that Oswald was guilty of using "provoking words" to a noncommissioned officer and sentenced him to twenty-eight days in the brig and forfeiture of fifty-five dollars. Furthermore, his previous suspension of sentence was revoked and Oswald supposedly went to the brig until August 13, a period of more than forty-five days.

Only one Marine who was in the Atsugi brig during this time recalled seeing Oswald and he said during this brief encounter Oswald was wearing civilian clothes.

After his release, several Marines commented that Oswald seemed different. Joseph D. Macedo said he found him "a completely changed person . . ." Others said that where "Ozzie Rabbit" had been extroverted and fun-filled, this new Oswald was cold and withdrawn.

It may well be right here that a new Oswald—an entirely different man—was substituted for the New Orleans-born Marine (see "Was Oswald Really Oswald?").

Meanwhile, a previously granted extension of overseas duty was canceled and it appeared that Oswald would soon be on his way home. However, on September 14, the Chinese Communists began making moves against the Nationalist islands of Quemoy and Matsu and there was a general mobilization. Oswald accompanied his unit to Formosa (now Taiwan). Not long after their arrival on the island, Oswald was assigned guard duty. About midnight, the officer of the guard, Lt. Charles R. Rhodes, heard several shots. Running to the scene, Rhodes found Oswald slumped against a tree holding his M-1 rifle in his lap. Rhodes recalled: "When I got to him, he was shaking and crying. He said he had seen men in the woods and that he challenged them and then started shooting . . . He kept saying he couldn't bear being on guard duty."

Almost immediately, Oswald was shipped back to Atsugi, arriving on October 5, 1958, according to official reports. Years later, Rhodes said he still believed that Oswald planned the shooting incident as a ploy to get himself transferred back to Japan. Rhodes was never given any explanation for the willingness of the Marine Corps to go along with this "ploy" except that Oswald was being returned for "medical treatment."

Recall the medical records concerning Oswald's gonorrhea contacted "in line of duty." However, this record is dated September 16, 1958, two days *after* Oswald officially left with his unit for Formosa.

There has been no explanation for this, as well as several other discrepancies in Oswald's military service records. This has caused some assassination researchers to believe that more than one man was using the name Oswald during this time.

Or could it be that even more time was needed to prepare Oswald for upcoming intelligence missions?

Back at Atsugi and with his unit gone, Oswald was temporarily assigned to a Marine squadron at Iwakuni, an air base about 430 miles southwest of Tokyo. Here, quite by accident, he came into contact with Owen Dejanovich, a Marine who had attended radar school with him. Dejanovich tried to renew the acquaintanceship but was rebuffed by Oswald, who made efforts to avoid the one man around who had known him previously. Dejanovich also found Oswald changed. He said Oswald kept referring to the Marines as "you Americans" and raving about "American imperialism" and "exploitation." He also noticed that Oswald was keeping company with locals again, this time with a ". . . round-eyed Russian girlfriend."

On November 2, 1958, Oswald boarded the U.S.S. *Barrett* for the two-week trip to San Francisco. On November 19, he took a thirty-day leave, traveling by bus to Fort Worth where he stayed with his mother, but he spent most of his time with his brother Robert hunting squirrels and rabbits.

On December 22, he was assigned to Marine Air Control Squadron No. 9 (MACS-9) at El Toro, California. Here he was one of seven enlisted men and three officers who formed a radar crew. According to the Warren Report:

This work probably gave him access to certain kinds of classified material, some of which, such as aircraft call signs and radio frequencies, was changed after his [attempted] defection to Russia.

It was here that Oswald's public embracing of communism reached new heights. He would answer questions with *"da"* or *"nyet"* and address fellow Marines as "Comrade." When playing chess, he always wanted the red pieces, which he referred to as the "victorious Red Army." His Marine companions began calling him "Oswaldskovich."

One of his fellow Marines, Kerry Thornley, was so impressed by this "eightball" that he later wrote a novel using a character based on Oswald. Here are some of his recollections:

I have never personally known an individual more motivated by what appeared to be a genuine concern for the human race than Lee Harvey Oswald . . . His concern for other people, not as individuals but as a mass, was real. Oswald was unselfish. He was so unselfish that he couldn't seem to concentrate on his own affairs. He would rather be busily solving the problems of mankind . . . [Once] I explained that I was an atheist.

"So am I," said Oswald, glancing up from his notebook. "I think the best religion is Communism."

"Yeah, Oswald's a Red," said one of the men, to me.

"No, I'm not a Communist. I just think they have the best system."

"Why?" I wanted to know.

"Because they have a purpose. And the Communist way of life is more scientific than ours. You don't have to believe in a bunch of fairy tales to accept it."

. . . What causes me to have second thoughts about his commitment to Communism is his enthusiasm for a book unpopular with the few self-admitted Communists I have known, for obvious reasons. The book is George Orwell's *1984*, a severe criticism in fiction form of socialist totalitarianism. . . . I read *1984* and for a while decided Oswald was not truly in sympathy with Marxism. It had to be a joke, I concluded. That explained his tight little smile. He was laughing to himself, I was sure. He saw all the fallacies in socialism that George Orwell saw. And, on this final point, I am still not convinced I was wrong . . . And, the one thing I remember most about Lee is that he was a comedian . . . his wit got him into the most trouble . . . One of his favorite games was to compare the United States Marine Corps to the society in *1984*. "Be careful, comrade, with Big Brother's equipment," he would say . . .

Thornley said he was greatly surprised when he read about Oswald going to Russia. He was even more surprised to learn that Oswald was identified as Kennedy's assassin. Although he was convinced of Oswald's guilt by the time he put down his recollections, thanks to the barrage of damaging information offered by the authorities through the news media, he nevertheless wrote:

From the moment I first heard of his arrest until after he was gunned down by Jack Ruby, I did not believe Oswald could be guilty. But, as the facts came in, as the evidence piled up, I decided there must have been more violence in him than I thought.

Another Marine, Nelson Delgado, also got along well with Oswald. Delgado, a Puerto Rican, said Oswald "treated him like an equal." Oswald and Delgado talked at length about Cuba and Fidel Castro's coming to power. After a while, Oswald began asking Delgado how he could get in touch with some Cubans.

Delgado said one day he handed Oswald a note saying he should write the Cuban embassy in Washington, D.C. Not long after that, Delgado noticed that Oswald, who previously received few letters, began receiving mail several times a week and that at least some of this mail came from the Cuban consulate.

Delgado also told investigators after the assassination that during this time, Oswald was often "gigged" for having a dirty rifle and that, when the unit went to the rifle range, Oswald got "Maggie's drawers"—a red flag signifying that he hadn't even hit the target.

If Oswald was a genuine Marine communist, it begs the imagination to think that his officers took no notice.

In fact, Thornley tells of an incident in which a young lieutenant did notice that Oswald was receiving a Russian newspaper in the mail. According to this story:

. . . the lieutenant grew very excited over his discovery and possibly made an open issue of Oswald's probable sympathy to the communist cause. Most of the troops . . . were very much amused at the lieutenant's having "pushed the panic button." Oswald, of course, didn't think it was so funny. But apparently the lieutenant's warnings were ignored by the command . . .

Were these warnings ignored or were higher-ups more knowledgeable about Oswald's communist activities?

Another hint as to Oswald's true allegiances may be found in an odd incident involving his friend Thornley, with whom Oswald spent many hours in ideological and philosophical discussions.

Thornley told the Warren Commission that one day while he and Oswald were preparing for a military parade and were remarking about the stupidity of the thing, Oswald said it made him angry. Thornley then said:

"Well, comes the revolution you will change all that." . . . at which time [Oswald] looked at me like a betrayed Caesar and screamed, "Not you, too, Thornley!" And I remember his voice cracked as he said this.

He was definitely disturbed at what I had said and I didn't really think I had said that much. . . . I never said anything to him again and he never said anything to me again.

This sounds more like a person deeply hurt that a good friend would seriously believe him to be a communist than like a communist sympathizer angered over an innocuous jibe.

James Botelho, today a California judge, was a roommate of Oswald's during his stay at El Toro. Botelho even once took Oswald home to meet his parents. He has never bought the idea that Oswald turned Communist. In an interview with Mark Lane, Botelho stated:

I'm very conservative now and I was at least as conservative at that time. Oswald was not a Communist or a Marxist. If he was I would have taken violent action against him and so would many of the other Marines in the unit.

Whatever his true beliefs about communism, Oswald at this time knew bigger things were looming on his horizon.

In the spring of 1959, he had applied to study philosophy at the Albert Schweitzer College in Switzerland and had been accepted. In a cryptic letter to his brother, he wrote: "Pretty soon I'll be getting out of the Corps and I know what I want to be and how I'm going to be it . . . ."

Years later, Marine Bucknell told Mark Lane that during 1959, both he, Oswald, and other Marines at El Toro Base were ordered to report to the military Criminal Investigation Division (CID). There a civilian tried to recruit those present for an intelligence operation against "Communists" in Cuba.

Oswald was selected to make several more trips to CID and later told Bucknell that the civilian was the same man who had been his intelligence contact at Atsugi. Some time later, Oswald confided to Bucknell that he was to be discharged from the Marines and go to Russia. Oswald said he was being sent to Russia by American intelligence and that he would return to America in 1961 as a hero.

Judge Botelho, the former roommate of Oswald, told of his reaction to Oswald's trip to Russia:

Well, when Oswald's presence in the Soviet Union was made public, it was the talk of everyone who knew him at the base. First of all, I was aware of the fact that the radio codes and other codes were not changed and that Oswald knew all of them. That made me suspicious. I knew Oswald was not a Communist and was, in fact, anti-Soviet. Then, when no real investigation about Oswald occurred at the base, I was sure that Oswald was on an intelligence assignment in Russia. . . . Two civilians dropped in [at El Toro], asked a few questions, took no written statements, and recorded no interviews with witnesses. It was the most casual of investigations. It was a cover-investigation so that it could be said that there had been an investigation. . . . Oswald, it was said, was the only Marine ever to defect from his country to another country, a Communist country, during peacetime. That was a major event. When the Marine Corps and American intelligence decided not to probe the reasons for the "defection," I knew then what I know now: Oswald was on an assignment in Russia for American intelligence.

*   *   *

Whether intelligence agent or true defector, Oswald obviously had plans made and the Navy seemed oddly obliging.

On August 17, 1959, Oswald applied for a dependency discharge on the grounds that his mother needed his support. This application was accompanied by affidavits from his mother, an attorney, a doctor, and two friends—all supplied by his mother—stating she had been injured at work in December 1958 and was unable to support herself. Later investigation showed a candy box had fallen on her nose and that she had not even bothered to see a doctor until well after the incident. Nevertheless, within two weeks, to the surprise of his fellow Marines, Oswald's request was approved and he was released from service on September 11.

On September 4, Oswald applied for a passport, plainly stating that he might travel to various countries including Russia and Cuba. This, of course, was in opposition to his claim that he was going home to care for his injured mother. His passport was "routinely" issued six days later, just in time for his exit from the Marines.

After a brief stopover in Texas with his mother, Oswald withdrew $203 from his only known bank account and continued on to New Orleans, where he purchased a ticket for Le Havre, France, on the freighter *Marion Lykes* for $220.75.

He had told his mother he was going to New Orleans to work for an import-export firm, but in a letter mailed just before he sailed, he wrote:

> I have booked passage on a ship to Europe. I would have had to sooner or later and I think it's best I go now. Just remember above all else that my values are different from Robert's or yours. It is difficult to tell you how I feel. Just remember, this is what I must do. I did not tell you about my plans because you could hardly be expected to understand.

On September 20, 1959, Oswald left on the first leg of a journey that would take him to his destiny—via Russia.

Summary

Lee Harvey Oswald had a childhood that was no better nor worse than that of millions of other Americans. He was bright and eager to learn, despite a disrespect for educational systems and authorities.

At age sixteen, after joining the Civil Air Patrol and meeting Captain David Ferrie, he suddenly made some public posturings as a procommunist, despite the fact that he tried to join the Marine Corps at this same time.

Once a Marine, several odd and troubling items appeared in his military record.

Despite prior-service statements indicating interest in Communist activities, Oswald was granted a security clearance and stationed at the Japanese base where supersecret spy flights were being launched. Further evidence of Oswald's involvement with undercover work can be seen in his off-duty activities at the Queen Bee and his strange case of venereal disease ''in line of duty.'' Fellow Marines and even a former CIA clerk have stated publicly that Oswald was recruited into U.S. intelligence while stationed in Japan.

Various discrepancies in Oswald's military records—notations made for the same date but different locations, unaccounted-for periods of time— support the idea that Oswald was given secret intelligence training.

And consider the circumstance of a Marine in 1959 who was vocally supportive of communism and Castro, yet was ''ignored'' by higher command—further evidence that Oswald was creating a cover story as a procommunist on orders.

The speed and ease with which he obtained a hardship discharge from the Marines and a United States passport raise questions regarding Oswald's possible relationship with U.S. intelligence.

Until the United States government decides to divulge all it knows about Oswald's career—there are still numerous files locked away until the year 2039 and Oswald's military files were reported ''routinely'' destroyed—it may be impossible to conclusively prove Oswald's intelligence connections.

Until the day she died, Oswald's mother maintained her son was an agent of the U.S. government, and the evidence of Oswald's spy work is there for anyone to see.

> . . . I believe [Oswald] worked for the American government.
> —Marina Oswald

Russians

Stretching from the Baltic to the Pacific, the Union of Soviet Socialist Republics, which many still refer to as Russia, covers the largest territory in the world. It contains a wide diversity of peoples, many with separate customs, traditions, and even languages.

Spreading from the duchies around Moscow and Kiev, Ivan the Great and his son ultimately brought areas from the Volga Steppes and the Caspian Sea under control during the sixteenth century.

Modern Russia was created by annexing or conquering a long string of small nations such as the Ukraine, Belorussia, Georgia, Lithuania, Moldavia, Kazakh, Armenia, Uzbek, Turkmen, Latvia, Estonia, and Azerbaijan.

By World War I, this giant collection of peoples was held together by the czarist monarchy. Battered by world war, famine, public discontent, a shattered economy, and political intrigues within the monarchy, Russia collapsed into revolution in February 1917. With the abdication of Czar Nicholas II and Czarina Alexandra, a provisional government was set up under Aleksandr Kerenski. Kerenski attempted to bring Western democratic ideals to his beleaguered nation, but the fury of the revolution continued unabated.

In the fall of 1917, hoping to pull Russia out of the war, the Germans encouraged the return of Vladimir Ilich Ulyanov, better known as Lenin, leader of the radical Bolsheviks. After the October Revolution, Russia fell under control of the Bolsheviks, who declared themselves dedicated to the ideals of communism.

In 1922, the Union of Soviet Socialist Republics was established in Russia. On January 21, 1924, after suffering three strokes, Lenin died. It has been rumored he may have been helped along by poison ordered by his successor, Joseph Stalin. Stalin, who may have murdered as many as twelve million people in his drive to power, held Russia in his dictatorial grip until his death in 1953.

In the five years following Stalin's death, there was a quiet but deadly struggle for power in the USSR, with former secretary of the Communist Party Nikita Khrushchev coming out on top. Khrushchev continued to take the offensive against Stalinist hard-liners, first by denouncing Stalin's purge of Secret Police Chief Lavrenti Beria in 1953 in return for Russian

Army support and then by staging a series of impressive foreign visits during the late 1950s.

Both Khrushchev and his Western counterpart, U.S. President Dwight Eisenhower, seemed sincere in wanting to ease the tensions between their two countries. In the summer of 1959, Khrushchev visited the United States. *Newsweek* described the results:

After two private days with Eisenhower at Camp David, Khrushchev lifted an ultimatum on Berlin, announced that the President had "captivated" him and praised [Eisenhower's] wisdom and love of peace in terms no cold-war Soviet leader has used either before or since. The stage was set for a full-fledged negotiation at the summit in Paris.

This summit, scheduled for mid-May 1960, might have produced a limited nuclear-test-ban treaty, already foreseen as the first major accord of the cold war.

But it was not to be. On May 1, traditionally celebrated in Russia as May Day, CIA pilot Francis Gary Powers was captured alive after his U-2 spy plane crashed in the Soviet Union following an explosion.

Khrushchev was furious, yet he tried to give Eisenhower latitude in disclaiming any knowledge of the incident. He stated that the U-2 flight may have been the work of "American aggressive circles" trying to "torpedo the Paris summit, or, at any rate, prevent an agreement for which the whole world is waiting."

After days of half-truths and evasions, Eisenhower finally admitted that the spy plane was acting on his orders and took responsibility for the fiasco, just as John Kennedy would take responsibility for the disastrous Bay of Pigs invasion a year later.

However, questions still surround the U-2 incident, and some students of history such as David Wallechinsky and Irving Wallace in *The People's Almanac* note: "It is possible that certain U.S. military leaders deployed Powers purposely to sabotage the peace talks which Eisenhower himself acutely desired."

Oswald and the U-2

Francis Gary Powers and his ill-fated U-2 spy plane were brought down six months after a former Marine named Lee Harvey Oswald arrived in Moscow and told an American embassy official he planned to give the Soviets classified information he had gained as a radar operator in the Marine Corps.

Richard E. Snyder, a CIA intelligence operative serving as senior consular officer at the Moscow embassy, recalled that Oswald went so far as to state that he knew something that would be of "special interest" to Soviet intelligence.

What "special interest" information did Oswald have? The Russians had known about the U-2 program for some time and their antiaircraft missiles were capable of shooting down the high-flying craft. What the Soviets lacked was detailed altitude information on the U-2 that would have allowed them to accurately control their missiles at great altitudes. Oswald, who served as a radar operator at Atsugi, Japan, one of the staging bases for the U-2 flights, had that information.

After being swapped for a Soviet spy, Powers returned to the U.S. and wrote a book about his ordeal entitled *Operation Overflight*. He pointed out Oswald's claim that he had information for the Soviets and implied that if indeed Oswald gave information pertaining to U-2 operational altitudes and radar techniques used during its flight, the Russians may have learned enough to enable them to shoot down the U-2. Powers also said his Soviet interrogators seemed to have special knowledge about the Atsugi base, although Powers maintained he had never been stationed there.

Files detailing Oswald's connection with the U-2 flights have been withheld from the American public for years by the Warren Commission.

Colonel Fletcher Prouty, who served as focal point officer between the CIA and the Air Force, was particularly concerned with the U-2 flights. He has stated that it is preposterous to assume that information Oswald might have given the Russians could have led to their shooting down the craft. Prouty told author Anthony Summers: "The Russians simply had nothing that could touch a plane flying that high." Prouty concluded that, based on his interpretation of U-2 technical evidence, Power's plane was flying below its operational altitude when brought down.

Some people familiar with the U-2 incident believe the plane may have been downed due to sabotage. In 1977, Powers told a radio audience that he believed his U-2 had been brought down by a bomb placed on board. Shortly after making this statement, he was killed when his helicopter, used to report news for a Los Angeles television station, ran out of gas and crashed.

There are two tantalizing clues that Oswald may have indeed had some connection with the U-2 incident. In a letter to his brother, Oswald wrote regarding Powers: "He seemed to be a nice bright American-type fellow when I saw him in Moscow." There is no explanation of how or when Oswald might have seen Powers, particularly since officially Oswald never returned to Moscow after being sent to Minsk in 1960.

Next, after his return to the United States, Oswald told Dennis Ofstein, a fellow employee of Jaggers-Childs-Stovall who had worked for Army security, that he had only seen Russian jets in Moscow on May Day. And of Oswald's three May Days spent in Russia, the only one unaccounted for is May 1, 1960—the day the U-2 was captured.

*   *   *

Because of the U-2 flights during this time, Soviet intelligence was extremely interested in American defectors, both because of the knowledge they might have and the suspicion that most, if not all, were spies.

Apparently American intelligence was equally curious in learning about the Soviets. According to author Anthony Summers, who studied documents from both the State Department and the House Select Committee on Assassinations, only two U.S. enlisted men defected to Russia between the years 1945 and 1959. Yet in the eighteen months prior to January 1960, no fewer than nine defected, five of them U.S. Army men from West Germany and two Navy men.

All these defectors, including at least three civilians, had backgrounds in the military or in sensitive defense work. It is known that, like Oswald, at least four of these returned to the United States after a few years.

Robert E. Webster—Another Oswald?

The case of Robert E. Webster, an American who told officials he was defecting to Russia less than two weeks before Oswald, is worth considering since there appear to be many similarities between the two.

Webster, a former Navy man, was a young plastics expert who simply failed to return home with colleagues after working at an American trade exhibition in Moscow. He had been an employee of the Rand Development Corporation, one of the first U.S. companies to sell technical products to Russia.

Although Rand Development was thought to be separate from the more notorious Rand Corporation—the CIA "think-tank" front where Daniel Ellsberg copied the Pentagon Papers—there is some evidence of connections between the two. The firms were at one time located across the street from each other in New York City; Rand Development held several CIA contracts and several top officials of Rand Development—President Henry Rand, George Bookbinder, and Christopher Bird—were later connected with the CIA.

While in Russia, Webster took a Soviet girl as common-law wife (he was already married to a woman in the United States) and the couple had a child.

Like Oswald, Webster claimed to have become disenchanted with Soviet life and he returned to the United States about the same time as Oswald. But now the story turns even stranger. Although Webster is said to have told American officials he never had any contact with Lee Harvey Oswald, when Oswald was arranging his return to the United States in 1961, he "asked [U.S. Embassy officials] about the fate of a young man named Webster who had come to the Soviet Union shortly before he did . . ."

Furthermore, there are some intriguing connections between Webster and Oswald's wife, Marina. Years later in America, Marina told an acquaintance that her husband had defected after working at an American exhibition in Moscow. This, of course, reflects Webster's story, not Oswald's. After the assassination, when American intelligence was looking into Marina's background, they discovered an address in her address book matching that of Webster's Leningrad apartment.

Were Webster and Oswald two of several fake defectors being sent into Russia during 1958 and 1959? The parallels of their stories are striking. Author Summers talked with former CIA officer Victor Marchetti, who analyzed the Soviet military during the time Oswald went to Russia, and was told:

> At the time, in 1959, the United States was having real difficulty in acquiring information out of the Soviet Union; the technical systems had, of course, not developed to the point that they are at today, and we were resorting to all sorts of activities. One of these activities was an ONI [Office of Naval Intelligence] program which involved three dozen, maybe 40, young men who were made to appear disenchanted, poor, American youths who had become turned off and wanted to see what Communism was all about. They were sent into the Soviet Union or into eastern Europe, with the specific intention the Soviets would pick them up and "double" them if they suspected them of being U.S. agents, or recruit them as KGB agents. They were trained at various naval installations both here and abroad, but the operation was being run out of Nag's Head, North Carolina.

This is particularly interesting because this Navy program sounds exactly like Oswald's experience.

During the years Oswald was in Russia, the State Department was engaged in a study of U.S. defectors to Russia. Otto Otepka, the official in charge of the study, said one of its goals was to determine which defectors were genuine and which may have been U.S. intelligence operatives.

In June 1963, five months prior to the Kennedy assassination, Otepka said he was ousted from his job and, in fact, barred from access to his study material on defectors, one of whom was Lee Harvey Oswald.

Asked if Oswald was a real or fake defector by a researcher in 1971, Otepka replied: "We had not made up our minds when . . . we were thrown out of the office."

This incident is especially troubling, for if the shutdown of the State Department investigation was because of Oswald, this is evidence of someone within the U.S. government having prior knowledge of the assassination.

*   *   *

Oswald's attempted defection to Russia was as strange as many other aspects of his life.

The *Marion Lykes* arrived in Le Havre, France, on October 8, 1959. Oswald arrived in Southampton, England, October 9 and, according to the Warren Commission, set off for Helsinki, Finland, arriving and checking in to the Torni Hotel that same day.

However, in Oswald's passport, the British immigration stamp reads, "Embarked 10 Oct. 1959."

This presents a real problem, since the only direct flight from London to Helsinki that day did not arrive in time for Oswald to have checked into the Torni Hotel at the hour shown in the hotel's register.

The discrepancy in times has led some researchers to believe that Oswald got to Finland by some means other than public transportation—perhaps in U.S. military aircraft. But this possibility, of course, smacks of intelligence work and has not been officially investigated.

Another oddity: throughout his life, Oswald was tight with money, usually staying in cheap rooming houses and apartments. However, once in Helsinki, he registered in the Torni Hotel, then moved the next day into the Klaus Kurki Hotel, two of the city's most expensive and luxurious lodgings.

The Warren Commission claimed Oswald then visited the Soviet consulate in Helsinki and obtained a visa in two days, which must have been some sort of record, as the commission also determined that the shortest normal time for obtaining a visa was one week.

Oswald's visa was issued October 14 and the Commission said Oswald left by train the next day for Moscow, arriving on October 16.

However, the leading Swedish newspaper *Dagens Nyheters* reported three days after the assassination information—which since has been confirmed by Swedish intelligence—that Oswald failed to get his Soviet visa in Helsinki. The paper said Oswald instead came to Stockholm, where he obtained a visa at the Russian embassy after two days. Curiously, neither the Warren Commission nor the House Select Committee on Assassinations mentioned this side trip.

Whatever the facts, the speed and ease with which Oswald journeyed to Moscow leaves one with the impression that there was more motivating this young man than the simple desire to experience a communist state.

Arriving in Moscow by train, Oswald was taken in tow by a representative of Intourist, the official state tourist agency, who placed him in the Hotel Berlin where he registered as a student. The next day Oswald went sightseeing with his Intourist guide, a young woman named Rima Shirokova, and promptly told her he wanted to defect.

Despite his proclamation that he was a "Communist" desiring to live in Russia, after several contacts with Soviet authorities Oswald was informed on October 21 that his visa had expired and he had two hours to leave Moscow. Faced with deportation, Oswald reportedly cut his left wrist in a suicide attempt. Conveniently, this was done just before a meeting with his Intourist guide. She found him in his hotel room and had him taken to a hospital. This act accomplished the same end result of the Marine shooting incident—he was out of sight in the hospital for eleven days.

He was released on October 28 and, accompanied by Rima Shirokova, he checked out of the Hotel Berlin and into the Metropole. The Warren Commission concluded: "The government undoubtedly directed him to make the change."

Oswald had, in fact, been in touch with Soviet government officials from the Pass and Registration Office.

He remained in his hotel room three days, apparently awaiting orders from someone. He told Shirokova he was impatient, but didn't say why.

By Saturday, October 31, 1959, Oswald was ready to make his move. Striding past the Marine guards at the U.S. Embassy, he plopped his passport down in front of a receptionist and declared he had come to "dissolve his American citizenship."

He was directed to Richard E. Snyder, the second secretary and senior consular official, who tried to dissuade the young ex-Marine from his planned course of action. Oswald handed Snyder an undated, handwritten note that displayed a sophisticated knowledge of the legal subtleties concerning the revocation of citizenship. It reflected the same type of knowledge that had allowed Oswald to make his journey to Moscow in a most unorthodox manner.

The note stated:

I, Lee Harvey Oswald, do hereby request that my present citizenship in the United States of America, be revoked. . . . I take these steps for political reasons. My request for the revoking of my American citizenship is made only after the longest and most serious considerations. I affirm that my allegiance is to the Union of Soviet Socialist Republics.

Present with Snyder was John McVickar, another senior consular officer. In later years, McVickar said he felt Oswald:

. . . was following a pattern of behavior in which he had been tutored by a person or persons unknown . . . seemed to be using words he had learned but did not fully understand . . . in short, it seemed to me there was the possibility that he had been in contact with others before or during his Marine Corps tour who had guided him and encouraged him in his actions.

In later years Snyder himself came under suspicion of aiding Oswald in an intelligence mission when it was revealed that he had worked for the CIA—although the Agency claimed it was only for a brief time in 1949.

When the House Select Committee on Assassinations looked into the matter, investigators found that Snyder's CIA file was unavailable ". . . [as] a matter of cover." The committee found this revelation "extremely troubling."

According to the Warren Commission, Snyder did not permit Oswald to renounce his citizenship. Since it was a Saturday, Snyder explained that Oswald would have to return on a normal business day to fill out the necessary paperwork. Oswald never returned and, therefore, technically never renounced his citizenship.

Could the three-day wait in his hotel room have been because he had been coached not to defect unless it was on a Saturday? How could a high school dropout know all of these legalistic subtleties without being briefed by someone much more knowledgeable?

Even American newswoman Priscilla Johnson, who interviewed Oswald a few days later in his hotel room, thought he "may have purposely not carried through his original intent to renounce [citizenship]) in order to leave a crack open."

On November 3, Oswald sent the embassy a letter protesting its refusal to accept his renunciation of citizenship. However, he never showed up in person to pursue that act. And when embassy personnel attempted to contact Oswald, he refused to see them.

During this time, Oswald granted two newspaper interviews, one to Aline Mosby of UPI and the other to Johnson, who said she represented the North American Newspaper Alliance syndicate. Oswald harangued both reporters with his fervent support of Marxism and its ideals and both dutifully reported his comments in newspaper articles that appeared back in the United States.

Johnson (now Priscilla Johnson McMillan) would later write the book *Marina and Lee,* which supposedly "reveals the innermost secrets of [Marina's] life with the man who shot JFK." She once was an assistant to Senator John F. Kennedy and went on to become an acknowledged expert on Soviet affairs. It is Mrs. McMillan who has been responsible for much of the information concerning Oswald's personal life shortly before the assassination.

There has been much speculation over the years that Mrs. McMillan was operating for U.S. intelligence when she was in contact with Oswald. She has testified that she never worked for the CIA. However, the House Select Committee on Assassinations reported that she had applied to work for the CIA in 1952, had been "debriefed" by that agency after a trip to Russia in 1962, and, in fact, had provided the CIA with "cultural and literary" information.

Suspicion about Johnson grew in light of an FBI memorandum dated November 23, 1963, in which a State Department security officer informed the FBI:

. . . one Priscilla Johnston [sic] and Mrs. G. Stanley Brown also had contact with Oswald in Russia. Both these women were formerly State Department employees at the American Embassy and their contact with Oswald was official business.

By December 1959, Oswald had dropped from sight in the Soviet Union and was not heard from again for more than a year. During that time, most of what is known about Oswald's activities come from his "Historic Diary," supposedly a day-to-day account of his life in Russia.

Even the Warren Commission had trouble with Oswald's diary, noting:

> . . . it is not an accurate guide to the details of Oswald's activities. Oswald seems not to have been concerned about the accuracy of dates and names and apparently made many of his entries subsequent to the date the events occurred.

For instance, Oswald notes in his entry for October 31, 1959—the day he visited the American embassy—that John McVickar had taken Richard Snyder's place as "head consul." This change did not take place until two years after that date, at a time Oswald was preparing to leave Russia.

In later years, experts hired by the House Select Committee on Assassinations concluded the "diary" was written entirely on the same paper and was most probably written in one or two sittings. In other words, it was intended as a chronicle of his time in Russia, but was by no means contemporary.

This fact further fuels the charge that Oswald, even while in the Soviet Union, was acting on orders from someone else. This charge was even voiced by Warren Commission general counsel J. Lee Rankin, who told commission members in executive session: "That entire period is just full of possibilities for training, for working with the Soviet, and its agents.

Aside from the "diary" there is precious little documentation about Oswald's stay in Russia.

In early 1964, the Soviet government provided the Warren Commission with fifteen pages of documents, including copies of Oswald's passport, a job application form from a Minsk radio factory, some hospital records, and a supervisor's report from the factory.

Comrade Oswald

Although much about Oswald's life in Russia is unknown, several tantalizing pieces of information tell a decidedly different story of his sojourn there from the one that has previously been told.

After spending New Year's Day 1960 in Moscow, Oswald reportedly was then sent to Minsk with five thousand rubles. The money supposedly came from the "Red Cross," although Oswald himself wrote that the money actually came from the Soviet MVD (the Soviet secret police) after he "denounced" the United States. He reported that he was greeted in

Minsk on January 8 by no less than the mayor of the city, who promised him a rent-free apartment.

And what an apartment it was—a spacious flat with a separate living room, tile floors, and modern furniture, accommodations far beyond the means of the average Russian worker. Two private balconies overlooked a picturesque bend in the Svisloch River.

It was here that Oswald entertained his newfound Russian friends, such as Pavel Golovachev. The son of Hero of the Soviet Union General P. Y. Golovachev and a man who reportedly traveled in Minsk's highest social circles, Golovachev was pictured in some of the snapshots Oswald made in his Minsk home.

Oswald was assigned duties as a "metal worker" in the Byelorussian Radio and Television factory. Here, between his wages and the continuing "Red Cross" allowance, Oswald reportedly was making more money than the factory's director.

In his "diary," Oswald wrote about affairs with at least five local girls, whom he would take to nearby movies, theaters, and opera. As he wrote in his "diary," he was "living big."

On a darker side, it should be noted that Minsk, along with being a somewhat cosmopolitan city by Russian standards, also was the site of an espionage training school made known to the CIA as far back as 1947.

In testimony to the Warren Commission on May 14, 1964, FBI director J. Edgar Hoover said:

> . . . just the day before yesterday information came to me indicating that there is an espionage training school outside of Minsk—I don't know whether it is true—and that he [Oswald] was trained at that school to come back to this country to become what they call a "sleeper," that is a man who will remain dormant for three or four years and in case of international hostilities rise up and be used.

Almost adjacent to this spy school is the Foreign Language Institute. Oswald in a manuscript about his life in Minsk wrote, "I was in the Foreign Language Institute." Perhaps realizing his slip, Oswald edited this remark to read, "I was visiting friends in the Foreign Language Institute."

In addition to his money and lavish apartment, there is evidence to suggest that Oswald was living a privileged life with his Soviet hosts.

Although officially he never left Minsk—in his manuscript, Oswald pointed out how most Soviet citizens were prohibited from traveling far from their home—Oswald apparently traveled extensively in Russia.

Jeanne DeMohrenschildt, who along with her husband befriended Oswald after his return to the United States, said he was quite interested in photography. She said he had photographs of various locations in Russia that he showed her with great pride. He also told her about his enjoyable weekends hunting. And found among his possessions was a Soviet hunting license showing he had been a member of the Belorussian Society of Hunters and Fishermen, which carried with it the privilege of owning a 16-gauge shotgun, another feat impossible for the average Russian.

About the only fact that can be stated without question concerning Oswald's life in Russia is that he lived well beyond the means of the ordinary Soviet citizen. To most researchers, this abundant life was indicative of some sort of special relationship with Soviet officials. The exact nature of this relationship is still unknown; however many assassination students believe two things: one, that Oswald's fake "defection" to Russia may have had something to do with the downing of the U-2 spy plane on May 1, 1960, and, second, whatever the purposes of his intelligence mission to Russia, it had nothing to do with the subsequent assassination of President Kennedy except to paint the accused assassin as a Communist operative.

*   *   *

Although Oswald was not heard from in Russia between December 1959 and February 1961, the wheels of the U.S. bureaucracy were turning.

As early as November 10, 1959, the FBI, upon learning of Oswald's attempted defection, placed a "flash" notice on his fingerprint card. This would serve to alert Bureau officials should Oswald's fingerprints turn up in any FBI investigation. It also placed his name on a "watch" list used in monitoring overseas communications.

By the summer of 1960, the FBI was fully alert to Oswald and to the possibility that some sort of espionage game was being played out. On June 3, 1960, FBI director Hoover wrote to the State Department's Office of Security, warning: "Since there is a possibility that an imposter is using Oswald's birth certificate, any current information the Department of State may have concerning subject will be appreciated."

About this same time, the Marine Corps, informed that Oswald had offered to tell military secrets to the Soviets, took action. After failing to reach Oswald with certified letters, the Marine Corps officially changed Oswald's "honorable discharge" to "dishonorable" on September 13, 1960.

But it was Oswald's mother who seemed to get the swiftest reaction from queries about her son. After phone calls to the FBI and letters to her congressmen failed to turn up information about her son, Mrs. Oswald spent her small savings on a train ticket to Washington. Arriving on January 28, 1961, she called the White House wanting to speak to President Kennedy, who had just been inaugurated eight days before.

Failing to reach the President, she asked to speak to Secretary of State Dean Rusk. Instead, she was granted an immediate interview with Eugene Boster, White House Soviet affairs officer. Although she had not heard from her son in more than a year and his trip to Russia allegedly was made entirely on his own, Mrs. Oswald quoted Boster as saying, "Oh, yes, Mrs. Oswald, I'm familiar with the case." As before, she charged that her son was working for the government of the United States and demanded that the government locate him in Russia. Memos were routinely sent to Moscow.

On February 1, 1961, less than a week after Mrs. Oswald's Washington visit, the State Department sent a "Welfare-Whereabouts" memo to Moscow.

On February 13, 1961, the U.S. embassy in Moscow received a letter from Oswald dated February 5, stating: "I desire to return to the United States, that is if we could come to some agreement concerning the dropping of any legal proceedings against me."

Secretary Snyder was understandably astonished that Oswald should write to him just after he had been asked to locate the ex-Marine.

Mrs. Oswald maintained that the rapidity of response from her son indicated that the U.S. government was in contact with Oswald while in Russia.

The Warren Commission attributed his sudden reappearance to coincidence, in light of the fact that routine queries about Oswald had not yet been initiated by the American Embassy.

In his letter, Oswald showed unusual knowledge of the legalities of citizenship. He pointed out that he had never "taken Russian citizenship" and added: "If I could show [the Soviets] my American passport, I am of the opinion they would give me an exit visa."

Perhaps recalling Hoover's memo of the previous summer, the State Department informed Snyder that Oswald's passport was to be delivered on "a personal basis only."

On May 16, 1961, after some written sparring with the embassy, Oswald further complicated the entire matter by writing:

> Since my last letter I have gotten married . . . My wife is Russian, born in Leningrad, she has no parents living and is quite willing to leave the Soviet Union with me and live in the United States . . . I would not leave here without my wife so arrangements would have to be made for her to leave at the same time I do.

Oswald was ready to return to the United States, but only with his new bride, Marina Nikolaevna Prusakova.

A Whirlwind Romance

A little more than a month after telling the American embassy that he wished to return home, Oswald met the Russian woman who would become his wife and a chief witness against him after the assassination.

Around March 17, 1961—nobody seems to be certain of the date, including Marina—Oswald attended a trade union dance at the Palace of Culture in Minsk. Here he met nineteen-year-old Marina Nikolaevna

Prusakova, who was the hit of the party in a red brocade dress and hairstyle "à la Brigitte Bardot." Oswald was introduced to her as "Alik" and soon they were dancing.

Marina said they spoke Russian and she believed "Alik" to be a Soviet citizen, but from the Baltic area—Estonia, Latvia, or Lithuania. She was greatly surprised to learn this man was really an American named Lee Harvey Oswald.

After the dance, Oswald and Marina visited in the home of friends, where Oswald spoke up in defense of the United States, saying that while there were defects such as unemployment and discrimination, there still was ". . . more democracy . . ."

According to Oswald's diary, the pair hit it off well and he obtained Marina's telephone number before going home. The following week they again met at a dance and this time Oswald was allowed to accompany Marina home, where he was introduced to the aunt with whom she lived. Marina then agreed to go out on a date with Oswald, but the appointment fell through. On March 30, the day before his scheduled date with Marina, Oswald entered the Fourth Clinical Hospital for an adenoids operation.

Although the hospital visiting hours were Sundays only, Marina was able to visit Oswald almost every day, perhaps because she wore the white uniform of a pharmacist. She felt sorry for Oswald and on Easter Sunday, the day after his operation, brought him a painted Easter egg. Oswald immediately asked her to become his fiancée and she agreed.

Oswald wrote in his diary: "We are going steady, and I decide I must have her, she puts me off, so on April 15 I propose, she accepts." They married on April 30, less than six weeks after first meeting.

In later years, Marina exhibited a strange memory loss about many aspects of their meeting, whirlwind romance, and wedding.

She told varying stories as to who first introduced her to Oswald, then finally stated she just couldn't remember. She also told the House Select Committee on Assassinations that Oswald had proposed to her "a month and a half" before their wedding. This would mean Oswald proposed the first night they met. However, this was by no means the only inconsistency in Marina's recollections.

Marina claimed to be born on July 17, 1941, in the northern seaside town of Molotovsk. A war baby, she never knew who her father was and took her mother's name. In the book *Marina and Lee,* she suddenly revealed that she had found out that her father was a Soviet traitor named Nikolai Didenko. This may be a small matter, but it was never revealed to the Warren Commission. Her mother left her as an infant with elderly relatives in Arkhangelsk, where she grew up until rejoining her mother at age seven. By then her mother had married an electrical worker named Alexander Medvedev and by 1952, the family was living in Leningrad. Here Marina attended a pharmacist school. She was a young student when her mother died. She said life with her stepfather became intolerable after the death of her mother.

Upon graduation from school in June 1959, she was assigned a job in a pharmaceutical warehouse, but quit after only one day and spent the rest of the summer on vacation. At the end of the summer, she went to Minsk to live with her maternal uncle, Colonel Ilya Vasilyevich Prusakov, a ranking officer in the MVD (the Soviet Ministry of Internal Affairs, portions of which function as secret police), a leading citizen in Minsk and a Communist Party member.

It was at her uncle's urging that she attended the dance where she met Oswald. Marina's uncle apparently never protested her marriage, although his position could have allowed him to study Oswald's KGB file, which must have shown that Oswald had written to the American embassy about returning to the United States since it is now known that the KGB was keeping him under surveillance.

Within a matter of days after their marriage, Oswald informed Marina of his desire to return to the United States. Soon Marina began to apply for the documents necessary to leave the Soviet Union. Her exit visas appeared to have been expedited despite the fact that there were several problems with her background information. She stated her name as "Marina Nikolaevna," which indicated her father's name was Nikolai. She insisted, however, that she never knew the name of her father. Her birth certificate identified her birthplace as Severodvinsk. This was the name given to Molotovsk, but not until 1957. Furthermore, since being a member of the Communist Party might cause problems in leaving Russia, she denied any membership. Actually, she was a member of the Komsomol, the Communist Party's youth movement.

These discrepancies did not escape the notice of the CIA. Shortly after the assassination, a CIA memorandum noted:

> . . . at the time [the Agency] was becoming increasingly interested in watching develop a pattern that we had discovered in the course of our bio[graphical] and research work: the number of Soviet women marrying foreigners, being permitted to leave the USSR, then eventually divorcing their spouses and settling down abroad without returning "home." . . . we eventually turned up something like two dozen similar cases.

Noting that the birth certificate Marina brought to the United States was issued July 19, 1961, and that she had to have one to obtain a marriage license, author Edward Epstein concluded: "It thus seemed that new documents—and possibly a new identity—were furnished to Marina after it was decided that she would accompany Oswald to the United States.

On July 8, 1961, Oswald had flown to Moscow to retrieve his passport at the American embassy. Since he had never technically defected, his passport was promptly returned, although the State Department cautioned the embassy to proceed carefully in Oswald's "involved case" and to make sure "that the person in communication with the Embassy is . . . Lee Harvey Oswald."

With all their applications made, the Oswalds settled down to wait for approval to leave Russia.

To further complicate the situation, a baby girl—June Lee Oswald—was born to Marina on February 15, 1962. On May 10, the Oswald's heard from the American embassy that everything was in order and that they should come to Moscow to sign the final papers.

It was during this time that Marina noted a cooling in Oswald's attitude toward her. This coolness was to increase after they left Russia. It was almost as if he had made up the story of his love and instead was simply following some sort of orders in his courtship. Afterward, with his assignment completed, he didn't bother to act like his love was real.

Accounts of Oswald's time during this period are filled with inconsistencies. For example, in his diary he claims to have returned to Minsk from Moscow on July 14. However, on August 1, Rita Naman and two other tourists reported meeting a young American in Moscow and snapping his picture. Two photos made by these tourists were displayed by the House Select Committee on Assassinations, which said the young American was Oswald.

On May 24, 1962, the Oswalds arrived in Moscow to attend to the final details of their departure from Russia. On June 1, Oswald signed a promissary note at the American embassy for a repatriation loan of $435.71, the money needed for his return, and the couple boarded a train that same evening.

Their trip home also has nagging indications of intelligence handling. The Warren Commission said they crossed out of Communist territory at Brest. Yet Marina's passport was stamped at Helmstedt, one of the major checkpoints on the East German border. Intriguingly, Oswald's passport shows no Helmstedt stamp at all, raising the possibility that he somehow traveled a different route from Marina's.

Arriving in Amsterdam, the Oswalds stayed—not in a hotel—but in a private establishment recommended by someone in the American embassy in Moscow, according to Marina. She described this place variously as a "private apartment" and as a "boardinghouse." While the official record shows they stayed here only one night, after the assassination Marina recalled a three-day stay and she reacted with confusion when questioned about this by the House Select Committee on Assassinations. She did note that advanced arrangements had been made at this place and that their hosts spoke English.

Many researchers suspect that Oswald, and perhaps Marina, were "debriefed" by U.S. intelligence during their Dutch stopover. Even the chief counsel of the Warren Commission called the episode "unexplained."

Furthermore, in a statement to the Secret Service just after the assassination, Marina gave a version of their trip from Russia that was totally different from that given in the Warren Report. She claimed they "then arrived in New York by air . . . stayed in some hotel in New York City for one day and then went by train to Texas."

The Warren Commission, backed by tickets, documents, and Marina's later testimony, stated that the couple arrived in Hoboken, New Jersey, on June 13, 1962 aboard the ship S.S. *Maasdam*. There they were met by Spas T. Raikin, a representative of the Traveler's Aid Society, which had been notified of the Oswald's arrival by the State Department. Raikin helped whisk the Oswald's through customs and then found them a place to stay in New York. He later arranged contact with Lee's brother, Robert, who sent the couple two hundred dollars for plane fare to Fort Worth, Texas.

According to BBC researcher and author Anthony Summers, Raikin was also an official with an anticommunist emigré group with links to both the FBI and U.S. military intelligence as well as anticommunist groups in New Orleans "headquartered in the very building where, in months to come, Oswald's name was to be linked with CIA-backed anti-Castro activists."

The Department of Health, Education and Welfare (HEW) had approved the financial aid to Oswald upon urging from the State Department. In Dallas HEW records, it states that Oswald went to Russia "with State Department approval," an allegation later repeated by Oswald himself on a New Orleans radio program.

When the Oswalds arrived in New York, they had seven suitcases. When they left by plane, they only had five. Asked about the dwindling number, Oswald stated he had sent them ahead by rail. However, when the couple arrived in Fort Worth, Robert stated they had only two suitcases.

The lost baggage may have something to do with their flight to Texas, which, although many direct flights were available, went by way of Atlanta. Atlanta was the home of Natasha Davison, the mother of Captain Davison, the U.S. attaché with intelligence connections who had met with the Oswalds in Moscow.

Yet, with all this evidence suggesting that Marina may have been part of some unrevealed intelligence program, she was accepted publicly by the Warren Commission as "a simple, devoted housewife . . ." Privately, commission members thought differently. At one point, they voiced the fear that she might be a KGB agent. Commission member Senator Richard Russell commented: "That will blow the lid if she testifies to that." One Warren Commission lawyer described Marina as "a very different person [from her public image] . . . cold, calculating, avaricious . . ."

Some believe that Marina lied in many instances during her testimony to the Warren Commission. And, keep in mind the fact that as Oswald's wife, her testimony would not have been admissible had Oswald come to trial.

Despite all this, some of Marina's testimony proved very damaging to Oswald. In the hours after the assassination, Marina was quoted as saying: "Lee good man. Lee not shoot anyone." But after being held for weeks by the federal authorities, her statements began to change. Instead of telling what a good husband Oswald had been, she began saying he was violent to her. After initially being unable to identify the Mannlicher-Carcano rifle as her husband's, she later described it as "the fateful rifle of Lee Harvey Oswald." She also began to tell stories of other attempts at assassination by Oswald—one against Richard Nixon and another against Gen. Edwin Walker.

Today Marina has reversed her statements of 1963–64 and publicly made several astounding admissions, including:

—How federal authorities forced her Warren Commission testimony by threatening deportation and ordered her not to read or listen to anything pertaining to the assassination.
—That today she believes a conspiracy resulted in Kennedy's death.
—Lee Harvey Oswald was an agent who "worked for the American government" and was "caught between two powers—the government and organized crime."
—Oswald was "killed to keep his mouth shut."
—That someone impersonated Oswald to incriminate him and "that's no joke."
—Lee Harvey Oswald "adored" President Kennedy.

In a 1988 interview published in *Ladies' Home Journal*, Marina said:

When I was questioned by the Warren Commission, I was a blind kitten. Their questioning left me only one way to go: guilty. I made Lee guilty. He never had a fair chance . . . But I was only 22 then, and I've matured since; I think differently.

*   *   *

By 1979, Marina—by then a mature woman with a good command of English—had begun to doubt the official explanation of the assassination and joined with British author Michael Eddowes in seeking to have Oswald's body exhumed.

Considering the background of both Lee and Marina and the length of time spent by Oswald in Russia, it seems inconceivable that they were not interrogated by U.S. intelligence after their return. Yet the official story is that no U.S. intelligence agency had any interest in this ex-Marine.

Considering the Marine career of Oswald and the military information available to him as a radar operator, it is equally unbelievable that the Soviets did not interrogate Oswald at great length, especially if they found out about his connections with the U-2 flights from Atsugi.

Yet, this is precisely what the Soviets claimed in what has to become one of the most bizarre aspects of the Kennedy assassination—an aspect kept from the American public by the Warren Commission.

A Soviet Defector's Story

The strange story of Yuri Nosenko began on January 20, 1964, just two months after the events in Dallas.

Nosenko, an officer in the American Division of the KGB, had contacted the CIA initially on June 3, 1962, just two days after Oswald left Russia for the United States. Nosenko offered to spy for the Americans. However, nothing further had been heard from him and U.S. analysts were highly suspicious of his offer.

Then on January 20, 1964, Nosenko landed in Geneva as part of a Soviet disarmament delegation. He soon made his way to a telephone and renewed his offer to American intelligence, but with a difference—this time he wanted to defect.

The defection of Yuri Nosenko set in motion a chain of events that would lead to bitter divisions between the CIA and FBI as well as within the CIA itself.

Once he was in American hands, CIA officials were shocked to learn that Nosenko claimed to have been the KGB official who had personally handled the case of Lee Harvey Oswald during his stay in Russia. Nosenko said—based on two mental examinations made of Oswald—the KGB found the would-be defector not very bright and even "mentally unstable." And that the KGB had never debriefed Oswald about his military background nor ever considered recruiting him as an agent.

That was exactly what many people in the CIA and on the Warren Commission wanted to hear. However, there were others in the agency who were immediately suspicious of this man. After all, it appeared Nosenko had forever left a ranking position and his family simply to assure the U.S. government that the man accused of killing the President was not a Soviet agent.

CIA chief of counterintelligence James Jesus Angleton was particularly wary of Nosenko. He observed that most of the information provided by Nosenko revealing Soviet agents and operations was already known to the CIA prior to his defection.

Furthermore, shortly after bringing Nosenko to the United States, CIA interrogators began to find errors and gaps in his testimony. For example, there was the question of Nosenko's rank. He initially told the CIA he was a lieutenant colonel in the KGB. But another KGB defector, Maj. Anatoli Golitsin, stated he had been in close contact with the KGB departments described by Nosenko but had never run across the man. Under pressure, Nosenko admitted that he had exaggerated his rank to make himself more attractive to the CIA. However, detailed KGB documents provided by Nosenko refer to him as a lieutenant colonel, the senior rank he had repudiated. This caused CIA officials severe concern because it appeared that this defector was being aided in his cover story by the KGB.

To make matters worse, Nosenko's story was corroborated by one of the FBI's deepest secrets—their own Soviet KGB defector referred to only by his code name Fedora. Thus, if Nosenko was lying, then Fedora, too, became suspect.

In a remarkable attempt to resolve the issue, Nosenko underwent "hostile interrogation." He was kept in solitary confinement for 1,277 days under intense physical and psychological pressure.

He was put on a diet of weak tea, macaroni, and porridge, given nothing to read, a light was left burning in his unheated cell twenty-four hours a day, and his guards were forbidden to speak with him or even smile. His isolation was so complete that Nosenko eventually began to hallucinate, according to CIA testimony before the House Select Committee on Assassinations. Toward the end of this ordeal, Nosenko was given at least two lie detector tests by the CIA. He failed both. But Nosenko did not crack.

The believers of Nosenko, headed by the CIA's Richard Helms and J. Edgar Hoover, took his intransigence to mean that he was telling the truth about the KGB having no interest in Oswald.

But doubts remained. So at the CIA's request, the Warren Commission obligingly made no reference to Nosenko.

Angleton retired from the CIA and later wrote:

The . . . exoneration or official decision that Nosenko is/was bona fide is a travesty. It is an indictment of the CIA and, if the FBI subscribes to it, of that bureau too. The ramifications for the U.S. intelligence community, and specifically the CIA, are tragic.

The counterintelligence faction, led by Angleton, still believes that Nosenko's defection was contrived by the KGB for two purposes: to allay suspicions that the Soviets had anything to do with the JFK assassination and to cover for Soviet "moles," or agents deep within U.S. intelligence.

Today, Nosenko continues to be an adviser on Soviet intelligence to the CIA and the FBI at a salary of more than $35,000 a year. He has been given a new identity as well as more than $150,000 as payment for his ordeal.

But questions remain. No researcher seriously believes the Soviets failed to question Oswald about his Marine background. When they learned that he served as a radar operator at the base where U-2 flights were launched, he must have undergone intense interrogation.

Furthermore, there appears to be evidence that Oswald continued to keep in touch with Soviet officials almost up until the time of Kennedy's assassination. According to CIA documents, Oswald visited the Soviet embassy in Mexico City on September 23, 1963, and met with Valery Vladimirovich Kostikov, who was described as "function[ing] overtly as a consul . . ." However, the CIA memorandum added: "[Kostikov] . . . is also known to be a staff officer of the KGB. He is connected with the Thirteenth, or 'liquid affairs' department, whose responsibilities include assassination and sabotage."

Of course, Oswald's contact with this man, who was operating as a normal member of the Soviet embassy, may have been coincidental. However, it is significant that the Warren Commission, aware of the implication of this contact, failed to pursue the matter or include this information in their report.

Years later, FBI agent James Hosty, who was connected to Oswald prior to the assassination, said he was unhappy with the revelation about Kostikov's KGB ties and that, had he been made aware of this connection by the CIA, he would have placed Oswald's name on the Bureau's "Security Index."

Two theories have emerged:

One, Oswald was recruited by the KGB while serving in Japan and encouraged to defect to Russia, then sent back to the U.S. to kill President Kennedy. This theory is rejected by most students of the subject, including author Edward Jay Epstein, whose book *Legend* studies the Oswald-Soviet connections in detail. Epstein reasons: "I think that the fact that Oswald traces so clearly back to the Russians makes it extremely unlikely that they would have recruited him as an assassin."

Second, that Oswald was recruited into U.S. intelligence as a spy and sent to Russia. There, the KGB attempted to turn him into their agent and sent him back to the United States, unaware that he would be blamed for Kennedy's death. This would explain the extraordinary lengths gone to by the Soviets to disavow any connection with Oswald.

In the overall view, it is probable that Oswald was mixed up in some sort of intelligence work. And, while it is likely that the Soviets would recruit this lowly Marine would-be defector, it is highly unlikely that they would consider using him in something so dangerous as assassinating the U.S. president. In murdering Kennedy, the Soviets would have been risking all. World War III would be the likely result should a Soviet assassination plot be uncovered. And what would they have gained by killing Kennedy? Virtually nothing except Lyndon Johnson as president, a man with far better anticommunist credentials than Kennedy and a man with closer ties to the military-industrial complex most feared by the Soviets.

Testifying to the Warren Commission on June 10, 1964, Secretary of State Dean Rusk said:

I have seen no evidence that would indicate to me that the Soviet Union considered that it had any interest in the removal of President Kennedy . . . I can't see how it would be to the interest of the Soviet Union to make any such effort.

In 1979, the House Select Committee on Assassinations, even after hearing the Nosenko story, concluded: "The committee believes, on the basis of the evidence available to it, that the Soviet Government was not involved in the assassination of President Kennedy."

But perhaps the best argument against Soviet involvement comes from the memoirs of the highest-ranking Soviet official ever to defect to the West. In his book, *Breaking With Moscow*, Arkady N. Shevchenko writes:

In November 1963, President Kennedy was assassinated in Dallas. Everyone in the [Soviet] mission was stunned and confused, particularly when there were rumors that the murder had been Soviet-inspired. . . . Our leaders would not have been so upset by the assassination if they had planned it and the KGB would not have taken upon itself to venture such a move without Politburo approval. More important, Khrushchev's view of Kennedy had changed. After Cuba, Moscow perceived Kennedy as the one who had accelerated improvement of relations between the two countries. Kennedy was seen as a man of strength and determination, the one thing that Kremlin truly understands and respects. In addition, Moscow firmly believed that Kennedy's assassination was a scheme by "reactionary forces" within the United States seeking to damage the new trend in relations. The Kremlin ridiculed the Warren Commission's conclusion that Oswald had acted on his own as the sole assassin. There was in fact widespread speculation among Soviet diplomats that Lyndon Johnson, along with the CIA and the Mafia, had masterminded the plot. Perhaps one of the most potent reasons why the U.S.S.R. wished Kennedy well was that Johnson was anathema to Khrushchev. Because he was a southerner, Moscow considered him a racist (the stereotype of any American politician from below the Mason-Dixon line), an anti-Soviet and anti-Communist to the core. Further, since Johnson was from Texas, a center of the most reactionary forces in the United States, according to the Soviets, he was associated with the big-time capitalism of the oil industry, also known to be anti-Soviet.

A final argument against Soviet involvement goes like this. While it is conceivable that the Russians somehow contrived Kennedy's death and that high-level U.S. government officials were forced to cover up this fact to prevent a devastating world war, it makes no sense that these facts would not have been leaked slowly to the American public in the late 1960s and early 1970s in an effort to gain support for the anticommunist war in Vietnam and blunt the growing antiwar movement.

The fact that this didn't happen goes far to prove that hard evidence of Soviet involvement in Kennedy's death is nonexistent.

But if the Russians had nothing to do with the assassination, the same could not be said for their protégés on the island of Cuba. Cubans—both communist and anticommunist—would not have shed tears over the death of the American president.

Summary

It appears obvious to most assassination researchers that Oswald's visit to Russia was a planned intelligence operation—perhaps he was one of the members of the Office of Naval Intelligence defection program. After all, the Marines are technically part of the Navy.

Oswald's suspicious manner of entering and leaving Russia reinforce the belief that he was an intelligence operative—as does the lavish lifestyle he enjoyed while living in Minsk.

His hurried romance and marriage to Marina is yet another aspect of his time in Russia that hints at intelligence undertones.

Then there are the tantalizing—though unproven—connections between Oswald, the ex-Marine radar operator, and the ill-fated U-2 spy plane incident.

And consider the men with whom Oswald came in contact and their U.S. intelligence connections—U.S. embassy second secretary Snyder, Traveler's Aid Society representative Raikin and embassy doctor Captain Davison. Recall that both embassy personnel and news reporters voiced the belief that Oswald was acting under orders from someone.

All this is capped by the strange defection and interrogation of Yuri Nosenko, who apparently went to great lengths to assure U.S. government officials that the Soviets were not responsible for Kennedy's death.

There is much to argue against Soviet intelligence involvement in the assassination.

However, the same cannot be said for Oswald's involvement with non-Soviet intelligence work—and the trail always leads back to the United States.

Cubans

On October 28, 1492, Christopher Columbus stepped ashore from the long boat of his flagship *Santa Maria* in the Caribbean to become the first Western European to land in the New World, which would come to be known as America. This landing was the first step in the building of a Spanish empire that included the island of Cuba, located on the northern edge of the Caribbean, and ninety miles south of what is now Key West, Florida.

During the centuries of Spanish rule, Cuba—the most westerly of the West Indies—suffered the same fate as most islands in that chain. During the unrelenting search for gold and other precious minerals, exploitation of the land and resources, and ongoing raids by pirates, the natives were decimated. Of the approximately one million Ciboney Indians living on Cuba when Columbus arrived, all but a handful were dead by 1600.

On July 15, 1895, a group of Cubans in exile, encouraged by business interests in the United States, proclaimed Cuba a republic and a long-standing revolt against Spain was intensified.

What followed was the Spanish-American War and in the summer of 1898—while Commodore George Dewey was conquering Manila Bay in the Philippines—Colonel Theodore Roosevelt led his Rough Riders up San Juan Hill as his part in subduing the island. A treaty was signed on December 10, 1898, and Spain was expelled from the Western Hemisphere.

The United States established a military occupation government that finally relinquished power to an elected Cuban government headed by Tomas Estrada Palma on May 20, 1902. However, Cuba remained a trusteeship of the United States, which directly or indirectly remained dominant in the decision-making process of that country.

In 1952, former army sergeant Fulgencio Batista seized control in Cuba by means of a military coup. A dictator and a despot, Batista nevertheless worked closely with many American groups, especially organized criminals.

By the late 1950s, Cuba was a mecca for American gamblers, tourists, investors, and off-shore banking speculators.

Only one man seemed determined to overthrow Batista—Fidel Castro.

Fidel Castro

Born the son of a Spanish-born plantation owner on August 13, 1926, Fidel Castro had an active boyhood in rural eastern Cuba. He once threatened to burn the house down if his parents didn't send him to school.

In 1952, he ran for Parliament but was blocked when the dictator Batista canceled the elections. From that time on, Castro devoted himself to ousting Batista.

Gathering some followers, Castro's first assault on Batista took place on July 26, 1953, when they attacked Batista's Moncada Barracks. The attack was a military disaster. About half of the rebels were caught, tortured, and killed. Castro was put on trial. Conducting his own defense, the youthful Cuban lawyer stated: "Condemn me. It does not matter. History will absolve me."

Sentenced to fifteen years in prison, Castro was released after twenty-two months. He then fled to Mexico where he began reorganizing his guerrilla fighters. He used the brutality displayed by Batista at the Moncada Barracks as a rallying point and named his revolution the "26th of July Movement" after the disastrous attack. Since 1959, this date has been celebrated as Cuban independence day.

In 1956, Castro swam the Rio Grande and entered the United States to arrange the purchase of a dilapidated yacht named the *Granma*. Returning to Mexico, he began planning the next stage of his revolution—the invasion of his homeland. Confident that he would rapidly gain followers, Castro even made his invasion plans public.

On December 2, 1956, when he and eighty-two guerrillas waded ashore on the swampy coast of his native Oriente Province, Batista's soldiers were waiting in ambush. Only twelve guerrillas, including Castro, survived and escaped into the Sierra Maestra mountains.

After Batista proclaimed his death, Castro invited a reporter for *The New York Times* to his camp to show he was very much alive and he predicted that final victory would be his.

After several years of basic survival in the mountains—during this time, Castro grew his now-famous beard—Castro and his followers began to take the initiative. By the summer of 1958, his guerrilla band had grown to more than eight hundred, and later that year a detachment led by Ernesto "Che" Guevara captured the provincial capital of Santa Clara in Central Cuba.

Although backed by an army of some thirty thousand, Batista panicked and decided to quit the island. Taking bags of cash, Batista fled to the Dominican Republic in the first few hours of 1959.

Castro's fantasy revolution had suddenly become a dream come true. For two weeks, Castro slowly moved toward Havana. The excitement and passions of the moment were almost overpowering. Veteran news correspondents could not recall a more jubilant scene since the liberation of Paris in World War II. For a period of weeks, the jublilation continued, but then became subdued in the wake of trials and executions of prerevolution "war criminals."

Castro began the formidable task of restructuring Cuban society.

*　　*　　*

With the defeat of the dictator Batista, Castro became the undisputed leader of Cuba, even proclaiming himself "Jefe Maximo" (maximum leader). And he began making drastic changes in the island.

Castro closed down the gambling casinos and houses of prostitution that had been the source of an estimated $100 million a year for organized crime in the United States. He nationalized the sugar industry, the back-bone of Cuba's economy, and by the summer of 1960, he had seized more than $700 million in U.S. property, including banks that had been accused of laundering money for American interests. (Even his parents' plantation was nationalized, angering his own mother and prompting his younger sister, Juanita, to leave Cuba and become an anti-Castroite.)

Some social gains were made on the island. Within a few years, illiteracy had been reduced from 24 percent to 4 percent.

But Castro also proclaimed that he was the leader of socialist revolution in South America, although he strongly maintained that he was not a communist. American interests were quick to respond. The U.S. govern-ment abruptly restricted sugar imports and began encouraging its allies not to trade with Castro.

With his trade restricted and hearing rumors that the U.S. might invade the island at any time, Castro turned to the Soviet Union for support. He began selling sugar to Russia in 1960 and soon Soviet technicians and advisers began to arrive on the island. This confirmed the suspicions of American interests, who began to brand Castro a communist and a sub-verter of the status quo in Central and South America.

As Castro's social, economic, and agricultural reforms continued, often with brutal effectiveness, Cubans began to split into two factions—the Fidelistas (supporters of Castro) and the anti-Castroites, many of whom fled Cuba. By the end of the first year of Castro's takeover, more than one hundred thousand Cubans were living in the United States.

As the United States stepped up its program of isolating Cuba—first with cutting off the island's sugar markets and oil supplies, then through diplomatic maneuvers with other South American countries, and finally by introducing arms and saboteurs into Cuba—Castro grew more and more fearful of an armed invasion by the United States.

In November, 1963, Castro was quoted as telling the United States: "Of course we engage in subversion, the training of guerrillas, propaganda! Why not? This is exactly what you are doing to us."

On January 3, 1961, the United States ended diplomatic relations with Cuba after Castro demanded the U.S. embassy staff be cut to only eleven persons. Castro charged that 80 percent of the staff were "FBI and Pentagon spies." Two weeks later, the United States forbade its citizens to travel to Cuba. In the same month, the month that John F. Kennedy took office as president, Castro placed his militia on twenty-four-hour alert, proclaiming that the "Yankee invasion" was imminent.

In February, Soviet deputy prime minister Andrei Gromyko arrived in Cuba to arrange large-scale economic and military assistance to Castro.

And on April 17, 1961, less than three months after Kennedy became president, Castro's fears were realized. A force of anti-Castro Cubans landed at the Bay of Pigs.

Disaster at the Bay of Pigs

The plans to destroy Castro and regain control of Cuba began while Eisenhower was in office, more than a year before Kennedy became president.

By early 1960, the thousands of Cuban refugees in the United States had begun forming small groups dedicated to regaining their homeland, each claiming to be the one true voice of the exiles. To bring order to this situation, the CIA in May 1960 assisted in the creation of a Cuban coalition that came to be known as the Cuban Revolutionary Council (CRC). Early on this task was handled by CIA officer E. Howard Hunt—later to be involved in the Watergate affair and to be accused of being in Dallas the day Kennedy was killed.

As the election year of 1960 moved on, so did the CIA's plans for an "upheaval" in Cuba. Once in the hands of CIA staffers and adventurous case officers, the plan seemed to take on a life of its own.

Secrecy was the prime concern of everyone involved. Even CIA director Allen Dulles did not know many details of the plan. He had simply turned the whole project over to a deputy director, Richard M. Bissell, Jr. Bissell, in turn, handed the project to the former CIA station chief in Caracas, who recruited various CIA personnel, such as Hunt, Tracy Barnes, and David Atlee Phillips.

Many of the CIA officers involved in the Bay of Pigs had participated in the 1954 overthrow of the popularly elected government of Jacobo Arbenz in Guatemala, and their intent was to stage a similar low-key coup in Cuba.

Unknown to these CIA officers who began to create a Cuban-refugee fighting force, Bissell was working on a concurrent project—the assassination of Fidel Castro.

Bissell's idea began to work its way through the CIA bureaucracy with unintended humorous results. Plans were conceived to poison Castro's cigar, to slip him a depilatory so his famous beard would fall out or administer an LSD-type chemical so that the Cuban leader would hallucinate. These schemes took on a more sinister aspect, however, with the suggestion that American gangsters be hired to do the job.

President Dwight Eisenhower knew none of this. All he knew was that on March 17, 1960, at the urging of a top-secret committee for covert operations—known as the 5412 Committee because it was authorized by National Security Council Directive 5412/2—he had authorized a CIA plan entitled "A Program of Covert Action Against the Castro Regime." This plan offered a four-point program—1) the creation of a Cuban government in exile, 2) a "powerful" propaganda offensive, 3) the creation of a "covert intelligence and action organization" inside Cuba, and 4) "a paramilitary force outside of Cuba for future guerrilla action."

The fourth point, the "paramilitary force," was to evolve into Brigade 2506, a Cuban-exile expeditionary force supported by air and sea power as well as U.S. military units.

One man who did understand what all this might mean was Eisenhower's vice president, White House action officer, and the head of the 5412 Committee—Richard M. Nixon. Nixon had several reasons for supporting action against Castro. A year earlier, the anticommunist Nixon had met with Castro and concluded: "Castro is either incredibly naïve about Communism or is under Communist discipline." And as one of the congressmen who passed the legislation creating the CIA, Nixon undoubtedly wanted to support the men who through the years had passed along information politically helpful to him. Then, too, the November election was approaching and Nixon was eager to have the Republican administration get the credit for ending Castro's reign.

Whatever the reason, Nixon kept exhorting his executive assistant for national-security affairs, General Robert E. Cushman, Jr., to press the CIA officers for action.

Meanwhile, Hunt and an associate, Bernard L. Barker (who later participated in the Watergate break-in under Hunt's guidance), were wheeling and dealing in the Miami Cuban exile community, sometimes carrying as much as $115,000 in a briefcase to secure agents. Training camps were located, arms secured, and Cubans recruited. The plan was advancing into broader and grander stages and still the lower-level operators were in charge.

On July 23, 1960, presidential candidate John F. Kennedy was first briefed by Dulles about the Cuban operation. Since at that time only guerrilla infiltration and air drops were contemplated, Kennedy did not learn of the full invasion plan until after his election.

In an ironical twist, some of Senator Kennedy's speechwriters encouraged him to speak out against Castro and urge U.S. support for Cuban exiles. Nixon was furious, believing that Kennedy had been told about the invasion and was compromising security by using this knowledge as a political weapon against him. Nixon, who encouraged the invasion, was forced to attack Kennedy's proposal as "wrong and irresponsible because it would violate our treaty commitments" to protect the covert operation.

Shortly after the election, Dulles—along with Bissell—again briefed Kennedy on the Cuban plan. This briefing, too, was long on vague generalities and short on details.

It was not until near the end of 1960 that anyone outside of the CIA officers in charge were told that the plan had been expanded to include an invasion with air support. Even military brass, who were being asked for material assistance, were sworn to secrecy. Most of those ranking military officers brought into the plan thought the whole thing sounded "impractical."

The invasion was indeed impractical, for: one, it was predicated on a massive revolt against Castro by the Cuban people, a concept loudly advanced by the CIA analysts but doubted by most others involved, and two, it was apparent that to succeed, the invasion had to have the support of U.S. naval and air power, a contingency both Eisenhower and Kennedy had opposed.

By mid-March, 1961—with the invasion only a month away—Kennedy was having second thoughts. The Trinidad Plan, an invasion proposal hastily put together by the Pentagon, was rejected by the new president as "too spectacular," with its amphibious assault, air strikes, and landing of a provisional government.

Kennedy wanted something quiet, something that would not reveal the involvement of the United States.

A week before the invasion, Kennedy left no doubt as to his position on using U.S. military forces to help the Cuban exiles. *The New York Times* carried a two-column headline reading: PRESIDENT BARS USING U.S. FORCE TO OUST CASTRO. The Cuban exiles were aghast, but their CIA officers quietly assured them that no one would stand by and watch them die. Miscommunication was rampant up and down the chain of command.

On Saturday, April 15, 1961, less than three months after Kennedy took office, a force of six B-26 bombers left a secret airfield in Nicaragua for Cuba. It was to have been sixteen, but Kennedy ordered a reduction to "minimum" scale.

This weekend air strike was a partial success. Castro's tiny air force was caught on the ground. Only three T-33 jets—considered good only as trainers—along with two B-26 bombers and a few decrepit British Sea Furies escaped the bombing raid. But it was enough.

On Monday, April 17, the Cuban Brigade landed at Bahia de Cochinos, or Bay of Pigs (named after the wild boars that inhabited this desolate area of Cuba). Ironically, Castro knew the area intimately since it was his favorite hunting spot. It was a good location for a landing, with only two main road arteries leading past swamps and dense undergrowth. But this same attribute also made it a formidable trap should Castro's forces arrive too soon.

A second air strike had been planned and, by most accounts, would have completed the destruction of Castro's air force. However, the CIA planners had failed to reckon with John F. Kennedy. Kennedy hesitated, growing more and more concerned that the entire world was realizing that the United States was supporting this invasion of another country.

United Nations ambassador Adlai Stevenson, who had been lied to by the CIA, was facing intense pressure after telling the General Assembly that the United States had nothing to do with the invasion.

Although the Cuban Brigade already was running into trouble on the beaches—one of their ships, the *Houston*, was set afire by Castro's planes—Secretary of State Dean Rusk was more concerned that the "international noise level" had risen to an intolerable degree. Rusk argued that no further air strikes be attempted until it could be made to look like the planes came from captured Cuban airfields. Kennedy concurred and ordered a halt to any air strikes. Castro's surviving planes were able to disrupt the landing, allowing his troops to bottle up the beaches. The Bay of Pigs had become a death trap for the Cuban Brigade.

Kennedy authorized U.S. Navy ships sitting offshore to help evacuate the Brigade, but the Cuban commanders didn't want evacuation. They wanted the ammunition, naval support, and the "umbrella" of air cover that had been promised to them. It never came. As the remnants of the Brigade called for help from the beaches, U.S. military men could only stand silent by their weapons and watch as the gallant Cuban Brigade was torn to bits.

As news of the debacle spread, everybody concerned was furious.

Kennedy believed he had been led down a primrose path by optimistic CIA officials. He felt betrayed. The CIA planners felt betrayed in that the actual invasion had been scaled down on Kennedy's orders. The military felt betrayed because they had not been allowed to help in the planning of the invasion. And the Cuban exiles felt betrayed most of all because they had been led to believe they had the full support of the U.S. government.

In Guatemala City, staging area for the Brigade, the CIA officers were devastated. Many were getting drunk. CIA station chief Robert Davis described them this way: "If someone had gotten close to Kennedy, he'd have killed him. Oh, they hated him!"

Of the 1,600 men of the Cuban Brigade, 114 were killed, 1,189 were captured by Castro's forces, and 150 either never landed or made their way back to safety. (The captured Brigade was finally freed on December 23, 1962, after the United States agreed to exchange them for $53 million worth of food and drugs.)

Infuriated by this disastrous defeat, Kennedy nevertheless took the burden of blame. He told reporters: "There's an old saying that victory has a hundred fathers and defeat is an orphan. What mattered was only one fact: I am the responsible officer of government."

No one—especially in the CIA, the military, organized crime, or in the Cuban exile community—was to forget this acceptance of responsibility.

*   *   *

Following a shake-up in U.S. intelligence over the Bay of Pigs disaster, Attorney General Robert Kennedy took responsibility for overseeing Cuban affairs.

Soon another war—this one much more secret—was being waged against Castro under the code name "JM/WAVE." JM/WAVE operated on the campus of the University of Miami under the cover of an electronics firm called Zenith Technological Services. By mid-1962, this operation involved nearly six hundred CIA case officers, as many as three thousand contract agents, and numerous fronts such as boat shops, detective and travel agencies, and gun stores. With nearly a quarter million Cuban refugees living in the United States, it was easy to find those with a burning passion to liberate their island and return home.

The JM/WAVE operation seemed inconsistent from the start. President Kennedy stated "all actions should be kept at a low key," while his brother, Robert told CIA officials "no time, money, effort—or manpower—should be spared."

The near nightly raids on Cuba—landing saboteurs, dropping propaganda leaflets, and occasional military-style raids—actually achieved very little except confirmation of Castro's accusations that the United States was guilty of aggression.

Today, several of the military and intelligence officials who were dealing with President Kennedy during this period say they believed that the assassination of Castro was to be a part of this "Cuban crusade." However there is no documentation of this and, in fact, the only documentation available shows quite the opposite.

Early in 1962, Robert Kennedy was trying to prosecute a top Mafia boss named Sam Giancana, when he found the CIA interceding on Giancana's behalf. Pursuing the matter, Kennedy was finally told about the earlier deals between the CIA and Mafia to kill Castro. According to CIA attorney Lawrence Houston, the Attorney General ordered a halt to dealings with the Mafia. The younger Kennedy later told aides, "I stopped it . . . I found out that some people were going to try an attempt on Castro's life and I turned it off."

However, the lethal partnership between the Agency and the crime syndicate didn't stop until after well after President Kennedy was assassinated, indicating the CIA continued to operate out of control even after the agency shake-up following the Bay of Pigs disaster.

Whatever the Kennedys' role in Castro assassination plots, they got nowhere. Castro outlived both Kennedys and there is now some evidence to suggest that the CIA-Mafia plots may have been nothing more than a "scam" on the part of organized crime.

The ongoing tension with Cuba took on a more serious and urgent tone when on October 22, 1962, Kennedy announced that U.S. reconnaissance aircraft—the same U-2 spy plane that had ended Eisenhower's hopes for the 1960 summit meeting—had photographed offensive missile sites with nuclear capability being constructed in Cuba.

President Kennedy called for emergency meetings of the United Nations Security Council and the Organization of American States. He also ordered a "quarantine" of Cuba and vowed full retaliation against Russia if a nuclear warhead was launched from Cuba.

As Soviet ships carrying missiles approached the U.S. naval blockade of Cuba, the world watched and trembled. Nuclear holocaust seemed imminent. Then the Soviets blinked. Their freighters turned back and everyone breathed a sign of relief. Only much later did the American people learn that Kennedy had accepted a proposal from Khrushchev that included a pledge not to invade or support any invasion of Cuba.

But even Kennedy's diplomacy that ended the missile crisis earned him further rebuke by military and CIA officers who believed the presence of missiles justified a United States invasion of Cuba and the elimination of the Castro regime.

These suspicions only made the military and intelligence officers, along with their Cuban protégés, more convinced that Kennedy was "soft on communism."

In Miami's Orange Bowl in late December 1962, Kennedy spoke to the recently returned survivors of the Bay of Pigs invasion. Lashing out at communism in general and Castro in particular, Kennedy accepted the Brigade's flag and pledged: "I can assure you that this flag will be returned to this brigade in a free Havana." Most of those present believed this statement indicated a continued commitment to overthrow Castro. But future events dictated otherwise.

In 1976, Cuban Brigade veterans had to hire a lawyer to get their flag back from the government, which had stored it away in the basement of a museum. Likewise, beginning in 1963, the Cubans found U.S. government support for their continuing efforts against Castro nonexistent. In fact, moves were soon under way to stop exile action against Cuba.

The clamp-down on exile activity—whether sincere or official window-dressing—marked the beginning of a new relationship with both Cuba and the Soviet Union.

Kennedy used Jean Daniel, a journalist with the French newspaper *L'Express* as an unofficial contact with Castro. On October 24, 1963, Kennedy met with Daniel and urged him to pass along his good intentions to the Cuban premier during a scheduled interview in Havana. Daniel did meet with Castro and reported that the Cuban leader said:

I believe Kennedy is sincere. I consider him responsible for everything, but I will say this . . . in the last analysis, I'm convinced that anyone else would be worse . . . You can tell him that I'm willing to declare [Sen. Barry] Goldwater my friend if it will guarantee Kennedy's reelection!

Ironically, Daniel was with Castro on November 22, when the Cuban leader received word of Kennedy's assassination. *"Es una mala noticia"* (This is bad news), Castro said three times, adding:

All will have to be rethought. I'll tell you one thing; at least Kennedy was an enemy to whom we had become accustomed. You watch and see . . . I know that they will try to put the blame on us for this thing.

Castro was correct. From the day of the assassination, there was an effort to lay the blame on him.

But the attempt to reconcile relations with Castro had not been strictly unofficial. On September 17, 1963, Ambassador Syedou Diallo of Guinea in West Africa brought word to William Attwood, then a special adviser to the United States delegation to the United Nations and a former U.S. ambassador to Guinea, that Castro wanted to reach some sort of understanding with the Kennedy administration. According to Diallo, Castro was unhappy at being forced to align closely with the Soviet Union and wanted to normalize relations with the U.S. Attwood reported Diallo's conversation to his superior, U.N. ambassador Adlai Stevenson, who telephoned President Kennedy. Kennedy directed Stevenson to have Attwood meet with Cuban U.N. delegate Carlos Lechuga. This led to discreet meetings between Attwood and Lechuga, where it was decided that Attwood would travel to Cuba for direct meetings with Castro.

Although these unprecedented approaches to Cuba were strictly secret, it is almost certain that people within U.S. intelligence were aware of the rapprochement. Attorney General Robert Kennedy himself told Attwood the secret maneuvering was "bound to leak."

Three days after Kennedy's assassination, Attwood was formally notified that Havana was ready to proceed with a meeting. President Lyndon Johnson was briefed on the situation, but he turned a cold shoulder. Attwood sadly told author Anthony Summers: "The word came back that this was to be put on ice for the time being, and the time being has been ever since . . ."

Outside Miami, the next largest operational area for militant anti-Castro Cubans was the city of New Orleans, Lee Harvey Oswald's birthplace. It was in New Orleans that numerous leads have been developed linking the CIA, the FBI, anti-Castro Cubans, and perhaps military intelligence with Oswald.

Oswald's interest in Cuba went back to his Marine days, when he and Marine buddy Nelson Delgado toyed with the idea of traveling to Cuba and assisting Castro in his war against Batista. There was nothing unusual here. That same idea had crossed the minds of thousands of daydreaming American schoolboys.

But in Oswald's case, this dream may have taken on some reality. According to Delgado, the Marine Oswald began receiving letters plainly stamped with the seal of the Cuban consulate in Los Angeles. Oswald once traveled to Los Angeles with Delgado, saying his purpose was to "visit the Cuban consulate." There also were reports of Oswald meeting with mysterious strangers, who Delgado believed had to do with "the Cuban business."

But whose side was Oswald really on?

Gerry Patrick Hemming, a Marine with Oswald who was recruited into the CIA, has told of meeting Oswald in the Cuban consulate. Hemmings, himself working for Naval intelligence, said Oswald seemed to be "an informant or some type of agent working for somebody."

On April 24, 1963, less than a year after arriving back in Fort Worth from Russia, Oswald packed a bag and bought a bus ticket for New Orleans, telling Marina and friends that he couldn't find a job in Texas.

Shortly before leaving for New Orleans, he had written a letter to the Fair Play for Cuba Committee (FPCC), a pro-Castro organization headquartered in New York City and the object of intense scrutiny by various U.S. intelligence agencies, including the FBI and Army intelligence. Oswald praised Castro and asked for FPCC pamphlets, membership applications, and advice on tactics. He also mentioned he "was thinking about renting a small office at my own expense."

The FPCC director, V. T. Lee, promptly answered, saying the committee faced serious opposition and warned Oswald against provoking "unnecessary incidents which frighten away prospective supporters." It was advice that Oswald was to totally ignore.

Staying with relatives in New Orleans, Oswald managed to get a job at the William B. Reily Co., Inc., a coffee manufacturer. The company's owner, William Reily, was a financial backer of the Crusade to Free Cuba Committee, one of the many front groups raising money for the Cuban Revolutionary Council.

Through the spring and summer of 1963, Oswald, an avid reader, checked out twenty-seven books from the New Orleans Library. His reading ran from Ian Fleming's James Bond novels to Aldous Huxley and science fiction. Library records show Oswald also read two books about John F. Kennedy, *Profiles in Courage* and *Portrait of a President*. Oswald checked out nothing about Cuba.

In fact, it was during this time that a strange incident occurred that throws further doubt on Oswald's sincerity as a communist sympathizer. In July 1963, Oswald accompanied his uncle, Charles "Dutz" Murret, to a Jesuit seminary in Mobile, Alabama, where a cousin was enrolled. Here Oswald made what audience members thought was a well-constructed speech against Soviet-style communism. He took the opposite position from his procommunist public posturing over the previous few months in New Orleans—further evidence that Oswald was living some sort of dual life.

Back in New Orleans, this duplicity continued. Although Oswald handed out leaflets for the FPCC and continued to write to the national organization, his New Orleans chapter was a complete fraud. He even had his wife sign the name "Hidell" as president of his New Orleans Chapter of the Fair Play for Cuba Committee.

While there has been no documented evidence that—letters aside—Oswald was in contact with any pro-Castro group, he definitely was in touch with anti-Castro Cubans. On August 5, 1963, Oswald entered a store owned by Cuban militant Carlos Bringuier, a man with connections to both the CRC and the CIA. Oswald told Bringuier and friends that he was a Marine veteran with experience in guerrilla warfare and offered to train Cuban exiles. Pushing his point, Oswald returned the next day with a Marine training manual that he left with Bringuier. He again repeated his desire to join the fight against Castro.

Bringuier already was on guard. In his Warren Commission testimony, he said that some time earlier he had been interviewed by FBI agent Warren De Brueys, who had told him the Bureau might try to infiltrate his anti-Castro organization.

Three days later, Bringuier was shocked when a friend rushed into his store and said that the same man who had wanted to train exiles was on the New Orleans streets passing out pro-Castro literature. Bringuier and others sought out Oswald and confronted him. A crowd gathered as Bringuier railed against this "communist" who had tried to infiltrate the exiles. Displaying a loss of temper, Bringuier cursed Oswald, threw his leaflets into the air, then drew back his fist as if to strike. Oswald, who kept smiling throughout this episode, said: "Okay, Carlos, if you want to hit me, hit me."

But there was no fight. Police arrived and took Oswald, Bringuier, and two others into custody. All were charged with disturbing the peace. Oswald tried to contact his uncle for the twenty-five dollars bail money but failed. His uncle's daughter, however, contacted a family friend, New Orleans gambler Emile Bruneau, who put up the money.

However, before leaving the New Orleans police station, Oswald oddly asked to speak to an FBI agent. Despite being outside normal business hours, Agent John Quigley soon arrived and spent more than a hour with Oswald.

It is interesting to note the impression of Oswald by the New Orleans police. Speaking of the Bringuier episode, Lt. Francis Martello later said: "He seemed to have them set up to create an incident." While Sgt. Horace Austin recalled: "[Oswald] appeared as though he is being used by these people . . ."

After this brush with the law, Oswald's pro-Castro stance became even more public. He was soon on New Orleans radio and television telling his pro-Castro story to a wider audience. The radio interview is significant in that it was widely used after the assassination to "prove" his procommunist credentials. One of these interviews may have provided an accidental peek at Oswald's real identity. Tipped off to Oswald by Bringuier, radio reporter William Stuckey allowed Oswald to expound about his thoughts on Cuba and South America.

A few days later, armed with information obtained from the FBI, Stuckey and right-wing broadcaster Ed Butler verbally ambushed Oswald in another radio interview. Oswald was suddenly confronted with his attempted defection to Russia. The pro-Castro Oswald, self-proclaimed secretary of the New Orleans Chapter of the Fair Play for Cuba Committee, was suddenly revealed to have been a communist sympathizer who had tried to renounce his American citizenship. Caught off guard, Oswald stammered: "I was under the protection of the . . . uh . . . that is to say, I was not under the protection of the American government . . . but I was at all times considered an American citizen."

Could this slip of the tongue have revealed Oswald's true role as an agent of the U.S. government while in Russia?

It is also interesting that the radio newsmen handily obtained this derogatory information on Oswald so quickly and from such sources as the FBI and, according to Butler, the House Un-American Activities Committee.

It has been documented that both the CIA and the FBI at that time were making efforts not only to penetrate the FPCC but also to discredit the pro-Castro organization. Was this revelation of Oswald's Soviet life part of this program?

But the most intriguing aspect of Oswald's stay in New Orleans centered around a meeting place for anti-Castro militants, CIA and FBI agents, and organized-crime figures—544 Camp Street.

544 Camp Street

It was at 544 Camp Street in an old, three-story office building that the paths of Lee Harvey Oswald, the FBI, the CIA, anti-Castro Cubans, and organized crime figures all crossed.

Until a few months prior to Oswald's arrival in New Orleans, the aging building housed the offices of the Cuban Revolutionary Council (CRC), the umbrella anti-Castro organization that was created by CIA officer E. Howard Hunt.

CRC members included Carlos Bringuier, the man who had the much-publicized street encounter with Oswald; Sergio Arcacha-Smith, a CRC top official with close documented ties to CIA operative and adventurer David Ferrie; and Carlos Prio Socarras, former president of Cuba under Batista and one of the leading Cuban exiles close to CIA agents E. Howard Hunt, Bernard Barker, and Frank Sturgis (all of later Watergate fame).

Prio—who had paid for the yacht *Granma* used by Castro to land his revolutionaries on Cuba—had turned on Castro and become a leading anti-Castroite. It is alleged that Prio was to become the new president of Cuba following the ill-fated Bay of Pigs invasion.

Prio once was arrested in a gun-running conspiracy along with a man named Robert McKeown. McKeown, according to evidence developed by the Warren Commission, had been involved in a deal "running jeeps to Cuba" and other smuggling operations with Jack Ruby, the man who killed Oswald.

In April 1977, before he was scheduled to testify for the House Select Committee on Assassinations, Prio was found shot in the chest in his Miami Beach garage. The wound was ruled self-inflicted.

Although the CRC had left 544 Camp Street by the time Oswald was seen there in the summer of 1963, there were still plenty of Cuban connections. A side entrance to 544 Camp Street was 531 Lafayette Street, the address of Guy Banister Associates, a private detective agency. Banister, whom the *New Orleans States Item* in 1967 claimed helped supply munitions to the Bay of Pigs invaders, was a former FBI man with connections reaching into the Bureau, the CIA, and organized crime as well as the Cuban exiles.

His secretary, Delphine Roberts, in 1978 told the *Dallas Morning News* that Oswald had worked for Banister as "an undercover agent" in the summer of 1963. During that same time, another of Banister's employees was Oswald's former Civil Air Patrol leader, David Ferrie.

In the Warren Commission exhibits are some of Oswald's Fair Play for Cuba Committee leaflets. They are stamped:

> FPCC
> 544 Camp Street
> New Orleans, La.

Another intriguing contact point between Oswald, 544 Camp Street, and the Cubans was Ernesto Rodriguez. Recall that in the summer of 1963 Oswald wrote the Fair Play for Cuba Committee stating he was going to get a small office. During this same time period, the owner of the 544 Camp Street building, Sam Newman, said he was approached by a Latin man who asked about renting an office and said he was an electrician by day and wanted to teach Spanish at night.

Shortly after the assassination and acting on a tip, authorities talked with Rodriguez, who did teach Spanish and whose father was in the electrical business.

Rodriguez, an anti-Castro militant, denied a rumor that he had tapes of Oswald speaking Spanish, but admitted that he had met Oswald, who apparently wanted to learn Spanish. Rodriguez also said that Oswald had offered to train anti-Castro exiles and, in fact, it was Rodriguez who had sent Oswald to meet Carlos Bringuier.

There was plenty of undercover activity going on at 544 Camp Street in the summer of 1963. The location may have had something to do with it. The building was located close to the New Orleans offices of both the FBI and the CIA, it was near the Crescent City Garage where Oswald was seen in the company of FBI agents and it was just around the corner from the William B. Riley Coffee Co., Oswald's employer.

According to New Orleans district attorney Jim Garrison, it was here—at 544 Camp Street—that plans were set in motion that culminated in Dealey Plaza.

*   *   *

It was reported to the Warren Commission by the CIA that Oswald's pro-Castro contacts included an attempt to secure a visa to visit Cuba during a trip to Mexico City in late September 1963. The Agency apparently went to great lengths to prove that Oswald was in Mexico City at this time, but the effort was not entirely successful. Photographs of a man entering the Soviet embassy and a tape recording made at the time were shown to be of someone other than Oswald.

To document Oswald's visit to the Cuban embassy, the CIA relied on the testimony of a Mexican who worked at the embassy, Silvia Tirado de Duran. Duran, however, is a dubious witness at best since it is now known that the twenty-six-year-old woman was arrested twice following the assassination on orders from the CIA and may have been coerced into giving false testimony.

But again, it is the connections between the assassination and anti-Castro groups that has always turned up the most intriguing evidence —evidence that has largely been ignored by U.S. authorities, particularly the Warren Commission.

Oswald and the Exiles

One of several incidents that tend to connect Lee Harvey Oswald with the anti-Castro Cubans involves one of the most violent of the exile groups, Alpha 66, and its founder, Antonio Veciana Blanch.

Veciana, a former Cuban bank accountant who turned against Castro, was conducting raids against the island during the missile crisis and has consistently maintained that he was working for the CIA.

In the spring of 1963, Kennedy publicly criticized the hit-and-run raids of Alpha 66, to which Veciana replied publicly: "We are going to attack again and again." The militant Cuban leader has claimed to have worked for a CIA officer known to him as "Maurice Bishop." According to Veciana, he met with Bishop more than a hundred times and the CIA officer helped guide the activities of Alpha 66, including plans to assassinate Castro. Veciana said his relationship with the Agency did not end until 1973, when Bishop paid him $253,000 as back pay for his services.

But Veciana's most astounding claim is that, during a visit to Dallas in late August or early September 1963, he saw his CIA case officer in conversation with a man he later recognized as Lee Harvey Oswald.

Although the House Select Committee on Assassinations failed to "credit" Veciana's story of the Oswald-Bishop meeting, it nevertheless went to great lengths in an attempt to locate the mysterious Bishop, including sending an artist's sketch of Bishop to U.S. newspapers. The committee also scoured CIA files in an effort to identify Bishop. The Agency, unsurprisingly, denied ever assigning a case officer to Veciana.

Veciana also told the committee that shortly after the assassination, Bishop contacted him and reminded him that he had a relative working for Cuban intelligence living in Mexico. According to Veciana, Bishop wanted Veciana to offer his relative a "large sum of money" to say that the relative and his wife met Oswald during his Mexico City trip. Veciana said he agreed to this scheme, but was unable to contact his relative.

The House Committee later developed information that Bishop may have been none other than former chief of the CIA's Western Hemisphere Division's Directorate of Operations' David Atlee Phillips. Phillips denied being Bishop and a fearful Veciana agreed. However, after arranging a meeting between Veciana and Phillips, the Committee staff reported it "suspected that Veciana was lying when he denied that the retired CIA officer was Bishop."

A prime example of interference with an investigation into links between anti-Castro Cubans and the assassination came just days after Kennedy was killed. The Chicago Field Office of the Secret Service reported to superiors that it had heard from an informant that a Chicago group "may have [had] a connection with the JFK assassination." The informant reported that on the day before the assassination, a Cuban militant named Homer S. Echevarria had stated that he had "plenty of money" for an illegal arms deal and would proceed with the plan "as soon as we take care of Kennedy."

The Secret Service checked on Echevarria and discovered he was an associate of the military director of the Cuban Student Directorate (the New Orleans chapter of the CSD was headed by Carlos Bringuier, who had squabbled with Oswald on the streets of that city) and that the munitions deal was financed by "hoodlum elements . . . not restricted to Chicago."

Although the Secret Service wanted to pursue the matter, the FBI—which on November 29, 1963, was designated to control the assassination investigation by President Johnson—"made clear that it wanted the Secret Service to terminate its investigation" of the Echevarria report. The case was closed.

One anti-Castro-Cuban–Oswald story that was not so easy to brush off is that of Cuban exile Silvia Odio. She and her sister, Annie, came from a distinguished and wealthy Cuban family. The sisters had been forced to flee Cuba after their parents were imprisoned by the Castro government. Their father, who intially had supported Castro's revolution, had turned against the bearded leader and was arrested for concealing a man named Reinaldo Gonzales, who was involved in a plot to kill Castro. Interestingly, Gonzales's co-conspirator was Antonio Veciana, the leader of Alpha 66 who operated under the instructions of Maurice Bishop.

Shortly before moving to Dallas, Silvia Odio had joined with other anti-Castro Cubans in Puerto Rico and formed Junta Revolucionaria (the Cuban Revolutionary Junta) or JURE.

One night in late September 1963—they believe it was the 26th or

27th—three men came to Odio's Dallas apartment. There were two Latins and one Anglo, described as weary, unkempt, and unshaved.

The leader of the trio identified himself as "Leopoldo" and introduced the other Latin as "Angel" or "Angelo." He introduced the American as "Leon Oswald."

The men said they had just arrived from New Orleans, were members of JURE, and were working with the Cuban Revolutionary Council (CRC). They knew her father's underground name and also many details of anti-Castro activities in Cuba, including recent plots to kill Castro. They told Silvia Odio that they were trying to raise funds for anti-Castro operations and wanted her help in translating solicitation letters to American businessmen. Something about the men, however, made Odio uneasy and she sent them away after warning them that she did not want to be involved in a campaign of violence. During their brief stay, her sister Annie also got a good look at the trio.

Within forty-eight hours, "Leopoldo" called Silvia Odio and asked for her thoughts on their American companion. She said the man then made a series of comments, saying:

Well, you know he's a Marine, an ex-Marine, and an expert marksman. He would be a tremendous asset to anyone, except that you never know how to take him . . . He's kind of loco, kind of nuts. He could go any way. He could do anything—like getting underground in Cuba, like killing Castro . . . The American says we Cubans don't have any guts. He says we should have shot President Kennedy after the Bay of Pigs. He says we should do something like that.

Apparently, that was all "Leopoldo" had to say, for he quickly hung up and Odio was never to hear from him again. She later told author Anthony Summers: 'Immediately, I suspected there was some sort of scheme or plot . . .''

Although the Odio's wrote of the incident to their father and told the story to friends well *before* Kennedy's assassination, they did not tell authorities of the strange visitors.

Both sisters were shocked and frightened to see photographs of Lee Harvey Oswald since, then and now, they both believe him to be the same man who was introduced to them as "Leon Oswald."

After the assassination, word of the Odio visit reached the FBI, which investigated the matter for the Warren Commission. The commission, having already accepted FBI and CIA evidence that Oswald was on his way to or in Mexico City at the time of the Odio visit, stated:

While the FBI had not yet completed its investigation into this matter at the time the report went to press, the Commission has concluded that Lee Harvey Oswald was not at Mrs. Odio's apartment in September 1963.

Another factor that enabled the commission to dismiss the Odio story was reports from the FBI concerning anti-Castro militant, Loran Eugene Hall.

Although Warren Commission staff lawyers asked the FBI to prove or disprove the Odio story in August 1964, it was not until September 26—just days before the report was finalized—that the Bureau reported on the matter. An FBI report stated that the Bureau had located Hall, who admitted traveling to Dallas with two other Cubans and that they had visited Odio. Hall said neither of his companions was Oswald. The matter was dropped.

Even before the Warren report was issued, FBI agents located Hall's two companions, Lawrence Howard and William Seymour. Both denied ever meeting Silvia Odio.

Confronted with their statements, Hall retracted his story. In fact, Hall denied he ever told the FBI any such thing. The Bureau failed to tell the commission about this development. Hall, who acknowledged being imprisoned in Cuba with Mafia leader Santos Trafficante, also was an associate of Frank Sturgis (Watergate burglar and CIA-Mafia-connected anti-Castroite) and was twice taken into custody for engaging in unauthorized exile activities.

The Odio story caused great problems with the Warren Commission Report. If Oswald was in Dallas, he couldn't have been traveling by bus to Mexico at the same time. And, if the Oswald in Odio's apartment was not the real Oswald, then it is clear that someone was impersonating him with an eye toward implicating Oswald in the assassination. Small wonder the Commission decided to let the matter rest.

There is even some evidence to suggest that Oswald was in contact with anti-Castro Cubans on the Sunday prior to the assassination. In 1979, the *Dallas Morning News* reported that a photographer in Abilene, Texas, recalled a Cuban friend receiving a note from "Lee Oswald" on Sunday, November 17, 1963. Harold Reynolds said he had been friends with a Pedro Valeriano Gonzales for some time and knew him to be involved in anti-Castro activities. Gonzales was president of the Cuban Liberation Committee, an exile organization in Abilene, where he worked as a school-system maintenance man. Reynolds said he was showing Gonzales some baby pictures that Sunday when the landlady knocked on the door and said she had noticed a note stuck in Gonzales's door for two or three days. Reynolds took the note. He recalled:

In handwriting, it said something like "Call me immediately. Urgent" and had two Dallas phone numbers written on it. I noticed the name "Lee Oswald" and asked Gonzales who he was. Seems like he said, "Some attorney from Dallas." He looked nervous and sweat started appearing on his forehead. So, I left to go up the street and deliver some photos. As I was coming back, I noticed his car a few blocks from his house and him standing in a pay phone booth.

Reynolds said he thought this unusual as Gonzales had a telephone in his home.

The Warren Commission could not account for Oswald's presence on the Sunday prior to the assassination.

At an organizational meeting of the Abilene Cuban Liberation Committee, Gonzales had read a letter from his friend in Miami, Manuel A. de Varona, who expressed his desire to visit his friends in Abilene.

Varona, the former Cuban prime minister under Carlos Prio Socarras, was involved in the CIA-Mafia plots to kill Castro. Varona also was coordinator of the Cuban Revolutionary Council.

In fact, the *Dallas Morning News* reported having obtained copies of letters from the owner of the building at 544 Camp Street in New Orleans to Varona asking for help in paying for the CRC's office space there. (Recall that some of Oswald's FPCC material was stamped "544 Camp Street.")

Reynold's wife said Gonzales came to her home just after the assassination and demanded all photos and negatives that Reynolds may have taken of him and his friends. Gonzales simply dropped from sight in Abilene a short time later.

Reynolds said Gonzales never admitted knowing Oswald, but that on at least one occasion, he asked his friend about Kennedy. Gonzales told him: "Somebody is going to kill him."

*   *   *

While many people, particularly those close to U.S. intelligence and military sources, claim that Kennedy may have been killed on orders from Castro as a reprisal for the CIA-Mafia-Cuban plots against him, the evidence seems to point more toward the anti-Castro Cubans.

One anti-Castro leader, John Martino, even spelled out the assassination plan to a Texas business friend in 1975. In a startling telephone conversation with Fred Claasen, repeated by author Summers, Martino admitted to serving as a CIA contract agent. He told Claasen:

> The anti-Castro people put Oswald together. Oswald didn't know who he was working for—he was just ignorant of who was really putting him together. Oswald was to meet his contact at the Texas Theater. They were to meet Oswald in the theater, and get him out of the country, then eliminate him. Oswald made a mistake. . . . There was no way we could get to him. They had Ruby kill him.

Others such as former senator Robert Morgan, a member of the Senate Intelligence Committee that looked into CIA-Mafia plots, continued to maintain that Kennedy brought about his own death. Morgan, differing from the conclusions of his own committee, stated flatly: "There is no doubt in my mind that John Fitzgerald Kennedy was assassinated by Fidel Castro, or someone under his influence, in retaliation for our efforts to assassinate him."

But most researchers today doubt seriously that Castro had a hand in Kennedy's death. Even the accused assassin couldn't buy it. During interrogation on the Sunday morning he was killed by Jack Ruby, Oswald was asked if his beliefs regarding Cuba played a role in the assassination. He replied: "Will Cuba be better off with the President dead? Someone will take his place, Lyndon Johnson, no doubt, and he will probably follow the same policy."

Also, while Castro eventually did learn of the plots against him, there is no firm evidence that he knew of these schemes in time to have launched a retaliatory strike by November 1963.

And again, there seems no serious motive for Castro to have Kennedy killed outside of simple revenge—and every motive against the idea.

In a 1977 interview with Bill Moyers broadcast on CBS, Castro denied any thought of trying to kill the U.S. president:

It would have been absolute insanity by Cuba . . . It would have been a provocation. Needless to say, it would have been to run the risk that our country would have been destroyed by the United States. Nobody who's not insane could have thought about [killing Kennedy in retaliation].

But if the evidence of Castro's involvement in the assassination is meager, it is more than made up for by the abundance of evidence of anti-Castro Cuban involvement, as we have seen in this chapter.

And behind the anti-Castro Cubans always lurked the shadowy hands of U.S. intelligence and the even darker spector of organized crime.

Summary

After leading a successful revolution in Cuba, Fidel Castro angered many interests in the United States by ridding his island nation of organized crime and American business domination.

Castro chose to turn to the Russians for help after the United States initiated sanctions against Cuba. This Moscow-Havana connection further incensed factions within the U.S.

Responding to urgings from these factions, Vice President Richard Nixon encouraged action against Cuba—resulting in the ill-fated Bay of Pigs Invasion.

This invasion was to be launched by a brigade of anti-Castro Cubans under the direction of the CIA and with the assistance of the U.S. military. But right from the start, President Kennedy let it be known that he would not use American military force against Castro.

Despite this knowledge, the CIA officials behind the invasion went ahead with their plans.

The invasion was launched on April 17, 1961—less than three months after Kennedy took office—and proved an utter disaster.

The invasion's failure was blamed on Kennedy's refusal to unleash military naval and air support. Everyone connected with the invasion—the anti-Castro Cubans, the CIA, the military, and organized crime—was bitter toward the new president. This acrimony only increased with Kennedy's attempts to bring tighter control over the CIA and with his decision not to order a second invasion of Cuba during the 1962 missile crisis.

More hatred toward Kennedy was generated as the secret war against Cuba was geared down after the missile crisis and with Kennedy's attempts at reconciliation with Castro.

Into this world of passionate anti-Castro Cubans, adventurous CIA agents, and Mafia soldiers was injected the odd ex-Marine Lee Harvey Oswald.

Oswald, while maintaining a posture as a pro-Castro Marxist, nevertheless was in continuous contact with several anti-Castro elements.

During the summer of 1963, Oswald was loose in a deceptive world of undercover agents while living in New Orleans.

And while it may never be positively determined exactly who Oswald was working for, it is safe to assume that his employers represented the anti-Castro Cubans and their CIA and mob allies.

Oswald's activities during this period of time—and particularly the Silvia Odio affair—point to a manipulation of Oswald and others in laying a trail of incriminating evidence connecting the ex-Marine and vocal Castro supporter to Kennedy's assassination.

Kennedy's not going to make it to the election. He's going to be hit.
—Miami Mafia boss Santos Trafficante

Mobsters

During the late 1800s and early 1900s, immigrants arrived in the United States from all corners of the world seeking the golden American dream. What most found was an impoverished and bleak existence in one of the many big-city ghettos, where they were trapped by their inability to speak English, lack of education, and class and cultural differences.

Just like the inner cities of today, these ghettos spawned a multitude of street gangs with names like the Whyos, the Dead Rabbits, the Bowery Boys, the Tenth Avenue Gang, the Village Gang, the Gas House Gang, the Midnight Terrors, and the Growler Gang. Despite their colorful names, these gangs were anything but funny. Young toughs would rob and beat their victims in broad daylight, with little to fear from the police—as long as they confined their illegal activities to the ghetto and its cowed population.

In the various ethnic communities there were those who had belonged to the secret societies of other countries—the Mafia of Sicily, the Camorra of Italy, and the Tongs of China. They brought the learned terror and intimidation of these societies to their new home, where it found fertile soil.

The Mafia used a technique involving the Black Hand. The victim, usually a successful businessman, would receive a letter demanding money. It would be signed with the imprint of a black hand. Rumors were spread that the Black Hand was a secret society of assassins that operated with impunity. Even the famous Italian singer, Enrico Caruso, was shaken down in this early-day protection racket.

If the demands for money were not met, the recipient's business might burn down or a relative might be kidnapped or beaten. The Mafia offered protection from the Black Hand—its own invention.

As America entered the twentieth century, the city gangs were becoming more adept at their profession and expanding operations to include gambling, prostitution, and lotteries. They also were the bankers for the poor, charging exorbitant interest rates from those who could borrow money nowhere else.

The Irish brought a new dimension of power to the gangs. Unhampered by a language barrier and experienced in politics in their homeland, the Irish gangs gained advantages by allying themselves with political figures. Initially it was the politicians who used the gangsters. Ballot boxes were stuffed, voters intimidated, and opposition rallies broken up. But as the gang leaders grew more wealthy, and thus more powerful, soon the politicians came seeking favors. Through the years that Tammany Hall controlled New York City, Irish gangsters provided the enforcement muscle.

Another source of power for Tammany was the twelve-hundred-member Eastman gang, run by a Jewish immigrant named Monk Eastman (real name: Edward Osterman). After a furious public gun battle in August 1903 between the Eastmans and a rival gang, the authorities stepped in—not to eliminate the gangs, but to arrange a truce.

As the fortunes of America soared between 1910 and 1929, so did those of the gangs, particularly those with far-sighted leadership. Another Jewish gangster from New York, Arnold Rothstein, became an example of the successful underworld leader. Nicknamed "The Brain," Rothstein grew from a small-time gambler into one of the most powerful men in the city. He even reportedly fixed the 1919 World Series. Rothstein moved in the most respectable circles, rubbing elbows with city and state officials.

Bootleggers and Boozers

For more than fifty years prior to 1920, American groups such as the Women's Christian Temperance Union, the Anti-Saloon League, and others had lobbied Congress and state legislatures to prohibit the manufacture and sale of distilled spirits. Finally, with many male voters off serving in the military and with the emotional exhaustion and moral primness following World War I, their dream became reality. In December 1917, Congress passed the eighteenth Amendment to the Constitution, prohibiting the sale of intoxicating beverages, and by January 1919, the necessary thirty-six of the forty-eight states had ratified it.

In October 1919—overriding the veto of President Woodrow Wilson—Congress passed the Volstead Act, which created the government bureacracy needed to enforce the eighteenth Amendment. On midnight January 16, 1920, Prohibition became the law of the land.

Less than an hour after midnight, six masked men drove a truck into a Chicago railroad switchyard, broke into two freight cars, and made off with $100,000 worth of whiskey marked FOR MEDICINAL USE ONLY. That was just the beginning of an era that witnessed rapid decay of public morality, disrespect for law, and the rise of a gigantic criminal empire that remains with us today.

The catalyst for all this change was money—the immense profits to be made from the sale of illegal alcohol. Before Prohibition, a single shot of uncut Scotch sold for fifteen cents. Quickly the cost of that same shot of Scotch rose to seventy-five cents with the quality of the alcohol making a comparative drop. Bootleggers bought a quart of quality Scotch at sea for four dollars, then diluted it into three quarts selling for as much as forty dollars a bottle.

And there was plenty of alcohol available at home. Homemade "hootch" was often the life of the party—provided it didn't blind or kill.

But—profits aside—the greatest impact of Prohibition was to make crime and criminals acceptable in the minds of the general public. City hoodlums who before would never have been allowed in genteel circles became the heroes of the hour. The enormous profits from selling illegal alcohol made respectable businessmen of men who months before had been thugs.

Because of the unpopularity of Prohibition, buying protection from city and police officials became an easy chore. Chicago police chief Charles Fitzmorris once stated: "Sixty percent of my policemen are in the bootleg business." Many people thought his estimate was too low.

Local governments, overwhelmed by the wealth and power of the gangs, increasingly turned to Washington for help. Federal authorities found their hands were tied since, at that time, crimes were under the jurisdiction of the states. To counter the growing crime rate, more and more federal laws were passed, giving authority to federal agents.

Now, in addition to the growing power of the criminal empire, Americans saw law-enforcement powers slowly shift from local officials to the national government. New power bases arose, such as the fledgling Federal Bureau of Investigation, begun in 1909, and a variety of Prohibition agencies, which were to evolve into such modern forms as the Bureau of Narcotics and Dangerous Drugs (forerunner of the Drug Enforcement Agency) and the Alcohol, Tobacco and Firearms agency.

Illegal booze was smuggled into the United States in every conceivable manner and from every conceivable point—across the Mexican and Canadian borders and offloaded from ships to small powerboats that moved out of remote bays almost at will.

The profits were enough to turn even erstwhile honest businessmen to bootlegging. One such businessman would seem to be Joseph P. Kennedy, patriarch of the Kennedy clan. Although no conclusive evidence of Kennedy's bootlegging is available—his business papers are still kept locked away in Boston's John F. Kennedy Library—it has been widely rumored that the elder Kennedy got started on the road to riches by importing illegal booze.

Rumors have it that Kennedy made a fortune bringing Canadian whiskey into Boston. This charge is supported by the fact that as soon as Prohibition ended, Kennedy immediately was in the Scotch, gin, and rum business through a firm he founded called Somerset Importers.

Everyone fared well by flouting Prohibition. "I admit quite frankly that I made a fortune from bootlegging, "Meyer Lansky told biographers, adding:

Everybody I knew treated Prohibition with contempt. The most important people in the country—respectable businessmen, politicians, senators, congressmen—they all bought illegal booze from me or from other men in the business.

After thirteen years of Prohibition, even its most ardent supporters were forced to concede that it simply didn't work. If enough people want a commodity, others will find a way to get it to them—for a price.

The price of prohibited alcohol—the massive corruption of the political and legal system, the enormous power wielded by the criminal gangs, and the deaths and maimings from toxic hootch and gangland wars—was too steep. On December 5, 1933, Prohibition was repealed.

After national Prohibition ended, each state created its own liquor authority, opening up avenues for bribery and payoffs that hadn't existed before.

Liquor and beer laws differed widely from state to state and even from city to city. Even today, liquor laws are a bewildering forest of statutes, regulations, and directives that defy any pretense of rationality.

And the gangsters didn't get out of the liquor business. Their illegal "speakeasies" simply became legitimate cocktail lounges and bars, often with frontmen to apply for the necessary licenses.

As the Prohibition era dawned, many gangsters recognized the opportunity that presented itself. In Chicago, Big Jim Colosimo was not one of them. Afraid of bringing federal lawmen down on him, Colosimo prevented his right-hand man, Johnny Torrio, from handling any alcohol other than what was needed for the gang's brothels and speakeasies. Torrio was frustrated. On orders from Torrio, an ambitious New York gangster named Frankie Yale came to Chicago and on May 11, 1920, put a bullet through Colosimo's head.

Colosimo's funeral lasted three days, with more than five thousand mourners including two congressmen, three judges, one soon-to-be federal judge, ten aldermen, a state representative, and many other community leaders. It became the prototype for subsequent gangster funerals.

By now, every section of Chicago was ruled by a gang. The illegal operators of these gangs were often intensely competitive and their rivalry was fueled by racial and ethnic prejudices.

Torrio tried to make peace. Calling the gang leaders together, he argued persuasively that peaceful cooperation would lead to higher profits for all concerned. During the early 1920s, the "united" Chicago underworld prospered.

Then, in 1923, a gang from the far South Side tried to muscle in on Torrio's bootlegging operation. This challenge was halted quickly with the murder of eight gang members.

But the bloodletting—along with a new reform-minded mayor—resulted in strong pressure on the gangs from the authorities. This prompted Torrio to move his entire headquarters to a suburb—Cicero, Illinois—

where by bribery and threats he became undisputed master of the town. This was the beginning of a movement out of the traditional cities into new and more controllable communities.

Opting for semiretirement, Torrio traveled to his native Italy, where he was greeted like a conquering hero. He left the Chicago operation in the hands of an underling, Al Capone. Where Torrio was quiet, debonair, and opposed to unnecessary violence, Capone was the distinct opposite. A gambler, bully, and womanizer, Capone's answer to every problem was to apply gangland muscle.

In mid-May 1929, a meeting of the nation's underworld leaders was held in Atlantic City. It was decided that Capone had to go and that the gangs had to start looking for other avenues of profits since it appeared that Prohibition was on its way out. This was one of the first major meetings between gangsters, who only years before would have been blood enemies. But times were changing and so were the methods of the criminals.

On his way home from the meeting, Capone was arrested for carrying a concealed weapon and sentenced to one year in prison. After serving that sentence, he soon was convicted of income tax evasion and sentenced to federal prison for eleven years. "You won't see me for a long time," he said while being led away. Capone was released in 1939, but died soon afterward, insane from the ravages of syphilis.

In New York, Arnold Rothstein, who intially had stayed aloof from bootlegging, became the largest supplier of illegal booze in the East.

Rothstein was considered a wealthy front man by New York's real Mafia leaders, which by the late 1920s were two large families run by Giuseppe Masseria and Salvatore Maranzano. These families were locked in a protracted blood feud known as the Castellammorese War (from Maranzano's Sicilian hometown of Castellammore del Golfo).

Eventually, gangsters from both New York and Chicago were drawn into the war. By 1931, the war was going against Masseria when one of his lieutenants, Charles "Lucky" Luciano (real name: Salvatore Lucania) decided to arrange a "peace." On April 15, 1931, Luciano, along with some Masseria men loyal to him, met with Masseria in a Coney Island restaurant. After lunch, everyone left except Luciano and Masseria. Moments later, after Luciano stepped out "to go to the washroom," three men entered and fired more than twenty rounds at Masseria. Six hit Masseria in the head and back.

Luciano immediately called a meeting with Maranzano ending the war. But, Maranzano declared himself *"capo di tutti capi"* (boss of all bosses) and announced a new family structure, which remained in place into the 1960s.

Soon Luciano and his underboss, Vito Genovese, learned that Maranzano was planning to eliminate them, so plans were set in motion to end Maranzano's rule. Maranzano had scheduled a meeting with Luciano and

Genovese in his office on September 10, 1931, but before it could take place, four men posing as police officers came in and murdered Maranzano. The murder of Maranzano was accompanied by the killing of several Maranzano henchmen—and, it has been alleged, as many as forty other Mafia chieftains across the country—thus breaking the power of the old Mafia guard.

Luciano was now the preeminent leader of the criminal mobs. Wisely, he declined the title of "boss of all bosses." Instead, Luciano created a commission of bosses and organized the old Mafia families into a national crime syndicate. It was Luciano who finally realized the dream of Torrio and Rothstein—the merging of the criminal gangs into a national crime syndicate.

Backed by the deadly power of Murder, Inc.—a group of killers organized by Louis "Lepke" Buchalter in 1927 whose sole client was the Mafia—Luciano continued to gain absolute control of the syndicate he created.

During this time, Luciano began to move control of crime away from the traditional Italian and Sicilian families. New faces were beginning to show up in the crime syndicate. The Jewish math wizard Meyer Lansky, Legs Diamond, Dutch Schultz, and Benjamin "Bugsy" Siegel were among those slowly being admitted to policy meetings. But Luciano was still the man in charge. After extensive investigation, Senator Estes Kefauver wrote: "The Mafia is the cement that binds organized crime and the man who perfected the cement was Luciano."

Lucky Goes to War

Next to Prohibition, one of the most far-reaching events in the history of organized crime came during World War II when Lucky Luciano became partners with the U.S. government.

By the mid-1930s, Luciano was a wealthy crook with interests in a wide variety of legal and illegal activities. However, he never gave up his original means of making money—prostitution. It proved his undoing.

In 1936, under special New York County prosecutor Thomas E. Dewey, Luciano's phones were tapped and his prostitutes brought in for questioning. On April 1, Luciano, along with several associates, was indicted on ninety counts of compulsory prostitution. His trial was a sensation. The public was entranced and appalled as one prostitute after another told tales of beatings, degradation, and drug addiction. Luciano was convicted and sentenced to thirty to fifty years in prison. He was first taken to Sing Sing, but later transferred to Clinton State Prison at Dannemora near the Canadian border.

It appeared Luciano was safely put away. But then came World War II. The war produced undreamed-of wealth for the mobs wherever they were. The friendly bootleggers of yesterday became the friendly black marketeers of today, supplying nylons, new cars, gasoline coupons, tires, food ration stamps, and even military commissions and discharges.

It was even unnecessary to counterfeit ration coupons. Gangsters simply obtained real ones from corrupt officials within the Office of Price Administration, a semi-volunteer organization that counted among its young lawyers an aspiring politician from California, Richard M. Nixon. One man who dealt with the OPA and became rich in the automobile tire business during the war was Charles G. "Bebe" Rebozo, who remained close friends with Nixon through the years.

Toward the end of 1942, the first year of war for the United States, things were not going well for the U.S. Navy. In March of that year alone, twenty-four American ships had been sunk by German U-boats.

Then on November 9, 1942, the former French liner *Normandie*, caught fire and rolled over in her North River moorings in Manhattan while being refitted as a troop carrier. It was plainly an act of sabotage—and later was attributed to mobster Vito Genovese, who returned to Italy during the war and supported dictator Benito Mussolini.

Furthermore, Naval intelligence was convinced that information about ship convoys was being transmitted to the Axis by longshoremen of German and Italian extraction.

In a desperate attempt to compensate for years of neglect in the intelligence field, U.S. military officers decided to contact the mob for help.

Navy Secretary Frank Knox created a special intelligence unit for the Third Naval District, which included the Port of New York, which handled nearly one-half of all U.S. foreign shipping. This unit was headed by Lt. Commander Charles Radcliffe Haffenden, who quickly opened an unobtrusive office in Manhattan's Astor Hotel, where he met with mob figures.

The Navy appealed to Manhattan District Attorney Thomas E. Dewey to put them in touch with Mafia leaders. A Dewey investigator, Murray Gurfein, contacted Mafia boss Joseph "Socks" Lanza as a first step. Lanza immediately went to Meyer Lansky, who had helped guide Luciano in organizing the national crime syndicate. Lansky, sensing an opportunity to build his prestige with the syndicate, met with Commander Haffenden and promised to get Luciano's support. Years later, Lansky told biographers:

> Sure, I'm the one who put Lucky and Naval Intelligence together . . . The reason I cooperated was because of strong personal feelings. I wanted the Nazis beaten . . . I was a Jew and I felt for those Jews in Europe who were suffering. They were my brothers.

Although officially no deals were made with Lansky and Luciano— they supposedly cooperated out of sheer patriotism—soon Luciano was transferred from the "Siberia" of Dannemora to the more genial surroundings of Great Meadow Prison near Comstock, New York. Although in subsequent investigations into the Mafia-Navy partnership, the government denied any deals were made, the alliance proved effective.

Union strikes and sabotage were practically nonexistent on the New York docks during the war. And when U.S. forces landed in Sicily, there were Mafia men waiting to show them the location of German positions and safe routes through minefields.

During this final phase of the war, the Mafia-military cooperation—known as Operation Underworld—moved from the Navy to the Office of Strategic Services, forerunner of the CIA.

On January 3, 1946, Dewey—by then governor of New York—forwarded to the state legislature an executive clemency for Luciano that noted Luciano's "aid" to the war effort. Luciano was freed from prison but promptly deported. He had never bothered to become a naturalized citizen. He sailed for Italy aboard the S.S. *Laura Keene* on February 3, 1946. Once ensconced in Italy, Luciano didn't accept retirement. He began to bring his formidable organizational abilities to worldwide crime. Later that year, he turned up in Havana, Cuba, where Lansky was busy consolidating the gambling and prostitution business. However, American authorities warned the Cubans that medical supplies would be shut off if Luciano was allowed to remain. He soon departed.

Returning to Italy, Luciano began to organize an international narcotics syndicate that remains with us today.

*   *   *

The contemporary awareness of organized crime dates back to a conference of law-enforcement officials called together by U.S. attorney general J. Howard McGrath in 1950. Officials from New Orleans, Dallas, and other cities testified to the brutal takeover of crime in their areas of jurisdiction. One dissenter was Otto Kerner, the U.S. attorney from Chicago, who maintained there was "no organized gambling in the city of Chicago . . ." In 1973, Kerner was convicted of accepting $150,000 in bribes from horse-racing interests.

One of the results of the 1950 conference was the creation of a Select Senate Committee to probe organized crime under the sponsorship of Senator Estes Kefauver of Tennessee. The Kefauver Committee hearings lasted well into 1951 and provided much more public knowledge about the national crime syndicate. While Attorney General McGrath—along with FBI director J. Edgar Hoover—had maintained that no crime syndicate existed, Kefauver and his committee provided the evidence that it did. The committee found that organized, professional gambling and bookmaking was widespread throughout the nation, that the narcotics industry was a "highly organized crime" and that the mob had infiltrated legitimate businesses ranging from advertising to transportation.

It also showed the amount of official corruption that was necessary for the syndicate to flourish. The committee's final report quoted a mobster named John Roselli, who later became embroiled in the CIA-Mafia assassination schemes:

> [T]he wire service, the handbooks, the slot machines, and the other rackets which have thrived in the city of Chicago cannot operate without local corruption; if the handbooks are open, the conclusion is inescapable that the police are being paid off.

The Kefauver Committee also found that organized crime had spread from the cities of New York and Chicago to new markets in places like Kansas City, New Orleans, and Dallas.

After visiting New Orleans, the committee described it as "one of America's largest concentrations of gambling houses." One of these houses, the Beverly Club, was found to be owned by Phil Kastel, Frank Costello, Jake Lansky (Meyer's brother), and a local Mafia leader, Carlos Marcello.

Carlos Marcello

Carlos Marcello (real name: Calogero Minacore) was born in 1910, the child of Sicilian parents living in Tunisia. That same year, the family came to New Orleans. At that time, the leader of the Mafia in New Orleans was Charles Montranga, who had escaped a mass lynching in 1891 following the murder of Police Chief David Hennessey.

In 1922, Montranga was succeeded by one of his lieutenants, Sam Carolla. Carolla became a bootlegger during Prohibition and consolidated the mob's control of New Orleans. In 1932, Carolla was convicted of shooting a federal agent and was sent to prison, where he continued to run his crime organization. That same year, New York Mayor-elect Fiorello LaGuardia was clamping down on mob operations there, so Frank Costello moved his slot machine business to New Orleans with the permission of Carolla. Carolla even supplied a young associate to run the newly arrived gambling operation—Carlos Marcello.

By 1947, Carolla and Marcello—with the aid of Costello and Meyer Lansky—had expanded their gambling operations to include a racetrack, wire service, and several plush casinos. That year, Carolla was deported to Sicily and, despite two illegal trips back, his control over New Orleans passed to Marcello.

By 1963, Marcello's empire was estimated by the New Orleans Metropolitan Crime Commission to range into the hundreds of millions of dollars, although Marcello claimed he made only about $1,600 a month as a tomato salesman. Much of Marcello's ownings had been put under the names of close relatives, thus hiding his true worth.

Marcello's national crime contacts included Costello, Joe Civello of Dallas, Sam Yaras of Chicago, Mickey Cohen of Los Angeles, and Santos

Trafficante, Sr., identified by the Kefauver Committee as Tampa's leading mobster.

Since the Kefauver Committee hearings, the U.S. government has tried unsuccessfully to deport Marcello, who holds only a Guatemalan passport obtained allegedly by bribes.

In the spring of 1961, Marcello found he was facing a new, and much tougher government opponent than in the past. Entering the offices of the Immigration and Naturalization Services in New Orleans for his regular quarterly appointment to report as an alien, Marcello found himself handcuffed and driven to Moisant International Airport on direct orders from the new U.S. attorney general, Robert F. Kennedy.

He was flown twelve hundred miles to Guatemala City, where he was dumped without luggage and with little cash. Forced to leave Guatemala because of the ensuing political uproar, Marcello somehow found his way back to Miami. House Select Committee on Assassinations chief counsel Robert Blakey claims wiretaps showed Marcello was flown back to the United States by a Dominican Republic Air Force plane, however, others claim he was flown back by pilot David Ferrie.

Although still fighting deportation, Marcello managed to remain in the United States. But his Sicilian pride must have been greatly injured at Kennedy's unceremonious actions. It was not long afterward that Marcello reportedly made threats against the attorney general.

Edward Becker, a Las Vegas promoter and corporate "investigator," told the House Select Committee on Assassinations that he was present at a meeting in September 1962, at Marcello's estate just outside New Orleans, Churchill Farms. Becker said at the mention of Kennedy's name, Marcello became angry and stated: "Don't worry about that little Bobby son-of-a-bitch. He's going to be taken care of." According to Becker, Marcello then uttered a Sicilian curse:

"*Livarsi na petra di la scarpa.*" (Take the stone out of my shoes.)

Marcello described President Kennedy as a dog and Bobby Kennedy as the tail. He then gave a startlingly accurate prophesy of what was to come. He said the dog will keep biting you if you only cut off its tail, but cut off the head and the dog will die, tail and all. The analogy was clear—with John Kennedy out of the way, Bobby Kennedy and his war on crime would come to an end.

Becker said Marcello even had a plan. Marcello said he would use a "nut" for the job, someone who could be manipulated so that the killing could not be traced back to him.

The House Select Committee on Assassinations determined that there were many connections between Marcello and the JFK assassination—Marcello's associate in Dallas; Joe Civello, was close with Jack Ruby; a Marcello employee, David Ferrie, was first Lee Harvey Oswald's Civil Air Patrol leader and said to have been in contact with Oswald during the summer of 1963; and Oswald's uncle, Charles "Dutz" Murret, was acquainted with Marcello's personal driver as well as other associates of Marcello.

It was just a few months after Marcello's reported threat that Lee Harvey Oswald arrived in New Orleans.

*   *   *

In 1957, a conflict over who would lead the American crime syndicate was resolved on October 25, when two gunmen shot Albert Anastasia out of a barber's chair in New York. Earlier that year, Frank Costello, Luciano's successor, was shot while entering his Manhattan apartment. He lived, but was charged with tax evasion after a note was found on him listing receipts from the recently built Tropicana Hotel in developing Las Vegas. Costello retired from the rackets.

Three weeks after Anastasia's death, a mob conference was called by Vito Genovese. It was held at the country estate of a Mafia lieutenant near the small town of Apalachin in upstate New York. On hand was a collection of almost every leader of the crime syndicate. The purpose of the meeting, according to later testimony of some of those present, was the demand that Genovese be named "boss of all bosses" after he justified the attacks on Costello and Anastasia. One argument presented was that Anastasia had tried to move in on the Cuban gambling operations of Santos Trafficante, Jr., of Florida.

But before business could be settled, the police arrived, tipped off by an alert New York State Police sergeant who had become suspicious of all the big black cars with out-of-state license plates. Police roadblocks and searches of surrounding woods netted fifty-nine of the crime leaders, most of whom claimed they had come to visit a sick friend. They included Joe Bonanno, Joseph Magliocco, Carlo Gambino, Carmine Lombardozzi, John Bonventre, and Joseph Profaci from New York; Anthony Magaddino from Niagara Falls; Vito Genovese, Gerardo Catena, Joseph Ida, and Frank Majuri from New Jersey; Frank DeSimone from California; Joe Civello from Dallas, Texas; and Trafficante. Carlos Marcello had wisely sent a surrogate while others, such as Sam Giancana of Chicago, escaped.

It was the first public look at organized crime since the Kefauver Committee hearings in the early 1950s. But some people were already aware of the serious threat posed by the mob's syndicate. One of these was young Robert Kennedy who, after making a nationwide fact-finding tour in 1956 and 1957, became most concerned with the mob's takeover of labor unions.

On January 30, 1957, the U.S. Senate unanimously created the Senate Select Committee on Improper Activities in the Labor or Management Field—which became known as the McClellan Committee after its chairman, Senator John L. McClellan of Arkansas. The committee's chief counsel was Robert F. Kennedy. One of the senators on the McClellan Committee was a young man from Boston, John F. Kennedy. Kennedy later said his brother wanted him on the committee to keep it from being overloaded with conservative, antilabor people.

Both Kennedys were highly active in the committee's work, which first took on the corrupt leader of the International Brotherhood of Teamsters, Dave Beck. Following the committee's investigation, Beck was convicted in a state court of larceny and then convicted of tax evasion in federal court. Beck went to prison in 1957. (He was granted a full pardon by President Gerald Ford in May 1975.)

With Beck gone the presidency of the Teamsters Union went to Jimmy Hoffa. Even before Hoffa could be brought before the McClellan Committee, he was indicted for attempting to bribe commission attorney John Cye Cheasty.

At his trial, the FBI showed a film of the men conversing and Hoffa being arrested right after the money was exchanged. However, the jury of eight blacks and four whites was more impressed with former World Heavyweight Champion boxer Joe Louis, who embraced Hoffa in court, and with Hoffa's defense attorney, Edward Bennett Williams (owner of the Washington Redskins).

Hoffa went free to testify before the McClellan Committee. But Hoffa said he had a faulty memory when it came to most questions concerning his association with underworld characters, such as Paul Dorfman. Dorfman was described by the McClellan Committee as "an associate of Chicago mobsters and the head of a local of the Waste Material Handlers Union." Dorfman also was connected to Jack Ruby, the man who silenced Lee Harvey Oswald.

Dorfman's stepson, Allen Dorfman, was to play a major role in Hoffa loans to the underworld using the Teamster's Central States Health and Welfare Fund.

In 1951, shortly after setting up the Michigan Conference of Teamsters Welfare Fund, Hoffa persuaded the fund's two trustees—one of whom was Hoffa's successor, Frank Fitzsimmons—to place the fund with a newly formed branch of Union Casualty Agency. Union Casualty was owned by Paul Dorfman's stepson, Allen, and the elder Dorfman's wife, Rose.

Later Hoffa also sent the Central States fund to the Dorfman-controlled agency. These two funds made up 90 percent of the branch company's contracts, according to author Dan Moldea.

Veteran mob observers have established the close ties between Hoffa and two of the underworld's most powerful men—Carlos Marcello and Santos Trafficante, Jr.

Santos Trafficante and Cuba

During the mid-1950s, with gunfire punctuating internal mob leadership disputes in New York and the various government panels revealing the extent of organized crime in the United States, crime bosses began to look south for relief.

As early as 1933, the mob's financial wizard, Meyer Lansky, had obtained gambling concessions in Cuba, located just ninety miles off the Florida coast. Lansky had originally visited Cuba seeking molasses to make rum but discovered a suitable climate for gambling operations. Befriending the self-proclaimed dictator of Cuba, Fulgencio Batista, Lansky soon opened several gambling casinos. But World War II brought a halt to his plans for turning the island into a haven for gamblers. There simply weren't enough planes and boats available to make the project profitable.

In 1944, the Cuban economy was sagging and Batista was forced to make concessions to his political opponents, who included procommunists. According to investigative reporter Howard Kohn, the Office of Naval Intelligence—already in contact with Lucky Luciano through Lansky—asked Lansky to pressure Batista into stepping down. On Lansky's urging, Batista called an election, was defeated, and left Cuba for an eight-year exile in Florida.

On March 10, 1952, Batista returned to Cuba and seized power in a bloodless military coup. Reportedly, it was large amounts of money placed in numbered Swiss bank accounts by Lansky that convinced Cuban President Carlos Prio Socarras not to resist Batista's comeback.

Under Lansky's manipulation, Batista's government agreed to match investments in Cuba dollar for dollar plus grant a gambling license to any establishment worth more than $1 million. Soon the island's economy was booming as hotels and gambling casinos were quickly built. Lansky built the Hotel Nacional, whose pit boss was his brother, Jake. He and other associates had interest in the Sevilla Biltmore and the Havana Hilton. Lansky himself built the $14 million Hotel Havana Riviera, which was run by Dino and Eddie Cellini, organized-crime figures from Ohio.

But Lansky, a Jew, was still not considered an official member of the Mafia-dominated American crime syndicate. Organized-crime authority G. Robert Blakey wrote: ". . . the undisputed Mafia gambling boss in Havana was Santos Trafficante, Jr."

When Trafficante, Sr., died in 1954, his family crime business—mostly narcotics trafficking and gambling—went to his namesake. By the late 1950s, Trafficante, Jr., was well situated in Cuba, owning substantial interest in the Sans Souci, a renowed night spot partly managed by a Trafficante associate, John Roselli, later a central figure in the CIA-Mafia plots against Castro.

Both Trafficante and Lansky also were part owners of the Tropicana

Casino in Havana, which was managed by former Dallas gambler Lewis McWillie, the "idol" of Jack Ruby.

In Cuba, Meyer Lansky and associate Bugsy Siegel used the same tactics they had used successfully in 1945 when they turned a dusty strip of Nevada desert into the Las Vegas strip—flying in high-rollers to stay at their hotel-casinos. In reviewing the Havana operations during those years, Blakey wrote: "Havana, in short, was a full-service vice capital, owned and operated by the Mob."

Others who had gambling interests in Cuba during this time were men connected to Teamster boss Jimmy Hoffa. Two New York underworld figures allied with the Tommy Lucchese family, Salvatore Granello and James Plumeri, were part owners of a Havana race track and a large gambling casino. Granello and Plumeri also helped Teamster officials get Miami Local 320 of the International Brotherhood of Teamsters started, according to *The Hoffa Wars* author, Dan Moldea. Moldea also wrote that Granello and Plumeri at the time were splitting kickbacks with Hoffa on loans made through the Central States Pension Fund.

One high-placed guest in Cuba at the time was Congressman Richard Nixon, who made frequent trips to the island, visiting both President Batista and the gambling casinos. According to Nixon biographer Earl Mazo, Nixon visited Cuba as early as 1940 to consider "the possibilities of establishing law or business connections in Havana."

But the glamorous nightlife of Havana came to an abrupt end on New Year's Day, 1959, when Fidel Castro entered the city and proclaimed a new Cuban revolution. Both Batista and Lansky fled Cuba that same day. Lansky later lamented that he caught one of the last planes leaving Havana and was forced to leave behind $17 million in cash that had been earmarked for his various partners via Swiss bank accounts.

Jake Lansky, left behind to hold together his brother's gambling and narcotics operations, was jailed by Castro along with Santos Trafficante. Castro loudly proclaimed:

"I'm going to run all these fascist mobsters, all these American gangsters, out of Cuba. I'm going to nationalize everything. Cuba for Cubans!"

By 1960, Castro had made good on his threat to expel organized crime. He had deported all syndicate members, closed the whorehouses and casinos, and shut down the drug labs.

Both the crime syndicate and some American government officials were appalled at this turn of events. The CIA particularly wanted something done since, according to Agency sources quoted by journalist Howard Kohn, the Agency had used the underworld's Havana casinos to hide payments to the crime figures it sometimes employed. Thus the idea of an invasion of Cuba may have been born. A murky alliance developed between the CIA, the crime syndicate, the U.S. military, and anti-Castro Cuban exiles, and this alliance produced the ill-fated Bay of Pigs Invasion.

Four ex-casino bosses—including Hoffa associates Salvatore Granello and James Plumeri—even supplied the CIA with intelligence reports gathered from trusted Cuban contacts.

Along with the plans to invade Cuba, there were concurrent schemes to eliminate Castro by assassination. Involved in these plots were Trafficante, Frank Sturgis, Robert Maheu (the ex-FBI man who was liaison between the CIA and the Mafia and later became manager of the Howard Hughes empire), and two Mafia chiefs, John Roselli and Sam (Momo) Giancana.

With the failure of the invasion, the mob joined with the CIA, the military, and the Cuban exiles in putting the blame squarely on President John F. Kennedy.

Although mob gambling activity quickly shifted to Las Vegas and the Bahamas, crime leaders did not forget who cost them their Havana "vice capital."

According to evidence gathered by House Select Committee on Assassinations, Trafficante was in touch with a wealthy Cuban exile living in Miami named Jose Aleman. Trafficante had offered to arrange a million-dollar loan for Aleman which was coming from the Teamsters Union and had "already been cleared by Jimmy Hoffa himself." Aleman said he met with Trafficante at Miami's Scott-Bryant Hotel in September 1962, and the talk turned to Hoffa. According to Aleman, Trafficante brought the conversation around to President Kennedy, saying:

> Have you seen how his brother is hitting Hoffa, a man who is a worker, who is not a millionaire, a friend of the blue collars? He doesn't know that this kind of encounter is very delicate . . . It is not right what they are doing to Hoffa . . . Hoffa is a hard-working man and does not deserve it . . . Mark my words, this man Kennedy is in trouble and he will get what is coming to him.

Aleman said when he disagreed, saying Kennedy was doing a good job and probably would be reelected, Trafficante replied: "You don't understand me. Kennedy's not going to make it to the election. He's going to be hit." Later Aleman said Trafficante "made it clear" he was not guessing and even gave "the distinct impression that Hoffa was to be principally involved in the elimination of Kennedy."

Unknown to Trafficante, Aleman was an informant for the FBI at the time of this alleged conversation. He promptly reported what he had heard to the Bureau, but said FBI officials would not listen or take him seriously. In 1978, when Aleman testified before the House Select Committee on Assassinations, his story became vague. He said perhaps Trafficante meant Kennedy was going to be "hit" by a lot of Republican votes in 1964. Aleman also admitted he was "very much concerned about my safety . . ."

*   *   *

Jimmy Hoffa survived the McClellan Committee hearings. But it was the start of a personal war between two of the nation's most powerful men—Bobby Kennedy and Teamster leader Jimmy Hoffa.

The War on Hoffa

James Riddle Hoffa was born on February 14, 1913, in Brazil, Indiana. After the death of his father when he was seven, young Hoffa moved to Detroit with his mother, brother, and two sisters.

By 1932, Hoffa was already involved in the union movement. Angered over low pay and working conditions at the Kroger Food Company, Hoffa helped organize a work stoppage. After several days of negotiation, the company signed a one-page contract. It was the start of a one-company union and was affiliated with the American Federation of Labor. By the mid-1930s, Hoffa's fledgling union was absorbed by bigger organizations. After being fired by Kroger, he joined Detroit Teamsters Joint Council 43 as an organizer and negotiator.

In the early 1930s, Hoffa had a love affair with Sylvia Pigano, a woman with family connections to organized crime figures. This was Hoffa's introduction to the underworld, which over the years became an invaluable source of support. From that point on Hoffa's rise to the presidency of the International Brotherhood of Teamsters continued unabated. He walked a thin line, maintaining contacts with mobsters on one hand and presenting the image of a respectable labor leader on the other.

Vincent Piersante, head of the Organized Crime Unit of the Michigan Attorney General's Office, told author Dan Moldea:

> There is little doubt about the fact that Hoffa, consciously and willingly, protected the rackets in Detroit by protecting their legitimate fronts with the Teamsters Union. And that included those gangsters who were deeply involved in the drug traffic.

In 1957, fresh from his victory in exposing Teamster president Dave Beck's embezzlement of union money, McClellan Committee chief counsel Robert Kennedy turned his sights on Beck's successor, Jimmy Hoffa. After the committee hearings, Hoffa was acquitted on charges of wiretapping and perjury. He was living a charmed life, but his hatred for Kennedy was increasing.

The McClellan Committee, in its first interim report, stated:

> The power of the Teamsters Union president is so extraordinary that the committee finds the fact this power is now lodged in the hands of a man such as Hoffa tragic for the Teamsters Union and dangerous for the country at large.

Kennedy elaborated in his book:

The Teamsters Union is the most powerful institution in this country—
aside from the United States Government itself. In many Metropolitan
areas the Teamsters control all transportation . . . between birth and
burial the Teamsters drive the trucks that clothe and feed us and provide
the vital necessities of life . . . Quite literally, your life—the life of
every person in the United States—is in the hands of Hoffa and his
Teamsters . . . But though the great majority of Teamsters officials and
Teamster members are honest, the Teamsters Union under Hoffa is
often not run as a bona fide union. As Mr. Hoffa operates it, this is a
conspiracy of evil.

The major concern seems to have been the threat of mob blackmail. If
organized crime so desired, it could have pressured Hoffa into calling a
nationwide Teamsters strike that could have disrupted the country. For the
Kennedys, this was an intolerable situation.

When the election year of 1960 arrived, Hoffa knew which side he had
to be on. He and the Teamsters threw their support behind Richard Nixon.
In fact Edward Partin, a Louisiana Teamster official and later a government informant, has revealed that Hoffa met with Carlos Marcello. He
related:

I was right there, listening to the conversation. Marcello had a suitcase
filled with $500,000 cash which was going to Nixon. It was a
half-million-dollar contribution. [Another half million] was coming
from the mob boys in New Jersey and Florida.

But money wasn't enough. Nixon lost and Robert Kennedy became
attorney general. After the election, Hoffa was quoted as saying: "Nobody
had to tell me that he was really going to go after my scalp now."

In 1958, U.S. attorney general William P. Rogers formed a special
group on organized crime to investigate the Apalachin meeting. Kennedy,
following that precedent, organized a special unit within the Organized
Crime and Racketeering Section to investigate the Teamsters Union. Headed
by Walter Sheridan, who had been an investigator for the McClellan
Committee, the unit became known as the "Get Hoffa Squad." The squad
managed to bring 201 indictments and 126 convictions against Teamster
officials.

On May 18, 1962, Hoffa was indicted for receiving a million dollars in
illegal payments through the Test Fleet Corporation, a trucking company
set up under his wife's name. His trial ended in a hung jury, but Hoffa was
indicted along with five others for jury tampering on May 9, 1963.

On June 4, 1963, Hoffa was indicted for fraudulently obtaining $20
million in loans from the Teamsters' Central States Pension Fund.

Earlier, in September 1962—about the same time that Marcello and Trafficante had hinted that President Kennedy was going to be assassinated —Ed Partin, the Teamster official turned informant, went to Louisiana law-enforcement officials to tell of a threat by Hoffa. Partin believed that Hoffa thought he was closely associated with Marcello since he lived in Louisiana. Visiting in Hoffa's Washington office in August 1962, Partin said Hoffa began talking about plans to kill Robert Kennedy. Thinking out loud, Hoffa discussed two schemes. One involved the firebombing of Hickory Hill, Kennedy's Virginia estate. The second involved shooting Kennedy with a rifle while he rode in an open car. The "ideal setup," Hoffa reportedly told Partin, would be to catch Kennedy somewhere in the South, where "segregation people" might be blamed for the crime. The "ideal time" would be to hit Kennedy while he rode in a convertible, said Hoffa. Partin quoted Hoffa as saying: "Somebody needs to bump that son of a bitch off. Bobby Kennedy [has] got to go."

Partin's story was passed along to Kennedy aides, who were highly skeptical until an FBI lie detector test indicated Partin was telling the truth. Further confirmation of the seriousness of the threat came when federal officials taped a conversation between Partin and Hoffa. Partin said he had obtained some plastic explosives and Hoffa asked him to bring them to Nashville.

President Kennedy confided to journalist Benjamin Bradlee in February 1963, that Hoffa's men intended to kill his brother with a "gun fitted with a silencer." Bradlee, in notes taken at the time, wrote he found the story "hard to believe, but the President was obviously serious."

It was in the middle of Hoffa's jury-tampering case that President Kennedy was shot in Dallas. Hoffa, upon learning that the flags were flying at half-mast at Teamster headquarters in Washington, regaled officials there, shouting: "Why the hell did you do that for him? Who the hell is he?"

On the day that Ruby murdered Oswald, Hoffa told a Nashville reporter: "Bobby Kennedy is just another lawyer now."

In the jury tampering and the fraudulent loan cases Hoffa was convicted, fined, and imprisoned. He received executive clemency from President Richard Nixon on December 23, 1971, without the customary consultation with the sentencing judge. However, the clemency contained a provision prohibiting Hoffa from seeking office in the union. Hoffa filed suit to have the restriction nullified and began making overtures to Teamster rank and file. Ironically, he pledged that, if elected Teamster president in 1976, he would purge the union of all mob influence.

On July 30, 1975, Hoffa was to meet Anthony "Tony Pro" Provenzano, a New Jersey Teamster official and reputed member of the crime syndicate. He never returned.

* * *

One of the biggest boosts to Robert Kennedy's anticrime campaign began in June 1962, when an underworld tough serving a prison term in

Atlanta for narcotics murdered a fellow inmate with an iron pipe. The convict's name was Joseph Valachi and he killed the man believing him to be an assassin sent from his long-time boss and cellmate, Vito Genovese. Genovese had slipped back into the United States after World War II to resume his narcotics operations.

Imprisoned, Genovese heard rumors—apparently false—that Valachi was cooperating with authorities and had given his veteran soldier the "kiss of death." Soon after, there were three attempts on Valachi's life. Valachi didn't want to wait for the fourth. So, believing a man in the prison courtyard was a Genovese killer, Valachi beat him to death. He picked the wrong man.

With both the government and the mob seeking his life, Valachi decided he had nothing to lose by cooperating with authorities. Over the next year, he provided federal agents with a bonanza of information on the national crime organization known as the Mafia, La Cosa Nostra (Our Thing), the Outfit, the Arm, the Syndicate, etc.

On September 25, 1963, Valachi took his story to the public, testifying before McClellan's Senate committee. He presented a wealth of detail about the organization of the mob, its codes, rules and regulations, and its most important members, including those who sat on the "Commissione," the board of directors.

Organized-crime authority and former New York Police official Ralph Salerno evaluated Valachi's testimony:

> The Valachi confessions are ranked next to Apalachin as the single greatest [intelligence] blow ever delivered to organized crime in the United States. This evaluation came from the lips of those most affected by it: members of the criminal network whose comments were over-heard through bug and wiretap. . . . Many of the incidents Valachi described had . . . been known to the police, but . . . [Valachi] was able to fill in the gaps and connect one incident with another. . . . The pattern that Valachi furnished made it possible for police intelligence men to begin to see the dimensions of syndicated crime and stop looking at it as a series of unconnected cases.

The Valachi revelations were a great embarrassment to FBI director J. Edgar Hoover. They forced him to grudgingly admit that such a thing as a crime syndicate must exist.

In his ever-increasing war against organized crime, Kennedy made use of the Treasury Department's Internal Revenue Service to go after mob members. John H. Davis, a Kennedy relative and author of *The Kennedys,* wrote:

"Given another five years in office, the Kennedys could conceivably have exterminated the Cosa Nostra entirely, or at least crippled it beyond repair." Crime bosses wanted something done about the Kennedys, especially since they felt "double-crossed" by the two brothers.

After all, the connections between crime and the Kennedys reportedly went back a long way. In 1927, a shipment of bootleg whiskey on its way from Ireland to Boston was hijacked in southern New England. Almost the entire guard was killed in the resulting shootout. The hijackers were part of the Luciano-Lansky mob, while it was rumored that Joseph P. Kennedy was involved in the shipment. Kennedy reputedly lost a fortune on the deal and was besieged by widows of the guards seeking financial assistance. Lansky later told biographers he was convinced that Kennedy held a grudge against him personally from that time on and, in fact, had passed the hostility on to his sons.

But the crime contacts didn't stop with Prohibition. According to crime author Ovid Damaris, Kennedy would likely have lost the state of Illinois— and possibly the 1960 presidential election—except for overlarge voting in Cook County, home of Chicago mayor Richard Daley. Following the election, Illinois Republicans made an unofficial check of 699 paper ballot precincts in Cook County and turned up enough irregular votes to shift the victory to Richard Nixon. However, demands for an official recount were blocked by Daley's political machine. And behind that machine was the real power in Chicago at that time—Sam Giancana.

Momo and His Girlfriends

Sam Giancana (real name: Momo Salvatore Guingano) born May 24, 1908, to poor Sicilian immigrants living in Chicago. He grew up in the ghettos and was street wise at an early age.

A member of a gang called the "42s," Giancana was first convicted of car theft in 1925. Before he was twenty, he was arrested in connection with three murders, including the slaying of Octavious Granady, a black who sought election as a committeeman.

In 1932, he came to the attention of Paul "The Waiter" Ricca (real name: Felice DeLucia) who worked for the notorious Genna brothers. Giancana became the personal driver for Ricca, who took over the Chicago syndicate after the suicide of Frank Nitti in 1943.

In 1944, Ricca went to prison for extortion and Anthony Accardo took over as Chicago's syndicate boss. Giancana became his chauffeur. Giancana helped Accardo consolidate the rackets and gambling operations in Chicago. In 1957, Giancana was one of those forced to flee from the ill-fated Apalachin meeting.

In 1960, when Accardo retired after an income tax evasion indictment, Giancana took over the syndicate. By 1963, Giancana had been arrested sixty times and had served time for burglary, auto theft, and moonshining. He also was one of the wealthiest and most powerful men in Chicago and in the syndicate.

After the death of his wife Angeline in 1954, Giancana became well-known as a ladies' man. While visiting Las Vegas in 1960, Giancana met Phyllis McGuire, the youngest of the McGuire Sisters singing group. According to Robert Blakey, chief counsel of the House Select Committee on Assassinations, McGuire had run up gambling debts of more than $100,000. Giancana—who along with Accardo secretly owned interest in the Desert Inn and the Stardust casinos although both were nominally owned by Morris "Moe" Dalitz—made good her debt. Soon afterward, Giancana made his Las Vegas headquarters at the nearby Green Gables Ranch, which records showed had been leased by McGuire.

During the 1960 election, Giancana and other mob leaders apparently thought they had bought some relief from growing government awareness and prosecution of the syndicate.

In addition to meeting mob leader Joseph Bonanno in the winter of 1959, Kennedy reportedly received campaign contributions from the syndicate channeled to his father by singer Frank Sinatra. Yet another conduit for these funds may have been a woman with connections to both Kennedy and Giancana. Ironically, evidence of these contributions to Kennedy were picked up by FBI phone taps that were part of an electronic surveillance program initiated by Attorney General Kennedy's war on crime.

But Giancana believed he had an even better hold on Kennedy—the beautiful dark-eyed brunette named Judith Exner. Exner, going then as Judy Campbell, said she was introduced to John F. Kennedy on February 7, 1960, by Frank Sinatra, whom she had been dating. In her 1977 book, *My Story,* she wrote that both John Kennedy and his brother Edward were sitting with Sinatra in the lounge of the Sands Hotel in Las Vegas. She said she and John Kennedy met again a month later, this time alone and in the Plaza Hotel in New York where, according to Exner, they shared a bed.

From that point on Kennedy was to see Exner on a regular basis. The pair exchanged telephone calls frequently, including some to the White House, which were noted by the FBI. Why the FBI? The Bureau had been monitoring the activities of Exner because of another man in her life— Chicago mob boss Sam Giancana. Exner claimed she was introduced to Giancana, again by Sinatra, a month after she had become Kennedy's lover. When Giancana discovered she was seeing the Democratic presidential candidate, he took an immediate and continuing interest in her. And soon Giancana—one of the top Mafia bosses in the nation—was bedding the paramour of the soon-to-be president.

In later years, Exner said: "I feel like I was set up to be the courier. I was a perfect choice because I could come and go without notice, and if noticed, no one would've believed it anyway."

What passed between Kennedy and Giancana in this extraordinary triangle is not known, but in 1988, Exner revealed that she had acted as a courier carrying sealed envelopes for the two men on at least ten occasions. Given only a short time to live by her doctors, Exner said she wanted to set the record straight. She said she did not tell about the envelopes during 1975 testimony to the Senate Intelligence Committee because she feared for her life. She also claimed that she never opened the envelopes nor knew their contents. Most of her courier activities took place during the tough 1960 campaign and Exner speculated that her actions may have been connected with attempts to influence the critical West Virginia Democratic primary.

Once, after being questioned by FBI agents, Exner complained to Kennedy. She claimed Kennedy—by then president—assured her: "Don't worry. They won't do anything to you. And don't worry about Sam. You know he works for us."

Kennedy continued to see Exner until a meeting with J. Edgar Hoover on March 22, 1962. It is now accepted that on that date Hoover revealed to the President the extent of Exner's ties with organized crime and the obvious fact that he knew about Kennedy's liaison with her. Shortly after Hoover left the White House, there was one more call to Judith Exner. No more were ever logged. Kennedy also broke off his friendship with Sinatra, perhaps suspecting that the singer had set him up.

But the worst was yet to come. Although still seeing Exner, Giancana became suspicious that Phyllis McGuire was seeing comedian Dan Rowan. Giancana asked his contact with the CIA, Robert Maheu, to place a wiretap on Rowan's telephone. This was done, but a maid discovered the tap and told Rowan, who brought it to the attention of the federal government. The Justice Department initiated proceedings against Maheu for illegal wiretapping.

In May 1962, a month after the Kennedy-Hoover meeting apparently ended the President's relationship with Exner, Robert Kennedy was asked by CIA officials not to prosecute Maheu for fear that Giancana's role in the incident would become known. They reminded Kennedy that Giancana had played a role in the clandestine effort against Castro's government.

Kennedy, thinking the plots against Castro had been stopped back in 1961, was adamant about pressing the charges. Then on May 7, CIA general counsel Lawrence Houston finally told Kennedy the whole ugly truth—that the Agency had contracted with Giancana and John Roselli to murder Fidel Castro. According to Houston, Kennedy fixed him with a cold look and said: "I trust that if you ever try to do business with organized crime again—with gangsters—you will let the attorney general know."

From that moment on, both Kennedys must have feared what Sam Giancana might reveal if he chose—the CIA-Mafia murder plots and Giancana's girl in bed with the President. However, this fear did not stop the younger Kennedy from going on with his war against targeted Mafia bigshots, including Giancana.

The FBI haunted Giancana day and night, watching his home and trailing his car. It was most effective. Crime associates wouldn't come near and Giancana couldn't go where he pleased. He was isolated.

In June 1963, Giancana caused chins to drop throughout the under-world by becoming the first mobster ever to go to court seeking an injunction against FBI surveillance. To gain the injunction required Giancana to swear in court that he was an honest businessman, which, in turn, would expose him to government cross-examination—an unprecedented hazard for a crime boss. Giancana must have felt confident that the government would not question him too closely. And he was right. To a stunned courtroom, the U.S. attorney announced that the government waived the right to cross-examination. The decision not to question Giancana had come straight from the attorney general.

But while one effort against Giancana was deflected, the Kennedy Justice Department's all-out war against the underworld continued. The top crime bosses were incensed. Hadn't they contributed to Kennedy's election? Hadn't they helped steal critical votes? Hadn't Kennedy dabbled with one of their women? It undoubtedly looked like double-cross to the mob chieftains. And in the underworld the only solution for a double-crosser is elimination—a ''hit.''

*   *   *

On November 22, 1963, Attorney General Kennedy met with about forty of his Organized Crime and Racketeering Section staff. They had been meeting regularly for the past two and a half years.

Interestingly, one of the young crime busters was G. Robert Blakey, who years later would become chief counsel of the House Select Committee on Assassinations created to investigate the murders of John and Robert Kennedy.

Just before they broke for lunch, the last topic of discussion was Sam Giancana and political corruption in Chicago.

The attorney general had just finished lunch at his McLean, Virginia, home when J. Edgar Hoover called to inform him: ''The President's been shot.''

Kennedy never met with the Organized Crime and Racketeering Section again. With the death of John F. Kennedy, the war on crime was lost. Organized crime was ecstatic, but on FBI wiretaps, older and wiser mob leaders urged caution in speaking about the assassination. One was over-heard explaining: ''. . . police spies will be watching carefully to see what we . . . think and say about this.'' Such caution was certainly justified. In the years following the assassination, more and more attention has been drawn to the mob as one of the most likely suspects.

Beginning with Jack Ruby right on through to David Ferrie and Jim Braden, crime figures keep cropping up throughout the assassination case.

There now can be no question that organized crime had the means, motive, and the opportunity to murder the President. But could the crime bosses have effectively covered their tracks without the help of federal government officials?

It now appears that the vocal wishes of the crime bosses to eliminate the Kennedys were echoed by certain powerful men in both government and big business. G. Robert Blakey, chief counsel of the House Select Committee on Assassinations, pulled no punches in his book, *The Plot to Kill the President*. Its subtitle stated: *Organized Crime Assassinated J.F.K.* Blakey once told this author:

> One reason no one realized organized crime's involvement [for many years] was that people never saw before . . . what was going on in Cuba. They failed to see the significance of men like Lewis McWillie and Russell Matthews [and] because they did not understand these men's connections.

Asked if the fact that organized crime has been connected with the assassination only in recent years might suggest some control in the government on the part of the mob, Blakey replied: "That's conceivable . . . I would find that troubling, but no more so than the fact that they killed the man and got away with it."

Following his brother's death, Robert Kennedy appeared to lose interest in prosecuting the mob and the Justice Department staff seemed to follow suit.

While there must have been the desire to protect the loving-husband image of his dead brother, the cooling of the attorney general's passion for fighting the mob likely was due more to the potential revelations of CIA-Mafia assassination plots.

In fighting what the Kennedys had perceived as a great internal evil, they had once again found themselves confronted with an intelligence agency—the CIA.

Summary

Since its inception in the 1930s, organized crime or the national crime syndicate has exerted malevolent influence in the United States.

Attorney General Robert Kennedy, backed by his brother the President, waged war against organized crime as never before, causing great fear and hatred in the ranks of crime leaders.

Every one of the major crime bossess—including the powerful Teamsters Union president Jimmy Hoffa—were reported to have issued threats against the Kennedys.

What the Kennedys learned were the connections between the mob and U.S. intelligence agencies. These connections dated all the way back to Lucky Luciano and World War II.

Hoover's FBI had always taken a laissez-faire attitude toward the syndicate, while the CIA actually had worked with crime figures in assassination plots. These CIA-Mafia assassination plots continued right up to Kennedy's assassination in Dallas.

Considering the Kennedy war against the mob as well as its vital interests in Cuba lost to Castro and Kennedy's failure to militarily support the Bay of Pigs Invasion, mob bosses had more than enough motive to want the President dead.

If Judith Exner is to be believed, there were contacts between Kennedy and Sam Giancana during the 1960 campaign that may have led to Kennedy winning the Democratic nomination and the election. With Kennedy's support of Robert Kennedy's "war on crime" it must have looked like a double-cross to the mob.

There most certainly existed the opportunity to utilize intelligence contacts in an assassination plot.

Many assassination researchers, including House Select Committee on Assassinations chief counsel Blakey, today believe that organized crime was responsible for Kennedy's death.

But is the American public expected to believe that the mob could kill a president and that the combined resources of the FBI, CIA, Secret Service, and military, and the nation's police agencies could not discover that fact?

If American crime bosses ordered the assassination, they may have received some assurance of protection before the fact. And such assurance would have had to come from persons in high government positions. Perhaps, in time, such connections between government leaders of the time and the mob will become more fully documented. Until such time, the American public is left with only tantalizing bits of information and common sense to suggest such complicity.

[I will] splinter the CIA into a thousand pieces and scatter it to the winds.
—President John F. Kennedy

Agents

Since the first conflicts of man, there has been a need for intelligence, or information on the activities and purposes of a perceived enemy. In modern America the growth of several intelligence organizations over the years has spawned an intelligence industry. Under acronyms such as CIA, DIA, NSA, ONI, and others, these intelligence power bases have grown far beyond their original charters.

The history of the Central Intelligence Agency—the most publicized of the spy agencies—reveals a government organization that does much more than merely collect and interpret intelligence. In less than ten years after its creation in 1947 this coordinating agency grew to oversee military operations, destabilization efforts in foreign countries, and the assassination of national leaders—and an unholy alliance with organized crime.

At the end of World War II, information on a wide variety of issues and activities was being handled by as many as a dozen various intelligence organizations, including those within the Army and the Navy. President Harry S. Truman and others perceived a need for a coordinating intelligence unit. This need was further reinforced by the Congressional Joint Committee on the Pearl Harbor Attack, which concluded that the fragmentation of U.S. intelligence prior to 1941 resulted in the Japanese taking this nation by surprise. The committee recommended a unified intelligence service. Creating such a hybrid would not be easy. None of the existing intelligence units wanted to relinquish power or authority.

During World War II, one of the organizations that proved most effective against the Axis powers was the Office of Strategic Services, headed by the colorful Gen. William "Wild Bill" Donovan. The OSS not only gathered a remarkable amount of information on the enemy, but also engaged in various covert activities. It was a rough-and-tumble wartime operation that provided the factual background for many a fictional spy novel or movie.

The OSS was closed down at the end of the war, and on January 22, 1946, just four months later, President Truman signed a directive creating the National Intelligence Authority (NIA) composed of the secretaries of state, war, and Navy as well as the President's personal representative. The operating arm of the NIA was the Central Intelligence Group (CIG), made up of veteran intelligence officers from the participating departments. These men were managed by a director appointed by the President. To limit the CIG, Truman specifically prohibited any clandestine or paramilitary activities. The CIG was to have "no police, law-enforcement or internal-security functions" nor conduct "investigations inside the . . . United States."

The veteran spies and operatives of the old OSS were soon transferred to this new organization, operating under the designation of the Office of Special Operations (OSO). And these men of action soon wanted more elbow room in their restricted world of intelligence gathering.

By 1947, the CIG's staff had grown to nearly two thousand, with about one-third operating overseas. But it continued to be only one of several intelligence organizations. This was changed on September 15, 1947, when Truman signed the National Security Act, creating the national Security Council (NSC), the Air Force as a separate branch of the services, and the Department of Defense, uniting the Departments of the Army, Navy, and Air Force. With little notice, this act also created the Central Intelligence Agency (CIA), giving the United States its first full-blown peacetime intelligence service.

In later years, Truman was to state:

I never had any thought . . . when I set up the CIA, that it would be injected into peacetime cloak-and-dagger operations. Some of the complications and embarrassment that I think we have experienced are in a part attributable to the fact that this quiet intelligence arm of the President has been so removed from its intended role.

Under the National Security Act—passed in the heat of the growing anticommunist hysteria sweeping the United States—the CIA was responsible only to the National Security Council, which was headed by the President, effectively giving the President absolute control over the new agency.

The CIA had its own budget and was authorized to hire and train its own personnel. Yet the same restrictions of the old CIG remained—no clandestine or paramilitary operations and no internal spying.

However, a catch-all phrase had been included in the CIA's charter that stated the Agency could perform "such other functions and duties related to intelligence affecting the national security as the NSC may from time to time direct."

Utilizing this phrase—and with the blessings of the National Security Council—the CIA in 1948 became active in suppressing Communist influence in the national elections in Italy. This marked the beginning of the Agency's career of meddling in the affairs of other nations.

In 1949, the Central Intelligence Act was passed, exempting the CIA from all laws requiring the disclosure of "functions, names, official titles, salaries and number of personnel employed by the Agency" and allowing the director to spend money from its secret budget simply by signing vouchers.

Now operating with secret funds and with the vague authority of " . . . other such functions and duties related to intelligence . . ." the CIA began to flex its muscles. Victor Marchetti, a former executive assistant to the CIA's deputy director, wrote:

From those few innocuous words the CIA has been able, over the years, to develop a secret charter based on NSC directives and presidential executive orders, a charter almost completely at variance with the apparent intent of the law which established the Agency. This vague phrase has provided the CIA with freedom to engage in covert action, the right to intervene secretly in the internal affairs of other nations. It has done so usually with the express approval of the White House, but almost always without the consent of Congress, and virtually never with the knowledge of the American people.

By 1955, Allen Dulles was director of the CIA, now more than fifteen thousand strong not including thousands of foreign agents and contract employees.

In addition to its enormous secret budget—often disguised as portions of other U.S. government budgets—the CIA created a number of wholly or partly owned properties, or "fronts," to provide cover for clandestine operations.

These fronts included airlines, import-export companies, "high tech" firms, advertising agencies, foundations, and many others. And these were not dummy businesses. In most ways they operated normally, generating additional money to fund Agency operations. Using these fronts, the CIA channeled money to academic, labor, youth, and cultural organizations.

Many foreign leaders—such as King Hussein of Jordan, Archbishop Makarios of Cypress, Luis Echeverria of Mexico, and Willy Brandt of West Germany—have been named as recipients of CIA funds over the years.

It has been charged that the CIA, whose leaders have been drawn from the highest circles of business and wealth in the United States, often has been more concerned with American big-business investment than with true national security questions. For example, in 1953 the popularly elected prime minister of Iran, Dr. Mohammed Mossadegh, whose government had nationalized the oil industry, was overthrown in a coup initiated by the CIA. The CIA man in charge of that operation was Kermit Roosevelt, who later became vice president of Gulf Oil. Gulf Oil benefited greatly from the new Iranian political situation.

On June 18, 1954, a CIA-financed right-wing coup in Guatemala over-
threw the popularly elected government of Jacobo Arbenz, which had nationalized the property of United Fruit Company. Secretary of State John Foster Dulles's law firm had written the United Fruit contracts with

Guatemala in the 1930s. Assistant secretary of state for Inter-American Affairs John Moors Cabot was a major United Fruit stockholder. And CIA director Allen Dulles had been president of United Fruit, while his predecessor as CIA director, Gen. Walter Bedell Smith, was soon to become a United Fruit vice president.

One reason the CIA succeeded in becoming a world-class force was the relationship of its long-time director, Allen Dulles, with his brother John Foster Dulles, the secretary of state. David Wise and Thomas B. Ross, authors of *The Invisible Government,* wrote:

> Uniquely, they embodied the dualism—and indeed the moral dilemma—of United States foreign policy since World War II. . . . Foster Dulles reflected the American ethic; the world as we would like it to be. While he took this position, his brother was free to deal with nastier realities, to overturn governments and engage in backstage political maneuvers all over the globe with the CIA's almost unlimited funds. He was, as Allen Dulles once put it, able to "fight fire with fire" . . . it was under Allen Dulles's stewardship that the CIA enjoyed its greatest expansion, particularly in the field of government-shaking secret operations overseas.

And during the time the Agency was expanding and initiating its activities across the globe, few Americans had ever heard of the organization. The Agency's anonymity was largely the product of a timid news media. Former CIA director William Colby wrote: "The press, by and large, willingly accorded the CIA a privileged position among government agencies and refrained from inquiring into and reporting on its activities as a self-imposed act of patriotism."

"Patriotism" and "national security" were the watchwords of the CIA and other intelligence organizations and were used effectively to keep secret a multitude of sins and questionable activities. Some CIA activities were clearly in violation of both the Agency's charter and United States laws. One Agency endeavor—the search for effective brainwashing and behavior-modification methods—is especially chilling.

The Manchurian Candidates

The way that German rocket scientists were brought to the United States after World War II to become the leaders of the U.S. space program is well documented. Not so well known is how German experimentation with mind control also was continued in America after the war.

Although U.S. judges at the Nuremberg War Crimes Trials sentenced seven German scientists to death for their part in human experimentation in the concentration camps, their research material was forwarded to the OSS and their work was continued. With the creation of the CIA, this work became part of the Agency's behavior-modification program, first called BLUEBIRD, then later changed to ARTICHOKE.

By 1954, the ARTICHOKE program was part of the CIA's Technical Services Staff (TSS), which also provided the Agency with weaponry, disguises, gadgets, forged documents, and codes. ARTICHOKE teams usually consisted of a psychiatrist, a drug expert, a technician, and a hypnotist, who sometimes posed as a polygraph operator.

The CIA was not alone in attempting to develop brainwashing techniques. The Navy in 1947 began a top-secret program, named Project CHATTER, designed to develop a truly effective truth serum.

Such programs to alter minds formed the basis of a 1959 book by Richard Condon entitled *The Manchurian Candidate*. The book, later a movie that reportedly was one of John F. Kennedy's favorites, concerned an American soldier captured in Korea who is brainwashed into becoming a remote-controlled killer for the purpose of assassinating the president of the United States.

On April 13, 1953, the CIA mind-control program—including "covert use of biological and chemical materials" proposed by Richard Helms and managed by Dr. Sidney Gottlieb—was authorized by Director Dulles under the overall name MK-ULTRA. Under MK-ULTRA, the CIA went beyond mind-control experimentation to develop deadly toxins capable of killing without leaving a trace. One such toxin was later used in pills given by Agency officials to a mobster in the CIA-Mafia plots to assassinate Fidel Castro.

Also in 1953, the CIA, with Dulles's approval, spent $240,000 to purchase LSD. LSD (D-lysergic acid diethylamide) had been discovered by a Swiss doctor in 1943 and was believed to be a potential mind-control substance. Back in America, samples of LSD were later sent to various universities staffed by scientists on the CIA payroll. Some of these schools included the University of Minnesota, Harvard, University of Washington, Baylor University, and the University of Maryland. However, LSD did not accomplish what the Agency experts had hoped—a means to extract information and service from individuals. In fact, even staunch CIA officals who took the drug experimentally found their perceptions altered in unusual ways.

Author John Marks, who made a major investigation into CIA mind-control experiments, quoted a CIA official who took LSD:

. . . you tend to have a more global view of things. I found it awfully hard when stoned to maintain the notion: I am a U.S. citizen—my country right or wrong . . . You tend to have these good higher feelings. You are more open to the brotherhood-of-man idea and more susceptible to the seamy sides of your own society . . . I think this is exactly what happened during the 1960s, but it didn't make people more Communistic. It just made them less inclined to identify with the U.S. They took a plague-on-both-your-houses position.

In one documented case, a CIA official named Frank Olson was given
LSD without his knowledge by Gottlieb in 1953. Olson was driven psychotic by the drug and a few days later killed himself by crashing through
a tenth-floor window of a Washington hotel. Olson's family was not told
the truth about his death until 1975, when reports gathered by the Rockefeller Commission studying CIA abuses appeared in the news media.

Interestingly, one of the two CIA field stations that was involved in
MK-ULTRA and had quantities of both LSD and other chemical mind-
altering agents was Atsugi in Japan, the same station where Lee Harvey
Oswald served as a Marine radar operator and apparently was mixed up in
undercover operations.

Since the CIA has admitted that their most convenient source of mind-
control guinea pigs were "individuals of dubious loyalty, suspected agents
or plants, subjects having known reason for deception, etc.," the question
has arisen if perhaps Oswald was part of the mind-altering program of the
Agency. In an article published in *Rolling Stone,* the authors claim to have
contacted a Marine from Oswald's unit who said he participated in some of
the LSD experiments.

The exact nature of Oswald's relation to the CIA mind-control program—if
there was one—will likely never be known. According to Marks, Gottlieb,
upon his retirement from the Agency in 1973 and with the agreement of
Helms, destroyed what they thought were the last remaining documents on
MK-ULTRA.

Since Oswald may have taken a mind-altering drug; since his killer,
Jack Ruby, was to tell Dallas police he had no recollection of shooting
Oswald; since Sirhan Sirhan, the presumed assassin of Robert Kennedy,
still claims he can't remember what happened in the Ambassador Hotel,
and since a San Quentin psychologist, Dr. Eduard Simson, proclaimed
that Sirhan had been "programmed" by drugs, hypnosis, or both, the
possibility of mind control in the JFK assassination—while admittedly
unlikely—cannot be totally ruled out.

But the techniques of using someone under mind control by drugs and
hypnosis as an assassin or decoy in an assassination had not yet been
perfected in 1963. It is more likely that conspirators at that time would
have resorted to a less sophisticated method—they would simply have
hired the mob.

*   *   *

For all the myths that have arisen about CIA prowess—the actual history
of the CIA reveals as many glaring errors as victories.

Agency analysts failed to foresee the 1967 Arab-Israeli War or the 1968
Tet Offensive in South Vietnam. They also failed miserably in appreciat-
ing the popular sport enjoyed by Fidel Castro at the time of the ill-fated
Bay of Pigs Invasion.

One CIA officer deeply involved in the Cuban adventures was William
Harvey, who established and managed the CIA's now-famous "Executive

Action'' program—a program of calculated assassination code-named ZR-RIFLE. Referring to Harvey's program, President Lyndon Johnson once commented: ''. . . we were running a damn Murder, Inc. in the Caribbean.''

It is in this area—assassination plots—that the U.S. intelligence community in general, and the CIA in particular, have created serious suspicions in the minds of researchers regarding possible complicity in the death of President Kennedy.

CIA-Mafia Death Plots

In September 1963, CIA officers again tried to hatch an assassination plot against Castro—this time using a Cuban government official named Dr. Rolando Cubela. His CIA code name was AM/LASH.

Some two years earlier, Cubela, a Cuban minister without portfolio, had contacted the CIA and offered to defect. The Agency had persuaded him to remain in place as a valuable conduit of inside information.

This time, meeting in a São Paulo, Brazil safe house, Cubela startled his CIA contacts by offering to assassinate Castro if he had the support of the U.S. government. This offer was sent to Desmond FitzGerald, a personal friend of Robert Kennedy and one of the CIA officials in charge of Operation MONGOOSE.

Despite cautions from CIA counterintelligence that Cubela might be a Castro agent testing U.S. government intentions, FitzGerald ordered that Cubela be told that his offer to eliminate Castro was under consideration at the "highest levels." This strange story has been related in both *Legend: The Secret World of Lee Harvey Oswald* by Edward Jay Epstein and *The Kennedys* by John H. Davis.

Toward the end of October Cubela made an extraordinary demand. He wanted personal assurance that his plan to kill Castro was to be actively supported by the Kennedy administration. On October 29, again against the advice of counterintelligence, FitzGerald personally met with Cubela and assured him that once Castro was gone, the Kennedy administration would support a new Cuban government. But when Cubela asked for a rifle with telescopic sights and the means to deliver poison, FitzGerald declined to speak of such specifics. Another meeting with Cubela was set and on that day, the CIA case officer supplied Cubela with a poison ballpoint pen. Cubela was told the rifle and some explosives would be delivered to him soon. Cubela received his assassination tools from the CIA on November 22, 1963.

Although no documentation of the AM/LASH plot has survived, some senior CIA officials now claim that the plot did have the support of both Robert Kennedy and his brother. Since both are now dead, there's no real way to be sure.

It was the knowledge of AM/LASH, however, that caused consternation among CIA officials when Castro made certain public statements concerning assassination plots. While attending a reception in the Brazilian embassy in Havana, Castro told an Associated Press reporter: "Kennedy is the Batista of our time and the most opportunistic president of all time." Castro went on to warn against "terrorist plans to eliminate Cuban leaders" adding: "United States leaders should think that if they assist in terrorist plans to eliminate Cuban leaders, they themselves will not be safe." This warning has for years been used to support the theory that somehow Castro had learned of the CIA plots against him and, in retaliation, sent assassins after Kennedy. But since Cubela was not caught by Castro until 1966, it is unlikely that AM/LASH was the impetus of his 1963 remarks.

While the CIA MONGOOSE program continued in Florida, similar operations were being conducted in New Orleans, long a hotbed of Cuban exile-CIA activity. One of the centers of this activity was the shabby, three-story office building at 544 Camp Street, a connecting point for the CIA, FBI, anti-Castro Cubans, and Lee Harvey Oswald.

New Orleans

Within days of Kennedy's assassination, the FBI questioned David Ferrie in New Orleans. Ferrie denied any knowledge of the assassination and the FBI agents let him go, apparently unaware of Ferrie's Civil Air Patrol connection to accused assassin Lee Harvey Oswald or to New Orleans crime boss Carlos Marcello. Neither apparently did the agents know that Ferrie had been working for Detective Guy Banister in the summer of 1963.

Whatever information Ferrie gave the FBI will never be known, since the interview was classified and locked away on orders of J. Edgar Hoover and in 1976, the National Archives reported that Ferrie's original statement was missing from its collection of assassination documents.

Both Ferrie and Banister were well-connected with the Cuban exiles living in New Orleans. Ferrie, as a contract agent for the CIA, claimed to have flown on hazardous missions into Cuba, including landing there on the night of the ill-fated Bay of Pigs Invasion.

Ferrie's role as CIA agent was confirmed in 1975 when former executive assistant to the CIA's deputy director, Victor Marchetti, stated that during high-level CIA meetings in 1969, CIA director Richard Helms disclosed that Ferrie and other figures in the Garrison investigation had indeed worked for the Agency.

Banister investigator Jack Martin and others have told investigators through the years of contact between CIA contract agent Ferrie and Oswald during 1963. He said he suspected that Ferrie "had taught Oswald how to purchase a foreign-made firearm . . ."

According to Beverly Oliver, the "babushka lady" Oswald and Ferrie were even seen together in Jack Ruby's Carousel Club shortly before the assassination.

Delphine Roberts also claims that Oswald and Ferrie were together. She said that on one occasion Ferrie even took Oswald to an anti-Castro guerrilla training camp outside New Orleans "to train with rifles." Once she saw Oswald handing out pro-Castro literature on a New Orleans street. Reporting this to her boss, Banister reassured her, "He's with the office." Roberts later said: "I knew there were such things as counterspies, spies and counterspies, and the importance of such things."

The day after Kennedy's assassination, Secret Service agents went to 544 Camp Street after seeing the address on some of Oswald's pamphlets. Guy Banister's office was closed. They learned that "Cuban revolutionaries" had had an office there. The agents brushed the whole thing off by reporting that they hadn't found a trace of the Fair Play for Cuba Committee at 544 Camp Street.

*   *   *

Throughout 1963 the CIA continued to work with anti-Castro Cubans and others such as Ferrie and Banister, who were in contact with Lee Harvey Oswald.

Considering all this, as well as Oswald's bizarre military record and his trip to Russia, one must wonder whether the ex-Marine was working in intelligence.

Was Oswald a Spy?

After reviewing all available evidence, the answer to the above question seems to be a resounding "yes."

The following is a quick look at some of the evidence pointing to Oswald's involvement with spy work:

—His childhood—a bright loner who read a wide range of books and was drawn to unpopular ideas, attracted by spy stories (The TV show "I Led Three Lives" and Ian Fleming's James Bond novels were among his favorites)—perfectly fits the profile of persons most desired for intelligence work.

—Oswald's Marine career is checkered with inconsistencies and unexplained events that suggest secret intelligence training.

—His assignment to Atsugi base in Japan, which housed a large CIA facility.

—Oswald's incredible ability with the Russian language. Several Russians, including his wife, said he spoke like a native, yet this high-school dropout reportedly taught himself Russian from books.

—The fact that several persons—including a former CIA paymaster, Oswald's Marine roommate, and fellow Marine Gerry Patrick Hemming—have suggested that Oswald worked for U.S. intelligence.

—The manner in which Oswald traveled so easily in and out of Russia as well as the unaccounted-for funds he used suggests intelligence guidance.

—The ability of this American "defector" to leave the Soviet Union with his Russian-born wife at a time when most Russians were being denied exit permits.

—The ease with which this would-be defector obtained passports both in 1959 and 1963.

—The fact that Oswald wrote a lengthy report on his activities in Russia and, later, made a detailed report to the FBI concerning his Fair Play For Cuba activities in New Orleans.

—Oswald's notebook contained the word "microdots," a common spy technique of photographically reducing information to a small dot.

—Oswald's nonbinding "defection" to Russia fit perfectly the profile of an Office of Naval Intelligence program to infiltrate American servicemen into the Soviet Union during the late 1950s.

—One of Oswald's closest contacts, George DeMohrenschildt, was himself an intelligence operative, first for the Nazis and later for the CIA.

One of the strongest pieces of evidence for Oswald's involvement in spy work concerns a small Minox camera found among his effects by Dallas Police. Information developed by the *Dallas Morning News* in 1978 revealed the camera was not available to the public in 1963. It may have been spy equipment issued to Oswald. This evidence was so explosive that the FBI tried to get Dallas detectives to change their reports regarding the camera and also kept photos taken by Oswald hidden for nearly fifteen years.

Dallas detectives Gus Rose and R. S. Stovall had reported finding the Minox camera loaded with film in Oswald's Marine seabag in the Irving home of Michael and Ruth Paine hours after the assassination. The three-inch-long German-made camera was famous for being used by spies on both sides during World War II. An inventory of Oswald's property taken from the Paine home was made on November 26, 1963. Listed under item 375 was "one Minox camera." This inventory list was witnessed by FBI Agent Warren De Brueys, the FBI man in New Orleans who had been assigned to monitor Oswald during the spring and summer of 1963. Later however, the FBI property inventory listed item 375 as a "Minox light meter."

Detective Rose told the *Dallas Morning News*:

[The FBI] were calling it a light meter, I know that. But I know a camera when I see it . . . The thing we got at Irving out of Oswald's seabag was a Minox camera. No question about it. They tried to get me to change the records because it wasn't a light meter. I don't know why they wanted it changed, but they must have had some motive for it.

The motive may have been that the existence of the camera pointed to Oswald's intelligence connections.

Dallas Morning News reporter Earl Golz contacted Minox Corporation and spoke to Kurt Lohn, formerly in charge of Minox distribution in New York City. According to Lohn, the serial number of the camera found in Oswald's belongings—number 27259—did not exist among any Minox cameras distributed for commercial sale in the United States. Lohn said all Minox cameras distributed in the U.S. carried six-digit serial numbers beginning with number 135000. Number 27259 was "not a registered number . . . not a valid number," said Lohn. Golz also determined that Minox did not sell a light meter in the U.S. in 1963.

A later FBI report stated that a Minox III camera was obtained on January 31, 1964, from Ruth Paine and that it belonged to her husband who worked for Bell Helicopter. However, Mrs. Paine told Golz she did not remember being asked to turn over such a camera. Michael Paine reportedly also had a Minox camera but it was damaged and "unworkable."

The Dallas detectives both claimed to have found a Minox camera in Oswald's possessions. The FBI later claimed no such camera existed and that they had actually found a Minox light meter.

Yet in 1979, acting on a Freedom of Information Act request by an assassination researcher, the Bureau released about twenty-five photographs and stated they were taken with a Minox camera belonging to Oswald. Michael Paine was unable to recall taking any pictures such as the ones released by the FBI.

On page 113 of a book published by Dallas police chief Jesse Curry in 1969 is a photograph of Oswald's property taken from the Paine home. Clearly pictured is various Minox camera equipment, including a binocular-type telephoto lens.

Where did Oswald get an unregistered Minox "spy" camera? More important, why did the FBI attempt to have Dallas police change their reports to indicate a light meter was found rather than a camera?

In 1976, a CIA document was released that showed that the Agency indeed considered Oswald for recruitment. This contradicted the sworn Warren Commission testimony of CIA official Richard Helms who stated the Agency had never had "or even contemplated" any contact with Oswald. This document, written by an unidentified CIA officer three days after Kennedy's assassination, states "we showed intelligence interest" in Oswald and "discussed . . . the laying on of interviews."

Then there are the questions concerning a CIA "201" file on Oswald discovered only in 1977. The existence of this file came to light after a Freedom of Information Act request was pressed by assassination researchers. Many persons knowledgeable about the Agency equate a 201 file with a personnel file, implying Oswald had worked for the CIA. CIA officials told the House Select Committee on Assassinations that the Agency's file on Oswald was nothing unusual and merely reflected that Oswald had "potential intelligence or counterintelligence significance." However, at least three former CIA officers have stated publicly that the mere existence of a 201 file on Oswald indicated a relationship between the ex-Marine and the Agency.

Victor Marchetti, formerly an executive assistant to the CIA's deputy director, said: "Basically, if Oswald had a '201' file, he was an agent."

Bradley E. Ayers, a CIA officer who trained anti-Castro Cubans: "[A 201 file meant Oswald was] . . . either a contract agent, working for them full time, or he was on some kind of assignment for the CIA."

Former CIA agent Patrick McGarvey: "If a guy has a '201' file, that means he's a professional staff employee of the organization."

The CIA went to great lengths to convince the House Committee that its having a 201 file on Oswald—and the fact that this information was kept secret for nearly fifteen years—was in no way suspicious.

The Committee, however, found many problems with the Oswald 201 file. For example, Oswald's file reportedly was opened on December 9, 1960, yet a confidential State Department telegram reporting Oswald's attempted defection to Russia—cause enough to open a file on him—was sent to the CIA back on October 31, 1959.

Other problems with the Oswald file are that one CIA employee gave a reason for an "AG" code on the file that was at variance with the official Agency explanation; the 201 file was under the name "Lee Henry Oswald" leading the Committee to wonder if dual files were kept (a suspicion the CIA denied); and one CIA memo indicated as many as thirty-seven documents were missing from the Oswald file, although Agency officials later claimed they were only missing at the time the memo was written.

Further, a recently obtained CIA document states that Oswald's 201 file filled "two four-drawer safes," yet the House Committee was given a virtually empty folder.

The whole question of Oswald's connection to U.S. intelligence is so full of claims and counterclaims, deceit and misinformation, it is unlikely the whole truth of the matter will ever be known.

What is known—or at least believed by most people who have studied the issue at any depth—is that the weight of the evidence suggests it is likely Oswald was in some way connected with U.S. intelligence work.

*   *   *

Even the FBI apparently believed that Oswald may have been involved in spy work.

In a report dealing with Oswald's possessions taken from the Paine home in Irving, FBI laboratory personnel listed the items—which included shoes, socks, a pair of cotton gloves, towels, shirts, soap, office supplies, and toiletries—then stated: "Nothing was noted . . . which would indicate that these specimens would be particularly useful in the field of espionage." The report went on to state that all of the items were checked carefully, but unsuccessfully, for microdots.

There has been no explanation of why the Bureau was so concerned about such spy methods at a time when its official position was that Oswald was only a discontented loner.

While at the time of the JFK assassination, the official story was that no U.S. government agency had been interested in Oswald or knew of his whereabouts, it is now known that both the CIA and the FBI were keeping a close watch on the ex-Marine's activities. Oswald's alleged trip to Mexico City between September 26 and October 3, 1963, is a case in point. According to the Warren Commission, Oswald was in Mexico City for the purpose of visiting the Soviet and Cuban embassies. Proof of these visits were in the form of the statement of a Cuban embassy employee, Silvia Duran, and from CIA operatives monitoring the Soviet embassy.

On October 10, 1963, more than a month before the JFK assassination, the CIA sent a teletype to the State Department, the FBI, immigration authorities, and the Department of the Navy regarding the "possible presence of Subject [Oswald] in Mexico City":

On October 1, 1963, a reliable and sensitive source in Mexico reported that an American male, who identified himself as Lee Oswald, contacted the Soviet Embassy in Mexico City . . . The American was described as approximately 35 years old, with an athletic build, about six feet tall, with a receding hairline . . . It is believed that Oswald may be identical to Lee Harvey Oswald, born on 18 October 1939 in New Orleans, Louisiana.

Obviously this description did not match that of the twenty-three-year-old, five-foot-nine, slenderly built Oswald in Dallas.

The Warren Commission, seriously concerned about the ties between Oswald and the Soviets and Cubans in Mexico City, asked the CIA for documentation of Oswald's activities. After months of foot-dragging, the Agency could only provide the unsupported statement of Duran as proof that Oswald was at the Cuban embassy.

Then on January 22, 1964, the CIA leaked to Commission members that Oswald had contact with a KGB officer, Valery Kostikov, while in the Soviet embassy. The Agency said Kostikov's responsibilities included "assassination and sabotage." This possible link between Oswald and a KGB assassination plot so frightened Commission members that they were content to take the CIA's word for Oswald's Mexico activities.

Not shown to the Warren Commission was a cable sent by the director of the CIA to its station in Mexico City urging the secret arrest of Silvia Duran on the day after the assassination. Duran, a twenty-six-year-old

Mexican national, had been employed at the Cuban embassy only one month before Oswald allegedly arrived in Mexico. Her predecessor had been killed in an automobile accident. The CIA cable regarding Duran's arrest, only declassified in recent years, stated:

Arrest of Silvia Duran is extremely serious matter which could prejudice U.S. freedom of action on entire question of Cuban responsibility . . . With full regard for Mexican interests, request you ensure that her arrest is kept absolutely secret, that no information from her is published or leaked, that all such info is cabled to us, and that fact of her arrest and her statements are not spread to leftist or disloyal circles in the Mexican government.

In a 1978 article, Mark Lane concluded:

This almost incredible cable reveals the extent of CIA control over Mexican police officials, many of whom had been trained by the CIA, and many of whom were engaged by the CIA while they ostensibly worked for the Mexican government. The CIA's willingness to order Mexican police officials to make false statements to their own superiors and to mislead the ''circles in the Mexican government'' provides an insight into the CIA's desperation to secure some evidence to prove . . . that Oswald had gone to the Cuban Embassy.

Apparently the statements that Duran gave to the Mexican authorities were not to their liking. She was not released for several days and only then after she had identified Oswald as the man who visited the embassy.

Once free, Duran began to speak of her experience. This prompted yet another CIA cable, which ordered CIA personnel to have Duran rearrested, but to conceal who was behind the action. A portion of this cable stated:

. . . to be certain that there is no misunderstanding between us, we want to insure that Silvia Duran gets no impression that Americans are behind her rearrest. In other words we want Mexican authorities to take responsibility for the whole affair.

Duran was rearrested and did not speak of her experiences afterward. She was never interviewed nor called as a witness by the Warren Commission, which never learned of her two arrests.

Since the Oswald in the Cuban embassy apparently made quite a scene when told he could not get a visa to Cuba in three days—he shouted and called the embassy personnel ''bureaucrats''—he should have been well remembered by Duran and others there. But in 1978, Cuban consul Eusebio Azcue told the House Select Committee on Assassinations that he was convinced the man who visited the embassy in 1963 was not the

Oswald arrested in Dallas. After viewing photos of Oswald, Azcue stated: "My belief is that this gentleman was not, is not, the person or the individual who went to the consulate."

Silvia Duran—perhaps due to her experience in the hands of the police— has maintained over the years that the man was Oswald. However, in 1979, author Anthony Summers arranged for her to watch films of Lee Harvey Oswald. Duran, who admitted that her identification of Oswald was more from the name than from the fuzzy newspaper photos printed at the time, watched the Oswald films and concluded: "I was not sure if it was Oswald or not . . . the man on the film is not like the man I saw here in Mexico City." To add to Duran's confusion, she recalled the man who visited the consulate was short, no more than five feet six inches in height—far shorter than the five-foot-nine Dallas Oswald.

While the CIA stated that both the Cuban and Soviet embassies were under photographic surveillance during Oswald's visits, they could offer no proof. Lamely, CIA officials explained to the Warren Commission that the camera at the Soviet embassy was turned off on Saturdays (the day Oswald supposedly was there) and that the camera at the Cuban embassy just happened to break down the day Oswald was there. However, the day of the assassination, CIA officials sent photos taken outside the Soviet embassy in Mexico City to the FBI, claiming they were of Oswald. They are obviously of someone else. This someone appears to be about thirty-five years old, six feet tall, with an athletic build.

Questioning the photos, the FBI reportedly showed one of them to Oswald's mother, who said she had never seen the man depicted before. Later she claimed the photo was that of Jack Ruby.

CIA officials admitted there had been a "mix-up" on the photos.

The House Select Committee on Assassinations noted that Oswald allegedly made at least five trips to the two embassies and found it hard to believe that he was not photographed even once. The committee expressed the belief that "photographs of Oswald might have been taken and subsequently lost or destroyed."

The absence of any photos of Oswald at the embassies raises suspicion that an imposter was posing as Oswald during these embassy visits. Further evidence of this comes from an episode involving tape recordings. In 1976, at the onset of the House assassinations investigation, CIA officer David A. Phillips, one of the Bay of Pigs organizers who at the time of Oswald's alleged visit was stationed in Mexico City, told the House Committee's general counsel that the CIA had tape-recorded conversations between Oswald and the Soviet embassy but had not so informed the Warren Commission. When pressed on why the tapes, clear proof of Oswald's Mexican visits, had not been given to the Commission, Phillips said they had been routinely destroyed about a week later since prior to the assassination Oswald was not considered important.

However, long after his 1976 testimony, a five-page FBI document dated November 23, 1963, became public and threw doubt on Phillips's story. According to this report, which was not seen by the Warren Commission, FBI agents who were questioning Oswald in Dallas were informed by CIA officers that Oswald had contacted the Soviet embassy in Mexico City. The report went on to state:

> Special agents of this Bureau, who have conversed with Oswald in Dallas, Texas, have observed photographs of the individual referred to above and have listened to a recording of his voice. These special agents are of the opinion that the above-referred-to individual was not Lee Harvey Oswald.

If this FBI report is correct, then the CIA wiretap tape of Oswald was not destroyed in October but was available to Bureau agents the day after the assassination. When then were the tapes destroyed and by whom?

One disturbing aspect of this is that either the CIA notified other agencies in October that Oswald was in Mexico City not knowing the man was an impostor, then failed to follow up on their mistake later. Or—more ominously—the Agency knowingly participated in a scheme to place Oswald in Mexico City at that time—nearly two months *before* the assassination!

It is equally disturbing that the House Select Committee on Assassinations made a three-hundred-page report on these mysterious happenings in Mexico City, then failed to put it into its published report claiming it was withheld to protect "sensitive sources and methods" of the CIA.

Another Mexico incident, which has been misreported for years, concerns a note from Oswald to a "Mr. Hunt."

A Message from Oswald

In August, 1975, JFK researcher Penn Jones, Jr., received a typewritten letter in Spanish from Mexico City signed only with the initials "P.S." Translated, the letter reads:

Dear Sir:

At the end of last year I gave Mr. [Clarence] Kelly, the director of the FBI, a letter from Lee Oswald. To my understanding it could have brought out the circumstances to the assassination of President Kennedy.

Since Mr. Kelly hasn't responded to that letter, I've got the right to believe something bad might happen to me, and that is why I see myself obligated to keep myself away for a short time.

Convinced of the importance of that letter mentioned and knowing that you have been doing some investigation independently of the assassination, I'm sending you a copy of the same letter.

Accompanying this typed letter was a copy of a handwritten note in English dated November 8, 1963 that reads:

Dear Mr. Hunt,

I would like information concer[n]ing my position.

I am asking only for information. I am suggesting that we discuss the matter fully before any steps are taken by me or anyone else.

Thank you,

Lee Harvey Oswald

Jones, too, sent this information to the FBI and he, too, received no reply.

A reporter for the *Dallas Morning News* later obtained a copy of the Oswald note from Jones. He had three handwriting experts in Dallas compare the note to known examples of Oswald's handwriting. The experts all agreed that the handwriting was the same. The *Dallas Morning News* carried an accurate account of the strange note and raised the question if "Mr. Hunt" might refer to Dallas oilman H. L. Hunt. In 1983, it was learned that the FBI studied the note with the idea it may have been intended for Hunt's son, Nelson Bunker Hunt. The results of the FBI probe, however, have never been made public.

Jones, then and now, points out that the note came from Mexico City and that allegedly CIA officer E. Howard Hunt, who was in charge of anti-Castro Cubans at the time, was stationed there during Oswald's reported visit.

Jones told this author: "To me, knowing Hunt's background with the Cuban Revolutionary Committee and the CIA, it makes more sense that the note is addressed to E. Howard Hunt."

But since neither the FBI nor the House Select Committee on Assassinations appears to have taken an interest in the note, there the matter rests.

The fact of the Oswald note and its accompanying letter leads assassination researchers to believe that Oswald's brief visit to Mexico City might provide help in understanding who was really behind the assassination.

*   *   *

Yet another contact with the CIA that has only become known in recent years involves a man who "coincidentally" obtained the Mexican travel permit number just before Oswald's—William George Gaudet.

When applying for a new passport in June 1963, Oswald did not try to hide his past or his intentions. On the application, he acknowledged he might travel to Russia and other European countries later that year. He also noted that his previous passport had been canceled. Despite these admissions—coupled with the fact that the State Department, which loaned him money to return from the Soviet Union, knew of his attempted defection and threat to give military secrets to the Soviets—Oswald received a new passport within twenty-four hours.

On September 17, a week after the alleged meeting between Oswald and

CIA case officer "Maurice Bishop" Oswald visited the Mexican consulate in New Orleans and applied for a tourist card. He was issued card number 24085, which was valid for fifteen days.

After the assassination, the FBI, with the help of Mexican authorities, identified every person who had applied for Mexican entry papers on September 17—all but one. The FBI reported they could not locate the record of the card holder immediately preceding Oswald, No. 24084. However, in 1975—apparently due to a bureaucratic mix-up in declassifying FBI documents—it was learned that card holder No. 24084 was Gaudet, who had worked for the CIA for more than twenty years.

Gaudet claimed that sheer coincidence placed his name just ahead of Oswald's on the Mexican tourist card application sheet.

Gaudet, who worked in the area of Latin America for the Agency, operated the *Latin American Newsletter* for a number of years. Shortly after the assassination, Gaudet said he was interviewed by FBI agents, but only after obtaining approval of his CIA boss in New Orleans. No record of that interview has been made public.

In a 1978 interview with author Anthony Summers, Gaudet admitted he had "known" Oswald in New Orleans, but then qualified this by saying he had only observed Oswald handing out leaflets. "He was a strange man, an unusual man," was Gaudet's description of Oswald to TV newsmen.

Gaudet did firmly state that while in New Orleans, Oswald was in contact with known CIA and FBI agents. Gaudet told Summers: "I do know that I saw him one time with a former FBI agent by the name of Guy Banister."

Gaudet also mentioned David Ferrie, saying "He was with Oswald . . ."

Angered by the connection of his name to Oswald's, Gaudet went on to say:

> I've given this a lot of thought. I am now convinced in my own mind that those who are truly behind the conspiracy to kill Mr. Kennedy have done things purposely to draw attention to me. There are too many coincidences that involve me, unless someone was behind all this.

Gaudet said he did not accompany Oswald on a bus to Mexico, but went by air. He now claims he cannot remember if his 1963 Mexican trip involved intelligence activity.

Gaudet said that, due to his experience with the CIA, he is not surprised that little information concerning Oswald's intelligence activities has been forthcoming: "[CIA officials] told me frankly when I did things for them that if something went awry they would never recognize me or admit who I was. If I made a mistake, that was just tough, and I knew it." The former CIA operative went on to say he finds it "extremely possible" that Oswald was working for some American intelligence agency and added: "I think he was a patsy . . . I think he was set up on purpose." Gaudet also agreed with many assassination researchers who believe that the anti-Castro Cubans were involved in a plot to kill Kennedy. However, asked by newsmen if he thought the Cubans could have carried out an assassination alone, he replied: "No, I don't think so."

But if Gaudet did not actually accompany Oswald to Mexico, one very suspicious man did—Albert Osborne. Although the passenger list for Continental Trailways bus No. 5133, which allegedly carried Oswald to Mexico City, is missing, the FBI managed to locate some of the travelers, including two Australian girls who told of a conversation with a man who told them of his experiences in the Marines and in Russia. These girls told the FBI that the man also had sat next to and talked at length with an older man.

FBI agents tried to locate a man named John Howard Bowen, who had been on Oswald's bus. However, they only found Albert Osborne, but Osborne seemed to know a lot about Bowen. After three visits from the FBI, Osborne finally admitted that he was the man they were seeking, having used the alias "John Bowen" for many years. He denied ever having met Oswald. Even the Warren Commission didn't buy that, stating "his denial cannot be credited."

Osborne claimed to be a missionary who traveled extensively all over the world, although he never said how these travels were financed. Also, no confirmation of his story could be found by checking border records in the countries he claimed to have visited. Despite his lies to the FBI regarding his name, no charges were ever brought against Osborne.

In recent years, several assassination researchers have claimed that Osborne worked for the CIA, but no hard evidence of this has been established.

It is interesting to note, however, that when Oswald ordered Fair Play for Cuba Committee materials printed in New Orleans, he used the name "Osborne."

Other intriguing connections between the CIA and the JFK assassination concern George DeMohrenschildt and the Mannlicher-Carcano rifle found in the Texas School Book Depository.

Demohrenschildt and the Agency

George DeMohrenschildt, along with his wife, Jeanne, were identified by the Warren Commission as the people closest to Lee Harvey Oswald just before the assassination. If anyone was guiding Oswald's activities during late 1962 and early 1963, it would have been DeMohrenschildt. DeMohrenschildt's son-in-law, Gary Taylor, even told the Warren Commission: ". . . if there was any assistance [to Oswald] or plotters in the assassination they were, in my opinion, most probably the DeMohrenschildts."

DeMohrenschildt undoubtedly is one of the most colorful and suspicious of all the persons connected to Oswald. Based on CIA memos now available, thanks to Freedom of Information Act suits, it is known that DeMohrenschildt had a relationship with the Agency dating back to OSS days. One memo by former CIA director Richard Helms states that DeMohrenschildt applied to work for the government as early as 1942, but was rejected "because he was alleged to be a Nazi espionage agent."

The charge had some substance. After a trip to Yugoslavia with his wife in 1957 (they were shot at by guards of Marshal Tito), DeMohrenschildt provided the CIA with "foreign intelligence which was promptly disseminated to other federal agencies in 10 separate reports," according to the Helms memo. Another Agency memo indicated DeMohrenschildt also furnished lengthy reports on travels he made through Mexico and Panama at the time of the Bay of Pigs Invasion.

Asked by a Warren Commission attorney if he believed the DeMohrenschildts may have been spying on the invasion preparations, Taylor replied, "Yes."

In fact, at the time DeMohrenschildt was befriending Lee Harvey Oswald, one of his close friends in Dallas was J. Walter Moore. Moore just happened to have been an agent of the CIA's Domestic Contacts Division. DeMohrenschildt publicly stated that before becoming involved with Oswald, he had checked with Moore. Moore, according to DeMohrenschildt, said unhesitatingly: "Yes, he's okay. He's just a harmless lunatic."

In a CIA memorandum written not long after Oswald returned from Russia, the CIA author wrote: "Don't push too hard to get the information we need, because this individual [Oswald] looks odd."

Much later it was learned how the CIA was to "debrief" Oswald—by using the genial George DeMohrenschildt. Author Edward Epstein interviewed DeMohrenschildt on the morning of March 29, 1977. That same morning, an investigator from the House Select Committee on Assassinations had attempted to contact DeMohrenschildt. Three hours later DeMohrenschildt was dead from a shotgun blast to the head. His death was ruled a suicide.

According to Epstein, DeMohrenschildt said Moore encouraged him to see Oswald and that, in fact, he was to question Oswald "unwittingly" about his stay in Russia. DeMohrenschildt said that after his first meeting with the ex-Marine, Oswald gave him a lengthy memo covering his activities in Russia.

DeMohrenschildt, a petroleum engineer, and Moore had offices in the same Dallas bank building and often ate lunch together, according to Jeanne DeMohrenschildt.

The CIA memos, Moore's closeness, and DeMohrenschildt's own testimony all confirm that a certain relationship existed between the CIA and the man closest to Oswald in early 1963. While this does not necessarily involve the Agency in a plot to kill Kennedy, it raises questions about what Agency officials might have known regarding such a plot.

*   *   *

In a related issue that belies the idea set forth in 1963 that the CIA was neither aware of Oswald nor interested in him, it is now known that the Agency was opening Oswald's mail while he was in Russia. In letters to his mother, Marguerite Oswald, written in 1976 by former CIA legislative counsel George L. Cary, Cary admitted that the Agency had opened mail from her to her son while he was in Russia. Cary said the admission was a result of an investigation into the CIA's mail intercept program—known as HT-Lingual—by the Government Information and Individual Rights Subcommittee of the House Government Operations Committee.

Another possible connection between the CIA and the JFK assassination concerns a former CIA operative named Robert D. Morrow. In his book, *Betrayal*, Morrow tells how he purchased four 6.5 mm Mannlicher-Carcano rifles on orders from a CIA superior. Morrow remains convinced that at least one of these rifles ended up in the hands of Dallas police on November 22, 1963.

Morrow even presents a plausible, though unproven, account of the assassination:

Oswald, who went to Russia for the CIA and was an FBI informant by the summer of 1963, was brought into an assassination plot led by CIA consultant Clay Shaw, using right-wing CIA operatives and anti-Castro Cubans headed by Jack Ruby in Dallas and Guy Banister in New Orleans. This group, operating outside Agency control, manipulated events to insure Oswald being named as the assassin. They also used an Oswald look-alike to incriminate the ex-Marine by firing shots from the Texas School Book Depository. Dallas policeman J. D. Tippit was killed by this Oswald substitute when he failed to go along with the group's scheme to have Tippit kill the real Oswald in the Texas Theater. With the capture of Oswald, Ruby was compelled to stalk and finally kill the accused assassin.

The Mannlicher-Carcano ammunition also raised questions about CIA involvement. According to FBI documents, the 6.5 mm ammunition found in the Texas School Book Depository was part of a batch manufactured on a U.S. government contract by Western Cartridge Corporation of East Alton, Illinois, which is now a part of Winchester-Western Division of Olin Industries.

In the mid-1950s, four million rounds of this ammunition was purchased by the Marine Corps, prompting the author of the FBI document to state:

The interesting thing about this order is that it is for ammunition which does not fit and cannot be fired in any of the United States Marine Corps weapons. This gives rise to the obvious speculation that it is a contract for ammunition placed by the CIA with Western Cartridge Corporation under a USMC cover for concealment purposes.

It is well known that the CIA had used "sanitized" weapons—that is, weapons that cannot be traced directly back to the Agency or the United States—in various missions around the world.

Most of the information available suggesting links between the assassination and the CIA is circumstantial—which is hardly surprising. After all, Agency officials could hardly be expected to reveal information possibly connecting them to the death of the President. However, at this time there can be little doubt that many persons connected to Oswald—David Ferrie, Guy Banister, Carlos Bringuier, and other anti-Castro Cubans—were also connected to the CIA. Some knowledgeable persons—such as former CIA operative Morrow and others—claim these CIA people were operating outside of Agency control.

One strange incident involved an intelligence operative named Gary Underhill, who had served in World War II and was considered one of the top U.S. experts on limited warfare. At the time of the assassination, Underhill performed "special assignments" for the CIA and was on close terms with officials of both the Agency and the Pentagon. Several days after the assassination, Underhill visited friends in New Jersey. He was badly shaken and fearful. He said that President Kennedy had been killed by a small group within the CIA and that he believed his life was in danger. A short time later, Underhill was found fatally shot in his Washington apartment. His death was ruled suicide although he was shot in the left side of his head and a pistol was found in his left hand—and it was well known that Underhill was right-handed.

There is also a real possibility that the assassins who killed Kennedy may have had no direct link with Oswald and his Cuban contacts at all. This intriguing possibility—which could go far in explaining why none of the trails leading backward from Oswald seem to connect firmly with the shooting in Dealey Plaza—became apparent several years ago with the revelation of a French connection to the assassination.

The French Connection to the Assassination

The House Select Committee on Assassinations concluded in 1979 what most Dealey Plaza witnesses said in 1963—that at least one gunman fired on Kennedy from the Grassy Knoll.

While the committee said it could not identify the Grassy Knoll gunman, that second gunman may well have been a premier French assassin with close contacts to the CIA, organized crime, and even an oblique connection with Jack Ruby. According to recently uncovered evidence, more than one French assassin may have been operating in Dealey Plaza.

Central to this possibility is CIA Document No. 632-796, which was released by the Agency in 1977 along with more than three thousand other documents. These documents were pried from the Agency by a Freedom of Information Act suit filed by Washington attorney and JFK assassination researcher Bernard Fensterwald. A poor-quality reproduction with numerous blanked-out spaces, the document was painstakenly deciphered by veteran Dallas researcher Mary Ferrell.

Dated April 1, 1964, the document carries a handwritten title, "Jean Soutre's Expulsion from U.S.," and the half-page paper reads:

8. Jean SOUTRE aka [also known as] Michel Roux aka Michael Mertz—On March 5, [1964] the FBI advised that the French had [withheld] the Legal Attache in Paris and also the [withheld] had queried the Bureau in New York City concerning subject, stating that he had been expelled from the U.S. at Fort Worth or Dallas 18 hours after the assassination. He was in Fort Worth on the morning of 22 November and in Dallas in the afternoon. The French believe that he was expelled to either Mexico or Canada. In January he received mail from a dentist named Alderson . . . Subject is believed to be identical with a Captain who is a deserter from the French Army and an activist in the OAS [a right-wing French militant group.] The French are concerned because of DeGaulle's planned visit to Mexico. They would like to know the reason for his expulsion from the U.S. and his destination. Bureau files are negative and they are checking in Texas and with the INS (Immigration and Naturalization Service] . . .

And the government did check—first with the dentist, who was still practicing in Houston, Texas, in the 1980s. Dr. Lawrence M. Alderson told researchers that FBI agents began watching him in early 1964. He said finally agents contacted him and said they were trying to find the Frenchman "under any circumstances under any conditions."

Alderson said, "They felt that Jean knew who, or he himself had, assassinated Kennedy. And they wanted to know who in Washington had had him flown out of Dallas. And, to my knowledge, nobody ever found out or nobody knew."

Alderson said he had not seen the Frenchman since serving as a security officer with him shortly after World War II. He confided that he was working for the CIA at the time. The dentist gave the following information about the Frenchman, Jean Soutre (pronounced Sweat-ra):

He's a career soldier. From what I can gather, he was in the French underground movement in Algiers. I do know he left the French Air Force . . . I believe he was in the Fourth French Air Force Headquarters in France. He was a very prominent and upcoming French security officer. When I knew him, he was a lieutenant . . . I lived with him so I knew him quite well. He was very well educated, very outgoing, forward, dynamic. He came from a very poor family. In France, you don't have a thing if you're from a poor family unless you have a military career behind you. So, he was very interested in his career and this is why I never did really understand why he left it. But, he very definitely left, I presume, his wife. I have not heard from her in many years. She was a well-to-do, beautiful woman from a Southern France wine family. The last I heard from her, she was the one who told me that he had left the French Army and had gone underground trying to save Algeria. So, evidently, he was rather committed, or felt committed, to leave his career, which was the only career he had. The next time I heard of him, quite truthfully, was when the CIA, or the FBI rather, had me tailed for about two months following the assassination . . . The last contact I had with the CIA was in France when I was working for him. So, the only contact I had in this country was with the FBI.

Alderson, after providing a snapshot of his French friend, said Soutre in the early 1950s was about twenty-five years old and spoke English, Spanish, and German without a trace of an accent. He was about six-foot-one, and weighed about 175 pounds. Soutre was a "sharp dresser," seldom seen in uniform, and had the reputation of being a "ladies' man," Alderson said.

An FBI report stated that three persons named John Mertz, Irma Rio Mertz, and Sara Mertz flew from Houston to Mexico City on November 23, 1963, according to records of Pan American World Airways. The FBI report concluded: "These records contain no further identifying data regarding these individuals."

Although Soutre could have flown out of the country by private or even military aircraft, it is interesting to note the coincidental departure of the Mertzes at a time corresponding to that in the CIA document. After all, even the FBI report noted that Soutre also was known as Michel Roux and Michael Mertz.

Today it is known that Roux and Mertz are the names of two real individuals, both of whom were connected to the shadowy world of intelligence work.

The name "Mertz" crops up in the 1974 Pultizer Prize winning investigative book," *The Heroin Trail*, compiled by the staff of *Newsday*. According to this book, Michael Victor Mertz was a World War II French Resistance hero and a captain in the French secret service after the war. Mertz operated in Germany, Turkey, and Morocco under the cover of his military title. In April 1961, Mertz was ordered to penetrate the terrorist group, L' Organisation de l'Armie Secrete (OAS). Posing as an OAS sympathizer, Mertz was arrested later in 1961 for distributing pro-OAS leaflets and sent to an internment camp. There he worked his way into the highest levels of the OAS and was able to break up a bomb plot against Charles de Gaulle.

However, security work was not the only activity in which Mertz became involved. Even before saving de Gaulle, Mertz had become one of France's biggest heroin smugglers, according to *Newsday*, which cites numerous French police and count records.

It is known in intelligence circles that de Gaulle often turned his back on drug smuggling, particularly if it involved people he was indebted to for their work against either the Nazis or the OAS.

One of Mertz's contacts in both heroin smuggling and the French secret service was a man named Christian David, a petty hoodlum who had escaped a French prison and later was recruited into French intelligence for use against the OAS. According to *Newsday* and other knowledgeable sources, David was one of the men involved in the 1965 murder of Moroccan opposition leader Mehdi Ben Barka. Barka was opposing Moroccan strongman General Oufkir, and French authorities wanted him out of the way.

In 1972, Barka's murder—which is still officially unsolved—was brought up when David was arrested in Brazil and charged with being a member of a smuggling ring that had imported more than one thousand pounds of heroin into the United States over a three-year period.

After his arrest in Brazil, David was extradited to the United States and sentenced to twenty years in prison for heroin smuggling. He didn't stay there long. In 1975, when the Senate Intelligence Committee began looking into the CIA's "Executive Action" program, David was ordered extradited back to France and was taken out of the country.

The committee was especially concerned with the Agency's Executive Action program because it was established for the purpose of committing assassinations. The program was part of the operational arm of the CIA's Technical Services Division and was code-named ZR/RIFLE.

Former CIA Director Richard Helms spoke at length about ZR/RIFLE to the committee. Two members of the ZR/RIFLE team were identified by Helms only by their CIA cryptonyms—WI/ROUGUE and QJ/WIN. According to evidence gathered by the committee, WI/ROUGUE was a French Corsican, a stateless soldier of fortune and a criminal. This man approached QJ/WIN and attempted to recruit him into the CIA's assassination program. Although it was never learned if this recruitment effort was successful, there is evidence that it was.

Declassified CIA notes concerning the ZR/RIFLE project state:

4. Operational assets:
(1.) Personnel: QJ/WIN is under written contract as a principal agent, with the primary task of spotting agent candidates. QJ/WIN was first contacted in [deleted by CIA], in conjunction with an illegal narcotics operation into the United States. For a period of a year and a half, he was contacted sporadically by CIS Lucien Conien [who later became chief of foreign intelligence for the Drug Enforcement Agency] on behalf of the Bureau of Narcotics. Files of this bureau reflect an excellent performance by QJ/WIN.

Helms said this about QJ/WIN: "If you needed somebody to carry out murder, I guess you had a man who might be prepared to carry it out."

Until the Senate hearings, the ZR/RIFLE program with its agents, WI/ROUGUE and QJ/WIN, were among the CIA's most closely guarded secrets. Several separate sources familiar with both intelligence operations and drug smuggling claim that WI/ROUGUE and Christian David are one and the same. This claim is further supported by David's own admission of intelligence associations and by his convenient extradition to France in 1985.

Based on the association of David and Mertz coupled with their descriptions and backgrounds, which match those of the CIA agents, it is suggestive to speculate that QJ/WIN was Michael Victor Mertz, who also used the name Jean Soutre.

It this isn't complicated enough, QJ/WIN even had a tenuous connection with Jack Ruby—in the person of Thomas Eli Davis III.

Tom Howard, Ruby's first attorney, asked his client if there were any persons the prosecution might produce who could be damaging to Ruby's defense of momentary insanity. Ruby unhesitantly came up with the name "Davis." Ruby said Davis had first approached him about using some of Ruby's strippers in pornographic movies, but that later the two had become involved in gun-running activities.

The FBI told the Warren Commission they could not locate such a person. However the CIA did—and still does—have a classified file on Thomas Eli Davis III.

Veteran newsman Seth Kantor details Ruby's connection to Davis in his book *Who Was Jack Ruby?* Born to a respectable Texas rancher couple on August 27, 1936, Davis was discharged from the Army in 1958 and attended the University of Michigan until he was asked to leave because of low grades.

In June 1958, Davis entered a Detroit bank and handed a teller a note that threatened her life if she didn't give him money. According to the teller, Davis then said, "I can't do it. I can't do it" then threw his thousand-dollar take on the floor. He fled from the bank only to be caught by police a block away. Due to his family's good reputation and his lack of a criminal record, Davis was given a five-year probated prison sentence.

While on probation, Davis obtained passport No. D236764, issued by the State Department on January 31, 1963, in New Orleans, a feat almost impossible for a convicted felon without highly placed and powerful help.

Davis's ensuing activities took him into the murky world of anti-Castro gun-running, and it was here Davis met Ruby. Ruby told his attorney that Davis had come to one of his nightclubs and that he had intended to go into the gun-running business with Davis on a regular basis. However, apparently Davis's activities were not limited to dealing with Cuban gun runners.

At the time of the Kennedy assassination, Davis was in North Africa, allegedly setting up a deal to supply arms to the OAS. Less than a month later, he was jailed in Tangiers in connection with the assassination.

His wife told authorities that her husband was a soldier of fortune who had operated in such diverse countries as Indonesia, Algeria, and Cuba, and in the months prior to his arrest they had traveled through London, Paris, and Madrid.

According to correspondence between J. Edgar Hoover and the State Department, Moroccan security police detained Davis "because of a letter in his handwriting which referred in passing to Oswald and the Kennedy assassination."

Kantor wrote that evidence showed Davis was freed from jail through the efforts of QJ/WIN, "the code name given by the CIA to an unsavory foreign agent with a network of Mafia contacts." Here could be the connection, not only between Davis and the CIA, but between Davis and Mertz (if indeed Mertz was QJ/WIN).

Through early 1963, Davis had contact with the anti-Castro Cubans, as confirmed by his wife and family. And he not only was in New Orleans during the same time as Oswald in the summer of 1963, but once admitted to reporter George Carter that he had used the name Oswald while in North Africa.

Based on similar statures, ages, and features, many researchers today believe that Davis may have posed as Oswald in the months leading up to the assassination.

Neither the Warren Commission nor the House Select Committee on Assassinations chose to investigate the Davis story. Whatever information Davis had was carried to his grave.

Former Wise County, Texas, Sheriff Eldon Moyers said that in September 1973 Davis was attempting to steal copper wire from a construction site when he cut into a 7,000-volt power line and was electrocuted.

Through his connection to QJ/WIN, Davis certainly was in the right circles to be involved in assassination attempts.

According to testimony given to the Senate Intelligence Committee, QJ/WIN's boss on the ZR/RIFLE team was the CIA's William Harvey. Harvey's specialty was anti-Castro activities in general and the attempts to assassinate Castro in particular. Harvey, of course, was in contact with Johnny Roselli and Florida Mafia chief Santos Trafficante.

A reporter from Dallas once queried the FBI about Jean Soutre and his presence in Dallas in 1963 and was told that man was not Soutre, but another Frenchman named Michel Roux, whose name just happened to coincide with one of Soutre's aliases.

However the Bureau, who could find nothing concerning Soutre/Mertz/Roux in 1964, could not offer any subtantiating documents to support their story about the Soutre namesake.

At the heart of this labyrinth of intelligence and mob intrigue is QJ/WIN, who appears to have been Michael Victor Mertz.

Soutre today has been located, working as the public-relations director for a French casino. He denied any inside knowledge of the assassination.

Soutre did suggest that Mertz, an old enemy, may have been in Dallas using his name.

Virgil Bailey, an inspector for the Immigration and Naturalization Service, has told Texas researchers he remembered being ordered to pick up a Frenchman in Dallas at the time of the assassination. Bailey complied but today cannot recall the man's name. However, Bailey described the Frenchman to researcher Gary Shaw as a man about forty-five years old with thin, graying hair.

In 1963, Soutre was about thirty-five years old and Roux was about twenty-five. Mertz, the agent connected to both intelligence and world-wide organized crime, was about forty-five years old.

The answers to questions raised by the French connection to the Kennedy assassination lie in locked files in Washington. But some assassination researchers feel the other gunman in Dealey Plaza just might have been the Frenchman known to the FBI as Michel Roux, to the French authorities as Jean Soutre, to the CIA as QJ/WIN and to the international crime syndicate as Michael Victor Mertz.

Further evidence of the French connection to the assassination came in 1988 when Los Angeles author Steve J. Rivele claimed that after several years of investigative work he had learned the names of three French gangsters who killed Kennedy. He cited one source for his information as the imprisoned Christian David. Rivele said David claimed to have been offered a contract to kill JFK by the chief of the Marseilles Mafia, Meme Guerini.

The three hitmen were Sauveur Pironti, who today still lives in Marseilles; Lucien Sarti, who was killed in Mexico in 1972; and a man named Bocognoni, who is believed to be living in Central or South America.

According to Rivele's sources, Sarti wore a police uniform and fired from behind the wooden picket fence on the Grassy Knoll. Pironti and Bocognoni reportedly fired on Kennedy from a nearby building—either the old Dal-Tex Building or perhaps the Dallas County Records Building.

Pironti, questioned by European newsmen after Rivele's book *The Murderers of John F. Kennedy* was published in France in 1988, denied any involvement. His denial was supported by French military authorities who said Pironti was serving at a sea post at the time of the assassination. However, later investigation failed to substantiate this alibi.

According to Rivele, David and another mobster, Michel Nicoli, claimed that Lee Harvey Oswald played no part in the assassination. Allegedly the three assassins—Pironti, Sarti, and Bocognoni—were hired to kill Kennedy by the French Union Corse—the European branch of the international crime syndicate—on orders from organized-crime figures in America. The trio of hitmen flew to Mexico where they were met at the Texas border by some Chicago mobsters who drove them to Dallas. After the assassination, the trio remained in a "safe house" for more than a week and then were flown out of the country.

Interestingly enough, when Rivele approached U.S. government officials with David's story, he was put in touch with Lucien Conein—the same man who was working with QJ/WIN, the shadowy CIA "asset." Conein, known in Vietnam as "Black Luigi," often bragged about his connections with the Union Corse. Conein claimed he was made an honorary member of this branch of the Sicilian Mafia after serving with Corsican partisans as an officer in the OSS and the French Foreign Legion.

It was Conein who, at the urging of Nixon aide Charles Colson, implicated President Kennedy in the assassination of Vietnam's Diem, telling newsmen that Kennedy knew in advance of the plot to overthrow Diem.

Asked to comment on the French connection to Kennedy's death, James H. Lesar, vice president of the Assassination Archives and Research Center in Washington, D.C., said: "I think that it's sufficiently serious that the Department of Justice and the U.S. Secret Service should investigate it further."

Today it appears that no such investigation has been forthcoming, the U.S. media has paid little attention to Christian David's admissions, and Rivele reportedly has gone into hiding after receiving death threats.

*　　*　　*

There is some evidence—the suspicious activities of the Agency in Mexico City; Morrow's purchaser of Mannlicher-Carcano rifles, and the ZR/RIFLE program, which may have included the French criminal Christian David, for example—that suggests a foreknowledge of the assassination within the CIA.

Even Kennedy's successor once voiced suspicion of the spy agency. According to the *Washington Post,* Marvin Watson of President Johnson's White House staff in 1967 confided to an FBI official who wrote that: "[Johnson] was now convinced there was a plot in connection with the assassination. Watson stated the President felt that CIA had something to do with this plot."

Naturally, the CIA long has maintained innocence in the assassination and the House Select Committee on Assassinations concluded that, while the Agency was "deficient in its collection and sharing of information both prior to and subsequent to the assassination," the CIA was not involved.

Many researchers today are not as certain as the House Committee. However most agree that the CIA—as a government agency—most probably did not plan or authorize Kennedy's death.

Summary

There is little question that by the time of the Bay of Pigs Invasion the Central Intelligence Agency was running out of control. It had gone far afield from the intelligence-gathering and coordinating agency envisioned when created in 1947 by President Truman.

Documented CIA abuses included the overthrow of governments, secret mind-control experiments on unsuspecting victims, and assassination plots— all wrapped in a blanket of "national security" secrecy with any information given out strictly on an individual "need-to-know" basis.

As evidenced by the Yuri Nosenko affair and the on-again, off-again anti-Castro MONGOOSE program, there appear to have been serious divisions within the CIA in the early 1960s. While some factions undoubtedly supported President Kennedy and his programs, others did not disguise their hatred of him.

The CIA had become highly compartmentalized. Often CIA employees working on one project would have no idea that people they came into contact with also were working for the Agency. And the Agency—for expediency—employed and used some very unsavory characters—such as David Ferrie.

There can be little doubt that many persons in contact with Oswald also were in contact with the CIA. These contacts, plus the abundant evidence that Oswald was involved in intelligence work, raise serious questions about who may have been maneuvering Oswald in the fall of 1963.

However, it seems highly unlikely that the CIA, as an organization, initiated the assassination of Kennedy.

What does seem possible is that persons within the CIA may have played roles in an assassination conspiracy that later compelled their superiors to cover up their activities for fear that their connection to the Agency might become public.

The possibility also exists that all of the Agency intrigues involving Oswald, Ferrie, and the Cuban exiles were only so much window dressing to draw attention away from the real assassins—French "hitmen" hired by the American mob with money and promises of protection from highly placed sources within the U.S. government.

They [the FBI] have tried the case and reached a verdict on every aspect.
—Warren Commission member Senator Richard Russell

G-Men

Anyone making a serious study of the JFK assassination must take a long hard look at the FBI and the Secret Service. The former—as we now know—monopolized the investigation of the tragedy while the latter failed to prevent it.

The contacts between accused assassin Lee Harvey Oswald and the FBI are many and troubling. No less than seven FBI agents were associated with Oswald during the year and a half between his return from Russia and the assassination.

While the Bureau has been especially sensitive about the JFK assassination, it also has been unintentionally helpful. During the past twenty years, nearly one hundred thousand pages of documents regarding the assassination have been released by the Bureau, often as the result of Freedom of Information Act suits. The occasional nuggets of information buried in the raw ore of these documents have helped piece together some of the more mysterious aspects of the case.

Increasingly the Bureau has been called to task for its handling of the JFK assassination. At least two government panels have chided the Bureau for inadequacies in its assassination investigation. The House Select Committee on Assassinations concluded that the Bureau ". . . failed to investigate the possibility of a conspiracy to assassinate the President." Likewise the Senate Intelligence Committee chastised the Bureau for shoddy work in the assassination investigation.

Ironically, it was government corruption that prompted the creation of the FBI in the first place. Just after the turn of the century, there was a growing demand in Washington to combat the "public-be-damned" attitude of the giant trusts—later to become multinational corporations—and corruption within a number of federal agencies. Such abuses were the province of the Department of Justice, which Congress had never seen fit to equip with investigators. When investigators were required, Treasury agents were called in on a temporary basis.

In 1907, Attorney General Charles J. Bonaparte, despite objections in Congress, went ahead with plans to create an investigative force, stating: ". . . a Department of Justice with no force of permanent police in any form under its control is assuredly not fully equipped for its work." With the approval of President Theodore Roosevelt, Bonaparte issued an order dated July 26, 1908, creating an investigative agency within the Justice Department.

Less than one year later, Bonaparte's successor, Attorney General George W. Wickersham, gave the new agency a permanent position and a name— the Bureau of Investigation.

But the new Bureau could only enforce federal crimes and—outside of counterfeiting—there were hardly any federal crimes at that time. The Bureau had little to do.

But in 1910, Congress, pressured by a public that was shocked and outraged by press accounts of world-wide prostitution, or "white slave" rings, unanimously passed the White Slave Traffic Act. This law became known as the Mann Act after its sponsor, Representative James Robert Mann of Illinois. The law gave federal agents authority in any case in which a woman was taken across state or national boundaries for immoral purposes.

The Mann Act was loosely written, applying to crime-minded women as well as innocent "slaves." In effect, it gave the fledgling Bureau an excuse to intervene in any case in which a woman crossed state lines.

World War I boosted the Bureau into national prominence. During 1914 and 1915 explosions, fires, and other acts of sabotage occurred at several war plants.

American public opinion slowly began shifting from neutrality to animosity toward Germany. The pace of this shift quickened in January 1917, when Germany resumed unrestricted submarine warfare on American shipping. War against the Central Powers, led by Germany, was declared by Congress on April 6 and President Woodrow Wilson ordered the Bureau to begin wartime activities.

Wisely noting that all Americans of German descent could not be interred for the duration of the war, Wilson nevertheless required more than one million "enemy aliens" to register. The Bureau, which had only three hundred agents by then, was expected to enforce this presidential edict.

The nation suddenly became aware of the danger of spies and a full-blown spy scare swept across the land—much of the suspicion directed at labor unions and anarchists.

Badly undermanned, Bureau chief A. Bruce Bielaski was agreeable to a suggestion by a Chicago advertising man that a private volunteer organization be formed to aid federal agents in national defense work. Thus was formed the American Protective League, which eventually numbered more than a quarter million members. These vigilantes carried hidden badges that identified them as "American Protective League, Secret Service Division."

The words "Secret Service" were dropped after Treasury secretary William McAdoo complained that league members were being confused with his Secret Service agents.

The league became the object of many complaints to Washington. Suspected enemy sympathizers were beaten, some were killed, and many people charged that the league was being used to intimidate labor organizations.

Smarting under criticisms of its connection with the league, the Bureau came under further attack after leading a roundup of "slackers," men who failed to register for the draft. Responding to congressional calls for action against slackers, Bureau agents had joined with local police and army units to round up more than fifty thousand men off the streets of New York and Brooklyn to check for draft registration papers in early September 1918. The offensive was roundly criticized. Senator Hiram Johnson of California told his colleagues, " . . . to humiliate 40,000 citizens, to shove them along with bayonets, to subject them to prison and summary military force, merely because they are 'suspects,' is a spectacle never before presented in the Republic."

The next year a bomb exploded at the home of the new attorney general, A. Mitchell Palmer, killing the two bombers. Palmer was incensed and immediately took action. He replaced Bureau director Bielaski with William J. Flynn, a former chief of the Secret Service. Palmer also created a General Intelligence Division under the command of his twenty-four-year-old special assistant who had come to the Bureau fresh out of the George Washington University Law School two years before—J. Edgar Hoover.

The Top G-man

No one man has held so much power for so long in the history of the United States as John Edgar Hoover.

In the 1950s, Hoover was an honors-encrusted hero, hailed as the foremost defender of American freedom and democracy. By the 1970s, he was being likened to Heinrich Himmler, Hitler's dreaded SS commander.

By the 1980s, knowledge of FBI abuses under Hoover's leadership had become widespread although the major news media—perhaps recalling the veneration it had lavished on Hoover for so long—seemed reluctant to spotlight his darker activities.

The truth of Hoover's place in the still-untold history of modern-day America lies in the man's background and motivations, about which much is still unknown to most writers and researchers.

One reason so little is known about him is that for so long everything printed about Hoover was either a product of FBI public relations or, at least, was approved by Hoover or a subordinate. Newsmen, in order to get any cooperation from the Bureau—a necessity for obtaining any information involving a federal investigation—were forced to stay on Hoover's good side. Any story criticizing the director was an excuse to place the writer on the Bureau's list of people to be ignored.

John Edgar Hoover entered the world on January 1, 1895, five years before the twentieth century began. He was the youngest of four children. Born in Washington, D.C., Hoover rarely left the city his entire life. Until her death in 1938, he lived with his mother in the family home at 413 Seward Square. Afterward he continued living there with his constant companion and the FBI's associate director, Clyde Tolson.

His father, Dickerson N. Hoover, was a minor bureaucrat who served as chief of the Coast and Geodetic Survey's printing division. His mother, Annie M. Scheitlin Hoover, was a plump housewife who faithfully instilled American middle-class virtues and Lutheran Christianity in her children.

As a schoolboy delivering groceries, young Hoover discovered the quicker he delivered, the more trips he could make, which meant more money. He soon was given the nickname "Speed." Active in athletics, Hoover was once hit in the nose by a baseball—the basis of his bulldoglike appearance. After graduating from Washington's Central High School, Hoover got a job as a clerk in the Library of Congress. At night he began attending George Washington University Law School, where he obtained his law degree in 1916 and a master of law in 1917.

With the world at war, there was frantic activity in the Department of Justice. Jobs were opening up every day.

On July 26, 1917, Hoover joined the department and was placed in the enemy alien registration section. Earning a reputation as a diligent and efficient worker, Hoover soon became an assistant to the attorney general, who placed him in charge of the General Intelligence Division. Soon after taking charge of the division, Hoover was instructed by Attorney General A. Mitchell Palmer to make a study of subversive groups within the United States. Hoover went at it with zeal.

As Hoover studied the background of Communism, he came to a studied conclusion—the teachings of Karl Marx, Friedrich Engels, and Nikolai Lenin encouraged a worldwide revolution by the workers. If this was taken literally and since the American Communist Party (actually there have been several) agreed to follow the dictates of the Soviet leadership in Russia, the Communists were guilty of advocating the violent overthrow of the United States government.

From that time onward Hoover fought an unyielding war against what he perceived as communist penetration of America.

In 1919, Hoover presented this argument with the aim of deporting several persons believed to be Communists:

> American Communists supported the Third International which was run by Soviet Communists who advocated the violent overthrow of the U.S. Government. Therefore American Communists were advocating the violent overthrow of the government and could be deported as "enemy aliens."

Two of the "enemy aliens" rounded up by Hoover's men in 1919 were the famous anarchists Alexander Beckman and Emma Goldman. Beckman had shot steel magnate Henry C. Frick during the 1892 Homestead Steel strike, blaming the industrialist for the deaths of ten workers. Goldman, a vibrant orator who is said to have influenced such notables as writers Henry Miller, George Orwell, and Edna St. Vincent Millay, was Beckman's lover. Furthermore, Leon Czolgosz, the assassin of President William McKinley, stated he had been greatly influenced by Goldman's talks. Beckman and Goldman, along with many Russian immigrants who had not applied for citizenship, were shipped to Russia aboard a ship dubbed "the Soviet Ark" in December 1919.

Their exile marked the beginning of the famous "Palmer raids," in which the legal cases were prepared by Hoover. Early in 1920, at the orders of Attorney General Palmer, the Bureau launched a series of raids on Communist meeting places in thirty-three cities, rounding up more than twenty-five hundred aliens. These raids drew both praise and condemnation. U.S. District Court Judge George W. Anderson, hearing one of these cases, stated:

> . . . [the Communist Party's] whole scheme is for propaganda by words, not by deeds. No weapons of the cutting or exploding kind, with which . . . revolutions are carried on, were found in this raid. There is therefore not a scintilla of evidence warranting a finding that the Communists are committed to the "overthrow of the Government of the United States by violence" . . . it is notorious that political platforms generally adopt the language of exaggeration. . . . Here . . . freedom and a saving sense of humor and of proportion, have, until recently, saved us from being frightened by crusaders' rhetoric.

However in another federal court, U.S. District Judge John C. Knox saw things quite differently, stating:

> I am of the opinion that the manifesto and program of the Communist Party, together with other exhibits in the case, are of such character as to easily lead a reasonable man to conclude that the purpose of the Communist Party is to accomplish its end, namely, the capture and destruction of the State as now constituted by force and violence . . .

These opposite views of two judges looking at the same evidence is indicative of the split in American opinion over the danger presented by communists. It is a divergence of opinion that persists today.

Whether there was a real danger or not, the Palmer raids drove the American Communist Party underground and reduced its membership from an estimated sixty thousand to a hard core of about ten thousand.

Through the years, Hoover continually used the communist threat to great personal advantage, even to putting his name on a popular book, *Masters of Deceit,* which helped fan the fires of the 1950s communist scare.

Was there any real threat from American Communists? In his resignation letter to Hoover, William C. Sullivan, at one time third-ranking official at the FBI, wrote:

> In the mid-Forties when the membership of the Party was about 80,000 and it had many front organizations, you publicized this widely month in and month out. In fact it was far too widely publicized to the point where you caused a Communist scare in the nation which was entirely unwarranted . . . I am just as opposed to Communism as you but I knew then and I know now that it was not the danger you claimed it was and that it never warranted the huge amounts of the taxpayer's dollars spent upon it . . . What happened when the Communist Party went into a rapid decline? You kept the scare campaign going just the same for some years. However, when the membership figures kept dropping lower and lower you instructed us not to give them to the public any more and not even to the Justice Department . . . At the time of my leaving the Bureau [1971] . . . the membership figures of the Communist Party are down to an amazing 2,800 in a nation of over 200 million people and you still conceal this from the people.

It has been said that of the small number of members of the Communist Party in those days, almost half were FBI informers.

But Hoover never let the facts stand in the way of his campaign to eradicate communism, even if it meant neglecting one of the true menaces to America—organized crime.

In the forty-eight years that Hoover controlled the United States' only national police organization, he served eight presidents and outlasted more than a dozen attorneys general.

Organized-crime investigator Peter Maas has reported that prior to Robert Kennedy becoming attorney general, only four FBI agents in the New York office were assigned to organized crime and those were kept busy with in-office "bookkeeping" duties. Yet about four hundred agents were on the streets of the city searching out communists.

As late as January 1962, Hoover was on record as saying: "No single individual or coalition of racketeers dominates organized crime across the nation." As with the communist threat, Hoover was not telling the truth.

Shortly after the aborted mob conference at Apalachin in 1957, Sullivan and other top FBI officials prepared a monograph on the Mafia that was sent to the top twenty-five government officials concerned with law enforcement. Learning of this, an angry Hoover recalled all twenty-five copies and had them destroyed. He denounced the monograph as "baloney" and this report on organized crime was never heard of again.

It was not until Mafia thug Joe Valachi was brought to Washington by Attorney General Robert Kennedy's Justice Department for testimony before a Senate committee that Hoover was grudgingly forced to admit to the existence of an organized-crime structure in this nation.

Why did Hoover act like there was no such thing as the Mafia when there was so much evidence to the contrary?

In his book *The Bureau,* Sullivan wrote:

> [Hoover] didn't want to tackle organized crime. He preferred his agents to spend their time on quick, easy cases—he wanted results, predictable results which produced the statistics Hoover thrived on. . . . Investigating the Mafia promised to be more difficult than rounding up juvenile auto thieves. Organized crime is far more complicated: the Mafia runs legitimate businesses as a front for their illegal operations. Mafioso are rich and can afford the best lawyers, while we have to use government lawyers, some of whom are excellent, some of whom aren't worth a damn. And the Mafia is powerful, so powerful that entire police forces and even a mayor's office can be under Mafia control. That's why Hoover was afraid to let us tackle it. He was afraid we'd show up poorly.

There were also other considerations. Hoover was well known for his ingratiating attitude toward Washington politicians. The more powerful the politician, the more Hoover tried to befriend him.

Of one thing there is certainty—by the time of World War II, the vast power of the FBI was centered solely in J. Edgar Hoover.

But if blame has to be laid for this situation, it may, as argued by Tom Wicker, associate editor of *The New York Times,* be laid on the American public. Wicker wrote:

> . . . the public—gulled, it is true by the Bureau's incessant propaganda —until recent years loved it all; and what considerable percentage of voters Washington believed were still devoted to J. Edgar Hoover at his death was suggested by the President's funeral oration and by Congress's decision that his body should lie in state, where Lincoln and Kennedy had lain. There was little or no outcry when the Director, guardian of liberty, spoke up for Joe McCarthy, called Martin Luther King a liar and for years singlehandedly held up congressional passage of a consular treaty with the Soviet Union. There was always a radio audience for "The FBI in Peace and War" and the G-man movies to which the Director invariably lent "technical assistance" and his seal of approval—as long as they pictured his men on the side of the angels. For decades, his turgid and moralistic articles appeared with the regularity of the seasons in "Reader's Digest" and "American" magazines, and publishers took turns presenting his self-aggrandizing books to the

waiting public. If J. Edgar Hoover passed eventually beyond the normal restraints of office, the American public seemed to view this process happily, and with a sense of gratitude.

*   *   *

But if Hoover's reputation grew overlarge in later years, it certainly had no such problem back in the 1920s. Public criticism had arisen over the Palmer raids. Federal agents were charged with unconstitutional searches and seizures, individual rights violations, and even using agents provocateur.

One federal judge, after hearing testimony of warrantless arrests and prisoners being held incommunicado, declared: "It may . . . be observed that a mob is a mob, whether made up of government officials acting under instructions from the Department of Justice, or of criminals, loafers, and the vicious classes."

Later a Senate committee looked into the raids, but divided on its views of the operation and no consensus was reached. It was the first—and last—congressional investigation of the FBI.

Fresh from the complaints over the Palmer raids, morale in the Justice Department went from bad to worse.

In an effort to demonstrate leadership in this moral crisis, newly elected President Calvin Coolidge appointed Harlan Fiske Stone, a former dean of the Columbia University Law School, attorney general.

Soon after taking control of what had become known as the "Department of Easy Virtue," Stone named twenty-nine-year-old Hoover acting director of the Bureau. Hoover moved rapidly to restore respect for the Bureau, which was in real danger of being disbanded due to the years of problems and criticism. His actions produced immediate results. Asked if one of his agents would investigate the activities of a senator's son, Hoover replied: "This Bureau cannot be used for partisan purposes."

Backed solidly by Stone, Hoover completely rebuilt the image of the Bureau of Investigation. And on December 10, 1924, Stone made Hoover director. Stone later told a friend:

> I took the responsibility of appointing Mr. Hoover . . . although many people thought that Mr. Hoover was too young a man and had been in too close contact with the Burns regime to be given the post. I thought I knew my man and the event has proved that I was right. . . . Mr. Hoover has steadily built up the Bureau . . .

Over the next fifteen years, Hoover was to move the Bureau from a few hundred unarmed investigators to a full-fledged national police agency. And all the while, he kept an eye open for favorable public relations opportunities.

By the early 1930s, Prohibition had propelled crime into the national spotlight and Hoover was there to share the glory. During the heyday of

Bonnie and Clyde and the Ma Barker Gang, hardly a day passed that Hoover wasn't being quoted in the nation's press. His legend grew.

In the early 1930s Hoover, a staunch Republican, was very cautious about his moves within Franklin Roosevelt's Democratic administration.

By 1933, kidnapping was added to the list of crimes under the jurisdiction of the FBI due to the famous abduction of Charles Lindbergh's infant son. This list grew longer the next year, with the addition of killing or assaulting a federal officer, fleeing across state lines, and extortion involving interstate commerce.

By 1935, Bureau agents were given the power to go beyond investigation. They were allowed to serve warrants and subpoenas, to make seizures and arrests, and to carry arms. The Bureau had become the very thing that Hoover had often spoken against—a national police force. Also that year, the word *Federal* was added to the Bureau's name, and soon the initials FBI were well-known all over the world.

By the beginning of World War II, the FBI boasted an Identification Division with thousands of fingerprint records, a complete and up-to-date laboratory, and a National Police Academy for training state and local law-enforcement officers.

Even today it is considered the peak of a lawman's career to be selected for training at the FBI Academy at Quantico, Virginia. And Hoover made use of this too. According to former Assistant Director Sullivan:

> . . . Hoover felt that the alumni of the FBI training course were his men. Thanks to this network of FBI-trained police officers, we had a private and frequently helpful line to most city and state police organizations throughout the country.

Hoover also used the FBI Academy against perceived enemies. On the day of the JFK assassination, a shocked Dallas FBI agent named James Hosty told Dallas police lieutenant Jack Revill that Lee Harvey Oswald was a Communist known to the FBI, and that the Bureau had information that Oswald was capable of committing the assassination. Since all government agencies were saying they had no knowledge of Oswald, this story was a bombshell.

As a result of this conversation, Dallas police chief Jesse Curry told TV newsmen that the FBI was aware of Oswald but had not informed the Dallas police. When challenged to prove his charge by the head of the Dallas FBI office, Curry qualified his statement by saying he had no personal knowledge of the issue. But the damage had been done.

Until Curry's retirement in 1966, Hoover conducted a vendetta against the Dallas police, according to FBI documents released in 1980. The documents show that under orders from Hoover, FBI officials were prohibited from conducting training courses for Dallas police, and policemen from that city were not invited to attend the FBI Academy.

Furthermore, Curry resigned as chief in February of 1966, less than a month after Dallas mayor Erik Jonsson had visited Hoover in Washington. After hearing Hoover's complaints against Curry, Jonsson told the petulant director he would "immediately instruct the city manager to have a stern talk" with the police chief.

Hoover did not gain such immense power overnight. After turning his Bureau into an anticrime force, he began to look into other areas.

Beginning with secret meetings between President Roosevelt and Hoover in the summer of 1936, the Bureau began moving quietly into the areas of intelligence gathering. It was all explained in a "Strictly Confidential" staff memorandum written by Hoover:

> In talking with the Attorney General today concerning the radical situation, I informed him of the conference I had with the President on September 1, 1936, at which time the Secretary of State [Cordell Hull] was present, and at which time the Secretary of State, at the President's suggestion, requested of me, the representative of the Department of Justice, to have an investigation made of the subversive activities in this country, including Communism and fascism. I transmitted this request to the Attorney General, and the Attorney General verbally directed me to proceed with the investigation and to coordinate, as the President suggested, information upon these matters in the possession of the Military Intelligence Division, the Naval Intelligence Division, and the State Department. This, therefore, is the authority upon which to proceed in the conduct of this investigation, which should, of course, be handled in a most discreet and confidential manner.

This new authority marked the beginning of this nation's multiagency intelligence establishment and marked a period of extraordinary growth for the Bureau. The FBI, which boasted only 391 agents in 1933, counted nearly 5,000 by the end of the war.

In 1939, on the eve of World War II, the Bureau was directed to investigate espionage, sabotage, and violations of neutrality regulations. It also handled draft evaders and the apprehension of enemy aliens.

It should be noted that Hoover was one of the few government officials who opposed the relocation and incarceration of Japanese Americans as a violation of their civil rights.

During the war, the FBI was called upon to gather intelligence on activities detrimental to U.S. interests in South America. And while this activity was ordered terminated with the creation of the Central Intelligence Agency in 1947, the FBI still retains a large office in Mexico City.

Also during the war, Hoover's path crossed that of a young Naval intelligence officer with unexpected and long-term repercussions. The FBI had been snooping after a suspected Nazi agent, a beautiful woman named Inga Arvad who had attended the wedding of Germany's Field Marshal

Hermann Goering and met with Adolf Hitler. A former Miss Denmark, she had no trouble attracting young men in wartime Washington. One of these men was Naval Ensign John F. Kennedy.

Hoover's FBI wiretapped an apartment shared by Kennedy and "Inga binga," as he called his paramour, and picked up the sounds of sexual play. They also picked up a few remarks by Kennedy concerning sensitive security matters. After both the Navy and his father had been alerted to the danger presented by Kennedy's involvement with a suspected agent, young Kennedy was quickly transferred to the South Pacific. It was there, of course, that Kennedy led the survivors of PT-109 back to safety, thus becoming a war hero and helping to launch his political career—all thanks to the diligent J. Edgar Hoover. It could thus be argued—with great irony—that it was Hoover who actually set young Kennedy on the course that ended in Dallas.

After World War II, FBI intelligence activities actually increased, thanks to the anticommunist hysteria of the cold war years.

In fact it was the FBI that launched Senator Joseph McCarthy on his ill-fated anticommunist crusade. In 1950, a one-hundred-page FBI document alleging Communist infiltration of the U.S. government was leaked to a military intelligence officer with instructions to pass it along to the Jewish American League Against Communism. The League offered the document to McCarthy, who was further encouraged to fight communism by Father Edmund A. Walsh, vice president of Georgetown University and an anticommunist author.

A top McCarthy assistant, Roy Cohn, later said: "Joe McCarthy bought Communism in much the same way other people purchase a new automobile."

Assistant FBI Director Sullivan wrote: "We gave McCarthy all we had, but all we had were fragments, nothing could prove his allegations."

While Hoover always claimed that information collected by the Bureau was never to be released to unauthorized persons, it was a rule that he bent for friends.

In 1948, when New York Governor Thomas Dewey ran for president, Hoover secretly agreed to put the resources of the Bureau at his disposal, hoping that he would be made attorney general upon Dewey's election.

In 1954 Attorney General Herbert Brownell used FBI material to chide the Truman administration about a questionable employee. That same year Vice President Richard Nixon was able to obtain information in FBI files to use in his attack against Representative Robert L. Condon of California.

It is well known now that Hoover deliberately leaked derogatory material on Dr. Martin Luther King during the 1960s as a part of his secret counterintelligence (COINTELPRO) program.

It was this ability, first to gather information and then to control it, that gave Hoover his extraordinary power. Former Assistant FBI Director Sullivan wrote:

Hoover was always gathering damaging material on Jack Kennedy, which the President, with his active social life, seemed more than willing to provide. We never put any technical surveillance on JFK, but whatever came up was automatically funneled directly to Hoover. I was sure he was saving everything he had on Kennedy, and on Martin Luther King, Jr., too, until he could unload it all and destroy them both. He kept this kind of explosive material in his personal files, which filled four rooms on the fifth floor of headquarters.

Perhaps the presence of these files, which still held information on Kennedy and Inga Arvad, explains why the reappointment of Hoover was one of JFK's first actions on becoming president.

It has been reported that Hoover's Personal and Confidential files were destroyed soon after his death by Tolson and Hoover's faithful secretary Helen Gandy.

Hoover's reappointment by Kennedy certainly wasn't due to Hoover's politics. A Republican who liked to boast that he had never voted, Hoover had quietly helped Nixon as much as possible during the 1960 campaign. According to Sullivan, Hoover did his best to keep the news media supplied with anti-Kennedy stories.

Hoover's methods of ingratiating himself both to presidents and attorneys general he served have been well documented. He would send them letters marked "Top Secret, Eyes Only" filled with juicy tidbits of gossip about congressmen and political enemies. Most presidents disdained this practice, but two—Lyndon B. Johnson and Richard Nixon—seemed to enjoy this unusual channel of information.

Nixon and Hoover were GOP Allies from the days when Nixon was a representative from California. Sullivan wrote: "I spent many days preparing material based on research taken from FBI files that I knew was going straight from Hoover to Congressman Nixon, material which Nixon used in speeches, articles and investigations."

Nixon had been rejected as an FBI agent in 1937—he was told later by Hoover that the Bureau wasn't hiring at the time, but the agent who rejected him reported that Nixon was "lacking in aggression." Despite this, Nixon and Hoover remained close friends. Hoover was a regular dinner guest at the Nixon White House in later years.

In White House tapes transcripts made during the Watergate era, Nixon said: "Edgar Hoover . . . I have seen socially at least a hundred times. He and I were very close friends . . . [expletive deleted]—Hoover was my crony. He was closer to me than [Lyndon] Johnson actually, although Johnson used him more." Later in the same conversation, Nixon laments that Hoover's 1972 death prevented the director from aiding his Watergate defense. He said: "Well, Hoover performed. He would have fought. That was the point. He would have defied a few people. He would have scared them to death. He has a file on everybody."

Lyndon Johnson had no such problem. With Hoover very much alive during his presidency, Johnson had a strong right-hand man. According to Sullivan, Johnson—worried that Robert Kennedy might make a grab for the Democratic presidential nomination in 1964—asked Hoover for a special security team of FBI men, headed by Cartha D. DeLoach. Sullivan wrote:

> Ostensibly, the agents would be there to guard against threats to the President, but this security force was actually a surveillance team, a continuation of the FBI's surveillance on Martin Luther King in Atlantic City. By keeping track of King, LBJ could also keep track of RFK.

Johnson and Hoover had much in common, according to Sullivan. He wrote:

> Johnson and Hoover had their mutual fear and hatred of the Kennedys in common—and more. As neighbors in Washington since the days when Johnson was a senator from Texas, they had been frequent dinner guests in each other's homes.

The Hoover-Johnson friendship dated back to 1945 when young Senator Johnson and his family moved onto the same block of Washington's Thirtieth Place where Hoover lived. In later years Hoover relished telling how he helped raise the two Johnson daughters and how he would help Johnson hunt for the family dog. The nearly two decades of closeness between Johnson and Hoover led Johnson's last attorney general, Ramsey Clark, to comment that their friendship "almost disqualified" Johnson from being able to properly supervise the dour Bureau director.

Hoover biographer Richard Gid Powers said Johnson would telephone Hoover regularly to chat about the issues of the day and noted that Johnson's diary listed some sixty such conversations during the Johnson administration.

Johnson cemented his friendship—and perhaps his power—over Hoover in January 1964, less than two months after Kennedy's assassination. In a ceremony conducted in the White House Rose Garden, Johnson praised his friend Hoover as "a hero to millions of decent citizens, and an anathema to evil men."

After noting Hoover's accomplishments through the years, Johnson said:

> Edgar, the law says that you must retire next January when you reach your 70th birthday, and I know you wouldn't want to break the law. But the nation cannot afford to lose you. Therefore, by virtue of and pursuant to the authority vested in the President, I have today signed an Executive Order exempting you from compulsory retirement for an indefinite period of time.

It was tantamount to installing Hoover as FBI director for life since it would have required a subsequent executive order to rescind this action.

This extraordinary action coupled with the timing—with both the Warren Commission and the FBI's assassination investigation just getting into full swing—has led more suspicious assassination researchers to suspect that this presidential exemption was a partial payment to Hoover for his lack of a penetrating probe of Kennedy's death.

Shortly after this event, Hoover replaced Courtney Evans as the Bureau's White House liaison man with Cartha DeLoach, who had been quite intimate with Johnson since his early days in the Senate. DeLoach figured prominently in the assassination investigation and revealed in the 1970s that Johnson had begun to suspect that the CIA may have had something to do with Kennedy's death.

According to Sullivan, once Johnson assumed the powers of the presidency, his relationship with the trusty Hoover began to change. He wrote:

> They remained close when Johnson served as Vice President, but there was a change in their relationship when Johnson became President. The Director was over 65 by that time, past retirement age for federal employees, and he stayed in office only because of a special waiver which required the President's signature each year. That waiver put Hoover right in Johnson's pocket. With that leverage, Johnson began to take advantage of Hoover, using the Bureau as his personal investigative arm. His never-ending requests were usually political, and sometimes illegal . . . And Hoover hot-footed it to Johnson's demands . . . he found himself very much in the back seat, almost a captive of the President . . .

There is also the possibility that Hoover actually liked and respected the lanky Texas politician. Speaking to newspaper editors in 1965, Hoover said: "Texans [like Johnson] don't like to be told what to do. This is characteristic of Texans. They are a separate breed of man. I admire the intelligence and fearlessness of a man of that kind."

In addressing the relationship between Hoover and Johnson, author Richard Gid Powers stated: "Because of the extraordinary rapport between them, there was no service Hoover would refuse Johnson, no matter how far removed it might be from his law enforcement or domestic intelligence responsibilities."

Some researchers have darkly hinted that LBJ may have had more leverage on Hoover than simply securing his job as director—that it may have had something to do with the JFK assassination.

There can be no doubt that Hoover had an abiding and intense hatred for both John and Robert Kennedy, because of their politics, their associates, their personal lives, and their style. Sullivan recalled hearing Clyde Tolson, Hoover's associate director, confidant, and roommate, once say: "Goddamn the Kennedys. First there was Jack, now there is Bobby, and then Teddy. We'll have them on our necks until the year 2000.'' Hoover reportedly nodded in agreement.

This hatred for the Kennedys makes the Bureau's numerous contacts with Lee Harvey Oswald all the more suspicious. The FBI was involved with Oswald from the time he went to Russia. Recall Hoover's 1960 memo to the State Department warning ''. . . there is a possibility that an impostor is using Oswald's birth certificate.'' Very much aware of Oswald and even suspecting that someone may have been posing as the ex-Marine, the FBI attempted to keep tabs on Oswald after his attempted defection to Russia.

On April 27, 1960, John W. Fain, a resident FBI agent in Fort Worth, interviewed Robert Oswald concerning his brother's activities in the Soviet Union. The older Oswald said his whole family was shocked at his brother's behavior and that Lee had never had any sympathy for or connection with communism before his trip to Russia. Fain also interviewed Marguerite Oswald the next day concerning a twenty-five-dollar money order she tried to send to her son.

Apparently the FBI was not the only U.S. agency with an active interest in Oswald. On July 3, 1961, more than a year before Oswald arrived back home from Russia, Fain prepared another report on Oswald. This report is rich in detail of Oswald's life history as well as his activities in the Soviet Union. According to this document, much of the information on Oswald came from the district office of the Office of Naval Intelligence in New Orleans.

Armed with this Naval Intelligence information, Fain and FBI Special Agent Tom Carter requested a meeting with Oswald at the Fort Worth FBI office on June 25, 1962, less than two weeks after the Oswalds arrived back in Fort Worth from Russia. According to their report, Oswald told of flying home with Marina and their child, but he failed to mention the stopover in Atlanta. He also told of borrowing $435 to get home, but he declined to talk about why he went to Russia, saying only that he didn't want to relive the past.

The agents said Oswald ''exhibited an impatient and arrogant attitude'' during the interview. He also denied that he had attempted to renounce his American citizenship and that he had offered the Russians any military information.

Interestingly, Oswald did tell the FBI agents that ''in the event he is contacted by Soviet Intelligence under suspicious circumstances or otherwise, he will promptly communicate with the FBI.''

Could this agreement have been the beginning of a special relationship between Oswald and the Bureau?

Oswald's next recorded contact with the Bureau was on August 16, 1962, when Fain and Special Agent Arnold Brown approached him near his home at 2703 Mercedes Street in Fort Worth, where he and Marina had lived for about a month. Believing that Oswald had been ''evasive'' during his first interview, Fain had decided to contact him again, only this time the agents sat with Oswald in a parked car near his home. Fain explained that they didn't want to embarrass Oswald in front of his wife, so they declined his offer to come into the house.

The more suspicious researchers view this unusual meeting in a car as a time when the FBI may have begun to recruit Oswald as an informant. But according to the agents, Oswald once again denied any misconduct in Russia, denied that he had tried to defect, and denied that any Soviet intelligence personnel had ever tried to contact him or offer any ''deals.'' Once again, Oswald agreed to contact the FBI if anyone connected with Soviet intelligence tried to meet with him.

After satisfying themselves that Oswald was not a member of the American Communist Party, Fain and Brown marked the Oswald file ''closed.'' Fain retired from the Bureau on October 29, 1962.

However, that was not to be the last contact between Oswald and the Bureau. After arriving in New Orleans in the spring of 1963, Oswald became the object of yet another security investigation by the FBI. This time the special agent in charge of Oswald's file was Milton R. Kaack, who prepared a detailed report dated October 31, 1963, on Oswald, his background, and his New Orleans activities.

But the strangest contact between Oswald and the Bureau came on August 10, 1963, the day after his arrest for disturbing the peace while handing out Fair Play for Cuba Committee leaflets on a New Orleans street corner.

It seems utterly outlandish that a man who had tried to defect to Russia and was a self-confessed pro-Marxist should request to see an FBI agent after being arrested in connection with pro-Castro activities—but that is exactly what Oswald did. This contact with the FBI, initiated by Oswald, has caused many people—not the least of whom were Warren Commission members—to speculate on whether Oswald might indeed have been acting as an informant for the FBI.

Did Oswald Work for the FBI?

Traces of intelligence work appear in the activities of Lee Harvey Oswald while in the Marines and in Russia.

If Oswald indeed participated in spy work, particularly for the United States, it was most likely known to the FBI. And what better prospect to recruit as an informant than an experienced American agent with a procommunist background or ''cover''?

The day after Oswald's arrest in New Orleans for disturbing the peace was a Saturday, hardly a time for a quick FBI response to the request of a police prisoner jailed for a minor infraction. Yet Special Agent John

Quigley soon arrived at the New Orleans police station and met with Oswald for an hour and a half.

The five-page report of that meeting written by Quigley reads like a comprehensive report on the Fair Play for Cuba Committee. Oswald gave the agent background information on himself, then detailed his activities since coming to New Orleans, including his attempt to form a Fair Play for Cuba Committee chapter and the squabble between Oswald and anti-Castro Cubans.

Quigley, who told the Warren Commission had had never heard of Oswald until that Saturday, had a faulty memory. He later admitted that on April 18, 1961, he had reviewed Oswald's Navy file at the nearby U.S. Naval Air Station in Algiers, Louisiana, at the request of the Dallas FBI office.

Quigley could give the commission no reason why Oswald had wanted to see an FBI agent in 1963, but an FBI document released in 1977 may give a clue. There Quigley reports being contacted by a New Orleans police intelligence officer who "said that Oswald was desirous of seeing an agent and supplying to him information with regard to his activities with the FPCC in New Orleans." Again this statement, along with the detailed description Oswald gave of his activities, seems to indicate that Oswald was trying to make some sort of report. In this "report," Oswald continually mentions the fictitious head of the New Orleans FPCC, A. J. Hidell, saying that he had talked with him several times by telephone but had never met him. Asked for Hidell's number, Oswald said he couldn't remember it.

In all, at least ten FBI agents filed affidavits with the Warren Commission stating unequivocally that Lee Harvey Oswald was never an informant for the Bureau. Could they have said the same for "Harvey Lee Oswald," or "A. J. Hidell"? During his Warren Commission testimony, Quigley made an odd slip of the tongue, referring to Oswald as "Harvey Lee Oswald" until corrected by Assistant Counsel Samuel Stern. It is well known that FBI informants, and even agents themselves, often use code, or cover names.

It is interesting to note that J. Gordon Shanklin and Kyle G. Clark, the FBI supervisors in the Dallas office, only mentioned the fact that no payment was made to Oswald for information in their affidavits. They did not specifically deny knowledge of Oswald as an informant, as had the other agents in their affidavits.

Other circumstances of Oswald's New Orleans stay also indicate the possibility of a relationship with the FBI. In 1975, a New Orleans bar owner, Orest Pena, claimed to have seen Oswald in his Habana Bar in the company of both Cubans and FBI Agent Warren De Brueys.

Pena, himself an FBI informant and a Cuban exile associated with the CIA-backed Cuban Revolutionary Council, said he remembered Oswald as a man who came into his bar with a Cuban and ordered a lemonade, then vomited it up. He said he saw Oswald together with De Brueys and other "government agents" on several occasions.

Pena also said about ten days before he was to testify before the Warren Commission, De Brueys threatened him, saying: "If you ever talk anything about me, I will get rid—I'll get rid of your ass."

Pena added that Commission staff counsel Wesley J. Liebeler did not let him speak freely, so he decided to keep his mouth shut.

Agent De Brueys denied both allegations and the House Select Committee on Assassinations chose to believe him.

Then there is the strange story of William S. Walter, who served as a security clerk for the New Orleans FBI office in 1963. Like CIA paymaster James Wilcott, Walter was a minor functionary who claims to have seen the wrong things. When he tried to tell what he knew, he found himself facing an official stone wall. Testifying to the House Select Committee on Assassinations, Walter said he was on duty the day that Quigley interviewed Oswald in the New Orleans Police Station. He said, in response to Quigley's request for a file check on Oswald that day, he found that the New Orleans FBI office maintained both a security and an informant file on Oswald. However, Quigley told the Committee that there was no informant file on Oswald, only the security file.

Walter's story apparently was echoed by Dallas FBI agent Will Hayden Griffin. According to a 1964 FBI memorandum, Griffin reportedly told people that Oswald was definitely an FBI informant and that files in Washington would prove it. Griffin later denied making any such comment.

But Walter had other information for the committee. He claimed that while serving night duty in the FBI office on November 17, 1963, the New Orleans FBI office received a teletype from FBI headquarters warning against a possible assassination attempt on Kennedy during the coming trip to Dallas on November 22. Walter said he was alone in the New Orleans FBI office in the early morning hours when the teletype came through. He said it was headed "urgent," marked to the attention of all special agents, and signed "Director."

The thrust of the teletype was that the Bureau had received information that a "militant revolutionary group" might attempt to assassinate Kennedy on his proposed trip to Dallas. It went on to say that all receiving offices should "immediately contact all CI's [Criminal Informants], PCI's [Potential Criminal Informants], local racial and hate-group informants and determine if any basis for threat. Bureau should be kept advised of all developments by teletype."

Walter said he telephoned the special-agent-in-charge, Harry Maynard, who ordered Walter to call special agents with CIs and PCIs. Walter said he did this, writing the names of five agents contacted on the face of the teletype. By 8 A.M., Maynard had arrived for work and Walter went home.

Five days later, on November 22, 1963, Walter said he was in a barber shop when he heard about Kennedy's assassination. Rushing back to the

FBI office, he showed the teletype to various agents and asked, "How could this have happened? We had five days notice!" Later that day, Walter said he typed a copy of the teletype and wrote the five agents' names on the copy, which he took home.

Walter said soon after the assassination, Director Hoover ordered all agents in the New Orleans office who had written reports dealing with the case to review those reports. The object was to make sure there was nothing in them that might "embarrass the Bureau." Originals of the reports were to be destroyed.

Checking the relevant file later, Walter discovered the teletype was missing. In 1975, Walter told his story and showed his copy of the teletype to Senator Richard Schweiker. Later the House Select Committee on Assassinations looked into the matter. The Committee checked with New Orleans agents, supervisor Maynard and even Walter's ex-wife, who also worked for the FBI. All claimed to know nothing about a teletype. The Committee, declaring that it "declined to believe that that many employees of the FBI would have remained silent for such a long time," concluded that Walter's story was "unfounded."

Unfounded or not, there were other stories in New Orleans that were even harder to dismiss—take, for example, Adrian Thomas Alba, operator of the Crescent City Garage. The Crescent City Garage was located next door to the William Reilly Coffee Company, Oswald's employer while in New Orleans. Alba, a quiet man who has not sought publicity, was both operator and part owner of the garage. Alba said the garage had a contract to maintain a number of cars for the nearby Secret Service and FBI offices.

Alba said Oswald made frequent visits to his garage during the summer of 1963 and he got to know the ex-Marine quite well. They talked about firearms and Alba would loan Oswald his gun magazines. He claimed to have helped Oswald fix a sling on his Mannlicher-Carcano rifle.

But Alba's best story concerns a visit in early summer 1963. He said a man he believed to be an "FBI agent visiting New Orleans from Washington" came to his garage and took a green Studebaker from the car pool, after showing his credentials. The next day Alba said he saw the same car parked by Oswald's work place about thirty yards away. According to Alba:

> Lee Oswald went across the sidewalk. He bent down as if to look in the window and was handed what appeared to be a good-sized white envelope. He turned and bent as if to hold the envelope to his abdomen, and I think he put it under his shirt. Oswald went back into the building and the car drove off.

Years later, Alba said he saw the same thing happen the next day, but was farther away and could not see what was passed to Oswald. He said he did not tell the Warren Commission about these incidents because he did not recall them until 1970 when he was reminded of them by a TV commercial depicting a man running to and from a taxi.

The House Select Committee on Assassinations checked garage records and found that two Studebakers had been signed out during that time in 1963, but by Secret Service agents.

Alba recalled seeing Oswald after he was fired from the coffee company allegedly for malingering. Alba said Oswald seemed pleased with the turn of events and said he expected to soon be working at the National Aeronautics and Space Administration (NASA) plant near New Orleans. Alba quoted Oswald as saying: "I have found my pot of gold at the end of the rainbow." Of course, this was not to be. Oswald's destiny lay in Dallas.

But oddly enough, five Reilly Coffee employees, all of whom were in contact with Oswald, did join the NASA facility shortly after Oswald's departure. Former New Orleans district attorney Jim Garrison came across these intriguing employment shifts during his ill-fated JFK assassination probe. Oswald left the coffee company on July 19, 1963, just a few weeks before he began his public show of handing out FPCC material. According to Garrison, Alfred Claude, the man who hired Oswald at Reilly, went to work for Chrysler Aerospace Division located at NASA's New Orleans facility. Emmett Barbee, Oswald's immediate superior at Reilly, followed Claude to the NASA center in a few days. And within a few weeks they were joined by John D. Branyon and Dante Marachini, both of whom worked with Oswald. Branyon and Marachini also began aerospace careers at the New Orleans NASA center. Marachini, who had gone to work for Reilly the same day as Oswald, also was a friend of CIA-Mafia agent David Ferrie.

To compound these oddities, Garrison found that two of Ferrie's friends also went to work for the NASA center about this same time. James Lewallen, a friend of Ferrie who lived in the same apartment house as Marachini, went to work for Boeing, located in the NASA complex. Melvin Coffee, who had accompanied Ferrie on his strange Texas odyssey the night of the assassination, was hired by NASA at Cape Kennedy.

Was all this coincidence or was there some connecting link between these occurrences? Garrison claimed these men were lured into government-connected jobs so as to make them unavailable during the subsequent assassination investigation. And in fact, none of these men were called to testify before the Warren Commission. Garrison wrote in *Heritage of Stone*:

> The fact that these transfers were being made not in direct support of the assassination, but looking far beyond that, in order to complicate further investigations which might afterward occur, serves to give some idea of the scope and professional nature of the entire operation.

Other Dallas FBI agents swore under oath that Oswald was never an FBI informant. However, the truthfulness of their statements has come under severe question in light of the saga of FBI agent James P. Hosty, Jr. Hosty, who worked in the Dallas FBI office, was assigned to check on Oswald prior to the assassination. Although Hosty claims to never have met Oswald in person, his name, address, telephone number, and car license number appeared in Oswald's personal notebook—a fact omitted from a December 23, 1963, FBI report to the Warren Commission.

In testimony to the Commission, Director Hoover explained that the omission was due to the fact that the report was not originally intended for the Commission. He said that the information on Hosty in Oswald's notebook was presented to the Commission in a February 11, 1964, report. Of course, by that time, the Commission was already very much aware of the connection between Hosty and Oswald.

Hoover also explained that it was not unusual for agents to leave their name, address, and telephone number for persons they were attempting to contact. He said Oswald's wife Marina probably jotted down Hosty's license number for her husband. Hosty, however, claimed he had parked his car some distance from the house where Marina was staying to avoid drawing attention to his visit.

On January 22, 1964, Texas attorney general Waggoner Carr called Warren Commission general counsel J. Lee Rankin to report that he had information that Oswald had been recruited as an informant for the FBI in September 1962. He further stated that Oswald was being paid two hundred dollars a month and assigned Informant Number S-179. Carr cited Dallas district attorney Henry Wade, a former FBI man, as the source of this information.

Carr's call prompted a special executive session of the Warren Commission that same day. The minutes of that meeting were classified "Top Secret" until March 1975. At this meeting Commissioners were tense. What could they do with this report that Oswald, already designated as JFK's assassin, was working for the FBI?

Commission general counsel J. Lee Rankin said:

. . . When the Chief Justice and I were just briefly reflecting on [the Oswald-FBI informant rumor], we said if that was true and it ever came out, could be established, then you would have people think that there was a conspiracy to accomplish this assassination that nothing the Commission did or anybody could dissipate.

Representative Hale Boggs mused: "Its implications are . . . are fantastic . . ."

Referring to the fact that the Commission had no independent investigators and was forced to rely on the FBI for its information, Rankin said: "[the FBI] would like us to fold up and quit. . . . They found the man.

There is nothing more to do. The Commission supports their conclusions, and we can go on home and that is the end of it."

Boggs remarked: ". . . I don't even like to see this being taken down."

Former CIA director and Commission member Allen Dulles agreed: "Yes, I think this record ought to be destroyed. Do you think we need a record of this?"

On January 27, the commissioners met again to consider this information. It is obvious from the transcripts that they feared approaching Hoover with the matter. Turning to the former CIA Director Allen Dulles, Boggs asked how the FBI could disprove that Oswald was an informant. Dulles replied:

> That is a hard thing to disprove, you know . . . I never knew how to disprove it . . . The record may not be on paper. But on paper you would have hieroglyphics that only two people know what they meant, and nobody outside of the agency would know; and you could say this meant the agent and somebody else could say it meant another agent.

". . . The man who recruited [the agent] would know, wouldn't he?" asked Boggs. "Yes, but he wouldn't tell," replied Dulles. "Wouldn't tell under oath?" asked an incredulous Earl Warren. Dulles replied:

> I wouldn't think he would tell under oath, no . . . He ought not tell it under oath . . . What I was getting at, I think, under any circumstances. I think Mr. Hoover would say certainly he didn't have anything to do with this fellow.

Exasperated, Boggs said: ". . . What you do is . . . make our problem utterly impossible because you say this rumor can't be dissipated under any circumstances."

During this same meeting Rankin revealed that he had received the same Oswald-informant information from yet another source—the Secret Service. He said the Secret Service named a Dallas deputy sheriff, Allan Sweatt, as its source.

It was here that the commissioners decided to just drop the entire matter. The FBI was informing them that Oswald was never an informant, and they could never prove or disprove it.

Furthermore, although it would be several weeks before the Commission began hearing witnesses and taking testimony, it now appears the verdict already was in. In the same Commission minutes, Senator Richard Russell commented: "They [the FBI] have tried the case and reached a verdict on every aspect."

If Oswald was working for the FBI, it could explain many things. It could explain his mysterious movements and associations in New Orleans, where he tried to join both pro- and anti-Castro groups. It could explain

why he asked for Agent Quigley after his arrest. It could explain his light
sentence after being found guilty of disturbing the peace. It could explain
the remarks—later denied—by Agent Hosty in Dallas that the FBI knew
about Oswald. It also could explain why the FBI did not pass along its
security file on Oswald to the Dallas police and it could explain why
Dallas FBI chief Shanklin demanded that Hosty be allowed to question
Oswald while in police custody.

It also might explain a well-documented instance of the FBI destroying
evidence after the assassination. In August 1975, the *Dallas Times Herald*
reported it had recently learned that two weeks before the JFK assassination, Oswald had delivered a note to the Dallas FBI office and that the note
had been destroyed after the assassination. This story prompted an investigation by the Justice Department and eventually became the center of
hearings before a subcommittee of the House Judiciary Committee.

It is now certain that two to three weeks prior to the assassination,
Oswald came to the Dallas FBI office and asked a receptionist to see
Agent Hosty. When told Hosty was not in, Oswald left a note. The
receptionist, Nancy Fenner, noted that Oswald asked for "S.A. [Special
Agent] Hosty . . . [in] exactly those words." It's surprising that Oswald
would be so familiar with Bureau jargon. Years later Fenner recalled the
note said something like: "Let this be a warning. I will blow up the FBI
and the Dallas Police Department if you don't stop bothering my wife—
Lee Harvey Oswald."

Hosty, who said he was told not to mention the note at the time of the
assassination, said the note was not violent in tone and that it said
something more like:

If you have anything you want to learn about me, come talk to me
directly. If you don't cease bothering my wife, I will take appropriate
action and report this to the proper authorities.

Hosty also said the note was folded and expressed doubts that Fenner
had read it properly.

He said that within hours of the assassination, he was called into the
office of the special-agent-in-charge, J. Gordon Shanklin. Hosty said
Shanklin was visibly "agitated and upset" and wanted to know about the
Oswald note.

After Oswald had been killed, Shanklin again called in Hosty. Hosty
said Shanklin produced the Oswald note from his desk drawer and said,
"Oswald's dead now. There can be no trial. Here, get rid of this." As
Hosty tore up the note, Shanklin cried: "No! Get it out of here. I don't
even want it in this office. Get rid of it!" Hosty said he took the pieces of
note to a nearby restroom and "flushed it down the drain."

Before the House subcommittee, Shanklin denied any knowledge of the
Oswald note. But assistant FBI director William Sullivan said Shanklin

had discussed an "internal problem" concerning a message from Oswald with him and that the presence of the note was common knowledge at FBI headquarters.

Another Dallas agent, Kenneth Howe, also testified he showed Shanklin the Oswald note the weekend of the assassination. Existence of the note also was talked about among some members of the Dallas Police Department.

Mrs. Ruth Paine even mentioned that Oswald had dropped off a note to the FBI in her testimony to the Warren Commission in 1964. She told the Commission: "[Oswald] told me he had stopped at the downtown office of the FBI and tried to see the agents and left a note . . ."

Why then did the Bureau only acknowledge the existence of the note after media reports in 1975? The House Select Committee on Assassinations said the incident concerning the note was a "serious impeachment of Shanklin's and Hosty's credibility," and that with the note's destruction, "it was not possible to establish with confidence what its contents were."

It seems unbelievable, however, that the FBI would knowingly destroy evidence, especially if it would have proven Oswald prone to violence. Some researchers say a more plausible explanation is that Oswald, as an FBI informant, tried to warn the Bureau about the coming assassination. This could explain the receptionist's insistence that the note contained threatening words. It also could explain why the FBI was so concerned and fearful of the note that it was ordered destroyed.

Hosty, incidentally, was one of seventeen FBI agents reprimanded for the way they handled the assassination case. He was suspended for thirty days without pay and transferred to Kansas City. However, after the Oswald-note matter was investigated by the House Select Committee on Assassinations and despite the contradictions between Hosty's testimony and that of his superior, Shanklin, Hosty was given more than a thousand dollars in repayment for the Hoover-imposed suspension.

"Rather than come out and admit [that I was wronged in 1963] . . . [the FBI] just gave me my money back," commented Hosty.

In light of the FBI's meticulously-worded denials that Oswald had never been paid as an FBI informant, it should be noted that all informants don't work for money. It is common practice for the FBI to gain information from people who have something to fear from the Bureau, perhaps the possibility of being charged with a past crime or even possible deportation.

Oswald's wife, Marina, had never become a U.S. citizen and therefore was subject to deportation at the government's pleasure. She even mentioned this to the Warren Commission, saying:

Sometimes the FBI agents asked me questions which had no bearing or relationship [to the assassination], and if I didn't want to answer, they told me that if I wanted to live in this country, I would have to help in this matter . . .

According to Dallas Police Captain Will Fritz, Oswald became angry when FBI agent Hosty confronted him. According to Fritz, Oswald "beat on the desk and went into a kind of tantrum," telling Hosty: "I know you. You accosted my wife on two occasions." Asked by Fritz what he meant by "accosted," Oswald replied: "Well, he threatened her . . . he practically told her she would have to go back to Russia." Perhaps Oswald was not recruited by the promise of money, but by the threat of Marina's deportation.

Finally, while it cannot be established with any certainty that Oswald was working for the FBI, it is now known that his killer definitely was. In early 1959, at a time when Jack Ruby may have been involved in smuggling activities with Cubans, he contacted the FBI and said he wanted to provide the Bureau with information. Accordingly, Agent Charles W. Flynn opened a Potential Criminal Informant (PCI) file on Ruby.

The relationship between Ruby and the Bureau was mentioned in a letter from Hoover to the Warren Commission dated June 9, 1964. However, this information was kept classified until 1975.

In the 1964 letter, Hoover stated that Ruby "furnished no information whatsoever and further contacts with him were discontinued." This disclaimer is difficult to swallow, since records show that agents met with Ruby on at least eight occasions between April and October 1959.

Since Ruby was an FBI informant, and considering the massive circumstantial evidence now available concerning Oswald's relationship to the Bureau, the possibility of Lee Harvey Oswald having worked for the Bureau cannot be ruled out.

*   *   *

And if by the spring of 1963, when Oswald arrived in New Orleans, he was indeed working with the FBI, it could explain his contacts with the characters at 544 Camp Street.

544 Camp Street

By the spring of 1963 the faded, three-story Newman Building at the corner of Camp and Lafayette streets in New Orleans had become known as the "Cuban Grand Central Station."

Housed in this building was the CIA-backed Cuban Revolutionary Council, as well as Sergio Archaca Smith's Crusade to Free Cuba, both virulently anti-Castro groups.

Also in the same building was the private detective firm of Guy Banister. In the summer of 1963, Banister's employees included Jack Martin and David Ferrie, Oswald's former Civil Air Patrol leader, and reportedly Oswald himself.

During the 1940s Banister was the special-agent-in-charge of the FBI office in Chicago, Jack Ruby's hometown. One of his FBI associates at that time was Robert Maheu, who left the Bureau in the 1950s and later became the chief go-between in the CIA-Mafia assassination plots against Castro.

According to Banister's family, he was also involved with Naval intelligence during the war and maintained contacts with that intelligence group throughout his life.

Banister left the Bureau and came to New Orleans in the 1950s at the request of the mayor to become chief of police. However, in 1957, he was forced to retire after an incident in the Old Absinthe House, where Banister allegedly threatened a waiter with a gun. He then formed Guy Banister Associates, which occupied a ground-floor office in the Newman Building with the address of 531 Lafayette Street, the side entrance to 544 Camp Street. This office was within walking distance of the New Orleans FBI office, Naval intelligence offices, and other government agencies.

It was here that Banister became embroiled in right-wing causes. A member of the John Birch Society, Banister also was a member of the Minutemen, the Louisiana Committee on Un-American Activities, and the publisher of a racist publication entitled *Louisiana Intelligence Digest*. Reportedly an alcoholic, Banister was later described as "a tragic case" by a member of the New Orleans Crime Commission.

With the advent of Fidel Castro, Banister threw himself into the anti-Castro Cuban activity in New Orleans. He helped organize such anti-Castro groups as the Cuban Revolutionary Democratic Front and Friends of a Democratic Cuba.

According to an April 25, 1967 story in the *New Orleans States Item*, Banister even served as a munitions supplier during the planning stages of the Bay of Pigs Invasion. In fact, Banister employees have said that as late as 1963, guns of every type littered Banister's office.

Banister also ran a network of young informants on the campuses of Tulane and Louisiana State universities, collecting what he hailed as the largest file of anticommunist intelligence in the South.

Jerry Milton Brooks, a former Minuteman who worked for Banister, said he would regularly take Banister's updated files to the New Orleans FBI office where they were integrated into the Bureau's files. Brooks also said Maurice B. Gatlin, another Banister employee who regarded the younger Brooks as a protégé, once said: "Stick with me—I'll give you a license to kill."

Although Banister's files were scattered after his sudden death in 1964—he reportedly died of a heart attack before authorities could question him about his contacts with Oswald and the assassination—some idea of their scope can be found in indexed titles made public by Louisiana lawmen. "Central Intelligence Agency," "Ammunition and Arms," "Civil Rights Program of JFK," and significantly, "Fair Play for Cuba Committee" and "International Trade Mart" are just a few of these titles.

Banister's operation was right in the thick of New Orleans intelligence activities, located near government offices and just around the corner from the Reilly Coffee Company, Oswald's employer and a supporter of anti-Castro Cuban exiles.

On at least two separate occasions, Banister employees saw Oswald handing out pro-Castro literature and reported it to their boss. In one instance Banister simply laughed, and on the other, he told his secretary Delphine Roberts: "Don't worry about him . . . He's with us. He's associated with the office."

Roberts also said she saw Oswald at 544 Camp Street, and that he filled out one of Banister's "agent" application forms. She later told author Anthony Summers: "Oswald came back a number of times. He seemed to be on familiar terms with Banister and with the office."

Roberts's daughter had a photography studio at 544 Camp Street and she, too, recalled Oswald:

> I knew he had his pamphlets and books and everything in a room along from where we were with our photographic equipment. He was quiet and mostly kept to himself, didn't associate with too many people. He would just tell us "hello" or "good-bye" when we saw him. I never saw him talking to Guy Banister, but I knew he worked in his office. I knew they were associated. I saw some other men who looked like Americans coming and going occasionally from the room Oswald used . . . I got the impression Oswald was doing something to make people believe he was something he wasn't. I am sure Guy Banister knew what Oswald was doing . . .

One of the things that Oswald and Banister might have been doing involves the small town of Clinton, Louisiana. Located about ninety miles northwest of New Orleans, Clinton was a small community of about fifteen hundred people in 1963. Like most small towns, it was difficult to keep the townspeople from knowing just about everything that went on there—especially if it involved strangers.

In 1963, the civil-rights program was gaining strength throughout the South. That summer would become known as "civil-rights summer" and tiny Clinton was one of the communities targeted for a black voter registration drive by the Congress of Racial Equality (CORE). Tension in Clinton was high. Earlier in the summer, several blacks were arrested there simply for writing appeals to the mayor and district attorney.

One morning, between August 22 and September 17—a time when Oswald's whereabouts remain officially unaccounted for—a long line of blacks waited to undergo the then-tedious process of registering to vote. Local police stood nearby, watchful for any breach of the peace. The incident that morning—pieced together from several witnesses—began with the arrival of a large, black Cadillac carrying three men. After parking near the registrar's office, one of the men—a slightly built white man—got out and joined the line of blacks. Later, witnesses were unanimous in identifying the man as Lee Harvey Oswald.

The registrar, Henry Palmer, had more to go on than just looks. He later recounted: "I asked him for his identification and he pulled out a U.S. Navy I.D. card . . . I looked at the name on it and it was Lee H. Oswald with a New Orleans address." Palmer said Oswald told him he wanted to get a job at a nearby East Louisiana State Hospital and thought he would have a better chance if he was a registered voter. Oswald was told he had not lived in the area long enough to qualify as a voter and, after thanking Palmer, he returned to the Cadillac.

Meanwhile, Town Marshal John Manchester had approached the car, but left after speaking to the driver, whom he later described as "a big man, gray-haired, with ruddy complexion."

New Orleans district attorney Jim Garrison later tried to prove that the driver was Clay Shaw, the defendant in Garrison's JFK assassination plot trial in 1967.

Today many researchers believe the driver might well have been Guy Banister. But what would Banister [or Shaw], Ferrie, and Oswald be doing in Clinton? One suggestion—that fits the facts—is that the trio were somehow involved in the FBI's Counterintelligence Program (COINTELPRO). It is now well established that COINTELPRO was a ruthless long-term Bureau program designed by Hoover to disrupt and discredit political groups he opposed. The notorious wire-tapping of Dr. Martin Luther King is just one example of this program.

It appears that by late summer 1963, Oswald was playing a dangerous game—caught up in a mixture of CIA- and FBI-related agents who were operating largely on their own and in touch with both anti-Castro Cubans and organized crime.

*   *   *

Despite the contacts between Oswald and both current and former FBI agents—plus the evidence of advance warnings of the assassination to the Bureau—the Dallas tragedy still occurred.

While no unquestioned case for FBI involvement in the assassination can be made, there is now no doubt that the Bureau manipulated the subsequent investigation. In fact, FBI activities after the assassination fall into the realm of criminal behavior. Consider:

Suppression of Evidence: Examples include the loss of Beverly Oliver's assassination film which she claimed was taken by FBI agents; the disappearance of an assassination bullet taken from under the noses of a police guard by an FBI agent; the suppression of testimony, such as Ed Hoffman's, which failed to support the lone assassin theory; and the failure of the Bureau to follow important leads, even when requested to do so by the Warren Commission.

Destruction of Evidence: Examples include the destruction of an Oswald note by FBI Agent Hosty; the destruction of a license-plate number on a photograph of General Edwin Walker's home found intact among Oswald's possessions; and the immediate cleaning of the presidential limousine, which effectively destroyed vital ballistic evidence.

Intimidation of Witnesses: Examples include Richard Carr, who saw two men run from the Texas School Book Depository but later was told by FBI agents, "If you didn't see Lee Harvey Oswald in the School Book Depository with a rifle, you didn't witness it"; Ed Hoffman, who was told by a Bureau agent, "You'd better keep quiet, you could get killed"; and Jean Hill, who said she was hounded by Bureau agents until she stopped giving media interviews.

In any normal criminal case, such behavior would constitute a jailable offense, but this was not an ordinary case, and the culprits were not ordinary citizens but FBI agents. If a local police agency proves to be corrupt, the FBI can be brought in to investigate. But in the case of the Bureau—who watches the watchers?

Also consider the documented matter of warnings that Oswald would be shot while being transferred from Dallas Police Headquarters. An anonymous telephone call was received at the Dallas FBI office at 2:15 A.M. Sunday, November 24, 1963. The caller warned that Oswald would be killed during the transfer to the county jail later that morning. The police were in charge of the transfer and apparently the Bureau decided not to step in. There was no significant change of plans and by that afternoon, Oswald was dead.

Since there can be no question that in 1963 the FBI was personified by J. Edgar Hoover, the questions of means, motive, and opportunity must fall on his shoulders. Did Hoover have the means of committing the assassination? Surrounded by countless informers, agents, and former employees—many of whom were in contact with Lee Harvey Oswald—Hoover's means were limitless.

Hoover's motives are obvious. First, his hatred of the Kennedys was notorious, and second, he was justly fearful that upon re-election John Kennedy would not allow him to continue as FBI director. This fear was well founded. Rumors in Washington were plentiful that Hoover would be eased out as FBI director after Kennedy's re-election in 1964.

William Hundley, former head of the Justice Department's organized-crime section, is quoted in *The Director* as saying the thing that finally destroyed the fragile relationship between Hoover and Attorney General Robert Kennedy was:

> . . . that Bobby mentioned to too many people who complained to him about Hoover that, "Look, just wait," and we all got the message that they were going to retire him after Jack got re-elected and Hoover hit seventy. And it got back to him.

Presidential aide David Powers stated he believes that the question of Hoover's retirement was the subject of one of the very few private meetings between Kennedy and the Bureau chief: "[Hoover] had a long lunch with the President and Bobby [on October 31, 1963,] and, as you know, three weeks later we went to Dallas."

But did Hoover have the opportunity? Hoover built his immense power base by currying favor with men more powerful than himself. It is extremely unlikely that Hoover—the ultimate bureaucrat—would have assumed the responsibility for initiating the assassination.

However it is certainly plausible that Hoover—once having discovered the assassination plot through his network of agents and informers—caused it to happen simply by not preventing it. Of course this is tantamount to criminal complicity and would have required substantial manipulation of testimony and evidence to prevent discovery of the Bureau's role.

Hoover would have needed help. And help he had—in the form of the new president, his former neighbor and dinner friend Lyndon B. Johnson— another man about to lose his job thanks to the Kennedys.

However the question of the protection of the President must be taken into account. Could this protection be circumvented? Could a plot to assassinate a U.S. president succeed without in some way neutralizing or involving the Secret Service?

The Secret Service

On the day of his inauguration, Thomas Jefferson walked from the Washington boarding house where he was staying to the Capitol without benefit of any protection.

It was symptomatic of the young Republic that presidents had not yet acquired the mantle of royalty and thus did not require protection.

This naïveté began to change after an assassination attempt on President Andrew Jackson on January 10, 1835. An English-born housepainter named Richard Lawrence aimed two pistols at Jackson as he walked out of the Capitol. However, both weapons misfired. Lawrence was determined to have been insane and was incarcerated for the remainder of his life.

In August 1842, a drunken painter threw some rocks at President John Tyler, who was walking on the White House grounds. Congress soon passed an act creating an auxiliary watch of the Washington Metropolitan Police for the protection of public and private property consisting of a captain and fifteen men. Although the act was primarily aimed at protecting property—particularly the White House—it was the crude beginning of presidential protection.

Protection was more pronounced for Abraham Lincoln, who guided the nation through the emotional years of the American Civil War. From the moment of his election in 1860, Lincoln was the object of hate mail and threats. During his inauguration, unprecedented protective measures were taken—especially in light of a threat to kill Lincoln as he passed through the city of Baltimore. Union soldiers guarded strategic points all along his way to Washington and the inauguration platform.

Even after Lincoln was fatally shot by actor John Wilkes Booth in Ford's Theater on April 14, 1865, there was no clamor to create official protection for the President. Americans thought his death was just a freak accident of the war.

The Secret Service, which was organized as a division of the Treasury Department the year Lincoln was killed, was meant only to pursue counterfeiters.

It was not until after the assassination of President James A. Garfield in 1881 that serious attempts at presidential protection were made.

While the number of White House policemen was increased to twenty-seven after mail threats increased against President Grover Cleveland, it was not until 1894 that Secret Service agents were informally assigned to the President.

Throughout the Spanish-American War, a small detail of Secret Service men were stationed at the White House. However, Secret Service protection of President William McKinley did not prevent his assassination on September 6, 1901. McKinley was attending a public reception at the Pan American Exposition in Buffalo, N.Y., when self-professed anarchist Leon F. Czolgosz fired two bullets into him despite the proximity of four Buffalo detectives, four soldiers, and three Secret Service agents. McKinley died eight days later and Czolgosz was executed.

The McKinley assassination finally provoked a response from Congress, which in 1902 ordered the Secret Service to assume full-time protection of the President. Two agents were permanently assigned to the White House. This onset of around-the-clock presidential protection prompted President Theodore Roosevelt to write: "The Secret Service men are a very small but very necessary thorn in the flesh."

Slowly over the years, the power and funding of the Secret Service was increased. Their jurisdiction eventually covered threats against the President and even security for presidential candidates.

By World War II, the White House detail of the Secret Service had grown to thirty-seven men.

Following an unsuccessful attack on President Harry S. Truman by Puerto Rican nationalists in 1951, legislation was passed permanently authorizing the Secret Service to protect not only the President, but also his immediate family, the President-elect, and the Vice President.

By 1963, the Secret Service remained a small and specialized group restricted by law. Nevertheless, the Secret Service had an average strength of more than five hundred and ran sixty-five field offices throughout the country.

Protecting President John F. Kennedy was no easy matter, as Kennedy had an active personal life, which included the desire to meet and be with people.

Kennedy assistant Kenneth O'Donnell was in charge of the White House staff and, as such, had control over the Secret Service. However, O'Donnell left security measures up to the special agent-in-charge of the White House detail, Gerald Behn. Sizing up the problems of protecting an active president such as Kennedy, O'Donnell once told Behn: "Politics and protection don't mix."

During his fateful trip to Texas, Kennedy was assigned no less than seventy Secret Service agents plus eight clerks. This was about 14 percent of the entire Secret Service force. Yet glaring deficiencies in the President's protection are now known.

First, although apparently there were at least three assassination attempts planned against Kennedy in the fall of 1963, information on them was not forwarded to either the agent in charge of Kennedy's protection or the special agent-in-charge of the Dallas Secret Service office.

An ex-Marine named Thomas Arthur Vallee, who was a member of the right-wing John Birch Society and a vocal Kennedy critic, was arrested by the Secret Service in Chicago. Vallee was discovered to have an M-1 rifle, a handgun, and three thousand rounds of ammunition in his car. It was also learned that Vallee had asked for time off from his job on November 2, the date Kennedy was to visit Chicago. Despite the weapons found, Vallee was released from custody on the evening of November 2 and was still considered a threat. Yet no word of the Vallee matter was transmitted to Dallas.

One of the strangest stories to come out of the Secret Service at this time, however, concerned the first black man to serve on the Service's White House detail. Abraham Bolden was personally selected by Kennedy, apparently in an attempt to integrate the previously all-white Secret Service detail.

Born in poverty, Bolden had been a police officer with an outstanding record before joining the Service. However, Bolden criticized the White House detail for laxity and was transferred to the Chicago office.

According to Bolden, the Chicago Secret Service office received a teletype from the FBI shortly before Kennedy's November 2 visit warning that an assassination attempt would be carried out in that city by a four-man Cuban hit squad armed with high-powered rifles. Bolden said the entire office was involved in this matter, but that it was kept top secret.

Years later, Bolden could not identify Vallee as a participant in this threat, and the belief among researchers is that Vallee played no part in the second assassination plan.

Kennedy's Chicago trip was canceled, although the House Select Committee on Assassinations could not determine the cause of the cancellation.

Three weeks after Kennedy's death, Bolden discovered that information on the Chicago threat was to be kept from the Warren Commission and he made a trip to Washington to tell what he knew. However, he was quickly taken back to Chicago, where he was later charged with discussing a bribe with two known counterfeiters. Brought to trial, Bolden was convicted of accepting a bribe—even after one of the two counterfeiters admitted perjury—and was sentenced to a lengthy prison term after his motion for a retrial was denied.

While the Secret Service had admitted the Chicago threat occurred, it has repeatedly refused to clarify the matter. Bolden, who had since been released from prison, claimed he was framed and convicted to silence him regarding the Kennedy threat. Whether the Chicago threat was real or not, the information again was not passed along to Dallas.

Likewise, the Service failed to follow up on another threat, this time from the volatile Miami area. Here a wealthy right-wing extremist named Joseph A. Milteer accurately predicted what was to happen to Kennedy in Dallas almost three weeks before the event. Again, while this information was forwarded to the Service's Protective Research Section (PRS) in Washington, it was never relayed to Winston G. Lawson, the advance agent in Dallas, or to Forrest V. Sorrels, the special agent-in-charge in Dallas.

And neither Lawson nor Sorrels got a preview of the zigzag turn that placed Kennedy under the Texas School Book Depository window on November 22.

The journey through Dealey Plaza itself was made necessary because of the selection of the Dallas Trade Mart as the site of the noon luncheon for the Kennedy entourage. And according to White House aide and advance man Jerry Bruno, this decision was made by Texas Governor John Connally after some questionable manipulations.

After reviewing possible luncheon sites, the Secret Service and White House advance men settled on two locations—the new Dallas Trade Mart on Stemmons Expressway and the Women's Building in Fair Park, home of the Texas State Fair, located south of the downtown area.

The Secret Service and the Kennedy people decided the Women's Building would be a preferable location because it displayed fewer security problems and could accommodate more people. However, Democrats headed by Lyndon Johnson and John Connally wanted the Trade Mart because it was more modern and would be more acceptable to Dallas's wealthy elite.

Bruno wrote:

> There was another point about the Women's Building site that didn't seem important to anyone at the time. If Kennedy had been going there instead of to the Trade Mart, he would have been traveling two blocks farther away from the Texas School Book Depository—and at a much faster rate of speed.

The struggle over the luncheon site continued until November 18, when Bruno got a call from White House aide Kenneth O'Donnell. Bruno quoted O'Donnell as saying: "We're going to let Dallas go, Jerry. We're going to let Connally have the Trade Mart site."

Bruno was flabbergasted. Despite the recommendations of the Secret Service, the Kennedy White House, and himself, Connally had managed to swing the decision to the Trade Mart. Bruno said he later learned that Johnson-Connally people had held up selling tickets to the fund-raising luncheon in an effort to force the site-location selection their way.

Bruno wrote that upon learning of Kennedy's death: ". . . I was angry, furious, at Connally and his demands to control the trip, where Kennedy should go, and now the President had been shot because we went here instead of there."

But if the Secret Service had no control over the luncheon site, they certainly were in control of the motorcade. And several strange things happened there.

Police Chief Curry originally had asked that the presidential limousine be flanked by eight motorcycle policemen, four on each side of the car. However, Curry told the Warren Commission that Secret Service Agent Lawson ordered the number of cycles reduced to four, two on each side, and that the cycles were told to stay by the rear fender of the limousine. This order seems unusual to persons familiar with motorcade security, since the purpose of motorcycle outriders is to form a screen for the limousine rider in the event of trouble.

Curry was puzzled, too, over this apparent lack of concern for security as well as the fact that Dallas authorities were kept in the dark about Oswald. Years later, he wrote:

In retrospect the physical security arrangements provided by the Dallas Police Force for the Secret Service were carried out exactly as they had requested. In my opinion all police officers involved gave their complete and wholehearted cooperation. Yet the Dallas Police Department was never given any information or asked to cooperate with the FBI or Secret Service in any attempt to locate possible conspirators. The Dallas Police Department was never informed of the presence of Lee Harvey Oswald in Dallas, of his connections with the Communist Party, or the fact that he "was capable of committing the assassination of President Kennedy." The enclosed sworn statement of Jack Revill, Lieutenant of the Criminal Intelligence Section, revealed later that FBI agents were aware of Oswald and his movements but made no attempt to communicate this to the Dallas Police Department.

Curry also had planned to have a car containing police captain Will Fritz and other Dallas detectives immediately following the presidential limousine, a traditional practice during similar motorcades in the past. However, again Lawson vetoed this plan, ". . . so Fritz and his men were not in the motorcade."

Curry said Fritz later told him: "I believe that had we been there we might possibly have got that man before he got out of that building or we would have maybe had the opportunity of firing at him while he was still firing."

And certainly the Dallas detectives could not have moved any slower than Kennedy's Secret Service protectors when the shots were fired in Dealey Plaza.

Photos taken several seconds after the first shots show almost a total lack of response by the agents riding in a backup car behind the presidential limousine. While Kennedy is clutching at his throat, two of his guards have begun looking toward the rear while the others are looking directly at the President. The only agent to react with speed was Clint Hill, who was not even supposed to be on the Dallas trip. Assigned to protect Jackie Kennedy, Hill had been brought along at the last minute due to a specific request by the First Lady.

But the one aspect of the Secret Service protection that raises the disturbing possibility of complicity concerns the actions of presidential limousine driver William Greer.

At age fifty-four, Greer was one of the oldest members of the White House detail. He had driven both President Harry Truman and President Dwight Eisenhower. On the evening of November 22, 1963, Greer drove Kennedy's body from *Air Force One* to Bethesda Naval Hospital for autopsy.

Greer testified to the Warren Commission that as the limousine cruised down the incline of Elm Street through Dealey Plaza, he heard a noise that he thought was a motorcycle backfire. Shortly he heard a second similar noise and glanced over his right shoulder long enough to see Governor Connally begin to slump to his left. Greer said he never caught sight of Kennedy.

Greer testified that he turned back forward and began to accelerate the limousine at the same time that Agent Roy Kellerman, riding to Greer's right, yelled, "Get out of here fast!" Then he claimed to have heard a third shot fired.

He said the presidential limousine was moving at between twelve and fifteen miles per hour the entire time.

However, based on films made during the assassination and eyewitness testimony, it is now known that immediately after the first shot, the brake lights on the limousine came on and the big Lincoln slowed to almost a standstill, causing the Secret Service follow-up car to move up and almost touch the rear bumper. Contrary to his testimony, films show Greer looking over his right shoulder in Kennedy's direction for several seconds—in fact, until after the fatal head shot is delivered. Only then does Greer face forward and the limousine begin to accelerate.

This discrepancy between Greer's testimony and reality has caused the more suspicious-minded researchers to suspect that some individuals within the Secret Service may have played a role in placing an underprotected president under the guns in Dealey Plaza.

Greer's testimony, like that of all government officials presented to the Warren Commission, was taken at face value and there was no real attempt at cross-examination. Likewise, testimony that indicated why the reaction of the Secret Service agents that day was so sluggish was not examined closely by the Warren Commission.

A Few Drinks at the Cellar

Within days of the assassination, it was common knowledge in the Fort Worth-Dallas area that Kennedy's Secret Service agents were drinking well into the morning hours of November 22 at a notorious Fort Worth club, the Cellar.

The story eventually spread nationwide when columnist Drew Pearson wrote about the incident, adding editorially: "Obviously men who have been drinking until nearly 3 A.M. are in no condition to be trigger-alert or in the best physical shape to protect anyone."

The stories set off an investigation within the Secret Service. Chief James J. Rowley, a former FBI man who had been with the Secret Service since 1938, obtained statements from the ten agents involved, plus some Fort Worth news reporters and Pat Kirkwood, the club's owner and an acquaintance of Jack Ruby.

Several Secret Service agents denied having any alcoholic drinks and the remainder stated they only had one or two drinks, including beers. Everyone, including Kirkwood, stressed that the Cellar had no license to sell alcoholic drinks. Rowley told the Warren Commission: "This is a place that does not serve alcoholic beverages."

Why the concern about alcohol? The Warren Commission cited Section 10 of the Secret Service Manual:

10. Liquor, use of—a. Employees are strictly enjoined to refrain from the use of intoxicating liquor during the hours they are officially employed at their post of duty, or when they may reasonably expect that they may be called upon to perform an official duty. *During entire periods of travel status, the special agent is officially employed and should not use liquor, until the completion of all of his official duties for the day . . . However, all members of the White House Detail and Special Agents cooperating with them on Presidential and similar protective assignments are considered to be subject to call for official duty at any time while in travel status. Therefore, the use of intoxicating liquor of any kind, including beer and wine, by members of the White*

House Detail . . . while they are in travel status, is prohibited [Emphasis added].

Paragraph c of this regulation states: "Violation or slight disregard of the above paragraphs . . . will be cause for removal from the Service."

Several of the agents involved, including four who were riding in the Secret Service follow-up car behind Kennedy, admitted drinking, but only two beers at the most. Of those who went to the Cellar, most said they had one or two drinks called a "salty dick" described as grapefruit juice and soda. Again, everyone concerned stressed that the Cellar did not sell alcohol, although alcohol brought in by a patron was allowed.

At least three agents guarding Kennedy's hotel suite took their "coffee break" at the Cellar, leaving two Fort Worth firemen behind to guard the President.

Since all the agents turned out at 7 A.M. that morning "sober, alert and ready for the performance of their duties," Rowley told the Warren Commission he did not punish them for the violation of regulations.

According to the Warren Commission:

Chief Rowley testified that under ordinary circumstances he would have taken disciplinary action against those agents who had been drinking in clear violation of the regulation. However, he felt that any disciplinary action might have given rise to an inference that the violation of the regulation had contributed to the tragic events of November 22. Since he was convinced that this was not the case, he believed that it would be unfair to the agents and their families to take explicit disciplinary measures.

Obviously, Rowley and others in the government were very much concerned that the public might recall that President Lincoln was killed when his guard left his post to have a drink next door and might attach some significance to the fact that Kennedy's agents were keeping late hours in a "beatnik" club owned by an associate of Jack Ruby.

The entire affair was toned down and quietly forgotten—except by Cellar owner Kirkwood. During the intervening years, Kirkwood has admitted that, while the Cellar had no license to sell liquor, nothing prevented him from giving it away. And give it away he did. In a 1984 article in the *Fort Worth Star-Telegram* recalling the wild days of the Cellar, Kirkwood said: "We had strange rules. We'd give drinks to doctors, lawyers, politicians, stag girls, policemen, anybody we thought we might need if something broke out . . ."

Kirkwood's mother recalled that sometimes her son would "give away five hundred dollars' worth of whiskey in a month."

In the newspaper article, Kirkwood mentioned the Secret Service incident:

After midnight the night before [the assassination], some reporters called me from the Press Club [of Fort Worth], which didn't have a license to sell drinks after midnight. [They] said they had about 17 members of the Secret Service and asked if they could bring them to my place. I said sure. About 3:30 [A.M.], these Secret Service men were sitting around giggling about how the firemen were guarding the President over at the Hotel Texas. That night got the Cellar mentioned in the Warren Report.

Jimmy Hill, who managed the Cellar for eleven years, was even more to the point in that same article:

After the agents were there, we got a call from the White House asking us not to say anything about them drinking because their image had suffered enough as it was. We didn't say anything, but those guys were bombed. They were drinking pure Everclear [alcohol].

It might be noted that no one saw the agents in a drunken revelry—although at least one unmarried female reporter tagged along with them for company. In fact, according to most present, the agents sat by themselves talking and drinking. However, the fatigue of the multistop Texas trip coupled with the alcohol and lack of sleep obviously left the agents in less-than-optimal condition to perform their duties.

During the wild ride to Parkland Hospital, presidential aide Kenneth O'Donnell thought about the interval between the final shots. Years later, he wrote:

. . . if there was an interval of at least five seconds between the second and third shots, as it seemed, that was long enough for a man to run 50 yards. If the Secret Service men in the front had reacted quicker to the first two shots at the President's car, if the driver had stepped on the gas before instead of after the fatal third shot was fired, would President Kennedy be alive today?

Former senator Ralph Yarborough echoed O'Donnell's concern when he wrote the Warren Commission:

. . . All of the Secret Service men seemed to me to respond very slowly, with no more than a puzzled look. Knowing something of the training that combat infantrymen and Marines receive, I am amazed at the lack of instantaneous response by the Secret Service when the rifle fire began.

The reaction-impairment issue aside, conspiracy-minded researchers, noting that throughout history a great man's bodyguards usually are the key to a successful coup d'etat, have suggested that Kennedy's guards may have been aware of the coming events in Dealey Plaza and were under too much stress to get a quiet night's sleep.

Interestingly, none of Vice President Johnson's Secret Service guards were in the entourage that drank at the Press Club and then moved on to the Cellar.

*   *   *

Aside from the sluggish reaction of the Secret Service agents in Dealey Plaza, other oddities occurred in the motorcade during the assassination.

One agent, John D. Ready, did start to react by jumping off the follow-up car (a 1956 Cadillac touring sedan convertible). However, he was recalled by Special Agent-in-Charge Emory Roberts.

Then there is the well-publicized story of Agent Rufus Youngblood, who reportedly threw himself on top of Vice President Johnson after the shooting began in Dealey Plaza. Youngblood was considered the hero of the hour. In his report of that day, Youngblood wrote that upon hearing the first shot: "I quickly looked all around again and could see nothing to shoot at, so I stepped over into the back seat and sat on top of the vice President."

Johnson, in a statement to the Warren Commission, mentioned the incident:

> I was startled by a sharp report or explosion, but I had no time to speculate as to its origin because Agent Youngblood turned in a flash, immediately after the first explosion, hitting me on the shoulder, and shouted to all of us in the back seat to get down. I was pushed down by Agent Youngblood. Almost in the same moment in which he hit or pushed me, he vaulted over the back seat and sat on me. I was bent over under the weight of Agent Youngblood's body, toward Mrs. Johnson and Senator Yarborough.

Years later in his book, *The Vantage Point*, Johnson elaborated:

> . . . it is apparent that there were many reactions to the first shot . . . I did not know what it was. Agent Youngblood spun around, shoved me on the shoulder to push me down and shouted to all of us, "Get down!" Almost in the same movement, he vaulted over the seat, pushed me to the floor, and sat on my right shoulder to keep me down and to protect me. Agent Youngblood's quick reaction was as brave an act as I have ever seen anyone perform. When a man, without a moment's thought or hesitation, places himself between you and a possible assassin's bullet, you know you have seen courage. And you never forget it.

However, former Texas senator Ralph Yarborough, who was sitting beside Johnson that day, told this author: "It just didn't happen. . . . It was a small car, Johnson was a big man, tall. His knees were up against his chin as it was. There was no room for that to happen.''

Yarborough recalled that both Johnson and Youngblood ducked down as the shooting began and that Youngblood never left the front seat. Yarborough said Youngblood held a small walkie-talkie over the back of the car's seat and that he and Johnson both put their ears to the device. He added: ''They had it turned down real low. I couldn't hear what they were listening to.''

It would be most interesting to learn what the men listened to, since Dallas Police radio channel 1 designated for the presidential party was blocked from radio traffic for about eight minutes beginning at 12:26 P.M., about four minutes before the shooting, by a transmitter stuck open. It may have been that Johnson and Youngblood were listening to a channel reserved for inter-vehicle radio traffic, but no transcripts of this channel have been made public.

Obviously, either Yarborough or Johnson and his Secret Service agents did not tell the truth of what happened in the motorcade.

In reviewing the Secret Service activity in the course of Kennedy's Dallas trip, even the gullible Warren Commission concluded that, while ''the detailed security measures taken at Love Field and the Trade Mart were thorough and well-executed, in other respects . . . the advance preparations for the President's trip were deficient.''

The House Select Committee on Assassinations was even harsher, stating:

> In summary, the committee concluded that the Secret Service did in fact possess information that was not properly analyzed and put to use with respect to a protective investigation in advance of President Kennedy's trip to Dallas. Further, it was the committee's opinion that Secret Service agents in the Presidential motorcade in Dallas were not adequately prepared for an attack by a concealed sniper. Finally, the committee found that the investigation by the Secret Service of a possible assassination conspiracy was terminated prematurely when President Johnson ordered that the FBI assume primary investigative responsibility.

Lastly, there is the mystery of men encountered by several people in Dealey Plaza—including at least one policeman—who claimed to be Secret Service agents and even displayed credentials. No government panel has ever adequately investigated this matter to determine if these men were bogus or real agents.

There is cause for suspicion that the Secret Service was somehow involved in the assassination of John Kennedy.

While the President's guards certainly had the opportunity to achieve Kennedy's death—either through direct action or through inaction—no motive has been established. And since the Service is a small agency within the federal government with relatively little power or influence, no one seriously believes that the Secret Service initiated or orchestrated the assassination.

However, the possibility remains that certain individuals within the Service may have been working for someone other than John Kennedy on November 22, 1963.

Summary

By 1963, the Federal Bureau of Investigation was tightly controlled by one man—the strange and officious bureaucrat J. Edgar Hoover. Even the Secret Service had become but a small and relatively powerless agency compared to the Bureau, although the Service was much older than the FBI. No one but Hoover has ever held so much power for so long in the history of the United States.

With the death of Kennedy, the power of the presidency fell to Hoover's long-time friend, Lyndon B. Johnson. Between Hoover, the tyrant of the FBI, and Johnson, who as commander-in-chief controlled the military, these men had the power to manipulate any investigation into the assassination.

The many and varied contacts between the FBI and the accused assassin cause great suspicion among assassination researchers. These suspicions are heightened in light of the numerous and well-documented instances of FBI mismanagement of the postassassination investigations. It can now be demonstrated that the Bureau suppressed evidence, destroyed evidence, fabricated evidence, and intimidated witnesses. Any of these acts committed by a private citizen in the course of a criminal investigation would result in severe penalties.

Both the FBI and the Secret Service were chided for inadequately protecting Kennedy by both the Warren Commission and the House Select Committee on Assassinations.

Due to the many connections between the Bureau and Lee Harvey Oswald, coupled with a wealth of circumstantial and anecdotal evidence, it appears almost certain to most researchers that Oswald was working as an informant for the FBI in the months preceeding the assassination—an allegation that even the Warren Commission took seriously. However, since the FBI furnished most of the investigative evidence to the Commission, the question of Oswald's involvement with the Bureau could not be resolved. Considering the Bureau's ability to substitute records, alter documents, lose important evidence, and intimidate witnesses, it would be most surprising if any concrete evidence of Oswald's connection to the FBI should surface at this late date.

Both the FBI and the Secret Service failed to respond to several warnings concerning the assassination and the subsequent slaying of Oswald.

While evidence suggesting that elements within both the Bureau and the Secret Service may have played some role in the actual assassination can be disputed, there is no question that serious and suspicious manipulation of evidence occurred after the event. This fact, coupled with the unresolved connections between Oswald and the Bureau and the well-known hatred of the Kennedys by both Hoover and Johnson, causes most researchers today to regard certain agents within both the FBI and the Secret Service as prime suspects in the plot to kill Kennedy.

[Who is] the one man who has profited most from the assassination—your friendly President, Lyndon Johnson.

—Jim Garrison

Rednecks and Oilmen

By the fall of 1963, President John F. Kennedy had acquired more domestic enemies than just irate anti-Castro Cubans, fearful mob bosses, and disgruntled intelligence operatives.

Both big business and supporters of states' rights felt threatened by the new Kennedy brand of federalism—the wielding of total power from Washington.

Hatred of Kennedy also was being fomented among those people opposed to the growing civil-rights movement, particularly in the old confederate states, which included Texas.

Into this caldron of century-old passions stepped Kennedy the politician, hoping to find a middle ground between the radical activists—both black and white.

Kennedy friend Theodore Sorensen wrote: "Jack Kennedy . . . knew comparatively little and cared little about the problems of civil rights and civil liberties."

However, during the presidential campaign of 1960, Kennedy found it expedient to chastise the Eisenhower administration for not doing more to end segregation, despite the fact that two civil-rights bills were passed during that time, the first such major legislation since the Emancipation Proclamation.

In his 1961 inaugural address, Kennedy spurred on the expectations of millions of black Americans when he said:

Let the word go forth from this time and place, to friend and foe alike, that the torch has been passed to a new generation of Americans . . . one unwilling to witness or permit the slow undoing of those human rights to which this nation has always been committed and to which we are committed today at home and around the world.

Such rhetoric was effective for Kennedy. During the 1960 election, blacks responded to the support of Kennedy by Dr. Martin Luther King. They turned out a hefty 78 percent vote for the Massachusetts senator.

By 1962, polls showed Kennedy ranked only behind King himself in popularity among black Americans despite the fact that immediate action by Kennedy on civil rights was limited.

Although Kennedy had promised to end segregation in federal housing, it was nearly two years after taking office, with violent racial incidents increasing across the nation, before he took action.

Kennedy dawdled until June 1963, before sending his own civil-rights bill to Congress and even this did not pass until after his death, when the measure was adroitly maneuvered through Congress by President Lyndon Johnson.

Furthermore, in an attempt to appease the anti-civil-rights forces, Kennedy made several appointments that greatly angered his black supporters. For example, he named William H. Cox to a federal judgeship. Cox, a close friend to conservative Mississippi senator James Eastland, immediately attempted to block a Justice Department-sponsored voter registration drive in Mississippi.

In May 1961, one month after the ill-fated Bay of Pigs Invasion and at a time when Kennedy was preparing to journey to Europe for an historic meeting with Soviet Premier Khrushchev, King and twelve other "Freedom Riders" left Washington, D.C., for New Orleans to test the desegregation of public facilities along the way.

According to Kennedy biographer John H. Davis, the President asked the activists not to go ahead with the ride for fear it might cause him embarrassment during his European trip. To which the black leaders replied: "But we have been embarrassed all our lives."

By the end of May, the riders had grown to fill two buses, which left behind a trail of violence: In Aniston, Alabama, one bus was firebombed, while in Birmingham the other was met by a gang of whites who beat the occupants with pipes for more than ten minutes before police arrived. After entering Montgomery, the riders were attacked by a mob of a thousand while a local police official looked on stating: "We have no intention of standing guard for a bunch of troublemakers coming into our city."

In both Birmingham and Montgomery, FBI agents were on hand jotting down notes while the passengers were beaten and clubbed. Even when one of Attorney General Kennedy's top aides, John Seigenthaler, was knocked unconscious by the angry Montgomery mob, the agents were not moved to action.

Angered and moved by the bloodshed, Robert Kennedy—with the reluctant approval of the President—ordered out several hundred federal marshals to protect the riders as interstate travelers.

On May 21, the National Guard was ordered into Montgomery after a black church meeting was beseiged by an angry white mob.

By May 23, the Freedom Ride was resumed with the addition of marshals, but ended in Jackson, Mississippi, where all of the riders were arrested and jailed for entering a "white" restroom and failing to obey local police officers. This historic "ride" was soon followed by "Freedom

Flights'' and ''Freedom Trains'' and the civil-rights movement continued to gain momentum.

By September 1961, acting on a request by President Kennedy, the Interstate Commerce Commission adopted rules banning segregation on buses and in terminals.

While the Kennedys certainly did not invent the problem and, in fact, joined the push for civil rights belatedly and reluctantly, they nevertheless were the first major American leaders to fully address the problem and appeal for wisdom and restraint from both blacks and whites.

And despite its faint beginnings, some of the most dramatic accomplishments of the Kennedy administration were in the area of civil rights. Blacks for the first time were appointed to major government jobs as well as judgeships; civil-rights laws aimed at ending voter discrimination and public segregation were vigorously enforced by the Kennedy Justice Department despite a recalcitrant J. Edgar Hoover, and an executive order was issued creating a Committee on Equal Employment Opportunity headed by Vice President Johnson.

But racial problems continued. One of those persons who may have been moved to action by John Kennedy's political rhetoric was a black Air Force veteran named James Meredith. The day after Kennedy's inaugural address, Meredith applied for enrollment to the segregated University of Mississippi but was rejected.

In his fourth attempt to enroll, Meredith arrived in Oxford, Mississippi, on September 30 accompanied by three hundred U.S. marshals. He was met by a crowd of about twenty-five hundred segregationists and students who turned Meredith and his supporters away with bricks and bottles. The marshals responded with tear gas, and a bloody night-long riot ensued— leaving two people dead and more than 375 injured, including 166 federal officers.

The violence was quelled by the arrival of three thousand Army and National Guard troops and Meredith was enrolled on October 1 under the protection of marshals who remained with him until his graduation in August 1963.

One of those involved in that bloody incident was a former Army general named Edwin A. Walker who was to later be connected with Lee Harvey Oswald.

A Bullet for the General

About 9:10 P.M. on April 10, 1963, Maj. Gen. Edwin A. Walker was narrowly missed by a rifle bullet that crashed through a first-floor window and slammed into a wall of his fashionable Dallas home.

Seventeen months later the Warren Commission concluded that Walker's assailant was none other than Kennedy's alleged assassin, Lee Harvey

Oswald. This conclusion has increasingly been called into question as more information about this event has become known.

By the fall of 1963, Walker was notorious in Dallas, a city known for the conservatism of its leadership. A native Texan born in 1909, Major General Walker was commander of the U.S. Army's 24th Division stationed in West Germany, where he used his position to indoctrinate his troops with right-wing propaganda, including the assertion that both the U.S. government and the military had come under "Communist control." The Korean War hero once declared: "We must throw out the traitors, and if that's not possible, we must organize armed resistance to defeat the designs of the usurpers and contribute to the return of a constitutional government."

Ordered to stop this practice, Walker instead resigned from the Army in 1961 and returned to the United States where he began making political speaking tours. He even made an unsuccessful bid for governor of Texas in 1962, losing to John Connally.

On September 30, 1962, Walker was in Oxford, Mississippi, aligned with those who were trying to prevent the university enrollment of James Meredith. After Walker was charged with being a ringleader of the violent Oxford mob, Attorney General Robert Kennedy ordered that he be held temporarily in a mental institution.

By 1963, Walker was back in Dallas and had become a prominent figure in right-wing political activity there, particularly in the John Birch Society. In a 1964 interview with this author, Walker outlined his beliefs:

> The United Nations charter, which is only eight pages, should have been placed before [the American public] to study. Very few . . . have even seen the Fulbright Memorandum or the Walter Reuther Memorandum submitted to Attorney General Kennedy upon his request. . . . very few had even seen these papers or the U.N. declaration on racial discrimination, the U.N. term for integration. This paper declares that the whole world will integrate. I do not know where such authority comes from or who it represents. I can realistically predict that no one living today will see six hundred million Chinese integrated with one hundred million Japanese, Turks integrated with Greeks, or Mohammedans with Israelis. . . . A cause for America first and last and always is essential to our existence. All organizations which are implementing such a cause are in the best interest of the country and are needed. The Birch Society is doing a great job in educating people and exposing such memoranda as I have referred to previously.

Walker's connections in the months preceding the assassination are both convoluted and intriguing.

A driver and aide to Walker in the fall of 1963 was the brother of Larrie Schmidt, who along with Bernard Weissman, authored the infamous "Welcome Mr. Kennedy to Dallas . . .'' ad that ran in the *Dallas Morning News* the morning of November 22. The ad, which carried a heavy black border, asked twelve loaded questions of Kennedy ending with ''Why have you scrapped the Monroe Doctrine in favor of the 'Spirit of Moscow'?'' Financial contributors to this anti-Kennedy ad included oilman H. L. Hunt's son, Nelson Bunker Hunt; Joseph Grinnan, volunteer coordinator for the local John Birch Society; and H. R. ''Bum'' Bright, former owner of the Dallas Cowboys. The ad was signed ''The American Fact-Finding Committee,'' but Weissman admitted to the Warren Commission that the group was ''formed strictly for the purpose of having a name to put in the paper.''

It is noteworthy that Nelson Hunt's interests apparently ran to violent extremes. A former Hunt family security man, ex-FBI agent Paul Rothermeil, has claimed he was approached by Nelson Bunker Hunt while working for H. L. Hunt. Rothermeil said the younger Hunt wanted help in forming a paramilitary organization that would eliminate opponents with a ''gas gun'' imported from Europe. (Victims of this exotic weapon reportedly appear to have suffered a heart attack.) Rothermeil said Hunt planned to recruit this private army from General Walker's Dallas Birch Society group. Hunt has denied Rothermeil's allegation, claiming, ''I think you'll find he's CIA.''

Another Walker aide, Robert Allan Surrey, produced the ''Wanted for Treason'' leaflets that were distributed along the Kennedy motorcade route.

Surrey later revealed to researcher Penn Jones that one of his close bridge-playing friends was none other than James Hosty, the FBI agent who, on orders, destroyed a note to the Bureau from Lee Harvey Oswald after the assassination.

But perhaps the most significant connection between Walker and other assassination-connected characters was his contacts with anti-Castro Cubans and New Orleans.

Carlos Bringuier, the anti-Castro Cuban who was arrested with Lee Harvey Oswald in New Orelans, was with Walker on the faculty of Christian Crusade Anti-Communist Youth University. According to researcher Gary Shaw, Walker was retained by the CIA to arm and train Cuban exiles some time after the Bay of Pigs Invasion.

One member of the militant Cuban exile group Alpha 66 was Filipe Vidal Santiago, who was frequently seen with Walker. Santiago was known to drive a 1957 Chevrolet. Such a car figured prominently in several aspects of the assassination case.

About an hour after the slaying of Dallas patrolman J. D. Tippit, police dispatchers broadcast a pickup order for a 1957 Chevrolet last seen at the intersection where Tippit was killed. The charge was investigation of carrying a concealed weapon. The license number given by police registered to a Dallas man who told researchers he sold the car prior to

September 1963, indicating the license plate reported on November 22 may have been stolen. This—and other instances of cars with illegitimate license plates around the Tippit slaying and Oswald's rooming house— were never adequately investigated.

Part of the evidence that led the Warren Commission to conclude that it was Oswald who shot at General Walker were three photographs made of Walker's Dallas home found in Oswald's belongings. Commission photo experts said backgrounds of the pictures indicated they were made no later than March 10, one month before the attack on Walker and two days before mail orders were sent off for Oswald's pistol and the Mannlicher-Carcano rifle.

In one of the photographs is a 1957 Chevrolet in Walker's driveway. This photo—as shown in Warren Commission Exhibit 5—has a hole in it obliterating the car's license number.

In FBI reports, R. B. Stovall, one of the Dallas detectives who confiscated Oswald's belongings from the Paine home in Irving, is quoted as saying:

> . . . at the time he observed this photograph [the detective] surmised that Oswald had evidently taken the license plate number area out of the photograph to keep anyone from identifying the owner of that automobile. He advised he is positive the photograph was mutilated as shown in Commission Exhibit 5 at the time they recovered it at the Paine residence.

According to the Bureau, Stovall's partner, Guys Rose, commented:

> . . . he had noted that someone had torn out a section on the automobile, which area contains the license plate for the 1957 Chevrolet . . . He stated . . . that it had been mutilated at the time they had recovered the box containing the photographs.

However, during her Warren Commission testimony, Marina Oswald made it clear that the hole was not there when she was shown the photo by the FBI.

She told Commission attorney Wesley Liebeler:

> When the FBI first showed me this photograph, I remember that the license plate, the number of the license plate was on this car, on this photograph. It had the white and black numbers. There was no black spot that I see on it now. When Lee showed me this photograph there was the number on the license plate on this picture . . . This black spot is so striking I would have remembered it if it were on the photograph that Lee showed me or the FBI. . . . There was no hole in the original when they showed it to me—I'm positive of it.

Someone is lying. If the license number was obliterated while in the hands of the FBI, as stated by Marina Oswald, this is firm evidence of official destruction of evidence.

The truth of the matter came in 1969 with the publication of Dallas police chief Jesse Curry's *JFK Assassination File*. On page 113 is a police photograph of Oswald's belongings and in the foreground is the Walker photograph with the Chevrolet's license-plate number intact.

This piece of evidence was altered while in the hands of the authorities.

Apparently this criminal action disturbed at least one Warren Commission staff member. In 1966, two years after the Warren Commission had concluded its work, Attorney Liebeler wrote a letter to Charles Klihr, a volunteer worker for General Walker, stating:

> The [Oswald] picture was mutilated by someone in such a manner that the license plate is no longer visible. When we noticed this during the investigation we asked the FBI to determine whose car it was. They asked [Walker aide] Surrey about it and he told them he thought it was your car. I find no indication that FBI agents talked with you about the matter, however . . . I would appreciate it very much if you would let me know whether or not the FBI did interview you about this and if you were able to identify the car as your own.

There is no record as to Klihr's responses to Liebeler's letter.

All of these strange connections take on more sinister tones when viewed with the possibility that General Walker may have even been in contact with Oswald, his assassin Jack Ruby, or both.

A tenuous tie may be a St. Paul, Minnesota man named John Martin, who was an acquaintance of General Walker's and filmed him in his Dallas home in the late summer of 1963. Incredibly, Martin journeyed on to New Orleans where, on September 9, he photographed Lee Harvey Oswald handing out Fair Play for Cuba material on the same roll of film.

Walker's connections in New Orleans were many and substantial, ranging from anti-Castro Cubans in touch with David Ferrie and Guy Banister to Louisiana political leaders. According to Louisiana State Police files, Walker was involved in several hurried and secret meetings in New Orleans during the two days prior to the assassination, including a conference with Judge Leander Perez, one of the state's most powerful men.

In fact, Walker was on a Braniff flight from New Orleans at the time of Kennedy's assassination. He reportedly became upset when word of the assassination was broadcast over the plane's loudspeaker and roamed up and down the aisle telling fellow passengers to remember that he was on that flight at the time of Kennedy's death.

According to *Farewell America*, a book authored by French intelligence agents, Walker later joined oilman H. L. Hunt in a secret hideaway in Mexico where "they remained for a month, protected by personal guards, under the impassive eyes of the FBI."

Also in this book, the authors state that Oswald was introduced to both General Walker and Clay Shaw, the director of the International Trade Mart tried by District Attorney Jim Garrison, in late summer of 1963 by David Ferrie.

Author Anthony Summers has reported that Walker gave a talk in Dallas that may have been attended by Lee Harvey Oswald. He quotes another member of the audience who claimed Oswald sat at the back of the room during a meeting of the Directorio Revolutionario Estudiantil (DRE), an anti-Castro Cuban group. Oswald reportedly said nothing during the fund-raising meeting.

Then there are disconcerting reports that Walker knew Oswald's killer, Dallas nightclub owner Jack Ruby. Researcher Penn Jones has stated that Ruby made no secret of his admiration for the resigned general and that he once stated that Walker was "100 percent right" in his belief that Cuba should be taken back from Castro. More significant are the statements of former Walker employee William McEwan Duff. According to Warren Commission Document 1316-B, Duff claimed that Ruby visited Walker's home on a monthly basis between December 1962 and March 1963, shortly before Walker was fired upon.

Many researchers feel it is also significant that General Walker's name and telephone number were found in Oswald's address book. They believe this may indicate a possible connection between the two. However, Walker still maintains he never met Oswald and the Warren Commission concluded:

> Although Oswald's notebook contained Walker's name and telephone number there is no evidence that they knew each other. It is probable that this information was inserted at the time Oswald was planning his attack on Walker.

Yet another odd connection between Walker and the assassination involved car salesman Warren Reynolds. Reynolds chased the murderer of Patrolman Tippit but initially was unable to identify Oswald as the killer. Two months later, Reynolds was shot from ambush and after recovering, was befriended by General Walker. After consulting with Walker, Reynolds was able to identify Oswald to the Warren Commission in July, 1964.

The Warren Commission concluded, without even bothering to talk to Walker, that his assailant had been Oswald. The evidence used to reach this conclusion was the testimony of Marina Oswald, a note discovered at the Paine home, photographs reportedly taken by Oswald of the Walker home, and identification of a bullet found at the crime scene.

Marina Oswald's testimony has been called into question in a number of matters, and her stories of murder attempts by Oswald on Walker and Richard Nixon are fraught with inconsistencies and omissions. It is also curious that her first statement that Oswald tried to kill Walker came on December 3, 1963, about a week after a West German newspaper reported there might be a connection between the Walker shooting and the assassination. The Warren Commission reported that the German news story was "fabricated by the editor," but then advanced the same allegation.

The note in question turned up only after the Kennedy assassination, when Secret Service agents showed the note to Mrs. Ruth Paine and asked her to identify it. The undated note reportedly fell out of a book found among Oswald's belongings.

Government handwriting experts declared that Oswald wrote the message and Marina conveniently told investigators she thought she saw it shortly after the Walker shooting.

Federal investigators concluded that Oswald had written the note, which was in Russian, and that it had been left in a Russian volume entitled *Book of Useful Advice* and was only discovered nearly two weeks after the assassination when it fell out of the book's pages.

However, Mrs. Ruth Paine told the Warren Commission about the Dallas police search of her home mentioning: "Before I left they were leafing through books to see if anything fell out but that is all I saw." Mrs. Paine's testimony fuels the suspicion that the note may have been planted by authorities.

In the note, Oswald detailed instructions to his wife on what to do in his absence. He told her where the mailbox key could be found, that the current bills had been paid and even said she could "throw out or give my clothing, etc. away." Two notable passages state:

> Send the information as to what has happened to me to the Embassy [undoubtedly the Russian embassy, which Oswald had been contacting periodically] and include newspaper clippings—should there be anything about me in the newspapers. I believe that the Embassy will come quickly to your assistance on learning everything.
>
> If I am alive and taken prisoner, the city jail is located at the end of the bridge through which we always passed on going to the city (right in the beginning of the city after crossing the bridge).

These two sections raise troublesome questions for the official version of the Walker shooting.

Since Marina reportedly knew nothing of her husband's attack on Walker in advance, how could she be expected to watch for stories on Oswald in the newspapers since any such account would only report that an unknown sniper fired on the general? Also, why would a supposed American defector to Russia who returned home expect assistance for his family from the Soviet embassy if he were charged with the attempted murder of a prominent right-wing Dallasite?

Warren Commission critic Sylvia Meagher wrote:

> I suggest that Oswald wrote the undated letter in relation to a project other than the attack on General Walker—one that also involved risk of arrest or death—and that Marina was informed about her husband's plans in advance.

As noted by the Warren Commission, Oswald's letter "appeared to be the work of a man expecting to be killed, or imprisoned, or to disappear." Yet at the time of the Walker incident, he had no money, no passport, and no reasonable expectation of escape.

The photographs of Walker's home also pose a time problem. If they were made prior to March 10, 1963, as believed by the Warren Commission, then it must be believed that Oswald was actively reconnoitering a sniper position at the Walker home even before ordering his weapons.

Finally, the bullet found in Walker's home also presents problems. Contemporary news stories of the April 10 incident quote Dallas police as saying the recovered bullet was "identified as a 30.06," not a 6.5 millimeter Mannlicher-Carcano.

In 1975, researcher George Michael Evica received FBI spectrographic analyses of a bullet (CE 399) and bullet fragments reportedly recovered in the assassination investigation. According to Evica, these scientific reports, termed "inconclusive" by Director Hoover when reporting to the Warren Commission, revealed:

> . . . the bullet recovered in the assassination attempt on General Walker does not match either CE 399 or two fragments recovered from President Kennedy's limousine; the Warren Commission's linking of Lee Harvey Oswald to the General Walker assassination attempt is seriously weakened.

Further confusion over the bullet has been raised by Walker himself, who today claims the bullet exhibited by the House Select Committee on Assassinations is not the same bullet recovered from his home in 1963. He said the original slug was so mangled as to be hardly recognizable as a bullet.

After studying the government's evidence carefully, author Sylvia Meagher concluded: "Despite the [Warren] Commission's reliance on the testimony of Marina Oswald, compelling evidence virtually excludes the use of the Carcano rifle in the attempt on the life of General Walker."

And even if Oswald was responsible for the Walker shooting, there is evidence that he did not act alone.

Walter Kirk Coleman, who in 1963 was a fourteen-year-old neighbor to Walker, told police he heard the shot and, peeking over a fence, saw some men speeding down the alley in a light green or light blue Ford, either a

1959 or 1960 model. Coleman also said he saw another car, a 1958 black Chevrolet with white down the side in a church parking lot adjacent to Walker's house. The car door was open and a man was bending over the back seat as though he was placing something on the floor of the car.

At the time of the Warren Commission, Coleman was not called to testify and, in fact, told Walker he had been ordered not to discuss the incident by authorities.

Just prior to the Walker shooting, two of the general's aides saw suspicious activity around the general's home. Walker aide Robert Surrey said on April 6, he saw two men prowling around the house, peeking in windows. Surrey said the pair were driving a 1963 dark purple or brown Ford with no license plates.

And Walker aide Max Claunch told researcher Gary Shaw that a few nights before the shooting incident he noticed a "Cuban or dark-complected man in a 1957 Chevrolet" cruise around Walker's home several times.

The problems with the official version of the Walker shooting as well as the many unfollowed leads in this area are troubling to assassination researchers.

*   *   *

On January 14, 1963, George Wallace was sworn in as governor of Alabama, pledging: "Segregation now, segregation tomorrow and segregation forever."

By late spring, a voter registration drive in Greenwood, Mississippi, had grown into full-blown civil-rights demonstrations through much of the South. Thousands of arrests were made. The volatile situation, inflamed by shooting and bombing incidents, reached a climax in August when Dr. Martin Luther King led some two hundred fifty thousand people in a Freedom March on Washington. Here he proclaimed: "There will be neither rest nor tranquility in America until the Negro is granted his citizenship rights."

The march took place less than three months after President Kennedy had finally submitted his own civil-rights bill in Congress. Resistance to Kennedy's plans was widespread although a June 1963 Gallup poll indicated 59 percent of the population approved of the President and his programs.

On June 12, 1963, Georgia senator Richard B. Russell promised other southern senators:

To me, the President's legislative proposals are clearly destructive of the American system and the constitutional rights of American citizens. I shall oppose them with every means and resource at my command. . . .

Within six months, Russell was sitting as a member of the Warren Commission charged with finding the truth of Kennedy's death.

One government employee who watched the famous Washington monu-

ments become surrounded by demonstrators was FBI Director J. Edgar
Hoover. The strange and obsessed Hoover was particularly anxious over
King and his civil-rights movement. The aging director not only saw his
essentially southern way of life threatened but was convinced that King's
organization was being directed by Communists.

William Sullivan, at the time Hoover's man in charge of intelligence
operations for the Bureau, wrote:

> Hoover told me that he felt that King was, or could become, a serious
> threat to the security of the country. He pointed out that King was an
> instrument of the Communist Party, and he wanted it proved that King
> had a relationship with the Soviet bloc. Hoover also made it clear that
> he wanted evidence developed that would prove that King was embez-
> zling or misusing large sums of money contributed to him and his
> organization.

According to Sullivan, FBI agents jumped to please the director. He
wrote: "We gave him what he wanted—under the threat of being out on
the street if we didn't agree."

Hoover's vendetta continued against King until the black leader was
himself cut down by an assassin's bullet in 1968. Behind this vendetta was
Hoover's secret counterintelligence program called COINTELPRO, one of
whose purposes was "to expose, disrupt, misdirect, or otherwise neutral-
ize" King and his Southern Christian Leadership Conference.

Also secretly targeted for careful scrutiny under this program was
President Kennedy and Hoover's own boss, Attorney General Kennedy.
According to Sullivan:

> Hoover was desperately trying to catch Bobby redhanded at anything
> . . . and was always gathering damaging material on Jack Kennedy,
> which the President, with his active social life, seemed more than
> willing to provide.

One of Hoover's chief fears was being fired by the Kennedys, a fear with
some substance. The Kennedys both hated and feared the powerful Hoover
and made little effort to conceal the fact that he was to be replaced after
Kennedy won the 1964 election. Robert Kennedy even told interviewer
John Bartlow Martin: "[Hoover] is rather a psycho . . . I think [the FBI] is
a very dangerous organization. . . . He's senile and frightening."

Both Kennedy brothers eventually supported King and the civil-rights
program as they came to realize that its adoption as official policy was
inevitable.

As Kennedy biographer John H. Davis pointed out: ". . . the most
potentially dangerous enemy to emerge from Kennedy's civil rights policy
was the FBI and its director."

From the ranks of angered segregationists came one man with a prophetic vision of Kennedy's death.

The Miami Prophet

On November 9, 1963, a Miami police informant named William Somersett met with Joseph A. Milteer, a wealthy right-wing extremist who promptly began to outline the assassination of President Kennedy.

Milteer was a leader of the arch-conservative National States Rights Party as well as a member of other groups such as the Congress of Freedom and the White Citizen's Council of Atlanta. Somersett had infiltrated the States Rights Party and secretly recorded Milteer's conversation.

The tape, later turned over to Miami police, recorded Milteer as saying, "(During Kennedy's impending visit to Miami) You can bet your bottom dollar he is going to have a lot to say about the Cubans, there are so many of them here. . . . The more bodyguards he has, the easier it is to get him . . . From an office building with a high-powered rifle . . . He knows he's a marked man."

Somersett said, "They are really going to try to kill him?" Milteer responded, "Oh, yeah, it's in the works . . . (An investigation) wouldn't leave any stone unturned there, no way. They will pick up somebody within hours afterward . . . just to throw the public off." Captain Charles Sapp, head of Miami's Police Intelligence Bureau, was concerned enough with Milteer's remarks to alert both the FBI and the Secret Service.

Again, apparently no word of this right-wing plot reached Secret Service agents involved in Kennedy's Dallas trip. Sapp in later years, however, recalled that plans for a Miami motorcade were scrapped and the President instead flew to a scheduled speech by helicopter.

On the day of the assassination, Milteer telephoned Somersett, saying he was in Dallas and that Kennedy was due there shortly. Milteer commented that Kennedy would never be seen in Miami again.

While the House Select Committee on Assassinations was unable to confirm Milteer's presence in Dallas during the assassination, it also failed to prove he was elsewhere. Texas researcher Jack White claims to have located a photograph of a man bearing a striking resemblance to Milteer standing in the crowd near the Texas School Book Depository.

Back in Miami after the assassination, Milteer again met with Somersett and said, "Everything ran true to form. I guess you thought I was kidding you when I said he would be killed from a window with a high-powered rifle. . . . I don't do any guessing." Milteer said not to worry about the capture of Oswald, "because he doesn't know anything." "The right-wing is in the clear," added Milteer. ". . . the patriots have outsmarted the communist group in order that the communists would carry out the plan without the right-wing becoming involved."

The FBI questioned Milteer on November 27 and he denied making any such statements. And while some information of the Milteer incident was belatedly turned over to the Warren Commission, there is no mention of Milteer in its Report or 26 volumes. Before the prophetic Milteer could be questioned further about his apparent foreknowledge of Kennedy's assassination, he died after receiving burns when a heater exploded in a vacation cabin.

The Milteer episode raises a number of questions, not the least of which is why his specific knowledge of a threat agianst the president—tape-recorded by a police agency—was not passed along to Bureau and Secret Service personnel in Dallas?

*   *   *

But the racial unrest that rocked the United States in the 1960s was not President Kennedy's only domestic problem. He was being verbally attacked not only by poor minorities with rising expectations, but also by wealthy businessmen who felt threatened by his announced social reforms.

Big business was already leery of Kennedy, who as a senator had opposed the Taft-Hartley law aimed at curbing the power of labor unions and who as president had failed to consult the business world before making certain appointments. The fears of big business increased in the spring of 1962 when Kennedy used the power of the presidency to force U.S. steel manufacturers to roll back recent price increases.

Kennedy already had served notice on the giant steel companies in September 1961, when he sent a letter to industry leaders warning them against any price increases. In his letter, Kennedy rationalized:

> The steel industry, in short, can look forward to good profits without an increase in prices. Since 1947, iron and steel common stocks prices have risen 397 percent; this is a much better performance than common stock prices in general.

On April 6, 1962, at the request of the federal government, the Steel-workers Union agreed to limit its wage demands to a ten-cents-an-hour increase beginning that summer. Then on April 11, U.S. Steel and five other major steel companies announced a 3.5 percent hike in the cost of steel.

Incensed, Kennedy told the news media:

> The American people will find it hard, as I do, to accept a situation in which a tiny handful of steel executives, whose pursuit of private power and profit exceeds their sense of public responsibility, can show such utter contempt for the interest of 185 million Americans.

Administration officials suggested an FBI investigation and on April 13, the Defense Department awarded a $5 million contract to a smaller steel firm that had not raised prices. The next day, the six major firms announced their price increase had been rescinded.

The denunciation of the steel executives by Kennedy sent shock waves through the business community. A *U.S. News and World Report* editor wrote:

What happened is frightening not only to steel people but to industry generally. . . . President Kennedy had the public interest at heart in acting as he did, but the results may not in the long run be what he intended them to be.

Other results of the Kennedy administration were infuriating corporate executives. Mergers were becoming widespread in the business world and Attorney General Kennedy and his trust busters were taking a dim view of them.

During 1963, the Justice Department's Antitrust Division won forty-five of forty-six cases; asked a federal court to force General Motors Corporation to dispose of its locomotive business while charging the firm with monopolizing the manufacture and sale of intercity buses; and ordered General Dynamics to drop a division dealing with industrial gases.

Business and political leaders began to regret that the winner of the 1960 presidential election had not been Richard M. Nixon.

Nixon and the JFK Assassination

Most Americans remember Richard Milhous Nixon as the only U.S. president to resign his office under the threat of certain impeachment.

Few know of or recall Nixon's connection with the Kennedy assassination, including the fact that Nixon was in Dallas the day Kennedy died but couldn't recall that fact three months later when interviewed by the FBI.

Born January 9, 1913, in Yorba Linda, California, Nixon was a self-made man who reached the pinnacles of power after struggling up from a background of meager financial circumstances.

Nixon wanted to attend Harvard like young Kennedy, but was forced to settle for California's Whittier College, where he honed his skills as a debater. He went on to graduate from Duke University Law School in Durham, North Carolina, then unsuccessfully tried to join the FBI.

Shortly after Pearl Harbor, Nixon took a job with the tire-rationing department of the Office of Price Administration in Washington. It is interesting that Nixon's lifelong friend, Florida entrepreneur Charles "Bebe" Rebozo, began his profitable career selling recapped tires. Although Nixon has claimed he did not meet Rebozo until 1948 while vacationing in Florida after the Hiss case, some researchers say the pair were in contact during the war.

Later in the war, Nixon enlisted in the Navy and served in the South Pacific, where on one island he built a small shack used for high-stakes gambling and drinking.

In 1946, Nixon successfully ran for Congress after labeling his opponent, incumbent congressman Jerry Voorhis, a "friend of the Communists." With his anticommunist credentials, Nixon was immediately named to the House Un-American Activities Committee where his name became nationally known due to his part in the Alger Hiss case.

By 1950, the ambitious Nixon was ready to run for a Senate seat. His opponent was a liberal former Hollywood actress named Helen Douglas. Nixon painted Douglas as a friend of communism and dubbed her the "pink lady." He accused her of voting with a "notorious Communist-line congressman" from New York, failing to mention that Nixon himself had voted with this same congressman 112 times. Such campaign tactics earned Nixon the epithet "Tricky Dick." But they also proved effective. Nixon beat Douglas by nearly seven hundred thousand votes.

The man most responsible for Nixon's smear tactics was his close friend and campaign manager Murray Chotiner, a lawyer who represented ranking mobsters and who had connections leading back to reputed New Orleans Mafia chief Carlos Marcello and Teamsters leader Jimmy Hoffa.

In 1952, after only six years in politics, Nixon became vice president under Dwight Eisenhower, thanks to the support of his political mentor, former New York governor Thomas Dewey, and his undermining of the favorite-son candidacy of fellow Californian, Earl Warren.

Throughout the Eisenhower years, the war-hero president snubbed Nixon both politically and socially. In 1960, when Eisenhower was asked what major decisions Nixon had participated in, he caustically replied: "If you give me a week, I might think of one."

But Nixon was busy building up his own power base with men of dubious backgrounds.

In his memoirs, mobster Mickey Cohen wrote that he gave Chotiner $5,000 for Nixon's 1946 congressional campaign and raised $75,000 from Las Vegas gamblers for Nixon's 1950 Senate race.

Furthermore, Ed Partin, a former aide to Jimmy Hoffa turned government informant, detailed a meeting between Hoffa and New Orleans mob boss Carlos Marcello at the height of the 1960 presidential campaign:

> I was right there, listening to the conversation. Marcello had a suitcase filled with $500,000 cash which was going to Nixon. It was a half-million-dollar contribution. The other half [of a promised $1 million] was coming from the mob boys in New Jersey and Florida.

Nixon's organized-crime contacts apparently continued even after he resigned the presidency in disgrace. During a 1975 golf tournament at La Costa Country Club in California, Nixon's golfing companions included Allen Dorfman, a mob-Teamster financial coordinator, and Tony Provenzano, a former Teamster official and convicted Mafia killer.

It has been revealed by investigative authors Carl Oglesby, Howard

Kohn, David Scheim, and others that Nixon was a frequent visitor to Cuba during the early 1950s and was in contact with confederates of organized-crime financial wizard Meyer Lansky.

When Fidel Castro gained power in Cuba, Lansky was one of those mob chieftains who wanted him overthrown. An attempt with CIA officers to plan an invasion of Cuba was initiated by Eisenhower's White House Political Action Officer, Richard Nixon. In his book *Six Crises,* Nixon wrote: "The covert training of Cuban exiles by the CIA was due in substantial part, at least, to my efforts. This had been adopted as a policy as a result of my direct support."

Before the invasion could be launched, a serious snag occurred for Nixon and his backers—he lost the election of 1960 to John F. Kennedy.

Rather than bide his time waiting for the next presidential election, Nixon ran against Pat Brown for the governorship of California in 1962. He was handily defeated, especially after news broke of a secret $200,000 loan from billionaire Howard Hughes to Nixon's brother.

Within two years, Nixon was back on the political stage, campaigning for Republican candidates. GOP stalwarts repaid this activity by again nominating Richard Nixon for president in August 1968. By then, of course, both John and Robert Kennedy were dead.

During the Nixon years, his friends in organized crime were not forgotten. The Nixon administration intervened in at least twenty trials of crime figures, ostensibly to protect "intelligence sources and methods."

In 1973, Nixon's attorney general, Richard Kleindienst, denied an FBI request to continue an electronic surveillance operation that was beginning to penetrate connections between the Mafia and the Teamsters.

Neither did Nixon forget his friend Jimmy Hoffa, whom he pardoned in 1971 despite recommendations against such action.

But of all Nixon's possible crime connections, the most intriguing involves Jack Ruby, the killer of Lee Harvey Oswald. In 1975, Trowbridge Ford, a political science associate professor at College of the Holy Cross in Worcester, Massachusetts, was poring over a stack of recently released FBI documents. Ford was astonished to discover a memorandum written by a Bureau staff assistant to a government panel looking into organized-crime activity in 1947. The memo stated:

> It is my sworn statement that one Jack Rubenstein of Chicago, noted as a potential witness for hearings of the House Committee on Un-American Activities, is performing information functions for the staff of Congressman Richard Nixon, Republican of California. It is requested Rubenstein not be called for open testimony in the aforementioned hearings.

Later in 1947, Chicago's Rubenstein moved to Dallas and shortened his name to Jack Ruby.

The idea that Jack Ruby had worked for Nixon should have set off the national news media. Instead, FBI officials told Ford that the document he discovered was a fake and the story was quickly dropped. Of course, in accepting the Bureau's explanation of the memo, one must wonder why a "fake" document was contained in FBI files and how many other such fakes are yet residing with the Bureau?

By the early 1980s, Ford told this author he had studied literally thousands of genuine FBI documents and had slowly come to the conclusion that the Nixon-Ruby memo was probably legitimate. Legitimate or not, the matter raises even more suspicion when viewed with Nixon's presence in Dallas the day Kennedy died.

On November 20, 1963, Nixon arrived in Dallas, where a Carbonated Bottlers' convention was being held. A newsman from the *Dallas Times Herald* interviewed Nixon and wrote:

The former Vice President arrived in Dallas Wednesday night to attend a board meeting of Pepsi-Cola Company, which is represented by his New York law partnership. He plans to leave Dallas Friday morning a few hours before the arrival of President Kennedy. Mr. Nixon said that although he planned to talk by telephone to several Dallas Republican leaders, he had no plans for a formal meeting with them.

Interestingly, researcher Richard Sprague examined Pepsi-Cola corporate records and found no board meeting was held in Dallas in 1963.

The connections and politics of Pepsi-Cola deserve serious attention from assassination researchers. The soft-drink company's advertising was handled by J. Walter Thompson, the giant public relations firm that also worked to sell the Pentagon's brand of "peace."

Nixon was longtime friends with Pepsi-Cola President Don Kendall and, as president, it was Nixon who opened the lucrative Soviet soft-drink market to Pepsi. A Justice Department investigation into this transaction revealed that a "high government official had all the red tape done away with so Pepsico could obtain the Soviet franchise without any competition."

Pepsi went on to help those who had helped the company. In 1973, President Kendall formed the Save the Presidency Committee, which sought to protect Nixon from the wrath of Watergate investigations.

It is especially interesting to note that Cartha DeLoach, the FBI official who was chief liaison between Director Hoover and President Lyndon Johnson, later joined Pepsi-Cola.

With Nixon in Dallas was Pepsi Cola heiress and actress Joan Crawford. Both Nixon and Crawford made comments in the Dallas newspapers to the effect that they, unlike the President, didn't need Secret Service protection, and they intimated that the nation was upset with Kennedy's policies. It has been suggested that this taunting may have been responsible for Kennedy's critical decision not to order the Plexiglas top placed on his limousine on November 22.

Nixon also caused a stir in Dallas when he suggested that Lyndon Johnson would be dropped from the 1964 Democratic national ticket. Quoted in the November 22, 1963, *Dallas Morning News*, Nixon said:

> . . . we must remember that President Kennedy and his advisers are practical politicians. . . . Lyndon was chosen in 1960 because he could help the ticket in the South. Now he is becoming a political liability in the South, just as he is in the North.

On the morning of November 22, Nixon was driven to Love Field in Dallas, where he boarded American Airlines Flight 82 for New York. Less than two hours after Nixon left, *Air Force One* landed at Love Field with the doomed Kennedy.

Three months later, the Warren Commission asked the FBI to investigate Marina Oswald's allegation that her husband had tried to kill Nixon during a visit to Dallas. The FBI report dealing with Nixon's interview stated:

> On February 28, 1964, the Honorable Richard M. Nixon, former Vice President of the U.S., was contacted by Assistant Director in charge of the New York Office, John F. Malone, and furnished the following information:
> Mr. Nixon advised that the only time he was in Dallas, Texas, during 1963 was two days prior to the assassination of President John F. Kennedy.

The question of whether Nixon was merely forgetful or dissembling in his comment to the FBI might have been cleared up by yet another Bureau report entitled "Letter of FBI of June 29, 1964, concerning Richard Nixon." However, this document was reported missing from the National Archives in 1976.

Nixon's recollection improved during a 1967 interview with journalist Jules Witcover. Speaking about the assassination, Nixon said:

> I was in a taxicab when I got the news. I had been in Dallas attending a meeting. I flew back to New York the next morning. It must have happened just as my plane was landing. My cab stopped for a light in Queens and a guy ran over and said, "Have you got a radio? The President's been wounded." I thought, "Oh, my God, it must have been one of the nuts." A half hour later I got to my apartment and the doorman told me he was dead. I called J. Edgar Hoover and asked him, "What happened? Was it one of the nuts?" Hoover said, "No, it was a Communist."

The supposed attack on Nixon by Oswald undoubtedly is one of the more ludicrous incidents of the Warren Commission investigation—and it is a prime example of the unreliability of Marina Oswald's testimony.

In early February 1964, when Marina Oswald first testified to the Commission, she failed to mention the incident when asked if her husband had expressed any hostility toward any official of the United States. In June, her memory jogged by an FBI report from Oswald's brother, Robert, she said that just a few days before Oswald left for New Orleans on April 24, 1963, he put on a good suit after reading a morning newspaper. She told the Commission:

> I saw that he took a pistol. I asked him where he was going and why he was getting dressed. He answered, "Nixon is coming. I want to go and have a look." . . . I called him into the bathroom and I closed the door and I wanted to prevent him and then I started to cry. And I told him that he shouldn't do this, and that he had promised me.

She told the Commission she locked him in the bathroom to prevent him from trying to shoot Nixon. However, as confirmed by an FBI investigation, the bathroom—like most others—locked from the inside. Accordingly, in a subsequent interview with the Commission, Marina amended her story by saying she held the bathroom door for hours to prevent Oswald from leaving.

The Commission, upon learning that Nixon was not even in Dallas at any time near this incident, decided that Marina may have been mistaken and that the target of Oswald's pistol may have been Vice President Johnson, who had visited Dallas on April 23.

In an Oval Office meeting on June 23, 1972—just five days after the Nixon-connected burglars were caught in the Watergate office complex— Nixon spoke with his chief of staff, H. R. Haldeman, saying:

> Of course, this Hunt [Watergate burglar and CIA liaison man with the anti-Castro Cubans E. Howard Hunt], that will uncover a lot of things. You open that scab, there's a hell of a lot of things, and we feel that it would be very detrimental to have this thing go any further . . . the President believes that it is going to open the whole Bay of Pigs thing up again.

Later that same day, Nixon spoke with Haldeman again, saying:

> . . . very bad to have this fellow Hunt, ah, he knows too damned much, if he was involved—you happen to know that? [Hunt was not with the Watergate burglars, but was in radio contact with them from across the street.] If it gets out that this is all involved, the Cuba thing would be a fiasco. It would make the CIA look bad, it's going to make Hunt look bad, and it's likely to blow the whole Bay of Pigs thing, which we think would be very unfortunate—both for the CIA, and for the country, at this time, and for American foreign policy. Just tell him to lay off . . .

After telling Nixon that the FBI was aware of CIA operatives' involvement in the Watergate affair, Haldeman tells his chief:

. . . the problem is it tracks back to the Bay of Pigs and it tracks back to some other, the leads run out to people who had no involvement in this, except by contracts and connection, but it gets into areas that are liable to be realized.

What could Nixon and Haldeman have been talking about? The "whole Bay of Pigs thing" had been over for more than ten years. Nixon was out of office when the actual invasion began and the assault's disastrous consequences were a matter of historical record. Could they have been circuitously referring to the interlocking connections between CIA agents, anti-Castro Cubans, and mobsters that likely resulted in the Kennedy assassination? Did they themselves have some sort of insider knowledge of this event?

Researchers are left guessing. However, it is significant to recall that when Hunt later demanded $2 million to keep quiet about what he knew, Nixon agreed and the money was raised.

It may also be significant to consider the number of people connected with the Warren Commission that were hired or considered for employment by Nixon's circle during Watergate.

John Dean's lawyer was Commission Administrative Aide Charles N. Shaffer; John Ehrlichman hired Commission Senior Counsel Joseph Ball as his lawyer; Nixon initially wanted Commission General Counsel J. Lee Rankin as Watergate Prosecutor then wanted Commission Member John McCloy but later accepted Commission Special Counsel Leon Jaworski (who represented Texas Attorney General Waggoner Carr); Nixon named Rankin to "edit" White House tapes; Nixon accepted Commission Senior Counsel Albert E. Jenner as chief minority counsel for the House Judiciary Committee considering Nixon's impeachment and Nixon asked Commission Counsel Arlen Specter to help with his defense.

Specter, now Senator from Pennsylvania, was the chief architect of the controversial "single-bullet theory" for the Warren Commission. He was a protege of Nixon's attorney general, John Mitchell, and had served as co-chairman of the Pennsylvania division of the Committee to Re-Elect the President (CREEP) in 1972.

Commission attorney David Belin—still its most ardent supporter—headed Lawyers for Nixon.

In the final days of Watergate, organized-crime investigator Dan E. Moldea revealed that military authorities, including Nixon's chief of staff, General Alexander Haig, began to connect their chief with several mobsters, including Florida's Santos Trafficante, believed responsible for setting up heroin routes from Vietnam and making payoffs to Nixon associates.

Moldea quoted a Justice Department official as saying:

The whole goddamn thing is too frightening to think about. We're talking about the President of the United States . . . a man who pardoned organized crime figures after millions were spent by the government putting them away, a guy who's had these connections since he was a congressman in the 1940s. I guess the real shame is that we'll never know the whole story, it'll never come out.

In a final nose thumbing to the American people, Nixon appointed former Warren Commission member Gerald R. Ford as vice president after the resignation of Spiro Agnew.

One of Ford's first public actions was to pardon Nixon of any crimes.

*   *   *

The question has been raised: If there was a plot to assassinate Kennedy, wouldn't someone have been aware of it?

There are many indications that someone was in the fall of 1963.

We already have learned of many incidents of people with foreknowledge of Kennedy's death—including racist J. A. Milteer and Rose Cherami.

It also appears that some corporate leaders may have been aware of Kennedy's pending fate.

A Killing on Wall Street

In the thirty minutes following Kennedy's assassination in Dallas, the Dow Jones average fell more than 21.16 points. An estimated six million shares of stock changed hands, wiping out about $15 billion in paper values on the New York Stock Exchange alone. It was the greatest Stock Market panic since 1929. The panic and confusion was such that the Securities and Exchange Commission closed the Stock Exchange shortly after 2 p.m., more than eighty minutes before normal closing time. It was the first emergency shutdown of the Stock Market since August, 1933.

A few sharp investors—or perhaps individuals with a knowledge of what was to come—had taken "short" positions in scattered areas of the market. That is, some stocks unaccountably were sold before the market dropped, indicating some people may have had advanced word that something momentous was about to happen.

Then when the Stock Market reopened on November 26, 1963,—just four days after the assassination—the New York Stock Exchange made a record $21 billion advance, more than regaining the losses incurred the day Kennedy died. It was the biggest single-day rise in the history of the Stock Market. More huge profits were made. No one has publicly indentified the men who made their own private killing in the Stock Market, but it has been estimated that the profits made just on November 22 alone totaled more than $500 million.

It has been suggested by at least one author that the immense amount of money which changed hands on November 22, 1963, was the motivation behind Kennedy's death. And while most researchers reject this idea, many do believe that certain individuals—using insider information on the impending assassination—could not resist the temptation to profit from their knowledge.

*   *   *

Another overlooked aspect of Kennedy's attempt to reform American society involves money.

Kennedy apparently reasoned that by returning to the Constitution, which states that only Congress shall coin and regulate money, the soaring national debt could be reduced by not paying interest to the bankers of the Federal Reserve System, who print paper money then loan it to the government at interest.

He moved in this area on June 4, 1963, by signing Executive Order 11,110 which called for the issuance of $4,292,893,815 in United States Notes through the U.S. Treasury rather than the traditional Federal Reserve System. That same day, Kennedy signed a bill changing the backing of one- and two-dollar bills from silver to gold, adding strength to the weakened U.S. currency.

Kennedy's comptroller of the currency, James J. Saxon, had been at odds with the powerful Federal Reserve Board for some time, encouraging broader investment and lending powers for banks that were not part of the Federal Reserve system. Saxon also had decided that non-Reserve banks could underwrite state and local general obligation bonds, again weakening the dominant Federal Reserve banks.

A number of "Kennedy bills" were indeed issued—the author has a five-dollar bill in his possession with the heading "United States Note" —but were quickly withdrawn after Kennedy's death.

According to information from the Library of the Comptroller of the Currency, Executive Order 11,110 remains in effect today, although successive administrations beginning with that of President Lyndon Johnson apparently have simply ignored it and instead returned to the practice of paying interest on Federal Reserve notes.

Today we continue to use Federal Reserve Notes, and the deficit is at an all-time high.

Considering that the battle over U.S. monetary control by a monolithic central bank is an issue that dates back to the founding of the Republic, some assassination researchers believe Kennedy's little-noted efforts to reform the money supply and curtail the Federal Reserve System may have cost him much more than just the enmity of the all-powerful international bankers.

President Kennedy inched farther out on a limb with big business on January 17, 1963, when he presented both his administration's budget and proposals for tax reform that included a tax cut.

Kennedy's tax proposals included relieving the tax burden of low-income and elderly persons, revising tax treatment of capital gains for a better flow of capital funds, and broadening the base of individual and corporate income taxes to remove special privileges and loopholes and even to do away with the oil depletion allowance.

This action brought the beleaguered President into direct confrontation with one of the most powerful and singleminded groups in America—wealthy oilmen.

Kennedy and Oilmen

The history of oil is replete with stories of unbounded greed, business chicanery, and even violence.

During 1923, the first major oil scandal occurred when it was discovered that President Warren G. Harding's secretary of the interior, Albert B. Fall, had accepted money from oilmen in exchange for secretly leasing drilling rights on government land in Wyoming known as the Teapot Dome.

By 1933, there were calls for making the vital oil industry a public utility with governmental controls. One of the men supporting this move was President Franklin Roosevelt's secretary of the interior, Harold Ickes. However, FDR was finally turned against the plan by Texas Congressman Sam Rayburn, Lyndon Johnson's mentor, who faithfully represented Texas oil interests in Washington.

After World War II, the Marshall Plan began turning recovering European nations away from coal to oil. Refining capacity in Europe tripled in just a few years.

In 1950, a secret agreement was reached between the State Department and major oil companies that allowed all royalties paid to Arab nations to be applied as tax credits.

Dwight Eisenhower was elected with strong support from the oil industry and, early in 1953, in one of his first actions, he stopped a grand jury investigation into the "international Petroleum Cartel" citing reasons of "national security."

The same year, a CIA-backed coup reinstated the Shah of Iran and new oil arrangements were made with Iran. Ironically, the Iranian coup was masterminded by Kermit Roosevelt, Teddy's grandson, who went on to become a vice president of Gulf Oil.

The Suez Crisis in 1956 signaled the end of British and French colonialism in the Middle East and the major oil companies moved to consolidate their power.

When John F. Kennedy became President in 1961, the oil industry felt secure.

But President Kennedy then began to assault the power of the oil giants directly, first with a law known as the Kennedy Act, and later by attacking the oil depletion allowance. The Kennedy Act, passed on October 16, 1962, removed the distinction between repatriated profits and profits reinvested abroad. Both were now subject to U.S. taxation. The measure also was aimed at preventing taxable income from being hidden away in foreign subsidiaries and other tax havens. While this law applied to industry as a whole, it particularly affected the oil companies, which were greatly diversified with large overseas operations.

By the end of 1962, oilmen estimated their earnings on foreign investment capital would fall to 15 percent, compared with 30 percent in 1955.

One of the most sacred of provisions in the eyes of oilmen was the oil depletion allowance, which permitted oil producers to treat up to 27.5 percent of their income as tax exempt. In theory this was to compensate for the depletion of fixed oil reserves but, in effect, it gave the oil industry a lower tax rate. Under this allowance, an oilman with a good deal of venture capital could become rich with virtually no risk. For example, a speculator could drill ten wells. If nine were dry holes and only the tenth struck oil, he would still make money because of tax breaks and the depletion allowance.

It was estimated at the time that oilmen might lose nearly $300 million a year if the depletion allowance was diminished.

Attempts to eliminate or reduce the depletion allowance were rebuffed year after year by congressmen, many of whom were the happy recipients of oil-industry contributions.

Speaking of his tax reform act of 1963, President Kennedy pointed the finger at the oil companies, saying: ". . . no one industry should be permitted to obtain an undue tax advantage over all others."

Included in Kennedy's tax package were provisions for closing a number of corporate tax loopholes, including the depletion allowance. Needless to say, oilmen both in Texas and elsewhere felt threatened by Kennedy and his policies. Kennedy's use of his personal power against the steel manufacturers had shown them that the young President meant to enforce his will in these matters.

John W. Curington, who for twelve years was special assistant to Dallas oil billionaire H. L. Hunt, reported in 1977: "Hunt was often heard by top aides and followers to say that America would be much better off without Kennedy." Curington, whose statements were assessed truthful by Psychological Stress Evaluator (PSE) analysis, also said the oilman sent him to check on Oswald's police security while in custody and was "elated" to find it was lax. Curington also is convinced that he saw Marina Oswald coming from Hunt's private offices several weeks after the assassination.

Hunt's former assistant said he believes that the wealthy oilman unwittingly influenced right-wing followers to participate in a conspiracy to kill Kennedy. He added that in later years, Hunt admitted that he knew an assassination conspiracy existed.

Angry talk in the corporate boardrooms may have grown into deadly plots on golf courses and at private parties. But oilmen, despite their unparalleled wealth and power, could not have moved against Kennedy on their own. They needed allies within government and within the intelligence community. Such allies were there—among the anti-Castro Cubans, in the CIA, organized crime, and within the federal government—all were most receptive to the idea of a change of leadership.

* * *

One man with connections to government, intelligence, and the oil industry was George DeMohrenschildt, identified by the Warren Commission as the last-known close friend to Lee Harvey Oswald.

Oswald's Friends

Perhaps the most intriguing person in the entire cast of characters connected with the Kennedy assassination was oil geologist George S. DeMohrenschildt—a man who was friends with both Jackie Kennedy's family and the alleged assassin of her husband, Lee Harvey Oswald.

Despite this fascinating link, little was said about DeMohrenschildt at the time of the assassination. Both he and his wife, Jeanne, were in Haiti during the events in Dallas.

A close study of DeMohrenschildt's life shows a string of intelligence connections, raising the possibility that DeMohrenschildt may have played a role—perhaps unwittingly—in furthering plans for the assassination. This possibility came to haunt DeMohrenschildt in the days just prior to his suspicious death in 1977.

DeMohrenschildt—his family, originally named Mohrenskuld, was of Swedish extraction—was born April 17, 1911, in Mozyr, a small Baltic town in czarist Russia near the Polish border.

An educated, sophisticated young man, DeMohrenschildt was introduced to many wealthy and influential Americans. He later told the Warren Commission:

[I met] lots of people, but especially Mrs. [Janet] Bouvier . . . Mrs. Bouvier is Jacqueline Kennedy's mother, also [I met] her father and her whole family. [Mrs. Bouvier] was in the process of getting a divorce from her husband [Jackie's father, John V. "Jack" Bouvier]. I met him, also. We were very close friends. We saw each other every day. I met Jackie then, when she was a little girl. [And] her sister, who was still in the cradle practically.

After failing in his attempts to sell insurance and perfume, DeMohrenschildt traveled by bus to Texas, where he got a job with Humble Oil Company in Houston, thanks to family connections. Despite being friends with the chairman of the board of Humble, young DeMohrenschildt was confined to working as a "roughneck" in the Louisiana oil fields. He quit after being injured and contracting amoebic dysentery.

Although for years he claimed to have worked for French intelligence during the early years of World War II—he said he was never an official agent but had helped a good friend, Pierre Freyss, the head of French counterintelligence—in later years he confessed to his wife that he had briefly worked for the Germans.

DeMohrenschildt also became closely connected with many exiled Russians who joined with the General Vlassov movement, anticommunist Russians who fought with the Nazis in hope of recovering their homeland. Springing up in cities where there were large Russian exile communities, these people referred to themselves as "solidarists," indicating the solidarity of their purpose. One of these groups existed in Dallas during the early 1960s, although DeMohrenschildt disclaimed being a member.

The Vlassov organization was eventually absorbed by the Nazi spy system under General Reinhard Gehlen, which at the end of the war became a part of U.S. intelligence. Many members of this apparatus ended up working for the CIA.

His oil-related travels took him to France, Nigeria, Ghana, and Togoland.

In 1957, despite an unflattering background check by the CIA, he journeyed to Yugoslavia for the International Cooperation Administration, a branch of the U.S. government's Agency for International Development. By this time, DeMohrenschildt apparently had some association with the Agency, according to documents which became public in the late 1970s.

Researcher Michael Levy obtained one CIA memo from former Agency deputy director Richard Helms that states that DeMohrenschildt's trip to Yugoslavia provided "foreign intelligence which was promptly disseminated to other federal agencies in 10 separate reports." Another CIA memo indicated that DeMohrenschildt also furnished lengthy reports on his later travels through Mexico and Central America.

Shortly before leaving for Yugoslavia, DeMohrenschildt met another Russian exile who lived in the same Dallas hotel with him. Jeanne Fromenke LeGon had already established a career as a dancer and clothing designer. Her family, too, had strong political and defense-related connections. Her Russian father had built the first railroads in China and was connected with Nationalist politics there while her brother, Sergio, had worked on the supersecret Manhattan atomic bomb project. Her former husband, Robert LeGon, was connected to security work for Douglas

Aircraft and their daughter, Christiana, was married to a vice president of Lockheed Aircraft Corporation.

Jeanne and the outgoing DeMohrenschildt hit it off right away and she joined him in Yugoslavia. In a curious incident there, the couple were boating when they were shot at by Communist guards who became anxious when they came too close to Marshal Tito's summer home. DeMohrenschildt claimed to have been simply sketching the shoreline.

Returning to the United States, George and Jeanne were soon married and shortly set off on an incredible odyssey through Central America.

Back in Dallas in late 1961, the DeMohrenschildts were at the center of prominent Dallasites. His business and social contacts read like a who's who of the Texas oil community. DeMohrenschildt knew Dallas oil millionaires H. L. Hunt and Clint Murchinson, John Mecom of Houston, Robert Kerr of Kerr-McGee, and Jean De Menil, head of the worldwide Schlumberger Corporation.

(According to former New Orleans district attorney Jim Garrison, arms and explosives supplied by the CIA to the anti-Castro Cuban exiles were hidden away in a Schlumberger facility near New Orleans in the summer of 1963.)

But most intriguing was DeMohrenschildt's friendship with J. Walter Moore, a member of the CIA's Domestic Contact Service.

Moore, whom DeMohrenschildt described to the Warren Commission as "a government man—either FBI or Central Intelligence," debriefed the geologist upon his return from Yugoslavia and thereafter met with the DeMohrenschildts socially on many occasions.

After DeMohrenschildt first met Lee Harvey Oswald, he checked on the ex-Marine with Moore, who he said described Oswald as simply a "harmless lunatic."

In another incident, DeMohrenschildt wrote to friends less than two months after the assassination expressing shock and disbelief over Kennedy's death. He wrote: ". . . before we began to help Marina and the child, we asked the FBI man in Dallas . . . about Lee and he told us that he was "completely harmless."

These letters are part of DeMohrenschildt's FBI file, indicating the Bureau was monitoring him during this time. His statements that he had checked on Oswald with the Bureau apparently caused great consternation. Dallas FBI chief J. Gordon Shanklin even ordered Agent James Woods to go to Haiti and obtained a lengthy statement from DeMohrenschildt denying that he had ever spoken about Oswald to the Bureau.

DeMohrenschildt himself may have been the object of a secret investigation in the months preceeding Kennedy's death. Once DeMohrenschildt noticed small pencil marks on some of his papers and, convinced his home had been secretly entered, questioned Moore about it. Moore denied that government people had broken into DeMohrenschildt's home.

Another close friend of DeMohrenschildt was Fort Worth attorney Max Clark, who at that time was connected with security at General Dynamics.

In later years, neither George nor Jeanne DeMohrenschildt could recall exactly who first mentioned the Oswalds to them. But in the summer of 1962, DeMohrenschildt and a Colonel Lawrence Orlov went to nearby Fort Worth on business and DeMohrenschildt decided to visit the Oswalds. He had heard through the Russian community in Dallas that the Oswalds had recently arrived in this country from Minsk and he was eager for news about the city of his youth.

DeMohrenschildt was appalled at the poorly furnished "shack" in which the Oswalds lived, but was impressed by Oswald's command of Russian. He told the Warren Commission:

. . . he spoke fluent Russian, but with a foreign accent, and made mistakes, grammatical mistakes but had remarkable fluency in Russian. . . . Remarkable—for a fellow of his background and education . . . he preferred to speak Russian than English any time. He always would switch from English to Russian.

He said both his first impression of Oswald and his last were the same:

I could never get mad at this fellow. . . . Sometimes he was obnoxious. I don't know. I had a liking for him. I always had a liking for him. There was something charming about him, there was some—I don't know. I just liked the guy—that is all. . . . with me he was very humble. If somebody expressed an interest in him, he blossomed, absolutely blossomed. If you asked him some questions about him, he was just out of this world. That was more or less the reason that I think he liked me very much.

The DeMohrenschildts soon embraced the Oswalds and visited them with an idea of helping the struggling couple.

It is interesting to note how the Dallas Russian community split in their reactions to the Oswalds. Most of them—being staunch anticommunists—wanted nothing to do with a man who had tried to defect to Russia. But some of the emigré members—especially those with intelligence connections, such as DeMohrenschildt—seemed quite at ease with the young would-be defector. Perhaps they, too, had been assured that Oswald was just a "harmless lunatic."

In October 1962, DeMohrenschildt managed to move Oswald to Dallas, where he dropped out of sight for nearly a month. Marina was left with DeMohrenschildt's daughter and son-in-law, the Gary Taylors.

Something was going on because Oswald did not even inform his mother of the move and he told friends he had been fired from his job at Leslie Welding in Fort Worth when actually he had quit.

Furthermore, during this time DeMohrenschildt was making regular trips to Houston, according to his friends Igor Voshinin and Paul Raigorodsky. Raigorodsky, a wealthy oilman and a director of the Tolstoy Foundation—an anticommunist organization of Russian exiles that was funded by the U.S. government—told the Warren Commission he asked DeMohrenschildt about his frequent Houston trips. Raigorodsky stated: "He told me he was going to see Herman and George Brown. They are brothers." The Brown brothers were owners of Brown and Root Construction and close friends and financial contributors to Lyndon Johnson.

Today, however, Jeanne DeMohrenschildt contends that her husband was conducting oil business in Houston with John Mecom and John De Menil. She said the only reason they didn't relocate to Houston during this time was because of her successful clothing business in Dallas.

At the time of the Cuban Missile Crisis, Oswald went to work for Jaggars-Chiles-Stovall, a Dallas printing and photographic firm that had contracts with the U.S. Army Map Service. Although clearances were required to work in some areas of the plant, testimony before the Warren Commission showed security was sloppy and apparently Oswald had access to sensitive material. It was here, it was believed, that Oswald manufactured false identification papers both for himself and in the name A.J. Hidell, using company photographic equipment.

He once asked fellow employee Dennis Ofstein if he knew what the term *microdot* meant. (It should be noted that the word "microdot" was found written in Oswald's address book next to the entry for Jaggars-Chiles-Stovall.) When Ofstein replied no, Oswald proceeded to explain that it was a special photographic process whereby a great mass of documents could be reduced to the size of a dot. He said this technique was used frequently in espionage work. Ofstein wondered why Oswald would discuss such a subject.

Oswald and DeMohrenschildt also may have discussed spy work. He told the Warren Commission that Oswald once told him: ". . . he had some contacts with the Japanese Communists in Japan, and they—that got him interested to go and see what goes on in the Soviet Union."

Through the Christmas holidays of 1962–63 DeMohrenschildt continued to try with only marginal success to get the Dallas Russian emigré community involved with the Oswalds.

He apparently tried to separate the Oswalds and, on at least two occasions, tried to find living quarters for Marina and her children. But Marina decided to reunite with Oswald, much to the disgust of her friends in the Russian community who had tried to help her despite their dislike for her husband.

On February 22, 1963, the DeMohrenschildts brought the Oswalds to the home of Everett Glover, where Marina was introduced to Ruth Paine. Mrs. Paine was separated from her husband Michael, an employee of Bell Helicopter, and expressed an interest in seeing Marina again for the purpose of learning the Russian language. Marina agreed and several visits between the women followed.

According to the Warren Commission, Oswald ordered the fateful Mannlicher-Carcano rifle from a mail order firm under the name "A. Hidell" on March 12, 1963, and it arrived in Dallas on March 25. Just sixteen days later, Oswald reportedly fired a shot at General Walker.

The Walker incident occurred on a Wednesday night. Oswald arrived back home that evening and, according to Marina's Warren Commission testimony, told her he fired at Walker and had then buried his rifle. (Recall that the rifle discovered in the Texas School Book Depository was clean and well oiled and that no gun-cleaning material was found among Oswald's possessions.)

Yet the following weekend, the rifle was observed in his home by Jeanne DeMohrenschildt during a visit. She and her husband brought a pink bunny toy to Oswald's young daughter and Marina was showing her around their new apartment when she saw a rifle in a closet.

As Mrs. DeMohrenschildt recalls the incident today, she asked Marina: "What on earth is that?" Marina replied: "A rifle. Lee bought it. I don't know why when we need money for food and things." Asked what Oswald did with the weapon, Mrs. DeMohrenschildt said Marina answered: "He goes to the public park with little June [Oswald's daughter] and shoots leaves with it."

Mrs. DeMohrenschildt recently explained:

Today that sounds very strange, but at the time, I was thinking of the times I had fired guns at small targets in amusement parks and I really didn't think too much of her answer. When I told George about the rifle I had seen in the closet, he immediately boomed out, "Did you take that pot shot at General Walker, Lee?" George then laughed loudly. Looking back on this incident today, Lee and Marina did not appear to be shocked or upset. They merely stood there in silence while George laughed.

However, DeMohrenschildt told the Warren Commission:

He sort of shriveled, you see, when I asked this question. . . . Became tense, you see, and didn't answer anything. . . . the remark about Walker ended the conversation. There was silence after that and we changed the subject and left very soon afterwards. . . . It was frankly a stupid joke on my part.

Marina told the Warren Commission that on another occasion, DeMohrenschildt asked Oswald, "Lee, how is it possible that you missed?" However both DeMohrenschildts denied such a question was ever asked.

This visit was to be the last meeting between the DeMohrenschildts and the Oswalds. On April 23, Marina moved in with the attentive Mrs. Paine, and the next day Oswald left Dallas by bus for New Orleans.

About a week later, the DeMohrenschildts left for a new business venture in Haiti. It is now obvious that this venture involved more than simply oil surveying and hemp growing as detailed by DeMohrenschildt to the Warren Commission.

During May 1963, as the DeMohrenschildts were preparing to leave for Haiti, they stopped in Washington where, according to CIA records, DeMohrenschildt met with a CIA representative and the assistant director of Army Intelligence. What specifically was discussed at this meeting is not known, but at this same time, another CIA document shows that an Agency officer "requested an expedite check on George DeMohrenschildt." At this meeting was DeMohrenschildt's Haitian business associate, Clemard Charles. Researchers have noted that Charles later was involved in the sale of arms and military equipment involving a gun runner named Edward Browder.

According to the House Select Committee on Assassinations, Browder leased a B-25 bomber under the name of a fictitious company and flew it to Haiti a year after the Kennedy assassination and later cashed a $24,000 check signed by Charles. Browder, a former Lockheed test pilot who is serving a twenty-five-year prison sentence for "security violations," told the Committee he had been working for the CIA. Browder, according to information gathered by author David E. Scheim, also was an associate of Jack Ruby in the 1950s when both men were arranging the sale of arms to Fidel Castro.

The DeMohrenschildts were in Haiti when they learned of Kennedy's death. Reportedly, DeMohrenschildt told friends there the FBI was behind the assassination. Whether or not he actually made such a comment, he did start to experience difficulties after Haitian president François "Papa Doc" Duvalier reportedly received a letter from the FBI telling of DeMohrenschildt's friendship with Oswald and labeling him as a "Polish Communist and a member of an international band."

The DeMohrenschildts were called to Washington to testify to the Warren Commission in April 1964. Oddly enough, when DeMohrenschildt tried to raise the issue of the damaging FBI letter with Warren Commission attorney Albert Jenner, Jenner quickly told him: "I would say you have been misinformed on that." DeMohrenschildt replied: "Well, he did receive some kind of letter." Jenner then said, "But, nothing that would contain any such statements. . . . It may have been a crank letter, but nothing official." DeMohrenschildt, catching the drift of Jenner's remarks depreciating the whole subject, suddenly agreed: "Yes, I am sure it is nothing official. I am sure it could not have been anything official."

Researchers are left with the question of how a Warren Commission attorney, supposedly searching for the truth of the Kennedy assassination, could have been so confident that the FBI letter was a "crank" and why he had closed the subject rather than trying to find out more about it.

Today, Jeanne DeMohrenschildt claims that the Warren Commission did not appear eager to hear from her and her husband and that they had to ask to testify. She told this author:

> Much of our problems with government authorities came from our refusal to slander Lee's name. The Warren Commission, along with the mass media, depicted Oswald as a complete loner, a total failure, both as a man and a father. This is not the impression George and I had of this man. Lee was a sincere person. Although from a modest educational background, he was quick and bright. . . . Lee obviously loved his daughter June. We could not possibly consider him as dangerous.

During their stay in Washington, the DeMohrenschildts visited in the home of Jackie Kennedy's mother, now Mrs. Hugh D. Auchincloss, who, according to an unpublished book by DeMohrenschildt, said; "Incidentally, my daughter Jacqueline never wants to see you again because you were close to her husband's assassin."

Returning to Haiti, the DeMohrenschildt's problems there increased to the point that in 1967 they were forced to sneak away from the island aboard a German freighter, which brought them to Port Arthur, Texas. Here, according to Jeanne in a 1978 interview with this author, the DeMohrenschildts were met by an associate of former Oklahoma senator and oilman Bob Kerr. The returning couple were extended the hospitality of Kerr's home.

By the 1970s, the DeMohrenschildts were living quietly in Dallas, although once they were questioned by two men who claimed to be from *Life* magazine. A check showed the men were phonies.

DeMohrenschildt seemed content to teach French at Bishop College, a predominantly black school in south Dallas. Then in the spring of 1976, George, who suffered from chronic bronchitis, had a particularly bad attack. Distrustful of hospitals, he was persuaded by someone—Jeanne cannot today recall who—to see a newly arrived doctor in Dallas named Dr. Charles Mendoza. After several trips to Mendoza in the late spring and summer, DeMohrenschildt's bronchial condition improved, but he began to experience the symptoms of a severe nervous breakdown. He became paranoid, claiming that "the Jewish Mafia and the FBI" were after him.

Alarmed, Jeanne accompanied her husband to Dr. Mendoza and discovered he was giving DeMohrenschildt injections and costly drug prescriptions. She told this author:

> When I confronted [Mendoza] with this information, as well as asking him exactly what kind of medication and treatments he was giving George, he became very angry and upset. By then, I had become

suspicious and started accompanying George on each of his visits to the doctor. But this physician would not allow me to be with George during his "treatments." He said George was gravely ill and had to be alone during treatments.

Jeanne said her husband's mental condition continued to deteriorate during this time. She now claims: "I have become convinced that this doctor, in some way, lies behind the nervous breakdown George suffered in his final months."

The doctor is indeed mysterious. A check with the Dallas County Medical Society showed that Dr. Mendoza first registered in April 1976, less than two months before he began treating DeMohrenschildt and at the same time the House Select Committee on Assassinations was beginning to be funded.

Mendoza left Dallas in December, just a few months after DeMohrenschildt refused to continue treatments, at the insistence of his wife. Mendoza left the society a forwarding address that proved to be nonexistent. He also left behind a confused and unbalanced George DeMohrenschildt.

During the fall of 1976 while in this unbalanced mental state, DeMohrenschildt completed his unpublished manuscript entitled, *I Am a Patsy! I Am a Patsy!* after Oswald's famous remark to newsmen in the Dallas police station. In the manuscript, DeMohrenschildt depicts Oswald as a cursing, uncouth man with assassination on his mind, a totally opposite picture from his descriptions of Oswald through the years.

The night he finished the manuscript, DeMohrenschildt attempted suicide by taking an overdose of tranquilizers. Paramedics were called, but they declined to take him to a hospital. They found DeMohrenschildt also had taken his dog's digitalis, which counteracted the tranquilizers.

Shortly after his attempted suicide, Jeanne committed her husband to Parkland Hospital in Dallas, where he was subjected to electroshock therapy. To gauge his mental condition at this time, consider what he told Parkland roommate Clifford Wilson: "I know damn well Oswald didn't kill Kennedy—because Oswald and I were together at the time." DeMohrenschildt told Wilson that he and Oswald were in downtown Dallas watching the Kennedy motorcade pass when shots were fired. He said that at the sound of shots Oswald ran away and DeMohrenschildt never saw him again.

This story, which was reported in the April 26, 1977, edition of the *National Enquirer* as "Exclusive New Evidence," is untrue since both George and Jeanne were at a reception in the Bulgarian embassy in Haiti the day Kennedy was killed.

But the incident serves to illustrate George DeMohrenschildt's mental condition at the time.

In early 1977, DeMohrenschildt, convinced that evil forces were still after him, fled to Europe with Dutch journalist Willems Oltmans, who later created a furor by telling the House Select Committee on Assassinations that DeMohrenschildt claimed he knew of Oswald's assassination plan in advance.

However, DeMohrenschildt grew even more fearful in Europe. In a letter found after his death, he wrote: ". . . As I can see it now, the whole purpose of my meeting in Holland was to ruin me financially and completely."

In mid-March DeMohrenschildt fled to a relative's Florida home leaving behind clothing and other personal belongings. It was in the fashionable Manalapan, Florida, home of his sister-in-law, that DeMohrenschildt died of a shotgun blast to the head on March 29, 1977, just three hours after a representative of the House Select Committee on Assassinations tried to contact him there.

Earlier that day, he had met author Edward J. Epstein for an interview. In a 1983 *Wall Street Journal* article, Epstein wrote that DeMohrenschildt told him that day that the CIA had asked him "to keep tabs on Oswald."

However, the thing that may have triggered DeMohrenschildt's fear was that Epstein showed him a document that indicated DeMohrenschildt might be sent back to Parkland for further shock treatments, according to a statement by Attorney David Bludworth, who represented the state during the investigation into DeMohrenschildt's death.

Although several aspects of DeMohrenschildt's death caused chief investigator Capt. Richard Sheets of the Palm County Sheriff's Office to term the shooting "very strange," a coroner's jury quickly ruled suicide.

It is unclear if Oltmans knew of DeMohrenschildt's mental problems at the time he made his statements, but in later years, Jeanne told the newsman:

. . . If George's death was engineered, it is because you focused such attention on my husband that the real conspirators decided to eliminate him just in case George actually knew something, just like so many others involved in the assassination.

One other matter that involved the DeMohrenschildts with the case has proven as unfathomable as so many others. According to Jeanne, when the DeMohrenschildts arrived back in the United States in early 1967, they discovered a photograph of Oswald in some Russian-English language records they had loaned to Marina Oswald prior to leaving for Haiti. The records had never been returned and they were surprised to find them among their belongings, which had been left with their friend Everett Glover. Glover later placed the DeMohrenschildts' things in storage. Ruth Paine, with whom Marina lived at the time of the assassination, also had access to the DeMohrenschildt belongings.

The picture is one of the famous backyard scenes depicting Oswald with his rifle and pistol while holding a communist publication. It is one pose of at least three photos believed by most researchers to be faked. On the back of the photo is one inscription in English reading "To my friend George from Lee Oswald." Beneath this is an inscription in Russian Cyrillic script which translates "Hunter of fascists Ha-ha-ha!!!"

The photo also bears the date "5/IV/63" apparently meaning April 5, 1963. The date is curious, mixing in Roman numerals as it does and written in the European style. The New Orleans-born Oswald more likely would have written "4/5/63" and, in fact, a check of dozens of other examples of dates in Oswald's mass of written material shows not one written in the earlier manner.

Today, Jeanne swears neither she nor her husband ever saw the photograph until discovering it upon their return in 1967.

Handwriting experts for the House Select Committee on Assassinations could not indentify Oswald, Marina, or the DeMohrenschildts as authors of the inscription.

And Marina gave mixed accounts of the photo, which surfaced just at a time when many assassination researchers were first beginning to question the authenticity of the backyard photographs.

While testifying to the Committee in 1978, Marina suddenly said:

> . . . I remember being surprised at [Oswald] showing pictures like that to George [DeMohrenschildt], so apparently I saw them at the apartment . . . something strikes my memory that—how dare he show pictures like that to a friend?

If her statement is true, and that's a big "if" since later in her testimony Marina suddenly could not remember much else about the episode, it would mean that George DeMohrenschildt—the man with numerous intelligence connections—was aware of Oswald's possession of weapons months before the assassination.

The DeMohrenschildts denied any knowledge of the photo with the incriminating inscription, and today Jeanne is convinced that the picture was planted among their possessions.

Looking over the fascinating life of George and Jeanne DeMohrenschildt, one is struck by the idea that this sophisticated couple may be one of the biggest "red herrings" of the assassination.

There is now no question that DeMohrenschildt had numerous and long-standing connections with intelligence—most notably the CIA and, perhaps, private intelligence groups connected with the oil industry and defense work.

Yet it is apparent that through DeMohrenschildt certain elements within oil, business, and intelligence circles could have become aware of Oswald who, with his pro-communist background, must have appeared to be a prime candidate for an assassination patsy.

After the assassination, DeMohrenschildt—with his connections to German, French, Polish, and United States intelligence, wealthy right-wing Texas oilmen, and Carribean business interests—provided a wonderful opportunity to draw investigators into a labyrinth of false leads.

The mental deterioration near the end of his life caused DeMohrenschildt to make untrue statements that further clouded the issue.

*   *   *

If George DeMohrenschildt had a genuine liking for President Kennedy, as he stated on several occasions, this fondness was not shared by his conservative oil and business associates. They felt threatened by the young president, who was making decisions on finances, taxation, and foreign policy outside their control.

Corporate leaders traditionally had sought out politicians who would look out for their interests in Washington. So in the days of Kennedy's Camelot, these oil and business titans may have looked to a man who they knew they could deal with, if not completely trust—Vice President Lyndon B. Johnson.

All the Way with LBJ

In Dallas on the day Kennedy died there were those people iconoclastic enough to suggest that Vice President Johnson was behind the assassination. These were mostly long-time Texas residents who had heard vicious stories about Johnson for years and who figured the Texas politician had more to gain from Kennedy's death than just about anyone. Even today, many serious students of the assassination cannot discount the idea that Johnson, in some way, played a role in the Dallas tragedy.

Johnson's actions following the assassination do little to stop such speculation. And a close study of the corruption and violence that dogged Johnson's political career only adds to the suspicions.

Lyndon Baines Johnson was born August 27, 1908, near Johnson City, Texas, which had been named for his grandfather, one of the area's original settlers. His father, Sam Ealy Johnson, who served in the Texas Legislature for twelve years, told neighbors: "A U.S. Senator is born today."

Young Johnson graduated from Johnson City High School as president of his senior class of six. After running away to California, he hitchhiked home and enrolled in Southwest Texas State Teachers College at San Marcos.

After graduating at age twenty-two, Johnson got a teaching job in Houston, but it failed to hold the interest of this ambitious young man. So, in 1931, Johnson was drawn into Texas politics, campaigning strenuously for conservative congressman Richard M. Kleberg. After Kleberg's victory, Johnson accompanied him to Washington as his secretary.

In 1934 Johnson was visiting in Austin when he met an attractive twenty-one-year-old journalism student named Claudia Alta Taylor, the daughter of an affluent merchant and landowner in Karnack, Texas. (As the story goes, a black "mammy" took one look at the infant Claudia and declared: "Lawd, she's as pretty as a lady bird," and from then on, she was known as "Lady Bird.") After a whirlwind courtship of two months, consisting mainly of daily telephone calls from Washington, Johnson returned to Texas and asked "Bird" to marry him, adding: "If you say no, it just proves that you don't love me enough to dare to marry me. We either do it now, or we never will."

She agreed and the couple drove to San Antonio for a rushed wedding in St. Mark's Episcopal Church. After a brief honeymoon in Mexico, the Johnsons moved to Washington, where they rented a one-bedroom apartment and Johnson resumed his political work for Kleberg.

Watching the energetic Johnson was a close friend of the Johnson family, Congressman Sam Rayburn, already a power on Capitol Hill. In August 1935, thanks to some help from Rayburn, President Franklin Roosevelt named Johnson as Texas director of the National Youth Administration, a New Deal Program for employing youth. Johnson resigned as Kleberg's secretary and flew to Texas where he told newsmen his "job was to work himself out of a job." One of the first persons Johnson hired to join the NYA was Jesse Kellam, a former San Marcos schoolmate who was then deputy state supervisor of education. Kellam later succeeded Johnson as NYA director and went on to manage the Johnson radio-TV station KTBC in Austin.

Capitalizing on his authority to award loans and jobs, Johnson created a formidable political base in south Texas. He also used his new position to ingratiate himself with President Roosevelt, who Johnson referred to as "my political daddy." By now, his career designs were set firmly in politics.

In early 1937, with the sudden death of Austin congressman James P. Buchanan, Johnson saw his chance. Others also saw their chance. At the same time Johnson was looking for financial and political support to make a bid for Buchanan's seat, Austin attorney Alvin Wirtz and his client, Herman Brown, were looking for help in Washington.

Brown's construction company, Brown & Root, had already spent millions building the Marshall Ford Dam in South Texas. But the project had not been officially authorized by Congress, rather it had begun as a government grant obtained by Buchanan. With his death, the entire $10 million project was in limbo.

Backed by Wirtz, Brown, and their well-heeled business associates, the indefatigable Johnson raced through nearly eight thousand square miles of Texas hill country pledging total support of Roosevelt and his New Deal, a theme that sat well with impoverished farmers and laborers.

The senatorial election, climaxed by a raging blizzard and sudden surgery for LBJ to repair a ruptured appendix, was a victory, with Johnson outpolling five opponents by three thousand votes.

Back in Washington, the twenty-nine-year-old Johnson managed to get authorization for the dam project as well as a contract for Brown & Root to build a huge Navy base at Corpus Christi.

Herman Brown and his friends were so pleased with Johnson's performance that in 1940 the young congressman was offered a share in very lucrative oil properties with no money down. Johnson was told he could pay for his share out of yearly profits. It was tantamount to a gift. Brown was shocked when Johnson, who had been complaining of lack of money, turned him down, saying the offer "would kill me politically."

Since both a House and Senate seat would come from Texas votes—a reliable oil and gas constituency—Brown realized even at that time that Johnson's true political goal was the presidency.

As a congressman, Johnson continued to perform for his oil and business mentors back in Texas. In 1941, Brown & Root obtained a lucrative Navy contract to build four sub chasers, although, as George Brown was to later recall: "We didn't know the stern from the aft—I mean the bow—of the boat."

Just two days after Pearl Harbor, Johnson—who had been commissioned a lieutenant commander in the Navy Reserve some months previously—was called to active duty, becoming the first congressman to leave for military service.

After serving less than a year, Johnson arrived back in Washington after Roosevelt called on all congressmen serving in the armed forces to return home.

His wartime service had won Johnson at least one solid ally. After a period of cool relations due to Johnson's blatant ambitiousness, he again was accepted by powerful House Speaker Sam Rayburn. Rayburn taught Johnson his political philosophy, which he often repeated: "To get along, you have to go along."

J. Evetts Haley, a critical biographer of Johnson, wrote: "Lyndon became Rayburn's protégé; their relationship a fusion of experience and political sagacity with youthful ardor and enthusiasm, with no appreciable enhancement of the ideals and ethics of either."

Johnson entered a race for the Senate in 1948. It was a close race between Johnson, still identified with Roosevelt and the New Deal, and conservative Texas governor Coke Stevenson, who managed to defeat Johnson in the Democratic primary. However Stevenson didn't have a clear majority, so a run-off election was called for August 28.

Due to slow communications and manual voting procedures, the election outcome was in doubt for several days. Finally on September 2, Johnson went on radio with a "victory speech," which shocked the confident Stevenson forces. Veteran Texas newsman Clyde Wantland wrote:

Their fears were validated the following day . . . when a source friendly to Stevenson reported from Jim Wells County that Precinct 13 had been recanvassed and a "correction" made favoring Johnson with 202 more votes. Johnson's radio broadcast on Thursday thus became a reality on

Saturday. Precinct 13 had been corrected from Johnson 765–60 to Johnson 967–61. This gave him a lead of 87 votes, with returns now complete and semi-official.

This eighty-seven-vote edge earned Johnson the sobriquet of "Landslide Lyndon" and began one of the longest legal feuds in Texas history.

Johnson's opponents claimed the 87-vote "correction" in the 1948 election came only after frantic phone calls between Johnson and George Parr, a powerful South Texas political boss known as the "Duke of Duval County".

The controversy continued into 1977, when Luis Salas, the local election judge, admitted to the *Dallas Morning News* the he had certified fictitious ballots for Johnson on orders from Parr, who committed suicide in 1975. Salas told newsmen, "Johnson did not win that election; it was stolen for him." But more troubling than this case of common political fraud was the series of deaths and federal government interference with investigations into Johnson's activities.

One of these deaths was Bill Mason, a South Texas newsman investigating the Duval incident, who was murdered by Sam Smithwick, a Parr associate who in turn was found hanged in his prison cell after saying he was willing to talk.

As far back as 1941, the IRS had initiated investigations of Johnson's finances, but had been blocked by orders from Johnson's mentor, President Roosevelt.

In 1954, the Austin District IRS Collector Frank L. Scofield was removed from office accused of forcing political contributions from his employees. Scofield was aquitted of these charges but in his absence, all of the IRS files relating to Johnson and Brown & Root were placed in a Quonset hut in South Austin, which mysteriously caught fire destroying the evidence.

In the late 1940s and early 1950s, both Johnson and his protégé John Connally had offices in Fort Worth. Johnson operated out of the Hotel Texas, the site of Kennedy's breakfast speech the morning of November 22, 1963.

It was here in Fort Worth that both Johnson and Connally came into contact with gamblers, who in turn were later connected to Jack Ruby as well as anti-Kennedy Texas oilmen.

W. C. Kirkwood was known as a "gentleman gambler" because he never allowed anyone in his high-stakes poker games who was on a salary. He did not want to be the cause of someone's children going hungry. Kirkwood conducted his big-time gambling at a luxurious sprawling Spanish-style complex known as The Four Deuces—the street address was 2222 on Fort Worth's Jacksboro Highway, notorious for its taverns and prostitution. It was here, under the protective eye of off-duty policemen, that men like H. L. Hunt, Clint Murchinson, and others joined Sam Rayburn and his protégé Johnson for hours of Kirkwood-provided hospitality.

Retired Fort Worth policeman Paul Bewley recalled for this author that while providing security for Johnson's Hotel Texas office suite, the one man who had unquestioned access to Johnson was W. C. Kirkwood.

Assassination researchers note that Kirkwood's son, Pat Kirkwood, hosted Kennedy's Secret Service guards the night before his trip to Dallas—and that both the Kirkwoods and Dallas nightclub owner Jack Ruby shared a common close friend in gambler Lewis J. McWillie.

Ruby and McWillie—who at one time operated his own gambling establishment in Dallas, the Top of the Hill Club—had tried to open a casino in Cuba in 1959 and had participated in gun-running schemes.

Yet, despite this link between Jack Ruby's friend McWillie through the Kirkwoods to oilmen and Lyndon Johnson, neither the Warren Commission nor the House Select Committee on Assassinations apparently felt the need to fully investigate these associations.

In 1951, Johnson had been elected Democratic whip in the Senate. Two years later, at only forty-four years of age, Johnson became the Senate's majority leader.

Johnson used his powerful position to best advantage, according to author Caro, who told the *Atlantic Monthly*:

For years, men came into Lyndon Johnson's office and handed him envelopes stuffed with cash. They didn't stop coming even when the office in which he sat was the office of the vice president of the United States. Fifty thousand dollars in hundred-dollar bills in sealed envelopes was what one lobbyist for one oil company testified he brought to Johnson's office during his term as vice president.

There is evidence that Johnson also profited from cash contributions from the mob. Jack Halfen—a former associate of Bonnie and Clyde, Frank Costello, Vito Genovese, and Carlos Marcello—was the mob's gambling coordinator in Houston. On trial for income tax evasion in 1954, Halfen revealed how Houston gambling netted almost $15 million a year with 40 percent going to Marcello, 35 percent to Halfen, and 25 percent to Texas police officials and politicians.

In talks with federal officials while serving a prison term, Halfen told how Johnson had been the recipient of more than $500,000 in contributions over a ten-year period while in the Senate. He said Johnson, in turn, had help the crime syndicate by killing antirackets legislation, watering down bills that could not be defeated, and slowing congressional probes into organized crime.

Halfen substantiated his close ties to Johnson with photographs of himself and Johnson on a private hunting trip and a letter from Johnson to the Texas Board of Paroles written on Halfen's behalf.

According to published reports Johnson also received large-scale payoffs from Teamster president Jimmy Hoffa. A former senatorial aide, Jack Sullivan, testified that he witnessed the transfer of a suitcase full of money from a Teamster lobbyist through a Maryland senator to Johnson's chief aide Cliff Carter.

Also recall that one of Johnson's "trusted friends," Bobby Baker, had long and documented mob connections. Baker once wrote:

"A New Orleans businessman rumored to be well connected with the Mafia had once sought me out to inquire whether President Lyndon Johnson might be willing to pardon Hoffa in exchange for one million dollars."

The Johnson administration's anticrime record is dismal. Racket busting came to a virtual halt. During the first four years following the assassination, Justice Department organized-crime section field time had dropped by 48 percent, time before grand juries by 72 percent, and the number of district court briefs filed by that section by 83 percent.

Yet another example of Johnson's willingness to circumvent the law for his career's sake came in 1960, when he decided to run for president despite continually denying this decision. At the urging of Johnson, Democratic legislators in Texas rushed through a law that superceded an old statute forbidding a candidate from seeking two offices at the same time.

Thus Texas voters witnessed the bizarre spectacle of Johnson running for vice president on Kennedy's liberal national ticket while also running for Texas senator on the state's conservative Democratic ticket.

One can easily imagine Johnson's anger and hurt when the Democratic Party in 1960 handed its presidential nomination not to this long-time standard bearer, but instead to John F. Kennedy, a relative newcomer. Johnson lamented to friends: "Jack was out kissing babies while I was passing bills."

Knowing how Kennedy's top supporters detested him, Johnson must have seen Kennedy's nomination as a major roadblock in his drive for the presidency. He was therefore pleasantly surprised when Kennedy offered him the vice president's position on the ballot. This offer, coming as it did after an often-bitter contest between the two men, has been the subject of much debate. It now seems clear that Kennedy never really believed that Johnson would swap his Senate power for the empty honor of being vice president. He made the offer as a conciliatory move, fully expecting Johnson to turn it down. But Johnson saw it as an opportunity to get one step closer to the presidency and promptly accepted. Reminded by friends that the office of vice president carried little importance, Johnson said: "Power is where power goes."

The Kennedy forces were shocked. How could Kennedy pick Johnson, who stood for almost everything they hated? It has been speculated that Kennedy accepted Johnson because it seemed necessary to have Johnson's help in swinging the 1960 election in southern and western states.

This proved prophetic. It was only through the tireless efforts of Johnson that six crucial southern states—including Texas—were kept in the Democratic column.

In Texas this was accomplished very simply. According to Haley, both Johnson and Rayburn warned the state's oilmen that if they voted for Nixon and the Democrats won, the oilmen could kiss the oil depletion allowance good-bye. So oil money helped swing the state for Kennedy-Johnson, despite a national Democratic platform that called for repealing the allowance—mute testimony to their belief in Johnson's power and hypocrisy.

As vice president, Johnson was a changed man. Gone were his power and his enthusiasm. There was almost constant friction between this old-style political powerbroker and the new breed of Kennedy men. Johnson's brother, Sam Houston Johnson, wrote about the treatment of his brother as vice president:

> . . . they made his stay in the vice presidency the most miserable three years of his life. He wasn't the number two man in the administration; he was the lowest man on the totem pole . . . I know him well enough to know he felt humiliated time and time again, that he was openly snubbed by second-echelon White House staffers who snickered at him behind his back and called him "Uncle Cornpone."

By the fall of 1963, rumors were rife that Johnson would be dumped from the 1964 Democratic national ticket. In fact, the day of Kennedy's assassination, the *Dallas Morning News* carried the headline: NIXON PREDICTS JFK MAY DROP JOHNSON. Consequently, Johnson made several trips abroad, most probably to escape the daily humiliations in the White House.

Soon after Johnson became vice president, yet another investigation into his financial dealings got underway. This time it involved a big-time Texas wheeler-dealer named Billie Sol Estes. Henry Marshall, a Department of Agriculture official, was looking into Estes' habit of acquiring millions in federal cotton allotment payments on land which was under water or actually owned by the government. Marshall was particularly interested in Estes' connections with his long-time friend, Lyndon Johnson. However, before any official action could be taken, Marshall was found dead in a remote section of his farm near Franklin, Texas. He had been shot five times in the abdomen. Nearby lay a bolt-action .22-caliber rifle.

Five days later, without the benefit of an autopsy, a local peace justice ruled Marshall's death a suicide.

(In 1985 Estes, after being granted immunity from prosecution, told Texas media that Johnson had ordered Marshall's death to prevent his connections with Estes from being exposed. Later that year, a Texas district judge changed the official verdict of Marshall's death from suicide to homicide.)

At least three other men connected with the Estes case died in unusual circumstances.

By the time of the Kennedy assassination, dead witnessess, missing evidence and interference with official investigations were nothing new to Lyndon Johnson.

It may also be highly significant that during the years of Johnson's rise to power in Washington, one of his closest friends—in fact, a neighbor who frequently was his dinner guest—was none other than FBI director J. Edgar Hoover, who also was no stranger to the manipulation of politically sensitive investigations.

After becoming president, Johnson was encouraged to retire the crusty Hoover. But Johnson—possibly aware of the damaging evidence Hoover could provide against him—declined, saying: "I'd rather have him inside the tent pissing out, than outside pissing in."

Although it was against established security practice for the president and the vice president to be together in public, Johnson was riding only two cars behind Kennedy in the fateful Dallas motorcade.

At Parkland Hospital, Johnson was informed of Kennedy's death and then urged to make a public statement by Kennedy's assistant press secretary Malcolm Kilduff. As reported by author Jack Bell, Johnson told Kilduff:

> No, Mac . . . I think I had better get out of here and get back to the plane before you announce [Kennedy's death]. We don't know whether there is a worldwide conspiracy, whether they are after me as well as they were after President Kennedy, or whether they are after Speaker McCormack or Senator Hayden. We just don't know.

It is significant to look at some of the circumstances surrounding Johnson and his reactions to the assassination.

Although Johnson mentioned his fears of a "worldwide conspiracy" loudly in the hours immediately after Kennedy's death, there appears to have been no action to counter such a threat.

While the Texas border was closed for a couple of hours, there was no widespread closing of United States borders and major airplane and ship terminals were not shut down. Furthermore, while some units were placed on stepped-up status, there was no full-scale military alert, despite the commander-in-chief's stated fear of a "worldwide conspiracy."

It has seemed strange to researchers that, while Kennedy's men wanted to leave Dallas as quickly as possible, it was Johnson who demanded that the entourage remain at Love Field until he could be sworn in as president by federal judge Sarah T. Hughes.

Hubert Humphrey, who later became Johnson's vice president, once correctly stated: "A vice president becomes president when there is no president. Later, when he takes the oath, he puts on the cloak of office. But that act is purely symbolic."

After arriving back in Washington, Jackie Kennedy explained to Robert Kennedy that the delay in returning was due to Johnson, who told her the attorney general had told him to take the oath of office in Dallas. Robert Kennedy was surprised and replied that he had made no such suggestion. Johnson compounded this lie months later in his deposition to the Warren Commission, when he again stated that it was Attorney General Kennedy who had urged him to take the oath immediately.

The new president was waiting on board presidential jet *Air Force One* when Kennedy's body reached Love Field. In his Warren Commission affidavit, Johnson said Kennedy's aide Kenneth O'Donnell specifically told him to take the presidential plane because it had better communication equipment. However, O'Donnell denied this, telling author William Manchester: "The President and I had no conversation regarding *Air Force One*. If we had known that he was going on *Air Force One*, we would have taken *Air Force Two*. One plane was just like the other."

O'Donnell later wrote that a Warren Commission attorney asked him to "change his testimony so that it would agree with the President's"—an offer O'Donnell declined.

While others were shocked into immobility by Kennedy's death, Johnson exhibited a strange—and perhaps suspicious—ability to press forward with his work. Johnson aide George Reedy commented that while "everything was chaotic, only the President knew what he was doing." While Kennedy's body still lay in state in the White House East Room, Johnson outlined to a flabbergasted John Kenneth Galbraith his 1964 election strategy, saying: "I want to come down very hard on civil rights, not because Kennedy was for it, but because I am for it."

Author Jack Bell noted: ". . . almost from the moment he took the Presidential oath, Johnson had been unfolding a master plan designed to win the Presidency in his own right and . . . to carve for himself a favorable place in history."

During the course of the assassination investigation, a number of incidents occurred involving Johnson that have been viewed with suspicion by researchers.

Within seventy-two hours of Kennedy's death—at Johnson's order—the presidential limousine SX-100, which carried Kennedy through Dallas, was shipped to Detroit where the body was replaced and the interior completely refurbished. In any other case, this would have been destruction of evidence, since bullet marks on the windshield and blood traces could have provided essential clues as to the number and direction of shots.

After the assassination, Governor Connally's clothing—also vital evidence—was taken from the office of Congressman Henry Gonzalez by Secret Service agents sent by Johnson aide Cliff Carter. Connally's clothing was cleaned and pressed by the time it was handed over to the Warren Commission and, hence, was useless for study as evidence.

One of Johnson's actions that caused researchers of the assassination no end of problems was Executive Order 11652, which locked an immense amount of assassination evidence and documents in the National Archives away from the American public until the year 2039. It was this act, more than any other, which has caused so much speculation about a possible role by Johnson in the assassination.

It is now becoming publicly known that Johnson's mental state deteriorated significantly in the years following his predecessor's assassination. Former aide and speechwriter Richard Goodwin, who helped fashion LBJ's "Great Society," has written that Johnson became obsessed with the idea that America was being taken over by his enemies—Communists and "those Kennedys." Goodwin said he and aide Bill Moyers even consulted psychiatrists about his boss's behavior.

Madeleine Brown, reported to have been Johnson's mistress for twenty years, has publicly stated that Johnson had foreknowledge of the assassination.

But did Johnson really have enough power to initiate the assassination and force literally dozens of government officials and agents to lie and cover up that fact? Probably not.

Furthermore, if Johnson played some role in an assassination plot, he would have taken great pains to distance himself from such a conspiracy. Evidence of such a role would certainly not be readily available. Therefore, today it is only possible to point out that Johnson—above everyone else—benefited most from Kennedy's death.

With the assassination, Johnson achieved his lifelong goal of gaining the presidency, his business and oil backers were rid of Kennedy's interference, and his supporters who wanted an Asian war—notably Brown & Root and ranking officers at the Pentagon—were free to pursue a widening conflict.

A final point is that Johnson—always conscious of his role in history—must have feared appearing to be a dunce by continuing to support the Warren Commission "lone assassin" myth.

In an interview with Walter Cronkite in the early 1970s, Johnson expressed the belief that the assassination involved more than one person, then asked network executives to delete his remarks from the broadcast—which they did.

Johnson was quoted in *Atlantic Monthly* in 1973: "I never believed that Oswald acted alone although I can accept that he pulled the trigger."

Johnson even voiced the suspicion that the CIA had a hand in the assassination, according to an FBI document released in 1977. The document quotes Johnson's postmaster general and close friend Marvin Watson as relaying to the Bureau: ". . . that [President Johnson] was now convinced there was a plot in connection with the assassination. Watson stated the President felt the CIA had something to do with this plot."

Yet this, too, was kept hidden from the public for years.

Was Johnson well aware of such a plot and only mentioned it in later years so that future historians would not classify him as dense and unaware?

While this ambitiously driven man from Texas most probably did not initiate a death plot against Kennedy, everything known about the man—from the deaths and coverups of Texas scandals to his continued prosecution of the unpopular Vietnam War—indicates that Johnson may have had the willingness to join in a conspiracy that would place him in the White House.

As commander-in-chief of the armed forces and close confidant to the powerful J. Edgar Hoover, Johnson certainly had the ability to erase or mask all evidence that might lead to the truth of the assassination.

Summary

Although his efforts were belated and timid, President Kennedy nevertheless did more to further the cause of civil rights in the United States than any of his predecessors. This human-rights activity earned him the undying hatred of racist conservatives.

One of the leaders of right-wing extremists in 1963 was Dallas-based Maj. Gen. Edwin A. Walker, who was the victim of a gunman's attack in the spring of that year. The Warren Commission confidently concluded: "Oswald had attempted to kill Maj. Gen. Edwin A. Walker (Resigned, U.S. Army) on April 10, 1963, thereby demonstrating his disposition to take human life." However, many facts of the Walker shooting—witnesses who saw several men in suspicious cars, early reports of a different type of ammunition, and a photograph of Walker's home that was mutilated while in the hands of federal authorities—raise serious questions about Oswald's guilt.

Meanwhile, Kennedy managed to anger the U.S. business community by the use of his office to compel steel manufacturers to roll back price increases and the introduction of tax-reform legislation that would have closed corporate tax loopholes and abolished or reduced the lucrative oil depletion allowance.

Former vice president Richard Nixon—who lost to Kennedy in 1960 and went on to become this nation's only president to resign under threat of impeachment—had many strange and troubling connections with the assassination. Nixon flew out of Dallas the day Kennedy was killed, yet was ambiguous when questioned by the FBI later in 1963. There is also the incident of an FBI document that indicates that Jack Ruby worked for Nixon in 1947. The Bureau claimed this document was a fake.

In the summer of 1963, Kennedy ordered the Treasury Department to print more than $4 billion in "United States Notes," thus bypassing the powerful Federal Reserve system, which undoubtedly angered international bankers.

It may be pertinent that a member of the Texas oil community— geologist George DeMohrenschildt—was the last-known close friend to Lee Harvey Oswald. DeMohrenschildt, with his background in Russia, oil, and intelligence work, adds greatly to the suspicion that Oswald was being manipulated by someone with intelligence connections in the spring and summer of 1963. It may be that the DeMohrenschildts were simply used to maneuver Oswald and then, over the years following Kennedy's death, offered as red herrings to draw researchers away from the real plotters.

It is significant that one of the strongest allies of the Texas oilmen who loathed Kennedy was Vice President Lyndon Johnson. Johnson's ties with Herman Brown of Brown & Root which grew to be the world's largest construction company thanks to lucrative government contracts in Vietnam, and with Texas oil interests are legend.

Several people close to the assassination—notably Jack Ruby and former New Orleans district attorney Jim Garrison—have accused Johnson of some role in an assassination conspiracy.

And there can be no question that Johnson, above all others, clearly benefited the most from Kennedy's death. Likewise, Johnson's close friend and neighbor, J. Edgar Hoover, also benefited.

Both Johnson and Hoover reportedly were about to lose their lifelong careers since it was rumored that the Kennedys were going to drop Johnson from the 1964 Democratic ticket and force Hoover's retirement.

Both Johnson and Hoover certainly had the power to subvert a meaningful investigation into Kennedy's death—and a wealth of evidence suggests just such subversion. Did Johnson and Hoover contract with the mob to kill Kennedy? Or did the mob approach them? Or did they simply turn a blind eye to a plot already activated? The truth of their involvement may not be proven for years. However, a conspiracy involving Lyndon Johnson and his buddy Hoover as an alternative to the Warren Commission's discredited lone-assassin theory goes farther in tying together the disparate bits of assassination evidence than any theory offered to date, and it cannot be easily dismissed.

As president and commander-in-chief, history will surely hold Lyndon Johnson responsible—if not for involvement in the assassination itself, at least for failing to uncover the conspiracy during his leadership.

> ". . . We must guard against . . . the military-industrial complex.
> —President Dwight D. Eisenhower

Soldiers

In more than two hundred years the military forces of the United States have accumulated a distinguished history. From the Revolution-era citizen who could become a fighting man ready to protect his community in a minute to the professional Marines who grimly stood between the warring factions in Beirut, Lebanon, the American soldier has proved his worth time and again. Even during the bitter dissension produced by U.S. policy in Southeast Asia, few people seriously questioned the ability or bravery of the individual G.I.

And American military use of technology and logistics during World War II contributed greatly to the defeat of Nazism and the Japanese militarists.

However, throughout world history, it has proven extremely difficult to return to peacetime, civilian-control of government once power has been invested in the military. From the takeover of the Roman Empire by the Praetorian Guard up until today, military leaders have tried to maintain their power and control.

This situation was aggravated in the United States during World War II by a combining of military and industrial power.

The Military-Industrial Complex

On January 17, 1961, three days before John F. Kennedy took office as president, President Dwight Eisenhower gave his farewell address to Congress. In this talk he coined the phrase "military-industrial complex" and warned against potential abuses by such an entity. He said:

> Our military establishment today bears little relation to that known by any of my predecessors in peacetime . . . Until the latest of our world conflicts, the United States had no armaments industry. American makers of plowshares could, with time and as required, make swords as well. But now we can no longer risk emergency improvisation of national defense; we have been compelled to create a permanent armaments industry of vast proportions. Added to this, three and a half

million men and women are directly engaged in the defense establishment. We annually spend on military security more than the net income of all United States corporations.

This conjunction of an immense military establishment and a large arms industry is new in the American experience. The total influence—economical, political, even spiritual—is felt in every city, every State House, every office of the Federal government . . .

In the councils of government, we must guard against the acquisition of unwarranted influence, whether sought or unsought, by the military-industrial complex. The potential for the disastrous rise of misplaced power exists and will persist.

We must never let the weight of this combination endanger our liberties or democratic processes . . .

Eisenhower's warning was especially timely. The role of the military-industrial complex in American life has continued to grow under the presidencies of his successors.

The rise of the military-industrial complex can be charted by annual military budget expenditures. In 1950 the military budget was $13 billion; by 1961, this had risen to $47 billion; and by the end of the Vietnam War in 1975, it was $100 billion. By 1986 annual expenses by the Department of Defense had risen to nearly $170 billion.

Few Americans even realize how much power is wielded by the military, which—since the disaster of the Vietnam War—has tended to take a low public profile.

A large part of the argument for maintaining an ongoing war economy has come from men and women who lived through the shock of Pearl Harbor. Vowing never to allow the United States to be caught unaware by an enemy again—although there is now substantial evidence available showing that the Japanese attack was not wholly unexpected in certain Washington circles—these people argue that assembly and production lines must be kept operating so that America can convert to war production quickly, if needed. This argument—plus the fact that millions of American jobs are dependent on defense contracts—has been instrumental in maintaining the war economy.

Critics, on the other hand, claim the permanent war economy has actually been a drain on America's economic life—with its production of nonusable goods and its penchant for inefficiency.

*　　　*　　　*

Even young Senator John Kennedy parroted the Pentagon line during the campaign of 1960, promising increases in military spending.

Once in the Oval Office—and with access to other sources of information—Kennedy changed his attitudes toward the military. Earlier he had echoed Pentagon figures showing that the Soviet Union possessed between five hundred and one thousand intercontinental ballistic missiles. According to later reports, the number was more like fifty. Kennedy complained that he had been ill-informed as to the actual number of missiles and suggested that this exaggeration was part of Pentagon strategy.

This complaint has been repeated over and over through the years, most recently by former CIA director William Colby in comments about the book *The Myth of Soviet Military Supremacy*, which he called, ". . . the greatest intelligence gap of all: the exaggeration of Soviet power in comparison with America's, which fuels the wasteful and dangerous nuclear-arms race."

Kennedy also became concerned with the $3 billion federal deficit of his time—a paltry sum compared to today's near $200 billion—and feared it would present a threat to the U.S. dollar. Accordingly, Kennedy named a Ford Motor Company executive, Robert McNamara, as his secretary of defense and changes began to take place.

On March 28, 1961, Kennedy told Congress:

> In January, while ordering certain immediately needed changes, I instructed the Secretary of Defense to reappraise our entire defense strategy, capacity, commitments, and needs in light of present and future dangers. . . .

Kennedy began to significantly modify the way defense and intelligence operated.

Presidents Truman and Eisenhower had depended greatly on the National Security Council (NSC), a creation of the National Security Act of 1947. In 1963 the NSC consisted of the president, the vice president, secretary of state, secretary of defense, and the director of the Office of Emergency Planning.

Theoretically, the CIA was to be controlled by the NSC. But Kennedy had another way of getting things done. Accustomed to the quick-acting, hard-hitting world of political campaigning, Kennedy neglected the NSC method. Instead, he would call upon his friends and family to get things done. While this may have been effective at the time, it left both the Pentagon and the CIA largely to their own devices—a circumstance Kennedy came to regret.

During this same period, the foreign policy of the United States was being greatly influenced by a new vision of the role of the military in the world. This vision was codified in a May 15, 1959 document written by Gen. Richard Stilwell as a member of a special presidential committee. Innocuously entitled "Training Under the Mutual Training Program," this document offered nothing less than a plan to protect the noncommunist world by having nations ruled by a military elite with training and ideology supplied by Americans.

Initially Kennedy was fascinated by this concept, since by nature he was a strong believer in negotiation and limited response rather than simply using military options. Words such as *counterinsurgency, pacification*, and *special forces* began to creep into our political language.

Following the disastrous Bay of Pigs Invasion, a special board of inquiry was convened to learn what went wrong. It was here that both John and Robert Kennedy began to learn what the new military doctrines of counterinsurgency, flexible response, civic action, and nation building really meant. They learned how the obsession with secrecy had completely changed the way the military and intelligence operated. Everything was on a "need-to-know" basis, with fewer and fewer responsible leaders included on the "need-to-know" lists.

After the Bay of Pigs inquiry Kennedy became convinced that the CIA and the Pentagon had misled him terribly, and from that point on he was highly skeptical of information from those sources.

Moreover, the inquiry showed the Kennedy brothers how powerful the military-industrial complex and its intelligence-security force had become.

Kennedy learned something from this coalition, too: how to concoct a "cover story"—which may account for his public support of the CIA at a time when his private comments and actions showed otherwise.

The blending of the military and the political was seen clearest in Vietnam, where it was the U.S. ambassador who was in charge, not the senior military commanders.

War should be the last resort of politicians. But once war is inevitable, then it should be fought by professional soldiers with clearly defined goals and objectives.

After the CIA-sponsored Bay of Pigs fiasco Kennedy began to see that this nation's paramilitary and undercover operations were getting out of hand. He made an attempt to stem this trend by issuing two National Security Action Memoranda (NSAM) in June of 1961. NSAM 55, signed personally by Kennedy, basically stated that he would hold the chairman of the Joint Chiefs of Staff personally responsible for all activity of a military nature during peacetime, the same as during wartime. In other words, Kennedy wanted all cloak-and-dagger operations as well as military expeditions under the control, or at least under the scrutiny, of the chairman— and hence under his control.

NSAM 57 attempted to divide paramilitary activity between the military and the CIA. Basically, this document stipulated that the CIA would be allowed only small covert operations, while any large operations must be studied and approved by the military. It seemed a reasonable division of responsibility. However, there were men in both the CIA and the Pentagon who did not appreciate this attempt to curb their power and prerogatives.

Not only did Kennedy attempt to curtail the power of both the military and intelligence. On November 16, 1961, Kennedy told a Seattle audience:

We must face the fact that the United States is neither omnipotent nor omniscient—that we cannot impose our will upon the other 94 percent of mankind—that we cannot right every wrong or reverse every adversity—and that therefore there cannot be an American solution to every world problem.

With his words and actions, Kennedy became the first U.S. president since World War II to address the myth of America's infallibility.

This did not sit well with the military-industrial complex, which had so much to gain—including profits—by controlling the raw resources of other nations.

In the midst of Kennedy's reappraisal of U.S. military and intelligence operations came the Cuban Missile Crisis.

In October 1962, it was learned from satellites and U-2 flights that the Soviets were preparing offensive missile bases in Cuba, only ninety miles from the U.S. The military and the CIA were adamant. They prescribed nothing less than immediate bombing of the missile sites and another invasion of the island.

Kennedy chose a different approach. He personally struck a deal with Premier Khrushchev that called for the removal of the missiles in return for Kennedy's pledge not to support a new invasion of Cuba. The Soviets backed down and Kennedy's popularity rose significantly, except in offices at the Pentagon and at Langley, Virginia.

The Kennedy administration continued its efforts to reduce military spending. On March 30, 1963, McNamara announced a reorganization program that would have closed fifty-two military installations in twenty-five states, as well as twenty-one overseas bases, over a three-year period.

Then on August 5, 1963, following lengthy negotiations, the United States, Great Britain, and the Soviet Union signed a limited nuclear test ban treaty forbidding the atmospheric testing of nuclear weapons.

On July 26, just prior to the signing of the Treaty of Moscow, Kennedy proclaimed:

> This treaty is not the millennium. It will not resolve all conflicts or cause the Communists to forego their ambitions, or eliminate the danger of war. It will not reduce our need for arms or allies or programs of assistance to others. But it is an important first step—a step toward reason—a step away from war.

As part of this "first step" toward what later would be termed "detente," Kennedy and Khrushchev agreed to the installation of a "hot line" telephone system between Washington and Moscow.

It was a serious deviation from the hard cold war policies of the past and military leaders—both retired and active—were not hesitant to voice their disapproval.

But for all his activities to reduce the risk of war and curtail the military and intelligence establishments, Kennedy's most momentous—and perhaps fatal—decisions came when he began to reevaluate United States policy in Southeast Asia.

Kennedy and Vietnam

From the time Lyndon B. Johnson took over the presidency the afternoon that Kennedy was assassinated in Dallas, the idea was encouraged that he would simply carry on Kennedy administration policies. In many ways he did. It has been acknowledged that Johnson was able to push Kennedy's civil-rights legislation through Congress where his predecessor may have failed. But one emerging Kennedy policy was not continued—that involved South Vietnam.

Early in his presidency, Kennedy simply went along with Eisenhower's policy which was to continue sending military "advisers" and matériel to South Vietnam. In fact, during 1961 and 1962, Kennedy actually increased the U.S. military presence in that war-torn nation. (This may have been due to his desire to avoid at all costs another foreign-policy disaster such as the Bay of Pigs.)

But by summer 1963, Kennedy had begun to reevaluate United States involvement in Vietnam.

By the time Kennedy became president in 1960, large-scale guerrilla warfare was being conducted against the South Vietnam regime. But because of Castro and Cuba as well as Soviet incursions in Berlin and the Congo, Vietnam was not an issue during the 1960 campaign. Kennedy barely noticed that, three days after his election in South Vietnam, President Diem was the object of an unsuccessful military coup d' etat.

In December 1960, the Communists announced the formation of the Vietnamese National Liberation Front, and the internal guerrilla war got under way in earnest.

During 1961 Kennedy, though distracted by the Bay of Pigs Invasion, continued to support further U.S. military assistance to Asia, particularly after Communist forces seized the city of Phuoc Vinh, only sixty miles from Saigon. On December 11, two helicopter companies arrived in South Vietnam. It was the beginning of an expanded role for U.S. advisers. By January 1962, total U.S. military personnel in Vietnam numbered 2,646. And on January 13, a memorandum from the Joint Chiefs of Staff, entitled "The Strategic Importance of the SEA Mainland," stated that if the Viet Cong (Vietnamese Communists) were not soon brought under control, the chiefs saw no alternative but the introduction of U.S. combat units.

Kennedy continued to hesitate about sending combat units to Vietnam. At a news conference on May 9, 1962, he said: ". . . introducing American forces . . . also is a hazardous course, and we want to attempt to see if we can work out a peaceful solution."

According to assistant secretary of state Roger Hilsman, one of Kennedy's key foreign policy planners, Kennedy confided:

The Bay of Pigs has taught me a number of things. One is not to trust generals or the CIA, and the second is that if the American people do not want to use American troops to remove a Communist regime 90 miles away from our coast, how can I ask them to use troops to remove a Communist regime 9,000 miles away?

By mid-1963 after receiving conflicting advice and intelligence regarding Vietnam from his advisers, Kennedy began to reassess his commitment there. He was especially concerned about the treatment of Buddhists under the Diem government. Thousands of Buddhists were demonstrating for freedom, and on June 11, the first Buddhist suicide by fire occurred.

Reflecting Kennedy's concern, the State Department notified Saigon: "If Diem does not take prompt and effective steps to re-establish Buddhist confidence in him, we will have to re-examine our entire relationship with his regime."

Diem became even more unmanageable as the year drew on, staffing his government with relatives and refusing to listen to the pleas of the Buddhists. Talk began about replacing Diem with leaders more agreeable to American policy. Disgusted, Kennedy even went so far as to approve a plan to withdraw one thousand U.S. military advisers from Vietnam by the end of the year.

The American government, including Kennedy, left no doubt of its displeasure with Diem, thus paving the way for yet another Vietnamese coup, which occurred on November 1, 1963, just twenty-one days before Kennedy arrived in Dallas.

Accompanied by CIA agent Lucien Conien, South Vietnam generals seized key installations and attacked the presidential palace. After hours of fighting Diem and his brother, Ngo Dinh Nhu, surrendered. While being taken to the generals' headquarters, both were murdered.

Kennedy, who had approved the coup, then rejected it, then okayed it again, was genuinely shocked at the murders.

Washington was forced to recognize the new military government in Saigon, but for the next twenty months, there were no less than ten changes of government as one general overthrew another.

It was time for a decision in Vietnam—to support a major American military expedition as desired by the Pentagon or to simply withdraw and take the criticism of the anticommunists.

The assassination of the Diem brothers may have strengthened Kennedy's decision to disengage from Vietnam, and there is evidence that he would have curtailed the Vietnam War.

Kennedy, forever the astute politician, also apparently was very much aware of the approaching 1964 elections.

Senator Mike Mansfield told newsmen that once, following a White House leadership meeting, Kennedy had confided to him that he agreed "on a need for a complete withdrawal from Vietnam," but he couldn't do it until after being reelected.

Kennedy explained to O'Donnell:

"In 1965 I'll be damned everywhere as a Communist appeaser. But I don't care. If I tried to pull out completely now, we would have another Joe McCarthy Red Scare on our hands."

The President also may have given a hint as to his plans in a broadcast on September 2, 1963. Speaking of Vietnam, he said: "In the final analysis, it is their war. They have to win or lose it."

The people within the Pentagon and the CIA—who had so much to gain by widening the Vietnam War—continued to put out their conflicting and often erroneous information.

Shortly before the Diem coup, McNamara and Gen. Maxwell Taylor had returned from Saigon and told Kennedy that things were looking better in Vietnam and that the United States would be able to withdraw all military personnel by the end of 1965.

Less than one month after Kennedy's assassination, McNamara and Taylor reported to President Johnson that conditions in Vietnam were grave and that a major effort—including American combat troops and a massive clandestine program—was needed to prevent a Communist victory.

On hearing the optimistic assessment from McNamara and Taylor on November 20, 1963, Kennedy had also approved an Accelerated Withdrawal Program, designed to carry out the promise to end American military presence by the close of 1965.

The withdrawal plan ended two days after Kennedy's assassination when President Johnson signed National Security Action Memorandum (NSAM) No. 273 which cancelled the troop withdrawal. This document also subtly changed the United States objective from simply assisting the South Vietnamese to assisting them "to win" against the Communists, and authorized plans for expanding the war into North Vietnam. The memorandum also ordered senior government officials not to contest or criticize the changes.

Kennedy aide Kenneth O'Donnell, in "Johnny We Hardly Knew Ye," wrote, "The President's orders to reduce American military personnel in Vietnam by one thousand before the end of 1963 was still in effect on the day he went to Texas. A few days after his death, during the mourning, the order was quietly rescinded."

Obviously, at this late date, no one wants to claim responsibility for a ten-year undeclared war that killed fifty-eight thousand Americans, caused domestic riots and demonstrations, engendered lasting hatreds between classes and age groups and, according to many, nearly wrecked the American economy.

Was Kennedy's embryonic move to disengage in Vietnam a catalyst for his assassination? Was it the straw that broke the back of the military-industrial camel?

*　　*　　*

As terrible as it is to contemplate the involvement of the U.S. military in the Kennedy assassination, there are many connections between the two.

Several other factors have raised suspicions concerning the military's role in the assassination.

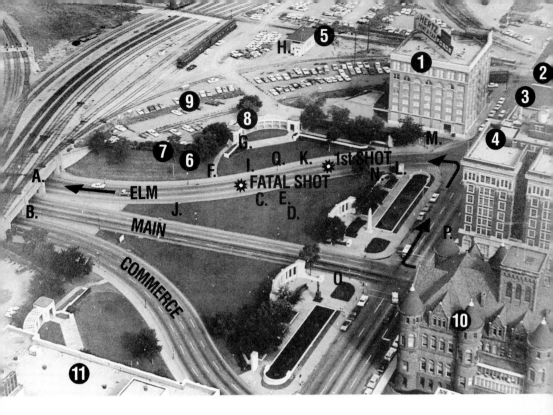

DEALEY PLAZA, DALLAS, TEXAS

1. Texas School Book Depository (now the Dallas County Annex)
2. The Dal-Tex Building (Now 801 Elm Building)
3. The Dallas County Records Building
4. The County Criminal Courts Building (which houses the County Jail and the Sheriff's Office)
5. The Union Terminal North Tower
6. The Grassy Knoll
7. Wooden, picket fence
8. Concrete pergola
9. Parking area
10. Old Court House
11. Union Terminal Building

LOCATIONS OF SELECTED WITNESSES

a. Policeman J.W. Foster, Sam Holland and other railroad workers.
b. James Tague
c. Jean Hill and Mary Moorman
d. Beverly Oliver (the "Babushka Lady")
e. Charles Brehm and son
f. Emmett Hudson
g. Abraham Zapruder
h. Railroad Supervisor Lee Bowers
i. The Bill Newman family
j. James Altgens
k. The John Chisms
l. The Phillip Willis family
m. Roy Truly, Billy Lovelady and other Depository employees
n. Howard Brennan
o. Charles Bronson
p. Roger Craig and other deputy sheriffs
q. The "Umbrella Man"

A smiling, robust-looking President John F. Kennedy is shown beginning his fateful motorcade through Dallas on November 22, 1963. He was accompanied by his wife, Jackie; Texas Governor John Connally; his wife, Nellie; and Secret Service Agents Roy Kellerman and William Greer. Kennedy made the trip to Texas despite warnings of danger and recent ugly right-wing demonstrations in Dallas.

As President Kennedy's limousine approaches the Texas School Book Depository (top), an arrow points to a man in the crowd. Researchers believe this man (blowup on left) may be Joseph Milteer (right), a Miami right-wing extremist who was tape recorded by a police informant telling of Kennedy's impending assassination in Dallas two weeks prior to the event. This same informant received a call from Milteer on the day of the assassination. Milteer said he was calling from Dallas. This is one of several documented incidents of persons with foreknowledge of the assassination.

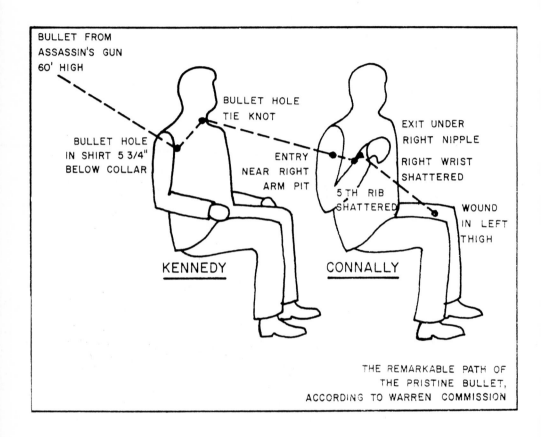

BULLET FROM
ASSASSIN'S GUN
60' HIGH

BULLET HOLE
TIE KNOT

EXIT UNDER
RIGHT NIPPLE

BULLET HOLE
IN SHIRT 5 3/4"
BELOW COLLAR

ENTRY
NEAR RIGHT
ARM PIT

RIGHT WRIST
SHATTERED

5TH RIB
SHATTERED

WOUND
IN LEFT
THIGH

KENNEDY

CONNALLY

THE REMARKABLE PATH OF
THE PRISTINE BULLET,
ACCORDING TO WARREN COMMISSION

The Government's lone-assassin theory rests on the idea of a single bullet acting in the manner described in this diagram and remaining virtually intact afterward.

JACK WHITE Photoanalysis

Above, Texas researcher Jack White has combined the left-hand side of a
photograph of Marine Lee Harvey Oswald with the right-hand side of a
photo reportedly made in Russia. He discovered that when all the facial
features are brought into alignment, the Russian Oswald's left ear and
head are significantly shorter than the Marine Oswald. Marine Corps
records report Oswald as 6'1" and the Oswald autopsy report stated he was
5'9". It is discrepancies such as these which have caused many researchers
to believe that the Oswald killed in Dallas may not have been the same
Oswald born in New Orleans in 1939.

In 1979, the House Select Committee on Assassinations recreated the JFK assassination gunshots at Dealey Plaza as part of acoustical studies which ultimately led to the conclusion that more than one gunman fired on the President. Notice at bottom right, the pile of sandbags has been placed near the south curb of Elm Street. The sharpshooter firing from the sixth floor of the Texas School Book Depository ordered the bags moved from the center of the street, the location of the first shots into Kennedy's limousine, because he could not get a line of sight through the intervening tree. The same problem existed in 1963. Two years earlier, this tree had been trimmed back to its 1963 configuration for the filming of a television docudrama on the assassination.

This view from the infamous sixth-floor "sniper's nest" window of the Texas School Book Depository shows several problems with the lone-assassin theory of the assassination. The height of the window sill, about a foot off the floor along with the half-opened window and the two pipes on the left, provide serious obstacles to anyone trying to sight down Elm street. Furthermore, the tree on the street below obscures a line of sight to the center of the street at about the position of the overhead highway sign which marks the location of the first shot which struck Kennedy. The author made this photo shortly after the tree was trimmed back to its 1963 configuration for a television docudrama in 1977.

Evidence of disappearing assassination clues can be found in this photograph of a sandy-haired man picking up what was described as a bullet slug which struck the grass on the south side of Elm Street. The man was identified by Dallas Police Chief Jesse Curry as an FBI agent. The policeman in the background, J. W. Foster, saw the bullet hit the ground during the assassination from his position on the Triple Underpass. A superior told him to guard this evidence, which he did until it was taken by the agent. No official explanation of this extraneous bullet has ever been made, although a photograph of its location was published in a Dallas-area newspaper the day after the assassination.

(left, bottom) Although more than a dozen persons were arrested in Dealey Plaza in the minutes following Kennedy's assassination, most were released without question after the capture of Lee Harvey Oswald. Over the years researchers have claimed that one of three "tramps" shown here being escorted to the Sheriff's Office under arrest may have been CIA officer E. Howard Hunt (man in rear with hat), a charge Hunt denied. Much evidence suggests that the taller "tramp" (on left) may have been convicted Texas hitman Charles V. Harrelson. Harrelson too denies any involvement. The truth of these suspects' identities may never be known because arrest records from the Dallas Police and Sheriff's Office for that day are missing from the National Archives.

(Above) Circumstances might well point to the truth of who was behind Kennedy's death. For example, two hours after the assassination Lee Harvey Oswald refused to tell Dallas police his real identity. He carried identification in the name of Oswald and of Alek James Hidell (seen above). The Dallas authorities were unsure of even the name of their recently-captured suspect. Yet, according to FBI documents released in 1977, at this same time, Bureau Director J. Edgar Hoover telephoned Attorney General Robert Kennedy with a full rundown on Oswald and his background in the Marines and in Russia. Hoover assured Kennedy that Oswald was the assassin and styled him as a "mean-minded individual . . . in the category of a nut."

Evidence of suppression of evidence by authorities is here in the backyard photos of Lee Harvey Oswald. Top left and center are the pictures reportedly discovered by Dallas Police on November 23, 1963 and soon sold to *Life* under unusual circumstances. These two photos were also published by the Warren Commission as evidence of Oswald's guilt (Commission Exhibits 133-A and 133-B). On the right, is a third backyard photograph which was only discovered in 1976. Notice that when Dallas police reenacted the backyard photograph for the Commission (bottom), they used the pose of the third photo which was kept from the public for 13 years.

Exhibit No. 37
Investigators restage the Oswald photographs for comparison purposes.

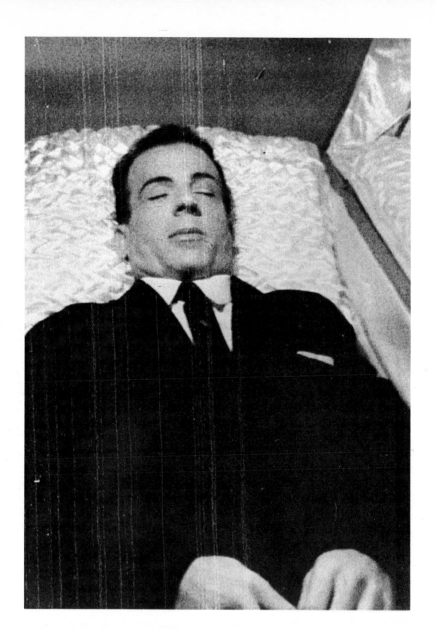

Questions about the identity of Lee Harvey Oswald arose immediately after his death at the hands of Jack Ruby. Police officials even opened his casket shortly before burial because of rumors that the casket was empty and his body spirited away. This picture of Oswald in his casket was made early on the morning of November 25, 1963, by a Dallas area police official. Although disputed as an authentic photo of Oswald when first made public in 1981, the FBI later released Bureau photos of Oswald in his casket which matched this picture. While the Oswald killed in Dallas was definitely buried in Rose Hill Cemetery in nearby Fort Worth and despite an official exhumation of his body in 1981, controversy over the true identity of Oswald continues today.

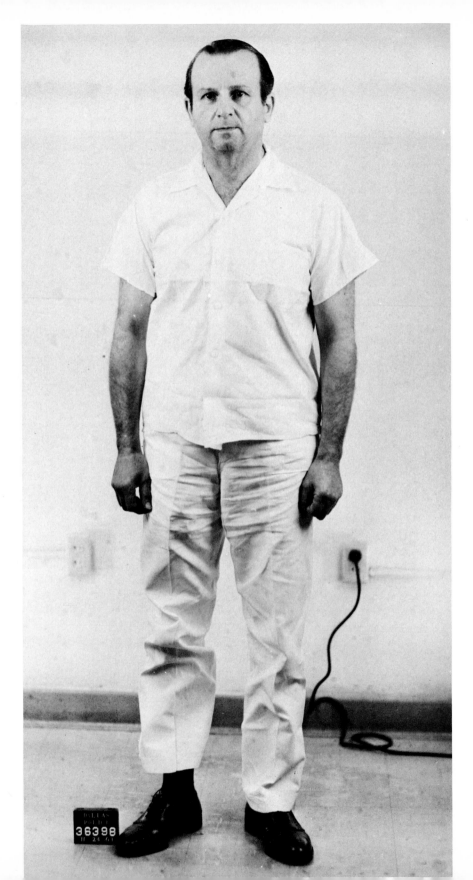

This 30.06 bullet has been fitted with an accelerator or "sabot", a small plastic device which allows a smaller caliber slug to be fired from a larger shell casing. Using such a device, the smaller slug will have increased velocity resulting in explosive striking power identical to what is viewed in the Zapruder film of the Kennedy assassination. The smaller slug also could have been previously fired and recovered, resulting in ballistic markings which match the original weapon and not the 30.06 which fired the "sabot" slug. Some researchers believe such a device was used to produce bullet fragments traceable to Lee Harvey Oswald's rifle. A 30.06 shell casing indicating the use of a "sabot" was found in the 1970s on the roof of the Dallas County Records Building overlooking Dealey Plaza.

(Right) Jack Ruby, shown here in Dallas Police custody, was far from being the insignificant nightclub owner described by the Federal Government. Ruby had solid contacts with many Dallas police and government authorities, including District Attorney Henry Wade as well as connections to organized crime figures in Chicago, New Orleans and Miami. In 1959, while involved with gunrunning activities involving Cuba, Ruby was an informant for the FBI.

Jean Hill, perhaps the closest bystander to Kennedy at the moment of the fatal head shot, claims to have witnessed a gunman fire from behind the picket fence on the Grassy Knoll. But when she tried to pursue the gunman, she was stopped by two men with Secret Service identification who forcibly took her to other agents in a building overlooking the assassination site. She said she was intimidated by a Warren Commission attorney and was kept under surveillance for years after by the FBI.

DICK BOTHUN from JACK WHITE Photoanalysis

(left, bottom)   Above are two of the most suspicious characters in Dealey Plaza at the moment of the assassination. The man on the right has become known as the "umbrella man" because just prior to Kennedy's arrival he stood in the warm sunshine with an open, black umbrella. As Kennedy was first shot, the man pumped the umbrella up and down as demonstrated in movie films made that day. Then seconds after the final shots, he joined this dark-complexioned man on the Elm Street curb. His folded umbrella lies on the ground by his left foot. In other photos, the second man on the curb appears to be speaking into a walkie-talkie. For almost twenty years the Federal Government failed to identify either of these men and made no mention of them in its official reports.

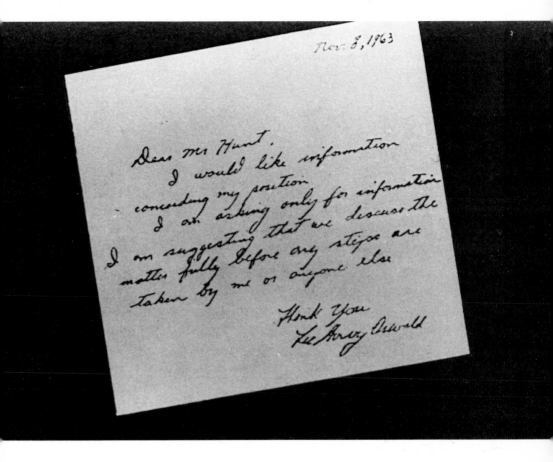

PENN JONES JR.

This handwritten note dated November 8, 1963, and signed Lee Harvey Oswald is addressed to a "Mr. Hunt" asking about "information concerding (sic) my position." The handwriting has been authenticated as that of Oswald. Some researchers believe the addressee may have been Dallas oilman H.L. Hunt. However, due to the fact that a copy of the note came from Mexico City, other researchers believe the addressee may have been Watergate scandal figure E. Howard Hunt, a CIA officer working with anti-Castro Cubans in 1963. By some accounts, Hunt was in Mexico City about the time the note was written. A CIA memo recently made public indicates that Hunt may have been in Dallas on the day of the assassination, an allegation Hunt steadfastly denied.

HEALTH RECORD	CHRONOLOGICAL RECORD OF MEDICAL CARE
DATE	SYMPTOMS, DIAGNOSIS, TREATMENT, TREATING ORGANIZATION (Sign each entry)

USNAS, Navy #3035, c/o FPO, San Francisco, California

A 9/16/58

Diagnosis: Urethritis, Acute, due to gonococcus #0303
Origin: In line of duty, not due to own misconduct.
CC: Urethral discharge

PI: Patient complains of a slight discharge and a stinging sensation on urination.

PH: Previous V.D.:

PE: Essentially negative except for a thick mucopurulent discharge from the urethra.

LAB: Smear reveals gram negative intra-and extracellular diplococci having the morphology of N. Gonorrhea.

RX: Procain Penicillin 900,000 Units I.M. X 3 days

D 9/16/58

To duty under treatment and observation:

PES-1421(VD) submitted: No B 754

SUBMITTED P. DERANIAN
CAPT.MC USN

APPROVED:

P. DERANIAN
CAPT MC USN
SENIOR MEDICAL OFFICER

SEX	RACE	GRADE, RATING, OR POSITION	ORGANIZATION UNIT	COMPONENT OR BRANCH	SERVICE, DEPT. OR AGENCY
M	C	PVT	MACS 1 MAG 11 USMC		

PATIENT'S LAST NAME—FIRST NAME—MIDDLE NAME	DATE OF BIRTH (DAY-MONTH-YEAR)	IDENTIFICATION NO.
OSWALD, Lee Harvey	10/18/39	1653230

CHRONOLOGICAL RECORD OF MEDICAL CARE
Standard Form 600

DONABEDIAN EXHIBIT No. 1—Continued

Tantalizing evidence that Lee Harvey Oswald participated in intelligence work is reflected in this Marine medical record dated September 16, 1958. Every branch of the U.S. military cautions troops against contracting venereal disease. Some elite units, such as the Marine Corps, actually punish members who are treated for the disease. However, Oswald's medical chart indicates that his case of gonorrhea was contracted "In the line of duty, not due to own misconduct." Researchers view this astonishing comment as evidence that Oswald was ordered to consort with prostitutes while serving in Japan.

Texas military intelligence units that normally were used to augment presidential security preparations were inexplicably told to stay home on November 22, 1963.

Col. Fletcher Prouty has reported that the 112th Military Intelligence Group at 4th Army Headquarters at Fort Sam Houston was told to "stand down" that day rather than report for duty in Dallas, over the protests of the unit commander, Col. Maximillian Reich. While apparently some elements of the MI unit did arrive in Dallas, their activities there remain obscure. One member may have been with FBI agent James Hosty the morning Kennedy was killed. In Warren Commission testimony, Hosty said that forty-five minutes before the assassination he was in the company of an Army intelligence officer, but he added the meeting had no connection with Kennedy's visit.

Recall that Agent Hosty's name, address, phone number, and license number were found in Lee Harvey Oswald's personal notebook (this was originally deleted from the material turned over to the Warren Commission) and it was Hosty who destroyed a message from Oswald days after the assassination apparently on orders from superiors.

Another Army intelligence officer to become involved in the assassination was Special Agent James Powell. Carrying a 35 mm Minolta camera, Powell had taken several photos in Dealey Plaza at the time of the assassination. He entered the Texas School Book Depository and his presence became public knowledge when he was forced to show his identification after Dallas police sealed the building. Powell told researcher Penn Jones he "worked with the sheriff's deputies at the rear of the Texas School Book Depository for about six or eight minutes" and that he had ordered a newsman to hang up a telephone on the building's first floor so that he (Powell) could use it.

No meaningful investigation has been made by the government to determine what intelligence agent Powell was doing in Dealey Plaza at the time of the assassination.

And the military connection becomes even more curious in light of two strange incidents that occurred in Dallas that day.

Dallas police lieutenant Jack Revill told the Warren Commission that an Army intelligence officer rode with him from Dealey Plaza to the Dallas Police Station. It was Revill, as head of the police criminal intelligence division, who submitted a list of Texas School Book Depository employees. Leading Revill's list was the name "Lee Harvey Oswald," with the address given as 605 Elsbeth in Dallas.

Oswald had lived at 602 Elsbeth in late 1962 and early 1963, but had since moved, and the Elsbeth address had never been given to his employers at the Depository. Where then did Revill get the Elsbeth address?

It was later revealed that the 112th MI Group, which maintained an office in Dallas, had possessed a file on a man named "Harvey Lee Oswald," identifying him as a procommunist who had been in Russia and had been involved in pro-Castro activities in New Orleans. This military file erroneously gave Oswald's address as 605 Elsbeth, the same mistake found on Revill's list.

Apparently military intelligence was swift in providing Dallas police with information on Oswald, the man who came to be labeled as the lone assassin of Kennedy.

Information on Oswald apparently came from the 112th MIG's operations officers, Lt. Col. Robert E. Jones, who was stationed at Fort Sam Houston in San Antonio. Testifying to the House Select Committee on Assassinations, Jones said the afternoon of the assassination he received a call from his agents in Dallas advising that a man named A. J. Hidell had been arrested.

Jones said he began a search of his intelligence indexes and located a file on A. J. Hidell that cross-referenced into one for Lee Harvey Oswald. He said he then contacted the FBI in both San Antonio and Dallas with his information.

However, nowhere in the vast documentation of Oswald's life did he ever actually use A.J. Hidell as an alias—the exceptions being when he mail-ordered the rifle allegedly used to kill Kennedy and the pistol allegedly used to kill Officer Tippit using the name Hidell and the use of the name Hidell on Fair Play for Cuba literature.

This raises two possibilities. Either military intelligence had some independent knowledge of Oswald's purchase of the weapons which took place long before he arrived in New Orleans (were they monitoring his Dallas post office box?) or someone, perhaps even Oswald himself, informed the military of his purchases.

The files on Hidell and Oswald gave detailed information about Oswald's trip to Russia as well as pro-Castro activities in New Orleans. Jones said he had become aware of Oswald in the summer of 1963 when information had been passed along by the New Orleans Police Department regarding his arrest there. He said the 112th MIG took an interest in Oswald as a possible counterintelligence threat.

The House committee, remarking on how quickly the military found files on Oswald, stated:

"This information suggested the existence of a military intelligence file on Oswald and raised the possibility that he had intelligence associations of some kind."

The Warren Commission specifically asked to see any military files regarding Oswald but were never shown the files mentioned by Jones or any others.

In 1978, when the House Select Committee on Assassinations learned of these files and requested them from the military, they were told the files had been "destroyed routinely" in 1973.

The committee concluded:

The committee found this "routine" destruction of the Oswald file extremely troublesome, especially when viewed in light of the Department of Defense's failure to make the file available to the Warren Commission. Despite the credibility of Jones' testimony, without access to this file, the question of Oswald's possible affiliation with military intelligence could not be fully resolved.

Even more troublesome is the military's file on A. J. Hidell. Jones stated that Hidell was an alias used by Oswald, which accounted for the fact that the two files were cross-indexed.

It appears that the U.S. military knew more about Oswald and his weapons than has yet been made public. But does that mean the military ordered the assassination?

It is ironic that of all our modern presidents, it was John F. Kennedy who received the only full military funeral in recent history.

Was this the military's way of making atonement?

Summary

While the U.S. military has attempted to keep a low profile in modern American life, there can be no question that the military-industrial complex is a force in the nation.

Obviously military and intelligence officers did not take kindly to Kennedy's attempts to restrain this powerful conglomeration. Kennedy angered these men by refusing to use U.S. military power to salvage the Bay of Pigs Invasion. Then he added fuel to the fire by rejecting recommendations by the joint chiefs to bomb the missiles emplacements in Cuba and to refrain from signing a nuclear test ban treaty with the Russians.

Vietnam may have been the straw that broke the generals' philosophic back. Viewed from the broadest perspective, it now seems possible to state that the opening shots of the full-scale war in Vietnam were in Dallas, Texas. Much evidence exists that Kennedy would have disengaged this nation from Southeast Asia had he lived—again in direct conflict with the wishes of the military-industrial complex.

Some generals—including Dallas mayor Earle Cabell's brother, Gen. Charles P. Cabell—even went so far as to brand Kennedy a "traitor." Cabell, after being fired by Kennedy as deputy director of the CIA, resumed responsibilities in the Pentagon.

The known connections between the military and the assassination—are many and troubling.

All this—along with the mysterious disappearance of military files on

Lee Harvey Oswald, who had many opportunities to work with military intelligence—makes many assassination researchers believe that at least some members of the U.S. military may have played a role in an assassination conspiracy.

If you didn't see Lee Harvey Oswald up in the School Book Depository with a rifle, you didn't witness it.

—FBI agent to witness Richard Carr

Part III
Aftermath

Dallas

The gunfire had barely died away in Dealey Plaza when an aftermath of odd and often unexplained events began in Dallas—and continued for more than two decades.

Dallas police blocking the nearby intersections—with no orders to the contrary (recall the eight-minute disruption of the Dallas police radio motorcade channel during the time of the shooting)—released traffic that began pouring through Dealey Plaza.

Spectators from blocks away, having heard the shots and sirens, ran to the scene. Some bystanders were in shock. Others were shouting, "They shot the President!" while others sobbed out the news. Pandemonium was the order of the day.

There was no shortage of lawmen as nearly twenty sheriff's deputies, following Sheriff Decker's orders, ran to the railroad yards behind the Grassy Knoll. Dozens of Dallas police officers also were flooding the area. But all were receiving conflicting information—witnesses on the west end of Dealey Plaza pinpointed the picket fence on the Grassy Knoll as the source of the shots, while many people on the east end said shots came from the Texas School Book Depository.

It is significant to recall that James Tague, who was slightly wounded when a bullet or bullet fragment struck the Main Street curb near the Triple Underpass, last spoke with Deputy Sheriff E. R. Walthers before having to move his car once traffic got moving. Tague said this occurred about 12:40 P.M.

Yet Walthers was among the first officers to seal off the Depository, indicating that the building was open for at least ten minutes after the shooting.

Actually the time may have been much longer. Dallas Police Captain Will Fritz, who headed the Dallas investigation, told the Warren Commission he began making detailed notes after hearing of the assassination at the Trade Mart. Fritz said he arrived at the Texas School Book Depository at exactly 12:58 P.M. Asked if the Depository exits were guarded at that time, Fritz replied:

I am not sure, but I don't—there had been some question about that, but the reason I don't think that—this may differ with someone else, but I am going to tell you what I know . . . After I arrived, one of the officers asked me if I would like to have the building sealed and I told him I would.

Recall that Ed Hoffman was able to drive from Stemmons Freeway to the railroad yards behind the Depository, circle the area, and leave unchallenged.

The point here is that there was absolutely no effective containment of the crime scene or of the Depository for at least ten minutes—and perhaps as much as twenty-eight minutes—after the shooting.

Officially it has been said that within an hour of the assassination, there was a roll call at the Texas School Book Depository. Employee Lee Harvey Oswald was the only person missing and authorities immediately began a search for him. Like so much other information in this case, this story is simply untrue.

To begin with, most Depository employees were outside viewing the motorcade at the time of the shooting and were prevented from returning to work by police. During the first roll call, dozens of Depository employees were missing. By the time it was determined that Oswald was gone—about 2:30 P.M.—he was already in police custody.

This was confirmed in 1981 by *Dallas Morning News* reporter Kent Biffle, who recalled that day in a lengthy article based on his notes of that day. Biffle wrote:

. . . only two of us [reporters] had arrived at the ambush building [the Depository] by this point. . . . Getting in was no problem. I just hid my press badge . . . and went in with the first wave of cops. . . . Hours dragged by. The building superintendent showed up with some papers in his hand. I listened as he told detectives about Lee Oswald failing to show up at a roll call. My impression is that there was an earlier roll call that had been inconclusive because several employees were missing. This time, however, all were accounted for except Oswald. I jotted down the Oswald information. . . . Neither the police in the building nor the superintendent knew that Oswald already was under arrest.

In the confusion following the assassination, there was ample opportunity for conspirators to escape and for vital evidence to be eliminated.

One such incident occurred minutes after the shooting on the south side of Elm Street. Dallas policeman J. W. Foster, from his vantage point on top of the Triple Underpass, saw a bullet strike the grass on the south side of Elm near a manhole cover. He reported this to a superior officer and was told to guard the area. Photographs taken that day show both Foster and Deputy Sheriff Walthers standing over the manhole cover.

Newsmen and spectators were kept at a distance and told that evidence—a bullet—was embedded in the grass inches from the manhole cover. News cameraman Harry Cabluck photographed the scene and recalled seeing more than one gouge in the ground. He, too, was told that a bullet had struck there. However, Cabluck said he took the photographs hours after the assassination and never actually saw a slug.

One photograph of the slug even appeared in the November 23, 1963, edition of the *Fort Worth Star-Telegram*, with the caption ASSASSIN'S BULLET:

> One of the rifle bullets fired by the murderer of President Kennedy lies in the grass across Elm Street from the building in which the killer was hiding and from where he launched his assault.

Inches from the bullet, which is circled in the newspaper photo, is the edge of the cement manhole.

On November 24, the *Dallas Times Herald* reported: "Dallas Police Lt., J. C. Day of the crime lab estimated the distance from the sixth floor window the slayer used, to the spot where one of the bullets was recovered, at 100 yards."

Richard Dudman wrote in the December 21, 1963, issue of *New Republic*:

> On the day the President was shot I happened to learn of a possible fifth [bullet]. A group of police officers were examining the area at the side of the street where the President was hit, and a police inspector told me they had just found another bullet in the grass.

Other witnesses to the bullet marks on the south side of Elm Street were Wayne and Edna Hartman, who were in Dallas for jury duty. After hearing shots in Dealey Plaza, the couple "ran like the devil" down to the grassy middle area of the plaza. Mrs. Hartman told this author:

> There were not many people in this area at the time, but a policeman was there. He pointed to some bushes near the railroad tracks on the north side of the street and said that's where the shots came from. . . . Then I noticed these two parallel marks on the ground that looked like mounds made by a mole. I asked "What are these, mole hills?"

and the policeman said, "Oh no, ma'am, that's where the bullets struck the ground."

On Sunday, the Hartmans again visited Dealey Plaza but found that the crush of people bringing memorials had obliterated the marks.

In the summer of 1964, the Hartmans contacted the FBI after learning that the Bureau was still seeking assassination information. Mrs. Hartman said FBI agents didn't seem too interested in what they had to say. One agent told them the marks had been made by bone fragments from Kennedy's head, an explanation that sounded "strange" to the Hartmans.

Both Hartmans told the FBI that the bullet marks did not line up with the Texas School Book Depository but rather with the picket fence on the Grassy Knoll. Mrs. Hartman recently recalled:

I don't see how what we saw down there could have come from those windows up there because they were not the right angle. So we have always felt that it came from across the street . . . that was the angle . . . across the street from where we stood . . . the Grassy Knoll, we've always felt it came from there. . . . And at that time people were telling us the bullets came from over there. There was somebody over there shooting also. And they pointed across the street, which was south of the Depository.

Yet in an FBI report dated July 10, 1964, agents stated:

[The Hartmans] said this gouged out hole was in line with the general area of the Texas School Book Depository Building. [They] said some bystander had mentioned that he believed the shots had come from the Texas School Book Depository Building.

If one or more bullet slugs were in the grass, what happened to them? What role did an extra slug play in the assassination? Was this proof that at least four shots were fired? The answers to these questions may never be known because, officially, this bullet never existed.

Within minutes of the shooting, a sandy-haired man in a suit—this man was identified in Dallas police chief Jesse Curry's book as an FBI agent—in full view of both Walthers and Foster, walked up, reached down, cupped some object in his hand, and stuck it into his left pants pocket.

The bullet was gone.

Later in 1964, when reports of this bullet reached the Warren Commission, the FBI was instructed to investigate the matter. Agents reported back that they had examined the manhole cover and there was no sign of a bullet striking it. There was no mention of the fact that the bullet in question landed inches away from the manhole cover. Apparently satisfied, the Warren Commission dropped the matter.

Later on the day of the assassination, the "Stemmons Freeway" sign, which according to some bystanders was struck by a bullet, disappeared. It is missing in photographs made in Dealey Plaza the next day. No explanation of this disappearance has ever been brought forth.

In 1974, Richard Lester, using a metal detector, discovered a bullet fragment on the far south side of Dealey Plaza just east of the Triple Underpass. Two years later, Lester turned the fragment over to the FBI. It was later studied by firearms experts of the House Select Committee on Assassinations.

This study showed the fragment was from 6.5-millimeter ammunition but, based on ballistics, it had not been fired through the Oswald rifle.

Rather than view this as evidence that perhaps multiple rifles were used in the assassination, both the FBI and the Committee left the impression that this discovery had no connection with Kennedy's death.

Yet another story of a bullet found may shed much light on how some bullet fragments were traced to the Oswald rifle.

Dean Morgan of Lewisville (a suburb of Dallas) has told Texas researchers that in 1975 his father was working on air-conditioning equipment on the roof of the Dallas County Records Building located just catercorner from the Texas School Book Depository. The Records Building's west side faces onto Dealey Plaza and there is a waist-high parapet along the edge of its roof.

According to Morgan, his father discovered a 30.06-caliber shell casing lying under a lip of roofing tar at the base of the roof's parapet on the side facing Dealey Plaza while searching for water leaks.

The shell casing is dated 1953 and marks indicate it was manufactured at the Twin Cities Arsenal. One side has been pitted by exposure to the weather, indicating it lay on the roof for a long time. The casing, which remains in Morgan's possession, has an odd crimp around its neck.

Rifle experts have explained to Morgan that this is evidence that a sabot may have been used to fire ammunition from a 30.06 rifle. A sabot is a plastic sleeve that allows a larger-caliber weapon to fire a smaller-caliber slug. The results of using a lighter-weight slug include increased velocity producing more accuracy and greater striking power. And the smaller slug exhibits the ballistics of the weapon it was originally fired from, rather than, in this case, the 30.06, as the sabot engages the 30.06's rifling.

In other words, assassination conspirators could have fired 6.5-millimeter bullets from the Oswald rifle into water, recovered them, then reloaded them into the more accurate and powerful 30.06 with the use of a sabot—which is held in place by crimping the cartridge.

By this method, bullet fragments found in the presidential limousine would have the ballistics of Oswald's rifle rather than the 30.06 from which they were actually fired.

Warren Commission Exhibit 399—the nearly intact slug found at Parkland Hospital the afternoon of the assassination—displays all the characteristics of a slug fired into nothing more solid than water. It is just such a slug that can be reloaded and refired using a sabot, which disintegrates on firing.

But bullets were not the only evidence found later in Dealey Plaza.

The day after the assassination, a college student named Billy Harper was taking pictures in the plaza when he found a piece of skull. It, too, was never acknowledged by the Warren Commission.

And while evidence was disappearing from Elm Street, men were seen fleeing the rear of the Texas School Book Depository.

Richard Carr, a steelworker who saw a heavyset man on the sixth-floor of the Depository minutes before the shooting, saw two men run from either inside or from behind the Texas School Book Depository minutes after the assassination.

He claimed the men got into a Nash Rambler station wagon facing north on the west side of Houston street by the east side of the Depository. He said the wagon left in such a hurry one of its doors was still open. He last saw the station wagon speeding north on Houston.

After reaching ground level from his seventh-story vantage point on the courthouse under construction, Carr said he saw the same man he had seen earlier in the Depository window. Carr said the man was "in an extreme hurry and kept looking over his shoulder" as he walked hurriedly eastward on Commerce Street.

Carr's story was corroborated by that of James R. Worrell, Jr., who told the Warren Commission that seconds after the shooting, he saw a man wearing a sportcoat come out of the rear of the Depository and walk briskly south on Houston (the direction of Carr's location). Worrell can't be questioned further about what he saw, as he was killed in a motorcycle accident on November 9, 1966 at age twenty-three.

Carr, however, told researchers about his treatment at the hands of the authorities. In a taped interview, Carr said:

> The FBI came to my house—there were two of them—and they said they heard I witnessed the assassination and I said I did. They told me, "If you didn't see Lee Harvey Oswald up in the School Book Depository with a rifle, you didn't witness it." I said, "Well, the man I saw on television that they tell me is Lee Harvey Oswald was not in the window of the School Book Depository. That's not the man." And [one of the agents] said I better keep my mouth shut. He did not ask me what I saw, he told me what I saw.

Not long after this encounter with the FBI, Carr's home was raided by more than a dozen Dallas policemen and detectives armed with a search warrant. Claiming they were looking for "stolen articles," they ransacked Carr's home while holding him and his wife at gunpoint. Carr and his wife were taken to jail but later released. The day after the police raid, Carr received an anonymous phone call advising him to "get out of Texas."

Carr finally moved to Montana to avoid harassment, but there he found dynamite in his car on one occasion and was shot at on another.

After testifying in the New Orleans Clay Shaw trial, Carr was attacked by two men in Atlanta. Although stabbed in the back and left arm, Carr managed to fatally shoot one of his assailants. After turning himself in, Carr was not indicted by an Atlanta grand jury.

Other witnesses also were later intimidated. Acquila Clemmons, who saw two men at the scene of the Tippit slaying, said a man with a gun came to her home and told her to keep quiet. Ed Hoffman, who saw two men with a rifle behind the picket fence on the Grassy Knoll at the time of the assassination, was warned by an FBI agent not to tell what he saw ''or you might get killed.''

A relative of Depository superintendent Roy Truly recently told researchers that due to intimidation by federal authorities, Truly was fearful until his death. Truly's wife, Mildred, still refuses to discuss the assassination—even with family members.

Sandy Speaker, the supervisor of Warren Commission star witness Howard Brennan, would not discuss the assassination until recently, after getting a phone call from his friend and co-worker A. J. Millican. Speaker said he got a call from Millican early in 1964. Millican was almost in tears and told him never to talk about the assassination. Millican said he had just received an anonymous call threatening not only his life, but the lives of his wife and her sister. He said the caller told him to warn Speaker to keep his mouth shut.

Recently Speaker told this author:

That call really shook me up because Millican was a former boxing champ of the Pacific fleet. He was a scrapper, a fighter. But he was obviously scared to death. And I still don't understand how they got my name because I was never interviewed by the FBI, the Secret Service, the police or anyone. They must be pretty powerful to have found out about me.

Whispered rumors, anonymous phone calls, and freakish ''accidents'' combined to create a tangible aura of fear in Dallas in the weeks following the assassination. Some of that fear still lingers there.

Mysterious Secret Service Men

One of the most puzzling aspects of the post-assassination confusion involves encounters between Dealey Plaza witnesses and ''Secret Service'' agents.

The most noted incident of this type was recounted by Dallas police-

man Joe M. Smith. Smith had run into the parking lot atop the Grassy
Knoll after a woman had told him, "They're shooting the President from
the bushes!" While searching through the parked cars, he encountered a
man who displayed Secret Service identification. Smith told author Anthony Summers:

> The man, this character, produces credentials from his hip pocket which
> showed him to be Secret Service. I have seen those credentials before,
> and they satisfied me . . . So, I immediately accepted that and let him
> go and continued our search around the cars.

Malcolm Summers was one of the bystanders who followed police up
the Grassy Knoll immediately after the shooting. He told Jack Anderson:

> I ran across Elm Street to run up there toward that knoll. And we were
> stopped by a man in a suit and he had an overcoat over his arm. I saw a
> gun under that overcoat. And his comment was, "Don't you'all come
> up here any further, you could get shot . . . or killed . . ."

It has subsequently been asserted by the Secret Service that none of their
agents on duty that day were anywhere near Dealey Plaza either before or
just after the assassination.

In retrospect, Smith doubted the legitimacy of the man he encountered.
In 1963 Secret Service agents, like their FBI counterparts, wore crewcuts,
dark suits, and narrow ties.

Smith described the man thusly:

> He looked like an auto mechanic. He had on a sports shirt and sports
> pants. But he had dirty fingernails, it looked like, and hands that looked
> like auto mechanic's hands. And, afterwards, it didn't ring true for the
> Secret Service. . . . At the time we were so pressed for time and we
> were searching. And he had produced correct identification and we just
> overlooked the thing. I should have checked the man closer, but at the
> time, I didn't snap on it . . .

In addition to Smith and Summers, GI Gordon Arnold also encountered
a man who claimed to be with the Secret Service just moments prior to the
assassination. Arnold said he was walking behind the wooden picket fence
on top of the Grassy Knoll when he was approached by a man who told
him he was with the Secret Service and that Arnold could not stay behind
the fence. Moments later, Arnold said shots came from behind the fence.

Sam Holland, who was standing with two Dallas policemen and other
railroad workers on the Triple Underpass, told the Warren Commission
that "a plainclothes detective or FBI agent or something like that" was
helping the police guard the railroad bridge. Holland told a Commission

attorney: "... there were two city policemen and one man in plain-clothes. I didn't talk to him. I talked to the city policemen."

Holland said after hearing shots and seeing a white puff of smoke come from behind the wooden picket fence, he and others ran to the Grassy Knoll. He later said that while they found no one behind the picket fence: "... somebody had been standing there for a long period. I guess if you could count them, about a hundred foot tracks [were] in that little spot, and also mud on the bumper of [a] station wagon."

Constable Seymour Weitzman, who had rushed behind the wooden picket fence, met men he believed were Secret Service. Warren Commission lawyer Joseph Ball asked Weitzman if there were others with him behind the fence. Weitzman replied:

Yes sir; other officers, Secret Service as well, and somebody started, there was something red in the street and I went back over the wall and somebody brought me a piece of what he thought to be a firecracker and it turned out to be, I believe, I wouldn't quote this, but I turned it over to one of the Secret Service men and I told them it should go to the lab because it looked to me like human bone. I later found out it was supposedly a portion of the President's skull.

It is not certain if this particular piece of bone was ever investigated by the proper authorities. There is no mention of it in official reports, although Commission Document 1269 is entitled "Location of Photos of a Bone Specimen." This document, however, is still classified.

Dallas police sergeant D. V. Harkness also encountered Secret Service men where none officially were supposed to be. Harkness told the Warren Commission that he ran to the rear of the Texas School Book Depository moments after the shooting and "there were some Secret Service agents there." Harkness told a commission lawyer: "Didn't get them identified. They told me they are Secret Service."

In later years Harkness told the *Dallas Morning News* that the men were dressed in suits and "were all armed." He told the newspaper: "[I] assumed they were with the Presidential party."

Dallas Secret Service agent-in-charge Forrest V. Sorrels was the only Secret Service agent to return to the scene of the assassination within an hour or so. Sorrels said he walked through a rear door of the Texas School Book Depository without showing any identification. His arrival was too late to have been that of one of the men encountered by Harkness.

In 1978, Sorrels, then retired, was asked by a Dallas newsman to comment on the stories of bogus Secret Service agents in Dealey Plaza. Sorrels said: "[I'm] not answering any questions about this thing. I gave all my testimony in Washington and I don't put out anything else. As far as I'm concerned, that's a closed incident."

Another odd incident involving Secret Service agents who may have been bogus occurred within an hour of the assassination in the small town of Ferris, located just south of Dallas. Two high-school students—Billy V. James and Ronnie Witherspoon—witnessed a speeding car being stopped by local police on Interstate 45. The students stopped to watch because they thought "we may have been witnessing the arrest of the assassins." However, according to the students, the men in the stopped car told police they were Secret Service agents "in a hurry to get to New Orleans to investigate something in connection with the assassination." James said the men were believed and allowed to go on without being ticketed.

No Secret Service agent reported leaving Dallas for New Orleans that day and the identity of the men in the car remains a mystery.

Incredibly, even the accused assassin apparently had an encounter with one of these bogus agents.

Secret Service inspector Thomas J. Kelley was one of the several officials who interrogated Lee Harvey Oswald on the Sunday morning he was shot by Ruby. In his report of that interview, Kelley wrote:

> . . . [Oswald] asked me whether I was an FBI agent and I said that I was not, that I was a member of the Secret Service. He said when he was standing in front of the Textbook Building [Texas School Book Depository] and about to leave it, a young, crew-cut man rushed up to him and said he was from the Secret Service, showed a book of identification, and asked him where the phone was. Oswald said he pointed toward the pay phone in the building and that he saw the man actually go to the phone before he left.

In later years, the theory was advanced that Oswald had merely mistaken a news reporter for an agent. Kelley's report dispels this notion.

In fact, when the sixth-floor museum of the assassination opened in 1989, a taped tour of the exhibit was narrated by newsman Pierce Allman, who claimed to have been the reporter encountered by Oswald. However, Allman apparently had no direct knowledge of this incident since he says government agents told him months after the assassination that he had met Oswald.

Considering the number of people claiming to have encountered agents in Dealey Plaza, it appears that Oswald may well have been correct in his identification of a Secret Service agent.

It seems incredible that the suspected killer of the President not only took the time to help someone he believed to be a Secret Service agent, but then stood around to watch him get to the telephone.

But perhaps the strangest—and most ominous—incident involving the Secret Service happened to witness Jean Hill. Jean Hill was standing beside her friend Mary Moorman on the south side of Elm Street at the moment Kennedy was killed. Moorman fell to the ground at the sound of the shooting, but Hill remained standing and watchful.

After seeing both a man fire from behind the wooden picket fence and a suspicious man rapidly walking west in front of the Depository, Hill ran across Elm Street and began to run up the Grassy Knoll. Hill told this author: "I don't know what I would have done if I had caught them, but I knew something terrible had happened and somebody had to do something."

As she ran up the Grassy Knoll, her attention was drawn to a "trail of blood in the grass just to the right of the steps." Thinking that "our guys had shot back and we got one of them," she followed the red droplets until she discovered they belonged to a Sno-cone—flavored ice packed in a cup. Someone had dropped a red-colored one that day on the Grassy Knoll.

After the distraction of the Sno-cone, Hill continued her run up the Grassy Knoll, but valuable seconds had been wasted. She looked in vain for either the suspicious man behind the fence or the man she saw by the Depository. She recalled: "All I saw in that parking area were railroad workers and police."

Walking to the west of the Texas School Book Depository, Hill said she encountered two men who identified themselves as Secret Service agents. She told interviewers in Texas:

I was looking around but I couldn't see anything, when these two guys came up behind me. One of them said, "You're coming with us," and I replied, "Oh, no I'm not. I don't know you." "I said you're coming with us," one of them said and then put this horrible grip on my shoulder. I can still feel the pain when I think about it. I tried to tell them, "I have to go back and find my friend Mary." But then the other guy put a grip on my other shoulder and they began hustling me past the front of the Depository. "Keep smiling and keep walking," one of them kept telling me. They marched me across the plaza and into a building. We entered from the south side and I think it was the sheriff's office. They took me to a little office upstairs and they wouldn't let me out of this room. It was all such a shock. There was a lot of tension and it was like a lot of it was focused on this one area. The two men that grabbed me never showed me any identification but, after we got to this little room, some men came in who were Secret Service. They began to ask me a lot of questions. One man told me they had been watching Mary and I out of the window. He asked me, "Did you see a bullet hit at your feet?" I told him I didn't realize that one had struck near my feet. "Then, why did you jump back up on the curb?" he asked me and I told him how I had started to run at the President's car but thought better of it. Then I heard some booming sounds and it startled me and I jumped back on the curb by Mary. I guess they were up there the whole time and watched the whole thing. Then they sent those two guys to come and get me. I mean, I wasn't too hard to find that day—wearing that red raincoat.

Hill said she was kept in the room for some time before rejoining Mary Moorman in a downstairs office. There were other assassination witnesses in the office, such as Charles Brehm and others who signed sheriff's depositions that day.

Hill said a Dallas newspaperman, whom the women at first believed to be a federal agent, took all of the Moorman snapshots. Later that day the photos were returned, but three of the six Moorman snapshots were taken by federal authorities, who returned them only after several weeks. Two of the returned photographs had the backgrounds mutilated.

Dallas police chief Jesse Curry summed up the import of a man with Secret Service identification when he told author Anthony Summers:

> . . . certainly the suspicion would point to the man as being involved, some way or other, in the shooting, since he was in the area immediately adjacent to where the shots were—and the fact that he had a badge that purported him to be Secret Service would make it seem all the more suspicious.

The House Select Committee on Assassinations briefly looked into the matter of men with Secret Service identification but came up with no real answers.

After establishing that "Except for Dallas Agent-in-Charge Sorrels, who helped police search the Texas School Book Depository, no [Secret Service] agent was in the vicinity of the stockade fence or inside the book depository on the day of the assassination," the Committee wrote off most of the sightings as people mistaking plainclothes police for agents.

However, the committee could not dismiss Smith's story so lightly. FBI agent James Hosty (whose name was in Oswald's notebook and who destroyed the Oswald note) told the committee that Smith may have encountered a Treasury agent named Frank Ellsworth. When deposed by the Committee, Ellsworth denied the allegation.

Despite its inability to determine who was carrying Secret Service identification on the Grassy Knoll on November 22, 1963, the Committee nevertheless concluded: "[We] found no evidence of Secret Service complicity in the assassination."

However, if Jean Hill's account is true, either men posing as federal agents were using offices in the Dallas county sheriff's building minutes after the assassination or genuine federal agents were monitoring the tragedy from an upper-story window.

* * *

Only one portion of Jean Hill's account of the assassination seems unbelievable—that of identifying the man she saw in front of the Depository as Jack Ruby. However, her story appears to have some corroboration.

First, recall the story of Julia Ann Mercer, who identified a man sitting in a truck just west of the Triple Underpass about an hour prior to the assassination as Jack Ruby. Also recall that both Mercer and Marguerite Oswald (Lee's mother) said authorities showed them photographs of Jack Ruby before Ruby killed Oswald.

Then there is the Warren Commission testimony of Depository employee Victoria Adams, who said she and a co-worker saw a man at the intersection of Elm and Houston minutes after the assassination "questioning people as if he were a police officer." She told the Commission that the man "looked very similar" to the photos of Jack Ruby broadcast after the Oswald slaying. Her companion, Avery Davis, was never asked for her opinion.

Mal Couch, a television cameraman for WFAA-TV in Dallas, also supported the idea that Ruby was in Dealey Plaza when he told the Warren Commission that another newsman, Wes Wise (who later became mayor of Dallas), had seen Ruby walking around the side of the Texas School Book Depository moments after the shooting. However, Couch was forced to admit his story was just "hearsay" by Commission lawyers who then declined to call Wes Wise to clarify the issue.

Jean Hill said she recognized the man who shot Oswald as being the same man she saw "walking briskly" in front of the Texas School Book Depository seconds after the assassination. The man she saw was almost running in a westward direction toward the Triple Underpass. However, after gaining the top of the Grassy Knoll, she lost sight of the man.

This story may play a part in the account of one Dallas policeman who chased a man leaving the area of the Triple Underpass.

The Black Car Chase

On November 22, 1963, Dallas policeman Tom G. Tilson, Jr., had taken a day off. A friend and fellow policeman. J. D. Tippit, was covering Tilson's regular beat that day. Three days later Tilson was a pallbearer at Tippit's funeral.

Tilson, now retired, has told Dallas newsmen of chasing a black car from the scene of the assassination that day and claims the man in the car bore a striking resemblance to Jack Ruby.

Tilson and a daughter, Judy, were going downtown to pick up another daughter who had been watching the presidential motorcade. As Tilson was turning east on Commerce from Industrial just west of the Triple Underpass, he said he learned from a police radio monitor he had in his car that Kennedy had been shot.

Tilson stated:

. . . I saw all these people running to the scene of the shooting. By that time I had come across under Stemmons. Everybody was jumping out of their cars and pulling up on the median strip. My daughter Judy noticed the [presidential] limousine come under the Underpass. They took a right turn onto Stemmons toward Parkland Hospital. Well, the limousine just sped past [this] car parked on the grass on the north side of Elm Street near the west side of the underpass. Here's one guy coming from the railroad tracks. He came down that grassy slope on the west side of the Triple Underpass, on the Elm Street side. He had [this] car parked there, a black car. And, he threw something in the back seat and went around the front hurriedly and got in the car and took off. I was on Commerce Street right there across from [the car], fixing to go under the Triple Underpass going into town. I saw all this and I said, "That doesn't make sense, everybody running to the scene and one person running from it. That's suspicious as hell." So, I speeded up and went through the Triple Underpass up to Houston . . . made a left . . . [came] back on Main . . . and caught up with him because he got caught on a light. He made a left turn and I made a left turn, going south on Industrial. I told my daughter to get a pencil and some paper and write down what I tell you. By this time, we had gotten to the toll road [formerly the Dallas-Fort Worth Turnpike, now Interstate 30] going toward Fort Worth. I got the license number and description of the car and I saw what the man looked like. He was stocky, about five-foot-nine, weighing 185 to 195 pounds and wearing a dark suit. He looked a hell of a lot more than just a pattern of Jack Ruby. If that wasn't Jack Ruby, it was someone who was his twin brother. Or pretty close. You know how Jack wore an old dark suit all the time? He always wore that old suit. He had that same old suit on. Anyway, I got the license number and all and exited off the turnpike and came back and picked up my other daughter down there at Commerce and Houston. Then I went to a phone and called in the information on the license number and what I had seen . . .

Tilson's story is corroborated by his daughter, now Mrs. Judy Ladner, although photos taken west of the Triple Underpass at the time do not show the black car.

Also, Dallas police radio logs for the day do not indicate any alert for such a car as described by Tilson.

Tilson maintains that he gave the license number and man's description to the police homicide bureau, "but they never contacted me or did anything about it." Believing he had done his duty, Tilson threw away the scrap of paper with the license number on it. It was only much later that he discovered that his information had been ignored.

Tilson recalled in 1978:

Homicide was that way. If you didn't have one of their big white hats on, they didn't even want you in the office. Here they were solving this case . . . here they had arrested a suspect [Oswald] in one day and cleared up the murder of a president in one day . . . They didn't want to have to look for anybody else and they didn't even want to know about it really. They wanted to clear up the case.

Tilson was never contacted by either the Warren Commission or the House Select Committee on Assassinations.

*   *   *

Another story regarding Jack Ruby's possible presence in Dealey Plaza comes from amateur photographer and assassination witness Phil Willis. Willis, who knew Jack Ruby by sight at the time of the assassination, still claims to have seen and photographed Ruby minutes after the shooting, standing near the front of the Texas School Book Depository.

In publishing Willis's series of assassination photos, the Warren Commission cropped the face of the Ruby figure out of the picture.

Was Jack Ruby at the scene of the assassination?

The Warren Commission established that Ruby was in the offices of the *Dallas Morning News* at the time of the shooting. The Commission stated that Ruby arrived at the newspaper between 11 and 11:30 A.M. (Some thirty minutes after the incident at the Triple Underpass involving Julia Ann Mercer.)

The Commission also determined that Ruby was with newspaper advertising employee Don Campbell until Campbell left for lunch about 12:25 P.M. About 12:45 P.M. Ruby was reportedly seen in the same spot Campbell had left him by another advertising employee, John Newnam. However, Newnam and other newspaper employees said once word came that Kennedy had been shot (probably no sooner than 12:40 P.M. and from employees who had been in Dealey Plaza returning to work), "confusion reigned" in the newspaper offices.

Employee Wanda Walker even today recalls vividly how Ruby sat quietly in the near-empty newspaper office that noontime. Walker told researchers in 1986:

The other secretary had gone to lunch and the ad salesmen were all gone and it was just me and Ruby up there. He was waiting for his regular ad man. He did an odd thing. I knew who he was, but we had never talked. But he got up and came over and sat by the desk where I was. It was like he didn't want to be alone. He said some things but I can't tell you what they were. Then some people started coming back in and they said the President had been shot. Jack Ruby got white as a sheet. I mean he was really shaken up.

Despite Walker's certainty that Ruby remained at the newspaper office during the time of the assassination, it is possible that Ruby could have slipped away for a few minutes.

No one was keeping exact times, and the *Dallas Morning News* offices are only two blocks from Dealey Plaza. It is conceivable that Ruby could have left the newspaper offices, been in Dealey Plaza and returned unnoticed within the space of ten or fifteen minutes.

In 1964 newsman Seth Kantor reported meeting and talking with Ruby at Parkland Hospital about 1:30 P.M. on November 22, 1963. This was supported by radio newsman Roy Stamps, also an acquaintance of Ruby's, who told this author he saw Ruby enter Parkland about 1:30 P.M. carrying some equipment for a television crew.

According to the Warren Commission, Ruby "firmly denied going to Parkland . . ." and "Video tapes of the scene at Parkland do not show Ruby there . . ." and so the Commission concluded "Kantor probably did not see Ruby at Parkland Hospital . . ."

The House Select Committee on Assassinations, in reviewing the evidence that Ruby was at Parkland Hospital an hour or so after the assassination, concluded: "While the Warren Commission concluded Kantor was mistaken [about seeing Ruby at Parkland], the Committee determined he probably was not."

So, if Ruby lied and the Warren Commission was wrong about Ruby's presence at Parkland, it is certainly possible that Ruby may have made his way—no matter how briefly—to the scene of the assassination.

Back in Dealey Plaza, while Sam Holland and other railroad workers were finding evidence of men waiting behind the picket fence and Jean Hill was being taken by Secret Service agents to the sheriff's office, Deputy sheriff Roger Craig thought he saw a suspect flee in a station wagon.

The Strange Saga of Roger Craig

In 1963 Roger Dean Craig was an ambitious young deputy sheriff who was going places.

Having run away from his Wisconsin home at age twelve, Craig had received a high-school diploma on his own and had served honorably in the U.S. Army. By 1959 he had married and taken a job as a sheriff's deputy in Dallas. Craig already had received four promotions within the Dallas County Sheriff's Department and in 1960 had been named Officer of the Year by the Dallas Traffic Commission.

But then came November 22, 1963.

Craig's account of his experiences that day caused considerable problems for the official version of the assassination's aftermath.

He later recounted that about 10:30 A.M. that morning, Sheriff Bill Decker called plainclothes men, detectives, and warrant men into his office and told them that President Kennedy was coming to Dallas and that the motorcade would come down Main Street. According to Craig, Decker then advised his employees to stand out in front of the building but to take no part whatsoever in the security of the motorcade.

Craig later said the crowd of deputies was hostile. "The men about me felt they were being forced to acknowledge Kennedy's presence," he said, adding the deputies voiced "bitter verbal attacks on President Kennedy." Craig said: "They spoke very strongly against his policies concerning the Bay of Pigs incident and the Cuban Missile Crisis and they seemed to resent very much the fact that Kennedy was a Catholic."

Craig said just after the motorcade turned on Elm Street, he heard a shot and began running toward Dealey Plaza. He ran down the grassy incline between Main and Elm Street and saw a Dallas police officer run up the Grassy Knoll and go behind the picket fence near the railroad yards. Craig followed, noting "complete confusion and hysteria" behind the fence. He began to question people when he noticed a woman in her early thirties attempting to drive out of the parking lot. Craig recalled:

I stopped her, identified myself, and placed her under arrest. . . . This parking lot was leased by Dallas deputy sheriff B. D. Gossett. He, in turn, rented parking space by the month to the deputies who worked in the courthouse, except for official vehicles. I rented one of these spaces . . . I paid Gossett three dollars a month and was given a key to the lot. An interesting point is that . . . the only people having access to it were deputies with keys . . . How did this woman gain access and, what is more important, who was she and why did she have to leave? I turned her over to deputy sheriff C. L. "Lummie" Lewis and . . . [he] told me that he would take her to Sheriff Decker and take care of her car. . . . I had no way of knowing that an officer with whom I had worked for four years was capable of losing a thirty-year-old woman and a three-thousand-pound automobile. To this day, Officer Lewis does not know who she was, where she came from, or what happened to her. Strange!

Meanwhile, Craig questioned people who were standing at the top of the Grassy Knoll, including Mr. and Mrs. Arnold Rowland. Craig said by approximately 12:40 P.M. he had turned the Rowlands over to Lummie Lewis and met E. R. Walthers back on the south side of Elm Street where "several officers and bystanders were looking at the curb on Elm Street where a nick caused by a bullet was reported to have hit."

He said his attention was attracted by a shrill whistle. In his report of November 23, 1963, Craig wrote:

. . . I turned around and saw a white male running down the hill from the direction of the Texas School Book Depository Building and I saw what I think was a light-colored Rambler station wagon with luggage rack on top pull over to the curb and this subject who had come running down the hill get into this car. The man driving this station wagon was a dark-complected white male. I tried to get across Elm Street to stop the car and talk with subjects, but the traffic was so heavy I could not make it. I reported this incident at once to a Secret Service officer, whose name I do not know, then I left this area and went at once to the [Depository] building and assisted in the search of the building. Later that afternoon, I heard that the city had a suspect in custody and I called and reported the information about the suspect running down the hill and getting into a car to Captain [Will] Fritz and was required to come at once to City Hall. I went to City Hall and identified the subject they had in custody as being the same person I saw running down this hill and get into the station wagon and leave the scene.

Craig later described the driver of the station wagon as a "very dark complected" man with short, dark hair wearing a white windbreaker-type short jacket. (Recall the witnesses who told of a dark man or Negro on the sixth floor of the Depository just before Kennedy's arrival.)

Craig said since the two men were the only ones he saw trying to flee the scene, he believed the incident "important enough to bring to the attention of the authorities at a command post which had been set up in front of the Texas School Book Depository."

Here Craig may have had a brush with one of the bogus Secret Service men. Craig later said he approached the front of the Depository and asked for someone involved in the investigation. He said a man in a gray suit told him, "I'm with the Secret Service" and listened to Craig's report on assassination witnesses. Craig later recalled:

He showed little interest in the persons leaving [the scene]. However, he seemed extremely interested in the description of the Rambler [station wagon]. This was the only part of my statement which he wrote down in his little pad he was holding.

On April 1, 1964, Craig described his confrontation with Lee Harvey Oswald at Dallas Police Headquarters to the Warren Commission:

I drove up to to Fritz's office about, oh, after five—about 5:30 or something like that—and—uh—talked to Captain Fritz and told him what I had saw. And he took me in his office—I believe it was his office—it was a little office, and had the suspect sitting in a chair behind a desk— beside the desk. . . . And Captain Fritz asked me was this the man I saw—and I said, "Yes" it was. . . . Captain Fritz then asked him about the—uh—he said, "What about this station wagon?" And the suspect [Oswald] interrupted him and said, "That station wagon belongs to Mrs. Paine . . . Don't try to tie her into this. She had nothing to do with it." . . . Captain Fritz then told him . . . "All we're trying to do is find out what happened and this man saw you leave from the scene." And the suspect again interrupted Captain Fritz and said, "I told you people I did." . . . Then he continued and he said, "Everybody will know who I am now."

In later years Craig said Oswald made the last statement in a dejected and dispirited tone, almost as if "his cover had been blown."

This was all explosive testimony since Oswald officially acted alone and made his way home that day by bus and by taxi. Therefore the Warren Commission stated it "could not accept important elements of Craig's testimony." It even went further, suggesting that the meeting between Craig and Oswald never occurred. According to the Warren Commission Report:

> Captain Fritz stated that a deputy sheriff whom he could not identify did ask to see him that afternoon and told him a similar story to Craig's. Fritz did not bring him into his office to identify Oswald but turned him over to Lieutenant Baker for questioning. If Craig saw Oswald that afternoon, he saw him through the glass windows of the office.

The truth of whether or not Craig was in Fritz's office came in 1969 with the publication of a book by Dallas police chief Jesse Curry. On page 72 is a photograph captioned "The Homicide Bureau Office under guard while Oswald was being interrogated." In the photograph, well inside the homicide office, stands Deputy Sheriff Roger Craig.

Craig also pointed out to Warren Commission attorneys that he had learned that Mrs. Ruth Paine, with whom Oswald's wife Marina was living, indeed owned a light green Nash Rambler station wagon.

His insistence on sticking with his story despite repeated attempts by authorities to have both Craig and Arnold Rowland change their testimony, began to cause problems for Craig within the Sheriff's Department. Initially, Sheriff Decker had backed Craig, calling him "completely honest." But later, Craig's credibility began to slip within the department and on July 4, 1967, he was fired by Decker. Some say the cause was laxity and improprieties in his work, while others say it was due to his unyielding position on the assassination.

In recent years there seems to be growing corroboration for Craig's story. First, a photograph taken in Dealey Plaza minutes after the assassination shows Craig in the exact locations as he described. There are even two photos of a Nash Rambler station wagon moving west on Elm.

In later years, researchers discovered Warren Commission Document 5, independent corroboration of Craig's story that was not published in the Commission's twenty-six volumes. In this document, an FBI report dated the day after the assassination, Marvin C. Robinson reported he had just past Houston Street driving west on Elm Street in heavy traffic when he saw a light-colored Nash station wagon stop in front of the Texas School Book Depository and a white man walk down the grassy incline and get into the vehicle, which drove west.

This is further evidence of the deceptive lengths to which the Warren Commission went trying to suppress any evidence that failed to fit its preconceived scenario.

In later years, Roger Craig—though vindicated in the controversy over his assassination testimony—continued to live with hard luck. His wife left him—some say due to pressure over his involvement in the assassination—and his back was injured in a car accident. He claimed to have been the object of murder attempts.

On May 15, 1975, Roger Craig, then only thirty-nine years old, was killed by a rifle bullet. His death was ruled a suicide.

*   *   *

Within an hour of the assassination, Dallas police sergeant D. V. Harkness had an encounter with three strange fellows, whom many researchers believe may have been involved in the shooting.

Union Pacific Railroad dispatcher Lee Bowers saw three men sneak into an empty railroad car in the train yards just behind the Texas School Book Depository a short time after the assassination. Bowers ordered the train stopped by radio and then summoned Dallas police. Several officers, including Harkness, rousted the trio from the rail car at gunpoint and marched them to the Dallas County Sheriff's Office. Their route took them past the Depository and across the eastern portion of Dealey Plaza. At least three news photographers took pictures of the three men as they were marched through the plaza under guard. These photographs are the only proof that this incident occurred.

For once in the sheriff's custody, the men officially disappeared. Although reportedly transferred later to the Dallas Police Station, they were never booked and any names, information, or fingerprints that were taken have never been made public.

The House Subcommittee on Government Information and Individual Rights discovered in 1975 that Dallas police arrest records for November 22, 1963, compiled for the Warren Commission, were missing.

These three men remain among those persons whom the FBI failed to identify and who were on the scene near the time of the assassination.

But were these "tramps" actually near the assassination site at the time of the shooting? In 1981 Kent Biffle, a reporter for the *Dallas Morning News* wrote an article detailing his experience that day:

Everyone was pointing toward a fence that connected with the Underpass. . . . I ran that way. Some teenagers followed. One of them darted ahead and hit the fence before I did. . . . Puffing, I followed him. The other side of the fence revealed no gunman. There was just a maze of railroad tracks and three dazed winos. "What happened?" I asked one. "What happened?" he asked me. People were still climbing over the fence. I ran east toward the Texas School Book Depository.

Were these three "dazed winos" the same three men later apprehended?

For more than twenty years the identities of the three men have been the object of speculation among assassination researchers. Although labeled "tramps," photos show the men had recent haircuts, shined shoes, and old, but unsoiled, clothing. In the photographs they hardly appear to be genuine tramps or winos.

In 1976 the three "tramps" drew national attention when comedian/social activist Dick Gregory and others claimed that two of the men were none other than Watergate conspirators E. Howard Hunt and Frank Sturgis. This allegation was quickly, though not conclusively, dismissed. (In the summer of 1985, E. Howard Hunt lost a libel court case based on a national article that claimed that CIA documents indicated Hunt was in Dallas the day of the assassination.)

After the 1980 arrest of convicted assassin Charles V. Harrelson, researchers took a fresh look at the "tramps," particularly the youngest of the trio. Many researchers now believe the tallest "tramp" may indeed be sitting in jail today.

The Role of Hitman Harrelson

Of all the people who have confessed to participating in the JFK assassination, convicted Texas hitman Charles V. Harrelson appears to have the most independent evidence to back up his claim.

Aside from being twice convicted of murder for hire, Harrelson has a long history of involvement with Dallas underworld characters linked directly to Jack Ruby. This connection first came to the attention of JFK researchers when Harrelson was arrested near Van Horn, Texas, September 1, 1980. He had been identified as a suspect in the death of federal judge John Wood of San Antonio who was shot from ambush by a high-powered rifle.

High on cocaine (well-known for loosening the inhibitions) and pointing a pistol to his head, Harrelson held lawmen at bay for six hours. During this time, according to the arresting officers, he not only confessed to the Judge Wood killing, but also claimed he participated in the Kennedy assassination. This statement, repeated in some Texas newspapers, sent assassination researchers to their files looking for confirmation.

Researcher Gary Mack already had noticed the resemblance of Harrelson to the youngest tramp. His search led to a review of the strange story of three "tramps" arrested near Dealey Plaza.

Harrelson was forty-seven years old in 1985, making him twenty-five at the time of the assassination. This corresponds with the age of the youngest "tramp," who was thought to have been between twenty-five and thirty years old.

In June 1981, Harrelson was interviewed by Chuck Cook, then a reporter for the *Dallas Morning News*. In a telephone interview with this author, Cook recalled:

> Because of his statements during his arrest, I felt obligated to ask him about that. I asked about the Kennedy assassination and he got this sly grin on his face. Harrelson is very intelligent and has a way of not answering when it suits him.

Cook said at a later interview he again brought the subject up and that Harrelson became very serious. Cook quoted Harrelson as saying: "Listen, if and when I get out of here and feel free to talk, I will have something that will be the biggest story you ever had."

Cook said when he asked what that story would be, Harrelson would only reply: "November 22, 1963. You remember that!"

Intrigued with the possibilities, Cook said he later showed photographs of the three "tramps" to Harrelson's wife, Jo Ann Harrelson, who "was amazed at the similarities." Cook added:

> Then I gave the photos to one of Harrelson's attorneys and he was supposed to show them to Harrelson. But that's the last I heard of it. He didn't want to talk about it because he felt his jail cell was bugged, and rightly so.

It was later revealed that Harrelson's jail conversations were indeed being monitored.

In an interview with Dallas TV newsman Quin Mathews, Harrelson offered further comments on the Kennedy assassination. "You said you'd killed President Kennedy?" commented Matthews. Harrelson replied:

> At the same time I said I killed the judge, I said I had killed Kennedy, which might give you an idea as to the state of my mind at the time . . .
> It was an effort to elongate my life . . . Well, do you believe Lee Harvey Oswald killed President Kennedy alone, without any aid from a rogue agency of the U.S. Government or at least a portion of that agency? I believe you are very naïve if you do.

Fort Worth graphics expert Jack White, who testified before the House Select Committee on Assassinations, is convinced that Harrelson is the youngest of the three "tramps." White told this author: "I have done various photographic comparison tests and everything matches . . . the hair, the nose, the ear, the profile. It's Harrelson."

But over and above the comparisons of Harrelson's photograph with that of the younger "tramp," further evidence indicates Harrelson very well may have played a role in the assassination.

When arrested, Harrelson was carrying the business card of R. D.

Matthews. In subsequent interviews, Harrelson admitted to being a close friend of Matthews. In fact, Harrelson said he looked up to Matthews as a father.

Russell Douglas Matthews, a former Dallas underworld character, is mentioned in the Warren Report, as a "passing acquaintance" of Jack Ruby and is obliquely connected there with a Ruby-backed jeep sale to Cuba in 1959.

The House Select Committee on Assassinations indicated Matthews' relationship with Ruby was more than "passing" and described Matthews as a man "actively engaged in criminal activity since the 1940s." The Committee also documented Matthews's connections to Dallas gamblers Lewis McWillie (close friend to the Kirkwoods of Fort Worth—and Benny Binion—all closely acquainted with Ruby. The Committee further developed evidence that Matthews was in contact with associates of Florida crime chieftain Santos Trafficante and was linked to Texas underworld characters such as Hollis de Lois Green, Jettie Bass, Nick Cascio, and James Todd, all acquaintances of Harrelson's.

In a strange sidelight, Matthews was best man at the wedding of a Dallas underworld character named George McGann to Beverly Oliver. Oliver, a friend to both Ruby and several of his employees, was in Dealey Plaza filming the Kennedy motorcade at the time of the assassination and became known to researchers as the "babushka lady".

The former chief counsel of the House Committee, G. Robert Blakey, in his book *The Plot to Kill the President*, reiterated the Committee's findings that Kennedy was assassinated as the result of a conspiracy and that more than one gunman was involved. Then Blakey went even further, stating that evidence compiled by the Committee indicated that organized crime played a major part in that conspiracy.

If organized crime in Dallas was involved—and Ruby's role would seem to justify that conclusion—then the entire spectrum of the Dallas underworld becomes suspect. And we come back to young Charles Harrelson.

But there is evidence that Harrelson's contacts went far beyond Dallas police characters. Indicted along with Harrelson in the plot to kill Judge Wood was the brother of reputed New Orleans crime boss Carlos Marcello, another of the organized-crime figures named by the House Select Committee on Assassinations as possibly involved in the Kennedy assassination conspiracy.

And then came the revelation of Harrelson's involvement with criminals connected to intelligence agencies and even the military.

In April 1982, Harrelson was identified by Florida law-enforcement officials as being a member of a shadowy group of hired gunmen, mercenaries, and drug smugglers known as "The Company."

The Company, which according to lawmen took its name from the CIA, involved more than three hundred persons, many ex-police or ex-military men. During one criminal trial involving members of the group, federal prosecutors claimed The Company owned more than $30 million in assets such as planes, ships, and real estate.

Federal drug agents said the group imported billions of dollars' worth of narcotics from Central and South America as well as conducting gun-running and mercenary operations.

Florida lawmen investigating this group claimed Harrelson was a member and that Jimmy Chagra, the man who allegedly hired Harrelson to kill the judge, also once hired The Company for protection.

Oddly enough, the very day that Harrelson was formally charged with the Judge Wood assassination—April 16, 1982—a Dallas news reporter and a JFK assassination researcher were scheduled to meet with Harrelson to discuss his role in the Kennedy murder. Although Harrelson had been jailed for more than a year and a half, when the formal charges were filed, all visits to him were canceled. JFK researcher and author J. Gary Shaw claimed: "I feel this was done at that particular time to prevent Harrelson from revealing what he knows."

During Harrelson's trial, Joe Chagra, brother of Jimmy, testified that Harrelson got the Wood contract after telling his brother that he had participated in the JFK assassination. (Researchers find it most revealing that a man reputed to be a high-ranking mobster by government agents should hire Harrelson on this claim rather than boot him out of his office—since everyone had been told the assassination was caused by only a lone nut.)

Harrelson, now serving a life sentence after being convicted of the Wood assassination, has not been interviewed recently about his role in Dallas, so researchers are left only with his cryptic reminder: "November 22, 1963. You remember that!"

* * *

The "three tramps" were not the only persons arrested on the day of the assassination. More than a dozen people were taken into custody, and it will forever remain puzzling that few records were kept on any of them. It seems that once Oswald was captured, the authorities totally lost interest in anyone else.

A Catholic priest told this author of observing the arrest of a young man wearing a three-piece suit and gloves who was then escorted from the Texas School Book Depository to the Dallas Sheriff's Office. He said he overheard the arresting officers say, "Well, we got one of them." There is no record of such an arrest.

Assassination witness Phil Willis told researchers that shortly after the shooting, police escorted a man in a black leather jacket and black gloves from the Dal-Tex Building—which lies directly east of the Depository and the building several researchers believe shots may have come from. Again there is no record of such an arrest. This man may have been Larry Florer, who was arrested in the Dal-Tex Building. In a statement to authorities,

Florer said he tried to use a telephone in the Dal-Tex Building but found they were all busy. He was taken into custody as he tried to leave the building.

Another man arrested in the Dal-Tex Building was a Mafia-connected police character with a record of more than thirty arrests.

The Mafia Man in Dealey Plaza

Moments after the assassination, an elevator operator in the Dal-Tex Building noticed a man he did not recognize. The operator summoned Deputy Sheriff C. L. "Lummie" Lewis, who arrested the man. He identified himself as Jim Braden.

Taken to the Sheriff's Office for questioning, Braden said he was visiting Dallas on oil business and was staying at the Cabana Motel (a motor inn built with Teamster money) on Stemmons Expressway. He said he had entered the Dal-Tex Building to use the telephone when he was taken into custody.

With no information to the contrary, authorities released Braden three hours later. It was an unfortunate decision. What is now known is that Braden had recently legally changed his name from Eugene Hale Brading. If the authorities had obtained that name on November 22, 1963, there perhaps would have been more interest in the man. Braden/Brading was a man with a police record stretching back to 1934 for such crimes as burglary, embezzlement, mail fraud, and conspiracy, including several arrests in Dallas.

Braden's story, which had been pieced together over the years by a variety of researchers and newsmen, indicates this man may have been more deeply involved in the assassination than was first suspected. On parole for mail fraud and interstate transportation of stolen property, Braden had informed his parole officer that he would be in Dallas from November 21 to 25, 1963. He said on November 21, 1963, he visited the offices of Texas oilman H. L. Hunt to meet with Hunt's son, Lamar. Interestingly, Jack Ruby also was at the Hunt offices about that same time, ostensibly to help a young woman get a job. (Both Braden and Ruby denied these visits although they have been verified by more than one office worker.)

And Braden, along with ex-convict Morgan Brown, was staying at the Cabana Motel, the same motel visited by Ruby the night of November 21.

Furthermore, in a book entitled *Legacy of Doubt*, CBS newsman Peter Noyes documented Braden's connections to a number of underworld figures, including Meyer Lansky. Apparently Braden was known as a Mafia courier.

Most sinister of all, Braden may have been in contact with the New Orleans Mafia-CIA man, David Ferrie, Lee Harvey Oswald's former Civil Air Patrol leader.

Noyes found that in the weeks immediately preceding the assassination, Braden was in and out of Room 1701 of the Pere Marquette Building in New Orleans, just down the hall from Room 1707, where Ferrie was working for an attorney of Mafia boss Carlos Marcello.

Another fascinating connection between Braden and the assassination concerns two New York businessmen, Lawrence and Edward Meyers. Lawrence Meyers was a personal friend of Jack Ruby. On November 20–21, 1963, Meyers also was staying at the Cabana Motel in Dallas. While in Dallas, Meyers told the FBI he was with Jean West, a "rather dumb, but accommodating broad." Edward Meyers was in Dallas to attend the bottlers convention—the same convention attended by Richard Nixon. Both brothers were visited by Jack Ruby briefly at the Cabana Motel on the night of November 21—the same night Braden was at the same motel.

While no direct connections between this group and Ferrie in New Orleans can be made at this time, it is fascinating to note that when New Orleans district attorney Jim Garrison began looking at long-distance telephone calls for David Ferrie he discovered something—the same day Oswald left New Orleans for his reported trip to Mexico City, Ferrie called a number in Chicago that belonged to Jean Aase West, Meyer's friend.

In Warren Commission Exhibit 2350—a listing of telephone calls made by Lawrence Meyers in November 1963—it was found that that same day he, too, called the Chicago number of Jean West, the woman who accompanied him to Dallas. While not conclusive, these documents, suggest possible connections between Jack Ruby and David Ferrie via Meyers/ West and Braden.

Meyers also told the Warren Commission that his friend Ruby had called him the night before shooting Oswald. The next day, upon hearing the news that Ruby shot Oswald, Meyers decided not to contact Dallas police because "in light of the apparent hectic activities then ensuing at the police station, it would be better if he did not do so."

All of this occurred in the context of Braden's visit to Dallas. The House Select Committee on Assassinations tried to sort out the truth of Braden's visit as well as his contacts, to little avail.

First Braden said he made the trip to Dallas from California and met with a Dallas parole officer at the moment of the assassination. However, the parole officer could not recall such a meeting. (If Braden had not notified his parole office that he was leaving California, he would have been in violation of parole and subject to arrest.) Braden told the Committee he walked as far as the Dal-Tex Building in an effort to find a telephone so he could call his mother and tell her about the assassination. He denied he ever was in Dealey Plaza.

However, due to statements made while in custody and the fact that Braden has definitely been identified in Dealey Plaza photographs, it is now widely accepted that Braden was among the spectators gathered in Dealey Plaza minutes after the shooting.

This fact alone—that a known felon with many ties to Mafia figures, New Orleans, and Jack Ruby would be hanging around Dealey Plaza just after Kennedy's death—creates deep suspicion about the immediate Dallas investigation and, even more particularly, the subsequent federal investigation. This suspicion is heightened in light of the fact that in 1976, the National Archives revealed that at least two documents relating to the Braden arrest were missing.

*   *   *

One of the oddest arrests that day was only reported in a Dallas newspaper.

The November 22, 1963 edition of the *Dallas Times Herald* reported that a policeman arrested a man wearing horn-rimmed glasses, a plaid coat, and a raincoat after Depository employees pointed to him from a third-floor window. The news account said the man was taken under protest to the Sheriff's Department, while members of the crowd shouted, "I hope you die!" and "I hope you burn!"

Three weeks later, the same newspaper reported that "an early suspect in the assassination of President Kennedy was still in jail—but no longer a suspect in the killing." This account said the man was arrested minutes after the assassination after police swarmed into the railroads yards where "a man was reported seen in that area carrying a rifle." The story said the still-unidentified man was being held on "city charges."

Who was this man and what, if anything, did he know about the assassination?

Another odd arrest—that of Jack Lawrence—deserves serious study. Lawrence was arrested late on the afternoon on November 22, 1963, after his actions caused suspicions among his co-workers at Downtown Lincoln-Mercury, located two blocks west of Dealey Plaza.

Lawrence had obtained a job as a car salesman at the dealership just one month before the assassination with job references from New Orleans that later were discovered to be phony. Lawrence never sold a car and on the day before the assassination, he had borrowed one of the firm's cars, after telling his boss he had a "heavy date."

On Friday, November 22, Lawrence failed to show up for work. However, about thirty minutes after the assassination, he came hustling through the company's show room, pale and sweating with mud on his clothes. He rushed into the men's room and threw up. He told co-workers he had been ill that morning, and that he had tried to drive the car back to the dealership but had to park it due to the heavy traffic. Later, employees found the car parked behind the wooden picket fence on top of the Grassy Knoll overlooking Dealey Plaza.

Lawrence's activities were so suspicious that employees called police, who picked up Lawrence that evening. Lawrence, who reportedly was an expert marksman in the Air Force, left Dallas after being released the next day. His current whereabouts are unknown.

Of course, the most prominent arrest of that day was when Dallas police nabbed Lee Harvey Oswald less than an hour and a half after the assassination. But such rapid police action was precipitated by yet another tragic incident—the slaying of Dallas policeman J. D. Tippit.

The Shooting of J. D. Tippit

Of all the aspects of the Kennedy assassination, the shooting of Dallas policeman Jefferson Davis Tippit has received less attention than most others. Allegedly Tippit was shot down while attempting to arrest Lee Harvey Oswald forty-five minutes after the assassination in Oak Cliff, south of downtown Dallas. And it was the slaying of this policeman that led to the arrest of Lee Harvey Oswald and, in many ways, became a cornerstone of the case for Oswald's guilt—Warren Commission attorney David Belin called the shooting the "Rosetta Stone to the JFK assassination." "After all," stated the conventional wisdom of 1963–64, "Oswald killed that policeman. Why would he do that if he hadn't killed the President?"

Yet today there is a growing body of evidence to suggest that Oswald did not kill Tippit—which, if true, destroys the argument above.

Little is known about Tippit or his life and personal contacts. This absence of information prompted researcher Sylvia Meagher to write:

Tippit, the policeman and the man, is a one-dimensional and insubstantial figure—unknown and unknowable. The [Warren] Commission was not interested in Tippit's life, and apparently interested in his death only to the extent that it could be ascribed to Oswald, despite massive defects in the evidence against him.

With no real knowledge of Tippit's background or associations and with a number of problems with several aspects of the evidence, the Warren Commission nevertheless concluded that Oswald was his killer based on four primary pieces of evidence.

• 1. Two witnesses who saw the shooting and seven who saw a man fleeing "positively identified Lee Harvey Oswald as the man they saw fire the shots or flee from the scene."

The chief witness for the Warren Commission was Helen Markham, whose credibility, even at the time of the Commission, was strained to the breaking point. Markham claimed to have talked for some time with the dying Tippit, yet medical authorities said he was killed instantly. She said she saw Tippit's killer talk with the policeman through his patrol car's right-hand window, although pictures taken at the scene show that window was shut.

She was in hysterics at the time and even left her shoes on top of Tippit's car. Later, in her testimony before the Warren Commission, Markham stated six times she did not recognize anyone in the police lineup that evening, before Commission attorney Joseph Ball prompted, "Was there a number-two man in there?"

Markham responded: "Number two is the one I picked . . . When I saw this man I wasn't sure, but I had cold chills just run all over me . . ."

Furthermore, other witnesses at the scene—William Scoggins, Ted Calloway, and Emory Austin—even today claim they never saw Mrs. Markham in the minutes immediately following the shooting.

Cabdriver Scoggins also identified Oswald that day, although Scoggins admitted he did not actually witness the shooting and his view of the fleeing killer was obscured because he ducked down behind his cab as the man came by. Scoggins and cabdriver William Whaley, who allegedly drove Oswald home that day, both viewed a Dallas police lineup composed of five "young teenagers" and Oswald. Whaley told the Warren Commission:

> . . . you could have picked [Oswald] out without identifying him by just listening to him because he was bawling out the policemen, telling them it wasn't right to put him in line with these teenagers. . . . He showed no respect for the policemen, he told them what he thought about them . . . they were trying to railroad him and he wanted his lawyer . . . Anybody who wasn't sure could have picked out the right one just for that . . .

If his protestations weren't enough to guide the witnesses in their identification of Oswald, the suspect had conspicuous bruises and a black eye. Furthermore, Oswald stated he was asked and gave his correct name and place of employment. By Friday evening, everyone in Dallas who attended the police lineups had heard that shots were fired from the Texas School Book Depository.

On Saturday, Scoggins again identified Oswald, although in his Warren Commission testimony he admitted seeing Oswald's photograph in a morning paper prior to viewing the police lineup. His identification of Oswald fell further into disrepute when he told the Commission that after the lineup, an FBI or Secret Service agent showed him several pictures of men, which Scoggins narrowed down to two. Scoggins recalled: ". . . I told them one of these two pictures is him [Oswald] . . . and then he told me the other one was Oswald."

These were the two star government witnesses. Other witnesses, including Domingo Benavides—the person closest to the killing—were never asked to view a lineup nor were they able to identify Oswald as the killer.

Several other witnesses, including Acquilla Clemons, who claimed two men were involved in the Tippit shooting but said she was threatened into silence by a man with a gun, were never questioned by federal investigators. The Warren Commission denied Clemons's claim, stating: "The only woman among the witnesses to the slaying of Tippit known to the Commission is Helen Markham."

Markham reportedly initially said that Tippit's killer was short and stocky with bushy hair. This is the same description given by Clemons, who in a filmed interview said the killer was "kind of a short guy . . . kind of heavy." Markham later denied giving this description.

Frank Wright lived near the scene of the Tippit shooting. He heard shots and ran outside. In an interview with private researchers less than a year later, Wright said he saw Tippit roll over once and lie still. He added:

I saw a man standing in front of the car. He was looking toward the man on the ground. . . . He had on a long coat. It ended just above his hands. I didn't see any gun. He ran around on the passenger side of the police car. He ran as fast as he could go, and he got into his car. His car was a little gray old coupe. It was about a 1950–51, maybe a Plymouth. It was a gray car, parked on the same side of the street as the police car, but beyond it from me. It was heading away from me. He got in that car and he drove away as fast as you could see . . . After that a whole lot of police came up. I tried to tell two or three people what I saw. They didn't pay any attention. I've seen what came out on television and in the newspaper, but I know that's not what happened.

Another witness was Warren Reynolds, who chased Tippit's killer. He, too, failed to identify Oswald as Tippit's killer until after he was shot in the head two months later. After recovering, Reynolds identified Oswald to the Warren Commission. (A suspect was arrested in the Reynolds shooting, but released when a former Jack Ruby stripper named Betty Mooney MacDonald provided an alibi. One week after her word released the suspect, MacDonald was arrested by Dallas police and a few hours later was found hanged in her jail cell. Neither the FBI nor the Warren Commission investigated this strange incident.)

• 2. The cartridge cases found near the Tippit slaying "were fired from the revolver in the possession of Oswald at the time of his arrest, to the exclusion of all other weapons," claimed the Warren Commission.

There are many problems with this evidence. First, Dallas police sergeant Gerald Hill, at the time of the Tippit shooting, radioed the police dispatcher, saying: "The shells at the scene indicate that the suspect is armed with an automatic .38 rather than a pistol." Oswald reportedly was captured with a .38 Special revolver. There is a significant difference between an automatic, which ejects spent shells onto the ground, and a revolver, which requires deliberate emptying of the weapon. These weapons also require different types of ammunition.

Other officers at the scene believed that an automatic weapon was used, based on the distance from Tippit's body to where the shells were found and what some perceived to be ejector scratches on the shells. If an automatic was used, then Oswald's revolver cannot be blamed for Tippit's death.

Then there's the problem of identification of the empty shells. Police man J. M. Poe received two cartridge cases from witness Benavides at the scene. In an FBI report, Poe firmly stated that he marked the cases with his initials, "J.M.P." before turning them over to Dallas Crime Lab personnel.

However, on June 12, 1964, the FBI showed Poe the four. 38 Special cases used as evidence of Oswald's guilt by the Warren Commission. The Bureau reported:

> . . . [Poe] recalled marking these cases before giving them to [lab personnel], but he stated after a thorough examination of the four cartridges shown to him . . . he cannot locate his marks; therefore, he cannot positively identify any of these cartridges as being the same ones he received from Benavides.

Testifying to the Warren Commission, Poe vacillated, saying he couldn't swear to marking the cases. However, asked to identify the cartridges, Poe also stated: "I want to say these two are mine, but I couldn't swear to it."

Poe's failure to find his initials on the cases, coupled with the fact that the cases were not turned over to the FBI until six days after other inventoried evidence, leaves many researchers with the suspicion that shell cases from Oswald's revolver was substituted for the ones marked by Poe.

To further confuse the issue, the Warren Commission discovered that the shell cases allegedly recovered at the scene of the shooting do not match up with the slugs that were recovered from Tippit's body. The four cases are made up of two of Winchester-Western manufacture and two of Remington-Peters, while of the bullets removed from Tippit, only one is Remington-Peters and three are from Winchester-Western.

Weakly, the Warren Commission attempted to explain this anomaly by surmising that perhaps a fifth shot had been fired but not recovered (most of the witnesses recalled no more than four shots) or that perhaps Oswald already had an expended Remington-Peters case in his pistol prior to shooting Tippit. The Commission even suggested that perhaps ". . . to save money . . . he might have loaded one make of bullet into another make of cartridge case."

This, of course, would require Oswald to own or have access to reloading equipment. It should be pointed out that when arrested, Oswald reportedly was carrying five live Winchester-Western bullets in his pocket in addition to the fully loaded revolver, which apparently was never tested to determine if it had been fired recently. With this exception, authorities found no other ammunition or gun-cleaning materials in any of Oswald's possessions.

• 3. The Warren Commission determined that the revolver in Oswald's possession at the time of his arrest was purchased by and belonged to him. While this segment of the evidence against Oswald may be true (some researchers are not convinced that the weapons order signed by A. J. Hidell can conclusively be traced to Oswald), it does not prove that the gun was used to kill Tippit.

For instance, even the resources of the FBI failed to prove that the slugs recovered from Tippit's body had been fired from Oswald's pistol. FBI officials claimed that since the Oswald revolver had been rechambered to accept .38 Special ammunition, the barrel was oversize for the bullet, causing inconsistent ballistic markings. Thus, ". . . consecutive bullets fired in the revolver by the FBI could not even be identified with each other under the microscope," stated the Commission in an appendix to its report. This statement is most odd, for several firearms experts have told this author that similar .38 Specials do fit the rifling grooves and can be checked ballistically.

If the slugs from Tippit's body cannot be matched to Oswald's revolver, perhaps it is because they did not come from that gun. Adding fuel to this speculation is the statement of Eddie Kinsley, the ambulance attendant who drove the mortally wounded Tippit to a hospital. In recent years, Kinsley told newsman Earl Golz of an extraneous bullet. According to Kinsley, as he unloaded Tippit from his ambulance: "I kicked one of the bullets out of my ambulance that went into his button . . . onto the parking lot of Methodist Hospital. It didn't go in the body . . . It fell off the ambulance still in this button."

Since Tippit reportedly was struck by all four bullets fired at him and these slugs were placed in evidence with the Warren Commission, what is the explanation for Kinsley's fifth slug? Kinsley told Golz he had never been questioned by the Warren Commission.

Recent work by Texas researchers indicate that the cases now residing in the National Archives and exhibited by the Warren Commission as the shells used in the Tippit slaying, may not have been fired by Oswald's pistol. Oswald's pistol was originally a Military and Police Smith & Wesson 1905 Model .38-caliber revolver, the largest-selling quality revolver ever produced. Originally shipped to England during World War II, more than eighty-eight thousand were shipped back to the United States in the late 1950s and early 1960s.

The pistol in question, serial number V510210, ended up in California, where it apparently was converted to a .38 Special Model. This involved cutting off the barrel from its original five inches to two-and-a-quarter inches. The Warren Commission said the pistol also was rechambered to accept .38 Special ammunition (slightly smaller in diameter but longer than. 38 Standard ammunition), although Commission testimony fails to establish this change.

Texas researcher and veteran hunter Larry Howard discovered after buying an exact duplicate of Oswald's .38 revolver that .38 Special cartridges, when fired in a rechambered weapon, bulge noticeably in the center. Howard told this author:

> I have checked this with several expert gunsmiths. Since the rechambering cannot change the diameter of the cylinder, but only makes it longer to accept .38 Special ammo, the bullet bulges in the middle when fired. I've done it time after time. My wife can notice the bulge. The case looks like it's pregnant. Studying the shells depicted in the Warren Commission volumes and also in a close-up clear photograph in the November 1983, commemorative issue of *Life* magazine, it appears to everyone that the shell cases in the National Archives (supposedly the casings found at the scene of Tippit's death) do not show any bulging at all. This indicates to me and other experts that those cases could not have been fired from the .38 Special that was supposed to belong to Oswald.

Until further testing can be done on the cartridge cases in question, this is hardly solid proof of Oswald's innocence in the Tippit shooting. But it is further proof of the wide gaps still open in the case against Oswald.

• 4. According to the Warren Commission, Oswald's jacket was found along the path of flight taken by Tippit's killer.

The Warren Commission wrote:

> . . . Oswald was seen leaving his roominghouse at about 1 P.M. wearing a zipper jacket . . . the man who killed Tippit was wearing a light-colored jacket, that he was seen running along Jefferson Boulevard, that a jacket was found under a car in a lot adjoining Jefferson Boulevard . . . when he was arrested at approximately 1:50 P.M., he was in shirtsleeves. These facts warrant the finding that Lee Harvey Oswald disposed of his jacket as he fled from the scene of the Tippit killing.

But did the facts warrant such a conclusion? Not really, since almost every aspect of the jacket story has since come under question. Oswald, it is known, had only two jackets—one blue and one a lightweight gray zipper jacket. At least two witnesses at the scene of Tippit's slaying reported his killer wore a white jacket.

One of these witnesses, Helen Markham, was shown Oswald's gray jacket by a Warren Commission attorney who asked, "Did you ever see this before?" Despite having been shown the jacket by the FBI prior to her testimony, Markham replied: "No; I did not . . . that jacket is a darker jacket than that, I know it was."

Witness Domingo Benavides was shown a jacket by Commission attorney David Belin, who said, "I am handing you a jacket which had been marked as 'Commission's Exhibit 163,' and ask you to state whether this bears any similarity to the jacket you saw this man with the gun wearing?" The accommodating Benavides responded: "I would say this looks just like it . . ."

The problem here is that Commission's Exhibit 163 is Oswald's dark blue jacket. The gray jacket is Commission's Exhibit 162. Here is yet another example of a witness obligingly providing the answers he felt were wanted.

Another example is cabdriver William Whaley, who reportedly drove Oswald home from downtown Dallas. Whaley identified the gray jacket as the one Oswald was wearing in his cab. Yet the Warren Commission, based on testimony from Oswald's landlady, stated that Oswald put on the jacket *after* arriving at his lodgings.

Testifying to the Warren Commission, Roberts said:

[Oswald] went to his room and he was in his shirtsleeves . . . and he got a jacket and put it on—it was kind of a zipper jacket. [She then was shown Commission's Exhibit 162, Oswald's gray jacket, and asked if she had seen it before] . . . Well, maybe I have, but I don't remember it. It seems like the one he put on was darker than that . . .

Barbara Davis, another witness at the Tippit slaying, also could not identify Oswald's gray jacket to the Warren Commission. In fact, she stated the killer wore "a dark coat . . . it looked like it was maybe a wool fabric . . . more of a sporting jacket."

Cabdriver William Scoggins also failed to identify Oswald's jacket, saying, "I thought it was a little darker."

Despite these problems of identification, the Commission went right on asserting that the jacket belonged to Oswald.

More Commission deception occurred in its reporting of the discovery of the jacket. The Warren Report stated: "Police Capt. W. R. Westbrook . . . walked through the parking lot behind the service station and found a light-colored jacket laying under the rear of one of the cars." However, in his testimony, Westbrook was asked if he found some clothing. He replied: "Actually, I didn't find it—it was pointed out to me by . . . some officer . . ." According to the Dallas police radio log, a "white jacket" was found by "279 (Unknown)" a full fifteen minutes before Westbrook arrived on the scene. The Commission made no effort to determine who really found the jacket, if a jacket was actually found, or if it was a white jacket that only later was transformed into Oswald's gray jacket.

Recently, the owner of the Texaco station where the jacket reportedly was found told Texas researchers that no one—neither the FBI, Dallas police, nor the Warren Commission—ever questioned him or his employees about this important piece of evidence.

In addition, the jacket identified by federal authorities as belonging to Oswald carried inside a laundry mark "30 030" and a dry-cleaning tag "B 9738." A full-scale search by the FBI in both Dallas and New Orleans failed to identify any laundry or dry cleaners using those marks.

Oswald's wife, Marina, testified she could not recall her husband ever sending his jackets to a cleaning establishment, but that she did recall washing them herself. Further investigation by the FBI turned up no laundry or dry-cleaning tags on any of Oswald's other clothing.

With all this, plus a broken chain of evidence, the jacket cannot be considered evidence of Oswald's guilt in the killing of Officer Tippit.

Then there is a matter of time and a strange incident at Oswald's lodging. Earlene Roberts, Oswald's landlady, told the Warren Commission she was watching television coverage of the assassination about 1 P.M. when Oswald—who had been registered at the rooming house as O. H. Lee—hurried in and went to his room.

She said next a Dallas police car pulled up in front of her house and honked. She explained: "I had worked for some policemen and sometimes they come by . . . I just glanced out, saw the number [on the car] . . . It wasn't the police car I knew . . . and I ignored it. . . ." She said the police car was directly in front of her home when the driver sounded the horn, like "tit-tit." She said the car then ". . . just eased on . . . and they just went around the corner that way."

According to Roberts, there were two uniformed policemen in the car, most unusual since daytime patrols in that area of the city were limited to one officer—such as Tippit. She could not recall the number of the car precisely, but said she did recall that the first two numbers of a possible three-digit combination were a 1 and a 0. Tippit was driving car No. 10 that day and Tippit failed to respond to a dispatcher call at the approximate time of the police-car incident.

Immediately following the police-car episode, Roberts said Oswald came out of his room and left hurriedly, zipping up a jacket. She said he left her house three or four minutes after 1 P.M.

Roberts said she looked out of the window and last saw Oswald standing at a nearby bus stop.

According to the Warren Commission, a man keyed a microphone at 1:16 P.M., saying, "Hello police operator . . . We've had a shooting here . . . it's a police officer, somebody shot him." This, of course, referred to Tippit, who lay dead about a mile from Oswald's residence.

The Commission tried to establish that the Tippit shooting occurred moments after 1:15 P.M., hardly enough time to allow Oswald to run from his rooming house to the scene of the Tippit slaying at 10th and Patton. The Commission could not locate even one witness who saw Oswald walking or running between his rooming house and the scene of the Tippit slaying.

This time frame becomes stretched to the breaking point when one considers the Tippit witnesses' testimony. Even Helen Markham, who was so confused about other matters, was certain of the time because she was on her way to catch her usual 1:12 P.M. bus for work. Asked by a Warren Commission attorney about the time she saw the Tippit shooting, Markham responded: "I wouldn't be afraid to bet it wasn't six or seven minutes after one."

In this instance, Mrs. Markham's recollection must be correct since another Tippit shooting witness, Jack Ray Tatum, told researchers that Mrs. Markham did not want to remain at the scene because she feared missing her bus for work.

T. F. Bowley, the man who made the call to the police dispatcher, was never called to testify to the Warren Commission. The reason may be that Bowley heard shots, saw Tippit's body lying next to his squad car, and looked at his watch. It was 1:10 P.M.

Other witnesses hid at the sound of the shots, afraid the gunman would turn on them. Only after the killer fled did they venture out.

One of the first persons to reach Tippit was Benavides, who told the Warren Commission he was in a truck across the street from the shooting. After hearing only three shots, Benavides said:

> . . . I sat there for just a few minutes . . . I thought maybe [the killer] had lived in there [the house where he last saw the gunman] and I didn't want to get out and rush right up. He might start shooting again. . . . That is when I got out of the truck and walked over to the policeman . . . The policeman, I believe, was dead when he hit the ground . . .

After checking on Tippit, Benavides said he tried to call on the patrol car's radio but got no answer. Another bystander, Bowley, then got in the car and was successful in raising the police dispatcher and reported the shooting.

Obviously, several minutes went by between the time of the shooting and 1:16 P.M. when the police radio log recorded the citizen's alert. This places the actual shooting closer to Bowley's time of 1:10 P.M.—a time frame that rules out the possibility that Oswald could have traveled on foot from his rooming house to the scene of the shooting.

The conversations of police regarding time sequences, orders, discovery of evidence, etc., were recorded on Dallas police radio recording equipment. These recordings should have provided accurate times and movement orders—in fact, they were relied on greatly by the Warren Commission and subsequent investigations.

Today there is evidence that the Dallas police radio recordings may have been edited. Soon after the assassination, the tapes may have been taken by federal authorities, who certainly have access to the most sophisticated audio equipment. Any police broadcasts not consistent with the lone-assassin theory could have been simply edited out and an edited copy returned to Dallas police for conveyance to the Warren Commission.

Is there any evidence that this occurred? Yes. Dr. James Barger, chief acoustic scientist for the House Select Committee on Assassinations, studied the "original" police tapes and discovered a break in the sixty-cycle hum background tone. He found two separate tones on the tape, which could only result from copying.

Although ignored publicly, the Ramsey Panel, studying the recordings for the National Academy of Science, did suggest in an appendix of its report that "The original Dictabelt could be studied more extensively for possible evidence . . . of being a copy . . ."

Researcher Gary Mack reported that in recent years, former Dallas police sergeant J. C. Bowles, the radio-room supervisor who prepared transcripts for the Warren Commission, stated that a few days after the assassination, federal agents "borrowed" the original police Dictabelt and at the time he was under the impression that they took them to a recording studio in Oklahoma.

Like so much of the Warren Commission's evidence, now the Dallas police radio recordings are open to question.

The House Select Committee on Assassinations supported the Warren Commission's conclusion that Oswald killed Tippit; however, it obliquely indicated that all is not known about the killing.

Committee investigators studied information developed by researcher Larry Harris that Tippit may have been killed as the result of personal problems.

They also talked with yet another witness who had not been interviewed by the Warren Commission. Jack Ray Tatum told Committee investigators that Tippit's killer, after shooting the officer from the sidewalk, walked toward the patrol car and shot Tippit once in the head at point-blank range. Correctly, the Committee wrote:

> This action, which is often encountered in gangland murders and is commonly described as a coup de grace, is more indicative of an execution than an act of defense intended to allow escape or prevent apprehension.

There is a problem with Tatum's story, however. Most of the witnesses stated that four shots were fired in succession—with no interval between the shots.

Several serious students of the Tippit incident now believe that his death may have had no connection with the Kennedy assassination. And of the researchers who still believe such a connection exists, few cling to the belief that Oswald was the killer.

*   *   *

Regardless of who actually killed Officer Tippit, that event was the catalyst that set off a flurry of police activity in Oak Cliff resulting in the arrest of Lee Harvey Oswald.

Prior to his arrest, there were at least two incidents in which police were obviously seeking a suspect. Sometime after 1 P.M., a number of policemen stormed the Oak Cliff branch of the Dallas Public Library. Unable to locate who they were looking for, they quickly left. Oswald was a frequent visitor to that library. Then, shortly before being called to the Texas Theater, the scene of Oswald's arrest, police surrounded a church near the scene of the Tippit slaying in the belief that Tippit's killer had hidden there. However, before they could conduct a search of the building, they were called to the theater.

The Arrest of Oswald

The arrest of Lee Harvey Oswald appears straightforward enough in the official reports, but there are some strange aspects when it is viewed objectively.

By 1:45 P.M. on November 22, 1953, the President of the United States had been murdered just seventy-five minutes earlier, and only about thirty minutes before, Policeman Tippit had been shot down on an Oak Cliff street. Dallas police were swarming about like angry bees.

A report came in to police dispatchers. It seemed a man had slipped into the Texas Theater without paying. Immediately carloads of officers, including one federal agent and an assistant district attorney, converged on the theater. The report had been instigated by a shoestore manager named Johnny Brewer. Brewer was listening to the radio when he learned of the Tippit murder. Hearing police sirens, he looked out the window of his store and saw a man duck into his doorway as a police car went by. Believing this to be suspicious activity, Brewer watched the man continue up the street to the Texas Theater, where he lost sight of him. Moments later, when Brewer asked the theater's ticket seller if she had sold a ticket to anyone, she replied she had not. Entering the theater, Brewer learned that the concession stand operator, W. H. "Butch" Burroughs, had heard the front doors open, but had seen no one enter the theater lobby.

Between the theater's front doors and a second set of doors were stairs leading to the balcony. Burroughs was convinced that whoever entered had gone up to the balcony since no one had passed his concession stand. Brewer asked the ticket seller to call police while he and another theater employee unsuccessfully looked for the suspicious man.

The authorities arrived quickly. Several policemen went to the theater's rear exit and waited with drawn guns. Inside, police, including Sergeant Gerald Hill, who had commanded the search of the sixth floor of the Texas

School Book Depository, turned up the house lights and moved to the front of the theater.

Officer M. N. McDonald had come in the rear door and was standing at the side of the movie screen. In an article written the day after the assassination for the Associated Press, McDonald recalled:

> I noticed about 10 to 15 people sitting in the theater and they were spread out good. A man sitting near the front, and I still don't know who it was, tipped me the man I wanted was sitting in the third row from the rear of the ground floor and not in the balcony [as reported to the police dispatcher]. I went up the aisle and talked to two people sitting about in the middle. I was crouching low and holding my gun in case any trouble came. I wanted to be ready for it. I walked up the aisle and turned in Oswald's row. We were no more than a foot from each other when he suddenly stood up and raised both hands. "It's all over now," he told me. Then he hit me a pretty good one in the face with his fist. I saw him going for his gun and I grabbed him around the waist. We struggled and fell around the seats for a few seconds and I got my hand on the butt of his pistol. But he had his hand on the trigger. I was pulling the gun toward me and I heard the hammer click. The primer [which detonates the bullet] was dented and it didn't fire . . . I'm sure glad that shell didn't fire.

McDonald's account of Oswald's gun misfiring was confirmed to the Warren Commission by theater patron John Gibson.

In his testimony to the Warren Commission, Brewer never mentions speaking to McDonald. In fact, he said he was standing by a rear exit when he was grabbed by a couple of policemen and asked what he was doing there. Brewer told them he was suspicious of a man in the theater. Brewer continued:

> And I and two or three other officers walked out on the stage and I pointed him out, and there were officers coming in from the front of the show . . . and officers going from the back. . . . I saw this policeman approach Oswald and Oswald stood up and I heard some hollering, I don't know exactly what he said, and this man hit Patrolman McDonald . . . I didn't know his name [McDonald], but I had seen him quite a few times around Oak Cliff.

Was the sitting man who tipped off McDonald to Oswald's location Johnny Brewer? Apparently not, since Brewer stated he was standing and then on stage with several policemen. Brewer also never mentioned talking to McDonald, whom he said he recognized from around Oak Cliff. Who then was the man who tipped off McDonald to Oswald's location?

Brewer also told the Commission that as Oswald struggled with police, he heard one of the officers cry: "Kill the president, will you?"

If members of the police department somehow knew that Oswald was an assassination suspect at this time, it is strong evidence that something was going on behind the scenes. The Warren Commission, while not contradicting Brewer's account, nevertheless felt compelled to add:

"It is unlikely that any of the police officers referred to Oswald as a suspect in the assassination." George J. Applin, one of only two theater patrons questioned by the Warren Commission, told the Warren Commission he was watching the movie when the lights came on and a policeman with a rifle or shotgun began moving down his aisle. Applin said he was sitting in the downstairs middle aisle about six rows from the back when the commotion began. He moved down the aisle to ask what was going on, when a policeman (apparently McDonald) passed him moving toward the rear. Applin then witnessed Oswald's arrest.

At the close of his Warren Commission Testimony, Applin said:

But, there is one thing puzzling me . . . And I don't even know if it has any bearing on the case, but there was one guy sitting in the back row right where I was standing at, and I said to him, I said, "Buddy, you'd better move. There is a gun." And he says—just sat there. He was back like this. Just like this. Just watching. . . . I don't think he could have seen the show. Just sitting there like this, just looking at me.

Applin told Commission attorney Joseph Ball twice he didn't know the man, but in 1979, he told a news reporter he recognized the man as Jack Ruby two days later, following the Oswald slaying. Applin told the *Dallas Morning News*:

At the time the Warren Commission had me down there at the Post Office in Dallas to get my statement, I was afraid to give it. I gave everything up to the point of what I gave the police there in town. . . . I'm a pretty nervous guy anyway because I'll tell you what: After I saw that magazine where all those people they said were connected with some of this had come up dead, it just kind of made me keep a low profile. . . . [Jack] Ruby was sitting down, just watching them. And, when Oswald pulled the gun and snapped it at [McDonald's] head and missed and the darn thing wouldn't fire, that's when I tapped him on the shoulder and told him he had better move because those guns were waving around. He just turned around and looked at me. Then he turned around and started watching them.

Ruby's identity only became known to Applin after his picture was broadcast following Oswald's death.

Yet more questions have been raised by recent statements of concession stand operator Burroughs. In a 1987 interview with this author, Burroughs, who is now an assistant manager at the Texas Theater, reiterated his story of someone slipping in the theater about 1:35 P.M. that day. However, Burroughs claims that it could not have been Oswald because Oswald entered the theater shortly after 1 P.M. Burroughs said Oswald entered only minutes after the feature started, which was exactly at 1 P.M.

He said several minutes later, about 1:15 P.M., the man later arrested by police and identified as Oswald came to his concession stand and bought some popcorn.

Burroughs said he watched the man enter the ground floor of the theater and sit down next to a pregnant woman. About twenty minutes after this, the outside doors opened and Johnny Brewer arrived.

Several minutes after the man—identified by Burroughs as Oswald—took his seat, the pregnant woman got up and went upstairs where the ladies' restroom was located, said Burroughs. He said he heard the restroom door close just shortly before Dallas police began rushing into the theater.

Burroughs said: "I don't know what happened to that woman. I don't know how she got out of the theater. I never saw her again."

The story of Oswald being in the Texas Theater at the time of the Tippit shooting is further supported by Jack Davis, who today hosts "Gospel Music Spotlight" on a Dallas Christian radio station.

Davis told this author that on the day of the assassination, he went to the Texas Theater to see the war movies. The eighteen-year-old Davis found a seat in the right rear section of the theater and recalled seeing the opening credits of the first film, which was only minutes past the 1 P.M. starting time for the feature movie.

He said he was somewhat startled by a man who squeezed past him and sat down in the seat next to him. He found it odd that this man would choose the seat adjacent to him in a nine-hundred-seat theater with less than twenty patrons in it. Davis said the man didn't say a word but quickly got up and moved across the aisle and took a seat next to another person. Then shortly, the man got up and walked into the theater's lobby. A few minutes later, Davis, whose attention had returned to the movie, vaguely remembered seeing the same man enter the center section of the theater from the far side.

After twenty minutes or so after this incident, according to Davis, the house lights came on and when he walked to the lobby to ask why, he saw policeman running in the front door. He recalled:

I was looking for the manager, but I never got to say anything because the policemen all came rushing past me. I did not see what went on in the theater, but I heard some scuffling going on. A few minutes later the police brought out this same man who had sat down next to me. He was shouting, "I protest this police brutality!" Later, of course, I learned that this was Lee Harvey Oswald.

If Oswald was already in the theater at the time of the Tippit slaying as claimed by Burroughs and Davis, then who slipped in about 1:35 P.M.?

Since it can be established that someone was impersonating Oswald in Dallas prior to the assassination, it can be suggested that someone besides Oswald lured police to the Texas Theater. But, if this were the case, what happened to the man who slipped in without buying a ticket? Initial police reports stated the suspect was in the theater's balcony, this information perhaps coming from Burroughs's belief that the man who sneaked in went upstairs.

The Dallas police homicide report on J. D. Tippit of that day stated: "Suspect was later arrested in the balcony of the Texas Theater at 231 W. Jefferson."

Was someone else arrested in the Texas Theater? Not according to the official record. However there is now evidence that perhaps another man was taken from the rear of the theater.

Bernard J. Haire owned Bernie's Hobby House, located two doors east of the Texas Theater on W. Jefferson.

On November 22, 1963, Haire, who was unaware of the assassination, saw the street in front of his business fill up with police cars. He went outside and saw a crowd gathered at the Texas Theater but could not see what was happening. Haire was captured in at least one photograph taken at the time Oswald was brought from the theater by police.

Walking through his store, Haire went into the alley, which he said was also filled with police cars. Walking toward the theater, Haire was opposite the rear door when police brought a young white man out. He said the man was dressed in a pullover shirt and slacks and appeared to be flushed as if having been in a struggle. Although Haire was unable to see if the man was handcuffed, he was certainly under the impression that the man was under arrest. Haire watched police put the man in a police car and drive off.

For nearly twenty-five years Haire believed he had witnessed the arrest of Lee Harvey Oswald. He was shocked to discover that Oswald had been handcuffed and brought out the front door of the theater. Recently he commented: "I don't know who I saw arrested."

Neither does anyone else, but it is eloquent testimony that apparently someone other than Oswald led police to the Texas Theater.

*   *   *

The arrested Oswald was taken from the Texas Theater shortly before 2 P.M. and driven downtown to police headquarters. He was quickly taken to the third-floor office of Captain Will Fritz, the crusty chief of the Homicide Bureau, and placed in a seat in the hallway.

Detective Gus Rose was already busy interviewing assassination witnesses. He soon took charge of Oswald. Rose recalled:

I took the man to an interrogation office. I removed his handcuffs. I asked him to identify himself. He refused. In his pockets I found two pieces of identification. One card was for Lee Harvey Oswald, the other was for Alek Hidell. "Which are you?" He said, "You're the cop. You figure it out." He told me a lot of lies. Captain Fritz called me out at sometime near 2:20 P.M. He said that the employees of the Texas School Book Depository were accounted for—except one. He told me to get some men together and get out to this address in Irving. I asked what the man's name was. He said, "Lee Harvey Oswald." I was stunned. "Captain," I said, "I think this is Oswald, right in there."

With a suspect in custody, the entire complexion of the assassination investigation changed.

Despite what was heralded as overwhelming proof of Oswald's guilt in both killings, it was not until late Friday, November 22, 1963, that he was charged with the murder of Officer Tippit. And it was well after midnight before he was reportedly charged with the murder of President Kennedy.

Dallas police and federal authorities quickly lost interest in any information, evidence, or detained suspects that did not fit in with the presumed activities of Lee Harvey Oswald.

An indictment was not even issued in the Tippit slaying, since the presumed killer—Oswald—was dead.

Yet many items of interest continued to crop up in the aftermath of the assassination. There were reports of a man seen with a rifle near Cobb Stadium, located on the Stemmons Freeway route from downtown to the Trade Mart. Nothing came of this report.

At Red Bird Airport, a private field located just south of Dallas, it was reported that federal officials seized a plane with its engine running the afternoon of the assassination and placed it in a closed hangar under tight security. Two days prior to the assassination, the airport's manager, Wayne January, said three men talked to him about renting an airplane on November 22 to fly to Mexico. He said one of the men remained sitting in a car and closely resembled Lee Harvey Oswald. None of these stories regarding possible escape plans were properly investigated.

But if unfollowed leads remained in Dallas, there was no official doubt in Washington as to Oswald's guilt. Less than two hours after the assassination—at a time when Dallas police were not even certain of the identity of the man they had in custody (recall Detective Rose's story of an uncooperative Oswald with two separate sets of identification)—FBI director J. Edgar Hoover called Robert Kennedy. In a Bureau document released to the public in 1977, Hoover wrote: "I called the attorney general at his home and told him I thought we had the man who killed the President down in Dallas . . ."

Hoover went on to describe Oswald as an ex-Marine who had defected to Russia, a pro-Communist and a "mean-minded individual . . . in the category of a nut." This incident raises the troubling question of how

Hoover could have had all this information on Oswald at a time when the Dallas authorities were not even certain of their prisoner's identity.

On November 24, less than two hours after Oswald was killed in Dallas, Hoover telephoned the Johnson White House, saying: "The thing I am most concerned about . . . is having something issued so we can convince the public that Oswald is the real assassin."

In 1976 a Senate Select Committee report stated:

> Almost immediately after the assassination, Director Hoover, the Justice Department and the White House "exerted pressure" on senior Bureau officials to complete their investigation and issue a factual report supporting the conclusion that Oswald was the lone assassin.

Over the assassination weekend, information on—and evidence against— Oswald continued to pile up. The news media was on around-the-clock alert. No bit of information was too insignificant to broadcast or publish.

The *Dallas Morning News* of November 23, 1963, carried a story stating:

> [District Attorney Henry] Wade said preliminary reports indicated more than one person was involved in the shooting which brought death to the President and left Gov. John Connally wounded . . . "This is the most dastardly act I've ever heard about," Wade said. "Everyone who participated in this crime—anyone who helped plan it or furnished a weapon, knowing the purposes for which it was intended—is guilty of murder under Texas law. They should all go to the electric chair."

But Wade's initial claim of evidence of a conspiracy quickly faded as official statements began to center more and more on Oswald. Years later, Wade recalled why:

> Cliff Carter, President Johnson's aide, called me three times from the White House that Friday night. He said that President Johnson felt any word of a conspiracy—some plot by foreign nations—to kill President Kennedy would shake our nation to its foundation. President Johnson was worried about some conspiracy on the part of the Russians. Oswald had all sorts of connections and affections toward Castro's Cuba. It might be possible to prove a conspiracy with Cuba. But it would be very hard to prove a conspiracy with Russia. Washington's word to me was that it would hurt foreign relations if I alleged a conspiracy—whether I could prove it or not. I would just charge Oswald with plain murder and go for the death penalty. So, I went down to the Police Department at City Hall to see Captain Fritz—to make sure the Dallas police didn't involve any foreign country in the assassination.

With an ever-growing pile of evidence of conspiracy in the assassination, the federal government began to assert itself.

Police Chief Curry told the Warren Commission:

The FBI actually had no jurisdiction over [the murder of Kennedy], the Secret Service actually had no jurisdiction over it. But, in an effort to cooperate with these agencies we went all out to do whatever they wanted us to do . . . We kept getting calls from the FBI. They wanted this evidence up in Washington . . . there was some discussion, [Captain] Fritz told me, he says, "Well, I need the evidence here, I need to get some people to try to identify the gun, to try to identify this pistol and these things, and if it's in Washington, how can I do it?" But, we finally . . . about midnight of Friday night, we agreed to let the FBI have all the evidence . . .

However, Curry said, to the best of his knowledge, no one from the Dallas police accompanied this evidence to FBI headquarters in Washington. This, of course, caused a serious break in the "chain of evidence."

Curry added:

We got several calls insisting we send this [evidence to Washington], and nobody would tell me exactly who it was that was insisting, "just say I got a call from Washington, and they wanted this evidence up there," insinuating it was someone in high authority that was requesting this, and we finally agreed . . .

Disjoined and incomplete as Curry's statements are, there now is no doubt that Washington authorities were putting extreme pressure on Dallas police as early as Friday night.

A thirty-four-page report on police activities that weekend, sent to Curry by his assistant chief and two deputy police chiefs, states:

At approximately 12:01 A.M. [other reports state an earlier time], Saturday, November 23, 1963, pertinent physical evidence in the case involving Oswald and the slaying of President Kennedy was turned over to Mr. Vince Drain of the Federal Bureau of Investigation to be delivered in person to the FBI Laboratory in Washington, D.C., for processing.

Persistent rumors among Dallas policemen have it that some of this pressure came in the form of a personal call to Captain Fritz from none other than President Lyndon Johnson. However, Fritz would never confirm this.

Public awareness of the federal takeover of the Dallas evidence did not come until November 27, 1963, when the *Dallas Morning News* reported: "The White House approved the decision that the FBI take charge of all evidence which officers assembled in their investigation of the murder of President Kennedy. . . .''

The assassination was now a federal government matter.

The next major shock came about 11:20 A.M. Sunday, November 24, 1963, when the prime suspect was fatally shot while in the basement of Dallas Police Headquarters.

Five days later, Lyndon Johnson moved to block any further investigation of the curious events in Dallas by appointing a "blue ribbon" commission to probe the entire affair. It was the beginning of total federal control over the evidence and witnesses in the assassination case.

As with any good investigation dealing with criminal violence, much of the work in the first hours after the assassination centered around the medical evidence—that should have clearly shown how many bullets struck Kennedy and from which direction they came.

Therefore, on the day of the assassination, attention was centered on two hospitals—Parkland Memorial Hospital in Dallas and Bethesda Naval Hospital near Washington, D.C.

Summary

Following the assassination there was total confusion and panic in Dealey Plaza. The Texas School Book Depository was not sealed by police for at least ten minutes, perhaps as much as twenty minutes—enough time for an entire squad of assassins to have escaped.

Security was nonexistent on the Grassy Knoll. Policemen, sheriff's deputies, spectators, and assassination witnesses mingled together in a confused mass behind the wooden picket fence. Despite this chaos, some unidentified man managed to give Dallas police a general description of the possible assassin—". . . a slender white male about 30, 5-feet-10-inches, [weight] 165, carrying what looked to be a 30-30 or some type of Winchester"—which was broadcast over the police radio at 12:43 P.M.

Even as evidence was being gathered by police, other evidence may have been disappearing—such as the bullet taken by an FBI man from the grass on the south side of Elm Street and the STEMMONS FREEWAY sign.

Despite later reports by federal authorities that Oswald left the scene by bus and taxi, several people—Deputy Sheriff Roger Craig, Richard Carr, and Marvin Robinson—saw someone matching Oswald's description get into a Nash Rambler station wagon near the Depository minutes after the assassination.

Some people in and around Dealey Plaza even believed they saw Jack Ruby near the scene of the assassination, although the Warren Commission concluded he was two blocks away at the *Dallas Morning News* at the time. These included Julia Mercer, Phil Willis, Jean Hill, and Dallas policeman Tom Tilson.

Many strange people were in the vicinity of the assassination. Some—such as the "three tramps" and Mafia character Jim Braden—were even taken into police custody. However, with the capture of Lee Harvey Oswald, official interest in those arrests ended. Arrest records for that day are missing from the National Archives.

Dallas police activity intensified following the shooting of Patrolman J. D. Tippit. Although never indicted for Tippit's slaying, Oswald has always been considered guilty of this crime. But an objective look at the evidence of Oswald's guilt in Tippit's death shows many deficiencies. The best witnesses to the Tippit shooting were not called to testify before the Warren Commission and many of the witnesses were unable to positively identify Oswald as the killer. The manner in which Dallas police lineups were conducted was unfair and weighted toward identifying Oswald as the guilty party.

There is still considerable question over the ammunition used as evidence in the Tippit shooting. Recent studies of the spent cartridges found at the scene increase the evidence of Oswald's innocence. With the absence of Policeman J. M. Poe's initials from the cartridges and without the customary bulge of .38 Special ammunition fired from a modified pistol such as carried by Oswald, it seems unlikely that the shell cases in the National Archives came from Oswald's revolver.

Many of the witnesses could not identify Oswald's gray jacket as the one seen on Tippit's killer. Furthermore, since Oswald was seen near his rooming house six or seven minutes after 1 P.M. and, by the best accounts, Tippit was killed around 1:10 P.M., it would have been impossible for Oswald to have reached the crime scene on foot in that span of time. Furthermore, the concession stand operator at the Texas Theater and theater patron Jack Davis contend that Oswald was in the theater at the time Tippit was killed.

The Dallas police recordings of dispatcher orders, responses, and times has been called into question, since the original police Dictabelt shows evidence of copying and the police sergeant in charge of the Dispatch Room recalled that federal agents took the original Dictabelt a few days after the assassination.

Even the arrest of Oswald is full of questions. For example, why would an assassin sneak into a theater without paying, thereby drawing attention to himself when he had enough money on him to buy a ticket? Did Oswald, in fact, enter without paying since Johnny Brewer last saw him in front of the theater but did not actually see him enter? Could someone other than Oswald have led authorities to the Texas Theater? Why didn't police rush Oswald once he was pointed out to them, rather than slowly working their way to him? Was Oswald being given an opportunity to flee? Was Oswald supposed to have been killed resisting arrest? Was Jack Ruby sitting in the Texas Theater crowd as claimed by George Applin? If so, was Ruby the man who "tipped" Sergeant McDonald to Oswald's location? Why did police reports state that the suspect was arrested in the theater's balcony, and who was the man taken from the rear of the theater seen by nearby businessman Bernard Haire?

These questions have not been addressed by the federal assassination investigations, leaving suspicious researchers to devise their own theories as to the role of Oswald, Tippit, and Ruby in the events of that day.

The key to the JFK assassination may be in the aftermath of the crime—the unfollowed leads, the presence of Secret Service agents (real or bogus) in Dealey Plaza where none should have been, the intimidation of witnesses, the destruction and suppression of vital evidence.

Furthermore, in light of the long-standing involvement of the FBI in Oswald's life, it is highly significant that Director J. Edgar Hoover telephoned Attorney General Robert Kennedy less than two hours after the assassination to give him a rundown on Oswald—this at a time when Dallas police were not even certain of the identity of the man they had in custody.

[Kennedy's autopsy was] the kind of examination that would not be tolerated in a routine murder case . . . in most major cities of America.

—Pathologist Dr. Cyril H. Wecht

Two Hospitals

As the echo of shots died away in Dealey Plaza, Dallas police chief Jesse Curry, riding in the lead car of Kennedy's motorcade, radioed his police dispatcher: "Looks like the President has been hit. Have Parkland stand by."

The motorcade sped up, reaching speeds of nearly eighty miles per hour during the four-mile race along Stemmons Freeway to the hospital.

Parkland Memorial Hospital remains the major public hospital in Dallas County today. Almost every victim of violence—from wrecks to gunshot wounds—is brought to Parkland. Its emergency room is constantly staffed with doctors and interns well experienced in trauma situations. President Kennedy could not have asked for more experienced and competent medical attention.

Yet following his autopsy that evening at the National Naval Medical Center at Bethesda, Maryland, numerous and continuing discrepancies in the medical evidence arose. These discrepancies have provided a source of controversy that continues even today.

If one assumes there was some sort of conspiracy involved in the assassination, the questions over the medical evidence provide a good starting point for determining its scope.

But before examining the tangled morass of medical evidence, there is a small question of the presidential limousine's arrival at Parkland. Secret Service driver William Greer testified to the Warren Commission that he did not know the way to Parkland and so followed Sheriff Decker and Chief Curry in the lead car. Greer's story is buttressed by the testimony of two other Secret Service officials, Forrest Sorrels and Winston Lawson. However, in his testimony, Chief Curry is strangely vague, saying only that the limousine went to the hospital under "siren escort."

What's the problem? During the time of the House Select Committee on Assassinations, a film taken by Dallasite Jack Daniel was seen widely for the first time. Taken just as the motorcade exited from the west end of the Triple Underpass and entered Stemmons Freeway, this film clearly shows that both the presidential limousine and the Secret Service backup car had passed Curry's lead car and were leading the race to the hospital.

How could Washington-based Agent Greer know how to find Parkland and, more important, why did he state in his Commission testimony, "I

361

never passed [Curry's car] . . . I was led to the hospital by the police car who was preceding me''?

Either these highly trained agents panicked and forgot what actually happened or they lied about it. Since the Daniel film can't lie, the question remains, how did Greer know how to reach Parkland?

Upon arrival at Parkland at 12:43 P.M., Governor Connally regained consciousness long enough to attempt to rise, but fell back into the car in great pain. Connally was lifted onto a stretcher and wheeled into the hospital. Secret Service Agent Clint Hill removed his suit coat and placed it over the President's gory head wound to prevent photographs.

However, several persons saw Kennedy's body, including Fort Worth newsman Roy Stamps. Stamps told researchers: "I rushed up and saw Kennedy lying in the car on his side. His foot was hanging over the side of the car. The back of his head was gone."

As other vehicles in the presidential motorcade began arriving at the Parkland emergency entrance and Connally was placed in Trauma Room 2, Secret Service agents Greer, Kellerman, and Lawson pulled the fatally wounded president away from Mrs. Kennedy, placed him on a stretcher, and pushed it into Trauma Room 1. There Kennedy was attended to by no less than twelve of Parkland's doctors—including four surgeons, the chief neurologist, an oral surgeon, and a heart specialist.

Dr. Charles J. Carrico, a resident surgeon, was the first doctor to examine Kennedy. He noted the President was ashen in color, his breathing lacked coordination, there were no voluntary movements, and his eyes were open with pupils dilated showing no reaction to light. However, a few chest sounds thought to be heartbeats were heard and immediately resuscitation efforts were begun. Carrico inserted a cuffed endotracheal tube in a small puncture wound just below Kennedy's adam's apple. The tube was connected to a respirator.

Other doctors began arriving and treating the President; fluids and stimulants were injected and oxygen administered. Cardiac massage was begun—to no avail.

President Kennedy was pronounced dead at 1 P.M. (CST) by Dr. Kemp Clark, Parkland's director of neurological surgery.

While one set of Parkland doctors worked on Kennedy, another worked feverishly to save Connally. A large sucking chest wound caused the greatest concern for Connally. A bullet had shattered the governor's fifth rib on his right side, sending bits of bone and metal tearing through his chest, collapsing one lung. And his right wrist had been broken, the bullet entering from the top and exiting from the bottom of his wrist. Doctors also discovered a wound in Connally's left thigh. This wound was cleaned and sutured shut, although, according to the Warren Report, "a small metal fragment remained in the Governor's leg."

Vice President Lyndon Johnson also had entered Parkland, but was kept secluded in a room near the area where efforts were being made to revive the President. About 1:20 P.M., presidential aide Kenneth O'Donnell informed Johnson that Kennedy was dead. According to the Warren Report, O'Donnell advised Johnson to return to Washington as soon as possible. However, Mrs. Kennedy refused to leave without her husband's body and Johnson refused to leave without Mrs. Kennedy.

It was finally decided to leave immediately and to return on *Air Force One* because the presidential plane had better communication equipment. The decision created one of the assassination's most enduring problems—with the President's autopsy performed at Bethesda, two sets of doctors viewed the body at different times and their descriptions of wounds differed so widely that controversy remains to this day.

The death of the President was legally a Texas homicide and by law, the body could not be removed until after an autopsy or a coroner's ruling, which also would have involved further medical investigation. Totally against prevailing law and despite the protest of Texas officials, a coffin was ordered from a Dallas funeral home and Kennedy's body was whisked away from Parkland Hospital.

After Kennedy's body left Parkland and while Dallas doctors worked on Connally in a second-floor operating room, another incident occurred in the hospital that was to have long-reaching effects on the official theory of the assassination: a hospital worker discovered an intact bullet in a hallway.

During the feverish activity in the emergency room, the hospital's senior engineer, Darrell C. Tomlinson, was asked to manually operate an elevator that connected the ground-floor emergency room to the second-floor operating theaters.

Despite efforts by Warren Commission attorney Arlen Spector to confuse the issue during testimony, Tomlinson was remarkably clear on what happened that day. Tomlinson stated that one hospital stretcher containing two rolled-up bloody sheets, some surgical instruments, and some sterile packs was sitting against a wall near the elevator.

No effort apparently was made by the Commission to determine where this stretcher came from. Some researchers believe it may have held Kennedy's body while in the emergency room. But this is doubtful since Kennedy's body remained on his stretcher until the Dallas casket arrived about 1:40 P.M. At this time, his body was placed in the casket and the stretcher was stripped of sheets and rolled across the hall to Trauma Room 2, according to Nurse Diana Bowron. Since Tomlinson claimed to have discovered a bullet at this same time and two nurses reported placing Kennedy's empty stretcher in Trauma Room 2, it is virtually impossible to believe that the hallway stretcher carried the President.

Today it seems more likely that this stretcher was used in the treatment of two-year-old Ronald Fuller, who entered the Parkland emergency room at 12:54 P.M. with a bad cut on the chin. The child's mother, Mrs. Ross Fuller, years later told the *Dallas Morning News* what happened:

I was watching the President's parade on television when they announced he had been shot. I knocked over the bottle of soda pop I was drinking and it broke into pieces. My little boy Ronnie fell on it and started bleeding badly. My husband and I ran to the car and headed for Parkland with the baby. When we reached Harry Hines Boulevard, traffic was at a standstill. I told my husband I couldn't just sit in the car like that [and that] I was going to take the baby in on foot. Then I jumped out of the car. [While running] . . . a man came up and asked if he could help. He saw the blood and he thought we'd been shot the same way the President had.

Mrs. Fuller finally reached the Parkland emergency room and handed her son to medical personnel. Then she fainted. She recalled:

When I came to, they told me Ronnie was all right. They were sewing him up. Then they told me the President was dead. It happened in the cubicle right next to us. The doctor said I was living a part of history.

The Fuller child was briefly placed on a stretcher and his cut was treated with sutures and gauze packs, which could have been left behind on the cart.

Considering both the condition—bloody sheets, instruments, sterile packs—and the location of Fuller's stretcher—the child originally was placed on a stretcher in the same hallway leading to Trauma Rooms 1 and 2—it is most likely this stretcher on which the bullet was found.

Tomlinson said a second stretcher was on the elevator—perhaps the one that carried Connally to the second-floor operating room—and that he pulled it out and placed it near the first stretcher. Specter designated the stretcher pulled off the elevator as stretcher A and the stretcher already in the hall near the elevator as stretcher B.

After making a few trips in the elevator, Tomlinson said someone—a doctor or an intern—moved one of the stretchers away from the wall so he could enter a men's restroom. Tomlinson told Specter as he pushed the stretcher back up against the wall to clear the hallway: "I bumped the wall and a spent cartridge or bullet rolled out that apparently had been lodged under the edge of the mat." "And that was from which stretcher?" asked Specter. "I believe that it was B," replied Tomlinson.

Later in his testimony, Specter tried to shake Tomlinson's recollections. Specter asked: "And at the time we started our discussion, it was your recollection at that point that the bullet came off of stretcher A, was it not?" "B," quickly responded Tomlinson.

Finally, after Specter continued to confuse the matter by telling Tomlinson that he had identified stretcher A during a Secret Service interview, the hospital worker said:

. . . I really don't remember. I'm not accustomed to being questioned by the Secret Service and the FBI and by you and they are writing down everything, I mean. . . . I'm going to tell you all I can, and I'm not going to tell you something I can't lay down and sleep at night with either.

From Tomlinson's testimony, it appears more than likely that the stretcher holding the bullet did not belong to Connally. However, the Warren Commission stated definitely: "A nearly whole bullet was found on Governor Connally's stretcher at Parkland Hospital after the assassination." It was this bullet—Commission Exhibit 399—that became the foundation of the single-bullet theory of the assassination. It has also become known as the "magic bullet."

Tomlinson turned the bullet over to Parkland's chief of security, O. P. Wright, who gave it to Secret Service agent Richard Johnsen.

Interestingly, Wright was the father-in-law of Dallas police sergeant Patrick T. Dean, the officer blamed by the Warren Commission for allowing Jack Ruby into the police department basement just prior to the slaying of Oswald. Dean's mother-in-law, Mrs. O. P. Wright, was director of nursing at Parkland and on duty when Kennedy was being treated.

Neither Wright nor Agent Johnsen were interviewed by the Warren Commission—perhaps because, in later interviews with researchers, neither man could positively identify CE 399 as the bullet found that day.

In fact, during a 1966 interview with author Josiah Thompson, Wright—a professional security officer—picked a pointed-tipped bullet shape as more nearly like the bullet discovered at Parkland. He rejected round-nosed bullet shapes similar to CE 399. Tomlinson, likewise, selected a pointed shape as resembling the bullet he found.

The whole bullet matter becomes even more clouded when the possibility of substitution and planting is considered. The hallway in which both stretchers A and B were left unattended was a public corridor. Although the Warren Commission apparently never considered that CE 399 may have been planted on one of the stretchers or later substituted for the found bullet, these possibilities find favor in the minds of most assassination researchers.

This possibility that the bullet was planted is especially strong since the evidence indicates that the stretcher containing the bullet belonged to neither Kennedy nor Connally.

Adding to this suspicion is the presence of Jack Ruby at Parkland Hospital while Kennedy's body was still there.

Jack Ruby at Parkland

Veteran newsman Seth Kantor told the Warren Commission that he encountered Jack Ruby at Parkland Hospital about the time Kennedy's death was publicly announced at 1:30 P.M. Kantor said he and Ruby even shared a brief conversation. Kantor recognized Ruby, having worked in Dallas for some time. He said he spoke to Ruby at 1:30 P.M. and recalled that Ruby asked if he should close his club out of respect for the slain President.

When asked about his presence at Parkland, Ruby denied ever being there, and the Commission chose to believe him and concluded that Kantor must have been mistaken.

Ignored by the Commission were FBI interviews with a Dallas woman whose experiences on the day of the assassination fully supported Kantor's account of his Parkland meeting with Ruby. Mrs. Wilma Tice was home when she heard the news of the Dealey Plaza shooting. Curious, she drove to Parkland Hospital arriving about 1:30 P.M., and joined the throng of bystanders awaiting word on the President's condition.

Some months later, she told the FBI she stood beside a heavily built man in a dark suit who was hitting his hat against his leg. She was only three or four feet from the man when another man approached him and said, "How are you doing there, Jack?" She said the two men had a brief conversation during which the man named Jack offered to donate a kidney to John Connally.

Two days later Mrs. Tice was astounded to see the man called Jack on television identified as Jack Ruby, the slayer of Oswald. However, she assumed that the authorities knew about his presence at Parkland and did not notify anyone until late in the spring of 1964.

Mrs. Tice had telephoned Ruby's sister, Ms. Eva Grant, to express her condolences over Ruby's death sentence when she mentioned her encounter at Parkland and learned that Ruby had denied being there. It was at this point that Mrs. Tice contacted the FBI and told her story.

On April 12, 1964, she received a call from a man claiming to be a newspaper reporter. He asked about her Parkland encounter and then advised her not to talk about the incident.

On July 19, Mrs. Tice received a letter asking her to testify for the Warren Commission. The next day she received an anonymous call from a man who warned her: "It would pay you to keep your mouth shut."

On July 22, Mrs. Tice called police because someone tried to break into her home while her husband was away. This incident was followed by other phone calls, but she had a fourteen-year-old niece answer the phone and the caller would hang up.

The account of Ruby at Parkland has been further supported in recent years by former radio newsman. Roy Stamps said he had met Ruby on about forty-five occasions prior to November 22, 1963. Stamps told Texas researchers that he was in the hall of Parkland holding open a telephone line to his radio station when he noticed Ruby enter the hospital. He said Ruby was carrying some television equipment and trailing behind a TV crew.

In 1979, The House Select Committee on Assassinations reversed the Warren Commission's decision that Kantor was mistaken about his Parkland meeting with Ruby, stating: "While the Warren Commission concluded that Kantor was mistaken, the Committee determined he probably was not."

With the presence of Ruby in Parkland, the possibility that CE 399—the "magic bullet"—was planted appears even more likely.

Of course, virtually anyone could have planted the bullet, since the stretcher in question lay unattended in the public hallway for some time. But even if the bullet were not planted—and there is some evidence to suggest that the bullet may have worked its way out of Kennedy's back wound—there is also the possibility that CE 399 was substituted for the bullet found on the stretcher. (Recall that neither of the men who initially handled the bullet could identify it later.)

Of course, if bullets were switched, it could only have been done while in the hands of federal authorities—a most ominous suspicion.

*　　*　　*

After Kennedy's body was returned to *Air Force One* at Love Field, Lyndon B. Johnson was sworn in as thirty-sixth president of the United States by federal judge Sarah T. Hughes.

On the plane flight back to Washington, it seems the original destination for Kennedy's body was to have been Walter Reed Army Hospital—long the major military medical facility for Washington. Examining U.S. Army Signal Corps transcripts of radio messages from *Air Force One* that day, researchers have found several references indicating that military officers were going to send the body to the Army hospital.

Agent Roy Kellerman radioed Secret Service headquarters saying: "Arriving Andrews [AFB] 6:05. The body will go to Walter Reed. Have an ambulance from Walter Reed to take the body there."

Later, Gen. Chester Clifton, senior military aide, radioed:

This is Gen. Clifton. We do not want a helicopter to go to Bethesda Medical Center. We do want an ambulance and a ground return from Andrews to Walter Reed, and we want the regular post-mortem that has to be done by law under guard performed at Walter Reed. Is that clear?

Even the official history of the 1001st Air Base Wing, which included *Air Force One*, reported: ". . . the body of the slain President was removed to Walter Reed General Hospital . . ."

So why the sudden change to Bethesda?

Kennedy's personal physician, Dr. George G. Burkley, wrote in his report of that day:

During the course of the flight [back to Washington], determination of the immediate action on arrival in Washington was made to assure complete compliance with Mrs. Kennedy's wishes. I spoke to her while kneeling on the floor so I would be at the level of her face rather than leaning forward, and expressed complete desire of all of us and especially of myself to comply with her wishes, stating that it was necessary that the President be taken to a hospital prior to going to the White House. She questioned why and I stated it must be determined, if possible, the type of bullet used and compare this with future material found. I stated frankly that I had no preference, that it could be any hospital, but that I did feel that, if possible, it should be a military hospital for security measures. The question was answered by her stating that she wanted the President taken to Bethesda Naval Hospital.

Oddly, having just received Mrs. Kennedy's wishes, Dr. Burkley then adds: "Arrangements were made on the ground for departure to Walter Reed Army Hospital or Bethesda Naval Hospital, as the case may be."

Why such confusion over military hospitals? Was Mrs. Kennedy's natural desire to take her husband, a former naval officer, to the naval hospital an unexpected hitch in a plan for an autopsy at Walter Reed?

It certainly appears that Bethesda was not prepared for this most important autopsy. The three military physicians who performed Kennedy's autopsy were clinical pathologists with little experience in gunshot wounds. Neither Navy Cdr. James J. Humes nor Navy Cdr. J. Thornton Boswell had practical, firsthand experience with bullet wounds. Army Lt. Col. Pierre Finck did have some such experience, but he later said he was hampered in his autopsy procedures by officials in the room. The military autopsy doctors apparently were surrounded by both military and civilian superiors who directed much of the autopsy—some of this direction going against normal autopsy procedures.

During the Clay Shaw trial in New Orleans, Dr. Finck was asked under oath if Dr. Humes had been in charge of the President's autopsy. He replied:

Well, I heard Dr. Humes stating that—he said, "Who's in charge here?" And I heard an Army general, I don't remember his name, stating, "I am." You must understand that in those circumstances, there were law-enforcement officers, military people with various ranks, and you have to coordinate the operation according to directions.

An unnamed Army general in charge? Directions to the doctors? Finck continued to describe the scene:

The autopsy room was quite crowded. It is a small autopsy room, and when you are called in circumstances like that to look at the wound of the President of the United States who is dead, you don't look around too much to ask people for their names and take notes on who they are and how many there are. I did not do so. The room was crowded with military and civilian personnel and federal agents, Secret Service agents, FBI agents, for part of the autopsy, but I cannot give you a precise breakdown as regards the attendance of the people in that autopsy room at Bethesda Naval Hospital.

New Orleans executive assistant district attorney Alvin Oser then pressed Finck on why, as an autopsy pathologist, he had not tracked the bullet wound through Kennedy's body to determine its exact path.

After dodging the question for a time, Dr. Finck finally was ordered by the court to answer Oser's question. Dr. Finck stated: "As I recall I was told not to, but I don't remember by whom." "Could it have been one of the admirals or one of the generals in the room?" asked Oser. "I don't recall," said Dr. Finck.

Finck, the only member of the autopsy team who was a member of the American Academy of Forensic Sciences, asked to examine Kennedy's clothing—a normal and acknowledged autopsy procedure. His request was denied.

Further, the autopsy doctors were ordered not to talk about what they had seen in the autopsy room. Finck again:

. . . when you are a lieutenant colonel in the Army you just follow orders, and at the end of the autopsy, we were specifically told—as I recall it, it was by Admiral [Edward C.] Kenney, the surgeon general of the Navy—. . . not to discuss the case.

In 1977 Dr. Humes appeared before a medical panel gathered by the House Select Committee on Assassination. Because of longstanding questions concerning the possibility that Kennedy suffered from Addison's disease (which can be detected by studying the adrenal glands), Humes was asked about the glands by Committee Medical Panel member Dr. Charles Petty ". . . because normally we examine adrenals in the general course [of an] autopsy, as we undertake it." Humes replied:

. . . Since I don't think it bore directly on the death of the President, I'd prefer not to discuss it with you, doctor. . . . I'd only comment for you that I have strong personal reasons and certain other obligations that suggest to me that it might not be preferable.

Certain other obligations? To whom?

But for all the puzzles and the directions of superiors, Humes had come to some definite conclusions by the end of the autopsy.

—One bullet entered the rear of Kennedy's head and exited from the top of his skull.

—Another bullet entered the President's back and apparently worked its way out during cardiac massage at Parkland.

The autopsy, which began at 8:15 P.M. the evening of the assassination, was concerned with only two of Kennedy's wounds. Humes studied the head wound and found about forty pieces of bullet metal, indicating a bullet had fragmented while passing through the skull area. He concluded that a high-velocity rifle bullet had entered the rear of the skull, fragmented, and then exited through the top of the skull. Death was attributed to the head wound.

Not so easily explained was a wound in the President's back. The Dallas doctors never saw this wound because they said they never examined Kennedy's back. However, the autopsy doctors studied this wound carefully and wrote clear records of it. On the autopsy face sheet diagram marked by Dr. Humes, a wound is depicted in Kennedy's back between the shoulder blades.

In Kennedy's death certificate, it states: ''. . . a second wound occurred in the posterior back at about the level of the third thoracic vertebra.'' The third thoracic vertebra is located almost midway between the shoulder blades.

Two FBI agents, Francis X. O'Neill, Jr., and James W. Sibert, were ordered to attend the autopsy and make a report. Their report, which was kept classified by the Warren Commission for several years, stated:

During the latter stages of this autopsy, Dr. Humes located an opening which appeared to be a bullet hole which was below the shoulders and two inches to the right of the middle line of the spinal column.

This description on the wound's location was supported by the testimony of Secret Service agents and bullet holes in Kennedy's clothing. Yet it presented a real problem to the Warren Commission. If the President's wound was between the shoulder blades, this was lower than the position of the neck wound making for an upward trajectory—totally inconsistent with the idea of shots from sixty feet above and behind the President.

The solution to this dilemma was simple—the Commission reported:

A bullet had entered the base of the back of [Kennedy's] neck slightly to the right of the spine. It traveled downward and exited from the front of the neck, crossing a nick in the left lower portion of the knot in the President's necktie.''

The Commission simply reported the back wound as located 5½ inches higher than determined by the evidence.

Later, when questioned about the location of the wound as marked on the autopsy face sheet, Dr. Boswell stated the drawing was a "diagram error." And Humes was quoted as saying the back wound was higher than the throat wound, although he had marked it well below the neck wound.

The issue of the autopsy diagram was resolved in 1975 when researcher Harold Weisberg obtained the original autopsy face sheet by means of a Freedom of Information suit.

Researchers discovered that the original sheet—depicting a wound in the low back—had been marked "verified" by Kennedy's personal physician, Dr. George Burkley. This verification of the autopsy sheet had been eliminated in copies of the document presented by the Warren Commission to the public. Curiously, Dr. Burkley was never called to testify to the Commission, although he was the only medical authority who rode in the motorcade, viewed Kennedy's body at Parkland Hospital, and was present at the autopsy. In 1982, Burkley reportedly told author Henry Hurt that he believed Kennedy's death was the result of a conspiracy. However, Burkley declined to elaborate further.

The Sibert-O'Neill FBI report further stated:

This opening [the back wound] was probed by Dr. Humes with the finger, at which time it was determined that the trajectory of the missile entering at this point had entered at a downward position of 45 to 60 degrees. Further probing determined that the distance traveled by this missile was a short distance inasmuch as the end of the opening could be felt with the finger. Inasmuch as no complete bullet of any size could be located in the brain area and likewise no bullet could be located in the back or any other area of the body as determined by total body X rays and inspection revealing there was no point of exit, the individuals performing the autopsy were at a loss to explain why they could find no bullets.

Commander J. Thornton Boswell, Humes's assistant, told author Josiah Thompson that all three doctors probed the back wound with their fingers but could not penetrate past an inch or so. According to Boswell, a thin metal probe also was used but no bullet track could be located.

After failing to find any bullet, agents Sibert and O'Neill called the FBI Laboratory and were informed of the bullet that had been found on a stretcher at Parkland Hospital. This information was relayed to Humes and the autopsy doctors and led them to a conclusion expressed in the FBI report of Sibert and O'Neill:

. . . since external cardiac massage had been performed at Parkland Hospital, it was entirely possible that through such movement the bullet had worked its way back out of the point of entry and fallen on the stretcher.

At the end of the autopsy, the military doctors concluded, as recorded in the Sibert-O'Neill report:

> . . . that the one bullet had entered the President's back and had worked its way out of the body during external cardiac massage and that a second high-velocity bullet had entered the rear of the skull and had fragmentized prior to exit through the top of the skull.

But if the back wound caused problems, they were nothing compared to the problems that arose after Humes learned that the autopsy doctors had completely missed one of the President's wounds.

On the day after the autopsy—with the President's body already prepared for burial and lying in state at the White House—Humes contacted the medical officials in Dallas. He was shocked to learn that they had observed a bullet wound in Kennedy's throat. The autopsy doctors had noticed an opening in the throat but had assumed it had been made at Parkland to facilitate a tracheal tube.

Here is one of the most suspicious of the differences recorded in Kennedy's wounds: Dr. Perry at Parkland described the throat wound as a small hole about 3 to 5 millimeters—or about ⅕ of an inch—in diameter that had the appearance of an entrance wound. Perry said he made a surgical incision laterally across this hole to facilitate a tracheotomy, but did not obliterate the bullet wound. But by the time the autopsy doctors examined Kennedy's throat, this wound had elongated to almost three inches—such a gash that they didn't realize it obliterated a wound from the assassination. Furthermore, all of the Dallas doctors said Kennedy had a large blasted hole in the right rear portion of his head—not at all like the gaping wound in the right top portion of his skull as reported by the autopists.

These differences in the descriptions of the throat and head wounds suggest only three explanations:

1. The Dallas medical personnel lied about what they saw.
2. The autopsy doctors lied about what they saw.
3. No one lied—thus indicating the wounds were altered between the time they were seen in Dallas and the autopsy.

The latter explanation is buttressed by the Sibert-O'Neill FBI report of the Bethesda autopsy which states:

> The President's body was removed from the casket . . . and placed on the autopsy table, at which time the complete body was wrapped in a sheet and the head area contained an additional wrapping which was saturated with blood . . . it was also apparent that a tracheotomy had been performed, as well as surgery of the head area, namely, in the top of the skull.

Surgery in the top of the skull? No such surgery was ever mentioned by the Parkland medical staff.

This oddity became one of the focal points of an investigation by researcher and author David Lifton, who reached some startling and well-publicized conclusions.

The David Lifton Investigation

David Lifton, a former NASA computer engineer who researched the assassination for more than fifteen years, was the first person to interview both medical personnel in Dallas and at Bethesda Naval Medical Center. What he discovered shocked him.

In his best-selling book, *Best Evidence*, Lifton reported that not only were there discrepancies in the descriptions of Kennedy's wounds, but there were discrepancies in reports of how the body was transported.

It has been well documented how Kennedy's body was wrapped in a sheet in Dallas and placed in an expensive bronze ceremonial casket for shipment to Washington. Yet Lifton found Bethesda technicians who said they removed Kennedy's body from a black zippered body bag that was inside a cheap, gray military-style shipping casket, similar to those used to transport bodies back from Vietnam.

Paul K. O'Connor, who was studying to be a medical technician, was working in Bethesda's laboratory when Kennedy's body arrived. He said the body arrived in a "shipping casket . . . kind of slate-type gray and a kind of light pinkish color on the edges." Asked by Lifton the condition of the body when the casket was opened, O'Connor replied: "He was in a body bag." O'Connor's recollection was confirmed by others, including Captain John Stover, Bethesda's commanding officer.

Just as startling was an interview with Bethesda X-ray technician Jerrol F. Custer. Custer said he had already made X-ray photographs of Kennedy's body, had gone to an upper floor to process them, and was returning to the morgue area of the hospital when he encountered a bloodstained Jacqueline Kennedy, surrounded by newsmen and Secret Service agents, entering Bethesda. Outside in an ambulance was the bronze Dallas casket supposedly containing the President's body.

Based on this and much more information gleaned from official reports and witnesses, Lifton concluded that the assassination was the result of a plot "involving the Executive Branch of the Government."

His hypothesis is this:

Since Lifton disbelieved that the doctors at both Parkland and Bethesda lied about their observations, the alternative belief was that Kennedy's body was altered. Lifton discovered a brief time period during the swearing-in ceremonies for Lyndon Johnson aboard *Air Force One* when everyone gathered forward, leaving Kennedy's body unattended. It was during this time that his body was taken from the bronze Dallas casket, placed in a military body bag, and stowed elsewhere in the plane [Autopsy photos showed several scratches on Kennedy's back that could be explained by the hasty handling of his body]. At Andrews Air Force Base, Kennedy's body was taken off the right side of *Air Force One* and placed in a helicopter, which immediately took off while the news media and officials concentrated on Mrs. Kennedy and the Dallas casket, which were unloaded from the left side of the plane. Either at Walter Reed or Bethesda, someone altered the President's wounds to conform to the shots-from-behind thesis and then the body was wrapped in a sheet and placed on the Bethesda autopsy table ready for Dr. Humes and the others.

Lifton's theory—incredible as it may seem—is supported by the available evidence. Further, attempts to discredit either Lifton or his sources have proven unconvincing.

There is no doubt that long-standing and serious questions have arisen over the medical evidence. Lifton's theory that Kennedy's body was altered while in the hands of federal officials goes a long way in explaining the puzzles and inconsistencies of the medical evidence.

*   *   *

Upon learning of the throat wound the day after the autopsy, Humes was forced to revise his autopsy report.

The autopsy doctors determined that the back wound was 4 to 7 millimeters in diameter and the Dallas doctors said the throat wound was 3 to 5 millimeters in diameter. Since the back wound was larger, this would normally suggest that the neck wound was one of entrance and the back wound one of exit—assuming both holes represented the path of a single bullet.

However, Humes saw it another way. Testifying to the House Select Committee on Assassinations, Humes said upon learning of the throat wound: ". . . lights went on, and we said, ah, we have some place for our missile to have gone."

After revising his autopsy report, Humes walked to his fireplace and burned autopsy material—alternatively described as original notes, a first draft, or other written notes. This highly-questionable practice preceded his final autopsy report, which stated definitely: "One missile entered the back of the President and exited in the front of the neck."

Considering that the wound in Kennedy's throat was too small to have been caused by a rifle slug and that FBI experts could not find any traces of metal on Kennedy's shirt or tie and that the Dallas doctors noted bruises on Kennedy's neck, it has been theorized that the neck wound may have been caused by bone fragments blasted downward at the time of the fatal head shot.

Author Josiah Thompson wrote:

If we suppose that a bullet (or more likely a bone) fragment was driven downward on a slight left-to-right trajectory through the midbrain, we have a hypothesis that accords with all the known facts surrounding the throat wound.

But Humes was not bothered by such theories. He now had a revised idea of how Kennedy died:

—One bullet entered Kennedy's back and exited from his throat.
—Another bullet struck the back of his head and exited from the top of the skull.

Even Kennedy's personal physician, Dr. Burkley, had problems accepting these findings, which may explain his belief in a conspiracy as revealed to author Henry Hurt.

Adding to this confusion is the possibility of yet another bullet being recovered from Kennedy's body during the autopsy. In *The New York Times* of November 27, 1963, Dallas doctor Kemp Clark stated one bullet struck Kennedy at the necktie knot "ranged downward in his chest, and did not exit." This statement was supported by Dr. Robert Shaw, who told *New York Herald-Tribune* reporter Martin Steadman on November 27 that a bullet entered the front of Kennedy's throat "coursed downward into his lung [and] was removed in the Bethesda Naval Hospital where the autopsy was performed."

The idea of a bullet being removed during autopsy gains additional strength in light of two government documents now available. One is a letter of receipt signed by FBI agents Sibert and O'Neill, who monitored the autopsy. The two-line letter, dated November 22, 1963, states: "We hereby acknowledge receipt of a missile removed by Commander James J. Humes, MC, USN on this date." The other is another letter of receipt, but this time from the Protective Research Section of the Treasury Department, dated November 26, 1963. Among the items it listed as received from Kennedy's personal physician, Dr. Burkley, is "One receipt from FBI for a missile removed during examination of the body." FBI agents normally would know the difference between bullet fragments and an intact slug. It is curious that both documents refer to a "missile" rather than fragments or pieces of bullet.

All of this suggests yet another bullet was discovered but kept secret, since another bullet would have destroyed the lone-assassin theory, which already was being strained to the limit.

Further evidence that more than two bullets struck President Kennedy came in 1968 when then Attorney General Ramsey Clark gathered a panel of physicians headed by Dr. Russell Fisher, a Maryland medical examiner, to study the JFK autopsy photographs and X-rays.

In addition to noting that the rear head wound had changed both size and shape from its description by the autopists, the Clark panel found at the base of Kennedy's skull ". . . a large metallic [bullet] fragment which . . . is round and measures 6.5 mm in diameter."

This could be construed as strong evidence against Lee Harvey Oswald, since he reportedly used a 6.5 mm rifle. However, recall that the official version states that one bullet—the "Magic Bullet"—traversed the President's neck, penetrated Connally, and was found intact at Parkland Hospital.

Since officially no large fragments had been noted by the autopsy doctors and no such fragments could have come from the whole bullet found at Parkland, it seems probable that either more than two shots struck Kennedy in the head area or that the autopsy materials viewed by the Clark panel were somehow faked.

Furthermore, yet another bullet base, about 6.5 mm in diameter, was said to be found in the front seat of the presidential limousine. All this goes far to prove that more than two bullets struck Kennedy.

A Navy officer who might have been able to clarify some of the questions about the President's autopsy is unavailable. He died under strange circumstances.

Over the years, as attempts have been made to clarify and substantiate the medical evidence, the wounds seem to take on a life of their own.

The head wound as seen by the Dallas doctors, consisted of a large blasted-out area in the right rear of the skull. Both medical and nonmedical persons in Dallas gave consistent descriptions of this wound.

Secret Service Agent Clint Hill told the Warren Commission:

The right rear portion of his head was missing.

Dr. Charles J. Carrico noted a large hole:

. . . in the posterior skull, the occipital region. There was an absence of the calvarium or skull in this area . . .

Dr. Malcolm Perry:

I noted a large avulsive wound of the right parietal occipital area, [The occipital is the large bone on the back of a human skull.] in which both scalp and portions of skull were absent . . .

Dr. William Kemp Clark:

I then examined the wound in the back of the President's head. This was a large, gaping wound in the right posterior part, with cerebral and cerebellar tissue being damaged and exposed. [The cerebellum controls muscle coordination and is located at the low rear portion of the head behind the occipital bone.]

Dr. Robert McClelland:

. . . I noted that the right posterior portion of the skull had been extremely blasted.

Yet the autopsy doctors saw a head wound that stretched from the upper side of the rear to the right front of Kennedy's head.

The autopsy doctors said a small entrance wound was located in the back of the skull at about the hairline, while the House Select Committee on Assassinations' medical panel placed the entrance wound four inches higher, near the top of the head.

Neither the Warren Commission nor the House Committee spoke of a hole blasted out of the right rear portion of the President's head. The House Committee even produced a drawing reportedly made from an autopsy photograph that depicts the rear of Kennedy's head. It is entirely intact except for what appears to be a small hole—the entrance wound—near the top.

Humes had problems with this drawing, stating he had never seen the small hole before. He suggested it might be dried blood. But he was certain that he had seen no entrance wound in that location.

Robert Groden, a researcher and photographic consultant to the House Select Committee on Assassinations, had a simple explanation for the mystery surrounding the autopsy photographs—after careful study, he decided several, if not all, were forgeries. After discovering evidence of retouching, Gordon wrote:

The vital autopsy photos of the back of the President's head were altered immediately after the autopsy in order to cover up the fact that the President received two bullets in the head, one from the rear and one from the front, and this second shot blew out the back of his head, as Jackie Kennedy testified to the Warren Commission.

Contemporary autopsy drawings and reports placed the location of the back wound in the middle of the back, between the shoulder blades—this description is corroborated by the bullet holes in Kennedy's clothing—yet the Warren Commission placed the back wound on the right shoulder near the base of the neck.

X-rays and other autopsy materials such as photographs, tissue samples, and blood smears—including Kennedy's brain, which was removed and preserved—could have provided definitive proof of the location of the wounds. However, much of this material is missing from the National Archives. (The House Select Committee on Assassinations hinted that the brain may have been taken by Robert Kennedy to prevent future public display, however, this has not been proven and Kennedy is not alive to comment.)

It also should be noted that the Warren Commission—the group officially charged with finding the truth of Kennedy's assassination—apparently never was allowed to view for themselves the President's autopsy photographs and X-rays. Commission attorney Arlen Specter, in an October 10, 1968, interview in *U.S. News & World Report* stated:

> The complete set of pictures taken at the autopsy was not made available to me or to the Commission. I was shown one picture of the back of a body which was represented to be the back of the President, although it was not authenticated. It showed a hole in the position identified in the autopsy report. To the best of my knowledge, the Commission did not see any photographs or X-rays. . . . The photographs and X-rays would, in the thinking of the Commission, not have been crucial, because they would have served only to corroborate what the autopsy surgeons had testified to under oath as opposed to adding any new facts for the Commission.

But they are crucial—if not in truthfully understanding Kennedy's wounds, then in understanding the manipulations surrounding the medical evidence. As Groden later told his author:

> The key to understanding who killed Kennedy lies with the autopsy photographs. These photographs may tell us more about the assassination than all of the official investigations. Perhaps the single most important question in the investigation was never asked: Why were the autopsy photographs and X-rays never officially shown to the numerous doctors and nurses in Dallas who treated President Kennedy? Had this question been pursued, the true nature of the conspiracy would then have been exposed, because the crucial pictures allegedly of the back of the President's head are forged! That forgery is one of the keys to the conspiracy. Who would have had that kind of access to the evidence in order to alter it? Who had the capability to alter it?

Summary

The medical evidence in the JFK assassination, which should be the basis for truthful determination of how many bullets struck Kennedy and from which direction, is hopelessly flawed. Some of it is still missing and other material has come under serious question as to its authenticity.

Kennedy was given an incompetent autopsy, with military and civilian authorities directing the three inexperienced and intimidated military doctors.

The late Dr. Milton Helpern, who as chief medical examiner for New York City supervised sixty thousand autopsies, once described Kennedy's autopsy thusly:

It's like sending a seven-year-old boy who has taken three lessons on the violin over to the New York Philharmonic and expecting him to perform a Tchaikovsky symphony. He knows how to hold the violin and bow, but he has a long way to go before he can make music.

Dr. Cyril H. Wecht, an experienced coroner and former president of the American Academy of Forensic Medicine, was more blunt:

[Kennedy's autopsy was] extremely superficial and sloppy, inept, incomplete, incompetent in many respects, not only on the part of the pathologists who did this horribly inadequate medical-legal autopsy but on the part of many other people. This is the kind of examination that would not be tolerated in a routine murder case by a good crew of homicide detectives in most major cities of America.

For whatever reasons—some innocent bumbling and some not so innocent—the medical evidence in the JFK assassination will forever be considered tainted, incomplete, and inconclusive.

And the question remains—who had the power to misdirect and confuse the official medical examination of the assassinated President?

> I know there is a terrible conspiracy going on in the world right now.
> . . . The world has the right to hear the truth.
>
> —Jack Ruby

Jack Ruby

On the day before Kennedy's assassination business appeared normal in the Dallas District Attorney's Office. There was a continuing parade of defendants, lawyers, and police officers as the office staff went about preparing causes. One officer, Dallas police lieutenant W. F. Dyson, later told the Warren Commission that it was here that he and other officers encountered a short, stocky nightclub owner who was going out of his way to make their acquaintance. Dyson overheard this man—Jack Ruby—tell the officers: "You probably don't know me, but you will."

The following Sunday the entire world knew Jack Ruby—the man who killed Lee Harvey Oswald.

When on November 24, 1963, Ruby silenced the one man whom authorities blamed for Kennedy's death, a rumble of discontent and suspicion began that still persists today. Many people could accept the idea of a "lone-nut assassin," but balked at the idea of two such characters.

Any serious probe of President Kennedy's death must include an in-depth look at the life and death of Jack Ruby, one of history's most unlikely candidates for fame.

In the months following the assassination, the American public was told—first by news media accounts and then by the Warren Commission—that Ruby was a small-time Dallas nightclub operator with no significant ties to organized crime or to Dallas authorities. It was said that his killing of Oswald was simply the spontaneous act of a man hoping to right the wrong of the President's death.

Today there is evidence that Ruby, a fixture on the Dallas scene in 1963, was more closely connected with organized-crime figures than earlier believed and that he, in fact, stalked Oswald throughout the assassination weekend.

It also is now known that Ruby tried to tell what he knew about the plot to kill Kennedy but was shrugged off by both government investigators and the news media. To a radio news reporter, Ruby said: "I know there is a terrible conspiracy going on in the world right now . . . I'm speaking the truth . . . The world has the right to hear the truth . . ."

Shortly after Ruby was granted a new trial, he was filmed by a Texas television station stating:

380

. . . everything pertaining to what's happened has never come to the surface. The world will never know the true facts of what occurred—my motive, in other words. I am the only person in the background to know the truth pertaining to everything relating to my circumstances.

Asked by the interviewer if this truth would ever come out, Ruby replied: "No. Because unfortunately these people, who have so much to gain and have such an ulterior motive to put me in the position I'm in, will never let the true facts come aboveboard to the world."

"Are these people in high positions?" asked the interviewer. Ruby answered, "Yes." In letters smuggled out of the Dallas County Jail, Ruby even named Lyndon Johnson as the person behind the assassination.

Ruby's mob connections stretched back over the years to his childhood in Chicago and were much more extensive than admitted by the Warren Commission. In 1964, one of Ruby's childhood friends told the FBI that as youths, he and Ruby had delivered sealed envelopes for Chicago gangster Al Capone.

Jack Ruby was born Jacob Rubenstein in 1911, the fifth of eight siblings. His exact birthdate is not known. Various documents show different birthdates, although Ruby himself used March 25, 1911, most frequently. Despite several moves, the family always remained in what was described by one brother as a "ghetto," complete with noisy streets filled with pushcarts and peddlers.

The elder Rubenstein was a violent man known for drunkenness, brawling, and associating with women of the street. He beat his wife and his children and was frequently arrested on assault charges. A coarse man, he objected to his children obtaining any sort of higher education.

Fannie Rubenstein, while desiring a better life for her children, nevertheless was herself a burden to the family. Illiterate and unpredictable due to mental problems, she would berate her husband for his lack of money and nag the children to improve themselves. The Rubenstein household constantly shook with violent and noisy fights.

When Ruby was ten years old, his parents separated and he, along with his three brothers and four sisters, was placed in various foster homes by the Jewish Home Finding Society. During this time, young Rubenstein was learning more on the streets of Chicago than in the schoolroom. Like young Oswald, Ruby was caught by truant officers after skipping school. Unlike Oswald, who found diversion in the local library and zoo, Ruby gravitated toward street gangs and amusement parks.

A 1922 psychiatric evaluation by the Illinois State Public Welfare Department's Institute for Juvenile Research, to which Ruby had been referred by the Jewish Social Service Bureau, characterized young Ruby as a boy with an "adequate" IQ but with "attention unsustained," "quick and careless" reactions, and an "egocentric" personality. This description of young Rubenstein of Chicago could have applied equally forty years later to Jack Ruby in Dallas.

On the streets, young Ruby was nicknamed "Sparky." According to his sister, Eva Grant, the name came from Ruby's swaggering walk, which reminded some people of the wobbling gait of Sunday comic strip character Barney Google's horse, "Sparkplug." Others believed "Sparky" was a tag reflecting Ruby's volatile temperament.

Ruby quickly found that holding a job was not for him. Years later, he recalled: "I tried to be an errand boy for a mail-order house but I couldn't be regimented. I couldn't get up in the morning."

So young street-wise Sparky got along selling novelties from a pushcart, after obtaining a vendor's license thanks to his brother Hyman's political pull in Chicago's 24th Ward. The license was soon revoked after nearby businessmen complained. Undaunted, Sparky scalped sporting event tickets, peddled carnations in dance halls and chocolates in burlesque shows, and even offered "hot" music sheets in violation of copyright laws. One close friend described Ruby's promotion schemes as "shady" but "legitimate."

Also on the street, Ruby gained a reputation with his fists, although the accounts of his aggressiveness differed with those who knew him. Barney Rasofsky, who gained fame in the 1930s as World Welterweight Boxing Champion Barney Ross, in 1964 told the FBI that he and Ruby along with other young toughs were paid one dollar per trip to deliver sealed envelopes for gangster Al Capone. (If this information was passed along to the Warren Commission, it was never reported.) Rasofsky also said Ruby was never a troublemaker, although he always was ready to defend himself against any attack. Others, too, recalled Ruby as one to avoid a fight if possible.

These recollections clash markedly with those of others who recalled Ruby as a street brawler, eager to take up any challenge, even to the extent of aiding someone else in trouble.

Ruby was also militantly proud of his Jewish ancestry. Although not particularly devout, he had nevertheless received some instruction in Orthodox Judaism.

In addition to fights with other street gangs because of racial and ethinic differences, Ruby reportedly joined with Jewish toughs in fights with the Pro-Nazi German-American Bund during the late 1930s.

In 1933, Ruby, along with several Chicago friends, went to Los Angeles and then San Francisco seeking employment. In 1936, he was still in San Francisco living for a brief time with his sister Eva and her husband.

Despite some evidence to the contrary, Ruby later told authorities he returned to Chicago in 1937—the same year his mother was committed to Elgin State Hospital with mental disorders. For more than twenty years, Fannie Rubenstein had frequented doctors and clinics reporting that a fishbone was lodged in her throat despite continuing reassurances that nothing organic could be detected.

Having returned to Chicago about 1937, Ruby began working for the Scrap Iron and Junk Handlers Union, according to Social Security Administration records. Chicago attorney Leon R. Cooke, a close friend to Ruby, had founded the union and was financial secretary. When gangsters connected to the Chicago underworld began taking control of the union and its funds, Ruby went along. Union president John Martin, who earlier had been indicted along with a major Chicago mobster for withholding tax information, named young Rubenstein union secretary. However, according to a statement Ruby made to police at the time, he was little more than a bagman for union thugs.

On December 8, 1939, Martin fatally shot Cooke in the union's offices after an argument over missing funds. Martin fled and Ruby was arrested. The incident was splashed all over the Chicago newspapers at the time. Although Cooke was shot in the back, Martin claimed self-defense and never served time for the murder.

While Ruby claimed such close friendship for the slain Cooke that he eventually took the name Leon as his own middle name, he nevertheless stayed on with the corrupt union after Cooke's brutal murder.

Following the bad publicity over Cooke's murder, the union was reorganized as the Waste Material Handlers Union, Local 20467, American Federation of Labor. Martin was replaced and the reorganized union was dominated by its secretary-treasurer, Paul J. Dorfman, a man with long-standing connections to Chicago racketeers.

In his book *The Enemy Within*, Robert Kennedy mentioned Dorfman while telling how Teamster president Jimmy Hoffa expanded his influence nationwide:

For [Hoffa], the key to the entire Midwest was Chicago, He needed a powerful ally there—and he found his man in Paul Dorfman. Dorfman, [the McClellan Committee] testimony showed, was a big operator—a major figure in the Chicago underworld who also knew his way around in certain labor and political circles . . . Dorfman took over as head of the Chicago Waste Handlers Union in 1939 after its founder and secretary-treasurer was murdered . . . Hoffa made a trade with Dorfman. In return for an introduction to the Chicago underworld, the Committee found, Hoffa turned over to him and his family the gigantic Central Conference of Teamsters Welfare Fund insurance.

Several months after Dorfman took over, Ruby suddenly left the union. In 1964, Ruby told the Warren Commission:

I was with the union back in Chicago and I left the union when I found out a notorious organization had moved in there. . . . I have never been a criminal . . . I am not a gangster . . . I had a very rough start in life, but anything I have done, I at least tried to do it in good taste.

Young Rubenstein went back to hustling—this time manufacturing and selling gambling punchboards. His punchboard "company" had no fixed address, but operated out of inexpensive hotels.

It was during this time, claimed Chicago attorney Luis Kutner, who both represented mob figures and worked for the Kefauver Committee, that Ruby became connected with Sam Giancana and his crowd.

By mid-1943, Ruby found a more permanent home—the U.S. Air Force. At the beginning of World War II, he had been granted a draft deferment for reasons not entirely clear. One version is that he feigned a hearing disability by wearing a hearing aid, while another is that he was granted a "economic hardship" deferment because he was the only Rubenstein child remaining at home. Whatever the reason, it was insufficient in 1943 when he was reclassified 1-A and, despite an appeal to his local board, inducted into the Air Force on May 21.

Upon his discharge from the Air Force in February 1946, Ruby returned to Chicago where he entered an unsuccessful sales business with his three brothers, Hyman, Sam, and Earl. As in their childhood, the four Rubenstein brothers constantly argued with each other—this time over how to run the business. One of the few things they agreed on was the need to obtain a more "American" name. After Hyman left the business, Sam, Earl, and Jack all shortened their name from Rubenstein to Ruby. Their stormy partnership lasted only one year, and by 1947 Jack Ruby had left Chicago for Texas.

Shortly after Jack arrived in Dallas his name change was made official by a decree from the 68th Judicial District Court of Dallas on December 30, 1947.

Although the official story of Ruby's move is that he went to help his sister operate a nightclub, several different sources—some within the mob—have claimed that Ruby was part of a plan to bring Dallas rackets under the control of the Chicago underworld. Shortly after the JFK assassination, Dallas businessman Giles Miller added support for this idea by telling the FBI that in 1959 Ruby had told him he wanted to go back to California in 1947 but "was directed" to go to Dallas.

But even more evidence of Ruby's move as part of a mob offensive into Texas came from former Dallas County sheriff Steve Guthrie. During the late 1930s and early 1940s, Dallas gambling operations were virtually wide open under the control of homegrown bosses like Benny "Cowboy" Binion and Herbert Noble. However, by the late 1940s a bloody feud between these two top gamblers had resulted in Noble's bombing death

and Binion's departure for the quieter environs of Las Vegas. It was then
that the Chicago mob made its bid for a takeover in Dallas.

In late 1946, an emissary from the Chicago syndicate named Paul
Roland Jones made contact with Dallas lawmen in an effort to open the
city for the mob. Jones held meetings with Sheriff Guthrie and an obscure
Dallas police lieutenant named George Butler, but later was indicted for
attempted bribery when Guthrie and Butler blew the whistle.

In their *Third Interim Report*, the Kefauver Senate Committee stated:

> Some indication of how modern crime syndicates operate and how they
> open new territory is apparent from . . . the extraordinary testimony of
> Lt. George Butler of the Police Department of Dallas, Texas. Lieutenant
> Butler was approached by a member of the Chicago Mob by the name
> of Paul Jones . . . Jones stated that he was an advance agent of the
> Chicago crime syndicate and was prepared to offer the District Attorney
> and the Sheriff $1,000 a week each or twelve-and-a-half percent cut on
> the profit if the syndicate were permitted to operate in Dallas under
> "complete protection." Jones also stated that syndicate operations were
> conducted by local people who "front" for the Chicago Mob.

At this time the two top Chicago mob leaders were Sam Giancana (the
coordinator of Mafia-CIA assassination plots) and Anthony Accardo.

Was Ruby one of the "fronts" mentioned by his friend Jones? Sheriff
Guthrie told the Warren Commission that Ruby was himself involved in
the bribery plan of Jones and that both Jones and his Chicago associates
"frequently mentioned that Ruby would operate a 'fabulous' restaurant as
a front for gambling activities."

The Commission went on to state, however, that since Ruby was not
mentioned in Jones's bribery scheme, the Commission "found it difficult
to accept [Guthrie's] report." The Commission also ignored a story by
Chicago newsman Mort Newman who reported that Butler told him that
"Jack Ruby came to Dallas from . . . Chicago in the late 1940s and was
involved in an attempt to bribe Sheriff Steve Guthrie."

The Warren Commission also ignored testimony that showed that Jones
met Ruby through two mutual friends, Paul "Needle Nose" Labriola and
Jim Weinberg—both well-known associates of Giancana.

In fact, to arrive at their conclusion that Ruby was not mob connected,
they had to ignore an FBI interview with Jones in which he stated that
when he first met Ruby, both Weinberg and Labiola told him Ruby was
"all right" as far as the syndicate was concerned. Weinberg and Labriola
were later found garroted and stuffed in a car trunk in a double gangland
slaying.

When interviewed for the Warren Commission in 1964, Jones said he
believed Butler was serious about accepting mob payoffs, changing his
position only after learning that the Texas Rangers were aware of the deal.

It was Butler—then assigned to the Juvenile Division—who was in charge of the fatal transfer of Lee Harvey Oswald on November 24, 1963. Butler apparently was also close to right-wing causes in Dallas. According to Penn Jones, former editor of the *Midlothian Mirror* and an early assassination researcher, Butler approached him in 1961 about publishing right-wing literature. Jones told this author:

"[Butler] offered me the job of printing a regional newspaper under the auspices of the Ku Klux Klan. He told me that half of the Dallas Police were members of the KKK."

Butler also was known to have provided personal police security for right-wing Dallas oil billionaire H. L. Hunt.

Butler's veracity comes into further question when one considers Commission Exhibit 2249, which includes the statements of two Dallas policemen who claim that shortly after Ruby killed Oswald, Butler approached them with the "important" information that young Oswald was actually the illegitimate son of Jack Ruby!

Whether or not Ruby participated in the 1947 bribe attempt, it is certain that his relationship with Jones continued.

On October 24, 1947, Jones was arrested and charged with smuggling opium into the United States from Mexico. In Chicago, both Ruby and his brother Hymie were questioned by Bureau of Narcotics agents investigating the case.

And over the next two years, while Jones appealed his narcotics conviction, he frequented Dallas's Singapore Club which by then was operated by Jack Ruby.

The Warren Commission and subsequent assassination investigations have attempted to portray Jack Ruby as a rambunctious, self-ingratiating nightclub owner simply striving for success in a rather shabby business— almost a Damon Runyan racetrack character.

It may also be significant that Ruby was much better connected socially in Dallas than has been publicly stated by federal investigations. As a man-about-town, Ruby was well known not only to police and law-enforcement officials, but also to the city and county officials and businessmen who frequented his clubs and attended area gambling parties.

One significant contact may be found in an account by Madeleine Brown, allegedly former mistress to Lyndon Johnson. She claimed to have first met Jack Ruby through Johnson attorney Jerome Ragsdale of Dallas. She told this author:

One day in the early 1950s, I was coming out of Nieman-Marcus in downtown Dallas when I encountered Jerome Ragsdale and another man talking on the sidewalk. They seemed to be good friends and Jerome introduced me to the man, who was Jack Ruby. Ruby told me he owned a club downtown and invited me to visit. He also gave me a card. Of course, later I saw Ruby frequently. A bunch of us would see him around town. Lots of people in town knew him, especially people in the downtown area like H. L. Hunt, Henry Wade, Earl Cabell, they all knew him. But after the assassination weekend, everyone was scared to say they knew him.

Furthermore the record shows Ruby a much more important criminal than previously believed.

Jack Ruby—Gangster

From the prewar union murder of Leon Cooke to the 1963 killing of Lee Harvey Oswald in Dallas, Jack Ruby's life was one of close association with gangsters and close calls with the law.
Consider these Ruby associates:

Barney Baker: Described by Robert Kennedy as one of Jimmy Hoffa's "roving organizer[s] and ambassador[s] of violence," Baker had moved from criminal activities involving mobsters Jake Lansky and Bugsy Siegel to Teamster organizer for the Central States Conference under Hoffa. According to the Warren Commission, Baker received at least two calls from Ruby in a three-week period preceding the assassination and Baker called Ruby on November 7, 1963. Three of Baker's phone numbers were found in Ruby's notebooks.
Joseph Campisi: An associate of Dallas Mafia member Joseph Civello, Campisi operated several businesses in Dallas, including a restaurant notorious as a gangster hangout, and has been linked closely to the New Orleans Marcello family. Both Ruby's sister, Eva Grant, and his business partner, George Senator, described Campisi as one of Ruby's closest friends. And, though trying to distance himself from Ruby, Campisi himself told the FBI in December 1963, that he had been in contact with Ruby the night before the assassination and had visited Ruby in jail on November 30, 1963.
Frank Caracci: Described by *Life* magazine as a "Marcello Mobster," Caracci was arrested by Houston police in 1969 with three members of the Marcello group who later attended the Dallas wedding of Joseph Campisi's son. One of these men was Frank "Tickie" Saia, a prominent Louisiana gambling and political figure who was close friends with Senator Russell Long. In the months preceding the Kennedy assassination, Ruby met with Caracci as least once and was in telephone contact on several occasions.
Frank Chavez: Another Teamster thug with arrests for obstruction of justice and attempted murder, Chavez told associates he had met with Ruby and other Teamster officials in the fall of 1961, including Richard Kavner, who was described by author Dan Moldea as "another key

member of the Hoffa circle.'' A Justice Department memorandum also linked Ruby and Chavez to mobster Tony Provenzano.

Joseph Civello: The Dallas Mafia chief who was one of those arrested at the 1957 Apalachin New York mob meeting, Civello admitted to the FBI after the assassination that he had known Ruby ''for about 10 years.'' Like Campisi, Civello tried to downplay his close connections with Ruby, and someone within the Warren Commission helped this effort by deleting an entire page covering Civello from Commission Exhibit 1536 and by blanking out several paragraphs within the document.

Mickey Cohen: A news reporter claimed that Ruby was acquainted with famed mobster Cohen through his girlfriend Candy Barr, a close friend of Ruby's who was jailed on a narcotics charge in the early 1960s.

Al Gruber: A former roommate of Ruby's from Chicago, Gruber told the FBI he had no mob connections. Yet in 1970, a two-page FBI report, which had been suppressed for years, showed Gruber had been arrested six times using two aliases in three states. Gruber, too, was associated with top Teamster officials as well as thugs working for Mickey Cohen. Gruber reportedly had not seen his old friend Ruby for ten years when he showed up in Dallas in mid-November, 1963, for an extended visit. Ruby called Gruber in Los Angeles three hours after the assassination.

Russell D. Matthews: An underworld character with a lengthy arrest record, Matthews has been linked to Campisi and Florida mob chief Santos Trafficante. He also was described as a father figure by convicted hitman Charles V. Harrelson. Several people told the Warren Commission that Ruby and Matthews were friends and on October 3, 1963, a call was placed from Ruby's Carousel Club to Matthews's former wife in Louisiana.

Murray "Dusty" Miller: A former secretary-treasurer of the Teamsters International who was associated with several underworld figures, Miller received a person-to-person call from Ruby on November 8, 1963, according to the Warren Commission.

Lenny Patrick: According to his sister, Ruby also placed calls to Patrick in late 1963. Identified in a 1965 U.S. Senate report as a high-ranking associate of the Chicago Mafia, Patrick reportedly was close to Chicago mob chieftain Sam Giancana.

Nofio J. Pecora: Described by various crime investigations as an ex-convict with several arrests, Pecora has been identified as one of Carlos Marcello's most trusted aides. As late as October 30, 1963, a call was logged between the Dallas phone of Ruby and a New Orleans phone listed to Pecora.

Johnny Roselli: A former associate of Al Capone, Roselli was one of the Mafia chiefs involved in the CIA-Mafia assassination plots against

Castro. His mutilated body was found in an oil drum in Florida's Biscayne Bay in 1976 just as Roselli was scheduled to testify before the House Select Committee on Assassinations. According to columnist Jack Anderson, Roselli knew Ruby and described him as "one of our boys." According to reports from federal sources in Florida, Roselli and Ruby twice met secretly in Miami motel rooms during the two months preceding the assassination. These meetings were monitored by the FBI, which was keeping Roselli under surveillance. However, no mention of these meetings were made to the Warren Commission.

Irwin S. Wiener: A close associate of both Hoffa and other Teamster officials, Wiener has been connected to mob bosses Trafficante and Giancana. On October 26, 1963, Wiener received a twelve-minute, person-to-person call from Ruby's Carousel Club. He later gave contradictory accounts of the content of this call.

Lewis McWillie: A notorious Dallas gambler, McWillie worked for several gambling houses there during the 1940s, including Benny Benion's Top of the Hill Club and W. C. Kirkwood's Four Deuces Club in nearby Fort Worth. McWillie then joined such famed gangsters as Santos Trafficante, Meyer and Jake Lansky, Dino Cellini, and others in gambling operations in Havana, Cuba, before being thrown out by Castro. One of Ruby's closest friends, McWillie was sent guns by Ruby while still in Cuba and, in fact, was sent a .38 Smith & Wesson by Ruby as late as May 10, 1963. Ruby told the Warren Commission, "I called him frequently . . . I idolized McWillie." The Kirkwoods, who conducted high-stakes poker games involving wealthy Texans such as H. L. Hunt, Clint Murchinson, and Amon Carter, Sr., also played host to Texas politicians Sam Rayburn, Lyndon Johnson, and John Connally. Kirkwood's son, Pat, served alcoholic drinks to President's Kennedy's Secret Service guards well into the morning hours of November 22, 1963. Kirkwood told the House Select Committee on Assassinations that "Chilly" McWillie was a close family friend. Warren Commission staffers saw several conspiratorial leads in McWillie and recommended that he be called to testify about Ruby's Cuban and mob connections, a recommendation that the Commission ignored.

Despite these revealing associations, the Warren Commission Report stated:

". . . the Commission believes that the evidence does not establish a significant link between Ruby and organized crime."

But Jack Ruby's connection to crime was not limited to simply his friends and associates. The record shows his involvement in a number of criminal activities including gambling, narcotics, prostitution, and gun running.

In an interview with FBI agents on December 6, 1963, a small-time bookie named William Abadie told how he had worked briefly for Ruby writing gambling "tickets" as well as serving as a "slot machine and jukebox mechanic."

According to this FBI report, only partially reported by the Warren Commission in Document 86 (the FBI first page containing the information about Ruby's gambling activities was inexplicably missing from the Commission document), Abadie stated:

> . . . it was obvious [to me] that to operate gambling in the manner that he [Ruby] did, that he must have racketeering connections with other individuals in the City of Dallas, as well as Fort Worth, Texas . . . [This] applied also to police connections with the two cities.

In fact, Abadie told agents that he had observed policemen coming and going while acting as a bookie in a Ruby establishment.

Another gambler, Jack Hardee, who was also interviewed by the FBI in December 1963, said when he tried to set up a numbers game in Dallas in 1962, he was told it would be necessary to obtain the approval of Jack Ruby since any "fix" with local authorities had to come through Ruby.

Harry Hall, yet another gambler who had participated in a scheme to bilk wealthy Texans including Dallas oil billionaire H. L. Hunt in the early 1950s, went on to become a credible informant for the Treasury Department and the FBI. He told the Secret Service that he once made a trip with Ruby through Oklahoma and Louisiana. Hall said Ruby had "good connections in gambling circles" there.

Hall, like Ruby, was from the same general Chicago neighborhood and had close connections with Teamster racketeers. He also was connected with mobster Johnny Rosselli, Eugene Hale Brading, and the La Costa Country Club.

According to Hall, he once won a large amount of money from H. L. Hunt after being introduced to the oilman by his friend Ruby.

According to Ester Ann Mash, a former employee who dated Ruby during the spring of 1963, Ruby was no stranger at the homes of some prominent Dallasities. She told this author:

> Several times he took me to big nice homes where there were important people in town, including District Attorney Henry Wade. I think he only took me so he didn't have to go alone. Once we got there, I never saw Jack. He would be off gambling.

There is simply no question of Ruby's connections to gambling and to gamblers, both local and national. In 1959 a Dallas gambler named Harry Siedband was arrested in Oklahoma City. On Siedband was a list of the top professional gamblers in the Dallas-Fort Worth area—including Jack Ruby.

Not so clear is Ruby's connection to drugs. As mentioned earlier, both

Ruby and his brother Hyman were questioned extensively by police following the arrest of one of Paul Jones's lieutenants on charges of smuggling hard narcotics.

In a later case, a drug offender named James Breen traveled to Dallas where he made contact with "a large narcotics setup operating between Mexico, Texas, and the East," according to Breen's female companion Eileen Curry. Curry told the FBI that Breen's contact with this drug ring was Jack Ruby.

After Ruby killed Oswald, Curry again was contacted by the FBI. She repeated her earlier contentions that Ruby and Breen had been mixed up in a narcotics smuggling ring.

There is also an abundance of evidence that Ruby was involved in other criminal activities, such as prostitution, pornography, and bribery.

And the fact that Ruby was a pivotal contact man for criminal activity in Dallas seems affirmed by his lack of prosecution by Dallas authorities.

Ruby's Dallas rap sheet showed he was arrested nine times in sixteen years—on charges ranging from operating his club after legal hours to using a gun to slug an off-duty Dallas policeman in a fight outside the Carousel Club—yet the toughest conviction shown in his criminal record was a thirty-five-dollar fine for ignoring a traffic summons.

*   *   *

Jack Ruby's criminal activity reached a peak in 1959, when he became even more closely connected to the mob and the Feds through their common interest in Cuba.

Jack Ruby—Gun Runner and Agent

The year 1959 was a busy time for Jack Ruby.

He made at least two trips to Cuba, which had just been taken over by Fidel Castro; he began making contact with gun runners who had been arming Castro but were beginning to turn against the bearded leader, and he began serving as an informant for the FBI.

Just prior to Castro's takeover, American mobsters had helped supply the revolutionary with arms for his fight with Batista. While the dictator Batista was friends with the mob, the gangsters were playing both sides of the fence, believing that if they helped Castro, they would be allowed to remain in Cuba should he succeed in his revolution.

The smuggling of arms to Castro was overseen by Norman "Roughhouse" Rothman, a burly associate of Miami mob boss Santos Trafficante who managed Trafficante's Sans Souci Casino in Havana. At the same time Rothman reportedly was splitting Havana slot machine revenues with Batista's brother-in-law.

After the assassination, the sister of a Cuban gun runner gave information indicating that Ruby was part of the Rothman operation. Mrs. Mary Thompson said she and her daughter traveled to the Florida Keys during June 1958, where her brother introduced them to a man named "Jack." The women were told that Jack owned a nightclub in Dallas and was a member of "the syndicate" who was running some guns to Cuba.

The women's story, which was reported to the FBI after the assassination, was later corroborated by Bureau informant Blaney Mack Johnson, who stated that in the early 1950s, Ruby had an interest in a notorious nightclub and gambling house in Hallandale, Florida, along with Meyer and Jake Lansky and other prominent mobsters. Johnson said Ruby was active in arranging illegal flights of weapons to Castro forces and named Edward Browder as one of the pilots operating for Ruby.

Browder, a flamboyant Miami arms dealer, was a central figure in Rothman's gun-running operation, according to federal court documents. Another soldier of fortune operating with Browder during this time was Frank Sturgis, who would much later be caught burglarizing the Watergate building along with men connected to the Nixon White House.

Although the FBI file on Browder reportedly contains more than a thousand pages, the Bureau only gave three small, innocuous reports to the Warren Commission.

And while there are reports that documents confirming Ruby's gun-running activities surfaced in both the State Department and Army intelligence files during the 1963–64 assassination investigations, these documents are said to be missing today.

Jack Ruby, like many other Americans who helped Castro seize power, lived to regret his actions. After Castro closed the mob's casinos and imprisoned gangsters, including Santos Trafficante, he quickly became persona non grata.

While awaiting a new trial shortly before his death, Ruby told his lawyers and a doctor that he feared people would find out about his Cuban activities and think him unpatriotic. He is quoted as saying: "They're going to find out about my trips to Cuba . . . and the guns and everything."

In another incident recorded in a letter smuggled out of the Dallas County Jail, Ruby wrote:

> They have found a means and ways to frame me, by deception, etc. and they have succeeded in same. My lawyers . . . were in on it. Now this is how they did it. They had a guard with me constantly . . . and he started to work on me with the Bible routine, and on his person unbeknownst to me he had one of these wireless speakers, which is very small and he kept it in his trousers pocket . . . I was very low and crying, and the guard knew I was at my lowest . . . I came to where he was sitting and I fell to the floor and broke down and said that I had sent guns to Cuba . . .

In an effort to repair this slip of the tongue, Ruby hastened to add that he had never really sent guns to Cuba but only had relayed a message from his friend Lewis McWillie to a Dallas gun store owner that McWillie wanted four pistols for personal protection.

However, this same lament was echoed to one of Ruby's employees not long after his murder conviction in 1964. According to Wally Weston, the Carousel Club's emcee who visited his former employer in the Dallas County Jail, Ruby said: ". . . Wally, you know what's going to happen now? They're going to find out about my trips to Cuba and my trips to New Orleans and the guns and everything."

In mid-1959, the Rothman gun-running operation was rocked when its chief was arrested in connection with an $8.5 million Canadian bank burglary. Federal authorities linked the bank job with a large theft of arms from an Ohio National Guard armory through a $6,000 airplane rental agreement by Rothman. Authorities agreed it appeared to all be part of a massive gun-running operation to Cuba.

And it was during this time that Ruby's travels to Cuba increased significantly, thanks to Ruby's mob idol, Lewis J. McWillie.

McWillie—potentially a key central character in this swirl of gun runners, drug smugglers, mob hitmen, CIA-Mafia assassination plots and Texas gamblers—has received scant attention from the two major government assassination investigations.

Yet, according to Elaine Mynier, who dated McWillie during his days in Dallas, the gambler and Ruby were close friends. In a December 5, 1963 FBI interview, she said McWillie was: ". . . a big-time gambler, who has always been in the big money and operated top gambling establishments in the United States and Cuba. He always had a torpedo [a bodyguard] living with him for protection." Mynier went on to say that Jack Ruby was: ". . . a small-time character who would do anything for McWillie, who was in the habit of being surrounded by people he could use."

In his Warren Commission testimony, Ruby made no secret of his closeness to McWillie. He said: "I called him frequently . . . I idolized McWillie. He is a pretty nice boy and I happened to be idolizing him. . . . I always thought a lot of him . . . I have a great fondness for him. . . ."

Despite Ruby's accolades, Commission members declined to follow through on a staff recommendation to call McWillie to testify about his relationship with Ruby and Mafia figures. The Warren Report mentioned McWillie only briefly, regarding Ruby's 1959 visit to Cuba, and concluded:

The Commission has found no evidence that McWillie has engaged in any activities since leaving Cuba that are related to pro- or anti-Castro political movements or that he was involved in Ruby's abortive jeep transaction.

As can be seen, there was no mention of McWillie's alleged mob ties or to McWillie's FBI record, No. 4404064, which gives a list of aliases and characterizes him as a gangland killer.

While the Warren Commission took Ruby and McWillie's word that the 1959 trips to Cuba were "purely social," the House Select Committee on Assassinations did not. After listing a number of visits to Cuba based on visas, airline tickets, and even a postcard, Chief Counsel Blakey wrote:

> . . . we established beyond reasonable doubt that Ruby lied repeatedly and willfully to the FBI and the Warren Commission about the number of trips he made to Cuba and their duration. . . . It was clear, for example, that the trips were not social jaunts; their purpose, we were persuaded, was to courier something, probably money, into or out of Cuba . . . the evidence indicated strongly that an association [with Trafficante] existed and that Ruby's trip was related to Trafficante's detention and release. We came to believe that Ruby's trips to Cuba were, in fact, organized-crime activities.

Lewis J. McWillie was born May 4, 1908, in Kansas City, Missouri. From 1940 until 1958, he lived in Dallas where he managed several gambling operations, including Benny Binion's legendary Top of the Hill Terrace and the Four Deuces in nearby Fort Worth owned by gentleman gambler W. C. Kirkwood. [Recall it was his son, Pat Kirkwood, who hosted Kennedy's Secret Service agents the night before the assassination.]

In the summer of 1958, McWillie relocated to Havana, Cuba, where he worked for Norman Rothman as a pit boss in Trafficante's Sans Souci casino. It was during this time that Ruby was encountered in the Florida Keys involved in gun-running schemes run by Rothman.

By September 1958, McWillie was manager of the Tropicana Hotel's luxurious casino, then styled as "the largest nightclub in the world." It was here that McWillie became a close associate of some of the mob's most powerful leaders. According to a March 26, 1964, FBI memo prepared for the Warren Commission:

> . . . it would appear McWillie solidified his Syndicate connections through his association in Havana with Santos Trafficante, well-known Syndicate member, for Tampa, Florida; Meyer and Jake Lansky; Dino Cellini and others who were members of or associates of "the Syndicate."

Yet over the years, McWillie maintained that he only knew these men "casually," but did admit an acquaintanceship with Dallas crime figures R. D. Matthews and Joseph Civello.

It is interesting to note that both McWillie—Ruby's "idol"—and Matthews—hitman Charles Harrelson's idol—were connected to Dallas gambling operations during the 1950s; both went to work gambling in

Havana, Cuba, in 1958–59; and in later years, both were employed at Benny Binion's Horseshoe Club in Las Vegas.

When Castro closed the Tropicana, McWillie became pit boss at the Capri Hotel's casino, another Trafficante property. The Capri was then run by Charlie "The Blade" Tourine, whose mistress later confirmed that she was assisting Frank Sturgis in an attempt to poison Castro.

McWillie finally left Cuba in January, 1961. According to Ruby and others, he was one of the last American mobsters to leave the island.

It is interesting to note that during the first half of 1961 McWillie was in Miami, the site of the CIA-Mafia assassination meetings involving Trafficante, Giancana, and Roselli.

Since that time, McWillie has worked at a number of Nevada gambling casinos including the Cal-Neva Lodge, the Riverside Club, Thunderbird Club, Carousel Club (Las Vegas), the Horseshoe Club, and the Holiday Inn Casino.

In early 1959, McWillie's boss Trafficante was arrested and jailed in the Trescornia Camp outside Havana. Within days of this incident, Jack Ruby contacted convicted Texas gun runner Robert Ray McKeown. In the 1950s, McKeown owned a manufacturing plant in Santiago, Cuba, but was forced to leave the island in 1957 after failing to pay kickbacks to Batista. In 1958, he received a two-year suspended sentence and five years on probation when convicted by U.S. authorities of conspiring to smuggle arms to Castro. His gun-running activities brought McKeown into close contact with two notable Cubans—one of whom was Fidel Castro. McKeown was photographed with the bearded leader during a visit to Houston in April 1959. He was also close to Carlos Prio Socarras, former president of Cuba, who quickly turned against Castro and became a leader of the anti-Castro Cubans in the United States.

It was due to this closeness to Cuban leaders that McKeown was contacted by telephone by a man who identified himself as "Jack Rubenstein of Dallas." The caller said he had obtained McKeown's phone number through a member of the Houston County Sheriff's Office and had thought his name was "Davis."

"Davis" was the same name that Ruby mentioned to his attorneys when asked if he knew of anyone that could damage their legal plea of momentary insanity for Ruby. Indeed, a gun runner named Tommy E. Davis not only was active in Texas at that time but during Ruby's trial showed up in Dallas and told Ruby's attorneys that he and Ruby had met several times to discuss the possibility of running arms to Cuba. However, Davis denied that anything came of this planning. Tommy Davis was linked to both U.S. intelligence and crime circles.

McKeown told the House Select Committee on Assassinations that Rubenstein—after Oswald was killed McKeown realized it was actually Jack Ruby—told him he represented Las Vegas interests that were seeking the release of three prisoners in Cuba. The caller offered $5,000 each for help in obtaining release of the prisoners. McKeown told the caller he would accept the offer if money were forthcoming. The man on the phone said he would think about it.

About three weeks later, McKeown said he was visited by a man at his business near Houston. The visitor was Ruby and this time Ruby said he had access to a large number of jeeps in Shreveport, Louisiana, which he was going to sell in Cuba. He offered McKeown $25,000 for a letter of introduction to Castro. Again, McKeown asked for money up front. He later claimed that Ruby "never returned nor did he ever see him again."

Of equal interest is McKeown's claim in later years that just weeks before the assassination, he was contacted by yet another man who wanted to buy weapons, particularly high-powered rifles with scopes. McKeown said this man indentified himself as "Lee Oswald."

In this story, which has been corroborated by a McKeown friend, Sam Neill, "Lee Oswald" and a man named Hernandez showed up at McKeown's home in late September or early October 1963, saying they were involved in planning a revolution in El Salvador.

Oswald, described as a "smart aleck" dressed only in shirtsleeves, then offered McKeown $10,000 for four .300 Savage automatic rifles each with a telescopic sight. McKeown said he refused to sell arms to "Oswald."

Both McKeown and his friend Neill independently recognized Oswald on November 22, 1963, as the man who had visited a few weeks earlier. However, both men decided to keep quiet about the Oswald visit, saying later they were "scared" to tell the FBI in 1964 what they knew. Indeed, a January 28, 1964, FBI document pertaining to McKeown's interview states: "To his knowledge, he has never seen or met Lee Harvey Oswald."

Although the House Committee pointed to inconsistencies in McKeown's various accounts of his contact with both Ruby and Oswald, on the whole—especially with the Neill corroboration—his story is suggestive to many researchers.

But there may be much more to it in light of the statements of a former poker partner of Ruby named James E. Beaird. Beaird told the *Dallas Morning News* in 1978 that he was an automobile dealer in Houston and knew that Ruby had been involved in arms deals near McKeown's home in Kemah, located southeast of Houston on Galveston Bay. Interviewed by the FBI in 1976, Beaird said he "personally saw many boxes of new guns, including automatic rifles and handguns" stored in a two-story house near the channel at Kemah. He said these arms were loaded onto what appeared to be a fifty-foot military-surplus boat nearby.

The FBI reported: "[Beaird] stated each time that the boat left with guns and ammunition, Jack Ruby was on board . . ." Beaird said Ruby would show up in Kemah usually on weekends and play poker to kill time until the boat was loaded. He told the FBI that he saw this operation take place at least twice while he was there.

Beaird said after the assassination, he contacted the FBI. In a newspaper article, he said he waited until 1966 and "nothing had come out [regarding Ruby's gun running], so I called them [FBI] just to find out why . . . I was curious. However, they didn't see fit to even mention it to me again, so I never heard of anything they ever opened up on it."

He said suddenly in 1976, an FBI agent showed up to talk to him. In his report, the agent wrote: ". . . there had been so much speculation as to possible foreign connections and [Beaird] thought it better not to mention his knowledge of Jack Ruby in Kemah." This FBI report made no mention of Beaird's attempt to tell the Bureau what he knew in 1966.

Yet another incident occurred in 1961 that indicates that Ruby's gun-running activities may not have ceased in 1959. Nancy Perrin Rich worked for Ruby and became involved in Cuban gun-running activities while married to Robert Perrin in Dallas. In interviews with both the FBI and Warren Commission, she related how her mob-connected husband met in 1961 with a group of anti-Castro Cubans. The meeting, which took place in a Dallas apartment, was presided over by a U.S. Army lieutenant colonel. During this meeting, her husband was offered $10,000 to bring a boatload of Cuban refugees to Miami. The couple demanded a cash retainer.

A few nights later, the Perrins met again with the Cubans, who apparently were expecting money. This time the Cubans mentioned taking stolen arms to Cuba and promised that more money was on the way. Rich told the Warren Commission: "I had the shock of my life. . . . A knock comes on the door and who walks in but my little friend Jack Ruby. . . . and everybody looks like . . . here comes the Savior."

Rich claimed to have detected a bulge in Ruby's jacket that disappeared quickly. That plus the fact that the Cubans' plans became more definite with Ruby's arrival led her to conclude that Ruby was the "bag man" bringing funds to the Cubans. She said she and her husband finally bowed out of the deal because they "smelled an element that I did not want to have any part of."

Less than a year after the meeting with the Cubans, Ruby, and the military officer, Perrin was found dead of arsenic poisoning. His death was ruled a suicide.

While McKeown claimed to have had no further contact with Jack Ruby and the Warren Commission proclaimed Ruby's jeep deal "abortive," something worked right, for shortly after a Ruby visit to Cuba in the summer of 1959, three Castro prisoners—Loran Hall, Henry Saavedra, and Santos Trafficante—were released from prison and ordered out of Cuba.

It may have all been due to Jack Ruby.

According to Elaine Mynier she was asked by Ruby to deliver a message to McWillie in Cuba not long after Castro took over. She told the FBI: "[It was] . . . a short-written message in code consisting of letters and numbers and including the word 'arriving.' "

On November 26, 1963, long before any in-depth investigation was done on Ruby's background, a British journalist, John Wilson, informed the American embassy in London that he had been held in the Trescornia Camp outside Havana with Trafficante in the summer of 1959. Wilson said there he "met an American gangster called Santos" and that "Santos was visited several times by an American gangster type named Ruby." Wilson claimed the man named Ruby would come to the prison with people bringing food to Trafficante.

Although Wilson is now dead, there is considerable corroboration to his story. In 1978, author Anthony Summers talked with the prison superintendent, who confirmed that the "English journalist" indeed was held in the same area as Trafficante. He also confirmed that Trafficante received special meals from one of the Havana hotels.

According to Ruby's travel documents, he stayed at the Capri Hotel, where Trafficante held a major interest.

This story is also corroborated by Gerry Hemming, a CIA agent who in 1959 was serving with Castro's forces. Hemming has said he saw Ruby in a meeting with Castro leader Captain William Morgan during this time and the talk centered around efforts to release Trafficante from prison.

There also is an intriguing mention of this matter in a confidential House Assassinations Committee briefing memorandum that stated: "Lewis J. McWillie, a close friend with Ruby and a man with many contacts among organized crime figures, indicates that in 1959 Jack Ruby traveled to Cuba and visited Santos Trafficante in jail."

Although during testimony before the House Select Committee on Assassinations, Trafficante plainly stated, "I never remember meeting Jack Ruby," the Committee concluded there was considerable evidence that such a meeting did take place.

Sources within the Dallas underworld claim Ruby was the middleman who, acting on orders of McWillie, bought Trafficante's freedom from Cuba with the sale of black-market jeeps to Castro.

While this has not yet been officially confirmed, it is certainly significant that there appears to have been much closer contact between Jack Ruby, Oswald's slayer, and Santos Trafficante, the mob boss who predicted that Kennedy would be "hit."

The fact that Ruby idolized the stylish, gray-haired McWillie and would do "anything" for his mentor is especially intriguing in light of the close association between McWillie and Trafficante.

And during those active days in 1959, Ruby made another astonishing contact—the Federal Bureau of Investigation. The Warren Commission was quietly notified in early 1964 that Jack Ruby had been contacted by the Bureau in 1959 as an informant but asked that the Commission keep this explosive fact a secret. The contents of this February 27, 1964 memo from Director Hoover to Warren Commission general counsel J. Lee Rankin was not made public until 1975. The memo, belatedly discovered through "a search of all files in the Dallas [FBI] office wherein references to Jack Ruby appeared," stated:

For your information, Ruby was contacted by an Agent of the Dallas Office on March 11, 1959, in view of his position as a nightclub operator who might have knowledge of the criminal element in Dallas. He was advised of the Bureau's jurisdiction in criminal matters, and he expressed a willingness to furnish information along these lines. He was subsequently contacted on eight occasions between March 11, 1959, and October 2, 1959, but he furnished no information whatever and further contacts with him were discontinued. Ruby was never paid any money, and he was never at any time an informant of this Bureau.

The Commission not only failed to see the significance of the nine meetings between the FBI and Ruby during the very time he was trying to free mob boss Trafficante, but also did not bother to question the FBI agent who had met with Ruby.

But many law-enforcement officers, both state and federal, have privately stated that both the frequency and duration of these Ruby contacts suggests there was more to the relationship than Hoover was admitting.

The House Select Committee on Assassinations did interview FBI Agent Charles W. Flynn, the agent who met with Ruby. According to Flynn, Ruby initiated the contacts on March 11, 1959, rather than the Bureau as stated in the Hoover memo. Flynn said Ruby told him he wanted to give information on a confidential basis and so Flynn opened a "Potential Criminal Informant," or PCI file on Ruby. Flynn said he closed the file on November 6, 1959, because Ruby had not been particularly helpful.

The House Committee staff also found this connection between Ruby and the FBI at the time Ruby was making trips to Cuba intriguing. The Committee's chief counsel later wrote:

Ruby could, of course, have contacted the FBI with no ulterior motive, and it could have been wholly unrelated to his Cuban activities . . . We [the Committee staff] believed, however, that Ruby's behavior was consistent with the pattern of seasoned offenders, who often cultivate a relationship with a law enforcement agency during a period when they are engaging in a criminal activity in the hope that, if they are caught, they can use the relationship to secure immunity from prosecution.

The House Committee also expressed interest in a post office box that Ruby used twelve times, coinciding with the times he met with Agent Flynn. Researchers have been equally intrigued by Ruby's purchase of miniature electronic bugging equipment during this time period, suggesting that Ruby's involvement with the Bureau was not as innocent as reported.

On April 27, 1959, shortly after his first contact with Agent Flynn and the day before their next scheduled meeting, Ruby rented safety deposit box 448 at Merchants State Bank in Dallas, where he maintained a small business checking account.

Sometime before he rented the bank box, Ruby bought more than $500 worth of tape-recording equipment. The saleswoman, contacted by Secret Service agents shortly after the assassination weekend, recalled that Ruby bought "a wristwatch which held a microphone for the equipment, and also an instrument to bug a telephone . . . [and a] tie clip and attaché case." An FBI agent also interviewed the saleswoman, but filed a meager two-paragraph report, omitting the descriptions of the electronic bugging equipment.

From the time Ruby acquired the safety deposit box through the fall of 1959, researchers have discerned a pattern—both before and after making a trip to Cuba, Ruby would enter this deposit box and then contact the FBI.

Flynn denied to the House Committee that he and Ruby discussed the Cuban visits, but in later years Flynn reportedly admitted to news reporters that Ruby may have mentioned one trip to Cuba.

And apparently Ruby was making no secret of his Cuban sojourns at the time. He sent a postcard from Havana to a girlfriend in Dallas and he was overheard telling one of his employees not to say where he was going "unless it were to the police or some other official agency."

It also should be noted that three days after Ruby shot Oswald, authorities in New Orleans received a tip that Jack Ruby had bought some paintings while in that city in the summer of 1959. While this information seemed hardly germane to the assassination, its source points to the involvement of U.S. Intelligence. For this bit of art news came from William George Gaudet, the CIA operative who accompanied Oswald to Mexico.

So apparently the CIA was tracking Ruby's movements in 1959, and after the assassination, Ruby was fearful that his activities in New Orleans— which obviously involved Cuba—would be found out.

The House Select Committee on Assassinations determined that Ruby may have made as many as six trips to Cuba, but most significantly, this issue was clouded and passed off by both the FBI and the Warren Commission.

When Warren Commission attorneys Leon Hubert and Burt Griffin— both assigned to the Ruby aspect of the investigation—requested further probing of Ruby's Cuban connections, they were rebuffed by both the CIA and other Commission staff members.

In later years, Warren Commission staffer Howard P. Willens—the liaison man with the Department of Justice—explained the Commission's reluctance to probe deeper by telling newsman Seth Kantor: ". . . these Cuban pursuits represented some kind of bottomless pit and our overall investigation had to be wrapped up."

Considered all together, the activities of Jack Ruby involving Cuba, Trafficante, McWillie, and the FBI represent a whole new dimension of the assassination—one that has yet to be fully explored.

But these connections, especially in light of the current theory of mob involvement in the assassination, certainly elevate Ruby far above the simple, emotional nightclub owner pictured by the Warren Commission.

The House Committee's chief counsel Robert Blakey, commenting on Ruby's connections with both mobsters and Cuba, wrote: "Our conclusion about Ruby in Cuba did not necessarily mean organized crime had a hand in the events in Dallas in 1963, but it did shift the balance in the careful process of weighing the evidence."

*   *   *

As the day of Kennedy's assassination approached, Jack Ruby remained in contact with a variety of mob figures both by telephone and in person.

One of the most intriguing incidents involved Johnny Roselli, the gangster involved with Santos Trafficante and Sam Giancana in the CIA-Mafia assassination plots.

It has now become known that beginning in the summer of 1963 and continuing into November, the FBI had Roselli under surveillance.

Researchers were surprised in later years that the Bureau had monitored two separate meetings between Roselli and Jack Ruby that occurred within two months of Kennedy's death. (Roselli, who later began to speak openly to columnist Jack Anderson, admitted to knowing Ruby, calling him "one of our boys.") What these meetings were about and why they were not reported to the Warren Commission is not known, but to most researchers this is yet another clear example of suppression of evidence by the FBI.

The Woman Who Foresaw the Assassination

One of the most intriguing stories to come out of the assassination case involved a woman who claimed to have worked for Ruby and who is on record as accurately predicting Kennedy's death.

On November 20, 1963, two days before the assassination, Louisiana State Police lieutenant Francis Fruge journeyed to Eunice, Louisiana, to pick up a woman who had received minor abrasions when she was thrown from a car. The woman appeared to be under the influence of some drug. She later was driven to the State Hospital in Jackson, Louisiana. On the way she told Fruge that she had been traveling with two men "who were Italians or resembled Italians" from Florida to Dallas. When Fruge asked her what she planned to do in Dallas, the woman replied: ". . . number one, pick up some money, pick up [my] baby and . . . kill Kennedy."

Thus began the strange saga of Melba Christine Marcades, better known as Rose Cheramie.

While at State Hospital, Cheramie told doctors there that Kennedy was to be killed in Dallas. She appeared quite lucid and hospital records studied by the House Select Committee on Assassinations reflect the woman was diagnosed as ". . . without psychosis. However, because of her previous record of drug addiction she may have a mild integrative and pleasure defect."

Dr. Victor Weiss told Committee investigators that Cheramie said she had worked for Jack Ruby and that her knowledge of the assassination came from "word in the underworld."

The day of the assassination, Lieutenant Fruge immediately remembered the woman and her apparent foreknowledge. He returned to State Hospital and took Cheramie into custody. During questioning she said the two men were on their way from Florida to Dallas to kill Kennedy. She said she was to receive $8,000 for her part in this activity and was then to accompany the two men to Houston to complete a drug deal and pick up her young son. She even gave Fruge the name of both a seaman and a ship that were involved in the drug deal and Fruge was able to verify this information through U.S. Customs.

Fruge also was able to verify the woman's story by talking to a Louisiana lounge owner. The owner related how two men and a woman had stopped at his lounge about November 20 and that the owner knew the men to be two pimps who regularly transported prostitutes from Florida. He said the woman became intoxicated and was taken outside after one of her companions "slapped her around."

Fruge said he soon contacted Dallas police captain Will Fritz, the man in charge of the assassination investigation, believing that he had uncovered valuable information. However, after Fritz told him he "wasn't interested," Fruge dropped his investigation.

Interestingly, the House Committee found that, while the FBI had no record of Cheramie's prognostication of the assassination, it did have reports that a Melba Marcades (Cheramie) had tipped Bureau agents that she was traveling to Dallas to deliver heroin to a man in Oak Cliff, then to Galveston to pick up a shipment of drugs. The Bureau had looked into the matter but decided that the woman's information was "erroneous in all respects."

On September 4, 1965, one month after yet another attempt to contact the FBI with similar information, Marcades/Cheramie was found dead by a highway near Big Sandy, Texas—a small town in East Texas about midway between Dallas and Louisiana. A man told authorities that Cheramie was lying in the roadway, apparently after being thrown from a car, and that he drove over her head while trying to avoid her. Police could find no relationship between the woman and the driver and the case was closed. However, Fruge later told researchers that when he attempted to contact the driver, he found the man's Tyler, Texas, address to be nonexistent.

While the entire Rose Cheramie episode was extensively covered in a staff report to the House Select Committee on Assassinations and essentially verified, oddly there was no mention of her in the Committee's report.

Did Ruby and Oswald Know Each Other?

Both federal investigations of the assassination announced publicly that they were unable to establish any link between Jack Ruby and Lee Harvey Oswald.

The Warren Commission flatly stated: "There is no evidence that Oswald and Ruby knew each other or had any relationship through a third party or parties."

Yet according to its own internal memos, Commission staffers were not all that certain. Arguing that further investigation was needed, Commission lawyers Burt Griffin and Leon Hubert wrote: "In short, we believe that the possibility exists, based on evidence already available, that Ruby was involved in illegal dealings with Cuban elements who might have had contact with Oswald."

The House Select Committee on Assassinations in its report seem to question the Warren Commission's conclusion by pointing out:

> The Commission also found no evidence that Ruby and Oswald had ever been acquainted, although the Commission acknowledged that they both lived in the Oak Cliff section of Dallas, [both] had post office boxes at the Terminal Annex, and had possible but tenuous third party links. These included Oswald's landlady, Earlene Roberts, whose sister, Bertha Cheek, had visited Ruby at his nightclub on November 18, and a fellow boarder at Oswald's roominghouse, John Carter, who was friendly with a close friend and employee of Ruby, Wanda Killam.

In fact, while leaving the impression that no link existed between Ruby and Oswald, the House Committee left the possibility open by stating:

> . . . the Committee's investigation of Oswald and Ruby showed a variety of relationships that may have matured into an assassination conspiracy. Neither Oswald nor Ruby turned out to be "loners," as they had been painted in the 1964 investigation.

And the body of evidence connecting Ruby and Oswald continues to grow.

As far back as 1964, Gen. Edwin A. Walker—himself a central figure in the assassination case—told this author:

> . . . the Warren Commission Report was ridiculous and a sham as well as an insult to the public's intelligence. Rubenstein knew Oswald; Oswald knew Rubenstein. The report would have to start all over on this basic fact.

Recall that Julia Ann Mercer identified both Ruby and Oswald as the men she saw near the Triple Underpass with a rifle shortly before the assassination and that Oswald's mother, Marguerite, claimed to have been shown a photograph of Jack Ruby by an FBI agent the night before Oswald was shot.

Stories have circulated around Dallas since 1963 about Ruby and Oswald being seen together. On November 26, 1963, the *Dallas Morning News* quoted Assistant D.A. Bill Alexander as saying: "[Investigators] have received at least a hundred tips [linking Oswald to Jack Ruby] and are checking out each one. As far as I know, none has panned out."

As early as Monday, November 25, 1963, newsmen were receiving information of a Ruby-Oswald link. Some were not easy to dismiss. Especially the number that grew out of experiences at Ruby's Carousel Club.

Madeleine Brown, the alleged mistress of Lyndon Johnson, worked for one of Dallas's leading advertising firms in 1963. She handled some of the agency's biggest accounts. After work, she and co-workers would unwind at various watering holes, including the Carousel Club. Brown recalled that in the spring of 1963 as she and her friends sat in the Carousel Club the conversation turned to speculation over who might have taken a shot at Gen. Edwin A. Walker. The group was surprised to hear Jack Ruby blurt out that the man who shot at Walker was Lee Oswald.

Brown took note of the name because she had never heard it before and because Ruby seemed so sure of the name of Walker's assailant. She was shocked the following November to see the names Ruby and Oswald tied to the assassination. She told this author:

I asked around and found out that many people knew that Oswald and Ruby knew each other. In fact, I just assumed that everyone knew this. I was surprised when, well into the 1980s, I learned that officially they were not supposed to be connected.

Another fascinating story was offered by former Dallas cabdriver Raymond Cummings. During the Garrison investigation, Cummings saw a news story with a photograph of David Ferrie and Ferrie's claim that he had never been in Dallas. Cummings contacted Garrison's office to tell how he had driven David Ferrie and Lee Harvey Oswald to Ruby's Carousel Club in the early part of 1963.

Even more convincing are the accounts of Ruby and Oswald together offered by employees of the Carousel Club. William D. Crowe, Jr., a magician and entertainer who was using the stage name Bill DeMar and performing in Ruby's Carousel Club at the time of the assassination, called a news media friend right after Oswald's arrest. He said Oswald had participated in his act just about a week prior to the assassination.

On November 25, Crowe told the Associated Press he was "positive" Oswald had patronized Ruby's club. He said:

I have a memory act in which I have 20 customers call out various objects in rapid order. Then I tell them at random what they called out. I am positive Oswald was one of the men that called out an object about nine days ago.

Crowe later told the *Dallas Morning News* that after the Associated Press story appeared, he was contacted by FBI agents who told him to check out of his Dallas hotel and go into hiding.

The Warren Commission Report went to great lengths to downplay Crowe's story, including quoting Crowe as saying: "... I never stated definitely, positively [that I saw Oswald], and they said I did, and all in all, what they had in the paper was hardly even close to what I told them."

Crowe was not asked why he told the same story of seeing Oswald to *Dallas Morning News* reporter Kent Biffle several days later.

The Warren Commission likewise brushed off the testimony of Dallas electronics salesman Robert K. Patterson, who said that Jack Ruby along with a man who looked like Oswald bought some equipment from him on November 1, 1963. Commissioners said Ruby's companion most likely was a Carousel Club employee named Larry Crafard who "bears a strong resemblance to Oswald."

The Commission noted that at least four other persons had told them of seeing Oswald in the Carousel Club, but these stories also were dismissed.

The Commission made no mention of Rose Cheramie or Beverly Oliver, the Dealey Plaza assassination witness who told researchers she was introduced to "Lee Oswald of the CIA" by Ruby a few weeks before the assassination.

Oliver, now a Christian evangelist using another name, told British television:

I purposely waited this long [to publicly tell the story] because I felt threatened . . . I didn't want to become another statistic. About two weeks prior to the assassination, between shows [She was a singer at the nearby Colony Club and would frequently visit Ruby's Carousel Club], I trotted over. There was this girl who danced there by the name of Jada. And she was sitting at a table with Jack Ruby and another man. I went and sat down with them to have a drink. As I sat down, Ruby introduced me to this man. He said, "Beverly, this is my friend Lee." And after Jack Ruby went into the police station and killed Lee Harvey Oswald, it was then I realized it was the man I had met in the club two weeks before the assassination . . . Jack Ruby and Lee Harvey Oswald were linked together but I don't know how . . . But I know in my heart that Lee Harvey Oswald, or the man shot in the police station, was the man I met in the club two weeks before the assassination.

She also told researcher Gary Shaw of meeting David Ferrie in the Carousel Club. She said Ferrie was there so often that she initially took him to be assistant manager of the club.

This story is buttressed by other Carousel employees who recalled seeing Ruby and Oswald together.

Karen Bennett Carlin, who danced in Ruby's club using the name

"Little Lynn," was the woman to whom Ruby mailed a twenty-five-dollar money order minutes before shooting Oswald. Interviewed by the FBI on November, 24, 1963, Carlin "seemed on the verge of hysteria." FBI agent Roger C. Warner reported:

> Mrs. Carlin was highly agitated and was reluctant to make any statement to me. She stated to me that she was under the impression that Lee Oswald, Jack Ruby, and other individuals unknown to her, were involved in a plot to assassinate President Kennedy and that she would be killed if she gave any information to the authorities.

Another Ruby dancer, Janet Adams Conforto, known as "Jada," told Dallas newsmen shortly after the assassination that she had seen Oswald in the Carousel Club. Likewise, Bill Willis, a musician at the club, reportedly recalled Oswald sitting "right in the corner of the [Club's] stage and runway."

Ruby stripper Kathy Kay told the *Dallas Times Herald* in 1975 that she recalled seeing Oswald in the club and even danced with him on one occasion.

This account is supported by Bobbie Louise Meserole, who danced at the Carousel club under the name Shari Angel. Meserole, now an ordained minister in Dallas who remembers Jack Ruby fondly, told this author she recalled conversations with Kathy Kay and others in which they laughingly told how Ruby had ordered Kay to dance a bump and grind to embarrass Oswald.

But the most ominous story of this kind came from Shari Angel's husband, Walter "Wally" Weston, who was the Carousel Club's master of ceremonies until five days before the assassination. In a 1976 interview with the *New York Daily News,* Weston said he had seen Oswald with Ruby in the Carousel Club at least twice prior to the assassination. Weston recalled:

> I was working in the club one night approximately three weeks before the assassination. I was on stage, doing my bit, and this guy was standing near the back wall. The club was pretty crowded. The guy walked up in the middle of the club, right in front of the stage, and for no reason he said, "I think you're a Communist." I said, "Sir, I'm an American. Why don't you sit down." He said, "Well, I still think you're a Communist," so I jumped off the stage and hit him. Jack was right behind him when I hit him. He landed in Jack's arms and Jack grabbed him and said, "You [son of a bitch], I told you never to come in here." And he wrestled him to the door and threw him down the stairs.

After the assassination, Weston said he recognized Oswald as the man in the club but did not say anything when questioned briefly by the FBI and a Dallas detective because he was afraid after discussing the matter with other Carousel employees. He said:

> [Carousel drummer] Billy Willis saw me hit [Oswald]. When I discussed it with him [and dancer Kathy Kay], he said, "Wally, the best thing to do is to stay out of it. Just keep your mouth shut. Don't say anything. That's what I'm going to do. I don't want any part of this."

Weston visited Ruby in jail several times. He recalled: "The one time I mentioned it to him, I said, 'Jack, wasn't that the guy I hit in the club?' He just looked at me and didn't say yes or no."

Another reason Weston decided to talk in 1976 was that he claimed to have "bumped into" a gangster in Fort Lauderdale, Florida, who had been at a meeting with Ruby in the Carousel Club five days before the assassination. In an published interview, Weston said: "[This guy] said to me, 'I know you, you were Jack Ruby's emcee.' I asked him when he had been at the Carousel Club and he told me he was at the table the night the gun went on the floor."

The shaken Weston vividly recalled that night:

> There was a meeting held at Jack Ruby's club the night I left there, which was five days before the assassination of President Kennedy. There were approximately six to eight guys from Chicago who came into the club—friends of Jack Ruby. I first really noticed them at about 1:30 in the morning, right before closing. Four of them were sitting at a front table, the rest hung around the bar. I was on stage telling jokes and while I was up there, the ones at the table were talking to each other. So I walked to the front of the stage where they were sitting and said, "Hey, you guys, cool it." One of them looked at the others and said, "Who is this son of a bitch?" and he pulled a gun out of his waistband. . . . It looked like a cannon pointed in my direction. At this precise time, two uniformed policemen came in the front door. They just happened to walk in—which was not unusual at Jack's club. I said to the four guys at the table, "The police are here." The gun went to the floor immediately and was kicked over to the side. Jack Ruby, in the meantime, was explaining to the policemen that everything was all right and that there was no problem. After the show, Jack introduced me to the men . . . He didn't introduce them to me by name, he just said, "These are friends of mine from Chicago."

Weston might not have thought too much about this incident except that he returned to the club after closing to retrieve his jacket. One of the men from Chicago opened the door but refused to allow him inside. When he asked the man to go get Jack Ruby the man also refused, saying "You can't come in now." Understanding that something very secret was going on in the club, Weston left.

After the assassination, Weston kept quiet, later explaining, "In the nightclub business, you take your money and you keep your mouth shut."

But in 1976, after encountering one of the Chicago toughs who had been at the meeting, Weston decided he should tell his story. Incredible as Weston's story seems, there are at least two people who have corroborated it. A convicted murderer and mobster named Myron Thomas Billet, also known as Paul Buccilli, admitted in 1976 that he attended just such a meeting in Ruby's club. Billet stated:

> I was at the Whitemarsh Valley Country Club back in the late part of 1963 when I was contacted by the Mob for a meeting in Dallas at Jack Ruby's Carousel Club. As I remember it, there was myself, Jack Ruby, Lee Oswald, Sam Giancana, John Roselli, and an FBI man. The meeting was to set up a "hit" on John F. Kennedy. I can't say what the arrangement was because Sam and I left. Sam told me he wanted nothing to do with it. Hell, he helped put Kennedy in office. But three weeks later, JFK was hit and we all knew it wasn't done by one man. Sam told me then that he figured this would get us all killed before it was over.

Then there is the experience of Ester Ann Mash, which was made public only recently. Mash, who still lives in the Dallas area, told this author she served drinks at a meeting in the Carousel Club that included "gangsters" from Chicago, Jack Ruby, and Lee Harvey Oswald.

She had been a waitress at a restaurant near Love Field when a Dallas detective introduced her to Ruby early in 1963. Shortly after their introduction, Ruby enticed her into working at the Carousel Club, but only as a waitress and champagne hostess. She explained: "He wanted me to strip, but I just couldn't bring myself to do that." In addition to her club duties, Mash became a lover to Ruby, who she said took her to gambling parties around Dallas.

In the late spring of 1963, she said Ruby asked her to serve drinks at a gathering in a meeting area of the Carousel Club. Mash said the meeting was composed of Ruby, five "gangster types," and a young man who only sipped beer. She described the meeting:

> I had to follow Jack's orders to the letter for that meeting. He demanded absolute privacy and no interruptions. I was the only person allowed to enter the room and that was just to serve the drinks and then get out. Five men dressed in suits, looking very businesslike, came in about ten thirty that night. They were all dark, swarthy men who looked like gangsters out of some movie. There was another man, dressed real casual—he didn't look like he fit in with the rest of the group at all.

There were seven all together [including Ruby]. They talked until about one o'clock in the morning. Then the men in suits left. Jack went to his apartment behind the club. And the other guy stayed until closing watching the strippers. He couldn't take his eyes off them. That man was Lee Harvey Oswald. I really remember him because he was so unusual from the rest. He kept ordering beer. Everyone else drank mixed drinks but this wimpy-looking little guy. I might not remember a name, but I always remember a face. It was a serious meeting and although I did not overhear what they were talking about at the time, I am convinced that they were discussing killing Kennedy. I knew it had something to do with the Mafia because everybody in town in those days knew Ruby had something to do with the mob. Also, Jack asked me to take care of these guys, so later I played up to them a little and discovered they were Mafia guys from Chicago.

About two months after this meeting, Mash had a falling-out with Ruby. She explained:

He accused me of bringing the vice squad to the club but I didn't. But he wouldn't listen to me. He cussed me out. It upset me, so I left. Also, it was real strange, but I had a very bad feeling, a premonition, that I had better get away from Dallas. So I moved to Euless and got a job in a restaurant, then later moved to Phoenix. I was not even in Dallas the day of the assassination. I did not pay much attention to the news after the assassination. But then on Sunday morning, my children were watching TV when they were showing them moving Oswald. Ruby shot him and I screamed, "Oh, my god!" I couldn't believe my eyes. I thought, "That's the weird little man who was at that secret meeting with Jack and those Mafia types. I saw that grin on Oswald's face on TV the day Jack shot him. He was smiling because Jack was his friend. I didn't want to be involved, so I kept quiet. But now I have a blood clot on the right side of my brain as a result of a car accident. I've already lived longer than I am supposed to. That's the reason I'm telling you this now. Somebody needs to know this before I die.

But an even more damning story concerning Ruby and Oswald comes from a credible, if eccentric, attorney named Carroll Jarnagin. Jarnagin explained to this author that he visited Ruby's Carousel Club on October 4, 1963, to discuss a legal case with one of Ruby's strippers. While seated in a booth at the club, Jarnagin overheard Jack Ruby—whom he knew well—talking with another man. Jarnagin heard the man tell Ruby, "Don't use my real name. I'm going by the name of O. H. Lee." This, of course, was the name used by Lee Harvey Oswald to rent a room on North Beckley in Oak Cliff.

Jarnagin described this meeting:

These men were talking about plans to kill the governor of Texas. Ruby explained, "He [Governor Connally] won't work with us on paroles. With a few of the right boys out we could really open up this state, with a little cooperation from the governor." Then Ruby offered Lee a drug franchise. Ruby also said that the boys really wanted to kill Robert Kennedy. Lee offered to go to Washington to do the job. They then discussed using public lockers and pay telephones as part of hiding their plot. Ruby assured Lee that he could shoot Connally from a window in the Carousel Club and then escape out a back door. Lee was asking for money. He wanted half of the money in advance, but Ruby told him he would get one lump sum after the job was done.

One thing that sets Jarnagin's story apart from the others is that he contacted authorities with his information prior to the assassination. The day after hearing Ruby's conversation, Jarnagin telephoned the Texas Department of Public Safety. Nothing came of this.

Jarnagin stated:

[After Ruby shot Oswald] I definitely realized that the picture in the November 23, 1963, *Dallas Times Herald* of Lee Harvey Oswald was a picture of the man using the name O. H. Lee, whose conversation with Jack Ruby I had overheard back on October 4, 1963.

After the assassination, Jarnagin again contacted the authorities, this time the Dallas police and the FBI. He was interviewed but his startling account of a Ruby-Oswald plot was buried deep in the volumes of the Warren Commission and never mentioned in its report.

In fact, the Warren Commission quickly dismissed rumors circulating throughout Dallas in 1963–64 that Ruby and Oswald knew each other by stating: "All assertions that Oswald was seen in the company of Ruby or anyone else at the Carousel Club have been investigated. None of them merits any credence."

Jarnagin said when he tried to tell the FBI what he knew, agents accused him of having hallucinations. The attorney said: "It was clearly abuse of a witness."

The disparate meeting times given in these reports—Mash said late spring 1963; Weston indicated about mid-October, while Jarnagin pinpointed October 4, 1963—and the people involved indicate the possibility that more than one meeting between Ruby and Oswald occurred.

And neither the FBI nor the Warren Commission ever talked to Rose Cheramie, Beverly Oliver, Ester Mash, Wally Weston, Shari Angel, or Madeleine Brown.

But there is tantalizing evidence that authorities knew more than they were telling about a relationship between Oswald and Ruby. In 1976, four Dallas deputy constables told the *Dallas Morning News* that shortly after the assassination they had examined a boxful of handwritten notes and other papers in the Dallas County Courthouse that linked Ruby and Oswald together.

Deputy Billy Preston said he and Constable Robie Love (now deceased) handed the box of documents over to Dallas D.A. Henry Wade in late 1963 or early 1964. Wade told the paper he didn't recall receiving the papers.

Preston, along with deputy constables Mike Callahan and Ben Cash, said the box of papers came from the apartment of a Dallas woman. Preston explained: "She was really scared because she had all that stuff. She wanted me to pick it up for her. And I just wished I had made some more copies now."

Preston could not recall the woman's name other than "Mary," but then and now he believes she had some connection with Oswald because most of the box's contents appeared to have been written by him.

Cash, however, recalled that the box came from the woman's roommate who had kept it for a Latin American boyfriend. Cash told reporter Earl Golz:

The impression I got [was that] the papers were from the Latin American because he mentioned Ruby and he mentioned Oswald in the writings. He didn't mention the third party but he kept referring to a third party. And the third party would have to be him.

Among the papers in the box, according to the deputies, were newspaper clippings from Mexico, a photocopy of a press card with the words "Daily Worker" issued to Ruby, a receipt from a motel near New Orleans dated several weeks before the assassination with both the names Ruby and Oswald on it and references to calls to Mexico City, papers pinpointing a landing strip somewhere in Mexico, and references to meetings with "agents" in the border towns of McAllen and Laredo. There was also a church brochure with markings indicating something about going to Cuba.

Preston said one handwritten note referred to a plan to assassinate President Kennedy during the dedication of a lake or dam in Wisconsin. (Law officials in Wisconsin had speculated in December 1963 about the existence of just such a plan after discovering what appeared to be Lee Harvey Oswald's signature on the registry of a restaurant in Hubertus, Wisconsin, dated September 16, 1963. Kennedy indeed had made a speech on September 24, 1963, in Ashland, Wisconsin, as part of a nationwide conservation tour. The FBI rejected the signature as Oswald's and this subject received little attention outside Wisconsin.)

Deputy Cash explained why the men had not made this story public earlier:

Because at that time it was a pretty hot issue, you remember. So we kept quiet and went along with the game. We figured it would be handled on a higher level [than us]. And when it didn't come out, we thought at that time possibly they [the Warren Commission] thought that kind of information tying it into the Cubans or Russians couldn't be released at that time because it might put us in World War III.

Wade finally admitted that the incident with the box of documents "might well have happened," but added, "but I know that whatever they had didn't amount to nothing." Whether it did or not may never be known because as far as any official investigation, the box simply never existed.

With the disappearance of any documentation of a Ruby-Oswald link, researchers are left with only a multiplicity of anecdotes and stories. But the number and consistency of these stories—coupled with the demonstrable efforts on the part of both Dallas and federal authorities to suppress and ignore such evidence—leads most researchers to conclude that the stories that still circulate in Dallas of a Ruby-Oswald relationship may have some basis in fact.

Even former Dallas police chief Jesse Curry seems to indicate such a relationship existed in his 1969 book by noting: "Witnesses to the shooting [of Oswald] wondered if there wasn't a gleam of recognition in Oswald's eye when Ruby stepped out from the newsmen. . . ."

*   *   *

Whether it can ever be conclusively proven that Ruby and Oswald were in contact, there is no doubt that Ruby was in touch with associates of mob and Teamster leaders—and that telephone calls with them markedly increased in the days leading up to the assassination.

In March 1963, Ruby made fewer than ten long-distance calls and from May to September this number averaged between twenty-five and thirty-five. But Ruby's toll calls climbed to more than seventy in October and almost one hundred in November.

This surge in phone traffic also intrigued Warren Commission investigators Hubert and Griffin, who asked the FBI to make a thorough examination of all calls by Ruby, his family, and associates. They also requested the Bureau to have phone companies in Texas, Nevada, Los Angeles, San Francisco, Chicago, Detroit, Boston, New York, Washington, Miami, and New Orleans freeze all records until they could be studied by the Commission staff.

Apparently this was never done. Griffin later told the House Select Committee on Assassinations that while the Bureau did compile some telephone information, it was not the comprehensive check he had asked for and that "no request to freeze records was made to telephone companies." When the House Committee got around to requesting these same records, most had been routinely destroyed.

Nevertheless, enough information on Ruby's calls has become available to paint a portrait of a man frantically touching bases across the nation as November 22, 1963 approached. Some of Ruby's calls could be dismissed as obviously personal or business communications, although some—such as frequent calls to Harold Tannenbaum, who ran several New Orleans nightclubs that were owned at least in part by mob boss Carlos Marcello—may have served double purposes.

For instance, Ruby made at least seven traceable calls to his "mentor," gambler Lewis McWillie, beginning in June 1963. He also was in touch with Irwin S. Weiner, a bondsman and insurance agent connected with Santos Trafficante, Sam Giancana, and several other crime-syndicate figures. He also placed a seventeen-minute call in early November to Robert "Barney" Baker, identified as "Hoffa's ambassador of violence" by Attorney General Robert Kennedy.

Near the end of October, Ruby placed a call to Nofio Pecora, one of Marcello's closest associates. The House Committee developed information that Pecora owned the Tropical Court Tourist Park, a New Orleans trailer court in which Tannenbaum lived.

When questioned by House investigators, all of these telephone contacts said the Ruby calls were innocuous and pertained only to some union problems Ruby was having with the American Guild of Variety Artists (AGVA).

The Committee concluded: "We were no more satisfied with [this] explanation than we were with McWillie's, Weiner's, or Baker's."

But union disagreements were not the only problem facing Ruby in the fall of 1963.

According to the Warren Commission:

In 1960, the government filed tax liens for more than $20,000 [against Ruby]. In November 1962, the government rejected Ruby's offer to pay $8,000 to compromise the assessed taxes of more than $20,000 because he had not filed returns for other federal taxes and had not paid these taxes as they became due. These other taxes . . . amounted to an additional $20,000.

The House Committee determined that Ruby's tax liability may have been closer to $60,000 than the $40,000 mentioned by the Warren Commission.

Testimony from Ruby's friends and acquaintances confirmed that he was complaining of his tax debts to anyone who would listen.

One June 6, 1963, Ruby's attorney, Graham R. E. Koch, informed the Internal Revenue Service that his client would settle his debts "as soon as arrangements can be made to borrow money . . ." However, an FBI check of more than fifty banking institutions revealed no attempt by Ruby to borrow money legitimately.

Did Ruby turn to the mob for help? His flurry of phone calls would seem to indicate this as well as a secret trip to Las Vegas two weekends prior to the assassination.

Recall that Marguerite Oswald claimed she was fired from her job after her employers made a trip to Las Vegas. The Warren Commission rejected the idea that Ruby visited America's gambling capital, but the House Committee found "credible evidence" that Ruby was there. Both a cashier and the credit manager of the Stardust Hotel recalled that a man named Ruby, who claimed to own a club in Dallas, attempted to cash a check one weekend in mid-November. The FBI confirmed this trip through "confidential information."

Ruby's lawyer later told newsman Seth Kantor that it was right after this alleged trip that Ruby told him "he had a connection who would supply him with money to settle his long-standing government tax problems."

Taking the long view, House Committee chief counsel Robert Blakey noted: "Ruby's business was in deep financial difficulty, complicated by the dispute with AGVA over 'amateur' strippers and serious tax problems."

After pointing out Ruby's union and tax problems as well as his capacity for violence, his underworld missions to Cuba, and his familiarity with the Dallas police, Blakey concluded: "Whatever else may be inferred from Ruby's conduct in the summer and fall of 1963, it at least established that he was an available means to effect Oswald's elimination."

The Shooting of Lee Harvey Oswald

The Warren Commission—and hence the news media—reported in 1963–64 that the shooting of Lee Harvey Oswald by Jack Ruby was the spontaneous act of a grief-stricken man who was concerned with the possibility of Mrs. Kennedy having to return to Dallas to testify against Oswald. Today that story, still repeated in the news media, has been shown to be a lie and a legal ploy.

Less than three hours after shooting Oswald, Ruby was visited by Dallas attorney Tom Howard. Months later during his trial, Ruby scribbled a note to attorney Joe H. Tonahill saying: "Joe, you should know this. Tom Howard told me to say that I shot Oswald so that Caroline and Mrs. Kennedy wouldn't have to come to Dallas to testify. Okay?"

Ruby also admitted this ploy to attorney Melvin Belli, as recorded in his book, *Dallas Justice*. Belli wrote that Ruby told him: "We know I did it for Jackie and the kids. . . . Maybe I ought to forget this silly story that I'm telling, and get on the stand and tell the truth."

These confessions coupled with the movements of Ruby during the assassination weekend all portray a man who consciously stalked Oswald—propelled by motives that were not his own—before finally shooting him in the basement of the Dallas Police Station.

According to information developed by both the Warren Commission and the House Select Committee on Assassinations, Ruby awoke about 9:30 A.M. on the day of the assassination and drove to the offices of the

Dallas Morning News, where he tried to visit entertainment columnist Tony Zoppi. Failing to find Zoppi, Ruby said he went to the paper's advertising office and began to compose ad copy for his club.

Ruby claimed to have remained at the paper from nearly 11 A.M. until well after the assassination and several *News* employees, such as John Newnam and Wanda Walker, confirmed this. However, all the accounts of Ruby at the newspaper contain gaps when he was out of sight. One reporter told the FBI that Ruby was "missed for a period of about twenty to twenty-five minutes" before reappearing shortly after the assassination.

Considering the *Dallas Morning News* is only two blocks from Dealey Plaza, there is every reason to believe that Ruby could have been there—as claimed by Julia Ann Mercer, Jean Hill, Phil Willis, and Policeman Tom Tilson—and still hurried back to the paper before 1 P.M.

If fact, many researchers and others have claimed that Ruby's presence at the *News* was a stratagem calculated to give him an iron-clad alibi for the time of the assassination. His visit certainly achieved this purpose, if it was so planned.

According to Ruby, he drove back to the Carousel Club after learning of the assassination at the newspaper. However, club employee Andrew Armstrong later stated that Ruby did not come to the club until nearly 2 P.M. and several witnesses—newsmen Seth Kantor and Roy Stamps and Wilma Tice—placed Ruby at Parkland Hospital.

Ruby made several phone calls from the Carousel Club that afternoon and was visibly upset, according to the accounts of employees.

He claimed he left the club late in the afternoon, but was reported seen in the crowded Dallas Police Headquarters between 4 and 4:30 P.M. Various persons, including a reporter and policemen, placed Ruby at the police station at different places and time between 4 P.M. and 7:30 P.M.

By 9 P.M., according to phone records, Ruby was back at his apartment, and at 10 P.M., he visited a Dallas synagogue.

Shortly after 11 P.M. Ruby was back at Dallas Police Headquarters armed with about a dozen sandwiches he had bought to give to officers.

One officer has even told Texas researchers he saw Ruby enter Captain Fritz's office while Oswald was undergoing interrogation.

Ruby was still there shortly after midnight when Oswald was taken to a basement assembly room for a news conference. Mingling with newsmen, Ruby ended up in the rear of the room, where he elbowed his way onto a table past news photographer Tony Record. Record later said he thought Ruby was a fellow newsman but could not understand his insistence on standing on the table when he didn't carry a camera.

It was during this news conference that a singular incident occurred that many researchers have pointed to as evidence of Ruby's intimate knowledge of Oswald and his activities. Dallas D.A. Henry Wade, in briefing newsmen about Oswald's background, stated he belonged to the Free Cuba

Committee. Whereupon Ruby corrected Wade by shouting out: "Henry, that's the Fair Play for Cuba Committee."

While Ruby later claimed to have heard of Oswald's Fair Play for Cuba Committee affiliation over a local radio station that afternoon, it nevertheless struck researchers as most odd that this nightclub owner with no known politics would note the difference between the anti-Castro Free Cuba Committee and the pro-Castro Fair Play for Cuba Committee. Of course, this knowledge would not seem at all odd if the accounts of a Ruby-Oswald relationship are true.

The midnight news conference was tumultuous and if Ruby's plan was to silence Oswald there, it is obvious there was never a clear shot.

Ruby contented himself by helping to set up an interview between Wade and radio station KLIF. Ruby later explained his actions by saying: "I think it is a childish thing, but I met Henry Wade some time back and I knew he would recognize me."

The remainder of the night Ruby was a nervous bundle of activity. He reportedly brought sandwiches and drinks to news personnel at KLIF radio and sometime after 2 A.M. drove around downtown encountering one of his strippers, Kay Coleman (known as Kathy Kay) with Dallas policeman Harry Olsen. During this supposedly chance meeting, Ruby was exhorted to move against Oswald, if his account can be believed. He told the Warren commission:

> . . . they talked and they carried on, and they thought I was the greatest guy in the world, and he stated they should cut this guy [Oswald] into ribbons, and so on. And she said, "Well, if he was in England, they would drag him through the streets and would have hung him." . . .
> They kept me from leaving. They were constantly talking and were in a pretty dramatic mood. They were crying and carrying on.

Ruby claimed he then went to the *Dallas Times Herald* where he delivered a twist board—one of his many sales gimmicks—to a composing-room worker. Returning to his apartment, he said he picked up his roommate, George Senator, then returned to his club.

At the club he claimed to have gathered up a Polaroid camera, some film, and employee Larry Crafard, and to have driven out on a Dallas expressway to photograph an IMPEACH EARL WARREN sign before returning to bed.

Later during the day Saturday, Ruby was back at the police station and he telephoned a local radio station asking for any news about when Oswald would be transferred to the county jail. He was seen about town by several people and even claimed to have visited Dealey Plaza where he ". . . saw the wreaths on the Plaza and started to cry again."

After brief stops at the Carousel Club and the Dallas Police Station, Ruby reportedly was at his apartment during the early part of the evening.

Then he drove to his club, made some phone calls, then visited the Pago Club. After stopping again briefly at the closed Carousel Club, Ruby claimed to have gone back to his apartment and gone to bed.

All in all, even considering that much of what is known of Ruby's movements during that weekend is confusing and contradictory, it is evident that the man was in a nervous, anxious condition and touching bases all over town—especially the Dallas Police Station where Oswald was being held.

The House Select Committee on Assassinations noted: "These sightings, along with the one on Friday night, could indicate that Ruby was pursuing Oswald's movements throughout the weekend."

And it was in the early morning hours of November 24, 1963, that Ruby may have tried to avert his rapidly approaching confrontation with Oswald. Even the Warren Commission noted this strange incident by reporting:

. . . between 2:30 and 3 A.M., the local office of the FBI and the sheriff's office received telephone calls from an unidentified man who warned that a committee had decided "to kill the man that killed the President." . . . The police department and ultimately Chief Curry were informed of both threats.

What the public was not told was that the man who took one of the calls recognized the voice of Jack Ruby! Dallas police lieutenant Billy R. Grammer was a young officer working in the communications room early on November 24, 1963. A man called and asked to know who was on duty that morning. After hearing Grammer's name, the caller asked to speak with him. Refusing to give his name—the caller said cryptically "I can't tell you that, but you know me,"—the man detailed to Grammer the plans to transfer Oswald, even to the use of a decoy vehicle, and added: "You're going to have to make some other plans or we're going to kill Oswald right there in the basement." Grammer and his superior took the warning seriously to the extent of writing up a report for Chief Curry.

Later in the morning Grammer was awakened by his wife who told him that Jack Ruby had just shot Oswald in the basement of the police station. A stunned Grammer told his wife that he suddenly realized that the familiar voice on the phone was Ruby's. In 1988, Grammer told British television that he remains convinced that the caller was Ruby—especially in light of a chance meeting and conversation that he had with Ruby in a restaurant near police headquarters only a week before the call.

Of course, if the caller was Ruby and if he did have inside knowledge of the Oswald transfer, then it is clear that the shooting of Oswald involved others besides Ruby.

Despite these clear warnings and a few minor changes in the transfer plans as a result, the execution of Oswald went off according to plan.

Ruby told the FBI and the Warren Commission that he remained at his apartment until after 10 A.M. on that Sunday morning when he left to mail a money order to Lynn Carlin, but several witnesses and a call from a cleaning lady seem to belie that notion.

Ruby's roommate Senator also tried to say that Ruby was home in the early morning but his story proved inconsistent and even the Warren Commission expressed suspicions about it.

As early as 8 A.M. Warren Richey, a cameraman for WBAP-TV in nearby Fort Worth, reported seeing a man that he was "positive, pretty sure in my own mind" was Jack Ruby in front of the Dallas Police Station. Richey's observation was corroborated by two other WBAP newsmen, Ira Walker and John Smith. Smith also saw the man about 8 A.M. and, with Walker, about 10 A.M. when the same man approached them and asked, "Has [Oswald] been brought down yet?"

The three newsmen were amazed a short time later when Ruby's mug shot was broadcast over the air. Walker told the Warren Commission: "Well, about four of us pointed at him at the same time in the [mobile broadcast] truck, I mean, we all recognized him at the same time." Characteristically, the Warren Commission downplayed their testimony and suggested they were all mistaken, choosing rather to believe Ruby.

The Commission also failed to seriously consider the statements of Ray Rushing, a Plano, Texas preacher who had tried to visit Oswald at the police station that morning. Shortly after Oswald's death, Rushing told Dallas police lieutenant Jack Revill that he had held a brief conversation with Ruby about 9:30 A.M. during a ride in a police station elevator. Revill, in his report, evaluated Rushing as "truthful," but noted that District Attorney Wade "didn't need [Rushing's] testimony, because he had placed Ruby there the morning of the shooting."

Was Ruby at his apartment as he claimed rather than skulking about the police station? A call from a cleaning woman has been used to show that he was indeed home. However, consider the call made by sixty-year-old Mrs. Elnora Pitts. Pitts, who had the ongoing job of cleaning Ruby's apartment every Sunday, called sometime just after 8 A.M. November 24. She told the Warren Commission she called each Sunday to verify if she should work that day.

She said a man answered and she identified herself but the man didn't seem to recognize her name or the fact that she was to clean the apartment. Finally the man said, "Yes, you can come, but you call me." "That's what I'm doing now . . ." replied the exasperated Mrs. Pitts. By now the woman was frightened by this man who didn't seem to know her. She also said the man "sounded terrible strange to me . . . he never did sound like hisself."

But regardless of where Jack Ruby was earlier on Sunday morning, he was definitely in the Western Union office located just down the street from the police station at 11:17 A.M. That is the time stamped on Ruby's receipt for twenty-five dollars, which he was sending to Karen Carlin in

Fort Worth. Carlin, who also had worked for Pat Kirkwood's Cellar in Fort Worth, told Dallas police she had talked to Ruby earlier that morning:

> I needed twenty-five dollars to pay my rent and he said he had to go downtown anyway, so he would send it to Western Union in Fort Worth. Jack seemed upset. I picked the money up at Western Union ten minutes after we heard he had shot Oswald. I was afraid they would keep my money or something, since Jack had sent it, but they gave it to me without question. When I talked to him that morning, he sounded like his voice was going to crack any minute and he did sound like he had been crying and was very upset. I had to keep saying, "Jack, Jack, are you there?" and he would say, "Yes."

The time Ruby sent the twenty-five-dollar money order was only four minutes from the time he shot Oswald.

For years, supporters of the official version of the assassination have argued that if Ruby intended to shoot Oswald he could not have known that the transfer would be delayed almost an hour and he would not have sent the money order. Therefore, they say, Ruby's shooting of Oswald must have been a spontaneous act.

Most serious researchers now understand that the shooting of Oswald was not predicated on Ruby knowing the exact time of his transfer, but rather conversely that Oswald was transferred only after Ruby was in a position to shoot him.

This idea of a conspiracy to silence Oswald is based on several known facts. One of the most tantalizing of these is the story told by respected reporter Seth Kantor, author of *Who Was Jack Ruby?* According to Kantor, George Senator, Ruby's roommate, was at the Eatwell Café near the police station the morning Ruby shot Oswald. Reportedly Senator went to a pay phone and called Dallas attorney Jim Martin and asked Martin to represent his friend Ruby for murdering the accused assassin, Lee Harvey Oswald.

Minutes later news came over the radio that Oswald had been shot. Yet, Ruby's roommate was arranging legal representation *before* the event.

Other facts pointing to a conspiracy to kill Oswald include the fact that Ruby was in and out of the police station the entire weekend, apparently stalking Oswald; Ruby (or someone) tried to warn the authorities of Oswald's death even relating specific police precautions; and both the mob and the federal government had enough leverage on Ruby to force him to such an act.

Only a minute or so before the Oswald shooting, Ruby's initial lawyer, Tom Howard—the one who cooked up his concern over Mrs. Kennedy as a motive—entered the police station and peered through the basement jail office window just as Oswald was being taken off the elevator. Dallas detective H. L. McGee later that day reported:

. . . At this time, Oswald was brought off the jail elevator and Tom Howard turned away from the window and went back toward the Harwood Street door. He waved at me as he went by and said, "That's all I wanted to see." Shortly after that I heard a shot.

Detective Jim Leavelle, one of the men handcuffed to Oswald, told this author he never understood the reason for the nearly one-hour delay in transferring Oswald, but that Capt. Will Fritz gave him the order to move just after conferring with FBI and Secret Service officials.

In 1963–64, the federal government in the form of the Warren Commission offered a simple explanation for Oswald's death. It stated that Ruby strolled down the police department's Main Street ramp to the basement minutes after mailing the money order and, by sheer happenstance, arrived within shooting distance of Oswald.

The House Select Committee on Assassinations was not so confident of this theory. It reported:

. . . Ruby probably did not come down the ramp, and that his most likely route was an alleyway located next to the Dallas Municipal Building and a stairway leading to the basement garage of police headquarters.

The Committee also turned history around by concluding:

. . . Ruby's shooting of Oswald was not a spontaneous act in that it involved at least some premeditation. Similarly, the committee believed it was less likely that Ruby entered the police basement without assistance, even though the assistance may have been provided with no knowledge of Ruby's intentions. . . . The Committee was troubled by the apparently unlocked doors along the stairway route and the removal of security guards from the area of the garage nearest the stairway shortly before the shooting. . . . There is also evidence that the Dallas Police Department withheld relevant information from the Warren Commission concerning Ruby's entry to the scene of the Oswald transfer.

Ruby himself appeared to support the idea of police aid in reaching Oswald when he told the Warren Commission:

. . . who else could have timed it so perfectly by seconds. If it were timed that way, then someone in the police department is guilty of giving the information as to when Lee Harvey Oswald was coming down.

Then there are the words of mob boss Johnny Roselli. According to columnist Jack Anderson, Roselli once told him:

When Oswald was picked up, the underworld conspirators feared he would crack and disclose information that might lead to them. This almost certainly would have brought a massive U.S. crackdown on the Mafia. So Jack Ruby was ordered to eliminate Oswald . . .

But how could Ruby have known the transfer plans in such detail as to be at the right place at the right time? Researchers have several explanations. The most obvious is that someone within the Dallas police tipped Ruby to the plans. However, it is equally possible that the tip came from federal authorities, who were being kept completely up to date on police actions.

Studying the films of the Oswald shooting has given researchers valuable insight into what happened—particularly a film still held by WBAP-TV in Fort Worth. WBAP-TV was (and still is) the NBC affiliate in the Dallas-Fort Worth Metroplex and on November 24, 1963 had a remote truck and cameras at the Dallas Police Station.

One camera was set up across the Main Street ramp driveway and was running more than thirty minutes prior to Oswald's arrival in the basement (The transfer, originally set for about 10:30 A.M., was delayed by further questioning of Oswald in Fritz's office. Oswald finally arrived in the basement about 11:20 A.M. He was shot moments later.) The camera continued filming long after the shooting.

This documentary of the incident is intriguing seen in its entirety:

About a quarter of an hour prior to Oswald's arrival, a car moves out of the basement garage area and up the Main Street ramp. Its horn is sounded loudly as a warning to people on the sidewalk above. Newsmen and police, both uniformed and plainclothes, mill about in expectation. Then more than a minute or so before Oswald arrives, another horn blows but the sound is more muted, indicating that the car may be farther back in the garage area. Moments later, the jail elevator doors open and Oswald is brought out. "Here he comes," shout the newsmen, crowding up toward the jail office door. Police push them back forming a corridor through the crowd.

One reporter jams a microphone near Oswald's face and shouts: "Do you have anything to say in your defense?" Just at that moment, Jack Ruby moves in from behind the camera and shoves his .38-caliber snub-nosed revolver into Oswald's stomach. The bang is quite audible and Oswald cries out in pain.

Police immediately swarm over Ruby, knocking him to the floor. One of them calls out: "Jack, you son of a bitch!"

Both Oswald and Ruby are hustled back into the jail office while stunned newsmen are reporting: "Oswald has been shot! Oswald has been shot!" Soon these reporters are interviewing the officers who, moments before, had been standing unnoticed beside them. Their questions tumble out: "What happened? Did you know that man? Where did he come from?"

Their responses are intriguing. More than a couple indicated that they indeed recognized Jack Ruby but they declined to give his name or say more.

More than one officer says he thought Oswald's assailant came from the vicinity of a green car parked in the police garage.

Taken in total, this film of the shooting indicates that Ruby came through the parked cars in the basement and may have paused near a green car, perhaps the very car that sounded its horn moments before Oswald was brought down. Some researchers believe this horn honk may have been a signal to move Oswald because Ruby was in position.

The film also indicates that many of the officers in the police basement recognized Ruby right away.

Detective Leavelle told this author he both recognized Ruby and saw the gun in his hand as he stepped from the crowd of reporters, but that he was powerless to do anything in the split second it took to shoot Oswald. Leavelle recalled the shooting:

Captain Fritz had been talking to some men with the FBI and Secret Service when he turned and said, "All clear, take him down." . . . We went down the elevator to the basement. An unmarked car was supposed to be right there for us but it wasn't. It was a few feet from where it was supposed to be. There was a pack of newsmen right close to us. We were heading for the car, L.C. [Graves] and I, with Oswald between us. Out of the corner of my eye I saw Ruby step out from the crowd. He was crouched and he had a pistol. He took a couple of steps and pulled that trigger. Ruby was aiming dead center at Oswald. I had a grip on the top of Oswald's trousers. When I saw Ruby, I tried to jerk Oswald aside to get him out of the way. I succeeded in turning him. The bullet hit him in the side rather than straight into the stomach.

Oswald was pushed to the floor by Leavelle while Graves grabbed Ruby. Graves told researcher Edward Oxford:

By the time Ruby got that shot off, why I had him down. His hand was still flexing. I was saying to him, "Turn it loose! Turn it loose!" I pried his finger off the trigger. He was still trying to work it. Empty the gun into Oswald, I expect, if he could. Officers were jumping on Ruby to get him to the floor. Oswald said, "Owww!" and fell back. That was the last thing he ever said.

Police Chief Curry, who had to face so much criticism after the death of his prisoner, wasn't at the scene of the transfer. He later wrote:

As I was walking down the corridor [toward the jail office] I was called to take a phone call from Dallas Mayor Cabell in my office. He was interested in the progress of the investigation. Since other officers were in charge of moving Oswald and everything was in order, I stayed in my office to give the report to Mayor Cabell.

Researchers over the years have been struck by an odd fact. Part of the plan for security in the transfer involved focusing attention on an armored car that newsmen were told would carry Oswald to the county jail. The armored car was a decoy. Oswald was to have been transported in an unmarked police car. This car was only feet from where he was shot.

Yet rather than load Oswald into the police car standing by and rush him to a hospital, the mortally wounded prisoner was taken back into the jail office where police gave him artificial respiration while waiting for an ambulance to arrive.

Ruby's one shot had been remarkably efficient. It tranversed Oswald's lower abdomen, rupturing two main arteries carrying blood to the heart, and tore through the spleen, pancreas, liver, and the right kidney.

Obviously, pumping Oswald's chest was the worst possible reaction to the internal bleeding caused by the abdominal wound.

Chief Curry, having finally arrived in the basement, noted that when the ambulance arrived: "Oswald was already white as a sheet and looked dead as he was loaded on a stretcher."

Oswald was taken to Parkland Hospital where he was pronounced dead at 1:07 P.M.

*   *   *

Meanwhile, Jack Ruby had been hustled out of the police basement and taken, ironically enough, to the jail cell that had been vacated by Oswald earlier that morning.

Ruby asked his captors: "What happened?"

From that point on Ruby displayed an odd inability to recall the Oswald shooting with any clarity.

One of the Auto Theft detectives in charge of placing Ruby in jail was struck by the oddness of his behavior immediately after the shooting: Don Ray Archer told British television in 1988:

His behavior to begin with was very hyper. He was sweating profusely. I could see his heart beating. We had stripped him down for security purposes. He asked me for one of my cigarettes. I gave him a cigarette. Finally after about two hours had elapsed . . . the head of the Secret Service came up and I conferred with him and he told me that Oswald . . . had died. This should have shocked [Ruby] because it would mean the death penalty. I returned and said, "Jack, it looks like it's going to be the electric chair for you." Instead of being shocked, he became calm, he quit sweating, his heart slowed down. I asked him if he wanted a cigarette and he advised me he didn't smoke. I was just astonished at this complete difference of behavior from what I had expected. I would say his life had depended on him getting Oswald.

On November 27, 1963, a Dallas grand jury indicted Jack Ruby for the murder of Oswald.

There was never any doubt that he did it. After all, only a handful of Americans failed to see what undoubtedly has been the most widely viewed homicide in history. The networks ran replays of the shooting over and over. Because of this publicity, a change-of-venue hearing was conducted on February 10, 1964, but changing the location of Ruby's trial was denied. Jury selection began on February 17 and ended on March 3. Ruby's trial began the next day.

Ten days later, on March 14, 1964, the jury—eight men and four women—returned a verdict of guilty, with the judge handing down a death sentence. The verdict was appealed.

Many people considered Ruby a hero for eliminating Kennedy's presumed assassin. Cards and letters—even money—came from all over. Ruby's attorney, Tom Howard, echoed their sentiment when he stated: "I think Ruby deserves a congressional medal."

But despite the favorable pretrial publicity, Ruby never had much of a chance in the Dallas of those days. As right-wing assistant district attorney Bill Alexander explained to newsman Seth Kantor: "Jack Ruby was about as handicapped as you can get in Dallas. First he was a Yankee. Second, he was a Jew. Third, he was in the nightclub business."

To appeal to the mindset of Dallas at that time, Ruby's brother Earl insisted that his brother's friend, attorney Joe Tonahill, take part in his defense. Tonahill had the East Texas drawl and the rural mannerisms more acceptable to a Dallas jury.

But the heavyweight of Ruby's defense was flamboyant San Francisco super-attorney Melvin Belli, who quickly set himself at odds with the downhome provincialism of Dallas.

Belli's avenue of defense was to have Ruby declared a victim of "temporary insanity" due to "psychomotor epilepsy." To this end, Belli put a string of psychiatrists on the stand to testify. It also meant that he would not allow Ruby to take the stand on his own behalf.

This failure to allow Ruby to testify, coupled with the tight security in the Dallas County Jail, effectively kept Ruby isolated from the news media and the public. Ruby even cautioned his few visitors to the jail that his conversations were being recorded and monitored.

One of the only reporters to get a private interview with Ruby during his trial was nationally syndicated columnist Dorothy Kilgallen, who prevailed on lawyer Tonahill to arrange the meeting with presiding Judge Joe B. Brown. She claimed to have a message for Ruby from a mutual friend who "may have been some kind of singer."

Judge Brown, impressed with the famous Broadway newspaperwoman, agreed and, according to Kilgallen biographer Lee Israel, the pair met in a small office behind the judge's bench without the presence of the four sheriff's deputies who were always at Ruby's side. Israel wrote: "They were together privately for about eight minutes in what may have been the only safe house Ruby had occupied since his arrest."

Although Kilgallen mentioned this unique private meeting with Ruby to close friends, she did not publicly write about it. The fact that she did not publicly disclose what she learned in this meeting prompted author Israel to write:

> That she withheld suggests strongly that she was either saving the information for her book, *Murder One,* a chapter of which she had decided to devote to the Ruby trial; that he furnished her with a lead which she was actively pursuing; that he exacted a promise of confidentiality from her; or that she was acting merely as a courier. Each possibility puts her in the thick of things.

Israel also records that toward the end of her life, Kilgallen may have obtained inside assassination information from yet another source. He wrote:

> Dorothy began to draw drinking companions to her. Joan Crawford . . . was among them. She tooled around with Crawford . . . they boozed abundantly together in the back of Crawford's touring car, which was well stocked with hundred-proof vodka.

Recall that, upon the death of her husband, Crawford became a principal owner of Pepsi-Cola, the firm that counted Richard Nixon as an attorney. Both Nixon and Crawford had been in Dallas the week of the assassination and may have been privy to more information than the public was receiving.

Whatever information Kilgallen learned and from whatever source, many researchers believe it brought about her strange death. She told attorney Mark Lane: "They've killed the President, [and] the government is not prepared to tell us the truth . . ." and that she planned to "break the case." To other friends she said: "This has to be a conspiracy! [The Warren Commission is] laughable . . . I'm going to break the real story and have the biggest scoop of the century." And in her last column item regarding the assassination, published on September 3, 1965, Kilgallen wrote: "This story isn't going to die as long as there's a real reporter alive—and there are a lot of them."

But on November 8, 1965, there was one less reporter. That day Dorothy Kilgallen was found dead in her home. It was initially reported that she died of a heart attack, but quickly this was changed to an overdose of alcohol and pills. Her death certificate, dated November 15, 1965, stated the cause of death was: "... acute ethanol and barbiturate intoxication—circumstances undetermined."

Biographer Israel wrote:

> After three years of investigating the events surrounding Dorothy's death, it is clear to me that she did not die accidentally and that a network of varied activities, impelled by disparate purposes, conspired effectively to obfuscate the truth.

No trace of her notes or writings about what she may have learned from Ruby or Crawford was ever found.

During Ruby's trial, Dallas D.A. Henry Wade made a strong case for premeditation but carefully skirted the issue of conspiracy. According to the *Fort Worth Star-Telegram* of March 18, 1964, Wade's "big decision" was not to call witnesses "who insisted they had seen Ruby and Oswald together at various times."

A parade of police witnesses recalled various remarks reportedly made by Ruby at the time of the shooting, such as:

> You rotten son of a bitch, you shot the President. . . . I intended to get off three shots. . . . I did it because you [the police] couldn't do it. . . . I did it to show the world that Jews have guts. . . . I first thought of killing him at the Friday night press conference.

It was such statements as these, as well as Judge Brown's refusal of a change of venue, that prompted the Texas Court of Criminal Appeals to reverse Ruby's conviction on October 5, 1966. The appeals court ordered a new trial but Ruby died before it could take place.

Although Ruby was not allowed to testify at his trial, he was interviewed by the Warren Commission on June 7, 1964. Representing the Warren Commission were Chief Justice Earl Warren and Representative Gerald R. Ford along with general counsel J. Lee Rankin, staff attorneys Arlen Specter and Joseph Ball. Also present were attorneys Leon Jaworski and Robert G. Storey, who were acting as liaison between the Commission and Texas authorities; Secret Service agent Elmer W. Moore; Dallas assistant district attorney Jim Bowie; Sheriff Bill Decker; Ruby attorney Joe Tonahill; and several Dallas police officers.

Oddly enough, due to an internal squabble over the handling of Dallas witnesses, the two Commission staffers who were in charge of the Ruby investigation—Leon Hubert and Burt Griffin—were not allowed to sit in on this important interview.

During this interview Ruby was vacillating. After about an hour of a rambling account of his activities prior to shooting Oswald and some rather innocuous questions—for example, Rankin asked, "Did you have this gun a long while that you did the shooting with?"—Warren appeared ready to wrap up the interview. Sensing this, Ruby said: "You can get more out of me. Let's not break up too soon."

Ford then began questioning Ruby about his trips to Cuba in 1959, but just as the answers appeared to be leading into fruitful territory, Warren cut Ford off and changed the subject.

Tonahill later told newsman Seth Kantor:

Ford never did finish his interrogation on Cuba. Warren blocked Ford out on it. That was very impressive, I thought. Ford gave him a hard look, too. I was sitting right there and saw it happen.

Ruby became desperate, saying:

Gentlemen, my life is in danger here. . . . Do I sound sober enough to you as I say this? . . . Then follow this up. I may not live tomorrow to give any further testimony. . . . the only thing I want to get out to the public, and I can't say it here, is with authenticity, with sincerity of the truth of everything and why my act was committed, but it can't be said here. . . . Chairman Warren, if you felt that your life was in danger at the moment, how would you feel? Wouldn't you be reluctant to go on speaking, even though you request me to do so?

Having previously voiced the suspicion that his words and actions were being monitored in Dallas, Ruby then began to ask to be taken out of his present circumstances, saying:

Gentlemen, if you want to hear any further testimony, you will have to get me to Washington soon, because it has something to do with you, Chief Warren. . . . I want to tell the truth and I can't tell it here. Does that make sense to you?

Ruby begged to be taken to Washington, away from Dallas, at least eight times. He complained that his "life was in danger . . . [My] whole family is in jeopardy." He was shrugged off by Warren, who replied: "There are a good many things involved in that, Mr. Ruby."

Asked to explain, Warren said:

Well, the public attention that it would attract, and the people who would be around. We have no place for you to be safe when we take you out, and we are not law enforcement officers, and it isn't our responsibility to go into anything of that kind. And certainly it couldn't be done on a moment's notice this way.

Ruby grew more blunt:

. . . If you don't take me back to Washington tonight to give me a chance to prove to the President that I am not guilty, then you will see the most tragic thing that will ever happen. And if you don't have the power to take me back, I won't be around to be able to prove my innocence or guilt. . . . All I know is maybe something can be saved. Because right now, I want to tell you this. I am used as a scapegoat. . . . Now maybe something can be saved. It may not be too late, whatever happens, if our President, Lyndon Johnson, knew the truth from me. But if I am eliminated, there won't be any way of knowing.

At another part of his interview, Ruby may have uttered an ironic truth. Asked if he knew Officer Tippit, he replied that "there was three Tippits on the force" but he knew only one and didn't think he was the murdered policeman. Incredibly, no one followed up on this to find out which Tippit Ruby did know and how he knew it wasn't the murdered officer. To this author's knowledge, there were no other Tippits on the police force at that time.

Then Rankin asked him about a rumor that Ruby had been seen in the Carousel Club shortly before the assassination with a Mr. Weissman—the man who had paid for an anti-Kennedy newspaper ad—Officer Tippit, and a rich Dallas oilman.

Ruby said the story was untrue; then, looking around the room, he proclaimed: "I am as innocent regarding any conspiracy as any of you gentlemen in the room . . ." In later years, the potential irony of this statement has not been lost on assassination researchers.

As early as December 1963, Ruby had asked to be given a lie detector test—perhaps reasoning that such a test would bring out the truth by revealing his account of events to be false. During his meeting with Warren he again begged to be given a polygraph test and the Commission dutifully agreed. A polygraph test was administered to Ruby on July 18, 1964, and his answers did not indicate he was lying: No, he had not known Oswald; No, he did not assist Oswald in the assassination; No, he did not shoot Oswald to silence him; Yes, he entered the police basement by the Main Street ramp; Yes, he told the Warren Commission the entire truth; No, he never did any business with Castro; No, he never met Oswald or Officer Tippit at his club.

This test has been used over the years—as late as November 1988, by Warren Commission apologist David Belin—to support the contention that Ruby was not part of any conspiracy and only shot Oswald out of personal motives.

Few people bothered to read the last page of the Warren Report, where in Appendix XVII, J. Edgar Hoover commented:

It should be pointed out that the polygraph, often referred to as "lie detector" is not in fact such a device. . . . During the proceedings at

Dallas, Texas, on July 18, 1964, Dr. William R. Beavers, a psychiatrist, testified that he would generally describe Jack Ruby as a "psychotic depressive." In view of the serious question raised as to Ruby's mental condition, no significance should be placed on the polygraph examination and it should be considered nonconclusive as the charts cannot be relied upon.

Apparently unwilling or unable to see that Ruby was desperately trying to tell them something outside the surveillance of Dallas authorities, the Warren Commission entourage prepared to leave Ruby's interview. Failing to fully question Jack Ruby was one of the commission's greatest mistakes—if it was a mistake.

A resigned Ruby told them: "Well, you won't ever see me again. I tell you that . . . A whole new form of government is going to take over the country, and I know I won't live to see you another time."

He didn't.

The Mysterious Death of Jack Ruby

In the days following his trial and interview by the Warren Commission, Jack Ruby's moods went from confident highs to suicidal lows. A prisoner with few opportunities to communicate with the outside, Ruby nevertheless was given the freedom of Sheriff Bill Decker's jail. He reportedly was able to roam freely, occasionally use the telephone, and even sleep in a corridor. But at all times he was under close guard, especially after several inept suicide attempts.

On one occasion he tried to hang himself but there was not enough time to rip his clothing and fashion a knot before a guard got to him. Another time, Ruby became so despondent he tried to split his skull by running headlong into a wall. This attempt merely left him with a large knot on his head.

His most pathetic attempt took place when a guard went off for a drink of water. Quickly Ruby unscrewed an overhead light bulb, then threw water from his own glass onto his feet as a conduit. However, he couldn't reach the light socket with his finger while standing in the water. His guard, Deputy Sheriff Jess Stevenson found him ineffectually jumping up and down trying to complete the circuit. The attempt was "something nearly comical," Stevenson told newsman Seth Kantor.

As time dragged on and his isolation began to take its toll, Ruby became more despondent. His mood worsened after he came to believe that Stevenson, who had chatted at length with the prisoner after preaching the Bible to him, actually was passing information gleaned through the conversations back to Dallas authorities.

Long after the Warren Commission had issued its report in the fall of

1964, while waiting for the outcome of his conviction appeal, Ruby apparently wrote a sixteen-page letter to a fellow prisoner who was leaving the jail. Ruby asked the prisoner to memorize names and facts in the letter, then destroy it. The prisoner, identified only as "John," decided instead to sell the letter, and it ended up in the hands of long-time researcher Penn Jones. Jones purchased the letter from New York autograph dealer Charles Hamilton, who had the document appraised as authentic.

The letter is disjointed, rambling, and full of references to Nazis, the death of Jews and, most intriguing, derogatory references to Lyndon Johnson. Many researchers, as improbable as it seems, feel Ruby's letter, though written in a state of questionable mental equilibrium, laid bare some of his secret knowledge and fears. He wrote:

> First, you must realize that the people here want everyone to think I am crazy, so if what I know is actually [*sic*], and then no one will believe me, because of my supposed insanity. Now, I know that my time is running out . . . they plan on doing away with [me]. . . . As soon as you get out you must read Texan looks at Lyndon [*A Texan Looks at Lyndon: A Study in Illegitimate Power*, by J. Evetts Haley; Palo Duro Press, 1964] and it might open your eyes to a lot of things. This man [Johnson] is a Nazi in the worst order. For over a year now they have been doing away with my people. . . . don't believe the Warren report, that was only put out to make me look innocent in that it would throw the Americans and all the European country's [*sic*] off guard. . . . There are so many things that have been played with success that it would take all nite to write them out. . . . There wouldn't be any purpose of my writing you all of this unless your were convinced of how much I loved my country. . . . I am going to die a horrible death anyway, so what would I have to gain by writing all this. So you must believe me. . . . Johnson is going to try to have an all-out war with Russia and when that happens, Johnson and his cohorts will be on the side-lines where they won't get hurt, while the Americans may get wiped out. The only way this can be avoided is that if Russia would be informed as to [who] the real enemies are, and in that way they won't be tricked into starting a war with the U.S. . . . One more thing, isn't it strange that Oswald who hasn't worked a lick most of his life, should be fortunate enough to get a job at the Book Bldg. two wks. before the president himself didn't know as to when he was to visit Dallas, now where would a jerk like Oswald get the information that the president was coming to Dallas. Only one person could have had that information, and that man was Johnson who knew weeks in advance as to what was going to happen because he is the one who was going to arrange the trip for president, this had been planned long before president himself knew about [it], so you figure that one out. The only one who gained by the shooting of the president was Johnson, and he was in a car in the

rear and safe when the shooting took place. What would the Russians, Castro or anyone else have to gain by eliminating the president. If Johnson was so heartbroken over Kennedy, why didn't he do something for Robert Kennedy? All he did was snub him.

In yet a second letter smuggled out of the Dallas County Jail, Ruby was more blunt in his accusations. Researcher Gary Shaw quotes Ruby as writing:

. . . they found some very clever means and ways to trick me and which will be used later as evidence to show the American people that I was part of the conspiracy in the assassination of [the] president, and I was used to silence Oswald. . . . They alone planned the killing, by they I mean Johnson and others. . . . read the book Texas Looks At Lyndon [another reference to Haley's book] and you may learn quite a bit about Johnson and how he has fooled everyone. . . . In all the history of the U.S. never has a president been elected that has the background of Johnson. Believe me, compared to him I am a Saint.

Not long before his death, Ruby was interviewed by psychiatrist Werner Teuter. Perhaps realizing his end was near, Ruby told Teuter the assassination was ''an act of overthrowing the government'' and that he knew ''who had President Kennedy killed.'' He added: ''I am doomed. I do not want to die. But I am not insane. I was framed to kill Oswald.''

These comments will always intrigue researchers. Was Ruby merely speculating or were his messages born of secret knowledge? Did he know that Johnson and the people behind him wanted war—only mistaking Russia for Asia? And were his warnings of Nazis taking over rooted somewhere in a knowledge of the mentality of the people he knew were behind the assassination?

Or were his missives only the delusions of a man unhinged by his captivity and the belief that forces were out to destroy him?

An answer may be found in a study of Ruby's mysterious death.

The Texas Court of Criminal Appeals overturned Ruby's conviction on October 5, 1966 and ordered a new trial. On December 7, 1966, his new trial was ordered moved from Dallas to Wichita Falls, a small Texas city near the Oklahoma border. There was every likelihood that within another month or two, Ruby would walk free after his time in jail was counted against a probable short prison term for murder without malice. He certainly would have been allowed to post bond.

On December 9, 1966, two days after his new trial site had been announced, Ruby was moved from the Dallas County Jail to Parkland Hospital after complaining of persistent coughing and nausea.

Doctors initially diagnosed his problem as ''pneumonia.'' The next day, however, the diagnosis was changed to cancer and within just a few more days, it was announced that Ruby's lung cancer was too far advanced to be treated by surgery or radiation.

On the evening of January 2, 1967, doctors suspected that blood clots were forming and they administered oxygen and Ruby seemed to recover. But about 9 A.M. the next day, he suffered a spasm and, despite emergency procedures, he was pronounced dead at 10:30 A.M. January 3, 1967.

One of his attorneys told newsmen: "His death was a merciful release."

Shortly before his death, Ruby's brother Earl smuggled a tape recorder into Parkland and later produced a short record that was sold to Capitol Records. The proceeds from this record, in which Ruby simply reiterated the official account of his actions—including his Cuban travels, which the House Select Committee on Assassinations proved false—was used to pay for his burial expenses. This record also once again put the public off guard by repeating the same story reported in 1963–64.

An autopsy by Dallas County medical examiner Dr. Earl Rose showed the heaviest concentration of cancer cells in Ruby's right lung. However, Dr. Rose determined the immediate cause of death was pulmonary embolism—a massive blood clot had formed in a leg, passed through the heart, and lodged in Ruby's lung. There were traces of white cancerous tumors coursing throughout Ruby's body. Ruby's doctors had said they believed his cancer had originated in the pancreas, but Dr. Rose found Ruby's pancreas perfectly normal.

With the announcement of his inoperable cancer, there was immediate and widespread suspicion that Ruby had been maneuvered into killing Oswald knowing he had only a short time to live. Dr. Rose was asked by the House Committee if there was any chance that Ruby could have known about his cancer in November 1963. He said no.

Yet questions remain—especially among those close to Ruby in his last months.

Deputy Sheriff Al Maddox told researchers in 1982:

We had a phony doctor come in to [the Dallas County Jail] from Chicago, just as phony and as queer as a three-dollar bill. And he worked his way in through—I don't know, whoever supplied the county at that time with doctors. . . . you could tell he was Ruby's doctor. He spent half his time up there talking with Ruby. And one day I went in and Ruby told me, he said, "Well, they injected me for a cold." He said it was cancer cells. That's what he told me, Ruby did. I said you don't believe that shit. He said, "I damn sure do!" I never said anything to Decker or anybody. . . . [Then] one day when I started to leave, Ruby shook hands with me and I could feel a piece of paper in his palm. . . . [In this note] he said it was a conspiracy and he said . . . if you will keep your eyes open and your mouth shut, you're gonna learn a lot. And that was the last letter I ever got from him.

Maddox was not the only lawman to suspect that Ruby's death was not entirely natural. Policeman Tom Tilson has told researchers:

> It was the opinion of a number of other Dallas police officers that Ruby had received injections of cancer while he was incarcerated in the Dallas County Jail following the shooting of Lee Harvey Oswald.

At least one former Dallas lawman offered a more mundane explanation for Ruby's sudden and rampant cancer. He told this author: "Hell, it wasn't any big deal. They just took Ruby in for X-rays and had him wait in the X-ray room. While he sat there for fifteen or twenty minutes or more, they just left the X-ray machine on him."

Bruce McCarty operated an electron microscope at Southwest Medical School near Parkland. He told this author that he was called back to work during the holidays in 1966 to make a study of Ruby's cancer cells. McCarty explained that there are two types of cancer cells—cilia, which indicate an origin in the respiratory system, and microvilli, indicating an origin in the digestive system. These cells are difficult to differentiate with a regular microscope, hence the need for his electron microscope.

McCarty confirmed that Ruby's cells were microvilli, indicating his cancer originated in the digestive system. He was shocked when it was announced that Ruby died from lung cancer.

Could Ruby have been injected with live cancer cells, which could account for the presence of the microvilli? Traditional medical science claims this is impossible.

While none of this information establishes beyond doubt that Jack Ruby was somehow eliminated through cancer, it certainly shows there is cause enough for researchers to be highly suspicious of his sudden and convenient death.

With the death of the two men who might have shed light on the lines of communication within a plot to kill the President—Oswald and Ruby—researchers were left only with a vast amount of evidence, much of which seems insubstantial when studied at close hand.

Summary

The background of Jack Ruby is laced with mob associates and contacts that lasted right up to the eve of the Kennedy assassination.

Beginning as a runner for Al Capone in Chicago, Ruby maintained connections with mobsters associated with top Mafia bosses—such as Carlos Marcello, Sam Giancana, and Santos Trafficante. He also was in touch with associates of Teamster president Jimmy Hoffa. All of these men are said to have issued death threats against President Kennedy and his brother, Attorney General Robert F. Kennedy.

Add to this the abundance of information linking Ruby to gun-running activities involving CIA agents, mercenaries, and anti-Castro Cuban exiles and his possible position as an FBI informant in 1959.

Obviously Jack Ruby was much more than simply an overwrought nightclub owner who shot Lee Harvey Oswald to save Mrs. Kennedy the trauma of returning to Dallas to testify at Oswald's trial. In fact, his note to lawyer Joe Tonahill proves this widely reported motive to be only a cynical legal ploy.

Since Ruby lied repeatedly both about his motive and his connection to Cuban gun running, it is reasonable to conclude that his statements claiming no prior contact with Oswald cannot be accepted without severe question.

The abundance of evidence available today leads most researchers to the belief that an ongoing relationship between Ruby and Oswald did in fact exist prior to the assassination.

The fascinating story of Rose Cheramie—a woman with improbable foreknowledge of the assassination—takes on some meaning in light of her claim to have worked for Ruby.

Evidence also has grown—and been accepted by House Select Committee on Assassinations chief counsel Robert G. Blakey—that Ruby stalked Oswald throughout the assassination weekend. This lends extra credence to the widely held belief that Ruby's shooting of Oswald was not a spontaneous act—but rather a deliberate move to silence the accused assassin.

The act may well have been ordered by someone who had significant power over Ruby.

It is also instructive to note the number of persons who had access to Ruby or his environs who died suddenly—such as newswoman Dorothy Kilgallen.

Ruby himself tried to warn Chief Justice Warren and others that a conspiracy was taking place and that "a whole new form of government is going to take over the country." He begged to be taken to Washington eight times claiming ". . . my life is in danger here." Later, in messages smuggled out of the Dallas County Jail, Ruby confessed, ". . . I was used to silence Oswald." He bluntly stated that "Lyndon Johnson and others . . ." were behind the assassination.

In the winter of 1967—just as a new trial had been ordered and it seemed that Ruby might become accessible to the news media—he developed a case of sudden cancer and died in less than a month.

It seemed that Ruby's fear of death in Dallas—as expressed to the Warren Commission—was justified.

We were told not to study those bullet marks by the FBI.
—Reenactment surveyor Chester Breneman

The Evidence

There was never a lack of evidence in the assassination of President Kennedy. In addition to the several hundred witnesses in Dealey Plaza, there was an abundance of film and still pictures as well as a great deal of physical evidence.

In the hours following the assassination, this pile of evidence grew to include a rifle, empty shell cases, a "sniper's nest" and even a convincing—if belated—palm print on the suspected murder weapon.

The rapid accumulation of evidence prompted Dallas County district attorney Henry Wade to proclaim to the media he had an open-and-shut case against Lee Harvey Oswald the day after the shooting. After Oswald's death on Sunday, Wade was even more adamant. The *Dallas Times Herald* of November 25, 1963, stated:

> The Red propaganda mills had been grinding out angry report after report declaring Oswald was being made a scapegoat for a crime he did not commit. "Oswald was the man who fired the gun that took the life of our President. History will record it as such," the district attorney said in answer to the Kremlin's propagandists.

However, a long and thoughtful look at most of the evidence reveals just as many questions and as much confusion as there is concerning the medical evidence.

The Warren Commission questioned 126 of the 266 known witnesses either by testimony of affidavit. Regarding the source of the shots, thirty-eight gave no opinion—most were not asked—thirty-two indicated the Texas School Book Depository, and fifty-one placed the shots in the vicinity of the Grassy Knoll. Several believed shots were fired from two different locations.

Even veteran law-enforcement officers, who should have been expected to provide expert opinions as to the source of the shots, were divided in their beliefs. Of the twenty sheriff's deputies watching the motorcade from in front of the Sheriff's Office, sixteen placed the origin of the shots near the Triple Underpass, three gave no opinion, and one implied the Depository. Of the Dallas policemen interviewed, four placed shots from the Grassy Knoll, four said shots came from the Depository, and four gave no opinion.

It is evident that different witnesses held different beliefs as to the source of the shots. Supporters of the official version of the assassination point to this as proof that eyewitness testimony cannot be counted on for accuracy. Skeptics of the official story say this difference of opinion indicates shots from different locations.

Today there is evidence that some witnesses were advised—even pressured—to make their version of the assassination conform to the official story.

In 1975 a CIA liaison man told congressional investigators that two of Kennedy's aides, Kenneth O'Donnell and David Powers, initially said shots came from other than the Depository, but later changed their story after being warned by J. Edgar Hoover or one of his top aides that such testimony would only arouse public passions and could lead to an international incident. Both O'Donnell and Powers denied this story when it appeared in a Chicago newspaper column, but in light of other known attempts to change witness testimony—that of Senator Ralph Yarborough, Jean Hill, Phil Willis, etc.—this story cannot be summarily dismissed.

While it is clear that eyewitness testimony cannot be relied on for unequivocal information, the statements of otherwise ordinary citizens regarding second gunmen, muzzle flashes, and smoke on the Grassy Knoll must be considered in any impartial desire to learn the truth.

The best evidence would have been the medical reports. With a competent autopsy, it should have been well established how many bullets struck Kennedy and from which direction. However, as discussed earlier in "Two Hospitals," the medical evidence in this case continues to be a source of controversy—filled with inconsistencies, errors, missing items, and photographs of questionable origin. About all one can say of the medical evidence is that Kennedy was shot at least twice.

So it remains for other pieces of evidence—ballistic and physical evidence—to prove the official version of the assassination. Unfortunately, this area, too, is filled with doubts, questions, deceit, and ambiguity.

Some of the first physical evidence to be found was in the Texas School Book Depository. Many of the press accounts at the time mentioned fingerprints traced to Lee Harvey Oswald being found on boxes on the Depository's sixth floor, the shield of boxes around a "sniper's nest" in the southeast corner of that floor, and the remains of a chicken lunch discovered nearby.

The presence of Oswald's fingerprints on the sixth floor means nothing, since he was a Depository employee and by all accounts had worked on the sixth floor that day.

The stacking of book boxes both around the sixth-floor window and on the windowsill cannot be used as proof of Oswald's guilt since there is no proof he placed them and since it is now known that the entire "sniper's nest" scene was staged for the official photographs.

At least three Warren Commission photographs of the scene—Commission Exhibits 509, 724 and 733—show three different versions of the boxes stacked near the sixth-floor window.

R. L. Studebaker, Dallas police photographer, told the Warren Commission that some of his photos were taken as late as the Monday following the assassination.

Jack Beers, a photographer for the *Dallas Morning News*, took pictures of the "sniper's nest" less than three hours after the assassination. His photos show yet a different configuration of boxes from that shown in the Commission photos.

Dallas police lieutenant J. C. Day of the Crime Scene Search Unit admitted to the Warren Commission that the boxes had been moved around. In Commission testimony, the following exchange took place between Day and Commission attorney David Belin:

BELIN: . . . Were those boxes in the window the way you saw them, or had they been replaced in the window to reconstruct it?

DAY: They had simply been moved in the processing for prints. They weren't put back in any particular order.

BELIN: So [the "sniper's nest" photograph] does not represent, so far as the boxes are concerned, the crime scene when you first came to the sixth floor, is that correct?

DAY: That is correct.

When Belin showed Day photos of boxes in the sixth-floor window taken by bystanders in the street moments after the assassination, Day expressed confusion over the obvious differences in the configuration. He said: "What I am getting at, this box doesn't jibe with my picture of the inside . . . I just don't know. I can't explain that box there depicted from the outside as related to the pictures I took inside." Later in his testimony, Day suggested that the boxes were moved by someone before he arrived.

So the evidence of the "sniper's nest" is virtually useless since even the Dallas Police crime scene official stated the boxes had been moved about.

Unfortunately, it was the same story with the three cartridge hulls reportedly found on the sixth floor. Day said he took two photographs of the three hulls lying near the sixth-floor window. Two hulls can been seen lying near to each other on the floor beneath the windowsill while a third is some distance away. It has been assumed that this was the position of the hulls. However, today there is evidence that they, too, were moved.

In a 1985 interview with researcher Gary Mack, Tom Alyea gave the following account:

In 1963 Alyea was a news cameraman for WFAA-TV in Dallas. He managed to get inside the Texas School Book Depository before it was sealed by police. As he entered the building, Alyea heard someone shout, "Don't let anyone in or out!" Alyea reached the sixth floor and filmed Dallas police searching for evidence. He said the federal authorities there were "bent on getting me out of the place" and did not want him taking any film but his friendly local police contacts allowed him to stay. Alyea said he noticed shells lying on the floor but couldn't film them because of book boxes in the way. Noting Alyea's predicament, Captain Will Fritz scooped up the shells and held them in his hand for Alyea's camera—then threw the hulls down on the floor. All of this occurred before the crime scene search unit arrived. Alyea said film of the shells lying in their original positions on the floor was apparently thrown out with other unused newsfilm on orders of his WFAA news director.

If Alyea's account is true (and there's no reason to believe it's not), then the shells as photographed by the Dallas police were not in their original positions—but rather where they landed when thrown down by Fritz.

Two lawmen on the sixth floor at the time—deputy sheriffs Roger Craig and Luke Mooney—have told researchers they saw the three hulls lying side by side only inches apart under the window, all pointing in the same direction. Of course this position would be impossible if the shells had been normally ejected from a rifle. So the evidence of the empty shell cases is now suspect.

Just as a matter of speculation, it seems incredible that the assassin in the Depository would go to the trouble of trying to hide the rifle behind boxes on the opposite side of the sixth floor from the southeast window and then leave incriminating shells lying on the floor—unless, of course, the hulls were deliberately left behind to incriminate Oswald.

There is yet another problem with the empty rifle hulls. Although the Warren Commission published a copy of the Dallas police evidence sheet showing three shell cases were taken from the Depository, in later years a copy of that same evidence sheet was found in the Texas Department of Public Safety files which showed only two cases were found. This is supported by the FBI receipt for assassination evidence from the Dallas police that indicates only two shell cases arrived in Washington just after the assassination.

Reportedly Fritz held on to one of the cases for several days before forwarding it to the FBI. This breach of the chain of evidence causes suspicion to be raised about the legitimacy of the third shell. This suspicion is compounded by the fact that while the FBI Crime Lab determined that two of the hulls show marks compatible with being loaded in Oswald's rifle, the third showed no such evidence.

In fact, the third hull—designated Commission Exhibit 543—had a dent on its lip that would have prevented the fitting of a slug. In its present condition, it could not have fired a bullet on that day.

The FBI determined that CE 543 had been loaded and extracted from a weapon "at least three times" but could not specify that the weapon belonged to Oswald. (Some researchers speculate this shell may have been the one used to fire the slug from the Oswald rifle that later turned up at Parkland Hospital and has been designated as CE399—the "magic bullet.")

However, FBI experts said CE 543 did show marks from the magazine follower of Oswald's rifle. What went unexplained was how these marks were made, since the magazine follower marks only the last cartridge in the clip. This position was occupied by a live round found that day, not by CE 543.

Again, too many questions arise to accept the shell cases as solid evidence.

The rifle reportedly belonging to Oswald also is surrounded by controversy and inconsistencies. The rifle found behind boxes on the sixth floor of the Depository was initially described as a 7.65 mm German Mauser. It was described thusly by Deputy Sheriff E. L. Boone, discoverer of the rifle, in his report of that day. Boone's report is supported by that of Deputy Constable Seymour Weitzman. Both lawmen reportedly had more than an average knowledge of weapons.

As late as the day after the assassination, Weitzman wrote in a report:

I was working with Deputy Boone of the Sheriff's Department and helping in the search. We were in the northwest corner of the sixth floor when Deputy Boone and myself spotted the rifle about the same time. This rifle was a 7.65 Mauser bolt action equipped with a 4/18 scope, a thick leather brownish-black sling on it. The rifle was between some boxes near the stairway. The time the rifle was found was 1:22 P.M.

This account was confirmed by Deputy Craig, who told Texas researchers he actually saw the word *Mauser* stamped on the weapon's receiver.

When asked about the make of rifle shortly after midnight the day of the assassination, Dallas District Attorney Henry Wade replied: "It's a Mauser, I believe."

However, by late Friday afternoon the rifle was being identified as a 6.5 mm Italian Mannlicher-Carcano.

While a German Mauser and the Carcano do look somewhat similar, anyone vaguely familiar with these weapons—Weitzman, Boone, and Craig should certainly qualify—can distinguish between them. Why the discrepancies? The Warren Commission indicated that Weitzman was simply mistaken in his identification of the rifle and that the others, including Wade, probably repeated this mistaken identification.

However, Wade never gave any indication as to the source of his idea that the rifle was a Mauser. And Boone told the Commission he thought it was Captain Fritz who termed it a Mauser.

Asked to identify the Mannlicher-Carcano by Commission Attorney Joseph Ball, Boone stated: "It looks like the same rifle. I have no way of being positive."

Weitzman, who managed a sporting-goods store and was considered an expert on rifles, had identified the gun as a Mauser. He testified to the Warren Commission only by affidavit and was not asked to identify the Carcano as the gun he held in the Depository.

Author Sylvia Meagher wrote: "The failure to obtain such corroboration from Weitzman leaves open the possibility that a substitution of rifles took place, or that a second rifle may have been found at the Book Depository, but kept secret."

And consider that Lieutenant Day and another Dallas policeman mentioned writing contemporary descriptions of the rifle, yet neither of these documents was included in the mass of Warren Commission materials.

Even the CIA had doubts as to the true identity of the assassination rifle. Five days after the assassination, in an internal report transmitted from Italy to Langley headquarters, CIA officials noted that two different kinds of Italian-made carbines were being identified as the single murder weapon. The CIA document stated: "The weapon which appears to have been employed in this criminal attack is a Model 91 rifle, 7.35 caliber, 1938 modification . . . The description of a 'Mannlicher-Carcano' rifle in the Italian and foreign press is in error."

The possibility of a rifle substitution was even admitted by Dallas police chief Jesse Curry in 1976. In an interview with *The Detroit News*, Curry agreed "it's more than possible" the rifle originally found in the Depository could have been exchanged for the gun now in the National Archives. Curry said anyone wanting to substitute one suspected murder weapon for another "could have gotten away with it at the time" because no special precautions were taken to isolate the weapon as historic evidence.

But even accepting that the Mannlicher-Carcano was the assassination rifle, it is hard to envision a worse weapon. In testimony to the Warren Commission—conveniently left out of its report—FBI reports quoted firearms experts as calling the rifle "a cheap old weapon," "a very cheap rifle [which] could have been purchased for $3 each in lots of 25," and a "real cheap, common, real flimsy-looking [gun] . . . very easily knocked out of adjustment."

The FBI also noted that the Carcano was part of a gun shipment that was the subject of "a legal proceeding by the Carlo Riva Machine Shop to collect payment for the shipment of rifles which Adam Consolidated Industries, Inc., claims were defective."

A defective gun managed to strike two men with three shots at a range of nearly two hundred feet within six seconds?

There are many other questions concerning the rifle and its purchase.

The Warren Commission published a "duplicate" of the ad from which Oswald reportedly ordered the rifle from Klein's Sporting Goods Co. of Chicago on March 13, 1963. According to Klein's records, a rifle bearing serial number C2766 was shipped to one A. Hidell, Post Office Box 2915, Dallas, Texas, on March 20, 1963.

Why publish a duplicate ad? Why not publish the original ad? The order form reportedly came from the February 1963 issue of *American Rifleman* magazine—yet the ad from that issue advertises a ''36″ overall'' rifle. Perhaps that is why the Commission chose to present a ''duplicate'' ad, which depicts a forty-inch-long rifle—the same length of the weapon identified as Oswald's.

Perhaps the discrepancy between rifle lengths had a logical explanation. But the manner in which the Commission tried to conceal this problem only furthers the suspicions of researchers that there was manipulation of the evidence.

This problem is heightened by the fact that no record exists to show that either Oswald or A. Hidell actually took possession of the rifle. Despite postal regulations that Form 1039, which lists those persons with access to a post office box, be kept a minimum of two years after a box is closed—the Commission was told Oswald's form was thrown away. Likewise, there are no official records to show that Oswald signed for the .38 caliber pistol that reportedly was shipped to him by Railway Express.

In fact, according to Warren Commission documents, Oswald told Capt. Will Fritz ''he had bought [the pistol] several months before in Fort Worth, Texas.''

The rifle experts employed by the Warren Commission made negative comments regarding the capabilities of the Carcano rifle.

But the strongest evidence that the Mannlicher-Carcano was not the assassination weapon came from Ronald Simmons, chief of the Infantry Weapons Evaluation Branch of the Ballistics Research Laboratory of the Department of the Army, who headed the team evaluating the rifle. During testimony to the Warren Commission, Simmons was asked if his team had experienced any difficulties sighting in the rifle. He replied:

Well, they could not sight the weapon in using the telescope, and no attempt was made to sight it in using the iron sight. We did adjust the telescopic sight by the addition of two shims, one which tended to adjust the azimuth and one which adjusted an elevation.

Moments later, the Warren Commission attorney stated: ''For the record, Mr. Chairman, these shims were given to me by the FBI who told me that they removed them from the weapon after they had been placed there by Mr. Simmons's laboratory.''

What an astounding admission—the Oswald rifle needed metal shims placed under the telescopic sight before the Army laboratory could test the accuracy of it. And this evidence was known to both the FBI and the Warren Commission, but never adaquately relayed to the public.

The experts also indicated that the telescopic sight was adjusted for a left-handed shooter, yet both Oswald's wife and brother told the Commission Oswald was right handed. Robert Oswald said: ''I would say without qualification . . . He [Lee] was instinctively a right-handed person.''

Added to the inferior quality and the inaccuracy of the rifle is Oswald's well-documented inability to achieve marksmanship standards while in the Marines.

In its Report, the Warren Commission stated flatly: ''. . . the number C2766 is the serial number. This rifle is the only one of its type bearing that serial number.'' Yet an FBI report dated April 30, 1964, and signed by J. Edgar Hoover, stated:

> . . . the Mannlicher-Carcano rifle was manufactured in Italy from 1891 until 1941; however, in the 1930's Mussolini ordered all arms factories to manufacture the Mannlicher-Carcano rifle. Since many concerns were manufacturing the same weapon, the same serial number appears on weapons manufactured by more than one concern. Some bear a letter prefix and some do not.

Plainly, there could be more Mannlicher-Carcanos around with the serial number C2766—a fact that further weakens the case against Oswald.

Without going into minute details, it should be noted that the sling on Oswald's rifle was not a standard rifle sling but instead seemed to come from a musical instrument or a camera carrying strap. No attempt was made to determine where this sling came from, although Commission experts, after explaining that the purpose of such a strap is to steady the aim, stated: ''The sling on the rifle was too short to use in the normal way . . .''

Despite two massive federal investigations, no one bit of evidence has been brought forward as to where or when Oswald might have purchased ammunition or the ammunition clip for the rifle.

Bear in mind that no gun-cleaning oil or other materials, including ammunition, were found in Oswald's belongings.

Another important piece of evidence involved a paraffin test made on Oswald the day of the assassination. The results of this test presented evidence that Oswald may not have fired a rifle that day, yet these results were downplayed and even suppressed by the federal authorities.

In this test, layers of paraffin are applied to a suspect's skin and the sticky warm wax opens the pores and then picks up any foreign material that may be present on the skin. When the wax cools, it forms a hard cast that is treated with chemicals that turn blue if nitrates are present. The idea is that the skin of someone who has recently fired a weapon will bear traces of nitrates. While the presence of nitrates is not conclusive evidence that a gun was fired—tobacco, urine, cosmetics, matches, soil, and certain drugs can cause a positive reaction—the absence of nitrates is compelling evidence that the person has not fired a weapon.

Oswald's hands both reacted positively to the paraffin test, indicating the presence of nitrates. But a cast of his right cheek showed no reaction. Any competent defense attorney would have pointed to this test as evidence that his client had not fired a rifle.

However in its report, the Warren Commission termed this routine police test "completely unreliable," adding that an FBI agent fired three rounds through the Oswald rifle in rapid succession and tested negative on both his hands and face afterward.

The odd part of this issue is that in printing the Dallas police documents, the Commission apparently deleted reference to the paraffin test at the bottom of the police evidence sheet.

Why obscure this test result—which appeared to present evidence of Oswald's innocence—if the test can be demonstrated to be faulty or unreliable?

In all criminal cases, police always hope for that most important piece of evidence linking the crime to the suspect—a fingerprint.

An Incriminating Palm Print

The sole piece of hard evidence linking Oswald to the Mannlicher-Carcano rifle was a palm print reportedly found on the underside of the gun's barrel when the rifle was disassembled.

It seems strong evidence until inspected closely. To begin with, the palm print would never have been admitted as evidence in any courtroom trial because it totally lacked a chain of evidence—the unquestioned and documented path from discovery to presentation in court.

Consider the chronology of events leading to the presentation of the palm print as evidence: According to Dallas police lieutenant John Carl Day, he discovered the palm print shortly before turning the rifle over to the FBI about midnight on November 22, 1963. Yet he mentioned it to no one and there is no record of his discovery. Day even admitted to the Warren Commission that "it was his customary practice to photograph fingerprints in most instances prior to lifting them." Yet this was not done.

About midnight, the rifle was given to FBI agent Vincent Drain, who flew with the gun to Washington in an Air Force plane.

Early on November 23, 1963, the rifle was turned over to the FBI laboratory and examined for fingerprints. A report made that day and signed by J. Edgar Hoover stated: "No latent prints of value were developed on Oswald's revolver, the cartridges cases, the unfired cartridge, the clip in the rifle or the inner parts of the rifle."

The FBI had no indication of any useful print. Before the Warren Commission, FBI expert Sebastian Latona stated:

We had no personal knowledge of any palm print having been developed on the rifle. . . . evidently the lifting had been so complete that there was nothing left to show any marking on the gun itself as to the existence of such—even an attempt on the part of anyone to process the rifle.

On the morning of November 24, Oswald was killed in the basement of the Dallas Police Station and that afternoon the rifle was flown back to Dallas by an FBI agent.

The next day after autopsy, Oswald's body was lying in Miller Funeral Home in Fort Worth when, according to a local newspaper: "An FBI team, with a camera and a crime lab kit, spent a long time in the morgue."

Miller Funeral Home director Paul Groody told this author that the FBI fingerprinted Oswald's corpse. Groody said: "I had a heck of a time getting the black fingerprint ink off of [Oswald's] hands."

In 1978, FBI agent Richard Harrison confirmed to researcher Gary Mack that he had personally driven another Bureau agent and the "Oswald" rifle to the Miller Funeral Home. Harrison said at the time he understood that the other agent intended to place Oswald's palm print on the rifle "for comparison purposes."

Oswald had been fingerprinted three times while alive and in Dallas police custody. There has been no explanation for this postmortem fingerprinting.

On Monday, while talking to reporters, District Attorney Wade casually mentioned: "Let's see . . . his fingerprints were found on the gun. Have I said that?" It was the first mention of any prints being found.

By Monday evening, the news was all over the media. The *Dallas Times Herald* proclaimed: OSWALD'S PRINTS REVEALED ON RIFLE KILLING KENNEDY.

Asked about the strongest evidence of Oswald's guilt, Wade responded: "If I had to single out any one thing, it would be the fingerprints found on the rifle and the book cartons which [Oswald] used to prop the weapon on."

On November 26, the rifle was again sent to Washington. But the incriminating palm print did not arrive at the FBI lab until November 29, three days after all other Dallas police evidence had been turned over to the Bureau on orders from President Johnson.

This time FBI officials were able to confirm that the palm print matched that of Lee Harvey Oswald.

Today, Day still maintains he found the print and failed to mention it, photograph it, or send it to the FBI quickly because he believed that "sufficient traces of the print had been left on the rifle barrel." Day told author Henry Hurt that he specifically pointed out the print to Agent Drain when he gave him the rifle. However, Drain denied this. According to Hurt, Drain told him:

I just don't believe there ever was a print. . . . All I can figure is that it was some sort of cushion, because they were getting a lot of heat by

Sunday night. You could take the print off Oswald's [arrest] card and put it on the rifle. Something like that happened.

Considering the movements of the rifle, some researchers believe Oswald's dead hand was placed directly on the rifle barrel. Others believe Oswald's palm print was taken either from jail records or the book Depository and superimposed over marks from the rifle barrel.

No serious researcher in the 1980s believes that Oswald's palm print was legitimately lifted from the rifle barrel on November 22, 1963.

Even the Warren Commission found this piece of evidence hard to swallow. An internal FBI memorandum made public in 1978 disclosed that on August 28, 1964:

[Warren Commission general counsel J. Lee] Rankin advised because of the circumstances that now exist there was a serious question in the minds of the Commission as to whether or not the palm impression that has been obtained from the Dallas Police Department is a legitimate latent palm impression removed from the rifle barrel or whether it was obtained from some other source and that for this reason this matter needs to be resolved.

Commission fingerprint experts admitted: ". . . it was not possible to estimate the time which elapsed between the placing of the print on the rifle and the date of the lift."

The FBI then attempted to have Lieutenant Day certify a statement concerning his lifting of the palm print, but Day declined to sign it.

The Commission apparently made no effort to resolve the matter. It instead presented the belated palm print as strong evidence of Oswald's guilt. Like so much of the "hard" evidence in this case, the closer one looks, the softer it becomes.

*   *   *

After considering the rifle, the empty shells, and palm print, one must again consider the "hero of the Warren Commission"—CE (Commission Exhibit) 399 or the "magic bullet."

The discovery of CE 399 has been dealt with earlier, in "Two Hospitals." Now consider the highly technical studies of this bullet and other bullet fragments involved in the assassination.

The Commission attempted to duplicate the feat of CE 399—passing through seven layers of skin and muscle, striking bones in two male adults, and emerging in near-perfect condition—but with no success. Similar ammunition fired into goat carcasses, human bodies, and gelatin blocks all showed more deformity than CE 399.

In an attempt to explain away the unscathed condition of this bullet, members of the forensic pathology panel of the House Select Committee on Assassinations argued that other bullets had done similar damage and remained in pristine condition.

However, one member of the panel, Dr. Cyril Wecht, challenged the group to produce even one single bullet that had broken two human bones and remained unchanged. Dr. Wecht concluded: "It is clear to me that their reluctance was based upon their knowledge that such studies would further destroy the single-bullet theory."

Since neither the Warren Commission nor the House Select Committee on Assassinations were able to convincingly prove the feat ascribed to CE 399, the emission spectrography tests assume more importance. These spectrographic tests are a scientific means of determining if the various bits of bullet metal taken from both Kennedy and Connally came from the same bullet. These tests could have provided what is missing from all assassination investigations—clear, irrefutable proof that metal found in the victims could be traced to CE 399. The tests failed to do this and the handling of this evidence raised a great deal of suspicion toward federal authorities.

Under such testing it is a simple matter to determine if two bits of metal do not have the same percentage of basic elements, such as lead, copper, atimony, etc. It is much more difficult to prove that such bits are from the same source.

Concerning the tests, the Warren Commission chose not to ask one single question of the spectrographic expert who conducted the tests. They were content to simply report that several bullet fragments were "similar in metallic composition," which proved nothing.

In the years following the assassination, researcher Harold Weisberg sought unsuccessfully to obtain the spectrographic test results from the U.S. government. Government attorneys argued that revealing the results was not in the "national interest," although they would not explain why it was not.

Then in 1973, a batch of Warren Commission documents were released to the public that contained letters from FBI director J. Edgar Hoover. In these, Hoover reported that composition of the fragments was "similar" and "that no significant differences were found."

The fact that differences—no matter how "significant"—were found means they are not from the same source.

The real significance in this matter is that the results of these spectrographic tests have been kept from the public all these years. Obviously, if the tests proved conclusively that the fragments and CE 399 all came from the same ammunition, the case against Oswald would have been strengthened considerably. In fact, the opposite occurred. And by concealing the tests results, the Commission raised further suspicion about government handling of the case.

Unreported in the Commission's report or volumes was an account of even further scientific testing—this time using neutron activation analysis, a sophisticated method of determining differences in composition by bombarding the test object with radiation.

In referring to this test in a letter made public in 1973, Hoover wrote:

While minor variations in composition were found by this method, these were not considered to be sufficient to permit positively differentiating among the larger bullet fragments and thus positively determining from which of the larger bullet fragments any given small fragment may have come.

This wording is suspiciously deceptive, since any difference in composition is evidence that the fragments are not from the same ammunition.

Faced with scientific evidence that Kennedy and Connally were not struck by the same bullet, the House Select Committee on Assassinations decided to conduct their own tests. But researchers' hopes for a final, clear determination on this matter dimmed with the Committee's selection of Dr. Vincent P. Guinn to conduct the tests. Guinn admitted he had been an informal consultant to the FBI even prior to the Kennedy assassination. And predictably, Guinn concluded that it was "highly probable" that fragments taken from Connally's wrist came from CE 399.

This seemed to be the strong clear evidence researchers had been looking for, even though it appeared to support the single-bullet theory. Guinn's conclusions were warmly embraced by the House Committee. But it was later learned that the wrist fragments originally tested in 1964 were missing. And Guinn admitted publicly that the fragments he tested were not the originals from the National Archives.

Author Henry Hurt quoted Guinn as admitting how fragments from CE 399 could have been substituted for the missing fragments:

Possibly they would take a bullet, take out a few little pieces and put it in a container, and say, "This is what came out of Connally's wrist." And naturally if you compare it with [CE] 399, it will look alike . . . I have no control over these things.

Guinn also reported that he had examples of the ammunition from the four production runs in 1954 made at Western Cartridge Company, manufacturers of the Mannlicher-Carcano bullets. ". . . Reportedly those are the only lots they ever produced, and we have boxes from each of those lots," Guinn told the Committee.

If this was indeed the only ammunition ever produced, the results of Guinn's tests gain credibility. However, a Warren Commission document dealing with an interview of a Western Cartridge representative reveals this comment:

The Western Cartridge Company . . . manufactured a quantity of 6.5 . . . Mannlicher-Carcano ammunition for the Italian government during

World War II. At the end of the war the Italian Carcano rifle, and no telling how much of this type of ammunition, was sold to United States gunbrokers and dealers and subsequently was distributed by direct sales to wholesalers, retailers and individual purchasers.

If the ammunition supposedly used in the Oswald rifle came from this World War II batch, then Dr. Guinn tested the wrong bullets. This is another example of how seemingly indisputable evidence in the assassination diminishes upon closer examination.

Another major piece of evidence against Oswald was a brown paper bag reportedly discovered in the Texas School Book Depository on the afternoon of the assassination—although it is not depicted in any of the crime scene photographs. The Warren Commission claimed the bag was used by Oswald to transport the Mannlicher-Carcano rifle from a home in Irving, Texas, to the Depository on the morning of November 22, 1963.

If this bag indeed belonged to Oswald and if it could be traced to the Depository, it becomes strong evidence of Oswald's guilt. But again, upon closer inspection, this piece of evidence becomes highly questionable. First, while the Oswald rifle was found to be well oiled, there is absolutely no trace of gun oil on the paper bag.

Second, federal authorities claimed to have found cloth fibers on the bag that matched those of a blanket used to wrap the rifle at the Irving home. However, a Dallas police photograph of assassination evidence shows the bag touching the blanket, thus producing the incriminating fiber evidence. To add credence to this idea, the FBI found no traces of paper bag particles on the rifle.

When the Dallas evidence was shipped to the FBI laboratory early on November 23, there is no mention of the paper bag. Instead, Dallas FBI agent-in-charge J. Gordon Shanklin mentioned the blanket, which he suggested was used to carry the rifle into the Depository.

Both Wesley Frazier and his sister, Linnie Mae Randle, testified that Oswald took a paper bag to work with him on the morning of the assassination. However, both said they did not believe the bag they saw was like the one showed them by the Warren Commission. Frazier said Oswald told him the bag contained curtain rods for his room in Dallas. Frazier also said Oswald carried the package into the Depository tucked under his arm, with one end cupped in his hand and the other under his armpit.

Since the disassembled rifle measured thirty-five inches long, it would have been impossible for someone of Oswald's height to carry it in this position.

Jack Dougherty, a Depository employee who saw Oswald arrive for work, said he had seen no bag.

Yet the paper bag was a necessary piece of evidence, for if Oswald did not carry the rifle into the Depository on November 22, then it must have gotten there in some other manner. This possibility opened too many areas of investigation. But if Oswald fashioned the bag from wrapping paper at the Depository—as the Warren Commission concluded—how did he get it to the Irving home, where he spent the night before the assassination?

Frazier, who drove Oswald to Irving, repeatedly said Oswald had no package with him at that time. The Commission decided Oswald must have hidden the paper bag in his jacket, although there was no reason to do so and despite the discomfort and rustling noise sure to have been made by a 42-inch-by-18-inch folded paper bag.

This whole issue is further clouded by the discovery of a duplicate FBI report that claims two opposite facts concerning the paper bag.

In a November 29, 1963 report released with other FBI documents in 1968, Agent Vincent Drain wrote:

This paper was examined by the FBI laboratory and found to have the same observable characteristics as the brown paper bag shaped like a gun case which was found near the scene of the shooting on the sixth floor of the Texas School Book Depository building.

In 1980, researcher Gary Shaw discovered what appeared to be this same FBI report in the National Archives. It bore the same dates and the same identification number—Dallas 89-43.

However, in this version of Drain's report, it stated: "This paper was examined by the FBI laboratory and found not to be identical with the paper gun case found at the scene of the shooting."

When pressed for an explanation of the two opposite versions of the same report, William Baker, the FBI's assistant director of the Office of Congressional and Public Affairs, told researcher Edgar F. Tatro the version that states Depository paper and the paper bag are not the same was "inaccurate." Baker said the inaccuracy in Drain's original report was caught at FBI headquarters and the Dallas office was instructed to "make corrections at that time." He added that the "inaccurate" report was mistakenly passed along to the Warren Commission. Baker concluded: "We hope the above explanation resolves the problem."

Far from resolving the problem of identical FBI reports that state opposite facts, this incident raises the question of how many other assassination documents stated one thing and were subsequently "revised." And if there do exist "revised" documents in federal files, how would anyone know unless the originals accidentally slip out, as in this case?

Considering all of the above and considering that not one of the lawmen who searched the Depository mentioned finding the bag in their testimony, the evidence of the paper bag must be viewed skeptically.

Two other observations should be made concerning primary pieces of evidence—the presidential limousine and the rifle.

Even while the limousine was parked at the emergency-room door of

Parkland Hospital, federal agents and even Dallas police apparently mopped up blood, picked up bullet fragments, and otherwise tampered with this important piece of evidence, contrary to basic crime scene protection procedures. Within forty-eight hours the limousine was shipped to the Ford Motor Company in Detroit and completely dismantled, thus destroying any important bloodstains, bullet holes, or more bullet fragments that could have shed light on the assassination.

While the Mannlicher-Carcano was checked for fingerprints, apparently it was never given the simple test by Dallas police or the federal authorities to determine if it had been recently fired. This normal testing might have proved conclusively whether the rifle had been used in the assassination. The failure to conduct such a test is viewed by researchers as strong evidence of fabrication in the case against Oswald.

Other vital evidence was destroyed. After receiving Governor Connally's bloodstained clothing at Parkland Hospital, Congressman Henry Gonzales kept this potential evidence in a closet in his Washington office. Several months later, while Gonzales was home in Texas, Clifton Carter, an aide to Lyndon Johnson, notified a Gonzales secretary that the Secret Service was coming to pick up Connally's clothing.

Some time later, this clothing was presented as evidence to the Warren Commission. But by this time, it had been cleaned and pressed, thereby eliminating metal traces at the bullet holes that could have been studied to determine the type of ammunition and the direction of shots.

(It was Gonzales who formally called for a reopening of the assassination investigation in 1975, which led to the forming of the House Select Committee on Assassinations.)

But the one piece of evidence that did more than all others to convict Oswald as the assassin in the minds of the American public was the famous backyard photographs depicting Oswald with a Mannlicher-Carcano rifle and communist publications.

Questionable Backyard Photos

Dallas police claim to have discovered two prints and one negative of pictures showing Lee Harvey Oswald standing in his backyard wearing a holstered pistol and holding a rifle and some communist literature.

According to police reports, these photos were found among Oswald's possessions in the garage of the Paine home in Irving, Texas, on Saturday, November 23, 1963, although a search the day before failed to turn up such photos.

One of these photos became the cover of the February 21, 1964 issue of *Life* magazine. This now-famous issue was seen by millions around the world.

The Warren Commission heard from Oswald's accommodating wife,

Marina, that she had taken the snapshots with a hand-held Imperial Reflex camera at the insistence of her husband. The Commission, based on Marina's testimony and the order form for Oswald's rifle, pinpointed the date as March 31, 1963. She said she took one shot then handed the camera back to Oswald, who advanced the film and had her take another picture.

The Commission asserted that the rifle in the picture is the same rifle found on the sixth floor of the Texas School Book Depository.

Yet when shown the photographs by Dallas police, Capt. Will Fritz said Oswald made the following comments:

> He said the picture was not his, that the face was his face, but that this picture had been made by someone superimposing his face, the other part of the picture was not him at all and that he had never seen the picture before. . . . He told me that he understood photography real well, and that in time, he would be able to show that it was not his picture, and that it had been made by someone else.

Of course, Oswald never got the time to explain the backyard photos. But various researchers have spent years studying this incriminating evidence, and today almost all are convinced Oswald was truthful about the pictures being fabricated.

To begin with, it appears there were actually four backyard pictures. One was described by Marguerite Oswald as depicting her son holding a rifle above his head with both hands. She was shown this photo by Marina at the Paine's Irving home the night of the assassination. On Marguerite's insistence, the incriminating photo was burned and flushed down a toilet.

In 1976 the Senate Intelligence Committee discovered yet a fourth backyard photo in the hands of the widow of a Dallas policeman. Mrs. Roscoe White said her husband once told her the picture would be very valuable some day. In this heretofore unknown version of the backyard photo, Oswald is depicted holding the rifle in his left hand and the communist material in his right. This is the same pose used by Dallas police in reenacting the photo for the Warren Commission—strong evidence that authorities were aware of the suppressed picture long before it became known to the public.

Photo experts told the House Select Committee on Assassinations that the most famous backyard picture—the one used on the cover of *Life* magazine—was obviously made from the original negative while in the hands of Dallas authorities. Yet this negative was never accounted for by the Dallas police. The Committee noted: "There is no official record explaining why the Dallas Police Department failed to give the Warren Commission the other original negative."

To further cloud this issue, two Dallas commercial photographic processors have told this author they saw copies of the backyard photo the night of the assassination—more than twelve hours before they were reported found in the Paine garage.

Robert Hester, who was called from home on November 22, 1963, to help process assassination-related photographs for the FBI and Dallas police at National Photo, said he saw an FBI agent with a color transparency of one of these pictures and that one of the backyard photos he processed showed no figure in the picture. Hester's claim was corroborated by his wife, Patricia, who also helped process film on the day of the assassination.

There is also considerable question regarding the camera reportedly used to make these photographs. Oswald's brother Robert claimed to have obtained the camera from the Paine home on December 8, 1963. He did not mention it to authorities because he didn't realize anyone would be interested.

Robert was only told the camera belonged to his brother by Ruth Paine and the FBI did not receive the camera until February 24, 1964. About that time, Marina was shown two cameras but failed to identify either as belonging to her husband.

When the government got the camera, it was inoperable. FBI photographic expert Lyndal L. Shaneyfelt told the Warren Commission: "In order to be able to make a photograph with the camera, I had to make slight repairs to the shutter lever, which had been bent. I straightened it and cleaned the lens in order to remove the dirt which had accumulated."

Finally, in June 1964, Marina identified the camera as the one she used to take the photographs. Marina, who originally claimed to have only taken one picture, revised this statement in her testimony to the Commission in February 1964. She said: "I had even forgotten that I had taken two photographs. I thought there was only one. I thought there were two identical pictures, but they turned out to be two different poses."

She, of course, never mentioned the other two photographs. But then this incident was not the only time Marina's testimony reflected inconsistencies and rehearsal.

An objective viewing of the three available backyard photographs reveals internal problems aplenty. Although all three pictures were reportedly taken with a hand-held camera, the background of all three is identical when brought to the same size. That is, though cropped differently in the three photos, the elements of the background—shadows, leaves, branches, stairs, etc.—are exactly identical. This sameness of background could be produced with a stationary camera on a heavy tripod but is almost impossible with a hand-held camera.

The V-shaped shadow under Oswald's nose remains the same in all three pictures, although his head is tilted in different directions.

And the photos all show a discernible line marking a break in the print's emulsion across Oswald's face just above a flat, broad chin. In Dallas police photos, it is clear that Oswald had a sharply pointed, cleft chin.

And when all three photos are brought to the same size and placed on top of each other as transparencies, nothing matches except the face of Lee Harvey Oswald—strong evidence that he was telling the truth when he said his face had been superimposed on another body.

Oswald's assessment that the photos are superimposed fakes has been confirmed by two foreign authorities. In 1977, Maj. John Pickard, commander of the photographic department at the Canadian Defense Department, made these statements after studying the backyard pictures:

> The pictures have the earmarks of being faked. The shadows fall in conflicting directions. The shadow of Oswald's nose falls in one direction and that of his body in another. The photos were shot from a slightly different angle, a different distance, with the gun in a different hand. So, if one photo is laid on top of another, nothing could match exactly. Yet, impossibly, while one body is bigger, in the other the heads match perfectly, bearing out Oswald's charge that his head was pasted on an incriminating photograph.

Author and British Broadcasting Corporation investigative reporter Anthony Summers had the photos studied by retired Detective Superintendent Malcolm Thompson, a past president of the Institute of Incorporated Photographers in England. Thompson said he detected retouching in the photos around the area of Oswald's head and on the butt of the rifle. He also noted inconsistencies in the location of shadows and the different chin on Oswald. Thompson stated: "One can only conclude that Oswald's head has been stuck on to a chin which is not Oswald's chin. . . . My opinion is that those photographs are faked. . . . I consider the pictures to be the result of a montage."

However, neither Pickard nor Thompson studied the original photos. The Photographic Evidence Panel of the House Select Committee on Assassinations, which did study the originals, concluded in 1978 that it could find no evidence of fakery in the backyard photos.

This conclusion rested primarily on studies that showed markings on the edges of the negative of one of the original photographs were identical to markings on other photographs made by the Imperial Reflex camera. This ballistics-type evidence convinced the panel that the photos must be genuine.

However, Texas graphics expert Jack White pointed out that if a knowledgeable person wanted to fake the backyard pictures, it would have been a simple matter to produce a high-quality montage photograph using one backyard scene, a figure with rifle and papers and a head shot of Oswald, which then could be photocopied using the Imperial Reflex camera. This procedure would produce a backyard photo that could be proven to have come from the camera traced to Oswald.

Another method to achieve the same results, according to White, would be to make an exposure through the Imperial Reflex camera that would include the markings on the edge but nothing else. Then, when the composite photo is combined with this, the markings become part of the negative.

Asked to study the sameness of the different photos' backgrounds, the House Committee's experts said they measured the distances between certain objects in the pictures—such as wooden fence posts—and determined differences in distance, indicating that the photos were indeed separate shots.

White, on the other hand, claimed that the differences were simply the result of "keystoning" or tilting the easel on which the photograph was exposed in an enlarger. He said he, too, had been concerned with what appeared to be differences in the photos but discovered that by simply tilting the photographic print in an enlarger's easel, the backgrounds of the supposedly separate pictures overlapped and matched perfectly.

Furthermore, in recent years White has discovered other problems with the backyard photos. In one picture, the tips of Oswald's fingers appear to be missing as does one end of the rifle's telescopic scope. White claims this is due to sloppy airbrushing on the part of whoever faked the picture.

In one photo, the figure can be seen to be wearing a large ring on his right hand, yet the ring is missing in the other photos.

Sameness of backgrounds and Oswald's face, conflicting shadows and distances, loss of portions of the photos—again, a vital piece of evidence remains in "controversy" despite the inconsistencies that can be viewed by any layman and the studied opinions of experts.

Yet the federal government continues to vouch for the authenticity of the incriminating photos. The reason for this steadfast support may have been voiced by House Committee chief counsel Robert Blakey, who told the Committee:

If [the backyard photographs] are invalid, how they were produced poses far-reaching questions in the area of conspiracy, for they evince a degree of technical sophistication that would almost necessarily raise the possibility that [someone] conspired not only to kill the President, but to make Oswald a patsy.

Reenactment Problems

In light of the many questions that surround the physical evidence attempting to link Lee Harvey Oswald to the assassination, the Warren Commission tried to strengthen the case against the ex-Marine through the use of reenactments.

However, the results of these reenactments has been questioned by at least two of the participants.

Chester Breneman, a surveyor who participated in two separate reenactments of the Kennedy assassination, said the studies proved that more than one man was involved in the shooting. Breneman, who went on to become county surveyor of Eastland County, Texas, told this author in 1978 that distance and time figures published by the Warren Commission were "at odds" with figures obtained in the reenactment staged for the FBI and Secret Service in 1964.

Breneman's story was confirmed by Dallas County surveyor Bob West, who also participated in both reenactments. Both men were in West's office on the Monday following the assassination when a man entered. Breneman recalled:

> [He] said he was a special investigator for *Life* magazine. He asked if we would make an investigation down there [in Dealey Plaza] and see if any other bullets were fired and from which direction they came. They were aware at that time that something was haywire. . . . So, we went down there and roped the area off. I stood on the parapet where [Abraham] Zapruder stood and took those pictures. They had still pictures of all the frames of Zapruder's film. [Reportedly *Life* did not take possession of the Zapruder film until that same day.]

Breneman and West took measurements of the plaza and distances from the Texas School Book Depository and matched everything against the Zapruder stills.

Later that day, Breneman accompanied *Life*'s investigators to the thirteenth floor of Dallas's Adolphus Hotel, where they were headquartered. He said at that time everybody involved agreed that no one man could have done all the shooting the day of the assassination.

Breneman said the magazine investigators also had obtained a Mannlicher-Carcano rifle and attempted to work the bolt in the time frame attributed to Oswald.

Breneman, a former Marine medal winner for marksmanship, said he, too, worked the rifle's bolt for hours. He said: "We came to the conclusion that it couldn't be done in the time limit they were trying to get me down to."

He also said a strange incident occurred during his time with the magazine people: "This [one] man told me, 'My life isn't worth a plug nickel on this investigation.' Then he pulled his shirt back and showed me this bullet-proof vest. I thought that was a little odd."

Breneman again was visiting his friend West on May 31, 1964, when the FBI and Secret Service reenacted the assassination for the Warren Commission. Both surveyors participated in the tests. Breneman recalled:

> We again measured distances and elevations by matching the frames of the Zapruder film. We examined a bullet mark on the curb on the south side of [Elm] street. This part of the curb was replaced shortly after the

assassination. Also, right after the assassination, they were mentioning a [highway] sign which had a stress mark from a bullet on it. It's my understanding that this particular sign was quickly taken down and no one has been able to locate it.

During the May reenactment, Breneman said the FBI used a big Cadillac as a substitute for Kennedy's Lincoln Continental. "It was in no way like Kennedy's limousine," said Breneman.

West said: "That was one thing that was always funny to me. They brought this big old Cadillac down to use in the tests, but it was thirteen inches higher than Kennedy's car."

Breneman added: "They were all crunched up in there, shoulder to shoulder. In that condition it could have been possible for one man to shoot two of them."

West said his study showed that one of the alleged shots from the Depository followed a path straight through a leafy tree. West said: "If he shot through a hole in that tree, it was absolutely fantastic." Breneman concluded:

I wish to state that both investigations led us to believe beyond any doubt that there were two assassins. *Life* magazine's special investigators believed this to be true. The Secret Service would not say. But at the time, that seemed to be the reason we were there and we felt the Secret Service felt that way too.

After the Warren Commission published the figures from the government reenactment, Breneman and West were shocked to find that the figures did not match those made by them at the time. Both Breneman and West retained copies of the Dealey Plaza reenactment figures.

Breneman said:

They [the figures] were at odds with our figures. After checking a few figures, I said, "That's enough for me," and I stopped reading. . . . For instance, on our map, we marked the spot corresponding to Zapruder film frame 171. The Warren Commission changed this to 166 before they used it in the report. The Warren Report shows a 210 where we show a 208. . . . It would seem to me that . . . these figures were changed just enough that the Warren Commission could come up with the idea that another shot came from the same direction as the first. But all I have been concerned with is, did another shot come from another direction? I know danged well it did.

Neither Breneman nor West—the actual surveyors used for the Commission's reenactment studies—were asked to testify. Further, the Commission declined to publish the map drawn by Breneman and West, claiming it was inaccurate.

This map indicates a bullet hit on the south curb of Elm Street. Breneman said: "We were told not to study those bullet marks by the FBI."

Again, any meaningful search for the truth of the assassination was ended by altered figures and orders not to note extraneous bullet marks—all from federal authorities.

Summary

The physical evidence compiled against Lee Harvey Oswald appears formidable at first glance—a rifle traced to him, three spent cartridges on the sixth floor of the building where he worked, his palm print on the rifle, and even photographs of Oswald holding the murder weapon. However, the closer one inspects this evidence, the more questionable it becomes.

One example of tunnel vision on the part of federal authorities can be found in studying the testimony of assassination witnesses. While many people indicated the Texas School Book Depository as the source of shots, the majority of witnesses in Dealey Plaza believed shots came from the Grassy Knoll. Yet the federal authorities simply asserted they were wrong, possibly confused by echoes. A much more plausible interpretation of this evidence is that shots came from at least two separate locations.

Other witnesses—such as Jean Hill, Senator Ralph Yarborough, Phil Willis, and James Tague—claim their testimony was altered by federal authority.

Photographs of the crime scene and the empty shells found on the Depository's sixth floor can be demonstrated to be inaccurate, making them virtually useless as evidence.

One of the three shell casings was bent and would not have been able to fire a slug in the condition in which it was found.

There are many questions concerning the Mannlicher-Carcano rifle reportedly used in the assassination, beginning with its make and model. Even CIA documents questioned the accuracy of its identification.

Military experts stated it required the placement of three metal shims to make the rifle accurate with the sight and that the rifle had been adapted for a left-handed person. Oswald, according to his mother and his brother, was right handed.

Oswald's palm print reportedly found by a Dallas policeman on the underside of the dismantled rifle barrel has no chain of evidence and would not have been permitted in a court of law. Further, it can be shown that the incriminating palm print was likely made at the Miller Funeral Home by placing the dead Oswald's hand on the rifle.

Even sophisticated spectrographic analysis failed to prove conclusively that pieces of bullet recovered from both Kennedy and Connally came from the same bullet as claimed by the Warren Commission.

Findings of the spectrographic analysis were misrepresented and perhaps even deceptive.

Further suspicion concerning the evidence was aroused with the discovery of two seemingly identical FBI reports concerning the brown paper bag authorities claimed was used to smuggle the rifle into the Depository. While one FBI document stated the paper bag matched paper in the Depository, the other stated the paper was different.

Other items—such as the presidential limousine and Connally's clothing— were destroyed as evidence by order of federal authorities.

The most incriminating evidence against Oswald was the photographs reportedly made in the backyard of his home in March 1963. Yet a careful study of the three available snapshots—one was hidden from the public for more than thirteen years—gives ample evidence of fakery. This conclusion is supported by photographic experts both in England and Canada. Oswald himself claimed the photos were composites—his face pasted on someone else's body.

Yet the FBI and a photographic panel of the House Select Committee on Assassinations claim the photos are genuine. If they are not genuine, this means some sort of deception has taken place at the level of the federal investigations.

It can be demonstrated that such deception took place with reenactments of the assassination. Two Texas surveyors who were employed to conduct a reenactment of the assassination in Dealey Plaza for the FBI and Secret Service in 1964 have said their distance and elevation numbers were altered when published by the Warren Commission, making all of the detailed computations of time and distance offered by the Commission invalid. They also said the FBI and Secret Service ordered them not to record extraneous bullet marks in the street and on the Elm Street curb— further evidence of the deceit practiced by federal authorities.

All in all, there is not one single piece of physical evidence used against Oswald that cannot be called into question. This evidence must be considered in light of the possibility that much of it could have been planted for the purpose of incriminating Oswald in the assassination.

Once all this is understood, the case against Oswald as the lone assassin seems to crumble.

I think the Warren Commission has, in fact, collapsed like a house of cards.
—Senator Richard Schweiker

The Warren Commission

The federal government—led by President Lyndon Johnson—began to assert itself immediately following Kennedy's death.

The day after the assassination, despite tremendous confusion in Dallas and elsewhere, FBI director J. Edgar Hoover forwarded to Johnson a preliminary report detailing the evidence supporting the idea of Lee Harvey Oswald's sole guilt.

Following the death of the accused assassin on November 24, there were growing calls for an investigation wider than that of the Dallas police, who were being held responsible for Oswald's death in many circles.

That same day, Hoover talked with Johnson aide Walter Jenkins, stating:

> The thing I am concerned about, and so is [Deputy Attorney General Nicholas D.] Katzenbach, is having something issued so we can convince the public that Oswald is the real assassin. Mr. Katzenbach thinks that the President might appoint a Presidential Commission of three outstanding citizens to make a determination.

On November 25, President Johnson ordered his friend Hoover to prepare a detailed report on the circumstances surrounding Kennedy's death. The news media were already reporting leaks from the Bureau including: ". . . rumors that will be spiked by the [FBI] report . . . is one that there was a conspiracy involved, and another one that shots fired at Kennedy came from different guns."

That same day, Katzenbach wrote a memo to Johnson aide Bill Moyers and outlined his thoughts on an assassination investigation:

> It is important that all of the facts surrounding President Kennedy's assassination be made public in a way which will satisfy people in the United States and abroad. That all the facts have been told and that a statement to this effect be made now.
>
> 1. The public must be satisfied that Oswald was assassin; that he did not have confederates who are still at large; that the evidence was such that he would have been convicted at trial.
>
> 2. Speculation about Oswald's motivation ought to be cut off, and we should have some basis for rebutting thought that this was a Com-

munist conspiracy or (as the Iron Curtain press is saying) a right-wing conspiracy to blame it on the Communists. Unfortunately the facts on Oswald seem about too pat—too obvious (Marxist, Cuba, Russian wife, etc.). The Dallas Police have put out statements on the Communist conspiracy theory, and it was they who were in charge when he was shot and thus silenced.

3. The matter has been handled thus far with neither dignity nor conviction; facts are mixed with rumor and speculation. We can scarcely let the world see us totally in the image of the Dallas Police when our President is murdered.

I think this objective may be satisfied and made public as soon as possible with the completion of a thorough FBI report on Oswald and the assassination. This may run into the difficulty of pointing to inconsistency between this report and statements by Dallas Police officials; but the reputation of the Bureau is such that it may do the whole job.

The only other step would be the appointment of a Presidential Commission of unimpeachable personnel to review and examine the evidence and announce its conclusions. This has both advantages and disadvantages. I think it can await publication of the FBI report and public reaction to it here and abroad.

Also on November 25, Texas attorney general Waggoner Carr announced he planned to conduct a court of inquiry concerning the deaths of both Kennedy and Oswald. Carr named two prominent Texas attorneys—Leon Jaworski (who went on to become the special Watergate prosecutor) and Dean Storey—as special counsel for the probe.

The next day, Senator Everett Dirksen announced that a Senate investigation of the assassination would be conducted by a special committee headed by Senator James O. Eastland, chairman of the powerful Judiciary Committee. One Republican senator told newsmen: "Too many people are disturbed about the strange circumstances of the whole tragic affair."

Not to be outdone by the Senate, an attempt to create yet another investigative committee was announced in the House of Representatives the next day.

The grief-stricken attorney general, Robert Kennedy, was never consulted about any of these attempts. But the next-ranking officials of the Justice Department—Deputy Attorney General Katzenbach and Solicitor General Archibald Cox (later of Watergate fame)—met with Johnson's close friend, Attorney Abe Fortas, who had blocked the 1948 election investigation of Johnson by obtaining a court order from Supreme Court Justice Hugo Black.

These men, aided by Yale law professor Eugene Rostow, Secretary of State Dean Rusk, and columnist Joseph Alsop, convinced President Johnson that his plan for a Texas investigation could by misinterpreted by the public as an attempt to cover up the crimes in Johnson's home state.

It was decided that a national commission headed by men of unimpeachable integrity was needed.

These attempts at independent investigations ended one week after the assassination when President Johnson announced the creation of a "blue ribbon" presidential commission to probe the events in Dallas.

In telling of the formation of what came to be known as the Warren Commission, the *Dallas Morning News* commented: "Creation of the Presidential commission appeared certain to head off several congressional inquiries into the slaying of President Kennedy in Dallas a week ago."

The newspaper was absolutely correct. With the creation of the Warren Commission, Johnson not only blocked any congressional investigations but, by the next week, Texas attorney general Carr had announced postponement of his state board of inquiry.

Despite massive media coverage of Oswald's arrest, his slaying, and the amount of evidence offered to the public by both Dallas and federal authorities, a Gallup poll taken the first week of December 1963, showed a majority of respondents—52 percent—continued to believe that Oswald had not acted alone.

Rumors were widespread in Texas that Johnson, in some way, had a hand in the assassination. A man of distinction and credibility was needed to stop such rumors. That man was Chief Justice Earl Warren.

The Reluctant Chairman

Earl Warren had no middle name. He once said, "My parents were too poor to afford the luxury of a middle name." Born to Scandinavian immigrants on March 19, 1891, Warren grew up in Los Angeles and nearby Bakersfield. By delivering newspapers, working for the railroad where his father was employed, and other odd jobs, Warren managed to save enough money to enroll in the University of California at Berkeley.

In June 1912, Warren received a bachelor of letters degree and entered law school. He also began working in a nearby law firm acquiring practical experience. Warren graduated from the University of California Law School near the bottom of his class on May 14, 1914.

His law practice was interrupted by World War I. After enlisting as an infantry private, Warren was accepted for officer training and became a lieutenant. However the Armistice was signed before Lieutenant Warren could leave the United States. After the war, Warren became an assistant attorney for the city of Oakland and later a member of the district attorney's staff. By the late 1920s, he had married Nina Palmquist Meyers and become one of the nation's youngest district attorneys.

The young D.A. began acquiring a reputation for the relentless, but honest, prosecution of crime.

Building a reputation for honesty, hard work, and court convictions,

Warren easily won reelection in 1930. As his family grew, so did his political reputation.

In the late 1930's, Warren campaigned for and won the office of California attorney general.

Almost immediately, Republican Warren was in a heated contest with the California Democrat Governor Culbert Olson. Adding to their political differences were Olson's support of unions and his outspoken isolationism on the eve of World War II. This conflict reached a breaking point when, after Pearl Harbor, Olson proclaimed a state of emergency in California. Warren as attorney general, challenged his authority to do so and shortly after declared himself a candidate for governor.

In a surprising upset—Roosevelt and the Democrats were still in firm control nationally—Warren was elected governor of California in late 1942 by more than three hundred forty-two thousand votes.

As long-time friends and fellow Masons, Warren and Democrat Harry S. Truman remained cordial after Truman became president following the death of Roosevelt on April 12, 1945.

In 1946, despite eroding support from both the extreme right and left, Warren handily won reelection as governor and began to look toward Washington. During the 1948 Republican National Convention, Warren reluctantly agreed to run for vice president with Thomas Dewey, the former governor of New York. He may have actually been relieved when the team was defeated by Truman in the greatest upset victory in American politics.

Turned down nationally, Warren announced he would seek a third term as California governor. But conservative forces were lining up against him and his progressive policies. Nonetheless, thanks to Warren's reputation and the looming conflict in Korea, California voters returned him to office by more than a million votes.

Still wishing for national office, Warren announced he would seek the GOP presidential nomination in 1952. He was chagrined to quickly find himself pitted against the war hero, Dwight "Ike" Eisenhower. Richard Nixon, who had signed a pledge to support Warren, nevertheless began to campaign for Eisenhower, hoping for the vice presidential nomination that he indeed later received. Eisenhower got the nomination and then the presidency. Nixon, who had only been in public office for six years, was the nation's number-two man.

Warren had been a strong contender and Nixon was fearful of his clout in the next election. According to Warren biographer Pollack:

Nixon . . . badgered Eisenhower to find a suitable appointment for Governor Warren which would effectively separate him from his electoral constituency. The ideal solution presented itself in September 1953, when a vacancy arose on the Supreme Court after Chief Justice Fred Vinson suddenly died. Warren, who already had decided not to seek a fourth term as governor, was offered the prized seat and, to Nixon's delight, accepted.

New on the job and with the naïve Eisenhower years as a backdrop, Warren's intital decisions as chief justice tended to support the status quo. But as he grew more comfortable in his position, his decisions began to reflect the progressive policies he advocated as California governor. It was under Warren's leadership that the Supreme Court—after years of foot dragging—finally ruled on the touchy desegregation issues raised by *Brown* vs. *Board of Education of Topeka, Kansas*. Using private discussions as well as judicial conferences where no positions were taken by the justices, Warren was able to guide the court to its unanimous decision in favor of Brown, which virtually eliminated the old "Jim Crow" separate-but-equal segregation laws and paved the way for racial equality in the United States.

Brown was a landmark decision and one that caused archconservatives to begin a campaign of bitter attacks against the chief justice. IMPEACH EARL WARREN signs were commonplace throughout the South as well as Texas. Later court opinions dealing with the rights of accused persons and the persecution of suspected communists added further fuel to the fires of Warren's opponents.

In the squeaky-close election of 1960, the Republican Warren found himself voting for young John F. Kennedy, apparently because he could not bring himself to vote for the ever ambitious Nixon. Displaying considerable foresight, Warren told a California friend: "Nixon is a bad man."

Warren and Kennedy voiced mutual respect for each other and the new President supported the Warren Court's progressive activism, even in such controversial cases as the June 1962, decision that outlawed compulsory prayer in public schools.

In a congratulatory letter to Warren in September, 1963, Kennedy wrote:

You have presided over the work of the Supreme Court during ten years of extraordinary difficulty and accomplishment. There have been few decades in our history when the Court calendar has been crowded with so many issues of historic significance. As Chief Justice, you have borne your duties and responsibilities with unusual integrity, fairness, good humor, and courage. At all times your sense of judicial obligation has been unimpaired by criticism or personal attack. During my time as President, I have found our association to be particularly satisfying and I am personally delighted that during this week you will receive not only the acclaim of Californians, but also the respect and affection of all Americans whose common destiny you have so faithfully helped to shape throughout your public career.

Two months later, Warren was being asked to head a federal panel to decide who killed Kennedy.

On November 29, the same day President Johnson announced his plans for a special commission, Warren was visited by Deputy Attorney General Nicholas D. Katzenbach and Solicitor General Archibald Cox (who gained fame during Watergate by being fired as special prosecutor by Nixon). As they began to speak of the Commission, Warren interrupted: "If you are asking my permission to have an Associate Justice of this Court serve, I have no intention of giving my approval."

Warren was told he was being asked to serve as chairman of the presidential commission. He declined, saying: "Please tell the President that I am sorry but I cannot properly undertake this assignment." Warren then explained that he did not feel it proper for a member of one branch of government to be employed by another branch.

Two hours later, Warren received a telephone call from President Johnson. The new President wasn't going to take no for an answer. He summoned Warren to his office. Dutifully, the chief justice reported to his president and was given the famous "Johnson treatment"—a combination of back patting and arm twisting. According to Warren biographer Pollack:

> The President spoke gravely of the desperate need to restore public confidence. He hinted darkly at the possibility of dangerous international repercussions. He invoked Warren's sense of duty and patriotism . . . By the end of the interview, he had succeeded in making Warren feel that to refuse the President would be a betrayal of a public trust. As a man-to-man persuader, Lyndon Johnson had no equal. His trump card was: "Mr. Chief Justice, you were a soldier in World War I. There's nothing you then did that compares with what you can do now for your country. As your Commander-in-Chief, I am ordering you back into service."

There may have been matters of more personal concern that Johnson transmitted to Warren. In an internal Warren Commission memorandum written on February 17, 1964, Melvin Eisenberg mentioned what Warren told fellow commissioners regarding how he had been "pressured" by Johnson. Eisenberg wrote:

> The President stated that rumors of the most exaggerated kind were circulating in this country and overseas . . . Some rumors went so far as attributing the assassination to a faction within the government wishing the presidency assumed by President Johnson. Others, if not quenched, could conceivably lead the country into a war . . . No one could refuse to do something which might help prevent such a possibility. . . . He placed emphasis on the quenching of rumors and precluding further speculation.

Warren left the emotional meeting with tears in his eyes, perhaps thinking of what had become of the country he loved. He had reluctantly agreed to chair the Commission. It is obvious that Warren's sense of patriotism outweighed his sense of legality in his acceptance of the Commission chairmanship.

Later that same afternoon, Johnson signed Executive Order 11,130 creating the seven-man Warren Commission.

*   *   *

Some Commission members saw their work as having a dual purpose— one, to find the facts of the Kennedy assassination, the other, to calm public fears and suspicions both at home and abroad. Allen Dulles told author Edward Jay Epstein that since an atmosphere of rumors and suspicion interferes with the functioning of the government, especially abroad, one of the main tasks of the Commission as to dispel rumors.

Other Commission members also thought it their duty to protect the image of the United States as reflected in these public statements:

JOHN MCCLOY: [It was of paramount importance to] show the world that America is not a banana republic, where a government can be changed by conspiracy.
JOHN COOPER: [An important purpose was] to lift the cloud of doubts that had been cast over American institutions.

When evidence presented to the Commission supported this duality of purpose there was no problem. But since so much evidence contradicted the official assassination theory and called into question certain government institutions, it must be asked which purpose became paramount to the commissioners.

Johnson's old friend, lawyer Abe Fortas, and Katzenbach had prepared a list of seven prominent persons to serve on the new presidential commission. This list was promptly approved by President Johnson without change.

Headed by Chief Justice Warren, the Commission members were:

Representative Hale Boggs (D-La.)—The most vocal critic among Commission members, Boggs became frustrated with the panel's total reliance on the FBI for information. Speaking of the "single-bullet theory," Boggs once commented, "I had strong doubts about it." On April 1, 1971, House Majority Leader Boggs delivered a blistering attack on J. Edgar Hoover, charging that under his directorship the FBI had adopted "the tactics of the Soviet Union and Hitler's Gestapo." Boggs, who undoubtedly would have become Speaker of the House and a powerful ally in any reopening of the JFK assassination investigation, vanished on October 16, 1972, while on a military junket flight in Alaska. Despite a massive search, no trace of the airplane or of Boggs has ever been found.

Senator John Sherman Cooper (R-Ky.)—A former member of the Kentucky General Assembly and county judge, Cooper served with the U.S. 3rd Army in Europe during World War II and helped reorganize the judicial system in Bavaria. He also was a former ambassador to India and Nepal in the mid-1950s. Like Boggs, Cooper later voiced dissatisfaction with the Commission's "single-bullet theory," stating he was "unconvinced."

Allen W. Dulles—Dulles had been fired as director of the Central Intelligence Agency by Kennedy following the ill-fated Bay of Pigs Invasion. Today it seems more than ironic that Dulles would have been selected to sit in judgment on Kennedy's death. Dulles also was tightly connected to the military, not only because of his years with the CIA, but because of his service in World War II, which included arranging the surrender of German troops in Italy. It is now acknowledged that Dulles withheld CIA information from the Warren Commission, particularly concerning assassination plots between the Agency and organized crime.

Representative Gerald Ford (R-Mich.)—Former President Ford is now recognized as the FBI's "spy" on the Warren Commission. This is confirmed by a memo from Cartha DeLoach, a close aide to Director Hoover, in which he noted:

> I had a long talk this morning [December 12, 1963] with Congressman Gerald R. "Jerry" Ford . . . He asked that I come up and see him . . . Ford indicated he would keep me thoroughly advised as to the activities of the Commission. He stated this would have to be on a confidential basis, however, he thought it should be done. He also asked if he could call me from time to time and straighten out questions in his mind concerning our investigation. I told him by all means he should do this. He reiterated that our relationship would, of course, remain confidential.

According to former New Orleans D.A. Jim Garrison:

> . . . Ford [also] enjoyed the reputation of being the CIA's best friend in the House of Representatives.

Ford's name as a member of the Warren Commission was recommended to President Johnson by Richard Nixon. A World War II Navy veteran, Ford became the Commission's most industrious member, hearing seventy out of the ninety-four witnesses who actually met with commissioners. He also profited from his time on the Commission. Ford had his first campaign manager and former Nixon for President campaign field director John R. Stiles hired as his special assistant. Ford and Stiles went on to write *Portrait of the Assassin*, a book that presented selective evidence of Oswald's guilt. When their publisher found the book dull reading, Ford and Stiles spiced it up with rewritten transcripts of the January 27, 1964 Commission meeting where Oswald's possible connection to the FBI was discussed. The minutes of this meeting were classified Top Secret and remained closed to the public. During confirmation hearings before the Senate Judiciary Committee in 1973, Ford was asked specifically about his use of classified Warren Commission material in his book. Ford replied:

> . . . we did not use in that book any material other than the material that was in the 26 volumes of testimony and other exhibits that were subsequently made public and sold to the public generally.

When it was discovered that the January 27, 1974, meeting transcripts were still classified, Ford belatedly said:

> I cannot help but apologize if the circumstances are such that there was this violation, but there certainly was no attempt to do it.

Despite being caught in perjury, Ford was dutifully confirmed by his old friends in Congress and sworn in as this nation's first unelected president. Six months later, Ford ordered the Commission material in question declassified.

John J. McCloy—As coordinator for the Kennedy administration's disarmaments activities since 1961, McCloy had a distinguished background. He had been assistant secretary of war throughout World War II, military governor and high commissioner for Germany from 1949 to 1952, and president of the World Bank from 1947 to 1949. He also help build the U.S. intelligence establishment after the war. Despite his continued defense of the Warren Commission, McCloy himself voiced a prophetic skepticism of its work on December 5, 1963, stating:

> The Commission is going to be criticized . . . no matter what we do, but I think we would be more criticized if we simply posed before the world as something that is evaluating Government agencies' reports, who themselves may be culpable.

In Commission arguments over the "single-bullet theory," it was McCloy who finally proposed that the evidence supporting this theory be called "persuasive," a term all members finally agreed upon.

Senator Richard B. Russell (D-Ga.)—As chairman of the powerful Senate Armed Services Committee, Russell carried much clout on Capitol Hill, usually employed to further the aims of the Pentagon. His work on behalf of defense projects brought sizable government contracts to Georgia. A former governor there from 1931 to 1933, Russell was elected to the Senate in 1933. Russell also sat on the watchdog Subcommittee on CIA Oversight. Russell, widely regarded as one of the most intelligent senators, became the first Warren Commission member to publicly question its conclusions. In a 1970 *Washington Post* article, Russell said he had come to believe that a criminal conspiracy had resulted in Kennedy's death. The senator even worked with assassination researcher Harold Weisberg in an effort to obtain Commission transcripts. In a court affidavit, Weisberg stated:

Privately Senator Russell told me that he was convinced that there were two areas in which Warren Commission members had been deceived by Federal agencies responsible for investigating the assassination of President Kennedy. These two areas were: (1) Oswald's background; and (2) the ballistics evidence.

As can be seen, all of the Commission members had long-standing ties to both the military and intelligence establishments of the United States. They also were men accustomed to the delicacy of dealing with highly sensitive political issues.

Each had received a copy of White House Executive Order 11130, which, after naming the seven members of the President's Commission, stated:

The purposes of the Commission are to examine the evidence developed by the Federal Bureau of Investigation and any additional evidence that may hereafter come to light or be uncovered by federal or state authorities; to make further investigation as the Commission finds desirable; to evaluate all the facts and circumstances surrounding such assassination, including the subsequent violent death of the man charged with the assassination, and to report to me its findings and conclusions.

The Commission is empowered to prescribe its own procedures and to employ such assistants as it deems necessary.

Necessary expenses of the Commission may be paid from the "Emergency Fund for the President."

In an effort to obtain fairness for her son, Marguerite Oswald wrote to Warren Commission general counsel J. Lee Rankin and even President Johnson, stating: "I [am] . . . imploring both in the name of justice and our American way of life to let my son Lee Harvey Oswald be represented by council [sic] so that all witnesses including my son's widow will be cross-examined."

Her request was denied.

In fact, every basic legal right guaranteed to even the lowliest street criminal—the right to legal representation, to face accusers, to cross-examine witnesses and evidence—was denied Lee Harvey Oswald. The Commission met behind closed doors, heard secret testimony, and emerged to announce its conclusions.

Armed with a mandate to ". . . uncover all the facts concerning the assassination of President Kennedy and to determine if it was in any way directed or encouraged by unknown persons at home or abroad," the Commission set to work.

The Warren Commission's first official meeting took place on December 5, 1963. The primary purpose of this meeting was to get the investigation organized. During this process, Warren suggested that the Commission need not hire its own investigators nor obtain subpoena powers from Congress. He was, however, overridden in this matter by other Commission members. McCloy stated:

> . . . I have a feeling that we have another obligation than the mere evaluation of the reports of agencies, many of which as you suggested, or some of them at least, may be interested, may be involved. There is a potential culpability here on the part of the Secret Service and even the FBI, and these reports . . . may have some self-serving aspects in them. And I think that if we didn't have the right to subpoena documents, the right to subpoena witnesses if we needed them, that this Commission's general standing might be somewhat impaired.

Not wishing to appear as simply a conduit for information from federal agencies, Commission members appealed to Congress for the right to issue subpoenas. This was granted on December 13, 1963, by the passage of Senate Joint Resolution 137. This law also authorized the Commission to compel testimony by providing immunity from prosecution—an authority that the Commission never once used.

During this meeting, Senator Russell noted the ongoing leaks of assassination information by the FBI while Commission members were still awaiting the Bureau's first full report. He asked pointedly: ". . . how much of their findings does the FBI propose to release to the press before we present the findings of this Commission?"

This was the beginning of a quiet—yet intense—feud between the Commission and Hoover's Bureau.

There followed a discussion of the hiring of a general counsel, with Dulles remarking: "I don't think it should be anybody from Texas."

Finally the members tried to decide on a time to reconvene. Ford asked Warren to clarify his plans for Commission meetings later in December because "we have a holiday season coming up, at least I have, with some family plans."

A meeting was scheduled for the next day, but McCloy begged off, saying: "I have this luncheon with the President, whatever it is. They made it clear to me it was a command performance."

The Commission's second meeting was on December 6. Both then as the day before there was considerable discussion about the proposed Texas court of inquiry.

State Attorney General Carr had traveled from Texas to Washington but was put off from meeting with Warren for three days because the chief justice wanted a formal promise that there would be no Texas hearings until after his Commission had completed its investigation. Warren read from a letter he had sent Carr stating: ". . . it is the view of this

Commission . . . that a public inquiry in Texas at this time might be more harmful than helpful in our search for the truth.''

Warren then told his fellow commissioners:

I think that we have to show a spirit of cooperation with these people and still . . . not reveal everything we have got or anything about our innermost secrets. . . . I've cooperated with the federal government in a thousand things when I was in state government and we didn't tell everything . . .

It was during this meeting that the name of J. Lee Rankin was advanced as a possible general counsel for the Commission.

Warren originally wanted Warren Olney III, head of the FBI Criminal Division from 1953 to 1957, as chief counsel. However, Olney, an outspoken critic of Director J. Edgar Hoover and most knowledgeable about the internal workings of the Bureau, was rejected after the powerful Hoover voiced fierce opposition to his appointment.

The Commission then recessed until December 16, when it reviewed the first formal report on the assassination issued by the FBI on December 9. Warren set the tone by commenting: "Well, gentlemen, to be very frank about it, I have read that FBI report two or three times and I have not seen anything in there yet that has not been in the press.''

Boggs commented: ''. . . reading that FBI report leaves a million questions.''

Dulles said the CIA couldn't finalize a report until the Agency received more documents from the FBI. He commented: "They've been working for a long while, I know. It started when I was there.'' This was the first admission that the CIA had been keeping an eye on Oswald since his trip to Russia in 1959.

On December 8, 1963, J. Lee Rankin, a fifty-six-year-old corporate attorney and U.S. solicitor general under Eisenhower, had accepted the appointment as general counsel for the commission and met for the first time with the commissioners. Rankin would take charge of the Commission's investigation, serve as the primary liaison between the Commission and both the FBI and CIA, and act as cordinator between Commission members and the staff. One Commission attorney said years later: "It was, very simply, a Rankin operation.'' And Rankin appeared more concerned with wrapping up the Commission's investigation swiftly than fully probing each assassination issue.

When Commission assistant counsel Wesley Liebeler submitted a twenty-six-page memorandum to Rankin carefully outlining the serious deficiencies of the evidence against Oswald as the lone assassin, Rankin reportedly replied: "No more memorandums. The report has to be published.''

On another occasion when Liebeler tried to address the problems arising from the Silvia Odio affair an angry Rankin said: "At this stage, we are supposed to be closing doors, not opening them."

Initially, even Rankin voiced the suspicion that the Commission might have to do more than simply evaluate FBI reports. During the December 16 meeting, he stated:

> The Chief Justice and I finally came to the conclusion . . . that we might have to . . . ask for some investigative help . . . because we might not get all we needed by just going back to the FBI and other agencies because the [FBI] report has so many loopholes in it. Anybody can look at it and see that it just doesn't seem like they're looking for things that this Commission has to look for in order to get the answers that it wants and is entitled to . . . [This] might be a tender spot. I am sure the FBI is certainly tender about the knowledge they had [concerning Oswald's presence in Dallas] and the fact that the Secret Service did not have that knowledge in order to do anything about it.

After discussing whether or not to forward the FBI assassination report to the CIA, Senator Russell summed up the problem of dealing with the various government agencies by saying:

> I have never been able to understand why it is that every agency acts like it's the sole agency in the government. There is very little interchange of information between the departments in the United States Government.

The Commission members then debated how soon to interview Mrs. Kennedy. All seemed loath to interview the widow, yet most agreed that she would constitute a most important witness. McCloy stated: "She's got it very definitely in mind now . . . She may not be the chief witness as to who did the job. She's the chief witness as to how those bullets hit her husband. She saw both of them."

On January 21, 1964, the Commission met for the fourth time. Warren optimistically predicted an early end to the investigation, although there continued to be debate over whether to hurry up the Commission's work prior to the election-year conventions or slow it down pending the outcome of the Texas trial of Jack Ruby, which was about to begin.

And again the issue of FBI reliability was raised, this time in connection with the conflicting information commissioners were getting concerning the President's wounds. McCloy said:

> Let's find out about these wounds, it is just as confusing now as could be. It left my mind muddy as to what really did happen. . . . why did the FBI report come out with something which isn't consistent with the autopsy . . . ?

Rankin urged avoiding embarrassment in questioning the FBI, saying: "... it would make our relations difficult and make it hard for us to get the other material if we needed it later."

Senator Russell even suggested double-checking the FBI studies, but no action was taken.

A lengthy discussion ensued regarding the Commission's responsibility to question Mrs. Kennedy and the new President, Lyndon Johnson. However, almost a dozen pages of this discussion were marked "classified" and kept from the public.

The Commission then discussed the possibility of moving Oswald's body, including another autopsy and even cremation. Although the transcripts make no mention that they suspected impersonation at this time, it is significant to note the Commission's interest in Oswald's body. McCloy said: "I don't think we ought to have on the record that we are moving in this thing [an Oswald exhumation]. We are not saying anything about it."

In response to news articles that Marina Oswald was being held against her will, Warren suggested allowing someone with the American Civil Liberties Union to meet with her. Rankin added: "We do have a little problem because the Secret Service came to us and said, 'Shall we quit our surveillance over her?' . . . I said we can't do that because she would slip right across the border and be gone . . ."

The Commission again grappled with the problem of interagency rivalries.

Oswald and the FBI

On January 22, 1964, the Warren Commission was hurriedly called into secret session because of the explosive news that Texas authorities were in possession of information that Oswald had been an undercover informant for the FBI. Reports of this meeting were not made public until 1975.

Rankin told members:

Yes, it was being rumored that [Oswald] was an undercover agent. Now it is something that would be very difficult to prove out. There are events in connection with this that are curious, in that they might make it possible to check some of it out in time. I assume that the FBI records would never show it. . . . or if their records do show anything, I would think their records would show some kind of number that could be assigned to a dozen different people according to how they wanted to describe them. . . . [Oswald] did use postal boxes practically every place he went, and that would be an ideal way to get money to anyone that you wanted as an undercover agent . . .

Rankin wondered aloud if Oswald had been operating for the FBI during his trip to Russia, but Warren pointed out ". . . they haven't any people in

Russia . . .'' Rankin was still wondering: ''One of the strange things that happened . . . is the fact that this man who is a defector, and who was under observation at least by the FBI . . . could [obtain] a passport that permitted him to go to Russia.''

Rankin then connected his musings to the Commission's problems with the Bureau:

> . . . the FBI is very explicit that Oswald is the assassin or was the assassin, and they are very explicit that there was no conspiracy, and [yet] they are also saying in the same place that they are continuing their investigation. Now in my experience of almost nine years, in the first place it is hard to get them to say when you think you have got a case tight enough to convict somebody. . . . In my experience with the FBI, they don't do that. They claim that they don't evaluate . . . secondly, they have not run out of all kinds of leads in Mexico or in Russia and so forth which they could probably. . . . But they are concluding that there can't be a conspiracy without those [leads] being run out. Now that is not [normal] from my experience with the FBI. . . . it raises questions.

The specter of Oswald being identified as an FBI agent caused great difficulty for the Commission. There appeared no way to fully resolve the matter, and, as Representative Boggs pointed out: ''[The] implications of this are fantastic, don't you think so? . . . I don't even like to see this being taken down.''

Dulles agreed: ''Yes, I think this record ought to be destroyed.''

Five days after this secret meeting, the Commission met formally. The minutes of this meeting, January 27, 1964, show that commissioners were still agonizing over the question of Oswald's possible involvement with the FBI. More than two hours of its three-and-a-half-hour afternoon session was spent trying to decide how to broach the subject with Director J. Edgar Hoover. The problem was compounded by rumors that added the CIA to Oswald's suspected intelligence connections.

The stories of Oswald's spy connections were traced back from Texas attorney general Waggoner Carr to Dallas D.A. Henry Wade and more specifically Assistant D.A. William Alexander. Alexander claimed he got the story from *Houston Post* reporter Alonzo Hudkins, who said he got it from Dallas deputy sheriff Allan Sweatt. Sweatt revealed his source for the story was none other than Alexander—who was on the scene of the Tippit slaying and reportedly also present at Oswald's capture at the Texas Theater.

Apparently no attempt was made to determine just where Alexander got his information that Oswald was FBI informant S-179 being paid two hundred dollars a month.

Rankin dismissed the possibility of approaching Attorney General Robert Kennedy with the problem, saying:

As the head of the [Justice] department, the FBI, of course, is under the attorney general, but I think we must frankly recognize amongst ourselves that there is a daily relationship there . . . and we wouldn't want to make that more difficult . . .

He then raised the possibility of going straight to FBI director J. Edgar Hoover. But since Hoover was already on record denying that Oswald had any connection with the Bureau, Commission members were hesitant to anger the dour Hoover by initiating their own inquiries. Senator Russell said: "There is no man in the employ of the federal government who stands higher in the opinion of the American people than J. Edgar Hoover."

Furthermore, Commission member Allen Dulles, former head of the CIA, while admitting that government agencies and even local police departments employed "terribly bad characters" as undercover agents, bluntly implied there was no way to prove such allegations during the following exchange:

REP. BOGGS: Let's say [someone] . . . was recruited by someone in the CIA. The man who recruited him would know, wouldn't he?

DULLES: Yes, but he wouldn't tell.

CHAIRMAN WARREN: Wouldn't tell it under oath?

DULLES: I wouldn't think he would tell it under oath, no . . . He ought not tell it under oath. Maybe not tell it to his own government but wouldn't tell it any other way.

MCCLOY: Wouldn't he tell it to his own chief?

DULLES: He might or might not. If he was a bad one then he wouldn't.

Dulles added that he would not reveal CIA business to anyone except the President and that questioning Hoover would not necessarily get to the truth. Dulles explained:

. . . if [Hoover] says no, I didn't have anything to do with it. You can't prove what the facts are. There are no external evidences. I would believe Mr. Hoover. Some people might not. I don't think there is any external evidence other than the person's word that he did or did not employ a particular man as a secret agent. No matter what.

Member McCloy voiced the Commission's exasperation with its total dependence on the FBI: ". . . the time is almost overdue for us to have a better perspective of the FBI investigation than we now have. . . . We are so dependent upon them for our facts . . ."

Commission members also were becoming suspicious that the Bureau was not being totally open with them regarding certains aspects of the assassination. For example, Rankin recalled that Marina Oswald told about her husband meeting with two FBI agents for nearly two hours shortly after their return from Russia, but said: ". . . we don't have any report that would cover anything like a two-hour conversation."

Senator Russell summed up the Commission's dilemma:

It seems to me we have two alternatives. One is we can just accept the FBI's report and go on and write the report based on their findings and supported by the raw materials they gave us, or else we can go and try to run down some of these collateral rumors that have just not been dealt with directly in this raw material that we have.

The Commission opted to allow Rankin to approach Hoover in the manner he thought best. But after all was said and done, the Warren Commission elected to accept the FBI's information and conclusions without independent verification.

*   *   *

During the same meeting that commissioners agonized over the question of Oswald's possible connection with the FBI, Rankin outlined at length the six major areas of the Commission's investigation.

Area 1 was "The Basic Facts of the Assassination," dealing with the number and source of the shots. In charge of this area were Commission assistant counsels Francis W. H. Adams, who had served as a special assistant to the U.S. attorney as well as police commissioner and chief assistant U.S. attorney in New York City, and Arlen Specter, a Yale Law School graduate and an assistant district attorney in Philadelphia. In March 1964, Adams announced he could not fulfill his responsibility in the investigation. Specter went on to singlehandedly manage this critical area.

Area 2 was to establish the "Identity of the Assassin." In charge were David Belin, an Iowa attorney with a distinguished academic record, and Joseph A. Ball, an Iowa-born attorney who was teaching criminal law and procedures at the University of Southern California. Belatedly, an investigation of the murder of policeman J. D. Tippit was added to this area.

Area 3 was a study of "Oswald's Background," an aspect of the probe that clearly indicated the Commission's predisposition toward Oswald's guilt.

Area 4 was to determine "Possible Conspiratorial Relationships." It was headed by William T. Coleman, Jr., a Pennsylvania attorney who had served as law clerk to U.S. Court of Appeals judge Herbert F. Goodrich and Supreme Court justice Felix Frankfurter as well as a consultant with the U.S. Arms Control and Disarmament Agency, and W. David Slawson, a Denver, Colorado attorney educated at Amherst College, Princeton, and Yale.

Area 5 was the study of "Oswald's Death." In charge were Burt Griffin and Leon Hubert, both former assistant U.S. attorneys.

Area 6 was added at a later date and dealt with "Presidential Protection," a study of the security precautions of the Secret Service and the FBI. Samuel Stern, a former law clerk to Chief Justice Warren, was assigned to the job, but Chief Counsel Rankin supervised this "politically sensitive area."

Rankin also outlined the questions already arising over the medical evidence. He said:

> . . . We think that the wound in the neck has to be related to one of these others, but the problem is difficult to determine because we have a statement from the hospital that the bullet that was more whole than the other was found on the stretcher which they brought the President in to the hospital on and then we have testimony later that goes back over the same ground . . . [saying] that this bullet was found under the blanket on the stretcher Gov. Connally was on.

It was the beginning of years of controversy over the basic medical and ballistic evidence.

As with the later House Select Committee on Assassinations, many experts with lengthy credentials were called upon by the Warren Commission to substantiate various assassination evidence, such as Oswald's fingerprints and ballistics. And, as with the House Committee, while these experts supported the government's conclusions, none of them could later state with any certainty that the materials they were given by the Commission were the original materials. But the possibility that someone within the government would substitute or fabricate evidence never seemed to have crossed the minds of the experts or commissioners.

There was also controversy over Oswald's connections. Rankin told the commissioners: "We have no evidence that is clear that Oswald was connected with anybody but we also have very great problems . . ." In regard to the Oswald's life in Russia, Rankin commented: "That entire period is just full of possibilities for training, for working with the Soviets, and its agents . . ."

Rankin also briefly discussed Jack Ruby and his associations with crime figures:

> He had all kinds of connections with the minor underworld, I think you would call it, in Dallas and in Chicago, but I don't—it isn't apparent that any of the important people in the underworld would have given him any consideration at all. . . . Now it would seem that he might have—he might be the kind of person they might try to use. He was a habitue apparently of the police department and was able to go to any part of it at any time, and they knew him . . .

On February 24, 1964, Warren, Senator Cooper, Representive Ford, Dulles, and Rankin met for about ten minutes. Rankin reported no significant progress in the problem area of Oswald's possible connection with the FBI. He said affidavits from Hoover, FBI agents, and even Dallas officials "show negative." However, he also reported one instance of the Bureau's lack of candor with the Commission, saying:

> As you recall, we informed you before that the address in the telephone book of Lee Oswald had in it the name of [FBI agent James] Hosty and his telephone number and his automobile license, and that it wasn't in the transcript of that information which was furnished to us by the FBI. And we have written to the FBI to ask them, an official inquiry, how that could happen, and to furnish us all of the information concerning that occurrence. And we have not received a reply yet.

On March 16, 1964, three and a half months after its inception, the Warren Commission met again. This three-minute session was to approve a resolution governing the questioning of witnesses by Commission staff members. Only Warren, Senator Cooper, Representative Ford, McCloy, and Rankin attended.

Jack Ruby's trial had ended on March 14, and at this point the real Warren Commission investigation began. On March 18, Commission staff attorneys flew to Dallas and set up a field station in the offices of U.S. attorney Barefoot Sanders.

Also in March the "more important" witnesses were called to testify over a period of fourteen days. By April, the number of days spent hearing testimony had dropped to seven.

On April 30, 1964, the Commission met again. Commissioners Ford, Boggs, and Russell were absent. Senator Cooper left the two-hour meeting after only thirty minutes.

Despite the passage of nearly five months, Commissioners were still concerned about the contradictions in the investigative material. The question of Oswald's involvement with the FBI and CIA remained unresolved.

Senator Cooper even expressed his concern over contradictions between the testimony of witnesses to Commission attorneys and news media reports of interviews with the same witnesses.

Conflicts in the Testimony

The questions raised by Senator Cooper remain valid today. Only a few assassination researchers have seen fit to study the problems between what some Commission witnesses actually said and what was reported.

Yet if basic conflicts exist in the Warren Commission testimony then all of it—used as primary evidence in all studies of the Kennedy assassination— must be reevaluated.

In fact, a close scrutiny of this issue brings out deeply troubling instances of suppression of evidence and intimidation of witnesses in this case.

The first problem with Warren Commission testimony is omissions. Despite what was hailed at the time as one of the most thorough investigations of all time, a review of the Warren Commission's performance reveals glaring deficiencies.

In their report, commissioners devoted more than a page to a detailed discussion of Lee Harvey Oswald's pubic hair. In their volumes, several pages are used to reproduce Marguerite Oswald's tax and house payment receipts, some dating back into the 1930s, and the dental records of Jack Ruby's mother.

Many other pages were filled with meaningless and irrelevant testimony, such as that of Mrs. Anne Boudreaux, who knew a woman who once babysat for the infant Oswald (Mrs. Boudreaux never met either Oswald or his mother); that of Mrs. Viola Peterman, a former neighbor of Marguerite Oswald who had not seen her for twenty-seven years; and that of Professor Revilo Pendleton Oliver, who took up thirty-five pages of testimony to discuss an article he had written that had no bearing on factual matters.

Yet many of the more pertinent witnesses were never asked to tell what they knew. These included:

JAMES CHANEY, the motorcycle policeman closest to Kennedy during the assassination who told newsmen he saw the President "struck in the face" by the final shot.

BILL and GAYLE NEWMAN, two of the bystanders closest to Kennedy at the time of the fatal head shot, who have consistently said that shots came from directly behind them on the Grassy Knoll.

CHARLES BREHM, a former U.S. Army Ranger combat veteran and one of the closest bystanders to Kennedy when he was shot.

J. C. PRICE, who from his bird's-eye perch on top of the Terminal Annex building witnessed the entire assassination and then told of seeing a man with a rifle running behind the wooden picket fence on top of the Grassy Knoll.

MILTON JONES, who told the FBI that he was on a Dallas bus that was boarded and searched by Dallas police after Oswald had gotten off, although at that time no one knew that Oswald was a suspect.

MARY DOWLING, a waitress at Dallas's Dobbs House restaurant who told the FBI that Policeman Tippit had been in the restaurant on November 20, when Oswald was there making a fuss over his food.

JAMES SIMMONS, a Union Railroad employee who supported Sam Holland in his contention that shots came from behind the picket fence on the Grassy Knoll.

RICHARD DODD, another railroad employee who told of hearing shots and seeing smoke come from behind the picket fence.

ALONZO HUDKINS, the Houston newspaperman who reported that Dallas officials told him that Oswald was an informant for the FBI.

RAY RUSHING, an evangelist who claimed to have ridden in an elevator at Dallas Police Headquarters with Jack Ruby about two hours before Ruby murdered Oswald and at a time when Ruby reportedly was at his home.

LT. GEORGE BUTLER, the Dallas police official in charge of Oswald's transfer November 24 and who was reported to have been in an extremely agitated condition by newspaperman Thayer Waldo.

ADMIRAL GEORGE BURKLEY, Kennedy's personal physician who rode in the motorcade, was with Kennedy at Parkland Hospital, rode with *Air Force One* on the trip back to Washington, was present at the Bethesda autopsy, and received all of the official medical evidence, much of which is now in controversy.

JOHN T. STRINGER and LT. WILLIAM PITZER, who photographed and X-rayed Kennedy's body at Bethesda Naval Hospital.

JAMES SIBERT and FRANCIS O'NEILL, two FBI agents who attended Kennedy's autopsy and made a report that contradicts some of the official conclusions.

RICHARD RANDOLPH CARR, a steelworker who reported seeing two men run from behind the Texas School Book Depository and drive off in a Rambler station wagon.

MARVIN ROBINSON, a motorist in Dealey Plaza who corroborated Deputy Sheriff Roger Craig's claim that Oswald entered a west-bound Rambler station wagon in front of the Depository minutes after the assassination.

SENATOR RALPH YARBOROUGH, who rode beside Lyndon Johnson in the motorcade and smelled gunpowder as they passed the Grassy Knoll.

The omission of these people's testimony appears to go far beyond inefficient oversight. It seems rather to support the charges by Warren Commission critics that the panel avoided information that conflicted with their preconceived determination that Oswald was the lone assassin.

Most of the conclusions reached by the Warren Commission—notably the single-bullet theory—were contradicted by medical evidence, the witnesses, and Governor John Connally. Therefore, the Commission chose to simply ignore them.

Some witnesses who were questioned by the Commission—either directly or by deposition—have told researchers and newsmen that their testimony was altered. Others simply shrugged off their superficial questioning. Railroad supervisor Lee Bowers later said: "I was there to tell them only what they asked and when they wanted to cut off the conversation, I figured that was the end of it."

Butch Burroughs, Jean Hill, Phil Willis, Orville Nix, James Tague, and others have stated that their testimony as presented by the Commission did not accurately reflect what they said.

While every Commission witness was given the opportunity to review his testimony for accuracy, as far as can be determined, few took advantage of the offer. As one person put it: "I trust you . . ."

One Warren Commission witness voiced her complaints to the FBI. Mrs. Nancy Powell, better known as Ruby stripper Tammi True, talked to agents in August of 1964. In their report, the agents stated:

Mrs. Powell complained that she did not feel that her testimony had been recorded accurately in the deposition. It was explained to Mrs. Powell that persons, while conversing, give meaning to their words through voice inflections, and that reading the words without inflections sometimes gives different meaning to the words which was not meant. . . . At that time she stated to me that the deposition as written was not acceptable to her, particularly in the area where she was questioned relative to Jack Ruby and to any part that Ruby may have played in the assassination. . . . Mrs. Powell stated it would be impossible for her to make corrections in the deposition as written because to make her testimony "sound right I would have to change the questions of [Commission attorney Burt] Griffin."

Witness Sam Holland was one of the few to attempt to correct his Warren Commission testimony. Holland told author Josiah Thompson he and his attorney attempted to correct the transcript: "We red marked . . . red penciled that statement from beginning to end because there were a lot of errors in it." Holland later told Thompson that apparently his corrections must have been lost somewhere along the line because "the statement that I made, as well as I remember, isn't in context with the Warren Commission." He told Mark Lane: "The Warren Commission, I think, had to report in their book what they wanted the world to believe. . . . It had to read like they wanted it to read. They had to prove that Oswald did it alone."

Ronald Fischer, one of the bystanders who saw a man in the sixth-floor window in the minutes preceding the assassination, later said he almost got into a fight with a Commission attorney who was trying to get him to change his story. In an interview with the *Dallas Morning News* in 1978, Fischer said Assistant Counsel David Belin tried to intimidate him:

[Belin] and I had a fight almost in the interview room over the color of the man's hair. He wanted me to tell him that the man was dark-headed and I wouldn't do it. [Oswald's hair] doesn't appear to me in the photographs as light as the man that I saw and that's what Belin was upset about. I see it now, but I didn't see it at the time.

Roger Craig, the Dallas deputy sheriff who claimed to see Oswald escape in a station wagon, years later wrote about his experience with the Warren Commission:

Combine the [harassment at his work] with the run-in I had with Dave Belin, junior counsel for the Warren Commission, who questioned me in April, 1964, and who changed my testimony fourteen times when he sent it to Washington, and you will have some ideas of the pressure brought to bear.

Julia Ann Mercer, the woman who claimed to have seen Jack Ruby behind the wheel of a truck in Dealey Plaza about an hour and a half before the assassination, subsequently told investigators for New Orleans district attorney Jim Garrison that several key portions of her statement were altered by the FBI and that even her signature was forged on a Dallas County sheriff's report that supported the altered FBI documents.

Phil Willis, who took a series of photographs of the assassination, was surprised when he was asked only to give a deposition rather than testify. He told this author:

This guy came to Dallas and took my deposition. He took down only what he wanted to hear. I tried to tell him about the shots and the echoes but he wasn't interested. He just seemed to want to get it over with. The Warren Commission never subpoenaed any photographer. They weren't interested in talking to me or Zapruder. It seems strange to me. It's not much of a way to conduct an investigation.

Willis's daughter, Mrs. Linda Pipes, also was a witness to the assassination. She said:

I very much agree [with Willis] that shots came from somewhere else other than the Depository. And where we were standing [across Elm from the Depository], we had a good view. . . . [Representatives of the Warren Commission] talked to me later, but they didn't seem to be investigating very thoroughly.

Phil Willis summed up his experience in a 1988 British TV interview:

All they wanted to know was that three shots came from the Book Depository. That's all that got into the Warren Commission [Report]. . . . I'm certain that at least one shot came from the right front. I'll stand by that to my grave!

Chester Breneman and Robert West, the two Dallas surveyors who produced the height and distance figures for the Commission's reenactment of the assassination in May 1964, were shocked to find their figures "at odds" with the figures published by the Warren Commission.

Breneman told this author:

Looking at [the surveyors' map of Dealey Plaza] you will notice small numbers with tiny circles by them. Each number represents a frame of the Zapruder film that we inked on in sequence. Our map shows 171. The Warren Report changed this to 166 before they used it in the report. The Warren Report shows a 210 where we show a 208. The Warren Report says that Kennedy and Connally were shot somewhere between Frame 206 and 225 (approx.). [Our] investigation shows Kennedy getting a rear entry wound at a place marked "K" on the map between frames 186 and 207.

The consequence of these altered numbers was to make the controversial single-bullet theory more plausible by simply moving back the time when both Kennedy and Connally were wounded.

The experience of former Texas senator Ralph Yarborough also sheds light on the manner in which the Commission allowed key witnesses to be handled. The fact that Yarborough was riding beside Lyndon Johnson in the motorcade may explain his treatment in the summer of 1964. He described it this way:

After I wrote them, you see, a couple of fellows came to see me. They walked in like they were a couple of deputy sheriffs and I was a bank robber. I didn't like their attitude. As a senator I felt insulted. They went off and wrote up something and brought it back for me to sign. But I refused. I threw it in a drawer and let it lay there for weeks. And they had on there the last sentence which stated "This is all I know about the assassination." They wanted me to sign this thing, then say this is all I know. Of course, I would never have signed it. Finally, after some weeks, they began to bug me. "You're holding this up, you're holding this up" they said, demanding that I sign the report. So I typed one up myself and put basically what I told you about how the cars all stopped. I put in there, "I don't want to hurt anyone's feelings but for the protection of future presidents, they should be trained to take off when a shot is fired." I sent that over. That's dated July 10, 1964, after the assassination. To my surprise, when the volumes were finally printed and came out, I was surprised at how many people down at the White House didn't file their affidavits until after the date, after mine the 10th of July, waiting to see what I was going to say before they filed theirs. I began to lose confidence then in their investigation and that's further eroded with time.

Yarborough also was shocked to find that all vital assassination information was sent to President Johnson before it ever went to the Warren Commission or even Attorney General Robert Kennedy.

Perhaps one of the most shocking statements regarding treatment at the hands of the Warren Commission came from witness Jean Hill. Fearful to speak out for years, Hill came forward in the spring of 1986 and told her story to a group of assassination researchers at the University of Texas at Arlington.

After witnessing a rifleman firing from the Grassy Knoll and immediately being grabbed by two men who claimed to be Secret Service agents, she was advised by friends in the Dallas Police Department to keep quiet about what she knew. Even after receiving a subpoena to appear before the Warren Commission, the same friends urged that she not go to Washington. She recalled: "They seemed to feel that there might be some danger if I was to leave Dallas. They told me I wouldn't come back."

After Hill refused to go to Washington, Commission attorney Arlen Specter sent FBI agents to take her to make a deposition. She recalled that experience for this author:

The FBI took me to Parkland Hospital. I had no idea what I was doing there. They escorted me through a labyrinth of corridors and up to one of the top floors of Parkland. I didn't know where we were. They took me into this little room where I met Arlen Specter. He talked to me for a few minutes, trying to act real friendly, then this woman, a stenographer, came in and sat behind me. He had told me that this interview would be confidential, then I looked around and this woman was taking notes. I reminded him that the discussion was to be private and he told the woman to put down her notebook, which she did. But when I looked around again she was writing. I got mad and told Specter, "You lied to me. I want this over." He asked me why I wouldn't come to Washington, and I said, "Because I want to stay alive." He asked why I would think that I was in danger and I replied, "Well, if they can kill the President, they can certainly get me!" He replied that they already had the man that did it and I told him, "No, you don't!" He kept trying to get me to change my story, particularly regarding the number of shots. He said I had been told how many shots there were and I figured he was talking about what the Secret Service told me right after the assassination. His inflection and attitude was that I knew what I was supposed to be saying, why wouldn't I just say it. I asked him, "Look, do you want the truth or just what you want me to say?" He said he wanted the truth, so I said, "The truth is that I heard between four and six shots." I told him, "I'm not going to lie for you." So he starts talking off the record. He told me about my life, my family, and even mentioned that my marriage was in trouble. I said, "What's the point of interviewing me if you already know everything about me?" He got angrier and angrier and finally told me, "Look, we can make you look as crazy as Marguerite Oswald and everybody knows how crazy she is. We could have you put in a mental institution if you don't cooperate with us." I knew he was trying to intimidate me. I kept asking to see that woman's notes, to see what she was putting down. I knew something was not right about this, because no one who is just taking a deposition gets that involved and angry, they just take your answers. He finally gave me his word that the interview would not be published unless I approved what was written. But they never gave me the chance to read it or approve it. When I finally read my testimony as published by the Warren Commission, I knew it was a fabrication from the first line. After that ordeal at Parkland Hospital, they wrote that my deposition was taken at the U.S. attorney's office in the Post Office Building,

Considering the information presented in this section, it appears the sins of the Warren Commission went far beyond a few omissions and distortions. Little wonder that the vast majority of Americans today place little credence in the Commission's findings of a lone assasin and no conspiracy. Once again the charge of coverup can be laid at the feet of the federal government.

*　　　*　　　*

During the April 30 Commission meeting Rankin openly admitted that the June 1 date for closing the investigation was unreasonable.

A brief discussion was held regarding Jack Ruby, who had been found guilty and had been sentenced to death. However, his attorneys were appealing the conviction on the grounds of his mental incompetence. When one member asked if Ruby would go to prison, Commissioner McCloy responded: "He goes to a mental institution. It is perfectly clear we cannot examine him at this stage." Warren, however, said the Commission probably had to interview Ruby, insane or not, but agreed ". . . not to do it at this stage."

Rankin again referred to the problems arising from the contradictory medical evidence and suggested that some Commission members and a doctor should study the autopsy photographs ". . . so that they could report to the Commission that there is nothing inconsistent with the other findings . . ." Warren added: ". . . But without putting those pictures in our record. We don't want those in our record . . . It would make it a morbid thing for all time to come . . ."

The inaccessibility of Kennedy's autopsy X-rays and photographs has been a cornerstone of criticism of the Warren Commission.

Before adjourning, commissioners agreed on the necessity of including a biography of Lee Harvey Oswald in their final report. At this time—five months before their final report—it is significant to read Rankin's explanation for the inclusion of Oswald's background: "Some of it will be necessary to tell the story and to show why it is reasonable to assume that he did what the Commission concludes that he did do."

Oswald's guilt was already decided—despite the questions, contradictions, and gaps in the evidence at hand.

The Single-Bullet Theory

The greatest problem for the Warren Commission was its attempt to reconcile the ballistic and medical evidence by supporting the idea that both President Kennedy and Governor Connally were struck by the same bullet.

The idea on its face is unpalatable. To believe the single-bullet theory, one must believe that a single, high-powered rifle slug penetrated two men causing seven wounds, shattering a rib and a wrist bone, then emerged almost totally unscathed to become the pristine Commission Exhibit 399.

Yet, to disbelieve the single-bullet theory means rejecting the Warren Commission's entire version of the assassination. Despite the testimony of many witnesses, the Warren Commission concluded that only three shots were fired during the assassination, solely on the basis that three spent shells were found on the sixth floor of the Texas School Book Depository.

Having concluded that only three shots were fired—the absolute maximum allowable for only one assassin—commissioners set about to determine the timing and effects of each shot.

In late 1963 and early 1964 there was no problem. Since the FBI early on had established an assassination time sequence by studying the Zapruder film and Zapruder's 8mm camera, the Commission had a certain time frame to work within.

The original FBI and Secret Service reports made it clear that Kennedy was struck in the back by the first shot, Governor Connally hit by the second, and the President's head wound caused by the third. While this stretched the allowable time for such shooting to the limit—and despite the contradiction of Connally, who testified he was hit after the first shot—this believable scenario was accepted by the Commission for a time.

Then came the problem of James Tague, the man who was struck by a piece of cement while standing near the Triple Underpass. Initially both the FBI and the Warren Commission tried to ignore Tague. But after an assistant U.S. attorney in Dallas sent commissioners both an account of the Tague wounding and a Dallas news photograph of the bullet mark on the curb, the Commission was forced to action.

In the spring of 1964—at a time the FBI was denying any curb shot in Dallas—Commission attorney Arlen Specter (today a U.S. senator from Pennsylvania) began conceiving the idea that both Kennedy and Connally were struck by the same bullet.

At this same time information from Dallas concerning the curb shot reached the ears of the Commission and invalidated the carefully constructed scenario of one lone assassin firing only three shots. Hence the only plausible explanation was that both Kennedy and Connally had been struck by the same bullet.

*   *   *

The presumption of Oswald's guilt was the first topic of the next Commission meeting on June 4, 1964. The Commission had met on May 19, 1964, but records of that meeting were kept from the public on the grounds that it only dealt with "personal and medical files."

Also in May, Rankin had told Commission attorneys to "wrap up" their investigations and submit their area chapters by June 1 so that the final report could be issued by June 30. By June 1, however, only two attorneys had completed a draft and the deadline had to be moved back.

Meanwhile in Dallas, a reenactment of the assassination, using surveyors, a limousine, and stand-ins for Kennedy and Connally, was conducted in Dealey Plaza on May 24.

Opening the June 4 meeting, Representative Ford denounced news reports that the Commission had already concluded that Oswald alone was responsible for the assassination as "obviously false" since the Commission had not yet reached any conclusions. (Only Warren, Ford, McCloy, Dulles, and Rankin attended this meeting.) In criticizing news media speculations regarding Commission conclusions, Representative Ford stated: "In my judgment, somebody somewhere is planting or leaking these stories."

Warren suggested making a statement to the media that while the taking of testimony was nearing an end, the Commission had not yet discussed any final conclusions.

On June 17, it was announced that Commission hearings were completed. On June 30, it was reported that the final report would not be issued until after the Republican National Convention set to begin on July 13.

Minutes of a Commission executive session held on June 23, 1964, were withheld from the public by the National Archives with the following explanation:

> . . . matters that are . . . specifically authorized under criteria established by an Executive Order to be kept secret in the interest of national defense or foreign policy and are in fact properly classified pursuant to such Executive Order.

The immense pressure to hurry up the investigation and close down the Commission may have accounted for the fact that five of the senior attorneys—Adams, Coleman, Ball, Hubert, and Jenner—returned to their private practices and made virtually no contribution in writing the final report.

On July 9, 1964, commissioners Dulles and McCloy met with three psychiatrists who had been asked to develop a psychological profile on Oswald. During the seven-hour meeting, the psychiatrists went over complex psychological conjectures regarding Oswald's motives, but their interpretations of his thinking were severely limited due to the fact that first, they were operating under the assumption of Oswald's guilt and, second, the material studied was based on Commission and FBI reports, which undoubtedly were one-sided. Even though the psychiatrists spent hours detailing their theories, they also cautioned against putting too much confidence in their psychological speculation since they had not had the opportunity to interview Oswald personally.

Dr. Howard P. Rome of the Mayo Foundation (connected with the Mayo Clinic) told commissioners:

As far as I am concerned, this is highly conjectural. It is purely speculative. I see it as being of no use to anyone beyond a staff level to help perhaps clarify your approach to the record. I should think it would be most unrealistic to use this in any way. I think you would be laughed right out by the public with this high-spun fantasy of inferences based on second- and third-hand hearsay information.

Yet in its final report the Warren Commission did use the psychiatrists' report to underscore the case against Oswald as a lonely and troubled man. And the public did not laugh them off. After all, the Warren Commission represented some of the most prestigious men in the nation.

Dulles suspected the truth of the matter when, during a discussion of whether or not to present the psychological material in the final report, he opened this dialogue with Commission counsel Albert Jenner:

DULLES: But nobody reads. Don't believe people read in this country. There will be a few professors who will read the record . . .
JENNER: And a few newspaper reporters who will read parts of it.
DULLES: The public will read very little . . .

In its final report, the Warren Commission made no specific reference to the psychiatric panel. Yet portions of the report presented ideas that originated with the doctors. In the report, after fully detailing Oswald's difficulty with human relationships, his discontent with the world, his search for personal truth and a place in history, his censure of certain aspects of American life and his professed commitment to Marxism, commissioners wrote: "Out of these and many other factors which may have molded the character of Lee Harvey Oswald there emerged a man capable of assassinating President Kennedy."

With its investigation winding down and most of the senior attorneys gone, the job of writing the Warren Commission Report fell to Assistant Counsel Norman Redlich and staff member Alfred Goldberg. Redlich was a law professor at New York University School of Law and Dr. Goldberg (a Ph.D.) was a historian for the U.S. Air Force Historical Division.

When Goldberg told Warren it was impossible to complete the report by mid-July, the deadline again was moved back, this time to August 1.

Through August, Goldberg and Redlich continued to rewrite the report's chapters—some as many as twenty times—and the deadline was moved back into September.

The Commission, well aware of the ever-nearing November presidential election, reportedly received increased pressure from Johnson aide McGeorge Bundy to hurry up and publish the report.

On September 4, galley proofs of the final report draft were circulated among commissioners and staffers for last-minute comments. Two days later, a dissatisfied Liebeler submitted a twenty-six-page memorandum highly critical of the "Identity of the Assassin" chapter. It had to be revised again.

On September 7, commissioners Russell, Cooper, and Boggs—still unsatisfied with the inevitable conclusion of Oswald's guilt—traveled to Dallas to reexamine Marina Oswald. Under questioning, she changed significant aspects of her story, prompting even more rewriting of the report.

The final Warren Commission session was on September 18, 1964, less than ten days before its final report would be issued to President Lyndon Johnson. According to the National Archives, no transcripts of this important final meeting exist. However, the minutes of the meeting show that great concern was being voiced to Chief Counsel Rankin that material within the report not conflict with its summary and conclusions chapter.

On September 24, 1964, the Warren Commission's report was submitted to President Johnson by Chief Justice Warren with the introduction:

Dear Mr. President:
Your Commission to investigate the assassination of President Kennedy on November 22, 1963, having completed its assignment in accordance with Executive Order No. 11130 of November 29, 1963, herewith submits its final report.

The report was signed by all seven commissioners although Senator Russell refused to sign until the wording regarding the single-bullet theory was softened to indicate the idea was only a probability.

Russell's dissension and skepticism of the report's conclusions may have been the topic of the September 18 meeting for which the transcripts are missing. Russell told researcher Harold Weisberg that several of the commissioners voiced doubts about the Commission's conclusions at that meeting and he was "shaken" by the discovery that the record of these doubts was missing.

The Warren Commission Report was made public on September 28, 1964, with the news media voicing virtually unanimous praise and support for the document.

Upon receiving the report from Warren, President Johnson's only comment was: "It's heavy."

Today it is intriguing to note that Johnson had refused to answer questions from his own Commission. According to *Newsweek*, August 15, 1966: ". . . a list of questions [concerning the assassination] for him was in fact prepared and submitted to Johnson's confidant, Abe Fortas. Fortas returned a veto of the idea." Instead, both Johnson and his wife submitted unsworn statements.

Johnson's action prompted Commission attorney David Belin to comment in later years:

> . . . if we could interrogate Mrs. Kennedy, whose husband has died before her eyes, there is no reason why President Johnson should not be examined in the same manner as every other witness [since] there was some speculation from abroad, however outlandish, that he might have had some indirect connection with the Dallas tragedy.

Two months after the Warren Commission Report was released with widespread publicity praising its thoroughness and conclusions, twenty-six volumes of Commission testimony and exhibits were quietly made public. It was only after years of diligent study that individual researchers finally were able to document the gross inconsistencies between these twenty-six volumes of material and the Commission's report. And by then they were largely ignored except by a few low-circulation periodicals. No one was in a position to receive new or clarified information regarding the assassination since—having completed its work on September 28—the Warren Commission had disbanded.

Researcher Sylvia Meagher, who, in *Accessories After the Fact*, produced a meticulous dissection of the Commission and its conclusions, stated:

> One of the most reprehensible actions of the Warren Commission is that it disbanded the moment it handed over its Report, leaving no individual or corporate entity to answer legitimate questions arising from demonstrable misstatements of fact in the Report.

After carefully researching both the activities and the conclusions of the Warren Commission, Meagher—who has never been successfully challenged in her assertions of the Commission's incompetence—wrote:

> Study has shown the Report to contain (1) statements of fact which are inaccurate and untrue, in the light of the official Exhibits and objective verification; (2) statements for which the citations fail to provide authentication; (3) misrepresentation of testimony: (4) omission of references to testimony inimical to findings in the Report; (5) suppression of findings favorable to Oswald; (6) incomplete investigation of suspicious circumstances which remain unexplained; (7) misleading statements

resulting from inadequate attention to the contents of Exhibits; (8) failure to obtain testimony from crucial witnesses; and (9) assertions which are diametrically opposite to the logical inferences to be drawn from the relevant testimony or evidence.

After reviewing Warren Commission meeting transcripts in the mid-1970s, author Tad Szulc wrote:

If the investigation was as inadequate and incompetent as is suggested by the Commission's own internal documents, once Top Secret and now declassified, it IS [emphasis his] legitimate to question the specific conclusions of the report. The transcripts of the Commission's executive sessions, staff memoranda . . . and other internal documents reveal the Commissioners to be consumed by doubts and fears; troubled by their own ignorance; suspicious of the investigatory work performed for them by the FBI and the CIA; lacking clear direction; worried about a competing inquiry in Texas; and finally suffering from a stunning lack of confidence in their own ability to produce a report that would be credible to the American people, the world, and, for that matter, credible to themselves. . . . So many of [their] doubts apparently were not resolved that the impression emerges from the private discussions among the Commissioners that, in the end, the Report was the only possible compromise they could produce—in terms of their knowledge and their conscience.

In the years following the release of the Warren Report, condemnation of its work and conclusions has only grown more widespread.

In 1976, the Senate Select Committee to Study Government Operations with Respect to Intelligence Activities, while claiming not to have found evidence of a conspiracy to kill Kennedy, nevertheless concluded:

The Committee has . . . developed evidence which impeaches the process by which the intelligence agencies arrived at their own conclusions about the assassination, and by which they provided information to the Warren Commission. This evidence indicates that the investigation of the assassination was deficient and that facts which might have substantially affected the course of the investigation were not provided the Warren Commission . . . Why senior officials of the FBI and the CIA permitted the investigation to go forward, in light of these deficiencies, and why they permitted the Warren Commission to reach its conclusions without all relevant information is still unclear. Certainly, concern with public reputation, problems of coordination between agencies, possible bureaucratic failure, and embarrassment and the extreme compartmentation of knowledge of sensitive operations may have contributed to these shortcomings. But the possibility exists that senior officials in both agencies made conscious decisions not to disclose potentially important information.

As has been demonstrated, in most cases, "potentially important information" meant any information that did not add to the evidence of Oswald's guilt.

The sins of the Warren Commission, the FBI, and the CIA go far beyond simple omission for face-saving purposes.

Senator Richard Schweiker, a member of the Senate Intelligence Committee's subcommittee that looked at the agencies' performance during the Warren Commission investigation, told newsmen in 1976 that both the CIA and the FBI deliberately lied to the Commission about significant assassination issues.

His charge was supported by statements from former Texas attorney general Waggoner Carr—whose own investigation was usurped by the Warren Commission—who told the *Houston Chronicle* in 1975: "All of the records were in the hands of the two agencies [the FBI and CIA] and, if they so desired, any information or files could have been destroyed or laundered prior to the time the Commission could get them.

Schweiker added that lies from the agencies, coupled with the numerous deficiencies seen by his panel, invalidated the Warren Commission's conclusions. He bluntly reported:

I think the Warren Commission has, in fact, collapsed like a house of cards. And I believe the Warren Commission was set up at the time to feed pablum to the American people for reasons not yet known, and that one of the biggest cover-ups in the history of our country occurred at that time.

Today it can be clearly seen that the sins of the Commission included investigating from a preconceived idea (Oswald's sole guilt), failing to substantiate evidence from the FBI, the intimidation of selected witnesses, the stifling of internal dissent, and the misreporting of its own information. These methods were actively employed to subvert a truthful investigation and to present flawed and inadequate conclusions to the unsuspecting public.

The evidence available today suggests the Commission slowly became aware of the massive power behind the assassination and simply could not—or would not—come to grips with it.

The Commission, like subsequent inquiries into the Kennedy assassination, released a slanted and timid version of the tragedy hoping to appease the public long enough so that commissioners would not have to face the full ramifications of a truthful and incisive investigation. And their plan worked well. For more than two decades much of the American public has been content with the palatable—but implausible—Warren Commission version of the assassination.

Only in recent years, with firm evidence of a second assassin available and a continuing history of government deceit, have growing numbers of citizens begun to reevaluate the official government assassination theory of one lone gunman.

Summary

The Warren Commission was in part the result of an attempt by President Lyndon Johnson and his close advisers to blunt independent assassination investigations both in Texas and in Congress.

Johnson hand-picked Commission members—all of whom had long-standing connections with either the military, defense industries, or U.S. intelligence.

Gerald Ford—who was selected at the insistence of Richard Nixon—became a "spy" on the Commission for the FBI. He heard more testimony than any other commissioner.

Supreme Court chief justice Earl Warren first rejected service on the Commission as unconstitutional, but was pressured into the job by Johnson, who told him that if he didn't find Oswald a lone assassin, World War III might result.

Johnson paid for the Warren Commission from an "Emergency Fund for the President."

At no time did the Warren Commission seem to consider the basic legal rights of Oswald—the assumption of innocence until proven guilty, the right to legal representation, or the right to cross-examine witnesses and evidence against him.

The Commission was acutely troubled by the FBI, beginning with Bureau leaks to the press that portrayed Oswald as the lone assassin prior to any Commission investigation through questions concerning the legitimacy of evidence presented by the Bureau. They also were at a loss as to how to determine the validity of allegations that Oswald worked for the Bureau as an informant.

And there were serious conflicts between the Commission's pat report and its attendant twenty-six volumes of testimony and evidence. Likewise, there were serious conflicts between witness testimony as published by the Commission and statements to newsmen and researchers by those same witnesses.

There is now firm evidence that not only the FBI and CIA lied about important assassination evidence, but that the Warren Commission itself participated in making serious omissions (more than a dozen critical witnesses); alteration of evidence (the reenactment surveyors' map figures); and intimidation of witnesses (Tammi True and Jean Hill).

The single-bullet theory of the Commission—necessitated by the wounding of bystander James Tague—prompted widespread skepticism of Commission findings. This theory—which flies in the face of most of the witness testimony and physical evidence—was obviously only necessary to maintain the official "lone assassin" theory.

Today—Gerald Ford and David Belin notwithstanding—national polls indicate most Americans have doubts about the basic tenets of the Warren Commission.

> Some long-cherished illusions of mine about the great free press in our country underwent a painful reappraisal during this period.
> —New Orleans district attorney Jim Garrison

The Garrison Investigation

On the afternoon of November 22, 1963, two men sat drinking in the Katzenjammer Bar, located in New Orleans next door to 544 Camp Street, where a puzzling parade of anti-Castro Cubans and intelligence agents—including Lee Harvey Oswald—were seen the previous summer.

One of the men was Guy Banister, the former FBI man who was running a private-investigation firm with intelligence connections out of an office at 544 Camp Street. The other man was one of his investigators, Jack Martin.

According to a police report prepared that day, the two men returned to Banister's office where an argument erupted. Banister, his irritability inflamed by alcohol, accused Martin of stealing files whereupon Martin reminded Banister that he had not forgotten some of the people he had seen in Banister's office that summer. Banister then beat Martin over the head with a heavy .357 magnum pistol.

In the heat of the moment, Martin screamed out: "What are you going to do—kill me, like you all did Kennedy?"

A police ambulance was called and carried the bloodied Martin to Charity Hospital.

An angered Martin soon whispered to friends that Banister had often been in the company of a man named David Ferrie, whom Martin claimed drove to Texas the day of Kennedy's assassination to serve as a getaway pilot for the assassins. He hinted at even darker associations.

Martin's words soon reached the ears of New Orleans district attorney Jim Garrison, who quickly arrested Ferrie and began an investigation into the JFK assassination that eventually turned into a worldwide cause célèbre.

Because of the Garrison investigation much new assassination information became known and the assassination was addressed for the first time in a courtroom—even though the defendant was finally acquitted.

Garrison claimed that the entire weight of the federal government was moved to block and ridicule his investigation, and indeed there were many strange aspects to this entire episode, including an attack by some in the national media before Garrison even had a chance to present his case.

A giant of a man, standing six-foot-six, Earling Carothers Garrison had shortened his name to simply "Jim," but was widely known to both friends and foes as the "Jolly Green Giant."

Born on November 20, 1921, in Knoxville, Iowa, Garrison grew up in New Orleans and enlisted in the U.S. Army a year before Pearl Harbor. In 1942, he was commissioned a lieutenant in the field artillery.

After the war, Garrison followed a family tradition in law by enrolling in the Tulane University Law School. He eventually earned bachelor of laws and master of civil laws degrees.

Garrison then joined the FBI, serving briefly in Seattle and Tacoma, Washington. He wrote:

I was very impressed with the competence and efficiency of the Bureau. However, I was extremely bored as I rang doorbells to inquire about the loyalty and associations of applicants for employment in a defense plant. So I decided to return to the law profession.

He served as an assistant district attorney in New Orleans from 1954 to 1958, resigning with a scathing attack on Mayor Victor H. Schiro. In 1961, Garrison decided to make a run for the district attorney's job, again blasting Mayor Schiro for corruption and failure to enforce the law. His attacks included incumbent district attorney Richard Dowling, whom he called "the great emancipator—he let everyone go free."

Not believing he had much of a chance, Garrison ran a meager campaign, comprised mostly of some television talks. To the surprise of many people Garrison managed to defeat Dowling in a run-off election, and he took office as district attorney on March 3, 1962.

Although Garrison did begin to clean up some of the more disreputable gambling and prostitution dens of New Orleans, his critics noted that he did not share that same enthusiasm against the leaders of organized crime—a force that Garrison has maintained did not exist during his years as New Orleans district attorney.

In 1962, Garrison was angered by the refusal of eight criminal-court judges to approve funds for investigating organized crime. He went so far as to publicly state that their refusal "raised interesting questions about racketeer influences." The judges sued him for defamation of character and won a $1,000 state court judgment. Garrison, however, fought this action all the way to the Supreme Court, which reversed the decision in a landmark case on the right to criticize public officials.

After hearing the remarks of Jack Martin, Garrison moved quickly enough. Over the assassination weekend, New Orleans lawmen vainly sought David Ferrie. On Monday, November 25, Ferrie turned himself in.

Garrison, who had met the bizarre Ferrie once before, could hardly forget the man. Ferrie suffered from alopecia, a rare disease that causes total baldness. He wrote:

The face grinning ferociously at me was like a ghoulish Halloween mask. The eyebrows plainly were greasepaint, one noticeably higher than the other. A scruffy, reddish homemade wig hung askew on his head as he fixed me with his eyes.

Ill at ease, Ferrie admitted his Friday trip to Texas, claiming he wanted to go ice skating in Houston. However, he had no adequate answer for why he had chosen to drive through one of the worst thunderstorms in years and why, instead of skating, he had spent his time at the rink's pay phone. Ferrie also denied knowing Lee Harvey Oswald.

Garrison was unsatisfied with Ferrie's story. He ordered him and two friends held in jail for questioning by the FBI. He later told interviewer Eric Norden:

When we alerted the FBI, they expressed interest and asked us to turn the three men over to them for questioning. We did, but Ferrie was released soon afterward and most of [the FBI] report on him was classified top secret and secreted in the National Archives . . .

In *On the Trail of the Assassins*, Garrison wrote:

I was 43 years old and had been district attorney for a year and nine months when John Kennedy was killed. I was an old-fashioned patriot, a product of my family, my military experience, and my years in the legal profession. I could not imagine then that the government ever would deceive the citizens of this country. Accordingly, when the FBI released David Ferrie with surprising swiftness, implying that no evidence had been found connecting him with the assassination, I accepted it.

Over the next three years, Garrison's attention was centered on his job and family. Vaguely aware of contradictions in the assassination story, Garrison nevertheless chose to believe the official version. He wrote:

By this time [1966] our military was deeply engaged in the war in Southeast Asia. Like most Americans, I took it for granted that our government had our troops over there to bring democracy to South Vietnam. Like most Americans, I also took for granted that our government had fully investigated President Kennedy's assassination and had found it to be indeed the result of a random act by a man acting alone. Certainly, it never crossed my mind that the murder of President Kennedy and the subsequent arrival of half a million members of the American military in Vietnam might be related.

Garrison's view began to change after a chance meeting with the powerful senator from Louisiana, Russell Long. Garrison said Long told him: "Those fellows on the Warren Commission were dead wrong. There's no way in the world that one man could have shot up John Kennedy that way."

It was a comment that was to put Garrison and his office back on the assassination investigation trail.

First Garrison went back and studied the Warren Commission Report and volumes in detail. He was aghast:

Considering the lofty credentials of the Commission members and the quality and size of the staff available to them, I had expected to find a thorough and professional investigation. I found nothing of the sort. The mass of information was disorganized and confused. The Commission had provided no adequate index to its exhibits. . . . The number of promising leads that were never followed up offended my prosecutorial sensibility. And, perhaps worst of all, the conclusions in the report seemed to be based on an appallingly selective reading of the evidence, ignoring credible testimony from literally dozens of witnesses.

Garrison, with his military background, was particularly shocked to read in the Commission volumes where a Lt. Col. Allison G. Folsom, Jr., reported on a grade made by Oswald in a Russian examination. Garrison knew that the mere fact that Oswald had been tested in Russian indicated intelligence training.

Fired by growing suspicions, Garrison took another look at Oswald's activities while in New Orleans in the spring and summer of 1963.

He began to discover the odd and mostly unexplained relationships between Oswald and anti-Castro Cubans, Oswald and intelligence agents including the FBI, and Oswald and 544 Camp Street.

Quietly he began to assemble some of his most trusted assistants, whom he dubbed his "special team," and his investigation grew.

Garrison reinterviewed Jack Martin and found that Oswald had been part of that strange entourage of agents in and out of Banister's Camp Street office. He found that Banister and his associates were involved in activities far afield from normal New Orleans activity—honest or otherwise. There were tales of burglarized armories, missing weapons, raided ammunition caches and gun-running operations. Garrison wrote: "The Banister apparatus . . . was part of a supply line that ran along the Dallas–New Orleans–Miami corridor. These supplies consisted of arms and explosives for use against Castro's Cuba."

By 1966, Banister was dead—he suffered a reported heart attack in June 1964—and Garrison was looking for a living person to prosecute in the conspiracy that he had begun to unravel.

One starting point was New Orleans attorney Dean Andrews, who told the Warren Commission that he had received a call from a "Clay Bertrand" the day after the assassination asking him to fly to Dallas and legally represent Lee Harvey Oswald. Andrews reiterated this story to Garrison and claimed that while he had "Clay Bertrand" as a client, he had never actually met the man.

As Garrison's investigators pried into the seamier areas of New Orleans nightlife, they began to piece together information from various sources that it was common knowledge in the homosexual underground that "Clay Bertrand" was the name used by none other than Clay Shaw, the respected director of the International Trade Mart in New Orleans.

Clay Shaw and Permindex

Clay Shaw, like Lee Harvey Oswald and Jack Ruby, was not simply a lone individual with no connections to persons and/or organizations that may have played a role in President Kennedy's death.

Shaw had some of the most intriguing and unprobed connections of any person involved in the assassination case. Even when some of these connections were brought to the attention of the House Select Committee on Assassinations, the Committee was either unable or unwilling to fully investigate them.

Shaw, a tall, distinguished man with silver hair and a polished manner, was born in Kentwood, Louisiana, on March 17, 1913. During the 1930s, Shaw was in New York City working as an executive for Western Union Telegraph Company and later as an advertising and public-relations consultant.

By 1941, Shaw was with the U.S. Army and, while his official biography states simply that he was an aide-de-camp to Gen. Charles O. Thrasher, Shaw later admitted he was working for the Office of Strategic Services (OSS) as a liaison officer to the headquarters of Winston Churchill. It was here that Shaw may have become entangled in the murky world of intelligence.

Although there is precious little reliable information on exactly what Shaw's wartime experiences included, he did retire from the U.S. Army in 1946 as a major—later he was made a colonel—with the Bronze Star, the Legion of Merit, France's Croix de Guerre, and Belgium's Order of the Crown.

After the war, Shaw returned to New Orleans where he was known as a wealthy real-estate developer. He also became director of the International House—World Trade Center, a "nonprofit association fostering the development of international trade, tourism and cultural exchange." Soon Shaw left this organization to found the International Trade Mart, which was quite profitable sponsoring permanent industrial expositions in the Carribean.

According to several separate sources—including Garrison's files and an investigation by the U.S. Labor Party—Shaw's International Trade Mart was a subsidiary of a shadowy entity known as the Centro Mondiale

Commerciale ("World Trade Center"), which was founded in Montreal, Canada, in the late 1950s, then moved to Rome in 1961.

The Trade Mart was connected with Centro Mondiale Commerciale (CMC) through yet another shadowy firm named Permindex (PERManent INDustrial EXpositions), also in the business of international expositions.

It is fascinating to note that in the 1962 edition of *Who's Who in the South and Southwest,* Shaw gave biographical information stating that he was on the board of directors of Permindex. However in the 1963–64 edition, the reference to Permindex was dropped.

In the late 1960s, both Permindex and its parent company, Centro Mondiale Commerciale, came under intense scrutiny by the Italian news media. It was discovered that on the board of CMC was Prince Gutierrez di Spadaforo, a wealthy aristocrat who had been undersecretary of agriculture under the dictator Benito Mussolini and whose daughter-in-law was related to Nazi minister of finance Hjalmar Schacht; Carlo D'Amelio, an attorney for the former Italian royal family; and Ferenc Nagy, former premier of Hungary and a leading anticommunist.

The Italian media reported that Nagy was president of Permindex and the board chairman and major stockholder was Maj. Louis Mortimer Bloomfield, a powerful Montreal lawyer who represented the Bronfman family as well as serving U.S. intelligence services.

Reportedly Bloomfield established Permindex in 1958 as part of the creation of world-wide trade centers connected with CMC.

According to a special report by investigative reporters David Goldman and Jeffrey Steinberg in 1981, Bloomfield was recruited into the British Special Operations Executive (SOE) in 1938, during the war was given rank within the U.S. Army, and eventually became part of the OSS intelligence system, including the FBI's Division Five. Reportedly Bloomfield became quite close with J. Edgar Hoover.

Attention began to be drawn to Permindex in 1962, when French president Charles de Gaulle publicly accused Permindex of channeling funds to the outlawed Secret Army Organization (OAS), which made several attempts on de Gaulle's life. De Gaulle identified several major and well-known international companies as investors in Permindex.

In tracing the money used to finance the assassination plots against de Gaulle, French intelligence discovered that some $200,000 in secret funds had been sent to Permindex accounts in the Banque de la Credit Internationale.

Researchers for years have been intrigued by information gathered by Jim Garrison early in his investigation, that in 1962 Guy Banister had dispatched an associate, Maurice Brooks Gatlin—the legal counsel to Banister's Anti-Communist League of the Caribbean—to Paris with a suitcase full of cash for the OAS, reportedly about $200,000.

As Garrison began to probe this area of interest, he discovered that

Gatlin had been killed when he fell or was thrown from the sixth-floor window of a hotel in Panama.

To further complicate this maze of business, finance, European money, holdover Nazis, and intelligence agents, various investigators—including some from *Life* magazine—found that some of the banking connections from this secret empire reached to Mafia chief Meyer Lansky and his Bahamas gambling operations.

Investigators Goldman and Steinberg, after noting the extensive and sophisticated satellite-computer system maintained by the World Trade Center Association, wrote:

> Among the fifty-plus world trade marts hooked into the [World Trade Center Association] satellite-computer complex is the Hong Kong World Trade Center. . . . [This] is the single largest and highest-priced chunk of real estate in Hong Kong. The international drug cartel, through this Hong Kong center, thus maintains a transnational tracking system [of international trade routes, carriers, inventories and rates] that is more sophisticated and technologically advanced than the capabilities at the disposal of any government attempting to combat its deadly traffic.

Whatever the truth behind Centro Mondiale Commerciale and its companion company, Permindex, the Italian government saw fit to expell both in 1962 for subversive activities identical to those in the much-publicized Propaganda-2 Masonic Lodge scandal of more recent years.

The news media in France, Italy, and Canada had a field day tying the two discredited firms to the CIA. And there is now evidence that Shaw indeed was CIA connected. Victor Marchetti, former executive assistant to the deputy director of the CIA and author of *The CIA and the Cult of Intelligence,* has revealed that in early 1969, he learned from CIA director Richard Helms that both Clay Shaw and David Ferrie had worked for the Agency.

Marchetti said Helms repeatedly voiced concern over the prosecution of Shaw and even instructed top aides "to do all we can to help Shaw." Further, a CIA memo dated September 28, 1967, to the Justice Department— finally made public in 1977—reveals that Shaw had provided the Agency with some thirty reports between the years 1949 and 1956.

It may also be pertinent that in May 1961, just after the disastrous Bay of Pigs Invasion, Shaw introduced CIA deputy director Gen. Charles P. Cabell to the Foreign Policy Association of New Orleans.

Garrison wrote:

> It would certainly have helped our case against Shaw to have been able to link him definitely with the CIA. Unfortunately, however, with our limited staff and finances, and many leads to follow, our investigation was not able to uncover any of this crucial background information when we needed it most.

*   *   *

By late 1966, Garrison had two suspects in mind in the murder of President Kennedy—the strange David Ferrie and the socially connected Clay Shaw.

David William Ferrie was a character straight out of some fictional novel, but he was frighteningly real. Ferrie looked like a clown with his painted eyebrows and reddish wig. Yet he was an aggressive homosexual with an appetite for young boys. Ferrie considered himself a master hypnotist, a philosopher, a psychologist, scientist, and a religious "bishop" in the Orthodox Old Catholic Church of North America.

Cashiered as a pilot for Eastern Airlines following publicity over a homosexual arrest, Ferrie continued his flying activities, which included work for both the CIA and reputed New Orleans mob boss Carlos Marcello.

Ferrie also was closely connected to anti-Castro Cubans. In 1961, Ferrie often was seen in the company of Sergio Archaca-Smith, New Orleans director of the virulently anti-Castro Cuban Democratic Revolutionary Front.

That same year, Ferrie was introduced to a meeting of the New Orleans Civic Club as one of the pilots involved in the ill-fated Bay of Pigs Invasion. Ferrie made a bitterly anti-Kennedy talk. Ferrie also made an anti-Kennedy talk to the New Orleans Chapter of the Military Order of World Wars in which he said Kennedy "double-crossed" the invasion force by failing to authorize needed air support. Ferrie's speech was so vitriolic that several members of the audience walked out.

As Garrison continued his investigations, he found abundant evidence that Ferrie—who had been in contact with Oswald—was connected to Clay Shaw.

Raymond Broshears, a long-time friend of Ferrie's, had seen Ferrie and Shaw together on several occasions. Furthermore, Broshears told Garrison how Ferrie once became intoxicated and detailed how he had driven to Houston the day of Kennedy's death for the purpose of meeting two members of the assassination team from Dallas. The pair were to have arrived in Houston in a single-engine airplane piloted by one of them, a Cuban exile known only as "Carlos." Ferrie was to have taken Carlos and his fellow assassin out of Houston in a four-engined plane. Ferrie told Broshears that something had gone wrong. The two men never showed up.

Whether the Broshears account of Ferrie's comments are accurate, Garrison soon found others who had known of the relationship between the pilot and Shaw. Jules Ricco Kimble, a member of the Ku Klux Klan, told Garrison of being introduced to Shaw by Ferrie, as did a Ferrie acquaintance named David Logan. Nicholas Tadin, the head of the New Orleans musicians' union, told Garrison that he and his wife had sought out Ferrie for flying lessons when they saw Ferrie and Shaw together at New Orleans Airport.

As Garrison's investigation broadened—including trips to Dallas, Houston, and Miami by members of his "team"—the secrecy surrounding his probe began to crumble. On February 17, 1967, the dam broke when the *New Orleans States-Item* published a story on Garrison's activities with the headline: DA HERE LAUNCHES FULL JFK DEATH PLOT PROBE. The story noted that the district attorney's office had spent more than $8,000 in travel and "investigative expenses." Countering the charge that he was simply seeking publicity, Garrison later wrote:

> We had operated as secretly as possible, assuming this was the most efficient and responsible way to handle such a potentially explosive situation. However, the voucher requests were public records, so they could not legally be concealed.

The local news story brought a deluge of media attention from across the nation. Reporters began arriving in New Orleans. The next day, Garrison was forced to come out in the open, announcing:

"We have been investigating the role of the City of New Orleans in the assassination of President Kennedy, and we have made some progress—I think substantial progress— . . . what's more, there will be arrests."

Also arriving in the city were some odd characters who were to add to the carnival atmosphere that was beginning to take shape. One such was a self-styled Denver oilman who told Garrison he could "guarantee" him a federal judgeship if he would drop his investigation into the President's death. Garrison showed him the door.

Not long after this attempt at bribery a more sinister plan came to light. A professional criminal from Philadelphia named Edward Whalen came to Garrison and said he had been approached by David Ferrie with a proposal to kill Garrison for $25,000. When Whalen declined the offer, he said Ferrie took him to Clay Shaw's apartment, where both men tried to persuade him to carry out the assassination of Garrison. This time Whalen not only was offered money but was told that if he did the job there would be top medical care and a college education for his daughter who suffered from polio.

Ferrie even went so far as to claim he had helped set up the JFK assassination and told Whalen that Lee Oswald was a CIA agent who had been well taken care of until he made some mistakes that necessitated his death. Whalen believed Ferrie's story to be unfounded boasts, and he again declined the murder contract.

By the time Whalen revealed this plot to Garrison in September 1967, it was too late to verify it. On February 22, 1967, less than a week after the newspapers broke the story of Garrison's investigation, David Ferrie—his chief suspect—was found dead in his cluttered apartment.

His death was not entirely unexpected by Garrison. The day the newspaper story first ran, Ferrie had telephoned Garrison aide Lou Ivon to say: "You know what this news story does to me, don't you. I'm a dead man. From here on, believe me, I'm a dead man."

Ferrie's nude body had been discovered lying on a living-room sofa surrounded by prescription medicine bottles, several completely empty. One typed suicide note was found on a nearby table while a second was discovered on an upright piano. Three days later the New Orleans coroner ruled that Ferrie had died from "natural causes," specifically a ruptured blood vessel in the brain.

Unconvinced, Garrison checked the empty medicine bottles found near Ferrie's body and discovered one had contained a drug designed to greatly increase a person's metabolism.

It is known that Ferrie suffered from hypertension. A physician friend confirmed to Garrison that if someone suffering from hypertension took a whole bottle of this specific drug, it would cause death very shortly. Garrison later wrote: "I phoned immediately but was told that no blood samples or spinal fluid from Ferrie's autopsy had been retained. I was left with an empty bottle and a number of unanswered questions."

Garrison also was left without the man he later described as "one of history's most important individuals."

And Ferrie was not the only person connected to the case to die. Banister reportedly died of a heart attack in June 1964, less than a month after his business partner, Hugh Ward—an investigator who had worked closely with Ferrie—died in a Mexico plane crash that also took the life of New Orleans mayor DeLesseps Morrison.

Yet another man closely connected to Ferrie was Eladio del Valle, a wealthy former Cuban congressman under Batista who had fled Cuba to become a well-known organizer of anti-Castro Cubans in Miami. Del Valle reportedly had paid Ferrie $1,500 a mission to make air raids against Cuba.

Three days before Ferrie's death, Garrison's investigators began trying to locate del Valle. Just twelve hours after Ferrie's death, del Valle's mutilated body was discovered in a Miami parking lot. Police reported that del Valle had been tortured, shot in the heart at point-blank range, and his skull split open with an ax. His murder has never been solved.

With Ferrie and del Valle dead, Garrison began to focus his attention on Clay Shaw. Fearing that Shaw might meet the same fate as Ferrie, Garrison moved rapidly. He and his "special team" had Shaw arrested on March 1, 1967.

Loud and long, Shaw protested his innocence, stating flatly: "I never heard of any plot and I never used any alias in my life."

The question of an alias came up as Shaw was being booked into jail. A police officer filling out forms asked Shaw if he had any aliases. Shaw replied, "Clay Bertrand," thus confirming the information that Garrison had been receiving from various sources around New Orleans. The officer duly noted this alias on his form.

Between the time of his arrest and his trial, Shaw was allowed to go free after posting a $10,000 bail bond.

As Garrison's men searched Shaw's house they found several interesting things such as two large hooks screwed into the ceiling of Shaw's bedroom along with five whips, several lengths of chain, and a black hood and cape. Shaw tried to shrug off this kinky collection as simply part of a Mardi Gras costume.

Harder to shrug off was Shaw's personal address book, which contained the names of important persons in Italy, Paris, and London.

But most intriguing was a listing for "Lee Odum, P.O. Box 19106, Dallas, Texas." What made this so intriguing was that the address "P.O. 19106" also appears in the address book of Lee Harvey Oswald.

Garrison announced that "P.O. 19106" actually was a code for Jack Ruby's unlisted Dallas telephone number and noted that the number was in the address books of both Shaw and Oswald.

Interest in this issue dissipated rapidly following a May 17, 1967, story in the *Dallas Times Herald* revealing that Lee Odum was a real person living in Dallas.

Odum, then thirty-one, told the newspaper that he had traveled to New Orleans in 1966 to promote a bullfight and had been sent to Shaw as a businessman who might be interested in his scheme. He said he gave Shaw the P.O. box number, which had been rented in the name of a barbecue company he operated at the time.

This seemed to clear up the issue, except that the *Times Herald* noted that P.O. Box 19106 did not come into existence until 1965, when the post office substation involved was remodeled. Therefore, it remains to be explained why that particular box number appeared in Oswald's address book in 1963.

To further titillate Garrison's interest, he found on an unused page of Shaw's address book the words "Oct" and "Nov" and, following an indecipherable scribble, the name "Dallas."

After the arrest of Shaw, the U.S. government "awakened like an angry lion," according to Garrison.

Attorney General Ramsey Clark told newsmen that Shaw had been checked out and cleared of any responsibility in the Kennedy assassination. But since Shaw's name had never before come up in connection with the assassination, questions arose over who had investigated Shaw in the federal government and why. Quickly a Justice Department spokesman tried to backpedal for Clark by issuing this statement: "The attorney general has since determined that this [report of Shaw's investigation] was erroneous. Nothing arose indicating a need to investigate Mr. Shaw."

This explanation was further clouded when a Justice Department official tried to explain that the department had been aware that Clay Shaw and Clay Bertrand were the same man and that the FBI had investigated a Clay Bertrand.

Despite the federal government's protest that Garrison was on a "witch hunt," when his evidence was presented to a New Orleans grand jury, a true bill was returned. Clay Shaw was indicted on a charge that he: ". . . did willfully and unlawfully conspire with David W. Ferrie, herein named but not charged, and Lee Harvey Oswald, herein named but not charged, and others, not herein named, to murder John F. Kennedy."

To assure the public that he was doing only his sworn duty, Garrison even took the unprecedented step of having himself—the prosecutor—file for a preliminary hearing for Shaw. This hearing took place on March 14, 1967, before three judges, who reviewed Garrison's evidence. After studying Garrison's case for three days, the three-judge panel upheld the indictment and ordered Shaw to a jury trial.

For the next year and a half, as the world waited for Garrison's case to be presented at Shaw's trial, the major news media of the United States lambasted the events in New Orleans. Garrison later wrote:

Some long-cherished illusions of mine about the great free press in our country underwent a painful reappraisal during this period. The restraint and respect for justice one might expect from the press to insure a fair trial not only to the individual charged but to the state itself did not exist. Nor did the diversity of opinion that I always thought was fundamental to the American press. As far as I could tell, the reports and editorials in *Newsweek, Time, The New York Times,* the *New York Post, The Saturday Evening Post,* and on and on were indistinguishable. All shared the basic view that I was a power-mad, irresponsible show-man who was producing a slimy circus with the objective of getting elected to higher office, oblivious to any consequences.

Garrison also commented on further efforts to give Shaw every consideration:

In this particular case, I've taken unusual steps to protect the rights of the defendant and assure him a fair trial. Before we introduced the testimony of our witnesses, we made them undergo independent verifying tests, including polygraph examination, truth serum, and hypnosis. We thought this would be hailed as an unprecedented step in jurisprudence. Instead, the press turned around and hinted that we had drugged our witnesses or given them posthypnotic suggestions to testify falsely.

This comment might have been aimed at James Phelan, a writer for *The Saturday Evening Post* who after hearing Garrison's account of his evidence, later reported that Garrison's key witness, Perry Russo, came up with his story of a Ferrie-Oswald-Shaw conspiracy only after being "drugged" and hypnotized by Garrison's people.

Phelan's account has been accepted by many researchers who failed to note that Russo told the press of the conspiracy meeting well before undergoing hypnosis. In fact, when Phelan appeared as a defense witness for Shaw, Russo soundly disputed his claims although Russo's conviction that Shaw was the man at the meeting appeared to weaken.

Particularly galling to Garrison was an account by *Newsweek*'s Hugh Aynesworth that Garrison had offered an unwilling witness $3,000 and an airline job to testify in the upcoming trial. The story added that the entire bribery attempt had been tape-recorded.

Aynesworth was a writer for the *Dallas Morning News* the day of the assassination and was at the scene of each important event. In 1988, Aynesworth wrote extensively for a special edition of the *Washington Times* commemorating the twenty-fifth anniversary of the assassination. While admitting "flaws" in the Warren Commission investigation, he nevertheless supported its conclusions by writing: ". . . that report has been proven to have been considerably more honest, more objective and of far greater depth than any subsequent 'probe' or 'inquiry' . . ."

When asked to present his evidence of Garrison's bribery attempt, Aynesworth failed to come forward with either a witness or the tape recording he mentioned.

During this time, the media made much out of a visit to Las Vegas by Garrison, where reportedly he was given a $5,000 credit line at the Sands Hotel.

In 1979, a report to the House Select Committee on Assassinations even stated that Garrison met with Mobster Johnny Roselli less than a month after Ferrie's death.

For his part, Garrison wrote to researcher John Judge: ". . . I have never even seen John Roselli in my life—nor have I ever had a 'secret meeting' with any racketeer anywhere."

An NBC program stated that one of Garrison's witnesses had lied under oath, but when requested to present their evidence to a New Orleans grand jury, news executives declined. In that same NBC program, Frank McGee claimed two of Garrison's star witnesses had failed their polygraph tests. Garrison publicly offered to resign if the network could substantiate this charge. Again, no proof was forthcoming.

CBS interviewed Garrison, but:

> When the CBS program was shown across the nation, my half hour had been reduced to approximately 30 seconds. This gave me just about enough time to be a discordant bleep in the network's massive four-hour tribute to the Warren Commission.

Shortly before the trial of Clay Shaw, Garrison believed he may have been the object of a setup to implicate him with a known homosexual and a former client. He escaped arrest and was shocked to learn that one of his "special team" members—a former FBI man—may have been responsible for the bizarre episode. However, before Garrison could question the man, he had hurriedly left New Orleans, taking many of the district attorney's files with him.

Garrison also claimed that someone had "bugged" the telephones of his office, his home, and even his staff.

The anti-Garrison media blitz coupled with the strange incidents surrounding his investigation prompted Garrison to claim that "a tremendous amount of federal power" had been arrayed against him in an effort to block his investigation of Kennedy's death.

He voiced his concern over a fair trial when he told interviewer Eric Norden:

. . . I'm beginning to worry about the cumulative effect of this propaganda blitzkrieg on potential jurors for the trial of Clay Shaw. I don't know how long they can withstand the drumbeat obligato of charges exonerating the defendant and convicting the prosecutor.

Garrison claimed this effort to stop him proved two things:

First, that we were correct when we uncovered the involvement of the CIA in the assassination; second, that there is something very wrong today with our government in Washington, D.C., inasmuch as it is willing to use massive economic power to conceal the truth from the people.

But Garrison was not without supporters. A group of New Orleans businessmen, going under the name "Truth or Consequences," gave Garrison both moral and financial backing.

Surprising solidarity came from Boston's Cardinal Richard Cushing, father confessor to the Kennedy family, who commented: "I think they [the investigation in New Orleans] should follow it through. . . . I never believed the assassination was the work of one man."

Another odd show of support for Garrison came years later from a most unlikely source. Shortly before his disappearance, Teamster boss Jimmy Hoffa stated: "Jim Garrison's a smart man . . . goddamned smart attorney. . . . Anybody thinks he's a kook is a kook themselves."

There is some evidence that Robert Kennedy also took Garrison's probe seriously. He indicated to his friend Arthur M. Schlesinger, Jr., that he believed Garrison might be onto something. But when his staff once began to tell him about Garrison's findings, he turned away, saying: "Well, I don't think I want to know."

By January 29, 1969, the day the Clay Shaw trial finally got under way, Garrison's case was already foundering. His chief suspect, Ferrie, was dead and others had fled New Orleans and were safe in other states that refused to honor Garrison's extradition requests.

Governor John Connally, himself a victim in Dallas, refused to extradite Cuban leader Sergio Archaca-Smith, while California governor Ronald Reagan declined to allow extradition for one Edgar Eugene Bradley.

Garrison, in a mistake that was to cost him further credibility, apparently had mistaken Bradley for Mafia man Eugene Hale Brading who was arrested in Dealey Plaza shortly after the assassination.

But Garrison's major "missing witness" was Gordon Novel, a young electronics expert who eventually became embroiled in some of this nation's most controversial cases. Novel first approached Garrison in early 1967 with information about David Ferrie and Cuban exile activities, but soon Garrison came to believe that Novel was a CIA "plant."

After Garrison subpoenaed Novel, he fled to Ohio where Governor James Rhodes—despite a personal call from Governor John McKeithen of Louisiana—refused to allow extradition. Likewise, the governor of Nebraska declined to honor an extradition order for Sandra Moffett, a former girlfriend of Perry Russo who was present at the gathering of Ferrie, Shaw, and Oswald in September 1963.

A note left behind in his New Orleans apartment, which was later authenticated as being written by Novel, mentioned his work for Double Check Corporation, a CIA "front" located in Miami. The letter stated: "Our connection and activity of that period [with Double Check] involves individuals presently . . . about to be indicted as conspirators in Mr. Garrison's investigation."

In 1974, Novel, who claimed to have worked for the CIA, met with President Nixon's special counsel Charles Colson and discussed developing a special "de-gaussing" machine that would erase Nixon's incriminating White House tapes from afar. Novel also cropped up as an electronics expert in the case of automobile magnate John DeLorean.

Despite the media attacks and missing witnesses, Garrison gamely moved ahead with his prosecution of Clay Shaw. His goals were twofold: 1) convince the jury that a conspiracy was behind President Kennedy's death and 2) prove that Clay Shaw was a part of that conspiracy. Garrison achieved the first goal but failed on the second.

After a string of witnesses from Dallas—including the Bill Newmans and railroadman James L. Simmons and others not called before the Warren Commission—told of shots to Kennedy's front and medical testimony pointed out the shortcomings of the President's autopsy, the jury became convinced of Garrison's charge that a conspiracy had existed.

This conviction solidified when the jury viewed the Zapruder film of the assassination—made available for the first time due to Garrison's subpoena power.

After the trial, every juror agreed that Garrison had convinced them that Kennedy had died as the result of a conspiracy.

However, the evidence of Shaw's involvement proved not as convincing. Despite several credible people who testified they had seen David

Ferrie and Lee Oswald with a man matching Clay Shaw's description—
including several prominent residents of Clinton, Louisiana—many jurors
remained skeptical.

Insurance salesman Perry Russo repeated his 1967 statements that he
was present when Shaw and Ferrie talked about assassinating Kennedy.
Russo said that Shaw had been introduced to him as Clem Bertrand.

He said Ferrie and the man he identified as Shaw talked of triangulation
of gunfire and the need to have alibis at the time of the assassination.

Defense attorneys pointed out that Russo had been given a truth serum
drug to help his recall and reiterated the charge that Garrison had im-
planted the entire Ferrie-Shaw story while Russo was under the drug's
influence.

One particularly compelling witness was Vernon Bundy, who testified
he had seen Clay Shaw meet with Lee Harvey Oswald at a seawall on
Lake Pontchartrain in June 1963. Bundy said he knew the man speaking
with Oswald was Shaw because he noticed the man had a slight limp.

A puzzled Shaw was asked to walk down the center isle of the courtroom and everyone—including an amazed Garrison—noticed for the first
time a nearly imperceptible limp.

Another credible witness was postman James Hardiman who testified
that during 1966 he had delivered letters addressed to ''Clay Bertrand'' to
a forwarding address for Clay Shaw. Hardiman said none of the letters
were returned.

Then came Charles Spiesel, a New York accountant who had suddenly
shown up in New Orleans to tell Garrison that he had met David Ferrie on
a visit and that they had been joined by Clay Shaw. Appearing to be a
credible witness, he had been belatedly added to Garrison's witness list.

Once on the stand, Garrison cringed at Spiesel's cross-examination. The
man rambled on about how he had been hypnotized on several occasions
by various unidentified people and how he regularly fingerprinted his
daughter upon her return from Louisiana State University to make sure she
was really his daughter.

Garrison's case also was not helped by several statements he made prior
to the Shaw trial, including the claims that Shaw had met with Ruby and
Oswald in the Jack Tar Capital House in Baton Rouge on September 3,
1963, and handed them money and that the man who killed President
Kennedy had fired a .45-caliber pistol then fled through the Dallas drain-
age system to another part of town. None of these claims were substantiated.

More harm came in the testimony of attorney Dean Andrews, who—
while under a perjury charge by Garrison—changed his story of being
called by a man named Clay Bertrand and asked to defend Oswald just
after the assassination. On the stand, Andrews said the name ''Clay
Bertrand'' was simply a ''figment of [his] imagination'' and that he had
never known Clay Shaw. Andrew's statements strongly affected the jury,

although later Garrison was to convict Andrews of perjury based on his testimony.

And when Assistant District Attorney James L. Alcock tried to discredit Andrews's testimony, it appeared he was impeaching the core of Garrison's charge that Shaw and Bertrand were one and the same.

So the crux of the case came down to whether Clay Shaw, the respected director of the International Trade Mart, and Clay (or Clem) Bertrand, the man overheard plotting against Kennedy, were the same man.

Garrison's strongest piece of evidence was Shaw's jail card, which showed he used the alias Clay Bertrand.

Yet Criminal District Court judge Edward Aloysius Haggerty refused to allow the jail card to be introduced as evidence, saying Shaw had not been allowed to have a lawyer with him during the booking procedure.

Garrison's "dramatic finale" then became New Orleans policeman Aloysius J. Habighorst, the man who filled out Shaw's jail form, and who was expected to testify that Shaw had told him his alias was "Clay Bertrand."

However, before Habighorst could take the stand, Judge Haggerty ordered the jury removed from the courtroom. He told stunned prosecutors that he was not allowing Habighorst's testimony to be admitted because again no attorney had been present and his alias story appeared to be a violation of Shaw's rights.

Judge Haggerty then said: "Even if [Shaw] did [admit the alias], it is not admissible. If Officer Habighorst is telling the truth—and I seriously doubt it . . ."

This remark brought Assistant D.A. James Alcock to his feet, saying: "Are you passing on the credibility of a state witness in front of the press and the whole world?"

To which Judge Haggerty responded: "It's outside the presence of the jury. I do not care. The whole world can hear that I do not believe Officer Habighorst. I do not believe Officer Habighorst."

With the judge's statements, Garrison's case—already severely weakened by dead, incredible, and unobtainable witnesses—collapsed.

Alcock moved to have a mistrial declared, but Judge Haggerty denied this, ordering the trial to proceed without the crucial testimony of Officer Habighorst.

Clay Shaw took the stand in his own defense claiming that he never knew Ferrie, Oswald, or Ruby and that he had not participated in a plot to kill Kennedy. Garrison's team was unable to provide any motivation for Shaw's involvement in such a scheme.

Just past midnight on March 1, 1969—two years to the day that Shaw had first been arrested—the jury filed into Judge Haggerty's courtroom to announce Clay Shaw's acquittal after less than an hour of deliberation.

Two days later, on March 3, Garrison filed perjury charges against Shaw for maintaining that he never met David Ferrie. Garrison later wrote:

We had more witnesses to prove this flagrant case of perjury than I had ever encountered as district attorney. . . . Given my personal choice, I would much rather have let the matter rest once and for all. . . . However, the choice was not mine. My decision had been made automatically when—contrary to the numerous statements in our files—Shaw had taken the witness stand and, in his grand and courtly manner, made a mockery of the law against lying under oath.

But again Garrison had not counted on the federal government.

According to federal law at the time, "A court of the United States may not grant an injunction to stay proceedings in a State Court except as expressly authorized by an Act of Congress, or where necessary in aid of its jurisdiction, or to protect or effectuate its judgments."

Garrison wrote:

Fortunately for Shaw, the federal judicial system shut its eyes to that federal law. The United States District Court DID [sic] enjoin me from prosecuting Shaw for committing perjury, and the federal appellate structure firmly backed up the District Court's ruling all the way. When the assassination of a dead president has been ratified by a live national government, details such as the law very quickly become irrelevant.

Clay Shaw, his finances depleted after the years of defending himself and despondent over the revelations of his homosexual connections, retired to his New Orleans home where he died on August 14, 1974.

Even Shaw's death did not pass without question. Neighbors saw some men carrying what appeared to be a body completely covered by a sheet on a stretcher into a carriage house belonging to Shaw. They called the coroner's office, which dispatched investigators. The coroner's investigators found Shaw's home empty and, after a day of searching, learned that Shaw had just been buried in his hometown of Kentwood. A death certificate signed by a Dr. Hugh Betson stated death was caused by lung cancer.

New Orleans coroner Dr. Frank Minyard—concerned over the circumstances of Shaw's death and the rapidity of burial—initially said he would seek a court order for the exhumation of Shaw's body. However, word reached the news media, which immediately editorialized against such a move, hinting that the exhumation was just another attack by Garrison, and Minyard dropped the whole matter.

Despite his courtroom loss and the tidal wave of negative publicity—*The New York Times* called the case "one of the most disgraceful chapters in the history of American jurisprudence" while the *New Orleans States-Item* demanded Garrison's resignation—the scrappy district attorney nevertheless handily won reelection later that year.

But his troubles with the federal government were not over. On June 30,

1971, Garrison was arrested at his home by agents of the Internal Revenue Service who charged him with accepting illegal payoffs from pinball machine operators.

After two years of more bad publicity, he was finally brought to trial. Several pinball machine operators told of making payoffs, but none of them could directly implicate Garrison.

Finally, a former Garrison investigator and Army buddy, Pershing Gervais, took the stand and told how Garrison had accepted $150,000 in payoffs. He even produced a tape recording of Garrison's voice reportedly made of the district attorney discussing the matter.

But on cross examination, Gervais admitted that he had told a television reporter that he had been forced by the Justice Department to lie and incriminate Garrison. Gervais had admitted the case against Garrison was "a total, complete political frameup, absolutely."

Furthermore, a speech expert testified that the incriminating tape had been created by splicing together several innocuous comments made by Garrison.

Garrison and two codefendants were quickly found not guilty, but enough damage had been done. Busy defending himself in court, Garrison failed to mount an effective campaign in 1973 and was defeated for district attorney by two thousand votes.

Furthermore, the federal government came at him again, this time alleging income tax evasion in connection with the discredited pinball payoffs. Again Garrison was found not guilty, but by this time the national audience had largely turned its back on the "controversial" lawman in New Orleans.

Even today many assassination researchers believe Garrison was far afield of truth about Kennedy's death. Many agree with House Select Committee on Assassinations chief counsel Robert Blakey, who bluntly wrote: "In short, the Garrison case was a fraud."

Blakey, who claims organized crime killed Kennedy, apparently fails to see any suspicious connection in the facts that David Ferrie was with New Orleans mob boss Carlos Marcello in court on the morning of the assassination; that Ferrie was the Civil Air Patrol leader of Lee Harvey Oswald; and that Ferrie and Clay Shaw both worked for the CIA and were connected to anti-Castro Cubans.

It should also be pointed out that critics of Blakey's work on the House Committee noted a cozy relationship between Blakey and government agencies such as the FBI and CIA.

Buried at the end of his "Principal Sources" section in his book, *The Plot to Kill the President*, Blakey gives evidence of precensorship as well as his relationship with certain government agencies by writing:

Pursuant to agreement with the House Select Committee on Assassinations, the Central Intelligence Agency and the Federal Bureau of Investigation reviewed this book in manuscript form to determine that classified information it contained had been properly released for publication and that no informant was identified. Neither the CIA nor the FBI warrants the factual material or endorses the views expressed.

Another Garrison detractor, author David E. Scheim—who also espouses the Mafia-did-it theory—cites the charges against Garrison made by NBC, *Newsweek, The New York Times,* and *The Saturday Evening Post* apparently without considering that few of their accusations were ever proven.

Citing Garrison's failure to loudly identify Jack Ruby as Mafia-connected, Scheim wrote:

Although Garrison made extravagant charges against an assortment of Cuban exiles, CIA agents, Minutemen, White Russians, and Nazis, he conspicuously avoided any reference to one prime assassination suspect: the Mafia.

Indeed, Garrison's failure to acknowledge Carlos Marcello and the mob's activities in New Orleans has caused many raised eyebrows among researchers otherwise kindly disposed toward the former D.A.

Scheim claims Garrison's former investigator, Pershing Gervais, was a Marcello associate and when Garrison cleaned up Bourbon Street nightspots, he "selectively avoided the clubs controlled by Marcello." The author also expressed the belief that Garrison's acquittal in the 1971 payoff case was the result of more bribes.

Scheim goes beyond Blakey by stating that Garrison's activities in New Orleans had a sinister design. Scheim wrote:

The purpose of the Garrison assassination probe [was that] Jim Garrison conducted a fraudulent probe of the Kennedy assassination, which deflected attention from Carlos Marcello and disrupted serious investigation of the case.

Stung by such suspicions, Garrison has written:

While I lay no pretense to being the epitome of virtue, with regard to connections with organized crime, I think you can safely place me as having approximately the same such connections as Mother Theresa and Pope Paul. What has been occurring here, quite obviously, is the CIA's disinformation machinery has been hard at work for a long time.

Further, Garrison has maintained that while elements within the mob undoubtedly played a role in Kennedy's assassination, they were certainly protected—and perhaps even encouraged and funded—by elements within the U.S. government.

To the charge that he was simply grandstanding, hoping for higher office, Garrison has stated:

A politically ambitious man would hardly be likely to challenge the massed power of the federal government and criticize so many honorable figures and distinguished agencies. Actually, this charge is an argument in favor of my investigation: Would such a slimy type, eager to profiteer on the assassination, jeopardize his political ambitions if he didn't have an ironclad case?

While charge and countercharge, claim and counterclaim, continue to surround Garrison—today he serves as an elected appeals court judge in New Orleans—he still speaks out for a truth he claims was denied nearly two decades ago.

Garrison still believes that President Kennedy was killed for one reason: because he was working for a reconciliation with Soviet Russia and Castro's Cuba. He wrote:

To anyone with a grain of intelligence, it should be apparent that John Kennedy was eliminated by forces desiring the continuation of the Cold War—an artificial conflict draining the assets of and greatly changing, for the worst, the character of our nation. The clandestine arm for those Cold War forces was the Central Intelligence Agency—the destructive talents of which run the gambit [sic] from deception to murder.

He has even identified those "forces," stating:

On the operative level of the conspiracy, you find anti-Castro Cuban exiles who never forgave Kennedy for failing to send in U.S. aircover at the Bay of Pigs. . . . They believed sincerely that Kennedy had sold them out to the Communists. On a higher, control level, you find a number of people of ultra-right persuasion—not simply conservatives, mind you, but people who could be described as neo-Nazi, including a small clique that had defected from the Minutemen because it had considered the group "too liberal." These elements had their canteens ready and their guns loaded; they lacked only a target. [After the secret agreements of the Cuban Missile Crisis] Kennedy . . . began to crack down on CIA operations against Cuba. As a result, on July 31, 1963, the FBI raided the headquarters of the group of Cuban exiles and Minutemen training north of Lake Pontchartrain and confiscated all their guns and ammmunition—despite the fact that the operation had the sanction of the CIA. This action may have sealed Kennedy's fate. . . . The link between the "command" level and the Cuban exiles was an amorphous group called the Free Cuba Committee (recall that it was this name which was tied to Lee Harvey Oswald the night of the assassination by Dallas district attorney Henry Wade, who was then corrected by none other than Jack Ruby), which with CIA sanction had been training north of Lake Pontchartrain for an assassination attempt on Fidel Castro. . . . Our information indicates that it was shortly after this setback [the July 31, 1963, FBI raid] that the group switched direction and decided to assassinate John Kennedy instead of Fidel Castro. . . .

Whether Garrison's assured assessment of such an assassination conspiracy can ever be fully documented, it nevertheless remains that his investigations in New Orleans did turn up much previously unknown evidence —another argument against his employment by the mob to deflect the truth.

Even the House Committee's Blakey—who termed his investigation a ''fraud''—conceded:

. . . Garrison might have been on the right track, at least up until Ferrie's untimely death . . . for evidence of an association between Ferrie and Oswald, presented at the Clay Shaw trial, was found by the Committee to be credible.

Summary

New Orleans district attorney Jim Garrison, the "Jolly Green Giant" did not go out trying to find a JFK assassination conspiracy—it found him.

Garrison certainly did not invent Guy Banister, David Ferrie, Clay Shaw, or that strange nexus of anti-Castro Cuban exiles, mob figures, and intelligence agents that collected at 544 Camp Street.

Even though rumors on the streets of New Orleans prompted Garrison to order the arrest of Ferrie the weekend of the Kennedy assassination, it was not until three years later that he began the investigation that would result in the trial of Trade Mart director Clay Shaw.

Contrary to reports that Garrison was simply out for publicity, the aggressive D.A. sought to keep his work quiet. It was only after an enterprising reporter discovered pay vouchers and travel request records that Garrison's efforts became public.

Once public, however, the story of his New Orleans investigation spread like wildfire—and a troubling dimension of the news media presented itself. Rather than simply report Garrison's activities or independently study his information, many media—particularly major national news outlets—chose to investigate the district attorney and make pronouncements on everything from his methods to his mental stability.

Even President Johnson's attorney general proclaimed that Garrison had no case—long before he presented his evidence. Obviously, both judges and grand juries in New Orleans did not feel the same way, since a grand jury indicted Clay Shaw and a three-judge panel upheld the indictment.

And in recent years, several studies of Shaw and his associations indicate a man who—through the shadowy company Permindex—was connected to the CIA, European Nazis and fascists, and international criminals. This cloudy area of Garrison's investigation deserves closer scrutiny.

However, by the time Shaw's case reached court, Garrison's case was fatally weakened by the death of key witnesses—Ferrie, Banister, Banister's partner Hugh Ward, and Cuban exile Eladio del Valle. Other witnesses—CIA operative Gordon Novel and anti-Castro Cuban leader Sergio Archaca-Smith—were given sanctuary in other states whose governors refused Garrison's lawful extradition orders.

In January 1969, Clay Shaw got his day in court. He declared himself innocent of the charge that he conspired with Ferrie and Oswald to kill President Kennedy.

Garrison was also hampered by some of his own witnesses—a self-admitted drug addict and a man who claimed mysterious men were constantly hypnotizing him.

Furthermore, Garrison's charges of a widespread conspiracy—involving President Lyndon Johnson, the FBI, the CIA, and the Cuban exiles—were considered so outlandish by most people that they refused to give his claims any credence.

Although Garrison convinced the New Orleans jury that a conspiracy—which included David Ferrie, Lee Harvey Oswald, and a man named "Clay Bertrand"—had existed to kill Kennedy, he failed to convince them that Clay Shaw was involved. Of course, he was not allowed to present his most potent evidence—the jail card showing Clay Shaw used the alias "Clay Bertrand" or Officer Habighorst. Shaw was found not guilty.

And Garrison's case was not helped by his lengthy statements to the media—some of which were misquoted or quoted out of context.

Garrison claimed the federal government tried to blunt his investigation, and there is much information to support this charge. However, it is also true that Garrison made many mistakes along the way—trusting the wrong people, talking too much about his case, and refusing to acknowledge the role of the Mafia.

It was the latter that had caused many researchers—who otherwise might have supported Garrison—to keep their distance.

Where the two major national assassination investigations exhibited a blind spot when it came to evidence of the involvement of U.S. intelligence agencies, Garrison showed the same blindness toward the mob and particularly toward the man whose connections to the assassination appear most strong—reputed New Orleans Mafia chieftain Carlos Marcello.

Despite the claim of some critics that Garrison was used to block any new investigation of the Kennedy assassination in the late 1960s, he most probably will be well remembered in the years to come as the one man who furthered knowledge of Kennedy's assassination at a time when many Americans were still accepting the lone-assassin theory.

Even House Select Committee on Assassinations chief counsel Robert Blakey—who termed Garrison's investigation a "fraud"—acknowledged that much of his information regarding Oswald, Ferrie, and the anti-Castro Cuban exiles was correct.

Despite continued efforts by the federal government to discredit Garrison—and even convict him of crimes—he still enjoyed a good reputation in New Orleans in the late 1980s serving as an elected judge of the state's Fourth Circuit Court of Appeals.

They [the House Committee] had their chance and they blew it.
—JFK autopsy Doctor James Humes

The House Select Committee on Assassinations

By the mid-1970s, national polls indicated that very few Americans still believed the "lone assassin" theory of the Warren Commission, despite the assurances of the national media and government spokesmen.

According to one Gallup Poll, 80 percent of the American public believed President Kennedy's death resulted from a conspiracy, while 70 percent believed the same regarding the death of Dr. Martin Luther King.

These nagging doubts prompted Congressman Henry Gonzalez of Texas to introduce a House Resolution in February 1975, calling for a select committee to study not only the death of John F. Kennedy, but also the deaths of Robert Kennedy, Martin Luther King, and the shooting of Governor George Wallace.

In remarks to fellow congressmen, Gonzalez said:

> . . . I have introduced this resolution after much consideration. It has not been a decision I have made hastily. . . . There are questions to be resolved. I was at Dallas the day that President Kennedy was killed and I suspended judgment on the questions that arose then and shortly thereafter until Watergate, August 1972, revealed possibilities heretofore considered not possible.

In an article published by St. Mary's School of Law two months later, Gonzalez added:

> There are a few who have offered criticism of my efforts . . . The attitude of these people is to "let sleeping dogs lie" . . . I say that this investigation is a need and has its proper place in our list of priorities. What future do we have as a nation if we let valid questions about these assassinations go unresolved and uninvestigated except by private individuals?

Gonzalez's House Resolution 204 was joined by a similar resolution, sponsored by lame duck Representative Thomas N. Downing of Virginia. In remarks to fellow congressmen on March 18, 1976, Downing complained of foot-dragging:

518

. . . in the past few weeks, certain events have transpired in this House which concern me deeply and which lead me to believe either I don't understand the House half as well as I thought I did, or that the House is undergoing a deep and fundamental transformation as a result of those tragic events which we collectively label "Watergate." Until now, it has seemed to me that, although Congress might not have dealt with all problems wisely, it has not been its policy simply and doggedly to refuse to look at a serious national problem, no matter how difficult, no matter how distressing. Yet, I fear that is precisely what it is doing today. It is simply and doggedly refusing to look at the problem of who executed our former President, John F. Kennedy, and why he was executed. I do not exaggerate. I have chosen my words carefully, and I mean precisely what I say. . . . However, we not only have failed to make any progress toward establishment of such an investigating committee, we also have not even been able to get a hearing on the merits before the Rules Committee. . . . I have been told informally that "the Leadership" is against reopening the Warren Commission's findings, and that is that. . . . Why would there be reluctance on the part of the Leadership and the committee? Have they been told by the Intelligence Community, which, incidentally, possibly acted as sole investigators for the Warren Commission, what really did happen to our young President, and why? Do they know who was behind the killing? Is it too horrible for the American people to face? . . . Someone apparently does not want us to see the evil, hear the evil and certainly does not want us to talk about it. . . . After all, if a President is eliminated, not by a "lone nut," but for political reasons, isn't the whole fabric of our form of government in direct danger if we cover up the political motivations and go on as if nothing happened?

Despite these passionate appeals for a reinvestigation into the assassinations, action stalled in the House for more than a year. The Rules Committee simply refused to even consider the idea.

Finally in mid-1976, the Black Caucus—at the instigation of Dr. King's wife, Coretta—put pressure on the House leadership and the Gonzalez and Downing bills were merged into House Resolution 1540 and passed in September 1976. However, the Committee would expire at the end of the congressional term on January 3, 1977.

Trouble began immediately. House tradition dictated that the author of a resolution creating a select committee be named chairman. Downing, who had not sought reelection in 1976, would soon retire and Gonzalez—a highly individualistic Mexican-American—was not liked by House power brokers.

Despite Downing's lame-duck status, he was named chairman of the House Select Committee on Assassinations by Speaker Thomas P. "Tip"

O'Neill—a decision that did not please Gonzalez, who began to operate as co-chairman.

Early on, Downing wanted Washington attorney Bernard Fensterwald to serve as the Committee's chief counsel and director. Fensterwald, who had formed a clearinghouse of assassination material called the Committee to Investigate Assassinations, was an early critic of the Warren Commission and thoroughly familiar with most aspects of the John F. Kennedy case.

Gonzalez objected and Fensterwald withdrew from consideration. But not before an article appeared in the *Washington Star* under the headline, ASSASSINATION INQUIRY STUMBLING—IS FENSTERWALD A CIA PLANT? Later it was learned that information for this attack came from Gonzalez's office.

In October 1976, Downing and Gonzalez settled on a former Philadelphia prosecutor, Richard A. Sprague, as the Committee's chief counsel. Initially, Sprague seemed like an excellent choice. He had a record of sixty-nine convictions out of seventy homicide cases, was well regarded as a tough and independent prosecutor. He had received national attention by his prosecution of United Mine Workers president Tony Boyle for the murder of UMW reformer Joseph Yablonski.

Sprague stated he planned to break his investigations into two separate areas—one for John Kennedy and one for Dr. King. He said these assassination inquiries would be treated as homicide investigations. This was a novel approach to the Kennedy assassination since, until that time, all investigation and deliberation had been done secretly by government groups.

Bypassing the FBI and the CIA, Sprague hired professional investigators and criminal lawyers from New York City. He made it clear that his investigation would not hesitate to look into FBI and CIA involvement and that he would use subpoena power and lie detector tests to get to the truth. Aware of the CIA connections to the Kennedy assassination, Sprague let it be known he planned to subpoena both Agency files and personnel.

Sprague also contacted many of the responsible Kennedy assassination researchers, including Jim Garrison in New Orleans, and privately told them he planned to use them as Committee consultants.

He was also truthful in projecting the costs of such a massive investigation, saying he needed a staff of at least two hundred and an initial budget of $6.5 million to start work.

Sprague's openness about both his needs and his goals prompted immediate outrage among congressmen who had never wanted the Committee in the first place. Many of these lambasted Sprague for his statements about using lie detectors, voice stress analyzers, and hidden tape recorders to learn the truth. Soon Sprague was almost too busy fending off media attacks to get his investigation rolling.

Other developments began to raise doubts in the minds of many assassination researchers, whose hopes had grown since creation of the Committee. To begin with, Sprague early on stated: "I have not, as of this date, read the Warren Commission Report or testimony. But I have never read any books by the critics, either.''

This unfamiliarity with the assassination was reflected in Sprague's selection of the prosecutors and lawmen as investigators and staff for the Committee. Many were agressive and able—but they did not understand the full ramifications of the case. Many had ties back to the FBI or CIA and none of them had the time to properly study the complex and convoluted assassination issues.

Furthermore, despite Sprague's wooing of the research community—the people with detailed knowledge of the cases—with few exceptions, they were excluded from the House Committee's staff.

Then there was the question of Sprague's close friendship with his former boss Arlen Specter, the Warren Commission staffer who created the ''single bullet'' theory of the assassination. Sprague was quoted as saying: ''I did not talk to Arlen before I took this thing.''

Sprague incensed Gonzalez immediately by renting a plush apartment in Washington's Watergate complex, then leaving for a vacation in Acapulco without informing the Committee's founder.

Almost singlehandedly, Gonzalez continued to work to save the Committee. Upon Sprague's return to Washington, Gonzalez was quoted in *Newsweek* as telling his chief counsel: ''If I had known in September what I know now, I would never have affirmed your appointment.''

With his pronouncements and absence, Sprague was making enemies everywhere. Representative Robert E. Bauman of Maryland charged that Sprague ''virtually assumed the role of chairman of the Committee.''

One of the only field investigators retained by the Committee during this time was Gaeton Fonzi, who was busy developing assassination leads among organized-crime and anti-Castro circles in Miami. In a 1980 article, Fonzi wrote:

After talking with Sprague, I was now certain he planned to conduct a strong investigation and I was never more optimistic in my life. . . . The Kennedy assassination would finally get the investigation it deserved and an honest democracy needed . . .

As 1976 drew to a close and Sprague found himself under attack by the media, including *The New York Times*, the Committee's reconstitution in January suddenly began to appear precarious.

Sprague was baffled at the hostility directed at him. He told Committee staffers: ''You know, I don't understand it. I've never been in a situation like this before where I am getting criticized for things I might do. It's nonsense, but I don't know why it's happening. . . .''

His proposed budget was targeted for attack, but Sprague held his ground, saying:

Several people around here who are familiar with the bureaucratic game told me to first present a smaller budget. They assured me that I could always go back later and plead for more. That's the way they do things in Washington, I was told. Well, I won't play that game.

The press attacks caused second thoughts in Congress. A resolution reconstituting the Assassinations Committee by a unanimous-consent voice vote on January 4, 1977, failed. It would take weeks of maneuvering before the Committee could officially be reconstituted. By this time, Downing had retired and Gonzalez had been named chairman of the Committee.

Suddenly the outside media attacks on Sprague were joined by an unexpected source—Committee Chairman Gonzalez. According to persons familiar with this situation, Gonzalez—already angered at not being named chairman until after Downing retired and at Sprague's early activities or lack of them—was further incensed that Sprague would not allow him to run the Committee the way he saw fit.

And there was the continuing problem of funding. Sprague had been told he had $150,000 a month for expenses until the Committee was reconstituted in January 1977. Later he found out that amount actually was only $84,000, which caused a cost overrun for which Gonzalez was taken to task by the House Rules Committee—the same committee that had stalled the Assassinations Committee in the first place. Gonzalez claimed Sprague had spent money without his knowledge or consent.

Gonzalez ordered Sprague to take a "number of steps," including giving written assurance that he would stay within the financial constraints of the Committee's funding and firing staff members recently hired. Sprague's refusal to bow to Gonzalez's demands, prompted the hot-tempered Texas representative to write:

Owing to an evident inability of the Committee in times past to adequately control the use of its letterhead and franked materials, and in the absence of any present controls on such materials, you are directed to return to me immediately any and all letterhead materials bearing my name.

Fonzi wrote:

Since all congressional committees use the postal franking privileges of its chairman, and every expense voucher, travel order, and most directives and requests are made under the chairman's signature, what Gonzalez was doing, in effect, was virtually stopping the operation of the Committee.

Next Gonzalez further subverted the Committee's work by asking the attorney general to deny Committee staffers access to FBI files and by cutting off long-distance phone calls by the Committee's staff.

Sprague reportedly remarked to co-workers: "Gonzalez went berserk."

Finally, in a hand-delivered letter, Gonzalez charged Sprague with being "engaged in a course of conduct that is wholly intolerable for any employee of the House" and ordered him to vacate his office that same day. However, within a few hours the other eleven members of the Committee had written their own letter, instructing Sprague to ignore Gonzalez. This in-fighting continued, with Gonzalez telling newsmen that Sprague was a "rattlesnake."

It appears that both Gonzalez and Sprague may have been the objects of secret personal smear campaigns—Sprague being told Gonzalez was trying to subvert the Committee's work while Gonzalez was being told that Sprague was a CIA plant on the Committee.

Early in March 1977, Gonzalez resigned from the Assassinations Committee claiming that Sprague had refused to cut costs and had tried to undermine his authority as chairman. Back home in San Antonio, Gonzalez told a reporter he had been forced out of the investigation by "vast and powerful forces, including the country's most sophisticated criminal element." Gonzalez told newsmen: "I am like a guy who's been slugged before he's got a chance to fight. . . . It was an exercise in futility. The fix was in."

While the life of the Committee had been extended for two more months in January, it was due to expire at the end of March 1977. Near that time, a new chairman was named—Representative Louis Stokes, a low-key, black Democrat from Ohio. With the more acceptable Stokes in charge, the Assassinations Committee was revived by the passage of House Resolution 433, which passed on March 30, 1977, reconstituting the Committee until January 3, 1979, and assigning it a pared-down budget of $2.5 million.

Just before the House vote to continue the Committee, Sprague was called to Stokes's office. Despite having been promised support by Stokes and other Committee members, Sprague could see the writing on the wall. He told them: "Gentlemen, it's clear it's in everyone's best interest if I resign." Sprague's resignation prompted several Committee members to state publicly that the chief counsel had been the victim of a McCarthy-like "witch hunt" and character assassination.

Although the Committee had been in existence for six months, the constant bickering and lack of funds prevented any meaningful work. Throughout its brief life, its focus so far had not been on assassinations, but on sheer survival.

Earlier in March, Fonzi—still on the job—had tried to contact the last-known close friend of Lee Harvey Oswald, George DeMohrenschildt, who was staying in Manalapan, Florida. Soon after arriving home and learning of Fonzi's visit, DeMohrenschildt was found fatally shot in his room. His death was ruled a suicide. Fonzi later wrote:

The inability of the Assassinations Committee to effectively react to the death of a key witness revealed that it was still—six months after it was formed—totally incapable of functioning as an investigative body. It reflected six months of political reality and how successful its opponents had been in keeping it distracted and off-balance.

Representative Gonzalez stated simply: "Strong organized forces have combined to stop the inquiry at any cost."

In June 1977, a new chief counsel was selected—G. Robert Blakey, a respected academician with impressive credentials.

Blakey at the Helm

No investigation can be better than its leadership, and the House Select Committee on Assassinations with its new chief counsel and director was no exception.

G. Robert Blakey, a professor of law and director of the Notre Dame Institute on Organized Crime, spent four years in the organized-crime and racketeering section of the Kennedy Justice Department; was former chief counsel to the Senate Subcommittee on Criminal Laws and Procedures; was principal consultant to President Lyndon Johnson's Commission on Law Enforcement and Administration of Justice; and a consultant to the publications *Time, Life,* and *Look.*

Upon becoming chief counsel and director for the House Select Committee on Assassinations, Blakey firmly took control of the panel and its investigation. He oversaw every aspect of the Committee's work, selecting witnesses, deciding which leads to follow and which to ignore, picked the expert panels, hired and fired staff members, and set the Committee's agenda.

It quickly became obvious that the Assassinations Committee was changing directions in key areas. Where Sprague had opted for openness in the Committee's inquiry, Blakey advocated secrecy. In fact, in his first statement to the news media, Blakey announced: "The purpose of this news conference is to announce there will be no more news conferences." Blakey also announced that the Committee would not be looking at any new evidence in the Kennedy-King assassinations, but would concentrate on evaluating the old evidence accumulated by the federal government.

His turnaround prompted assassination researchers to take a closer look at the new chief counsel, with some disturbing results.

Having worked for both President Johnson and President Nixon, Blakey had close contact with other ranking government persons involved in the Kennedy assassination case, among them:

NICHOLAS KATZENBACH—the deputy attorney general, who in 1964 put strong pressure on the Warren Commission to quickly endorse the premise that Lee Harvey Oswald acted alone.

LEON JAWORSKI—the Watergate special prosecutor who served as a special counsel to the Warren Commission charged with determining if Oswald had any ties to U.S. intelligence. (Jaworski found none, but some years later it was discovered that a foundation of which Jaworski was a trustee secretly used CIA funds.)

LEWIS F. POWELL—the attorney named by the American Bar Association as an observer to the Warren Commission to protect Oswald's rights, but who spent much of his time trying to have Commission critic Mark Lane disbarred.

Although considered an expert in the "war against crime," Blakey apparently had a strange connection with a reputed big-time gambler. When *Penthouse* magazine was sued for libel by Rancho La Costa, it was Blakey who sold his expertise and provided an affidavit condemning the magazine's charges of mob ownership while conceding ignorance of the truth of the charges. Any questions concerning this odd support of a resort built by Teamster pension-fund money were referred to Blakey's own attorney, Louis Nizer.

Furthermore, Blakey was recommended as chief counsel by HSCA member Representative Christopher Dodd, the former law partner of former FBI director L. Patrick Gray, who was indicted during the Watergate scandals.

While these connections don't prove compromise on Blakey's part, they do serve to cast a shadow over his credentials as an uncompromising crimebuster. They also raised doubts in many minds about Blakey's motives.

But is there any evidence that the findings of the assassinations Committee were undermined?

Apparently so. The main weapon used by Blakey to stop a meaningful investigation was a "nondisclosure agreement," which Blakey insisted everyone connected with the Committee sign. Signing this agreement, which was instituted within one week of Blakey's arrival, was mandatory for continued employment with the Committee. Even independent researchers who attempted to share assassination information with the panel were made to sign it.

The agreement bound the signer not to reveal that he or she even worked for the Committee; not to reveal anything learned while serving with the committee; gave the Committee the power to take legal action against the signer in the event of disclosures, even long after the Committee ended; and made the signer agree that all legal fees would be paid should the signer lose such a court suit.

Many persons who have seen this agreement, including attorneys, claim it is in violation of the U.S. Constitution and therefore illegal. However, it stopped most of the Committee's personnel and hired consultants from discussing the workings of the HSCA. It also effectively muzzled many of the assassination researchers.

(Evidence of the weak legal standing of this agreement may be found in the fact that Gaeton Fonzi has written scathing articles against the Committee and its operation in apparent violation of this agreement—yet there has been no prosecution.)

Blakey invited ten prominent critics of the Warren Commission to Washington for an exchange of assassination information. All were required to sign the "nondisclosure agreement," and all presented their information. Blakey reciprocated with nothing of value. After their departure, Blakey instructed the Committee staff to have no further contact with these researchers without his personal and specific authorization.

Even aides to Committee members were barred by Blakey from viewing the Committee's progress.

In explaining his zeal for secrecy, Blakey wrote:

> . . . it was resolved, then and there, that the Committee would conduct its investigation in private until it was appropriate to hold public hearings, and it would do its best to remain immune from the fever of assassination demonology.

Blakey also said such secrecy was necessary to protect the reputations of people involved in the investigation—the "innocent associates."

Even more disquieting to researchers was Blakey's accommodating attitude toward the FBI and the CIA—the two agencies that have become suspects themselves over the years in the minds of many. Earlier, Sprague had put both agencies on notice that subpoenas might be issued for access to assassination material withheld from previous investigations. Probes into CIA activity in Mexico City and the connections between Ruby and Oswald and the FBI had been initiated.

Under Blakey, Committee investigators had to sign a CIA secrecy oath before examining any classified files, thus giving the Agency the authority to "clear" any information, including investigators' notes.

A January 25, 1978, Committee report states:

> All staff members on the Committee have received or are in the process of receiving "Top Secret" security clearances. The FBI, as an accommodation to the Committee, conducts the background investigations for these security clearances. The CIA then reviews the background investigations done by the FBI. After consultation with the FBI and CIA, the full Committee makes the determination regarding an individual's security clearance.

In other words, both intelligence agencies had direct control over who participated in the Committee's investigation. This situation did nothing to ease the minds of researchers who already were convinced of intelligence involvement in the Kennedy assassination.

Several persons were fired from the Committee staff for failing to receive a security clearance, including one person who reportedly was told by Blakey: "The CIA would be more comfortable if you were gone."

It also has never been explained how this clearance review was made to conform with the CIA charter prohibition against domestic activities.

In a TV interview, original counsel Sprague stated he had refused to yield to CIA and FBI demands for security clearances, as such agreements would have given these agencies authority to decide what the Committee could disclose. Sprague argued: "What's the point of getting material in the first place, if they are going to control who sees it and what we can do with it?"

Blakey showed no such insight. In fact, in an article by writer Jerry Policoff, Blakey is quoted as saying: "I've worked with the CIA for twenty years. Would they lie to me?"

And there is evidence that Blakey's trust in the Agency went beyond simple naïveté. After it was discovered that the CIA held a "201 file" on Lee Harvey Oswald—evidence that he worked for the Agency according to several former CIA agents—Blakey retrieved the file from CIA headquarters. According to the House Committee, it was virtually an empty folder. Agency officials explained that the file was actually just a "Personality" file that had contained a few news clippings on Oswald after being opened on December 9, 1960.

Yet researchers today have a copy of a CIA "Memorandum For The Record" dated April 27, 1979, which states:

On 27 April, 1979, Mr. G. Robert Blakey, Chief Counsel and Staff Director of the House Select Committee on Assassinations (HSCA), visited CIA Headquarters. . . . Mr. Blakey examined only that material held [Blanked out]. He apparently did not go elsewhere within the Agency, [Blanked out] to examine their holdings. . . . Comment: Files reviewed by HSCA staff members fill nine four-drawer safes. The files include the Lee Harvey Oswald 201, which fills two four-drawer safes. Oswald's 201 file was not completely reviewed by HSCA staff members.

Despite not reviewing all of the CIA's held material—including the Oswald 201 file—the House Committee confidently concluded: "The Secret Service, Federal Bureau of Investigation, and Central Intelligence Agency were not involved in the assassination of President Kennedy."

Some investigators resigned from the Committee because of the control by intelligence agencies and because they felt the investigation had become too narrow in focus.

Other staff members—twenty-four of them investigators—were discharged on grounds that the Committee had no money. Yet in February of 1978,

Blakey returned $425,000 to Congress, saying the funds were not needed.

Whether or not the charges that Blakey sidetracked any meaningful investigation are true, the seeds of doubt were sown. This is reflected in a magazine article by Jerry Policoff and William Scott Malone, who wrote in 1978: "So poisoned has the atmosphere become from months of bitterness that whatever conclusions the Committee comes up with will be suspect."

According to assassination researchers who followed the HSCA closely, Blakey forced out or fired some of the most able investigators, severely restricted areas of investigation, hand-picked scientific experts who mostly denied any hint of conspiracy, and then locked Committee investigative material away for fifty years.

If Blakey wanted to restrict and misdirect the investigations of the House Select Committee on Assassinations—although at this point there is no definitive evidence to demonstrate that this was his wish—he could not have done a better job.

*   *   *

With Blakey's arrival as chief counsel and staff director, many aspects of the HSCA changed dramatically.

Under Sprague, Committee investigators had been running down promising leads in Dallas, Miami, New Orleans, and Memphis. Under Blakey, these field investigations—far from the oversight of Washington power— were severely restricted.

The focus of the Kennedy probe moved away from looking at intelligence and anti-Castro Cuban involvement and began scrutinizing the organized-crime aspects.

Somewhere along the way, the Committee dropped any investigation into the Robert F. Kennedy assassination and the shooting of Governor Wallace, despite the abundance of evidence raising serious questions about the official versions of both those events.

By October 1977, a Scripps-Howard article stated: "The Committee's investigation of the assassination of President John F. Kennedy has been scaled down and the panel's professional staff apparently has been spending virtually all its time exploring new leads in the King case."

On March 13, 1978, the HSCA received House approval for $2.5 million in funding to last until January 3, 1979. The final vote—204 to 175—was achieved despite objections from some Republican representatives who claimed the Committee had accomplished little in its year and a half of existence.

Scaled down and with a restricted agenda, the Committee nevertheless went to work. According to Blakey, the Committee spent a total of $5.5 million during its thirty-month investigation. Blakey wrote in an introduction to the Committee's report: "[This] may sound like a lot, but it should be contrasted with the fact that the Warren Commission spent the equivalent in 1977 dollars of over $10 million in ten months.''

Blakey admitted that early on the HSCA experienced "some rough sailing," and that the period of "rigorous factfinding" lasted only six months—from January to July of 1978. However, this fact finding was "intense and wide ranging," wrote Blakey. He claimed that Committee members and staffers made trips to Mexico, Canada, Portugal, England, and Cuba. There were a total of 562 trips to 1,463 points for more than 4,758 days of field investigation. More than 4,924 interviews were conducted and 335 witnesses heard, some in public hearings and some in executive session. There were 524 subpoenas issued and 165 witnesses were granted immunity for their testimony.

Beginning in late July 1978, the HSCA conducted a series of public hearings that lasted until September 28, 1978. There was a parade of technical and scientific experts, but no one cross-examined them—no one asked the obvious follow-up or embarrassing question. And the testimony of each witness seemed designed to further cement the idea that Lee Harvey Oswald was the lone assassin of Kennedy.

Some witnesses, such as Louie Steven Witt—who claimed to have been the "umbrella man" in Dealey Plaza—gave an implausible story that went unchallenged.

Dr. James Humes, the leader of the Kennedy autopsy team, was never asked why he waited fifteen years to become convinced that a bullet entered near the top of Kennedy's head well above where the other two autopsy doctors still place it. Humes also could have given more details about the military authorities present at the autopsy who directed the doctors in their inadequate work, but he was never asked in public. Humes even quipped: "They had their chance and they blew it.''

Many of the researchers watching the televised hearings felt the testimony was orchestrated and that it followed carefully selected lines of interrogation. This perception prompted a group of researchers who had formed an Assassination Information Bureau to comment:

[There was] no one to remind the on-looking press and the nation that Blakey's case against Oswald looks as good as it does primarily because no one with equal staff, budget and time has had the opportunity to take it in hand, pull open its seams and show the world what it is really made of. Blakey and the Committee may at the moment enjoy a certain sense of victory, but their decision to shut down the other side's chances at rebuttal and rejoinder will eventually work against the credibility of their results. Another one-sided trial of an undefended Oswald is not what the people paid $6 million to see.

The Committee also failed to mention the amount of medical evidence that is still missing.

And—more ominously—some material given to the Committee also turned up missing. Bill O'Reilly was a news reporter for WFAA-TV in Dallas. He recalled:

> . . . a guy who was [in Dealey Plaza] at the time watching the motorcade. His son found [a bullet]. I can't remember his name. . . . But he wanted to remain anonymous . . . He gave me this little cylinder. He said that his son had found it on the ground that day. . . . It was definitely a slug. And the guy said he definitely dug it out of there. . . . It was something I came across and held. And then when the Committee started, I handed it over to Gaeton [Fonzi]. . . . and I don't think anything ever came of it. It was a pistol slug, I'm pretty sure. But again, I'm not positive. . . . But again I am no ballistics expert so it could have been a rifle slug.

Fonzi recalled getting the slug from O'Reilly. He said:

> I wound up with the slug just prior to going with the Committee. I gave the slug to the chief investigator, Cliff Fenton, with the Committee and never heard any more of it. I kept asking Cliff whether he turned it over for analysis or what he did with it. I kept getting noncommittal answers.

Asked about the slug in 1982, Fenton said: "I don't know nothing about that. The best thing I can tell you is to talk to Rep. Stokes. I don't make any comment on the Assassinations Committee. . . . You got to forgive me for that but that's the way I am."

As the Committee closed its public hearings and moved toward presenting its final report in the late fall of 1978, it was apparent that its findings in regard to the JFK assassination were to parallel those of the Warren Commission—that Kennedy had been killed by two bullets fired by Lee Harvey Oswald from the sixth floor of the Texas School Book Depository and that Oswald had acted alone.

But then Blakey—who had carefully restricted the JFK assassination investigation to simply a reevaluation of previous evidence—was hoisted on his own petard.

A scientific study of a Dallas police radio recording revealed solid evidence that more than one gunman fired on Kennedy in Dallas.

The Dallas Police Radio Recording

Even before asking for more funding in March 1978, the House Select Committee on Assassinations already had uncovered a bombshell in the JFK investigation.

Sophisticated scientific studies of a Dallas police radio recording indicated that more than one assassin was involved in Kennedy's death. This evidence, which prompted immediate controversy, destroyed the Warren Commission's theory of a lone gunman and forced the Assassinations Committee to completely reverse its findings at the last moment.

The episode began with a problem very familiar to assassination researchers—an eight-minute "gap" in Dallas police radio broadcasts during the assassination gunfire.

Apparently a Dallas policeman—a motorcycle officer by the sound of a nearby motorcycle engine—opened his microphone about two minutes before the shooting started and left it open for about eight minutes.

In late 1976, researcher Gary Mack—believing that the open microphone had been in Dealey Plaza—obtained a copy of the Dallas police radio recording. He began studying it for sounds of gunfire. He reasoned that if the microphone was indeed open in Dealey Plaza, it must have picked up the sounds of the shots.

By September 1977, he had enhanced the quality of the tape and concluded there were as many as seven shots indicated in the recording.

In a newspaper interview, Mack said: "I managed to get a tape of the police broadcasts and I worked on it. . . . There was some distortion because it was about a 13th-generation tape . . . but it was then that I realized that the shots were in the tape."

Mack next obtained a copy of the tape closer to the original. He explained: ". . . finding the precise location of the shots, then, was easy and [after filtering out much of the motorcycle engine noise] we heard the first shot . . . a very loud, sharp crack immediately following some conversation between two policemen.

The existence of the police recording became known to the Assassinations Committee, which then obtained what was thought to be the original police recording from Dallas police officials. They located it in the possession of a retired police lieutenant.

This original recording—termed a Dictabelt—was turned over to the acoustics firm of Bolt, Beranek & Newman Inc. for sophisticated scientific tests. Dr. James Barger, the firm's chief scientist, converted the sounds on the tape into digitized waveforms to produce a visual picture. The study also looked into "sequence of impulses," which could determine sharp, loud noises such as gunshots and subsequent echoes. Barger determined there were at least six such impulses and asked for further tests, including an on-site test in Dealey Plaza.

By summer 1978, Blakey was aware that the acoustical scientists supported Mack's contention that the tape showed gunfire from more than one location. In fact, during their public testimony, the acoustical scientists stated that there were as many as nine sounds on the Dallas recording which could not be ruled out as gunshots.

But after the Dealey Plaza testing from two locations, they could only confirm four shots—one from the Grassy Knoll.

Additionally, the tape showed that one shot came only 1.6 seconds behind another. Since the FBI had carefully determined that it required at least 2.3 seconds to fire the Mannlicher-Carcano rifle twice, this was further evidence of more than one assassin.

Blakey shocked Committee members with this information, and staff members began to reconsider their conclusions. But not until after the police tape was turned over to yet another team of acoustical scientists. Blakey wrote: ". . . it was deemed judicious to seek an independent review of Barger's analysis before proceeding with the acoustical reconstruction."

The tape was then studied by Professor Mark Weiss of Queen's College of the City University of New York and his associate, Ernest Aschkenasy. Weiss and Aschkenasy agreed with Barger's findings and also encouraged on-site testing.

The idea was to create computerized graphic pictures of the sound patterns of rifle shots in Dealey Plaza and to match them against the patterns discovered in the police recording.

Beginning at dawn, on Sunday, August 20, 1978, three Dallas police sharpshooters fired a total of fifty-six live bullets into three piles of sandbags located along the motorcade route on Elm Street. Rifles were fired from two locations—the southeast corner of the sixth floor of the Texas School Book Depository and from behind the wooden picket fence on the Grassy Knoll.

Interestingly, a .38-caliber pistol also was fired from the Knoll, leading many researchers to speculate that the Committee must have received information leading them to believe a pistol may have been used in the assassination. However, at the time no one could explain why the pistol was test fired. Dallas police commented they were unaware of the Committee's desire to test fire the pistol until the day before the tests.

It also should be noted that two of the three piles of sandbags were located in the middle lane of Elm Street, exactly where films show the presidential limousine. However, one pile—apparently representing one of the early shots—was located in the far left lane. Asked why it was in this location, Dallas police sharpshooter Jerry Compton said he could not get a line of sight on the bags when it was in the center lane due to intervening tree branches.

Less than a year before these tests, a film crew had worked in Dealey Plaza producing a network movie entitled *The Trial of Lee Harvey Oswald*. The tree that prevented a line of sight between the sixth-floor Depository window and the location of the first shot had been pruned back to its 1963 size, based on photographs taken the day of the assassination. Compton's inability to fire at the center lane because of the obstructing tree gave strong support to researchers who have long claimed that a gunman on the Depository's sixth floor would have no line of sight to this location.

After the policemen fired their weapons, a line of microphones was moved along the motorcade route recording 432 impulse sequences or "acoustical fingerprints."

Later, matching up the tape sounds with the test sounds, two of the six possible shots were ruled out as having been fired from the Depository or the Knoll—leaving the possibility that shots came from other locations.

This still left four sounds that did match.

After refining their acoustical tests, Weiss and Aschkenasy concluded: ". . . with a certainty factor of 95 percent or better, there was a shot fired at the presidential limousine from the Grassy Knoll." Barger agreed with this assessment and added that sound from the Knoll was preceded by an N-wave, or supersonic shock wave, proving that the sound was that of a rifle bullet, which is a supersonic missile.

The Assassinations Committee studied photographs taken on November 22, 1963, as well as Dallas police assignments and concluded that the microphone that recorded the shots was on the motorcycle of Patrolman H. B. McLain.

Testifying before the Committee, McLain said his was the first motorcycle to the left of Vice President Johnson's car. He acknowledged that his motorcycle was in the correct location to record the shots, based on the acoustical studies, and that his microphone often got stuck in the "on" position.

However, a week after the Committee was disbanded, McLain suddenly reversed his position, claiming it could not have been his microphone that relayed the sounds. Stating that he had accompanied the presidential limousine to Parkland Hospital, McLain told newsmen: "That wasn't my motorcycle. There would have been a siren on that Channel 1 all the way to the hospital. Everybody had their sirens on . . . you would have heard that on Channel 1." McLain said he came to this conclusion belatedly because when he testified to the Committee, he had not listened to the police recording. However, an assassination photograph showed McLain had lagged behind and was still in Dealey Plaza after the presidential limousine raced off.

But McLain's criticism of the acoustical findings was just the beginning of a controversy over the acoustical studies and their conclusions. Not long after the Committee issued its report citing at least four shots at Kennedy, the FBI publicly disputed the acoustical studies. The Bureau, in news stories carried nationwide, stated that the findings of the acoustical scientists and the Committee were "invalid." This announcement prompted Blakey to term the FBI report "a sophomoric analysis . . . superficial, shoddy and shot full of holes."

However, the controversy was not over.

At the request of the Justice Department—under which is the FBI— the National Science Foundation authorized a $23,360 study of the acoustical evidence by a National Academy of Sciences panel headed by Harvard University physics professor Norman S. Ramsey.

The Ramsey panel decided—on the basis of apparent sounds from police Channel 2 (the motorcade security channel) being found on Channel 1 (the regular police channel)—that this "cross talk" meant the police recordings were unreliable. Ramsey's Committee on Ballistic Acoustics concluded: "the acoustic analyses do not demonstrate that there was a Grassy Knoll shot . . . [and] do not support a conclusion that there was a second gunman."

However, in the months following the Ramsey panel's announcement, its findings were called into question by researcher Gary Mack—the originator of the recording study—who pointed out that Ramsey had based his studies on problems involving the Automatic Gain Control (AGC) on police Channel 1. The Dallas police radios had no AGC circuitry at that time, Mack pointed out. Two members of Ramsey's panel admitted that, if there was no AGC in the Dallas police radios, their analysis of the tapes would have to be redone.

Well into the mid-1980s the controversy over the acoustical tests continued, with one expert challenging another expert and one technical argument being resolved only to find yet another waiting.

Keep in mind that there is now evidence to suggest that the Dallas police recordings may have been edited or otherwise altered while in the hands of federal authorities in the days following the assassination. If the tapes were altered, then the entire acoustical controversy has to go back to square one.

Despite the continuing controversy, the acoustical evidence prompted a complete turnabout in the official version of the JFK assassination.

* * *

The House Select Committee on Assassinations issued a preliminary report on December 30, 1978.

Out of time and money, but faced with the acoustical tests results, it could only conclude that President John F. Kennedy "was probably assassinated as a result of a conspiracy," but that the Committee was "unable to identify the other gunman or the extent of the conspiracy."

The Committee, under Blakey, had gone right to the finish trying to find Oswald the lone assassin. Then at the eleventh hour, they were forced to conclude that at least two assassins were involved.

Assassination researchers were greatly pleased with the revelation of more than one gunmen in the Kennedy murder. Others were not so impressed by the Committee's findings. A sampling of reactions include:

MARGUERITE OSWALD: . . . the select committee has done its work, tried hard, they are men of integrity, but they made the same mistake as the Warren Commission. My late son, Lee Harvey Oswald, was framed for the murder of President Kennedy. . . . They are saying in effect that Lee Harvey Oswald was one of the gunmen and I will emphatically say they are wrong.

DALLAS DISTRICT ATTORNEY HENRY WADE: I have no idea if there was a conspiracy or not. I doubt the Committee knows. If they bring us a body and say he is a conspirator, we'll prosecute him . . .

DAVID BELIN (Warren Commission attorney): Congress is just plain wrong. There was no second gunman firing from the Grassy Knoll. I've seen lots of expert testimony where people differ.

So the controversy over President Kennedy's assassination, far from being settled by the House Committee, continued anew. Only this time, researchers and critics of the Warren Commission had gained new ammunition through information gained by the Committee, and they were now supported in their conspiracy theories by a governmental body.

Even after the Committee had concluded its work, controversy about its operation continued. Five months later, Robert Groden, who had served as staff photographic consultant to the HSCA, told the news media the Committee had pulled its punches:

The direction of the entire House Assassinations Committee rested on one piece of evidence from the beginning—the autopsy photographs. And, from the beginning until the introduction of the acoustical evidence, the autopsy panel assumed the autopsy evidence was genuine. I was not allowed to study the autopsy photographs until December [1978—less than a month before the Committee disbanded] and when I did study them, I found at least two were phonies, which can be proved to any reasonable person.

Groden's charge has been backed by several of the Dallas doctors who worked to save President Kennedy's life. Interviewed by *The Baltimore Sun* in 1979, the Dallas physicians unanimously agreed that the photograph made public by the House Committee was not remotely like the wounds they saw in 1963.

Dr. Marion Jenkins, poking a point at the right rear of the head depicted in the photo, said: "This is where the wound was."

Dr. Charles Baxter: "It was a large, gaping wound in the occipital area, a tangential wound."

Dr. Jackie Hunt, after describing the large wound in the right rear of Kennedy's head and then being shown the House Committee's photo: "I can do a lot of funny things in this darkroom, too."

Dr. Robert Shaw: "If the body hadn't been stolen away from us and had Dr. [Earl] Rose performed a proper autopsy, there would be no question these fifteen years."

Dr. Fouad Bashour: "[The Committee photo] is not the way it was. . . . Why do they cover it up?"

In addition to the doctored autopsy photographs, Groden was openly critical of some of the Committee's experts. He said:

The man who did the ballistic analysis arbitrarily moved the position of Kennedy's back wound up one vertebra, making the whole angle off. . . . The man who concluded the back wound was between the shoulder blades had viewed the same material for the Rockefeller Commission and, at that time, said the wound was on Kennedy's right shoulder.

Groden concluded: "The biggest problem with the Committee is that they gave us a conspiracy, but the wrong one."

Veteran newsman Seth Kantor, who, because of his years working in both Dallas and Fort Worth prior to and during the assassination, may be one of the most knowledgeable media persons on that event told this author the entire House Committee episode was "strange and unusual."

The Committee tried to play to Congress . . . by not touching certain bases because certain congressmen didn't want it. . . . The original chairman [Downing] was about to retire . . . the committee was loaded with second-echelon House members, not leadership quality and with not much clout. . . . When Blakey came in, he wiped out the leadership of the [Committee's] staff and the new people that came in had to start from square one. The investigators sent to Dallas had no working knowledge of the case . . . My biggest grievance with the Committee is that they did not investigate the Dallas police force. Blakey said he had no mandate to investigate the Dallas police. More than half the life of the Committee was frittered away . . .

Many researchers' view of the Committee's work was summed up by Groden, who wrote:

In the end, the Committee consumed millions of dollars and accomplished little. The Select Committee never did the simple things required to get to the truth. Reluctantly, the Committee identified the existence of a "conspiracy" in the Kennedy and King assassinations. But the admission of "conspiracy" was a small breakthrough—the public had suspected it for years. The real truth about who was behind the conspiracies was left undisturbed.

Having totally reversed the government's view of the JFK assassination by stating publicly that a conspiracy "probably" resulted in Kennedy's death and that at least two gunmen fired at him, Chief Counsel Blakey, writing in an introduction to the Committee's report, said: "Realizing that there would be an opportunity for others to fill in the details—that there might be indictments and trials as a result of future investigation—we decided to present an understated case. We chose a cautious approach." An understated case? Consider these points as determined by the Committee:

- A conspiracy involving at least two gunmen resulted in the death of President Kennedy.
- Jack Ruby's killing of Oswald was not spontaneous and Ruby likely entered the Dallas Police Station basement with assistance.
- The Dallas police withheld relevant information about Ruby's entry to the Oswald slaying scene from the Warren Commission.
- The Secret Service was deficient in the performance of its duties in connection with the assassination.
- The FBI performed with varying degrees of competency and failed to investigate adequately the possibility of conspiracy.
- The CIA was deficient in its collection and sharing of assassination information.
- The Warren Commission failed to investigate the idea of conspiracy adequately, partly because of the failure of government agencies to provide the Commission with relevant information.
- Investigation of conspiracy of the Secret Service was terminated prematurely by President Johnson's order that the FBI assume investigative responsibility.
- Since the military 201 file on Oswald was destroyed before the Committee could view it, it could not fully resolve if Oswald had been affiliated with military intelligence.

All of these startling conclusions—and this was the "understated case."

The Committee ended by recommending that the Justice Department pick up where it left off and attempt to unravel the conspiracy that led to the deaths of John F. Kennedy and Martin Luther King. To date, the only action on the part of Justice has been the Ramsey panel, which has called into question the acoustical evidence of multiple gunmen.

An internal Justice Department memo made public only in 1988 revealed what researchers had suspected all along—despite the findings and requests by the House Committee, Justice officials had let the whole thing drop.

Summary

The House Select Committee on Assassinations was born out of political pressure to learn the truth about this nation's assassinations, yet it suffered from this same political pressure throughout its existence.

The Committee not only was susceptible to pressure from Congress—upon which it was dependent for funding—but also from agencies such as the FBI and CIA.

The largest part of the Committee's life was devoted to simply keeping the panel alive and funded.

There can be little doubt that the original chairman, Representative

Henry Gonzalez, and the original chief counsel, Richard A. Sprague, disrupted Committee unity.

And while the political games were being played out in Washington, important Kennedy assassination witnesses—such as George DeMohrenschildt, Carlos Prio Soccaras, Sam Giancana, and former FBI officials—were dying.

After Gonzalez was replaced by Louis Stokes and Sprague by G. Robert Blakey, the Committee's investigations finally got under way—but the depth and scope was severely limited. Blakey quickly announced that there would be no comments to the news media and that only "old" evidence would be studied to see if it withstood the test of time. He also instigated a stringent secrecy oath that effectively muzzled both assassination researchers who worked with the Committee and dissident staff members. Blakey also exhibited a friendly working relationship with the FBI and CIA—both agencies that had become highly suspect in the minds of most researchers. In fact, Blakey removed some of the Committee's most able investigators, restricted areas of study, hand-picked the scientific "experts" to study assassination material, and then locked away the Committee's investigative material for fifty years.

During its public hearings, the Committee was exceptionally gentle with critical witnesses like Marina Oswald and autopsy doctor James Humes, yet unexpectedly harsh with Warren Commission critics and private researchers. Some dubious witnesses—such as Louie Steven Witt, the "umbrella man"—were allowed to tell questionable stories without serious cross-examination.

Right up to the end of its existence, the Committee appeared ready to support the Warren Commission's conclusion that the Kennedy assassination was the work of one lone gunman, Lee Harvey Oswald. But due to two separate scientific studies on a Dallas police radio recording, the Committee was belatedly forced to conclude that Kennedy was fired upon by at least two gunmen.

Out of time and funding, the Committee reversed the official government theory of the assassination by concluding that Kennedy "was probably killed as the result of a conspiracy" but added, "The Committee was unable to identify the other gunman or the extent of the conspiracy."

The House Select Committee on Assassinations, while furthering the public's knowledge of the assassination by studying previously unavailable or ignored material, nevertheless failed to fully pursue its investigations. It left behind more questions than it answered, preferring to place the burden of finding the truth on the U.S. Department of Justice, which to this date has failed to take any positive action in the matter.

> . . . there is a possibility that an imposter is using Oswald's birth
> certificate . . .
> —FBI director J. Edgar Hoover in 1960

Was Oswald Really Oswald?

One of the most misunderstood issues surrounding the JFK assassination involves questions about the identity of Lee Harvey Oswald. This issue can be broken into two segments—one is the evidence pointing to someone impersonating Oswald in the weeks prior to the assassination and the second concerns the identity of the man killed by Jack Ruby.

This whole question of Oswald doppelgangers—or lookalikes—is admittedly bizarre. However, once the evidence suggesting such duplication is studied closely, one finds it worthy of serious consideration.

Questions about Oswald's identity did not suddenly surface years after the assassination as many people believe. As has been noted, J. Edgar Hoover expressed concern over Oswald's identity as far back as June 3, 1960, when he wrote: "Since there is a possibility that an impostor is using Oswald's birth certificate, any current information the Department of State may have concerning subject will be appreciated."

Despite assurances by government agencies at the time of the assassination that they were unaware of Oswald or his background, there is now evidence that people within the government were checking frequently on the ex-Marine.

On March 31, 1961, the deputy chief of the Passport Office wrote to the Consular Section of the State Department regarding Oswald, stating:

> . . . this file contains information first, which indicates that mail from the mother of this boy is not being delivered to him and second, that it has been stated that there is an impostor using Oswald's identification data and that no doubt the Soviets would love to get hold of his valid passport, it is my opinion that the passport should be delivered to him only on a personal basis and after the Embassy is assured to its complete satisfaction that he is returning to the United States.

Another State Department communication, this time to the United States embassy in Moscow, on July 11, 1961, stated:

> The Embassy's careful attention to the involved case of Mr. Oswald is appreciated. It is assumed that there is no doubt that the person who has been in communication with the Embassy is the person who was issued a passport in the name of Lee Harvey Oswald.

Only two weeks before the assassination, someone signing for the State Department checked out Oswald's military records.

The New Orleans FBI Office apparently kept close tabs on Oswald while he was in that city and then shipped its file on him to Dallas in the fall of 1963, where Agent James Hosty made an effort to reach Oswald. At the same time, a military intelligence unit in Texas was receiving information on Oswald for its files.

After the assassination, literally hundreds of people claimed to have seen Oswald in the days preceding the tragedy. This outpouring of sightings is normal in a case of this magnitude.

In every significant crime, police hear from many people who claim to have knowledge of it. Many of these are disturbed people seeking to insinuate themselves in a major news event. Others are honest citizens simply mistaken as to identities or activities. While this phenomenon is to be expected, there were many reputable people who encountered a Lee Harvey Oswald at a time when Oswald was reported elsewhere and whose stories cannot be easily dismissed.

However, the Warren Commission found it easy enough to dismiss these people. The Commission's rationale was simple: If someone saw Oswald at a time when the Commission had determined him to be elsewhere, then the observer was mistaken in his identification.

Consider a few instances.

One such encounter with a bogus Oswald is especially intriguing since it occurred long before Oswald reportedly arrived back in the United States from his sojourn in Russia. Oscar Deslatte, manager of a Ford dealership in New Orleans, contacted the FBI immediately after the assassination. He told the Bureau that a man identifying himself as "Joseph Moore" had tried to buy ten trucks on January 10, 1961. He said the man was accompanied by a Cuban and had said he wanted Deslatte to "give a good price because we're doing this for the good of the country."

Deslatte said "Moore" asked that the name "Oswald" be placed on the purchase estimate sheet. The man said "Oswald" would be paying for the trucks on behalf of an anti-Castro Cuban organization.

In 1979, the FBI released a copy of Deslatte's estimate sheet and it showed the anti-Castro organization involved was "Friends of Democratic Cuba," which just happened to have been the anti-Castro group that included in its membership ex-FBI agent Guy Banister. Banister, of course, was the fervent anti-Castro agent who was connected to Oswald in the summer of 1963 at 544 Camp Street.

At this time the CIA and its Cuban allies were preparing for the April 17 Bay of Pigs Invasion of Cuba.

Was Oswald or someone using his name involved in the Bay of Pigs activity?

Another story involves testimony heard by the Senate Intelligence Committee from a former immigration inspector in New Orleans. While keeping the man's identity secret, the Committee reported:

> . . . he is absolutely certain that he interviewed Lee Harvey Oswald in a
> New Orleans jail cell sometime shortly before April 1, 1963. Although
> the inspector is not now certain whether Oswald was using that particu-
> lar name at that time, he is certain that Oswald was claiming to be a
> Cuban alien. He quickly ascertained that Oswald was not a Cuban alien,
> at which point he left Oswald in his jail cell.

According to the Warren Commission, Oswald did not arrive in New Orleans until the end of April, nearly a month after the inspector's meeting with the jailed "Oswald."

During his time in New Orleans, Oswald was seen in many and varying situations. He was handing out pro-Castro literature on New Orleans streets, while at the same time approaching anti-Castro Cuban leaders with proposals to help train their followers.

He was reported seen in Clinton, Louisiana, during a civil-rights voter registration drive.

Some of the people who encountered Oswald in New Orleans described him as a clean and well-kept, courteous young man, while others said he was dirty and disheveled and a swearing hard-drinker. It is difficult to believe these people were talking about the same individual.

As the assassination drew closer, the strange reports of second Oswalds began to increase.

On September 25, 1963, Mrs. Lee Dannelly, an official with the Selective Service system in Austin, Texas, reported that a young man came to her office for help. He said his name was Harvey Oswald and that he wished to get his military discharge with "other than honorable conditions" changed to an honorable discharge. The man said he was living in Fort Worth. Mrs. Dannelly said she could find no such person in her files and she told the man to check with Selective Service in Fort Worth. She next saw Oswald on television after the assassination and promptly reported her experience. Oswald did have a dishonorable discharge and he had lived in Fort Worth, but on September 25, he was on his way to Mexico City, according to the Warren Commission.

After the assassination, Leonard Hutchinson came forward to say that he had been asked to cash a check for Oswald earlier in November. Hutchinson, who owned Hutch's Market in Irving, Texas, said the man asked him to cash a two-party check made out to "Harvey Oswald" for $189. He refused to accept the check, but said he saw the man in his store several more times. He said on one occasion the man and a young woman spoke in some foreign language. Hutchinson said he recognized both Oswald and Marina when their photographs were broadcast over television after the assassination. Near Hutchinson's store was a barbershop where a man identified as Oswald came for haircuts. The barber also said he saw the same man entering Hutchinson's store. Despite all this, the Warren Commission concluded: "Oswald is not known to have received a check for this amount from any source. . . . Examination of Hutchinson's testimony indicates a more likely explanation is that Oswald was not in his store at all."

Next is the well-documented story of Oswald's wild car ride weeks before the assassination. Albert G. Bogard, a salesman for Downtown Lincoln-Mercury—located just west of the Triple Underpass in Dealey Plaza—told the Warren Commission that before the assassination—"ninth day of November, I think it was, to be exact"—a man came into the dealership and introduced himself as "Lee Oswald." Bogard told the Commission:

I show him a car on the showroom floor, and take him for a ride out Stemmons Expressway and back, and he was driving at 60 to 70 miles an hour and came back to the showroom. And, I made some figures and he told me he wasn't ready to buy, that he would be in a couple or three weeks, that he had some money coming in. And when he finally started to leave I got his name and wrote it on the back of one of my business cards, and never heard from the man any more.

Bogard said on the day of the assassination, he heard Oswald had been arrested and threw the business card with Oswald's name on it away, saying: "He won't be a prospect any more because he is going to jail." His story was supported by two other dealership employees, Eugene Wilson and Frank Pizzo.

However, the Warren Commission concluded:

Several persons who knew Oswald have testified that he was unable to drive, although Mrs. Paine, who was giving Oswald driving lessons, stated that Oswald was showing some improvement by November. Moreover, Oswald's whereabouts on November 9, as testified to by Marina Oswald and Ruth Paine, would have made it impossible for him to have visited the automobile showrooms as Mr. Bogard claims.

In a 1977 *Dallas Morning News* story, Wilson said the FBI and the Warren Commission dismissed the story of Oswald's drive because they had it occurring on November 9.

Wilson told the newspaper the man was Oswald and that he did know how to drive and that the incident actually occurred on November 2, a more plausible date. He also said he recalled that when Oswald was turned down for a credit purchase, he said: "Maybe I'm going to have to go back to Russia to buy a car." Wilson said he could pinpoint the date because later the day of Oswald's drive, he used the same car to carry his wife and some friends home after a meeting of the Lone Star Bulldog Club. Wilson said the next day at a Dallas dog show, he won some ribbons that carried the date.

The Warren Commission indeed published a copy of an unsigned application for a Texas driver's license in the name of Lee Harvey Oswald.

If the car buyer was Oswald, he was expecting to come into money at the exact time of the assassination. If it wasn't Oswald, it was someone impersonating him.

Another incident involved the night manager of Western Union in Dallas. C. A. Hamblen told Bob Fenley, a reporter for the *Dallas Times Herald* that Oswald had collected money orders in small sums during the early part of November. Hamblen said he remembered Oswald because he "would give the girls [Western Union employees] a hard time. He was a cantankerous individual." These statements appeared in the Dallas newspaper on November 30.

Another Western Union employee, Aubrey Lee Lewis, said he recalled the man resembling Oswald as a "feminine, very slender-built fellow" who sent a small money order to the Dallas YMCA and was accompanied by a "man of Spanish descent." The man used a "little Navy ID release card" and a library card for identification.

This story of Oswald receiving money just before the assassination caused a minor uproar within both the Warren Commission and Western Union. Western Union's officials were quick to remind employees that they were not to discuss customers, their money orders, or amounts.

In his Warren Commission testimony taken on July 23, 1964, Hamblen suddenly was unclear on many aspects of his story. He told the Commission:

Yes; I did tell [Reporter Fenley] that I had saw Oswald. I may have told him that. I don't recall what all was said . . . we never discuss any telegrams . . . [Hamblen was shown a copy of his signed statement of December 2, 1963 telling of the Oswald encounter] Well, now, if I gave Bob any information like that, I don't recall it now. I might have at the time I wrote the statement. . . . I wouldn't say that it was Lee Oswald. I would say it was someone that resembled him from the picture that I had seen in the paper and on TV.

It is apparent that the Western Union employees were under pressure not to tell more about the money order incidents. In fact, in his testimony to the Warren Commission, Reporter Fenley said he sent the *Times Herald* police reporter to talk to Hamblen and that he was told the same story. Fenley added: ". . . I am still very curious about this . . . I don't mean this for the record, but I frankly heard that [Hamblen] recanted the tale."

A check by Western Union failed to turn up any money orders in the name of Lee Harvey Oswald. But if it was not the Marine Oswald using a

Navy ID and library card to receive money orders, then who was it? The Warren Commission apparently was unable to find out.

It is interesting to note the Western Union workers mentioned someone they believed to be Oswald sending money orders to the Dallas YMCA. According to the Warren Commission:

Oswald did not contact his wife immediately when he returned to Dallas [supposedly from a trip to Mexico City in late September 1963]. . . . He spent the night at the [Dallas] YMCA, where he registered as a serviceman in order to avoid paying the membership fee.

YMCA records showed an Oswald staying there on October 3 and 4. The records also indicated that Oswald lived at the YMCA between October 15 and 19, 1962.

The Dallas YMCA also had a member who frequented its health-club facilities quite often during this time—Jack Ruby.

A man resembling Oswald was seen by Dallas police handing out pro-Castro literature on downtown streets in the months preceding the assassination. Was it really Oswald?

Then there are the strange incidents involving Oswald or someone resembling Oswald using a foreign-made rifle in the weeks preceding the assassination. On November 1, a "rude and impertinent" man bought rifle ammunition in Morgan's Gunshop in nearby Fort Worth. Three persons recalled this incident after the assassination and claimed the man was Oswald. The Warren Commission however determined that Oswald was elsewhere at the time.

After the assassination, a British reporter checked with gun shops in Irving and discovered a furniture store where a gunsmith had earlier conducted business. The manager of the store told of a man who looked like Oswald visiting her store along with his wife and two small children. The manager recalled that the man spoke a foreign language to his wife and had asked about repairing a firing pin. Marina Oswald told the Warren Commission she had never been in the furniture store. The man resembling Oswald was directed to another nearby gun store—the Irving Sports Shop.

Dial Duwayne Ryder, the service manager at the Irving Sports Shop, recalled working on a rifle but it was not an Italian weapon. He even gave the FBI an undated check stub for six dollars that bore the name "Oswald." The stub indicated that work done on the rifle was "drilling and tapping and boresighting." Ryder said the work was probably done during the first two weeks of November.

However, since there was a $1.50 charge for boresighting and the drilling and tapping was $1.50 per hole, it indicated to Ryder that three holes were drilled in the rifle for a telescopic sight.

The Mannlicher-Carcano identified as Oswald's rifle had only two holes for the sight and the telescope sight came already fixed to the rifle.

Furthermore, neither Ryder nor his boss could readily identify pictures of Oswald as the man ordering the work. Thus it would appear that someone using Oswald's name ordered work on a rifle which was not the Oswald rifle.

The Warren Commission, never willing to admit the possibility that someone might have been fabricating evidence against Oswald, hinted that Ryder had made up the story about working on the rifle.

Again in early November, shooters at the Sports Drome Rifle Range recalled a young man who was there sighting in a foreign-made rifle. One of these shooters, Malcolm Price, helped adjust the rifle sight for the man shooting and another, Garland Slack, argued with the man on another occasion because the man was shooting at Slack's target. Both Dr. Homer Wood and his son, Sterling Wood, recalled the man and both were shocked to see his photograph on television in the days following the assassination. They are still convinced the man was Lee Harvey Oswald.

However, the Warren Commission noted that these witnesses were not consistent in their descriptions of the rifle-range gunman or of the rifle and scope. In addition, some of the gun-range witnesses said Oswald was accompanied by a man in a late-model car. Since Oswald reportedly could not drive and did not know anyone with a late-model car, the Commission concluded:

Although the testimony of these witnesses was partially corroborated by other witnesses, there was other evidence which prevented the Commission from reaching the conclusion that Lee Harvey Oswald was the person these witnesses saw.

Furthermore, Price remembered helping "Oswald" sight his rifle on September 28, 1963, a time when Oswald reportedly was in Mexico City.

In October 1963, Mrs. Lovell Penn heard shooting on her property located just outside Dallas. Accosting three men shooting a rifle in a field, Mrs. Penn ordered them to leave. After they left, she found a 6.5 mm Mannlicher-Carcano rifle shell near where the men had been target shooting. After the assassination, she turned the shell casing over to the FBI and told them that one of the men looked like Oswald while another was "Latin, perhaps Cuban." However, the FBI reported that laboratory tests showed the shell had not been fired from the Oswald rifle.

The reports of Oswald accompanied by Cubans came from many different sources.

Recall the incident of three anti-Castro Cubans—one by the name of Leon Oswald—visiting Silvia Odio shortly before the assassination.

It becomes possible that someone was posing as Oswald in the days preceding the assassination, carefully laying out a pattern of an irritating young man who was in possession of and practicing with a foreign-made rifle.

As the Warren Commission itself pointed out: "In most instances, investigation has disclosed that there is no substantial basis for believing that the person reported by the various witnesses was Oswald."

Of course, if the man in question was not Oswald, it means that someone was laying a trail of evidence to the real Oswald. This gives great credence to Oswald's cry to newsmen in the Dallas Police Station: "I'm just a patsy!"

But the question of Oswald's identity leads to even stranger areas.

In recent years, questions have even arisen concerning the man killed by Jack Ruby.

Was the Oswald killed in Dallas the same Oswald born in New Orleans in 1939? Bizarre as it may sound, there is considerable evidence to suggest that the man killed by Ruby was not the original Lee Harvey Oswald.

The first major publicity over this issue came in 1977 with the publication of *The Oswald File* by British author Michael Eddowes. Eddowes, who acknowledged to this author his connections with British intelligence dating back to World War II, advanced the following theory: "Lee Harvey Oswald was captured by the Soviets after traveling to Russia in 1959 and a look-alike substitute was returned to the United States in his place."

Eddowes said that after studying the issue of Oswald's identity, he became "one-hundred-percent convinced" that President Kennedy was killed by a Soviet KGB agent impersonating the real Oswald. The British attorney offered the following evidence for his theory:

- A mastoidectomy scar that was noted on Oswald's Marine Corps medical records was not mentioned in Oswald's autopsy report.
- Oswald's Marine records showed a vaccination scar on his arm, along with other scars. No vaccination scar was noted in Oswalds autopsy report and the location of scars differed from those in his military records.
- In Warren Commission documents, including Marine and passport application papers, at least eleven give Oswald's height as five-foot-eleven, while at least thirteen documents—all produced after Oswald's return from Russia—give his height as five-foot-nine.
- During Oswald's twenty-month disappearance in Russia, U.S. government agencies—including the FBI and the State Department—expressed suspicions regarding Oswald's identity.
- When Marina met Oswald at a dance in Minsk, she believed him to be a native Russian with a Baltic area accent. Since there is no doubt that the man she met in Russia was the man killed in Dallas, it should be understood that Marina knew only the one Oswald. But this fact does not eliminate the possibility that a substitution took place prior to their meeting.

There are a number of other intriguing hints that point toward substitution.

Just weeks before leaving Russia for home, Oswald wrote his mother and asked her to send him pictures of her and himself. Some researchers wonder if he needed such photos so he would know which woman to greet at the airport.

Jeanne DeMohrenschildt claimed that Oswald's knowledge of Russia extended beyond just its language. (Recall that native Russians thought he spoke the language better than they did.) She said her husband George and Oswald would have lengthy discussions about Russian literature, including such authors as Tolstoy and Dostoevski—an incredible feat for a high-school dropout whose Russian was self-taught.

She said Oswald even subscribed to a Soviet satirical journal entitled *The Crocodile* and had a large collection of photographs he claimed to have taken in several different areas of Russia. (Officially, Oswald never ventured outside Moscow and Minsk.)

Researcher Gary Mack has reported that three language experts at Southern Methodist University in Dallas studied tape recordings made of Oswald. They were not told the identity of the man whose voice they heard. All agreed that the English words spoken seemed acquired later in life—that English was not the native tongue of the man on the tape.

This startling conclusion was supported by Mrs. DeMohrenschildt, who told this author she was more amazed by Oswald's English than his Russian. She said he spoke in deliberate and precise terms, rarely ever using slang or curse words. She said: "Everybody always talks about how good his Russian was. I was always surprised at the English coming from this boy who was brought up in the South. I wondered, 'Where did he learn such proper English—certainly not from his mother.' "

A particularly intriguing hint at impersonation came in the fall of 1963, when a letter was sent to the Russian embassy in Washington. It was signed by Lee Harvey Oswald, who was writing about his alleged travel to Mexico City.

The second sentence of the letter—the Warren Commission published both his handwritten draft and the typed letter—reads:

I was unable to remain in Mexico indefinitely [*sic*] because of my mexican [*sic*] visa restrictions which was [*sic*] for 15 days only. I could not take a chance on requesting a new visa *unless I used my real name* [emphasis added], so I returned to the United States.

Since his passport and visa forms—as well as the November 9, 1963, embassy letter—were in the name of Lee Harvey Oswald, researchers are left to wonder about the meaning of having to use "my real name."

Based on these points, Eddowes went into a Texas court on January 10, 1979, and asked that the grave of Oswald be opened. He had the support of the Dallas County Medical Examiner's Office, which was convinced there was enough question about the identity of the body to warrant an exhumation.

Soon after Eddowes asked to have Oswald's body exhumed, political fights sprang up between conflicting jurisdictions. Oswald had been killed in Dallas County, but his body was buried in Rose Hill Cemetery, which is in nearby Tarrant County. While the Dallas Medical Examiner's Office had authorized an exhumation, Tarrant County officials balked.

On June 1, 1979, Texas District judge James Wright denied Eddowes's exhumation request. Dallas County assistant medical examiner Dr. Linda Norton told newsmen. "I feel it would be in the public interest to conduct the exhumation. However, there are apparent legal disagreements . . . and political forces who do not want this body dug up."

Norton said her efforts to exhume the body were being thwarted by Tarrant County district attorney Tim Curry, an elected official. The case dragged on.

Eddowes was not the first person to seek an exhumation of Oswald's body. A Warren Commission document declassified only in 1975 revealed that CIA officials were suspicious of Oswald's true identity as early as 1964. In a Commission memorandum dated March 13, 1964, staff member W. David Slawson wrote about a letter from FBI director J. Edgar Hoover on February 26, 1964. In this memo, Slawson quoted Hoover as writing: "The CIA is interested in the scar on Oswald's left wrist . . . The FBI is reluctant to exhume Oswald's body as requested by the CIA." In this same memo, Slawson expressed his own questions about what may have happened to Oswald in Russia:

> This whole aspect of Oswald's life and especially our attempt to authenticate it are highly secret at this point. . . . [Slawson mentions the reported suicide attempt by Oswald shortly after arriving in Russia] Therefore, if the suicide incident is a fabrication, the time spent by Oswald recovering from the suicide [attempt] in a Moscow hospital could have been spent by him in Russian secret police custody, being coached, brainwashed, etc.

Funeral director Paul Groody—who buried Oswald in 1963—told this author that Secret Service agents came to him three weeks after Oswald's burial asking questions about marks on the body. Groody said: "They told me, 'We don't know who we have in that grave.' "

Furthermore, Oswald's own mother asked for an exhumation in 1967, expressing questions as to the identity of the body in her son's grave. Marguerite Oswald told local news reporters that she did not believe her son had scars on his body as described by the Warren Commission. She said: "I think now would be the time to exhume this boy's body and see if he has these scars."

Mrs. Oswald previously had told the Warren Commission how her son had seemed changed after arriving back in Forth Worth from Russia. She said she noticed he was losing his hair and that Oswald told her he was going bald "because of the cold weather in Texas." She also noted: "And Lee was very, very thin when I saw him."

Oswald's brother, Robert, also noted changes in Oswald when he arrived back in the United States. He told the Warren Commission:

> His appearance had changed to the extent that he had lost a considerable amount of hair; his hair had become very kinky in comparison with his naturally curly hair prior to his departure to Russia. . . . He appeared the first couple of days upon his return . . . to be rather tense and anxious. I also noted that his complexion had changed somewhat to the extent that he had always been very fair complected—his complexion was rather ruddy at this time—you might say it appeared like an artificial suntan that you get out of a bottle, but very slight—in other words, a tint of brown to a tint of yellow. . . . he appeared to have picked up something of an accent.

Oswald's half-brother, John Edward Pic, was even more pointed in his comments to the Warren Commission concerning Lee's appearance after returning from Russia:

> I would have never recognized him, sir. . . . He was much thinner than I remembered him. He didn't have as much hair. . . . His face features were somewhat different, being his eyes were set back maybe, you know like in these Army pictures, they looked different than I remembered him. His face was rounder . . . when he went in the Marine Corps [Oswald had] a bull neck. This I didn't notice at all. I looked for this, I didn't notice it at all, sir.

Pic went on to tell how he became angered when Oswald introduced him to a visitor as his half-brother. He said Oswald had never previously mentioned the fact that Pic was only a half-brother.

In the book *The Two Assassins* by Renatus Hartogs, Pic was quoted as saying: "The Lee Harvey Oswald I met in November 1962, was not the same Lee Harvey Oswald I had known ten years previously."

In August 1979, Dallas medical examiner Dr. Charles Petty formally called for an exhumation and asked for his counterpart in Tarrant County to order it. However, this request, along with Eddowes's offer to pay the premium on a $100,000 indemnification bond to allow the exhumation to proceed, was rejected by District Attorney Curry.

Then in February 1980, Dr. Petty reversed himself and said he would not order an exhumation. Meanwhile the court found that Eddowes, being a British citizen, lacked any legal standing in a Texas court.

By the summer of 1980, Eddowes was joined in his exhumation efforts by Marina Oswald, who provided the necessary "legal standing."

As the foot-dragging of Tarrant County officials to an Oswald exhumation began to wane, another roadblock was thrown in the way of an exhumation—this time by Oswald's brother Robert. On August 15, 1980, Robert Oswald won an injunction against the exhumation, saying it would cause his family anguish. This was considered very odd by assassination researchers because if the exhumation showed the man in the grave was not Oswald, it would have exonerated his brother as a presidential assassin. If the exhumation proved the body was Oswald, nothing would have changed. So what harm could be done?

The case dragged on for more months. Finally, on August 20, 1981, Marina filed suit to have the grave opened. And on October 4, 1981—nine months after Marguerite Oswald died from cancer in a Fort Worth hospital and was quietly buried alongside her son Lee—the exhumation of the Oswald grave took place. Opposition to the exhumation had suddenly vanished. Robert Oswald said he could not afford to fight the issue further in court.

The body was taken from Rose Hill Cemetery in the early morning hours and driven to Baylor Medical Center in Dallas for study. A team of four forensic pathologists compared the teeth of the corpse brought from the Oswald grave with Oswalds Marine Corps dental records.

Almost four hours after the study began, the results were in. Dr. Norton, who headed the exhumation study, stated: "Beyond any doubt, and I mean any doubt, the individual buried under the name Lee Harvey Oswald in Rose Hill Cemetery is in fact Lee Harvey Oswald."

Within hours, local newspapers carried the headlines:

—DOCTORS IDENTIFY BODY AS OSWALD,

—AUTOPSY PROVES BODY IS OSWALD'S and

—OSWALD ISSUE FINALLY AT REST

While some discrepancies were found between the corpse's teeth and Oswald's military dental records, the doctors were satisfied that enough similarities remained to warrant their conclusion. Also, a hole was discovered behind the left ear, which corresponded to Oswald's known mastoid operation.

The issue appeared to be settled. But—as so much else in the Kennedy assassination—this was not to be.

New Questions on Oswald

A few weeks after the Oswald exhumation, the two funeral home directors who prepared Oswald's body for burial in 1963 got together and talked. Paul Groody and Alan Baumgartner were troubled. They were not supposed to have been at the postexhumation examination. But at the last minute, Marina Oswald had asked them to be present and identify rings on the corpse.

Entering the autopsy room in Dallas, both men confirmed that the rings were on the corpse in the same location they had placed them in 1963. However, as the forensic examination continued, both Groody and Baumgartner noticed that the skull of the corpse under examination was in one piece—completely intact.

Weeks later, after discussing the matter between themselves, the funeral home directors discussed the situation with Texas assassination researchers and gave startling information—the body that was exhumed in 1981 was not the same body they buried in 1963!

What confirmed this idea in their minds was the absence of signs of a craniotomy, a normal autopsy procedure. A craniotomy involves drawing the skin off the human skull and cutting off the top of the skull with a bone saw, usually in a V-shaped cut. This allows forensic pathologists to view the brain. There can be no question that this procedure was performed on Oswald's body since the weight of his brain was recorded in the autopsy report. Furthermore, both funeral home directors recalled the craniotomy in preparing the body for burial. Groody said: "I put the skull back together and sewed up his scalp."

Yet both men have said they noticed no sign of the craniotomy on the skull they viewed during the 1981 exhumation study. If there was no craniotomy performed on the skull in Oswald's grave, it is proof that the body is not the same one buried there in 1963.

There are other indications that some manipulation may have taken place with the body. To begin with, Marina Oswald told newsmen that she received a telephone call around Easter 1964, from government officials asking her to sign papers authorizing the installation of an electronic alarm system at the Oswald grave. She said a "respectful" man in a gray suit came to her home shortly after the call and had her sign some papers. She told United Press International: "I signed lots of papers and they were never translated or explained to me. I didn't even speak English. I just did what I was told."

Prior to the exhumation, Marina was nearly convinced that Oswald's body had been removed from the grave, most probably after the signing of the papers in 1964.

As far as is known, no electronic alarm system was ever installed at the Oswald grave.

Prior to the exhumation, mortician Groody told newsmen how carefully Oswald had been embalmed. He also described how the body was placed in an airtight coffin that was placed inside an airtight cement vault. Groody said that upon exhumation Oswald's body should look exactly as it had the day he was buried.

However, when workers exhumed the grave on October 4, 1981, they found the cement vault in pieces and the seal on the coffin broken. Water and air had gotten into the coffin and Oswald's body had deteriorated to skeletal remains.

While the rupture of seals on both the vault and the coffin is not an impossible occurrence, several morticians interviewed by this author said such an event is highly unusual. It could be explained by movement of the earth, although North Central Texas is regarded as a very stable area. The broken seals also could be explained by someone having opened the grave prior to the 1981 exhumation.

Another logical time for a pre-exhumation grave opening would have been earlier in 1981, when Marguerite Oswald was buried next to Oswald's grave. The presence of earth-moving equipment and a canopy covering both graves provided an opportunity for covertly opening Oswald's adjacent grave.

So, the question has been asked—was a substitution made for the body in Oswald's grave?

The answer may be found in a four-hour videotape made of the 1981 exhumation study. The tape was commissioned by Marina Oswald and Eddowes and was produced by Hampton Hall, the son of a Texas state politician.

Once the craniotomy question became known to Marina, a friend and neighbor was asked to view the tape. The neighbor, along with his personal physician, viewed the videotape and reported that there was no sign nor mention of a craniotomy. This added further suspicions about the exhumation.

Finally, in 1984—four years after the exhumation—a detailed report on the exhumation findings was published in the *Journal of Forensic Sciences*. In the report, it stated:

A previous autopsy saw cut in the usual fashion was present on the calvarium with an anterior inverted V-notch in the right frontal region. The calvarium was maintained in continuity with the remainder of the skull by virtue of decomposed mummified tissue. The previously sawed calvarium was not separated nor was it easily dislodged.

In other words, decomposed jellylike skin had coated the Oswald skull, which made it appear to be in one piece.

Researchers were skeptical of this information and turned to Marina for confirmation of the craniotomy by viewing the videotape of the exhumation. Oddly enough, photographer Hall refused to give up the tape, claiming that so much time had elapsed that ownership of the tape had reverted to him.

In February 1984, Marina was forced to go to court in an effort to retrieve the videotape she had commissioned. By the summer of 1986, an out-of-court settlement resulted in a promise to return the tape, but by mid-1989 it had still not been returned.

The issue should have been a simple one. View the tapes and photos of the exhumation and resolve whether or not the craniotomy marks were visible on the Oswald skull. But with the tapes still not available, this issue remains in controversy, like so much else in the JFK assassination case.

And researchers remain intrigued. If the body exhumed in 1981 was indeed that of Oswald—as confirmed by the forensic pathologists and his Marine dental X-rays—but the exhumed corpse was not that of the man buried in 1963—as claimed by the two morticians—then it is possible that an impostor Oswald was killed in Dallas and his body exchanged for Oswald's sometime prior to the exhumation.

And who might have the power and authority to accomplish such a momentous task? The idea that the Soviets, Castro agents, or mobsters could switch bodies is ludicrous.

All this only reinforces the knowledge that in the JFK assassination, not one piece of evidence or issue of fact can be taken for granted.

Summary

There is an abundance of evidence to suggest that one or more persons were impersonating Lee Harvey Oswald in the weeks and months prior to the assassination of President Kennedy.

The U.S. government has studiously avoided addressing this evidence since to admit impersonation would be to admit the possibility that Oswald was framed for the assassination—exactly as he claimed.

Chief Counsel Robert Blakey of the House Select Committee on Assassinations even told newsmen that the Committee purposely failed to look at such evidence "to avoid publicizing issues the Committee concluded were of dubious importance."

Blakey said questions over impersonation distracted the public from the central question: Who killed President John F. Kennedy?

Researchers, however, point out that discovering who may have been impersonating Oswald could go far in answering that question.

The idea that someone posed as Oswald to incriminate him in the assassination is supported by a wide and diverse amount of evidence—from a 1960 warning of impersonation from none other than FBI director J. Edgar Hoover to a woman who caught a man who looked like Oswald firing a 6.5 mm rifle near her home outside of Dallas.

There were several instances of Oswald being reported in two separate places at the same time—an anomaly that the Warren Commission and the House Committee simply disregarded.

A second impersonation possibility has it that the Oswald killed by Jack Ruby in Dallas was not even the same man who was born to Marguerite Oswald in 1939.

British author Michael Eddowes—who first publicized the possibility of a substitute Oswald in 1977—charged that a Soviet agent was substituted for Oswald while he was out of sight in Russia.

Other researchers claim that evidence supports the idea that someone was substituted for Oswald while he was in the Marines in preparation for his mission to Russia.

Even Oswald's mother and brothers noted how changed he appeared after his return from the Soviet Union. In 1967, his mother publicly raised questions over the identity of the body in Oswald's grave and asked to have his body exhumed. But when Eddowes—later joined by Oswald's widow, Marina—went to court to have an exhumation ordered, they were blocked for years—first by Texas political figures and later by Oswald's brother Robert.

When Oswald's grave was finally opened in the fall of 1981, a panel of four forensic pathologists declared the body that of Oswald—based on comparing the corpse's teeth to one set of Marine dental records.

But even today the controversy won't die. The two funeral directors who buried Oswald—both of whom were present at the exhumation—claim the man dug up in 1981 was not the same man they buried in 1963. They claim there was no sign of a craniotomy—a standard autopsy procedure known to have been performed on Oswald's body—on the corpse in 1981. The medical official in charge of the autopsy disputed this charge and the one piece of objective evidence—a videotape of the exhumation examination that should settle the issue—has yet to be returned to Marina Oswald, who commissioned and paid for the taping.

The impersonation of Oswald would appear to be an issue that could be resolved easily by a truthful government investigation. Instead, it is another area of the assassination full of omissions, inconsistencies, and possible deceit.

And in the final analysis, Blakey might be right in saying that the questions over Oswald's identity are distracting.

The issue of Oswald impersonation may be a moot point, since the preponderance of evidence suggests that the Oswald in Dallas—whether lone nut, American agent, Soviet operative, real, or substitute—did not kill President Kennedy.

> . . . bodies left with no hope of the cause of death being determined by the
> most complete autopsy and chemical examinations.
>
> —CIA letter on disposal of victims

Convenient Deaths

In the three-year period which followed the murder of President Kennedy and Lee Harvey Oswald, 18 material witnesses died—six by gunfire, three in motor accidents, two by suicide, one from a cut throat, one from a karate chop to the neck, five from natural causes.

An actuary, engaged by the *London Sunday Times*, concluded that on November 22, 1963, the odds against these witnesses being dead by February 1967, were one hundred thousand trillion to one.

The above comment on the deaths of assassination witnesses was published in a tabloid companion piece to the movie *Execution Action*, released in 1973. By that time, part of the mythology of the Kennedy assassination included the mysterious deaths of people who were connected with it.

By the mid-1960s, people in Dallas already were whispering about the number of persons who died under strange or questionable circumstances. Well into the 1980s, witnesses and others were hesitant to come forward with information because of the stories of strange and sudden death that seemed to visit some people with information about the assassination.

Finally, in the late 1970s, the House Select Committee on Assassinations felt compelled to look into the matter.

But aside from discrediting the *London Sunday Times* actuarial study, the Committee was unable to come to any conclusions regarding the growing number of deaths. The Committee said it could not make a valid actuarial study due to the broad number and types of persons that had to be included in such a study.

In response to a letter from the Committee, *London Sunday Times* legal manager Anthony Whitaker stated:

Our piece about the odds against the deaths of the Kennedy witnesses was, I regret to say, based on a careless journalistic mistake and should not have been published. This was realized by The Sunday Times editorial staff after the first edition—the one which goes to the United States . . .—had gone out, and later editions were amended. There was no question of our actuary having got his answer wrong: it was simply that we asked him the wrong question. He was asked what were the odds

555

against 15 named people out of the population of the United States dying within a short period of time, to which he replied—correctly—that they were very high. However, if one asks what are the odds against 15 of those included in the Warren Commission Index dying within a given period, the answer is, of course, that they are much lower. Our mistake was to treat the reply to the former question as if it dealt with the latter—hence the fundamental error in our first edition report, for which we apologize.

This settled the matter for the House Committee, which apparently made little or no attempt to seriously study the number of deaths that followed the JFK assassination.

Jacqueline Hess, the Committee's chief of research for the JFK investigation, reported:

Our final conclusion on the issue is that the available evidence does not establish anything about the nature of these deaths which would indicate that the deaths were in some manner, either direct or peripheral, caused by the assassination of President Kennedy or by any aspect of the subsequent investigation.

However, an objective look at both the number and the causes of death balanced against the importance of the person's connection to the case, still causes raised eyebrows among those who study such a list.

In this section, people who were connected—no matter how tenuously—with the assassination and who are now dead are listed according to date of death.

This is dealing only with deaths, not with the numerous persons—such as Warren Reynolds, Roger Craig, and Richard Carr—who claim to have been shot at or attacked.

This chapter has been entitled "Convenient Deaths" because these deaths certainly would have been convenient for anyone not wishing the truth of the JFK assassination to become public.

The CIA has gone to some lengths to discredit the idea of mysterious deaths plaguing assassination witnesses.

A 1967 memo from CIA headquarters to station chiefs advised:

Such vague accusations as that "more than 10 people have died mysteriously" can always be explained in some rational way: e.g., the individuals concerned have for the most part died of natural causes; the [Warren] Commission staff questioned 418 witnesses—the FBI interviewed far more people, conducting 25,000 interviews and reinterviews—and in such a large group, a certain number of deaths are to be expected.

Testifying before the Church Committee in 1975, CIA technicians told of a variety of TWEP technology—Termination With Extreme Prejudice—that cannot be detected in a postmortem examination.

One recently declassified CIA document, a letter from an Agency consultant to a CIA officer, states:

> You will recall that I mentioned that the local circumstances under which a given means might be used might suggest the technique to be used in that case. I think the gross divisions in presenting this subject might be:
> (1) bodies left with no hope of the cause of death being determined by the most complete autopsy and chemical examinations
> (2) bodies left in such circumstances as to simulate accidental death
> (3) bodies left in such circumstances as to simulate suicidal death
> (4) bodies left with residue that simulate those caused by natural diseases.

The letter goes on to show that undetected murders do not have to be the result of sophisticated chemicals. It states:

> There are two techniques which I believe should be mentioned since they require no special equipment besides a strong arm and the will to do such a job. These would be either to smother the victim with a pillow or to strangle him with a wide piece of cloth such as a bath towel. In such cases, there are no specific anatomic changes to indicate the cause of death . . .

While it is obvious that the CIA—and hence the mob through operatives who work for both—has the capability of killing, it is less well known that the Agency has developed drugs to induce cancer.

Recall that Jack Ruby died of sudden lung cancer just as he had been granted a new trial.

A 1952 CIA memo reported on the cancer-causing effects of beryllium: "This is certainly the most toxic inorganic element and it produces a peculiar fibrotic tumor at the site of local application. The amount necessary to produce these tumors is a few micrograms."

Local law-enforcement officers and coroners are not equipped, either by training or by inclination, to detect deaths induced by such sophisticated means. They look for signs of a struggle, evidence of a break-in, bruises, or marks on the victim.

With no evidence to the contrary, many deaths are ruled suicide or accident. Others are ruled due to natural causes, such as heart attack.

It is interesting to note how the deaths are grouped. Many of the earliest deaths came during the time of the Warren Commission investigation or just afterwards.

More deaths took place in the late 1960s as New Orleans District

Attorney Jim Garrison was launching his investigation. Other suspicious deaths occurred during the mid-1970s, as the Senate Intelligence Committee was looking into assassinations by U.S. intelligence agencies. And finally, another spate of deaths came around 1977, just as the House Select Committee on Assassinations was gearing up its investigations.

These deaths are listed below in chronological order. An asterisk means the death is a particularly suspicious one. They also are grouped according to which investigation was being conducted at the time.

The possibility of convenient deaths leads one into a well of paranoia, yet this long list cannot be summarily dismissed.

Obviously, many of these deaths—particularly in recent years—can be ascribed to the passage of time. But others cannot—especially when viewed in the context of the assassination inquiries taking place at the time.

Read for yourself and consider . . . When does coincidence end and conspiracy begin?

List of Deaths

Date	Name	Connection with Case	Cause of Death
11/63	Karyn Kupcinet*	TV host's daughter who was overheard telling of JFK's death prior to 11/22/63	Murdered

The Warren Commission Investigation

Date	Name	Connection with Case	Cause of Death
12/63	Jack Zangretti*	Expressed foreknowledge of Ruby shooting Oswald	Gunshot victim
2/64	Eddy Benavides*	Look-alike brother to Tippit shooting witness, Domingo Benavides	Gunshot to head
2/64	Betty McDonald*	Former Ruby employee who alibied Warren Reynolds shooting suspect	Suicide by hanging in Dallas jail
3/64	Bill Chesher	Thought to have information linking Oswald and Ruby	Heart attack
3/64	Hank Killam*	Husband of Ruby employee, knew Oswald acquaintance	Throat cut
4/64	Bill Hunter*	Reporter who was in Ruby's apartment on 11/24/63	Accidental shooting by policeman

5/64 Gary Underhill*	CIA agent who claimed Agency was involved	Gunshot in head, ruled suicide
5/64 Hugh Ward*	Private investigator working with Guy Banister and David Ferrie	Plane crash in Mexico
5/64 DeLesseps Morrison*	New Orleans mayor	Passenger in Ward's plane
8/64 Teresa Norton*	Ruby employee	Fatally shot
6/64 Guy Banister*	Ex-FBI agent in New Orleans connected to Ferrie, CIA, Carlos Marcello, and Oswald	Heart attack
9/64 Jim Koethe*	Reporter who was in Ruby's apartment on 11/24/63	Blow to neck
9/64 C. D. Jackson	*Life* magazine senior vice president who bought Zapruder film and locked it away	Unknown
10/64 Mary Pinchot Meyer*	JFK mistress whose diary was taken by CIA chief James Angleton after her death	Murdered
1/65 Paul Mandal	*Life* writer who told of JFK turning to rear when shot in throat	Cancer
3/65 Tom Howard*	Ruby's first lawyer, was in Ruby's apartment on 11/24/63	Heart attack
5/65 Maurice Gatlin*	Pilot for Guy Banister	Fatal fall
8/65 Mona B. Saenz*	Texas Employment clerk who interviewed Oswald	Hit by Dallas bus
?/65 David Goldstein	Dallasite who helped FBI trace Oswald's pistol	Natural causes
9/65 Rose Cheramie*	Knew of assassination in advance, told of riding to Dallas with Cubans	Hit/run victim
11/65 Dorothy Kilgallen*	Columnist who had private interview with Ruby, pledged to "break" JFK case	Drug overdose

11/65	Mrs. Earl Smith*	Close friend to Dorothy Kilgallen, died two days after columnist, may have kept Kilgallen's notes	Unknown
12/65	William Whaley*	Cabdriver who reportedly drove Oswald to Oak Cliff	Motor Collision (the only Dallas taxi driver to die on duty)
1966	Judge Joe Brown	Presided over Ruby's trial	Heart attack
1966	Karen "Little Lynn" Carlin*	Ruby employee who last talked with Ruby before Oswald shooting	Gunshot victim
1/66	Earlene Roberts	Oswald's landlady	Heart attack
2/66	Albert Bogard*	Car salesman who said Oswald test drove new car	Suicide
6/66	Capt. Frank Martin	Dallas police captain who witnessed Oswald slaying, told Warren Commission, "There's a lot to be said but probably be better if I don't say it."	Cancer
8/66	Lee Bowers, Jr.*	Witnessed men behind picket fence on Grassy Knoll	Motor accident
9/66	Marilyn "Delilah" Walle*	Ruby dancer	Shot by husband after one month of marriage
10/66	William Pitzer*	JFK autopsy photographer who described his duty as "horrifying experience"	Gunshot, ruled suicide
11/66	Jimmy Levens	Fort Worth nightclub owner who hired Ruby employees	Natural causes
11/66	James Worrell, Jr.*	Saw man flee rear of Texas School Book Depository	Motor accident
1966	Clarence Oliver	D.A. investigator who worked Ruby case	Unknown
12/66	Hank Suydam	*Life* magazine official in charge of JFK stories	Heart attack

The Garrison Inquiry

1967 Leonard Pullin	Civilian Navy employee who helped film *Last Two Days* about assassination	One-car crash
1/67 Jack Ruby*	Oswald's slayer	Lung cancer (He told family he was injected with cancer cells.)
2/67 Harold Russell*	Saw escape of Tippit killer	Killed by cop in bar brawl
2/67 David Ferrie*	Acquaintance of Oswald, Garrison suspect, and employee of Guy Banister	Blow to neck, ruled accidental
2/67 Eladio Del Valle*	Anti-Castro Cuban associate of David Ferrie being sought by Garrison	Gunshot wound, ax wound to head
3/67 Dr. Mary Sherman*	Ferrie associate working on cancer research	Died in fire (possibly shot)
1/68 A. D. Bowie	Assistant Dallas D.A. prosecuting Ruby	Cancer
4/68 Hiram Ingram	Dallas deputy sheriff, close friend to Roger Craig	Cancer
5/68 Dr. Nicholas Chetta	New Orleans coroner who ruled on death of Ferrie	Heart attack
8/68 Philip Geraci*	Friend of Perry Russo, told of Oswald/Shaw conversation	Electrocution
1/69 Henry Delaune*	Brother-in-law to coroner Chetta	Murdered
1/69 E. R. Walthers*	Dallas deputy sheriff who was involved in Depository search, claimed to have found .45-cal. slug	Shot by felon
1969 Charles Mentesana	Filmed rifle other than Mannlicher-Carcano being taken from Depository	Heart attack
4/69 Mary Bledsoe	Neighbor to Oswald, also knew David Ferrie	Natural causes

4/69 John Crawford*	Close friend to both Ruby and Wesley Frazier, who gave ride to Oswald on 11/22/63	Crash of private plane
7/69 Rev. Clyde Johnson*	Scheduled to testify about Clay Shaw/Oswald connection	Fatally shot
1970 George McGann*	Underworld figure connected to Ruby friends; wife, Beverly, took film in Dealey Plaza	Murdered
1/70 Darrell W. Garner	Arrested for shooting Warren Reynolds, released after alibi from Betty McDonald	Drug overdose
8/70 Bill Decker	Dallas sheriff who saw bullet hit street in front of JFK	Natural causes
8/70 Abraham Zapruder	Took famous film of JFK assassination	Natural causes
12/70 Salvatore Granello*	Mobster linked to Hoffa, Trafficante, and Castro assassination plots	Murdered
1971 James Plumeri*	Mobster tied to mob-CIA assassination plots	Murdered
3/71 Clayton Fowler	Ruby's chief defense attorney	Unknown
4/71 Gen. Charles Cabell*	CIA deputy director connected to anti-Castro Cubans	Collapsed and died after physical at Fort Myers

The Church Committee Investigation

1972 Hale Boggs*	House majority leader, member of Warren Commission who began to publicly express doubts about findings	Disappeared on Alaskan plane flight
5/72 J. Edgar Hoover*	FBI director who pushed "lone assassin" theory in JFK assassination	Heart attack (no autopsy)
9/73 Thomas E. Davis*	Gun runner connected to both Ruby and CIA	Electrocuted trying to steal wire
2/74 J. A. Milteer*	Miami right-winger who predicted JFK's death and capture of scapegoat	Heater explosion

1974 Dave Yaras*	Close friend to both Hoffa and Jack Ruby	Murdered
7/74 Earl Warren	Chief justice who reluctantly chaired Warren Commission	Heart failure
8/74 Clay Shaw*	Prime suspect in Garrison case, reportedly a CIA contact with Ferrie and E. Howard Hunt	Possible cancer
1974 Earle Cabell	Mayor of Dallas on 11/22/63, whose brother, Gen. Charles Cabell, was fired from CIA by JFK	Natural causes
6/75 Sam Giancana*	Chicago Mafia boss slated to tell about CIA-mob death plots to Senate committee	Murdered
1975 Clyde Tolson	J. Edgar Hoover's assistant and roommate	Natural causes
7/75 Allan Sweatt	Dallas deputy sheriff involved in investigation	Natural causes
12/75 Gen. Earl Wheeler	Contact between JFK and CIA	Unknown
1976 Ralph Paul	Ruby's business partner connected with crime figures	Heart attack
4/76 James Chaney	Dallas motorcycle officer riding to JFK's right rear who said JFK ''struck in the face'' with bullet	Heart attack
4/76 Dr. Charles Gregory	Governor John Connally's physician	Heart attack
6/76 William Harvey*	CIA coordinator for CIA-mob assassination plans against Castro	Complications of heart surgery
7/76 John Roselli*	Mobster who testified to Senate committee, was to appear again	Stabbed and stuffed in metal drum

1977—A Terrible Year for Many

The year 1977 produced a bumper crop of candidates for listing under convenient deaths connected to the JFK assassination—including the deaths of six top FBI officials all of whom were scheduled to testify before the House Select Committee on Assassinations.

Topping this list was former number-three man in the FBI, William C. Sullivan, who had already had a preliminary meeting with the investigators for the House Committee. Sullivan was shot with a high-powered rifle near his New Hampshire home by a man who claimed to have mistaken him for a deer. The man was charged with a misdemeanor—''shooting a human being by accident''—and released into the custody of his father, a state policeman. There was no further investigation of Sullivan's death.

Louis Nicholas was a special assistant to J. Edgar Hoover as well as Hoover's liaison with the Warren Commission. Alan H. Belmont also was a special assistant to Hoover. James Cadigan was a document expert with access to many classified assassination documents, while J. M. English headed the FBI laboratory where Oswald's rifle and pistol were tested. Donald Kaylor was the FBI fingerprint expert who examined prints found at the assassination scene. None of these six Bureau officials lived to tell what they knew to the House Committee.

Other key assassination witnesses, such as George DeMohrenschildt and former Cuban president Carlos Prio Soccaras, died within weeks of each other in 1977, just as they, too, were being sought by the House Committee.

The ranks of both organized crime and U.S. intelligence agencies were thinned by deaths beginning in 1975, the time of the Senate Intelligence Hearings, and 1978, the closing months of the House Committee.

Charles Nicoletti, a mobster connected with the CIA-Mafia assassination plots, was murdered in Chicago, while William Pawley, a former diplomat connected with both organized crime and CIA figures, reportedly committed suicide.

Adding to rumors that ''hit teams'' may have been at work, a *Time* magazine article reported that federal agents had initiated a nationwide investigation into more than twenty gangland assassinations constituting what agents believed was an ''open underworld challenge to governmental infiltration of Mafia activities.''

One FBI source was quoted as saying: ''Our main concern is that we may be facing a revival of the old 'Murder, Inc.' days.''

A *New York News* story concerning this official fear of roving assassination squads even mentions the death of Sam Giancana, who was killed one day before he was to testify about mob-CIA connections and while under government protection.

Prior to the House Committee investigation into the JFK assassination, the news media reported the following deaths:

Date	Name	Connection with Case	Cause of Death
1/77	William Pawley*	Former Brazilian ambassador connected to anti-Castro Cubans, crime figures	Gunshot, ruled suicide
3/77	George DeMohrenschildt*	Close friend to both Oswald and Bouvier family (Jackie Kennedy's parents), CIA contract agent	Gunshot wound, ruled suicide
3/77	Carlos Prio Soccaras*	Former Cuban president, money man for anti-Castro Cubans	Gunshot wound, ruled suicide
3/77	Paul Raigorodsky	Business friend of George DeMohrenschildt and wealthy oilmen	Natural causes
5/77	Lou Staples*	Dallas radio talk show host who told friends he would break assassination case	Gunshot to head, ruled suicide
6/77	Louis Nichols	Former number-three man in FBI, worked on JFK investigation	Heart attack
8/77	Alan Belmont	FBI official who testified to Warren Commission	"Long illness"
8/77	James Cadigan	FBI document expert who testified to Warren Commission	Fall in home
8/77	Joseph C. Ayres*	Chief steward on JFK's *Air Force One*	Shooting accident
8/77	Francis G. Powers*	U-2 pilot downed over Russia in 1960	Helicopter crash (He reportedly ran out of fuel.)
9/77	Kenneth O'Donnell	JFK's closest aide	Natural causes
10/77	Donald Kaylor	FBI fingerprint chemist	Heart attack
10/77	J. M. English	Former head of FBI Forensic Sciences Laboratory	Heart attack
11/77	William Sullivan*	Former number-three man in FBI, headed Division 5, counterespionage and domestic intelligence	Hunting accident
1978	C. L. "Lummie" Lewis	Dallas deputy sheriff who arrested Mafia man Braden in Dealey Plaza	Natural causes

9/78 Garland Slack	Man who said Oswald fired at his target at rifle range	Unknown
1/79 Billy Lovelady	Depository employee said to be the man in the doorway in AP photograph	Complications from heart attack
6/80 Jesse Curry	Dallas police chief at time of assassination	Heart attack
6/80 Dr. John Holbrook	Psychiatrist who testified Ruby was not insane	Heart attack, but pills, notes found
1/81 Marguerite Oswald	Mother of accused assassin	Cancer
10/81 Frank Watts	Chief felony prosecutor for Dallas D.A.	Natural causes
1/82 Peter Gregory	Original translator for Marina Oswald and Secret Service	Natural causes
5/82 Dr. James Weston	Pathologist allowed to see JFK autopsy material for HSCA	Died while jogging, ruled natural causes
8/82 Will H. Griffin	FBI agent who reportedly said Oswald was "definitely" an FBI informant	Cancer
10/82 W. Marvin Gheesling	FBI official who helped supervise JFK investigation	Natural causes
3/84 Roy Kellerman	Secret Service agent in charge of JFK limousine	Unknown

The power source that arranged [Kennedy's] murder was on the inside.
—Former Pentagon-CIA liaison officer Col. L. Fletcher Prouty

Conclusions

Since November 22, 1963, a massive amount of information has become available concerning the assassination of President John F. Kennedy. Some of it was made public immediately, but most of this information leaked out only after the passage of many years. Much has proven erroneous, incomplete, and misleading in light of later developments.

This book has been an effort to present the best available up-to-date information in a truthful and comprehensive manner. Keep in mind that much assassination information remains beyond public scrutiny—locked away in government files.

What does the information available today tell us about Kennedy's assassination? What conclusions may be drawn from the existing record?

Based on all currently available information, researchers have concluded:

1. Lee Harvey Oswald was involved in intelligence activities. He was—or at least he believed he was—working on behalf of the United States.

2. It is entirely possible that Lee Harvey Oswald did not fire a gun on November 22, 1963, thus making him innocent in both the death of President Kennedy and Police Officer Tippit.

3. If Lee Harvey Oswald did participate in the actual assassination—and much evidence indicates he did not—he certainly did not act alone.

4. An abundance of evidence indicates that Lee Harvey Oswald was framed for the assassination of President Kennedy.

5. This framing—plus a wealth of information revealing an attempt to cover up vital evidence in the case—proves the existence of a conspiracy to kill Kennedy.

6. Because this cover-up went far beyond simple face saving and was conducted at the federal level, it is apparent that people within the federal government of the United States were both involved in and aware of such a conspiracy.

7. The two most powerful men in the federal government in 1963—next to the President and his brother—were Vice President Lyndon B. Johnson and his close friend, FBI director J. Edgar Hoover. Both men were facing the end of their careers because of Kennedy.

Consider these conclusions point for point.

Lee Harvey Oswald was a bright young man whose father and brother had both served honorably in the U.S. military. At age fifteen, Oswald joined the New Orleans Civil Air Patrol and expressed a deep desire to be a Marine, evidence, perhaps, of a patriotic streak. He was in contact with David Ferrie, a man with documented connections to both the CIA and organized crime, who may have groomed young Oswald for future intelligence work during this time.

While in the Marines, Oswald was stationed at Atsugi base in Japan where some of his fellow Marines, such as Gerry Hemming, were recruited into the CIA. During his stay in Japan Private Oswald was seen frequenting the Queen Bee, an expensive night spot normally serving only ranking officers and pilots. It was also in Japan that Oswald was treated for gonorrhea "In line of duty, not due to own misconduct." And it was here that Oswald later told George DeMohrenschildt he was in contact with "Japanese Communists."

Since a Marine officer was told by higher authority not to be concerned about Marine Oswald receiving Communist publications and spouting Marxist theory in the Marine barracks, it is obvious that Oswald had become involved in intelligence work by the end of his Marine career. Although disbelieved by the House Select Committee on Assassinations, it should be noted that former CIA finance officer James Wilcott testified that he learned that Oswald was paid by the CIA while still stationed at Atsugi.

Other evidence of Oswald's connection with intelligence includes the ease with which he obtained passports both in 1959 and particularly in 1963, after he had returned from attempting to defect to Russia; his lengthy "reports" on his activities in Russia and his Fair Play for Cuba Committee work in New Orleans, which he gave to FBI agent John Quigley; the spy term "microdots" found in Oswalds address book; expensive miniature optical equipment found among Oswald's belongings, including a small Minox camera that carried a serial number not available to the general public, and the fact that in 1977, it was discovered that the CIA had a personnel file, or 201 file on Oswald.

Some researchers, notably British author Michael Eddowes, claim that Oswald either became a Soviet agent while in Russia or that a Soviet agent returned to the United States impersonating Oswald. While possible—and there is much information to support this thesis, especially J. Edgar Hoover's 1960 memo to the State Department warning that someone may have been using Oswald's birth certificate—it is apparent that whoever was claiming to be Oswald in the summer and fall of 1963 was in contact with U.S. intelligence rather than Soviet or Cuban.

Considering discrepancies in his Marine records and his reported intelligence connections, other researchers believe that an impostor Oswald was created and sent to Russia. This impostor—using Oswald's identity—then returned to the United States where he was selected as the fall guy in the assassination.

Even if Oswald—real or impersonator—was recruited as a Soviet agent, he was playing double—acting under orders from persons he believed to be in U.S. intelligence.

Evidenced by his contacts with Guy Banister and David Ferrie in New Orleans and George DeMohrenschildt in Dallas, it is apparent that in the months just prior to the assassination, Oswald was in contact with people connected to U.S. intelligence.

Once it is understood that Oswald was—or believed he was—working as an intelligence operative, assassination evidence takes on a new meaning.

It is apparent to many researchers that while Oswald most probably did order a rifle and a pistol through the mail and may have made some sort of trip to Mexico, he likely was following orders from persons he considered to be his superiors in intelligence.

Thus, many of Oswald's activities in the weeks prior to the assassination were carefully calculated to both incriminate him and to link him with foreign governments.

While it is probable that Oswald was in some way connected with persons involved in a plot against Kennedy, he may have felt secure in the belief that he was reporting on that plot to the U.S. government—most likely through the FBI.

While it cannot be stated with absolute assurance that Oswald never fired a weapon on November 22, 1963, there is an abundance of supporting evidence that he did not. The Dallas police paraffin test showed no nitrates on Oswald's cheek, court-admissible evidence that he had not fired a rifle, particularly the loose-bolted Italian Mannlicher-Carcano. Nitrate traces on both his hands is not conclusive evidence that he fired a pistol, since printer's ink and other material found at his workplace could account for nitrates on his hands.

The intimidated Howard Brennan notwithstanding, no one who claimed to have seen the assassin on the sixth floor of the Texas School Book Depository could positively identify Oswald as the gunman.

Oswald maintained he was in the Depository lunchroom at the time of the shooting and correctly named two co-workers who indeed ate in the lunchroom. Testimony of fellow employees indicates that Oswald was seen on a lower floor shortly before the assassination.

All this—coupled with the fact that less than ninety seconds after the shots were fired Depository superintendent Roy Truly and Dallas policeman Marion Baker encountered a calm and collected Oswald standing in the lunchroom with a soft drink in his hand—tends to support Oswald's alibi.

Then there is Oswald's documented mediocre marksmanship added to the extremely poor quality Mannlicher-Carcano rifle, which Army test personnel had to equip with metal shims after the assassination to make it accurate enough for testing. Also there is the consideration that due to an evergreen tree in front of the Depository building, there was no line of sight from the sixth-floor window to the point where films established that the first shots struck. The improbability of Oswald shooting as described by the federal government is supported by the fact that not one single person ever has been able to duplicate the feat.

Additionally there has always been evidence indicating that more than one gunman fired on President Kennedy's limousine.

This evidence was supported in 1979 by the House Select Committee on Assassinations' scientific study of acoustical material suggesting that at least one shot came from the Grassy Knoll. These acoustical studies are now supported by the photographic enlargement of the Moorman snapshot depicting the "badgeman" figure.

These pieces of evidence are enhanced by the witnesses in Dealey Plaza, the majority of whom said shots also came from the Grassy Knoll.

Today it is obvious to many researchers that multiple gunmen were shooting at Kennedy and that the three shots fired in Dealey Plaza were actually three volleys fired simultaneously—probably coordinated by radio.

Evidence of the radio coordination can be found in photographs of a man with what appears to be a hand-held radio and in the Garrison testimony of Jim Hicks, who also is pictured in Dealey Plaza with a radiolike object in his rear pocket.

The presence of Secret Service agents in Dealey Plaza at a time when all official agents were accounted for elsewhere is a particularly pertinent piece of evidence. Either these men were bogus agents carrying identification good enough to fool Dallas policemen or they were real agents carrying out some activity as yet unexplained.

Recall that witness Jean Hill was taken immediately after the shooting to the Dallas County Sheriff's Office where men identifying themselves as Secret Service asked her questions indicating that they were observing her throughout the assassination.

The medical and ballistic evidence, much of which bears the earmarks of tampering and is thus still controversial, apparently shows that Kennedy was struck by at least three shots—one in the middle of the back which did not penetrate his body, one in the throat, and one in the head (although there is some evidence that two shots may have struck his head almost simultaneously).

Most probably at least two shots struck Governor Connally—one penetrating his chest and lung while a separate bullet shattered his right wrist.

At least one shot definitely missed the limousine altogether, striking the curb near the Triple Underpass, slightly wounding bystander James Tague—although there is evidence that another bullet struck the grass on the south side of Elm Street and yet another hit in the street near the presidential limousine.

This count would mean at least six shots were fired in Dealey Plaza—

perhaps as many as nine—which argues against the idea of a lone gunman. (It is significant to note that acoustical experts testified before the House Select Committee on Assassinations that they had discovered as many as nine sound signals that they could not rule out as gunshots—but only four were confirmed since only two sites for comparison tests were used.)

It is apparent to some researchers that the assassination was the result of a well-executed military-style ambush utilizing multiple gunmen firing from hidden positions—perhaps using fragmenting or "sabot" bullets and even silencers.

To attempt to pinpoint each gunman's location and calculate the number and effect of each shot is an exercise in futility since actions were taken immediately to eliminate evidence and confuse investigators.

A spent slug found on the south side of Elm Street was apparently taken by a man identified later as an FBI agent. A highway sign, thought to have been struck by a bullet, later disappeared. Films and photographs that might have pictured the assassins were confiscated by federal authorities and much of this material was never returned to the rightful owners.

The presidential limousine—a vital piece of evidence—was taken from Dallas and destroyed as evidence on orders from President Johnson before investigators could inspect the car's interior and windshield.

On the other hand, it is astounding how fast a wealth of evidence incriminating Lee Harvey Oswald became public. Most researchers now consider much of this evidence highly questionable.

The Mannlicher-Carcano rifle found on the sixth floor of the Texas School Book Depositor could only be linked to Oswald by a poor-quality palm print that lacked a court-admissible chain of evidence and was most probably obtained while Oswald's body was being prepared for burial.

Authorities claimed to have found three spent rifle cartridges on the Depository's sixth floor, although a copy of the original Dallas police evidence sheet states only two were found.

A Dallas police captain later claimed he kept one of the cartridges for a time. While this explains why only two cartridges were listed on the evidence sheet, it also indicates a break in the chain of evidence, meaning the third cartridge would not have been admissible in a trial.

The fact that Oswald's palm prints were found on boxes on the Depository's sixth floor is meaningless since he had worked there earlier that day.

In fact, much of the material evidence becomes meaningless once the idea that it could have been planted to incriminate Oswald is considered.

The idea that Oswald was framed for the crime—recall his cry "I'm just a patsy!" to newsmen in the Dallas Police Station—is supported by several things.

Recall that the CIA was reporting internally that Oswald entered the Soviet and Cuban embassies in Mexico City in early October, but photographs of the man seem to prove he was an impostor. This would mean someone was posing as Oswald to link him to the Communists two months prior to the assassination—and the CIA was aware of it.

Also recall that instances of Oswald being seen in two places at once, target practice in South Dallas and test driving a car at high speed on a Dallas freeway at a time Oswald was still trying to learn to drive.

In light of these incidents, it is apparent that someone was laying a trail of incriminating evidence right to Oswald.

The famous backyard photographs of Oswald with his weapons have been labeled clever forgeries by virtually everyone who has studied them, except those connected with the federal government. With the discovery of a suppressed third backyard photo in the mid-1970s, the fakery became undeniable.

If these photos are composite fakes—as claimed by Oswald himself—it is evidence that someone with sophisticated photographic capabilities was working to incriminate Oswald prior to the assassination.

Recall that Dallas police claimed to have found only two backyard photos in the Paine garage the day after the assassination, while two Dallas photo processors, Robert and Pat Hester, claim they saw the backyard pictures in the hands of the FBI the night of Kennedy's death.

Since there would have been efforts to eliminate any evidence of foreknowledge of the assassination, it is not surprising that the proof of the framing of Oswald is meager and largely circumstantial.

What is obvious and demonstrable is the coverup perpetrated after the assassination.

Herein lies the real key to understanding the truth of Kennedy's death.

While anyone could have engineered the assassination—Castro agents, KGB assassins, mob hitmen, anti-Castro Cuban exiles, dissident CIA or FBI agents, even the infamous "lone nut"—who had the power to subvert and misdirect any meaningful investigation after the assassination had occurred?

Consider that in the wake of the assassination there has been:

—A continuing and consistent pattern of suppression of evidence, destruction of evidence, and intimidation of witnesses on the part of federal authorities, especially the FBI and the Warren Commission.

—A continued unwillingness on the part of the Justice Department—of which the FBI is a part—to pursue and prosecute assassination leads, even after being urged to do so by Congress.

—Revelations concerning the presence of Secret Service agents encountered in Dealey Plaza at the time of the shooting, when no agents were present according to official records.

—The questionable activities of the CIA in providing false evidence to the Warren Commission while suppressing other vital evidence, such as the existence of assassination plots involving the Agency and organized-crime members.

—The disconcerting pattern of communications blackouts occurring at the time of the assassination which involved the Dallas police radio channel dedicated to presidential security, the missing code book in the airplane carrying Kennedy's cabinet, and the virtual shutdown of the Washington, D.C., telephone system at a time when most Americans were only just becoming aware that something had happened in Dallas.

—The revelation that Kennedy's autopsy was performed by inexperienced Navy doctors who were ordered by higher authorities present not to follow established autopsy procedures such as examining the President's clothing and probing his wounds. It was this flawed autopsy that has been most responsible for the continuing controversy over the medical evidence.

—An effort on the part of federal authorities to lock assassination evidence away from the public. President Johnson ordered evidence locked up until the year 2039, while the House Select Committee on Assassinations sealed up its evidence for fifty years.

These sins of coverup and suppression of evidence can be laid squarely at the feet of officials of the federal government.

No agents of the Dallas police, organized crime, Fidel Castro, or Nikita Khrushchev could have accomplished these documented efforts to hide the truth of the assassination.

The argument has been offered that government agencies—notably the FBI and CIA—suppressed and altered some evidence in an understandable effort to keep themselves from looking incompetent during the public outcry following the assassination. For example, the Secret Service lied about its agents drinking the night before Kennedy died and the FBI lied in denying it had any knowledge of Oswald's whereabouts just prior to the assassination.

But other examples of official misconduct are harder to explain away. For instance, the destruction of the Oswald note to the FBI is blatant destruction of evidence. An average citizen found guilty of this offense in a criminal case is subject to both jail and fine.

Other documented instances of destruction of evidence involve the cleaning of the presidential limousine and Governor Connally's clothing, and the destruction of Dr. Humes's original Kennedy autopsy notes.

Evidence altered while in the hands of federal authorities include the General Walker home photograph, the location of Kennedy's back wound, the nature of Kennedy's throat wound, the Dallas police evidence sheet, the location of book boxes in the "sniper's nest" and the testimony of several key witnesses, such as Phil Willis, Jean Hill, Roger Craig, Julia Ann Mercer, and the reenactment surveyors.

Instances of suppressed evidence include Kennedy's autopsy X-rays and brain, missing bullets, the actual results of spectrographic and neutron activation tests, Oswald's photographic and optical equipment (including the Minox camera), Oswald's paraffin test, the third Oswald backyard photograph, the incidents involving Sylvia Odio and Yuri Nosenko and a variety of crucial assassination witnesses, including Bill and Gayle Newman, Charles Brehm, James Simmons, J. C. Price, Beverly Oliver, Ed Hoffman, Dallas policeman James Chaney, and many others.

The intimidation of witnesses runs the full gamut from simple pressure to alter portions of their testimony to strange and unnatural deaths.

Witnesses Charles Givens, James Tague, Phil Willis, and former senator Ralph Yarborough were pressured to alter their statements, while others—including Ed Hoffman, A. J. Millican, Sandy Speaker, Acquilla Clemons, and Richard Carr—were threatened into silence.

People with pertinent assassination information turned up dead under strange circumstances. Lee Bowers and taxi driver William Whaley were killed in odd crashes. Reporter Bill Hunter and Ruby acquaintance Betty McDonald died in separate police station incidents.

Witness Jean Hill said harassment by federal authorities—including surveillance and telephone taps—continued well into the 1970s.

All of these examples of official misconduct go far beyond any innocent attempt to prevent tarnish to an agency's reputation. Many of these incidents were obvious attempts to misdirect an impartial investigation and to incriminate Oswald.

Even before Oswald was killed, the FBI—aided by Dallas authorities—was leaking information that he was the sole assassin. This came at a time when most members of the Dallas police felt Kennedy's death involved a conspiracy of some magnitude.

The government had strong allies in perpetrating a coverup in the Kennedy assassination—a news media that seemed incapable of looking past official pronouncements.

Assassination Coverage

From the moment the Kennedy assassination occurred, coverage of the tragedy involved government manipulation of a news media, which appeared only too willing to be manipulated.

The established media allowed themselves to be set up by official leaks and pronouncements about the assassination to the point where later official findings had to be accepted, and defended.

In the days following the assassination, Dallas area newspapers were filled with factual, if contradictory, information—Dallas district attorney Henry Wade voiced suspicion of a plot, various people told of seeing Oswald and Ruby together prior to Kennedy's death, and information concerning more than three shots fired from more than one location was published.

Outside Texas however, wire-service reporting was limited to the official version of one lone assassin firing three shots.

Information on Oswald's procommunist background was leaked by the FBI and transmitted nationwide. Immediately media speculation was turned from whether or not Oswald acted alone to speculation on his motives.

Despite the insertion of the word *alleged* before the word *assassin,* the entire thrust of news coverage was aimed at Oswald's guilt.

The New York Times proclaimed:

EVIDENCE AGAINST OSWALD DESCRIBED AS CONCLUSIVE

While the *New York Post* simply headlined:

ASSASSIN NAMED

Even the Dallas-Fort Worth papers were not immune to this rush to judgment.

The day after the assassination, the *Dallas Morning News* told readers:

PRO-COMMUNIST CHARGED WITH ACT

And the nearby *Fort Worth Star-Telegram* carried a front-page headline reading:

PARAFFIN TESTS OF OSWALD SHOW HE HAD FIRED GUN

This story quotes Dallas police chief Curry as saying: ". . . he could not at this time state whether paraffin tests on Oswald's face also were positive."

Dallas police documents show that the test was negative on Oswald's face. This evidence of innocence was suppressed by both the Dallas police and the federal authorities.

After Oswald's death, with no one except his mother to contradict them, the media began going further in their presumption of his guilt.

A *New York Times* headline stated:

PRESIDENT'S ASSASSIN SHOT . . .

Life magazine profiled:

ASSASSIN: THE MAN HELD—AND KILLED—FOR MURDER.

A *Time* magazine article combining Oswald's obituary and biography was entitled:

THE MAN WHO KILLED KENNEDY

The presumption of Oswald's guilt was cemented in the minds of the American public by the February 21, 1964, edition of *Life*, which carried one of the infamous backyard photos on its cover with the caption: "Lee Oswald with the weapons he used to kill President Kennedy and Officer Tippit."

This issue was in the hands of the public nearly eight months before the Warren Commission emerged from behind closed doors and proclaimed Oswald the assassin.

Later, *Life* devoted much of its October 2, 1964 issue to coverage of the just-released Warren Report. Rather than assigning a staff member to evaluate the report, *Life* editors chose Representative Gerald Ford, himself a Commission member, to review his own work.

In that same issue, a still frame from the Zapruder film depicting Kennedy's rearward fall at that moment of the head shot was substituted with an earlier frame that gave no indication of the direction his head moved. Interestingly, the caption read: "The assassin's shot struck the right rear portion of the President's skull, causing a massive wound and snapping his head to one side."

This caption, which only vaguely contradicted the official version, was nevertheless changed twice until it read: "The direction from which shots came was established by this picture taken at the instant a bullet struck the rear of the President's head and, passing through, caused the front part of his skull to explode forward.

One *Life* editor, Ed Kearns, was later asked about the changes. He told assassination researcher Vincent Salandria:

I am at a loss to explain the discrepancies between the three versions of *Life* which you cite. I've heard of breaking a [printing] plate to correct an error. I've never heard of doing it twice for a single issue, much less a single story. Nobody here seems to remember who worked on the early Kennedy story . . .

Of course it was *Life* that paid Abraham Zapruder $150,000 in $25,000 installments, then proceeded to lock this vital piece of evidence away from the American public, which only got access to the film after it was subpoenaed for the Clay Shaw trial in New Orleans.

Government officials made great use of planned leaks to the media to assure the public that no conspiracy existed in the assassination.

On December 3, 1963, just eleven days after the assassination, the *Dallas Times Herald* reported:

Meanwhile, Washington sources said the extensive FBI report now being completed will depict Oswald as a lone and unaided assassin. The report also will point out that there was no connection or association of Oswald with any night club operator, sources said.

It is fascinating to consider how such assurances could be made by the FBI just one week after the "crime of the century"—a time when federal investigators supposedly were just beginning to unravel Oswald's life and associations.

On June 1, 1964, four months prior to release of the Warren Report, this headline appeared in *The New York Times*:

PANEL TO REJECT THEORIES OF PLOT IN KENNEDY DEATH

On September 27, 1964, the Warren Report was released to near-unanimous praise from the national news media. *The New York Times* even went to the expense of publishing the entire report as a supplement to its September 28 edition. The paper then published both a hardcover and paperback edition of the report in collaboration with Bantam Books and the Book of the Month Club.

Two months later, *The Times* again sought to lead the public's understanding of the assassination by helping publish *The Witnesses*, consisting of "highlights" of Warren Commission testimony. Assassination researcher Jerry Policoff, after studying this publication, wrote:

The selection and editing of testimony for this volume showed a clear understanding of that evidence which supported the Warren Commission findings and that which did not. Testimony which fit into the latter category was edited out in a manner which could hardly have been accidental. References to shots from the front, for example, were consistently edited out, as was the admission by one of the autopsy surgeons that he had burned his original notes. Deleted from the testimony of three Secret Service agents present at the autopsy was . . . a description at significant variance with the official autopsy report. . . . In short, a volume purporting to be an objective condensation of relevant testimony compiled by America's "newspaper of record" was little more than deliberately slanted propaganda in support of the Warren Commission Report.

Respected researcher Sylvia Meagher wrote: "*The Witnesses*, therefore, was one of the most biased offerings ever to masquerade as objective information. In publishing this paperback, *The Times* engaged in uncritical partisanship, the antithesis of responsible journalism."

In 1966, a great deal of controversy had been generated by researchers critical of the Warren Report. This prompted Richard Billings, then *Life*'s associate editor in charge of investigative reporting, to order a look into certain aspects of the assassination, particularly the "single-bullet" theory.

Billings's staff concluded after analyzing the Zapruder film that the one-bullet theory was untenable and, in its November 25, 1966, issue, *Life* called for a new investigation.

However, in its November 25, 1966, issue, *Time* magazine—also a part of Time-Life Corporation—editorialized against the "phantasmagoria" of Warren Commission critics and concluded: ". . . there seems little valid excuse for so dramatic a development as another full-scale inquiry."

Asked about these conflicting editorial postures, Hedley Donovan, editor-in-chief of both *Time* and *Life*, responded: "We would like to see our magazines arrive at consistent positions on major issues, and I am sure in due course we will on this one."

This reconciliation occurred two months later when Billings said he was told by a superior: "It is not *Life*'s function to investigate the Kennedy assassination." (Similar admonitions have been echoed in newsrooms throughout America over the intervening years.) Billing's investigation was terminated and the November 25 article, which was to have been the first of a series, became the last.

The one television network that continually backed the Warren Commission version of the assassination was CBS, where newsman Dan Rather has served as one of the anchormen on assassination reports since 1967. Rather was one of the only newsmen who managed to see the Zapruder film in the days following the assassination.

In a 1967 assassination documentary, CBS conducted a series of tests designed to prove that Oswald could have fired his rifle in the time established by the Warren Commission. When these tests essentially failed to support this contention, narrator Walter Cronkite nevertheless reported:

> It seems reasonable to say that an expert could fire that rifle in five seconds. It seems equally reasonable to say that Oswald, under normal circumstances, would take longer. But these were not normal circumstances. Oswald was shooting at a president.

Cronkite's mistake was the same as that of the Warren Commission and later the House Select Committee on Assassinations—a presumption of Oswald's guilt guided the investigation.

Of course, a presumption of Oswald's innocence would have led investigators into a confrontation with government agencies, the military, big business, and powerful politicians.

Therefore the major news media have been content to let sleeping assassination conspiracies lie, compounding this timidity by characterizing anyone who dared looked hard at the case as a "buff," "fantasist," "paranoid," or "sensationalist." In the Dallas area, for instance, diligent reporters were warned off the assassination story by superiors despite a continuing spate of new developments and information.

Early on there was some excuse for this pathetic media track record. Newsmen in the early 1960s were used to getting their information from official sources and had no real idea that these same sources might lie to them. Questioning the word of J. Edgar Hoover was tantamount to blasphemy.

When newsmen from all over the world descended on Dallas, they were at the mercy of local and federal authorities. They didn't know the city or its leaders and they didn't know how to talk to its residents. So the bulk of reporters waited in the police station for the next official pronouncement.

Oswald's brother Robert commented in his book, *Lee*:

> It seemed to me that the police, who should be conducting a careful investigation to discover just what had happened and how deeply Lee might be involved, had instead surrendered to the mob of reporters, photographers and television cameramen. I knew that these men from the newspapers, magazines and television networks were workingmen, just like I was, and I could not blame them for carrying out their assignments. But I could and did blame the Dallas Police Department for its failure to retain any control over the situation. The most casual

remark by any of the investigators or police officers was broadcast to the world immediately, without any effort being made to determine whether it was somebody's wild speculation, a theory that deserved further investigation or a fact supported by reliable evidence.

Independent investigating was virtually nonexistent. The few reporters who dared investigate quickly moved on to another topic after realizing the power arranged against them.

Author Leonard Sanders was a young reporter in the Dallas area at the time. He told this author that he discontinued investigating the assassination after becoming convinced that his telephone was tapped and his movements monitored.

Dallas investigative reporter Earl Golz was actually ordered not to write about the Kennedy assassination again in the late 1970's. This order was ignored in the wake of revelations made public by the House Select Committee on Assassinations.

In this type of atmosphere, it is no wonder that the public remains confused about the facts of Kennedy's death.

As researcher Jerry Policoff wrote: "The Kennedy Assassination cover-up has survived so long only because the press, confronted with the choice of believing what it was told or examining the facts independently, chose the former."

*   *   *

The major news media—like other official segments of American society—simply failed to function properly in response to the assassination of President Kennedy.

The normal police function was subordinated to pressure from the federal government. The usual legal precautions to protect against wrongful conviction—such as a presumption of innocence until proven guilty, cross-examination of evidence and witnesses, and the securing of defense counsel for the accused—were bypassed in the case of Lee Harvey Oswald.

The possibility of wrongdoing at the top of this nation's political structure panicked otherwise honest leadership in local, state, and federal government. Major business leaders, sensing the enormity of what had happened, kept their peace.

Never had the old saying "Who will watch the watchers?" carried more meaning.

As a result of this turmoil, what essentially had been a plot by a few fearful and greedy men grew into a full-scale palace revolt—aided by business, banking, industrial, media, and defense communities that played no active role in the plot. The results of this revolt were accepted by the "status quo"—the "Establishment"—after the fact.

But who plotted against Camelot and how was this plot realized?

A Likely Scenario

Since so much information concerning the plot to kill Kennedy has been destroyed, altered, or masked by false leads, it remains impossible to state with authority details of the plan. Even those involved were probably not informed of every aspect of the plot.

However there is enough information available today to begin to construct a likely scenario of what happened:

By the beginning of 1963, serious talk against President Kennedy was circulating within many groups—organized crime, the anti-Castro Cubans, the CIA, business and banking, the oil industry, and even the military.

There were many connections among all these groups and, once word of this pervasive anti-Kennedy feeling reached the ears of certain members of the Southwestern oil and business communities, secret meetings were held where money was raised and tacit approvals given.

From this point on, there would be no further contact between the individuals who initiated the plot and those who carried it out. Consequently, there is little likelihood that the originators of the plot will ever be identified or brought to justice. However, the broad outlines of the plot can be discerned by diligent study of all available assassination information.

Because of his family's great wealth, John F. Kennedy was incorruptible by bribes. He also was the only president since Franklin Roosevelt who was an intellectual. Kennedy had a rich sense of history and a global outlook. He apparently had an idealistic vision of making the world more peaceful and less corrupt. In other words, he really believed he was president and he set out to shake up the status quo of Big Banking, Big Oil, Big Military-Industrial Complex with its powerful Intelligence Community, and Big Organized Crime, which had gained deep inroads into American life since Prohibition.

There were—and most certainly remain—numerous ties among all of these powerful factions. It is now well documented that the mob and the CIA worked hand in glove on many types of operations, including assassination. The various U.S. Military intelligence services are closely interwoven, and in some cases, such as the National Security Agency (NSA), are superior to the FBI and CIA.

Therefore, when Kennedy and his brother, Attorney General Robert Kennedy, began to wage war on organized crime, it quickly became a matter of self-defense to the mob and the banks and industries it controlled.

Officials of the FBI and CIA, likewise, were fearful of the Kennedys, who had come to realize how dangerously out of control these agencies had become.

The anti-Castro Cubans felt betrayed by Kennedy because of his last-minute orders halting U.S. military assistance to the Bay of Pigs invaders and were quite willing to support an assassination.

However, no matter how violent or powerful these crime-intelligence-industrial cliques might be, they never would have moved against this nation's chief executive without the approval of—or at the very least the neutralization of—the U.S. military.

Already angered by Kennedy's liberal domestic policies, the Bay of Pigs fiasco, and his signing of the Nuclear Test Ban Treaty with the Soviet Union, top military brass undoubtedly were incensed in late 1963 when Kennedy let it be known that he planned to withdraw all U.S. military personnel from Vietnam by the end of 1965.

With that decision, the military turned against him and, even if they wouldn't openly plot against him, the military leadership would not be sorry if something were to happen to Kennedy.

The stage was set. Gen. Charles Cabell, the CIA deputy director fired by Kennedy after the Bay of Pigs, was back in the Pentagon, and his brother, Earle Cabell, was mayor of Dallas.

It was widely rumored that Vice President Lyndon Johnson—long associated with dirty politics, gamblers, and defense officials—was to be dropped from the Democratic ticket in 1964. Texas oilmen, staunch friends of Johnson and the military-industrial complex, were dismayed that Kennedy was talking about doing away with the lucrative oil-depletion allowance.

International bankers were shocked when Kennedy ordered the Treasury Department to print its own money, rather than distributing the traditional Federal Reserve notes, which carry interest charges.

Soldiers, mobsters, and conniving businessmen feared their apple cart was about to be upset by this youthful president.

So the decision was made at the highest level of the American business-banking-politics-military-crime power structure—should anything happen to Kennedy, it would be viewed as a blessing for the nation.

And simply voting him out of office wouldn't suffice. After all, what was to stop someone from carrying on his policies? Two more Kennedys were waiting in the wings for their turn at the presidency. A Kennedy "dynasty" was in place.

Therefore the decision was made to eliminate John F. Kennedy by means of a public execution for the same reason criminals are publicly executed—to serve as a deterrent to anyone considering following in his footsteps.

And the men at the top of this consensus didn't even have to risk getting their hands bloody.

Col. L. Fletcher Prouty—a former Pentagon-CIA liaison officer and long-time assassination researcher—has said that most assassinations are set in motion not so much by a specific plan to kill as by efforts to remove or relax the protection around a target.

Prouty has written:

No one has to direct an assassination—it happens. The active role is played secretly by permitting it to happen. That was why President Kennedy was killed. He was not murdered by some lone gunman or by some limited conspiracy, but by the breakdown of the protective system that should have made an assassination impossible. . . . Once insiders knew that he would not be protected, it was easy to pick the day and the place. . . . All the conspirators had to do was let the right "mechanics" (professional assassins—perhaps the French Corsicans?) know where Kennedy would be and when and, most importantly, that the usual precautions would not have been made and that escape would be facilitated. This is the greatest single clue to the assassination— Who had the power to call off or reduce the usual security precautions that are always in effect whenever a president travels? Castro did not kill Kennedy, nor did the CIA. The power source that arranged that murder was on the inside. It had the means to reduce normal security and permit the choice of a hazardous route. It also had the continuing power to cover that crime for . . . years.

Once such a consensus was reached among the nation's top business-crime-military leadership, the assassination conspiracy went into action. Operational orders most probably originated with organized-crime chieftains such as Carlos Marcello and his associates Santos Trafficante and Sam Giancana—who already were involved with the CIA.

But these mob bosses were smart. They realized the consequences if their role in Kennedy's death should ever become known.

Therefore a world-class assassin was recruited from the international crime syndicate—perhaps Michael Victor Mertz, the shadowy Frenchman with both crime and intelligence connections who may have been in Dallas on November 22, 1963, according to a CIA document. Armed with a contract from the world crime syndicate, this premier assassin was given entree to the conspiring groups within U.S. intelligence, the anti-Castro Cubans, right-wing hate groups, and the military.

Slowly, several assassination scenarios utilizing agents already involved in a variety of plots were constructed.

As the true assassination plot began to come together, word must have reached the ears of J. Edgar Hoover, a power unto himself with plenty of cause to hate the Kennedy brothers. Hoover was in contact with his close friend Lyndon Johnson and with Texas oilmen such as H. L. Hunt and Clint Murchinson of Dallas. His agents and informers were in daily contact with mob figures. This was only one cross point for mobsters, politicians, the FBI, and wealthy Texans. There were many others in New York, Washington, Las Vegas, and California.

Aided by ranking individuals within federal agencies and organized crime, agents from both intelligence and the mob were recruited. Many were like Watergate burglar Frank Sturgis in that they had connections to criminal circles as well as to U.S. intelligence and anti-Castro Cubans. It was a military-style operation in that overall knowledge of the plot was kept on a strict need-to-know basis. Many people on the lower end of the conspiracy truthfully could say they didn't know exactly what happened.

To keep public attention away from the real conspirators a scapegoat—or patsy—was needed. Enter Lee Harvey Oswald, a patriotic young man who followed the tradition of his father and brothers by voluntarily joining the U.S. military.

After being sent to Atsugi Air Base in Japan—the CIA's largest Asian training center—Oswald's real activities become clouded. Apparently he was recruited into U.S. intelligence, first through the Office of Naval Intelligence and then on to the CIA.

At Atsugi, in addition to his intelligence work while serving as a radar operator monitoring the supersecret U-2 flights over the Soviet Union, Oswald began concocting his "legend" of being a communist sympathizer.

After a quick and curious release from service, Oswald left for Russia— most probably on some sort of intelligence mission unrelated to the assassination.

Here is where the scenario becomes even more complicated.

There is abundant evidence that author Michael Eddowes (a former member of British intelligence) may be correct in charging that a duplicate Oswald returned to the United States. Photo and voice analyses, differences in height and physical markings, and several other discrepancies all tend to support the theory of a bogus Oswald.

However, based on contradictory Marine records that seem to indicate that Oswald was in two places at once while in the service, there exists the possibility that a U.S. agent was substituted for the real Oswald prior to his trip to Russia. Many oddities in Oswald's records and habits may be better understood using this theory, especially if the patriotic Oswald agreed to the switch.

If the Dallas Oswald was a Soviet agent or a U.S agent posing as a procommunist, he would have made the perfect patsy for the assassination. As an intelligence agent, he would have been eager to follow orders and easily could have been manipulated into incriminating himself as the assassin. Furthermore, his position as a spy would have prevented the Russians from proclaiming the truth of the assassination, since they could hardly be expected to admit their knowledge of Oswald.

If the Dallas Oswald was the real Oswald he still could have been ordered to build up an incriminating trail of evidence.

The question of Oswald's true identity—intriguing as it may be—is nevertheless only a peripheral one. The preponderance of evidence now clearly indicates that the Dallas Oswald did not kill Kennedy. Real Oswald or impostor, this man was maneuvered about by the assassination conspirators who—knowing or suspecting him of being a Russian agent—had obtained him from U.S. intelligence.

Acting on orders, Oswald was put into contact with unsuspecting FBI and CIA agents, anti-Castro Cubans, and others to confuse investigators after the crime.

Oswald was a perfect fall guy. His capture or death eliminated a possible Soviet agent and implicated Russia, Cuba, and leftists—drawing attention away from the true right-wing perpetrators. Naming Oswald as the assassin also implicated the FBI and CIA as organizations, thus forcing uninvolved agency officials to help cover up incriminating evidence.

One of Oswald's managers in late 1962 and early 1963 may have been George DeMohrenschildt, himself connected to Texas oilmen and various intelligence agents. While it now seems clear that DeMohrenschildt had no inkling of what was to become of his young friend, it is entirely possible that it was through DeMohrenschildt that the assassination conspirators learned of Lee Harvey Oswald.

It was just at the time of DeMohrenschildt's departure to Haiti that Oswald left for New Orleans, where he became embroiled with anti-Castro Cubans, ex-FBI agent Guy Banister, his old friend David Ferrie, and others involved in assassination plotting.

On November 22, 1963, there were many people in Dealey Plaza who were not just innocent bystanders.

There were cars roaming the area behind the famous Grassy Knoll with out-of-state license plates and extra radio antennas, men brandishing Secret Service identification when officially there were no agents in the vicinity, and an odd assortment of people pumping umbrellas in the air, waving fists, speaking into walkie-talkies, and even one man firing a rifle who apparently was wearing a uniform similar to that of the Dallas police.

Professional gunmen—the "mechanics"—quietly moved into position, secure in the knowledge that security was minimal.

Only three police officers were stationed at the critical points in Dealey Plaza—two on the Triple Underpass and one in front of the Depository. Police were under orders not to allow anyone onto the grassy area on the south side of Elm Street—exactly where bullets were reported striking the grass. Sheriff's deputies were ordered not to interfere with motorcade security no matter what.

It was a textbook ambush, and President Kennedy rode right into the middle of it in an open limousine that violated security regulations by making a 120-degree turn in front of the Texas School Book Depository and by slowing almost to a halt when shots first rang out. In fact, Kennedy's entire security force exhibited a startling lack of preparedness and response.

Three volleys of shots were fired—at least six and perhaps as many as nine—most probably using fragmenting bullets or "sabot" slugs which could be traced to Oswald's 6.54 mm rifle.

Shots were fired from the Depository building to draw attention there while other gun teams were on the Grassy Knoll and perhaps even at other locations, such as the Dallas County Records Building.

It appears there may have been two serious slip-ups for the conspirators during the assassination. First, it appears unlikely that as many as three shots were intended. More likely the assassination was to have been constructed so that it would appear that Kennedy was killed by one lucky shot from the Depository. The conspirators, of course, would have been prepared to fire another volley if necessary. Second, it is equally likely that their scapegoat, Oswald, was to have been killed by a conspirator during return fire by Kennedy's security men. However, there was no return fire and Oswald managed to slip away from the Depository.

The first shot, described by many bystanders as sounding different from the rest, may have been a bad round. Instead of striking Kennedy in the back of the head, this old wartime ammunition may have dropped, striking him in the middle of the back and failing to penetrate more than an inch or so.

This necessitated visual signals that more shots were needed—perhaps these came from the "umbrella man" or perhaps the dark-complected man near him.

The final volley—planned for but not anticipated by the real assassins— was ragged, resulting in many witnesses claiming that more than four shots were fired. This created a problem for subsequent investigators, who resolved it by proclaiming that three shots had been fired—the absolute maximum allowable for one gunman.

When the shooting started, confusion was rampant. No one except the conspirators knew what was happening, and the Dallas police radio channel used for the presidential motorcade security was blocked for more than eight minutes due to an open microphone.

The true assassins simply strolled away, after dumping their rifles into nearby car trunks or passing them to confederates.

Oswald most probably was exactly where he said he was during the shooting—safely out of sight in the lunchroom of the Depository. Perhaps he had been told to wait for a telephone call at that time by an intelligence superior.

Since there is evidence that Oswald may have been reporting to the government on the activities of the assassination conspirators, he must have been shocked when he learned that Kennedy had been shot as planned.

Shortly after his encounter with Officer Baker, Oswald may have begun to realize what was happening. He then left the Depository and made his way to his South Oak Cliff rooming house. His landlady said that within minutes of his arrival, he hurried from his room after a Dallas police car stopped out front and beeped its horn twice.

Whatever plans Oswald had at this point, he most probably was slated to be killed by police for "resisting arrest"—a backup plan in the event he escaped Dealey Plaza alive.

The slaying of Officer J. D. Tippit may have played some part in this scheme to have Oswald killed, perhaps to eliminate coconspirator Tippit or simply to anger Dallas police and cause itchy trigger fingers.

There is evidence to suggest that Tippit was killed by someone other than Oswald. However, if Oswald was responsible it may have been that he simply got the drop on Tippit, who—since his pistol was found lying near his body—was approaching his suspect with a drawn weapon.

When cornered in the Texas Theater, Oswald was given every opportunity to flee through a rear exit.

Whatever the plan, it backfired. Oswald was captured alive, creating a bad situation for the conspirators. Oswald could not be permitted to stand trial and reveal his true connections.

Jack Ruby—the mob's "bag man" in Dallas and the man who apparently handled funds for the local activities of the assassination conspirators—received his orders to kill Oswald from organized-crime leaders eager to protect the secret of their contract, and there were no alternatives for a mob directive.

The key to understanding the Oswald slaying is not that Ruby somehow knew when Oswald was to be transported from the police station, but rather, that the Oswald transfer was delayed until Ruby was in position—thanks to mob influence in the Dallas Police Department, one of the nation's most corrupt at that time. (The House Select Committee on Assassinations even stated that Ruby most likely entered the police basement down a back stairway with the assistance of one or more policemen.)

One shot and Oswald was dead, leaving only his mother to question the official version of the assassination.

While this assassination scenario cannot be undisputably proven at this time, it nevertheless represents the only theory to date that conforms to all of the known facts.

* * *

Lyndon B. Johnson was sworn in as president within two hours of the assassination.

His first act as president was to order the removal of Kennedy's body from Parkland Hospital over the objections of the Dallas medical examiner—thus violating the laws of his own state. By that evening, Johnson was exerting undue influence over the Dallas investigation both directly and through his aides.

Within two weeks, Johnson had coerced a reluctant Chief Justice Earl Warren into heading a special presidential commission charged with finding Oswald alone guilty of the deed. The creation of the Warren Commission effectively blocked several other assassination investigations both in Texas and Washington.

The Warren Commission, composed of captains of both intelligence and big business—and with Representative Gerald Ford spying on behalf of Hoover's FBI—paid precious little attention to anything that did not tend to prove the "lone-nut assassin" theory. The Commission had no staff of independent investigators. It relied for information almost entirely on the

FBI and CIA. Both agencies today have been officially chastised for hiding evidence from the Commission.

Government investigators found a virtual smorgasbord of assassination evidence available in Dallas and New Orleans. By carefully selecting data that fit the official version of one lone gunman, they were able to present a believable—if untruthful—account of Kennedy's death.

Meanwhile a documented campaign of intimidation of witnesses began in Dallas. Some were simply told to keep quiet while others died under strange circumstances. While some of this suppression might be blamed on mob thugs, many people in Dallas have claimed that it was FBI agents who warned them not to talk about the assassination—an odd admonition since officially it was the work of just one lone, troubled man.

Some of the only independent investigative work occurred in Texas, where embarrassing evidence was found indicating that Oswald was an informant for the FBI.

There is now abundant evidence that Hoover's FBI destroyed critical evidence in this case, suppressed other evidence, and intimidated witnesses. The FBI solely directed the verdict that Oswald acted alone.

But many others contributed to clouding the truth of the assassination.

President Kennedy's wounds were altered between Parkland Hospital and his autopsy at Bethesda Naval Hospital, making it appear that all wounds were to the rear of his head and body and forever confusing the medical evidence. Here lies another key to the Kennedy assassination. Who had the power and the impunity to have the President's wounds altered and to misdirect the national investigation? These accomplishments could only have come from the very pinnacles of power in the United States. Power such as that wielded by Lyndon Johnson and his friend J. Edgar Hoover, backed by the business-banking-defense communities.

There was never a real cover-up of the assassination, only official pronouncements for the major media and lots of red herrings for devout investigators.

Once the Zapruder film became available to the American public in the mid-1970s, the direction of the shots became obvious. Photographs surfaced showing other gunmen. Reticent witnesses came forward fleshing out the assassination story. Even a local district attorney tried to prosecute some of the lower-level conspirators, but he was belittled in the national media, thanks to unethical statements by ranking government officials.

Despite an ever-growing amount of contradictory evidence, the U.S. government and those closely connected to it, have remained intransigent in their original position that the assassination was the work of a lone gunman. For example, although Canadian and Scotland Yard photographic experts have both concluded that the incriminating photos of Oswald in his backyard with a rifle and communist newspapers are fakes—just as Oswald himself told Dallas Police Captain Will Fritz—the FBI still maintains the photos are genuine.

The FBI also got national headlines in 1980 by claiming that the House Assassinations Committee's acoustical evidence indicating that more than one gunman had fired at Kennedy was inaccurate and its conclusions wrong. Little attention was paid months later when the Bureau had to admit that its study of the acoustical tests was insufficient and that the basic findings were accurate.

The House Select Committee on Assassinations recommended that the Justice Department conduct further investigation in the John F. Kennedy case. No such activity was forthcoming.

As long as the U.S. government refuses to seek and reveal the truth of what happened on November 22, 1963, it will be up to individual Americans to cull through the mounds of Kennedy assassination material and find the elusive truth for themselves.

Who done it?—A consensus of powerful men in the leadership of U.S. military, banking, government, intelligence, and organized-crime circles ordered their faithful agents to manipulate Mafia-Cuban-Agency pawns to kill the chief.

President Kennedy was killed in a military-style ambush orchestrated by organized crime with the active assistance of elements within the federal government of the United States.

Pressure from the top thwarted any truthful investigation.

As the years go by and further information becomes available, a more detailed assassination scenario can be constructed.

Even today there is still pressure from the top of the American power structure to keep the lid on this sordid affair.

When reputable Americans mention the assassination, they are often laughed at by those who refuse to be made uncomfortable by the truth.

During a gathering in November 1980, which included former British prime minister Harold MacMillan, famed conductor Leonard Bernstein noted that the anniversary of Kennedy's assassination again went unreported in the media and stated: "We don't dare confront the implications. I think we're all agreed there was a conspiracy and we don't want to know. It involves such a powerful high force in what we call the high places, if we do know, everything might fall apart." ". . . Rubbish," commented one listener.

Some people were told that to reveal Oswald's connections to the Communists would result in nuclear war and must be avoided at all costs. Others feared their involvement might become known through any meaningful investigation of their agency.

Many officials who still seek to obscure the Kennedy case played no part in the assassination conspiracy. They simply do not want the American public to become alerted to the interconnections between the government, big business, the military, intelligence, and the mob. It might prove bad for business.

This is why the truth still has been kept from the American public.

What then is the legacy of President John F. Kennedy? The fact is that we will never know. His presidency always will be remembered, not for what he did, but for what he might have done.

But it may be worth considering what kind of America we might have today if President Kennedy had lived. Imagine the United States if there had been no divisive Vietnam War, with its attendant demonstrations, riots, deaths, and loss of faith in government. There may not have been the scandals of Watergate, other political assassinations, or the Iran-Contra Pentagon-CIA attempt at a "secret government." Detente with Communist Russia and China might have come years earlier, saving hundreds of millions of wasted defense dollars—dollars that could have been put to use caring for the needy and cleaning up the environment. Picture a nation where no organized-crime syndicate gained control over such divergent areas of national life as drugs, gambling, labor unions, politicians, and even toxic waste disposal.

Is it possible to consider that we might have a nation where peace and prosperity might have been achieved without the need for a massive military buildup, or that we might have experienced a kinder and gentler nation all along.

John F. Kennedy was no superman. Today there seems to be a movement to focus attention on the "morality" of his private life. But history will eventually record that Kennedy truly believed he had the best interests of his nation at heart. He wanted to lead America forward.

Kennedy was in the mold of Mikhail Gorbachev, complete with his own American brand of "glasnost," or openness with the public—but he was premature.

America—at least the backstage rulers of America—was not ready for such innovation. So they killed him.

In the 1960s, many young people sensed what was happening. They tried to warn of the sins of "Amerika." But most people—this author included—didn't listen to them, just as many reading these words won't listen now. In hindsight, they were right. But how many of us can admit we were wrong?

Members of Kennedy's inner circle also came to understand what had really happened. But this knowledge came too late. The proof had been taken up and they realized the extent of the power arrayed against them. Some kept their peace, some soon retired from government, and others left the country.

Robert Kennedy, too, came to understand the tremendous power behind the events in Dallas. On June 3, 1968, just two days before his own assassination, the younger Kennedy told close friends: "I now fully realize that only the powers of the presidency will reveal the secrets of my brother's death." He obviously had come to realize that the truth of John Kennedy's death could only come after he gained control over the FBI,

CIA, Secret Service, and the Pentagon—all of which had become powers unto themselves.

But today all this is nothing new. We Americans have learned much about the connections of crime and spy agencies to the government and business communities in many cases such as Watergate, the John DeLorean affair, the Iran-Contra scandal, the assassination of Federal Judge John Wood and others.

The emperor has no clothes on—or in this case, American business and political emperors wear bloodstained clothing—but no one of any prominence wants to be the first to say so.

As we have seen, J. Edgar Hoover had experience in controlling major criminal investigations. By the early 1960s, Hoover had undisputed power over the FBI and undue influence over other government agencies. Lyndon B. Johnson had long since perfected the art of using the federal bureaucracy to block and impede investigations into his dealings. And this time there were plenty of people willing to go along with them—people who wanted Kennedy out of the way.

Camelot was killed from within, by men whose fear and ambition overpowered their faith and loyalty to the United States Constitution and the people it was designed to protect.

An apt precedent for the Kennedy assassination can be found in William Shakespeare's immortal *Julius Caesar*, where Roman leaders—"all honorable men"—plotted to kill Caesar out of fear that they were losing total power in their country. Brutus defended his participation by explaining: "Not that I loved Caesar less, but that I loved Rome more." Or to paraphrase the American officer in Vietnam who defended the destruction of a village: "In order to save the country, they had to destroy it."

The Kennedy assassination was a true coup d'etat—a sudden and violent shift of power to the right in this country. And that power—though weakened by revelations of corruption and unachieved goals—remains with us today.

Few people have shown a willingness to confront and accuse this power. But until the people of the United States confront the reality of Kennedy's death and face the power behind it, the wars, near-wars, the wasteful military buildup, foreign adventurism, death, squandered millions, trampled human rights, moral decline, and environmental pollution will continue.

The way to this confrontation lies within each individual citizen—in our minds and—perhaps more important—in our hearts.

One can almost hear the sad spirit of John F. Kennedy whispering from Dealey Plaza:

Et tu, Lyndon?

SOURCES AND NOTES

In a work such as this, extensive footnoting within the text can often impede the flow of ideas, reducing comprehension.

There are further problems in the case of the JFK assassination. Neither the Warren Commission's twenty-six volumes or the volumes and appendices of the House Select Committee on Assassinations—a total of fifty-five volumes— were adequately indexed, creating a time-consuming nightmare for serious researchers. Additionally, too often official government reports do not accurately reflect the actual evidence or statements of witnesses. This situation complicates effective documentation.

Major statements in this work or ones that contradict the official version of the assassination are attributed in this section. Usually only one reference is given although multiple sources may be found for most points.

Any statements without attribution or a source listing indicate historical fact or issues which are undisputed among the majority of credible assassination researchers. For example, it is unnecessary to document Richard Nixon's crucial role in initiating the Bay of Pigs invasion since various historians have already documented that role and Nixon himself has written about it.

In the case of controversies—such as the identity of a man photographed in the front doorway of the Texas Schoolbook Depository during the assassination— every effort has been made to present both sides of the issue.

Accounts of witnesses sometimes represent a synthesis of their words from more than one source. It should be pointed out that just because a statement is attributed to some source does not make that statement true. People's accounts can result from mistakes as well as lies due to fear and intimidation.

Many sources in this section are cited simply by author, title, and page number. Complete data on the books cited can be found in the Selected Bibliography.

WC Report refers to the Warren Commission Report, while its attendant hearings and exhibits will be referred to by volume and page—for example XXII.644. Similarly, the House Select Committee on Assassinations volumes will appear as HSCA VIII.64.

It is significant to add that while all assassination works—including this book—must rely heavily on official government reports and publications, such reports can often be called into question. Therefore the burden of separating fact from fiction must unfortunately fall on the reader. This sad fact necessitates access to the broadest amount of information, often going far beyond official sources.

PART I
THE KILL ZONE
Dallas—The Stage Is Set

Page

3 JFK's affair with Inga Arvad captured on tape: Davis, *The Kennedys,* pp. 111–112.

Joe Kennedy quote: Ibid., p. 135.

4 Talk to ministers in Houston: Wallechinsky and Wallace, *The People's Almanac,* p. 313.

5 Slim margin of 1960 election: Ibid., p. 314.

Comparison to Eisenhower: Ibid., p. 316.

6 Yarborough: telephone interview with author, summer, 1986.

Dealey Plaza—November 22, 1963
The Motorcade

9 Organization of motorcade: WC Report pp. 43–46.

Press car moved: author's interview with Dallas researcher Mary Ferrell, 1986. Her husband had loaned his station wagon for press use in the motorcade.

10 Hollingsworth: "Rapid Bang of Gun Changes History's Course," *Dallas Times Herald,* Nov. 23, 1963.

11 Truly: III.220.

Lawson: IV.351.

12 Kellerman: II.73–74.

Mrs. Connally: IV:147.

Greer: II.117.

Connally: IV.133.

13 Connally's cry: WC Report p. 50.

Mrs. Kennedy: Ibid., p. 49.

Hill: II.138–139.

14 Decker: "President Dead, Connally Shot," *Dallas Times Herald,* Nov. 22, 1963 (Final Edition). "The sheriff said he heard two shots and 'may have seen one of the bullets hit the concrete and bounce.' He said he did not see the other bullet."

Ellis: HSCA XII.23.

Landis: XVIII.758.

Bennett: XXIV.542.

15 Hill: II.138–141.

Powers: VII.473.

16 Mrs. Cabell: VII.486–487.

Yarborough: author's interview, summer, 1986.

17 Atkins: "JFK Assassination Film No One Wanted to See," *Midnight,* March 1, 1977, pp. 21–22.

The Crowd

Hathaway, Lawrence, and Owens: XXIV.211, 214 and 220.
18 Mercer: XIX.483.
19 Smith: XIX.516.
20 West: author's interview, April, 1978.
   Walther: Summers, "Conspiracy," p. 74; *Dallas Morning News,* Nov. 28, 1978.
21 Carr: interview with researcher Gary Shaw, April, 1975; HSCA XIII.8–9.
22 Bronson film: "JFK Film May Reveal Two Gunmen," *Dallas Morning News,* Nov. 26, 1978.
   Prisoners: "Witnesses Overlooked in JFK Probe," *Dallas Morning News,* Dec. 19, 1978. Johnny L. Powell said "maybe more than half" of the 40 inmates in his holding cell were looking across to the Texas School Book Depository and saw the two men. Powell said the pair "looked darker" than whites and were wearing "kind of brownish looker or duller clothes . . . like work clothes."
   Similas: Harold Weisberg, "Photographic Whitewash," pp. 223– 235; J. Gary Shaw with Larry R. Harris, *Coverup,* p. 51.
23 Edwards: VI.204.
   Fischer: VI.195.
   Betzner: XIX.467–468.
24 Willis: VII.493–497; "JFK Killing Witness Not Surprised Tests Indicated 2nd Gunman," *Fort Worth Star-Telegram,* Dec. 22, 1978.
25 Brennan: XXIV.203.
26 Speaker: author's interview, July, 1987.
   Terry: author's interview, 1978.
27 Truly: III.220.
   Campbell: XXII.638.
   Mrs. Reid: III.273.
   Arce: VI.365.
   Baker: VII.508–509.
28 Woodward: "Witness From The News Describes Assassination," *Dallas Morning News,* Nov. 23, 1963.
   Millican: XIX.486.
   Speaker: author's interview, July, 1987.
29 Mrs. Chism: XIX.472.
32 Witt: HSCA IV.432–433.
33 Kounas: XXII.659.
   Altgens: VII.517–518.
34 Brehm: Mark Lane's film of assassination witnesses, *Rush to Judgement,* 1966.
35 Nix: Ibid.
36 Oliver: "Area Woman To Testify In JFK Slaying Probe," *Lubbock Avalanche-Journal,* April 10, 1977; Interview with researcher J. Gary Shaw 1970; Nigel Turner documentary, *The Men Who Killed Kennedy,* Central Independent Television, Birmingham, England, 1988.

38 Hill: VI.207; author's interviews, 1986.
39 Newman: XIX.490; author's interview, April, 1988.
Price: XIX.492; Lane, *Rush to Judgement*.

The Texas School Book Depository

40 Oswald's job: WC Report, pp. 737–738.
41 Truly: III.237.
Frazier: II.225–228.
42 Oswald's denial: WC Report, p. 604.
Dougherty: VI.376.
43 Belknap: Jerry D. Rose, "The Epileptic Seizure," Penn Jones' *The Continuing Inquiry*, Feb. 22, 1984, pp. 8–22.
44 Wilson: XXII.685.
Dorman: XXII.644.
Garner: XXII.648.
Adams: VI.388.
Styles: XXII.676.
Frazier: II.234.
45 Lovelady: VI.338–339; "Time Gives Back Identity," *Dallas Times Herald*, Nov. 21, 1971.
46 Shelley: VI.329.
47 Curry's quote: " 'Not Sure' on Oswald Author Curry Indicates," *Dallas Morning News*, Nov. 6, 1969.
Oswald: WC Report, p. 600.
Williams: III.175.
48 Norman: III.191.
Jarman: III.205.
49 Arnold: XXII.635; Summers, p. 108.
51 Baker: III.246.
Reid: III.273.
52 Oswald tells of Coca-Cola: WC Report, p. 600.
53 Mooneyham: XXIV.531.
54 Molina: VI.371.

The Triple Underpass

55 Foster: VI.251.
56 White: VI.255.
57 Holland: VI.243; Lane, *Rush to Judgement*.
58 Simmons, Dodd, etc.: Lane, *Rush to Judgement*.
59 Skelton: XIX.496.
Miller: XIX.485.
60 Brown: VI.233.
Tague: VI.553; author's interviews, 1977 and 1988.
61 Haygood: VI.297.
Walthers: XIX.518.
62 Stroud: Sylvia Meagher, *Accessories After the Fact*, pp. 6–7.

The Grassy Knoll

65 Zapruder: VII.571.
66 Timing of shot: WC Report, p. 105.
69 Film compromised: David S. Lifton, *Best Evidence: Disguise and Deception in the Assassination of John F. Kennedy,* footnote p. 557.
70 Newman: XXII.842; Author's interview, April, 1988.
71 McKinnon: *San Diego Star News,* Nov. 20, 1983.
   Hudson: VII.559.
73 Hargis: VI.294.
74 Weitzman: VII.106.
   Smith: VII.535.
75 Smith smells gunpowder: Summers, p. 62.
77 Bowers: VI.287; Lane's *Rush to Judgement.*
78 Arnold: "SS 'Imposters' Spotted by JFK Witnesses," *Dallas Morning News,* August 27, 1978; author's interview, summer, 1985.
80 Attempts to study "badgeman": author's interview with Jack White and Gary Mack, 1984; Turner documentary.
81 Hoffman: author's interview, summer, 1985; FBI Airtel and memorandum, June 28, 1967 and April 5, 1977. (These FBI documents were obtained Dec. 2, 1985, after a FOIA request was filed with the Bureau by researcher J. Gary Shaw.)

PART II
Means, Motives, and Opportunities
Lee Harvey Oswald—Assassin or Patsy?

91 Marguerite Oswald's reaction to HSCA: "Panel's Finding Pleases Mother of Lee Oswald," *Fort Worth Star-Telegram,* Dec. 31, 1978.
   Marguerite Oswald background: WC Report, pp. 669–681; author's interviews, 1974-1979.
93 Complaints on son's death: "Mother of Oswald Blames Officers," *Fort Worth Star-Telegram,* Dec. 2, 1963.
94 FBI shows her picture: I.152–153.
95 Marguerite Oswald on Watergate: "Marguerite Oswald Not Bitter After 10-Year Infamy," *Fort Worth Star-Telegram,* Nov. 18, 1973.
96 Marguerite on payment: author's interview, 1974.
97 Lee's bed: E. Graham Ward, *Transcripts 1: An Interview With Marguerite Oswald,* Boston, Houghton Mifflin Company, 1973, p. 35.
98 Lee's favorite TV show: Robert L. Oswald, *Lee: A Portrait of Lee Harvey Oswald,* p. 47.

99 Lee's Marxism: Ibid., p. 71–72.
100 Ferrie asks about card: Summers, p. 497.
Secret Service questions Ferrie: Jim Garrison, *Heritage of Stone*, New York. Berkley Medallion Books, 1975, p. 103.
Letter of intent: WC Report, p. 680.
101 Oswald on communisim: Ibid., p. 384.
102 Oswald's military service: Ibid., pp. 681–689.
Oswald's absences: Edward J. Epstein, *Legend: The Secret World of Lee Harvey Oswald*, p. 65.
103 "Race Car": Ibid., pp. 53–55.
"secrets" interest: Ibid., p. 68.
Oswald and "Queen Bee": Ibid., pp. 71–72.
104 Bucknell: Interview with Mark Lane, April, 1978; "The Assassination of President John F. Kennedy—How the CIA Set Up Oswald," *Hustler*, October, 1978, p. 50.
Hemming: Summers, p. 172.
Wilcott: "Couple Talks About Bad Days in CIA," *San Francisco Chronicle*, Sept. 12, 1978; HSCA Report, pp. 198–199.
105 Oswald's VD: IX.603; VII.313; XIX.601.
Executive session: Transcript of Warren Commission proceedings, January 27, 1964. (This transcript was classified "Top Secret" and made public only in 1974 after suit was filed by a private researcher.)
Bagshaw and Connor: Summers, p. 155.
106 John Wayne: Epstein, p. 76.
Rodriquez: Ibid., p. 78.
107 Rhodes: Ibid., pp. 81–82.
Dejanovich: Ibid., p. 82.
108 "Oswaldskovich": WC Report, p. 686.
Thornley: Kerry Thornley, "Oswald," p. 23–32.
109 Thornley: Ibid., p. 47.
Officer's reaction: Ibid., p. 21.
110 Thornley's comment: WC Report, p. 389.
Botelho: Lane, op. cit., p. 94.
Bucknell: Ibid., p. 94.
111 Oswald's letter and trip: WC Report, pp. 689–690.

Russians

114 Powers deployed: Wallechinsky and Wallace, p. 650.
115 Prouty: Summers, p. 205.
Oswald's letter: XVI.871.
Ofstein: X.203.
116 Defectors: Summers, p. 176.
Webster: Ibid., pp. 177–178.
117 Marchetti: Ibid., p. 174.
Otepka: Bernard Fensterwald with Michael Ewing, *Coincidence or Conspiracy?*, p. 231.
118 Sweden: Summers, p. 557, Note 38.
Shirokova: WC Report, pp. 690–691.

119 Attempted defection: Ibid., p. 392–393.
   McVickar: XVIII.155.
120 Johnson: FBI Memorandum from A. Rosen to Mr. Belmont, November 23, 1964.
121 "Historic Diary": WC Report, p. 258.
   Rankin: Warren Commission Executive Session transcript, January 27, 1964.
   MVD funds: WC Report, p. 272.
122 Life in Russia: WC Report, pp. 697–712; author's interview with Jeanne DeMohrenschildt, 1978.
123 Hoover warning: Summers, p. 409.
   Marguerite Oswald: author's interviews, 1974-1979.
125 Didenko: Priscilla Johnson McMillan, *Marina and Lee,* p. 205.
126 CIA concerns: Addendum to CIA document, Nov. 25, 1963; Epstein, p. 138; Summers, p. 192.
   New identity: Epstein, p. 139.
127 Relationship cooled: WC Report, p. 395.
128 Raikin: Summers, p. 217.
129 Marina Oswald: Myrna Blyth and Jane Farrell, "Marina Oswald— Twenty-Five Years Later," *Ladies' Home Journal,* November, 1988.
130 Nosenko: Epstein, pp. 3–50, 257–274; Summers, pp. 194–202; "How the CIA Tried to Break Defector in Oswald Case," *The Washington Star,* Sept. 16, 1978; Edward Jay Epstein, "The War of the Moles: Russian Spies Inside the CIA and the FBI," *New York,* Feb. 27, 1978, and March 6, 1978; G. Robert Blakey and Richard N. Billings, "The Plot to Kill the President," pp. 118–134.

Cubans

139 Nixon pushes Cushman: Peter Wyden, *Bay of Pigs: The Untold Story,* pp. 29–30.
   Hunt and Barker: Ibid., p. 33.
140 U.S. Force barred: *New York Times,* April 12, 1961.
   "Minimum" scale: Wyden, p. 170.
141 "Orphan" quote: Ibid., p. 305.
142 JM/WAVE: Blakey and Billings, p. 159.
   RFK "stops" Mafia dealings: *New York Times,* March 10, 1965.
144 Daniel: Summers, pp. 431–434; Blakey and Billings, p. 144.
   Attwood: Ibid., p. 453.
145 Mobile visit: WC Report, p. 728.
146 Martello and Austin: Summers, p. 301.
   CRC at 544 Camp Street: Blakey and Billings, p. 165.
148 Banister "agent": Summers, p. 324; Henry Hurt, *Reasonable Doubt,* p. 291–292.
   Rodriquez: Summers, p. 318.
149 Veciana: Ibid., pp. 353–392, 508–513; Hurt, pp. 327–337.

150 Echevarria: Blakey and Billings, pp. 170–171; Hurt, p. 327.
Odio: WC Report, pp. 321–325; Hurt, pp. 372–374; Summers, pp. 411–418.

151 Oswald not at Odio home: WC Report, P. 324.

152 Hall: Ibid., p. 301; Meagher, p. 387.
Gonzales: "Cuban's Friend Believes Oswald Contacted Exile Leader," *Dallas Morning News*, June 10, 1979.

153 Martino: Summers, p. 451.
Morgan: *Washington Post*, May 2, 1976.

Mobsters

162 Lansky: Dennis Eisenberg, Uri Dan and Eli Landau, *Meyer Lansky: Mogul of the Mob*, p. 184.

165 Becker: Summers, pp. 287–288; Blakey and Billings, pp. 244–245; Davis, *The Kennedys*, pp. 379–380.

167 Dorfman: Blakey and Billings, pp. 193 and 206.

168 Lansky and Trafficante: Howard Kohn, "The Hughes-Nixon-Lansky Connection: The Secret Alliances of the CIA from WWII to Watergate," *Rolling Stone*, May 20, 1976; Blakey and Billings, pp. 227–229.

170 Aleman: Ibid., p. 246; Davis, p. 490; Summers, p. 284.

171 Piersante: Dan R. Moldea, *The Hoffa Wars: Teamsters, Rebels, Politicians and Mob*, p. 51.

172 Marcello cash to Nixon: Moldea, p. 108.

173 Hoffa threat: Ibid., p. 148; Fensterwald, pp. 351–352; Blakey and Billings, p. 202; Summers, p. 282.
Bradlee: Moldea, p. 149.

174 Valachi evaluated: Blakey and Billings, p. 200.
Mob eliminated or crippled: Davis, *The Kennedys*, p. 484.

176 Exner: Judith Exner as told to Ovid Demaris, *My Story*, pp. 86–89 and 100–105; Kitty Kelly, "The Dark Side of Camelot," *People*, Feb. 29, 1988.

179 Blakey: author's telephone interview, June, 1981.

Agents

182 Truman: Victor Marchetti and John D. Marks, *The CIA and the Cult of Intelligence*, p. 304; David Wise and Thomas B. Ross, *The Invisible Government*, New York, Bantam Books, 1965, p. 101.

183 Marchetti and Marks, pp. 33–34.
Dulles: David Wallechinsky and Irving Wallace, *The People's Almanac #2*, p. 309.

184 Allen and John Foster Dulles: Wise and Ross, p. 104.

185 LSD and MKULTRA: John D. Marks, *The Search for the "Manchurian Candidate,"* pp. 53–67.
LSD description: Ibid., p. 70.

186 Olson: Ibid., pp. 73–86.

188 Ferrie statement missing: Fensterwald, p. 297.
Marchetti: Robert Sam Anson, *They've Killed The President! The Search for the Murderers of John F. Kennedy*, p. 122.
Martin: HSCA IX.104.
189 Roberts: Summers, pp. 333 and 324–325.
190 Rose: "Oswald Camera Disappeared During FBI Investigation," *Dallas Morning News*, June 15, 1978.
Lohn: Ibid.
191 Minox photos released: "Oswald Pictures Released by FBI," *Dallas Morning News*, August 7, 1978.
CIA document: HSCA IV.210; "Paper Shows Oswald Eyed," *Fort Worth Star-Telegram*, Oct. 1, 1976.
Oswald as CIA agent: Yet another former CIA man, Harry Dean, has claimed that Oswald was recruited into the Agency while stationed at Atsugi ("JFK Exclusive: Oswald was U.S. Agent!," *Argosy*, October, 1976.) Dean, who said he participated in undercover operations against Castro as well as the infiltration of such organizations as the Fair Play of Cuba Committee, the Minutemen and the John Birch Society, claimed Oswald shot no one in Dallas, but was incriminated in the assassination by a conspiracy headed by an unnamed U.S. congressman and general.
192 CIA "201" document: HSCA Report, pp. 200–205.
FBI on espionage: NOTE: In Oswald's pocket when arrested was a 3" x 2" top of a department store box labeled "Cox's. Ft. Worth" (XXIV.345). Intelligence agents have been known to carry such innocuous but unusual items to identify themselves to other agents. The box top's significance is enhanced by the fact that it was not included in the Warren Commission exhibits which presented thousands of less relevant items.
194 "Incredible cable": Mark Lane, "CIA Conspired to Kill Kennedy," *L.A. Free Press*, Special Report Number One, 1978, p. 5.
195 Azcue: Summers, p. 374.
Duran: Ibid. pp. 376–377.
Phillips: Summers, p. 384.
197 Oswald note: Penn Jones, Jr., *The Continuing Inquiry*, Feb. 22, 1977; "Alleged Oswald Letter Checked for its Authenticity by FBI Agents," *Dallas Morning News*, Feb. 6, 1977.
198 Gaudet: Summers, pp. 363–365.
199 Osborne/Bowen: Fensterwald, pp. 232–235; Summers, 369–370.
Taylor: IX.100.
200 DeMohrenschildt and CIA: "Oswald Friend Labeled CIA Informant in Memo," *Dallas Times Herald*, July 27, 1978.
J. Walter Moore: HSCA XII.53–54; author's interviews with Mrs. DeMohrenschildt, 1978-1979.
201 CIA mail opening: "Letters Reveal CIA Opened Mail to Oswald," *Fort Worth Star-Telegram*, Sept. 12, 1978.
202 Underhill: Robert J. Groden and Harrison Edward Livingston, *High Treason*, p. 124.
203 Alderson: researcher J. Gary Shaw's interview, Oct. 6, 1977; Hurt, p. 418.

206 Helms: "Senate Intelligence Committee Report on Foreign Assassinations," p. 142.
207 Davis in Algiers: Seth Kantor, *Who was Jack Ruby?*, p. 16.
Moyers: author's interview, spring, 1986.
208 Bailey: interview with researcher Gary Shaw, spring, 1980; Hurt, p. 416.
Rivele: "A New Theory: 3 French Gangsters Killed JFK, New Book Alleges," *Dallas Morning News,* Oct. 26, 1988; Turner documentary.
209 Conein: Henrik Kreuger, *The Great Heroin Coup: Drugs, Intelligence & International Fascism*, pp. 133–135.
Watson: "Senate Intelligence Committee Report" (1976), Vol. 6, p. 4.

G-Men

216 Sullivan on communists: William Sullivan, *The Bureau: My Thirty Years in Hoover's FBI*, p. 266.
Mafia monograph: Ibid, p. 121.
217 Sullivan: Ibid, pp. 117–118.
Wicker: Editors Pat Watters and Stephen Gillers, *Investigating the FBI*, p. 14.
218 Stone: Don Whitehead, *The FBI Story*, New York, Pocket Books, Inc., 1958, p. 84.
219 FBI alumni: Sullivan, p. 115.
220 FBI and Dallas Police: "Hoover's Vendetta Targeted Dallas Police, Memos Reveal," *Dallas Morning News*, Dec. 30, 1980.
FBI growth: Richard Gid Powers, *Secrecy and Power*, p. 218.
Arvad: Davis, p. 111; Powers, p. 359.
222 Hoover and JFK: Sullivan, p. 50.
Files destroyed: Powers, p. 266.
223 Hoover and Johnson: Sullivan, p. 60.
Retirement waived: Powers, p. 396; NOTE: Hoover's retention as FBI director was assured by Executive Order 11154.
224 Relationship changed: Sullivan, pp. 60–61.
225 Tolson quote: Ibid, p. 48.
227 Quigley: WC Report, pp. 436–437; IV.431–432.
Pena: CBS Reports Inquiry, *The American Assassins*, Part Two, Nov. 26, 1975.
228 Walter: "Never Before Published Documents Prove: FBI Had Five-Day Warning," *L.A. Free Press*, Special Report Number One, 1978, p. 10.
Alba: Summers, pp. 312–313; Hurt, pp. 296–298.
230 Coffee company employees: Garrison, *A Heritage of Stone*, pp. 128–130.
Garrison: Ibid, p. 131.
231 Oswald as agent: Warren Commission transcripts, meeting of Jan. 22, 1964; meeting of Jan. 27, 1964.
233 Hosty note destroyed: "Senate Intelligence Committee Report on the Kennedy Assassination," p. 95; Davis, pp. 550 and 560; Summers, pp. 394–396.
234 Marina: WC I.79.

237 Roberts and daughter: Summers, pp. 322–326.
    Clinton incident: Jim Garrison, *On the Trail of the Assassins*, pp. 105–108;
    Hurt, p. 280; Summers, 333–337.
238 Palmer: Registrar Henry Palmer subsequently stated on a New Orleans
    radio program that he had known Guy Banister in the Army and that the
    man driving the Cadillac in Clinton was definitely not Banister, thus
    providing further impetus to Garrison's charge that the man was indeed
    Clay Shaw.
240 Powers: Ovid Demaris, *The Director*, New York, Harper's Magazine
    Press, 1975, p. 175.
242 Bolden: Fensterwald, pp. 560–562; Groden and Livingston, pp. 136–137;
    Shaw with Harris, p. 22.
243 Luncheon site decision: Jerry Bruno and Jeff Greenfield, *The Ad-
    vance Man*, New York, William Morrow and Company, 1971, p.
    90.
244 O'Donnell: Ibid., p. 92.
    Angry at Connally: Ibid., p. 94.
    Incomplete information: Jesse E. Curry, *Retired Dallas Police Chief
    Jesse Cury Reveals His Personal JFK Assassination File*, p. 17.
245 Greer: II.117.
247 Rowley: WC Report, p. 451.
248 Kirkwood and Hill: "Remembering the Cellar," Startime Section, *Fort
    Worth Star-Telegram*, May 25, 1984, p. 14; author's interviews with Pat
    Kirkwood, 1978 and 1984.
249 Yarborough: author's telephone interview, summer, 1986.
250 Secret Service deficiencies: HSCA Report, p. 237.

Rednecks and Oilmen

254 Freedom riders: Davis, p. 412.
258 Stovall and Rose: XXII.583.
    Marina: XI.294.
260 Walker's name in Oswald's notebook: WC Report, p. 663.
261 Paine: III.87.
262 Meagher: Meagher, p. 287.
    Bullets don't match: George Michael Evica, *And We Are All Mortal*,
    West Hartford, University of Hartford, 1978, p. 75.
    "compelling evidence": Meagher, p. 62.
264 King as instrument: Sullivan, p 135.
    Hoover gathered material: Ibid, p. 50.
    Martin: Davis, p. 420.
    Davis: Ibid., p. 427.
265 Milteer: Ibid., p. 513; Shaw with Harris, pp. 169–170; Hurt, pp. 410–411;
    Summers, pp. 429–430, 606–607.
266 Kennedy and steel industry: Wallechinsky and Wallace, *The People's
    Alamanac*, p. 246.
268 Nixon-Marcello connection: Moldea, p. 108.

269 Rubenstein FBI memo: author's interview with Ford, 1977; Shaw with Harris, p. 54; Groden and Livingstone, p. 254.
271 Nixon interview: Warren Commission Exhibit 1973.
Nixon's version: Jules Witcover, *Saturday Evening Post,* Feb. 25, 1967.
272 Marina's statements: WC Report, p. 188.
Nixon-Haldeman: June 23, 1972, White House Transcript, meeting between President Richard Nixon and H.R. Haldeman.
273 Watergate figures: Fensterwald, p. 550.
274 Justice official: Moldea, p. 352.
Wall Street: *Book of the Year, 1964,* Chicago, Encyclopedia Britannica, 1964, p. 847; Lincoln Lawrence, *Were We Controlled?,* New York, University Books, Inc., 1967 p. 146; Theodore H. White, *The Assassination of the President,* Year Book Special Report, Chicago, The 1964 World Book Encyclopedia, 1964, p. 64; "Stocks Take Record Rise," *Dallas Morning News,* November 27, 1963.
275 "United States Note": Author's interview with the librarian of the Comptroller of the Currency, winter, 1988; "The Spotlight," Oct. 31, 1988, p. 2.
277 Curington: "JFK Assassins Got $$ From Kennedy-Hating Billionaire," *National Inquirer,* June 14, 1977.
278 DeMohrenschildt: IX.179.
279 CIA reports filed: "Oswald Friend Labeled CIA Informant in Memo," *Dallas Times Herald,* July 27, 1978.
283 Mrs. DeMohrenschildt: author's interviews, 1978 and 1983.
284 Browder with Ruby: David E. Scheim, *Contract on America,* p. 201.
FBI letter: IX.167.
285 Mendoza: author's interview with Mrs. DeMohrenschildt, 1978.
291 LBJ and Rayburn: J. Evetts Haley, *A Texan Looks at Lyndon: A Study in Illegitimate Power,* Canyon, Texas, Palo Duro Press, 1964, p. 14.
"Correction" made: Clyde Wantland, *The Texas Argus,* San Antonio, April, 1962.
292 Salas: "Man Admits Fixing LBJ's '48 Election," *Forth Worth Star-Telegram,* July 31, 1977.
IRS files burned: Haley, p. 92.
293 Envelopes with cash: Robert A. Caro, *The Atlantic Monthly,* October, 1981.
Halfen: Scheim, p. 169.
294 LBJ pardon for Hoffa: Bobby Baker with Larry L. King, "Wheeling and Dealing," p. 17.
Oilmen threatened: Haley, p. 238.
295 LBJ dumped: "Nixon Predicts JFK May Drop Johnson," *Dallas Morning News,* Nov. 22, 1963.
LBJ's treatment: Sam Houston Johnson, *My Brother Lyndon,* New York, Cowles, 1969, p. 108.
Marshall: "Suicide Changed to Murder in Billie Sol Estes Case," *Fort Worth Star-Telegram,* August 14, 1985; "Estes Claims LBJ Had Slush Fund, Sources Say," *Dallas Morning News,* March 24, 1984; "Estes

Cited Electric Chair in Refusal to Discuss Deaths,'' *Dallas Times Herald*, March 26, 1984; Haley, pp 134–135.

296 LBJ to Kilduff: Jack Bell, *The Johnson Treatment: How Lyndon B. Johnson Took Over the Presidency and Made It His Own*, New York, Harper & Row, 1965, p. 12.

297 O'Donnell: William Manchester, *The Death of a President*, p. 235.
LBJ to Galbraith: Ibid., p. 472.
LBJ's master plan: Bell, p. 22.
Connally's clothing: Shaw with Harris, p. 78.
Goodwin: "Was Lyndon Johnson Unstable?," *Time*, Sept. 5, 1988, p. 22.

298 Brown: author's interviews, 1988 and 1989.
Watson quotes LBJ: Senate Intelligence Committee Final Report, 1976, Vol. 6, p. 182.

Soldiers

304 NSAM 55 and 57: L. Fletcher Prouty, *The Secret Team: The CIA and Its Allies in Control of the United States and the World*, pp. 114–116 and 116–119.

306 Hilsman: Michael Maclear, *The Ten Thousand Day War—Vietnam: 1945-1975*, p. 60.

308 Military withdrawal: National Security Action Memorandum No. 263 (Copy available at the John Fitzgerald Kennedy Library, Boston) states: "At a meeting on October 5, 1963, the President considered the recommendations contained in the report of Secretary McNamara and General Taylor on their mission to South Vietnam. The President approved the military recommendations . . . but directed that no formal announcement be made of the implementation of plans to withdraw 1,000 military personnel by the end of 1963."
NSAM 273: Peter Dale Scott, Paul L. Hoch, and Russell Stetler, "The Assassinations: Dallas and Beyond," pp. 406–442.
JFK's order rescinded: Kenneth P. O'Donnell, David Powers, and Joe McCarthy, *Johnny, We Hardly Knew Ye: Memories of John Fitzgerald Kennedy*, New York, Pocket Books, 1973, p. 18.

(309) Nagell: William Turner, "The Garrison Commission on the Assassination of President Kennedy," *Ramparts*, January, 1968, pp. 56–58; Richard Russell with Dave Navard, "The Man Who Had A Contract to Kill Lee Harvey Oswald Before the Assassination of President John F. Kennedy," *Gallery*, March, 1981, pp. 37–38, 88–95; Garrison, *On the Trail of the Assassins*, pp. 182–186.

309 Hosty and agent: IV. 461.
Powell: Warren Commission Document 354; Shaw with Harris, p. 194.
Revill: Ibid., p. 194; V.57.

310 Jones: HSCA Report, pp. 221–222.

311 Oswald and military intelligence: HSCA Report, p. 224.

PART III
AFTERMATH

Dallas

314 Fritz: IV.205.
   Biffle: "Reporter Recalls the Day Camelot Died in Dallas," *The Dallas Morning News,* April 5, 1981.
315 Cabluck: author's interview, 1976 and 1986.
316 Hartman: author's interview, summer, 1986.
317 Lester: Associated Press, Jan. 5, 1978; Yet another bullet—this one a whole .45-caliber—was discovered in May, 1976, by Hal Luster buried in dirt by the four-foot-high cement retaining wall near the place where Abraham Zapruder stood filming ("Man Claims He Found Live Bullet Buried Under Top of Grassy Knoll," *Dallas Morning News,* Dec. 23, 1978).
   Morgan: author's interview, spring, 1989.
318 Carr: Shaw with Harris, p. 13.
319 Speaker: author's interviews, July, 1987.
320 Smith: Summers, p. 81.
   Summers: Jack Anderson TV Documentary, *Who Murdered JFK?,* aired Nov. 2, 1988.
321 Weitzman: VII.107.
   Harkness: VI.312.
   Sorrels: "SS 'Imposters' Spotted by JFK Witnesses," *Dallas Morning News,* August 27, 1978.
322 Oswald and agent: WC Report, p. 629.
323 Hill: author's interviews, 1986 and 1989.
326 Tilson: "Ex-Officer Suspects He Chased '2nd Gun' ," *Dallas Morning News,* August 20, 1978.
329 Craig: Roger Craig, *When They Kill a President* (unpublished manuscript, 1971), p. 7; XIX.524.
332 Biffle: "Reporter Recalls the Day Camelot Died in Dallas," *Dallas Morning News,* April 5, 1981.
333 Harrelson's confession: "Events Turn Sour . . .," *Dallas Morning News,* March 20, 1981; "Is Kennedy's Assassin Sitting in Texas Jail?," *The News Tribune,* Fort Worth, Texas, June 11, 1982.
334 Cook: author's telephone interview, spring, 1982.
   Matthews: KDFW-TV (Channel 4, Dallas) interview with Harrelson, aired Feb. 14, 1982.
335 "The Company": "Story of Spies, Stolen Arms and Drugs," *San Francisco Chronicle,* April 28, 1982.
336 Trial testimony: "Chagra Says Harrelson Told Him He Also Killed JFK," *Fort Worth Star-Telegram,* Nov. 2, 1982.
337 Braden: Summers, pp. 476–477; Hurt, pp. 123–124; Fensterwald, pp. 287–289.

340 Tippit "unknown": Meagher, p. 253.
341 Markham: III.311.
Whaley: II.261.
Scoggins: III.335.
342 Clemons: Lane, *Rush To Judgement,* New York, Dell Publishing Co., 1975, p. 194.
Wright: George and Patricia Nash, "New Leader," Oct. 12, 1964.
343 Poe: XXIV.415.
344 Kinsley: Notes of interview by *Dallas Morning News* reporter Earl Golz, spring, 1979.
345 Howard: author's interview, 1987.
Oswald's jacket: WC Report, p. 164.
346 Benavides: VI.453.
Roberts: VI.439.
Davis: III.347.
Scoggins: III.328.
Westbrook: WC Report, p. 175.
347 Roberts: VI.443–444.
349 Bowles: Interview with Gary Mack, winter, 1981; Gary Mack, "NAS Panel Stuck On Channel 1, Report Delayed," *The Continuing Inquiry,* March 22, 1982, p. 5; Gary Mack, "J.D. Tippit: The 'Missing' Broadcasts," *Coverups,* September, 1984, p. 2.
"coup de grace": HSCA Report, p. 59–60.
351 McDonald: "Officer Recalls Oswald Capture," *Dallas Morning News,* Nov. 24, 1963.
Brewer: VII.6.
352 Applin: VII.91; "Man Believes He Saw Ruby At Scene of Oswald's Arrest," *Dallas Morning News,* March 11, 1979.
353 Burroughs: author's interview, summer, 1987.
Davis: author's interview, fall, 1988.
354 Haire: author's interview, summer, 1987.
355 Rose: VII.228; Nigel Turner documentary.
January: Shaw with Harris, p. 111.
Hoover: "Hoover Called Oswald 'A Nut' FBI Files Show," *Fort Worth Star-Telegram,* Dec. 7, 1977.
356 Preliminary reports of conspiracy: "Wade Calls Killing A 'Dastardly Act,' " *Dallas Morning News,* Nov. 23, 1963.
Wade to say no conspiracy: Edward Oxford, "Destiny in Dallas," *American History Illustrated,* November, 1988, p. 24.
357 Curry: IV.195.

Two Hospitals

363 Fuller: "7 Shared Emergency Room With JFK," *Dallas Morning News,* Nov. 22, 1973.
364 Tomlinson: VI.133–134.
366 Tice: XV.389; Seth Kantor, *Who Was Jack Ruby?,* p. 192–194.

368 Burkley: XXII.96.
 Finck: Garrison, *On the Trail of the Assassins,* pp. 246–249.
370 Sibert-O'Neill Report: Edward Jay Epstein, "Inquest," pp. 166–170.
373 O'Connor: David Lifton, *Best Evidence,* p. 598–599.
 Custer: Ibid., p. 620.
375 Bone fragment: Josiah Thompson, *Six Seconds in Dallas* (Berkley Edition), p. 65.
 Burkley on conspiracy: Hurt, p. 49.
379 Helpern: Thompson, p. 254.
 Wecht: HSCA I.358.

Jack Ruby

380 ". . . a terrible conspiracy": Taped interview with Bob Huffaker of KRLD News, Dallas, following hearing for a new trial, Sept. 9, 1965.
381 ". . . the true facts of what occurred,": Turner documentary.
 Young Ruby: WC Report, pp. 779–786.
384 Ruby and union: V.200; Kantor, pp. 99–100.
385 Guthrie: Kantor, pp. 105–106.
386 Brown: author's interviews, 1988 and 1989.
387 Ruby's associates are discussed in the HSCA Report and volumes; Kantor; Fensterwald; Blakey with Billings; Summers; Scheim, op. cit.
390 Abadie: CE 1750 and 1753; Scheim, p. 105.
 Hardee: Ibid., p. 105.
 Hall: Ibid., pp. 81 and 105; Kantor, p. 111.
 Mash: author's interview, spring, 1988.
391 Breen-Curry: Scheim, p. 82.
392 Thompson: Ibid., p. 201.
 Browder: William Scott Malone, "The Secret Life of Jack Ruby," *New Times,* January 23, 1978, pp. 47–48.
 Ruby letter: Penn Jones, Jr., *The Continuing Inquiry,* December 22, 1978, pp. 4–5.
393 Weston: "Ruby-Oswald Link Cited By Witness," *Fort Worth Star-Telegram,* July 18, 1976.
 Mynier: CD 84, p. 215.
 WC on McWillie: WC Report, p. 370.
394 Ruby lied repeatedly: Blakey and Billings, pp. 293–294.
 McWillie: Malone, pp. 50–51; Fensterwald, pp. 285–286; Kantor, pp. 131–132; Blakey and Billings, p. 293.
395 McKeown: Kantor, p. 137; Scheim, pp. 202–203; Fensterwald, pp. 364–366.
396 Beaird: "Jack Ruby's Gunrunning To Castro Claimed," *Dallas Morning News,* August 18, 1978.
397 Perrin: Scheim, p. 206.
398 Wilson: Kantor, p. 132.
399 Flynn: Ibid., p. 128; Malone, p. 49; Fensterwald, p. 260; Blakey and Billings, pp. 295–296.
 ". . . no ulterior motive": Ibid, p. 296.

400 Ruby buys "bugging" devices: Malone, p. 49.
     Willens: Kantor, p. 127.
401 Ruby and Roselli: Malone, p. 51.
402 Cheramie: HSCA X.199–205.
403 "no evidence": WC Report, p. 650.
     Griffin-Hubert: Blakey and Billings, p. 82.
     Ruby-Oswald connections: HSCA Report, p. 148.
     Oswald-Ruby not "loners": Ibid., p. 180.
     Walker: author's interview, fall, 1964.
404 Alexander: "Any Oswald-Rubenstein Tie In Dallas Sought by Police,"
     Dallas Morning News, November 26, 1963.
     Brown: author's interviews, spring and fall, 1988.
     Cummings: "Oswald-Ferrie Link Made by Ex-Cabbie," *Fort Worth
     Star-Telegram,* March 10, 1967.
     Crowe: "Magician Says Oswald Was Patron in Ruby Night Club,"
     Dallas Morning News, November 25, 1963.
405 Oliver: Turner television documentary.
406 Carlin: XV.620.
     Kay: "FBI Eyes On Ruby Strippers in JFK Case," *Dallas Times Herald,*
     May 22, 1975.
     Meserole: author's interviews, spring and summer, 1988.
     Weston: "Ruby-Oswald Link Cited by Witness" (Copyright 1976, New York
     News), *Fort Worth Star-Telegram,* July 18, 1976; "JFK Murder Hatched
     in Ruby's Club—Oswald Was There," *Midnight,* November 15, 1976.
408 Billet: Ibid.
     Mash: author's interviews, summer and fall, 1988.
409 Jarnagin: author's interview, summer, 1988; XXVI. 254–257.
411 Box of documents: "Papers Link Ruby, Oswald," *Dallas Morning News,*
     March 28, 1976.
412 "Gleam of recognition": Curry, p. 133.
     Ruby's phone contacts: Blakey and Billings, pp. 302–305.
413 Tax liens: WC Report, p. 705.
414 Tax "connection": Blakey and Billings, p. 308.
     Ruby's business: Ibid., p. 309.
     Ruby's note to Tonahill: Ibid., p. 333.
     "this silly story": Melvin Belli, *Dallas Justice,* p. 39.
416 Ruby: V.191.
417 "sightings": HSCA Report, p. 158.
     Authorities warned: WC Report, p. 209.
     Grammer: Turner documentary.
418 Richey-Smith-Walker: WC Report, pp. 352–353.
     Rushing: XII.75–79; Shaw with Harris, p. 21.
     Pitts: WC Report, p. 353; Kantor, pp. 59–60.
419 Carlin: XIX.306.
     Senator's call: Kantor, p. 217.
420 Howard: CE 2002, p. 73.
     Leavelle: author's interview, fall, 1988.

Alleyway: HSCA Report, p. 157.
"some premeditation": Ibid., 157.
Ruby: V.206.
421 Roselli: Malone, p. 51.
422 Graves: Edward Oxford, "Destiny in Dallas," *American History Illustrated,* November, 1988, p. 47.
423 "I stayed in my office": Curry, p. 127.
Curry: Ibid., p. 130.
Archer: Turner documentary.
424 Alexander: Kantor, p. 114.
425 Kilgallen "possibility": Lee Israel, *Kilgallen,* New York, Dell Publishing Co., 1979, p. 358.
Crawford: Ibid., p. 361.
Lane: Ibid., p. 378.
"Story isn't going to die": Ibid., p. 388.
426 "Dorothy's death": Ibid., p. 395.
427 Tonahill: Kantor, p. 4.
Ruby: V.203–213.
428: Hoover: WC Report, p. 815.
429 Stevenson: Kantor, p. 167.
430 Ruby letter: Penn Jones, *The Continuing Inquiry*, November 22, 1978 and December 22, 1978.
431 Second letter: Copy in files of researcher J. Gary Shaw.
432 Maddox: Unpublished interview with *Dallas Morning News* reporter Earl Golz, winter, 1982.
433 Tilson: Unpublished interview with reporter Earl Golz, summer, 1978.
McCarty: author's interview, spring, 1988.

The Evidence

435 Witnesses: Shaw with Harris, pp. 8–9.
436 O'Donnell and Powers: Their changed testimony is confirmed by former House Speaker Thomas P. "Tip" O'Neill in his book, *Man of the House* New York, Random House, 1987, p. 178: "I was never one of those people who had doubts or suspicions about the Warren Commission's report on the president's death. But five years after Jack died, I was having dinner with (former JFK aide) Kenny O'Donnell . . . I was surprised to hear O'Donnell say that he was sure he had heard two shots from behind the fence. 'That's not what you told the Warren Commission,' I said. 'You're right,' he replied. 'I told the FBI what I had heard, but they said it couldn't have happened that way and that I must have been imagining things. So I testified the way they wanted me to. I just didn't want to stir up any more pain and trouble for the family.' Dave Powers was with us at dinner that night, and his recollection of the shots was the same as O'Donnell's. Kenny O'Donnell is no longer alive, but during the writing of this book I checked with Dave Powers. As they say in the news business, he stands by his story."

437 Day: IV.265.
438 Craig: Roger Craig, *When They Kill a President* (Unpublished manuscript: 1971), p. 18. NOTE: Craig wrote: "We (Mooney and Craig) immediately found three rifle cartridges laying in such a way that they looked as though they had been carefully and deliberately placed there—in plain sight on the floor to the right of the southeast corner window. . . . The three of them were no more than one inch apart and all were facing in the same direction, a feat very difficult to achieve with a bolt action rifle—or any rifle for that matter."
439 Weitzman: XXIV.228.
    Wade: XXIV.831.
    Boone: III.294.
440 "substitution of rifles": Meagher, p. 100.
441 Pistol bought in Fort Worth: WC Report, p. 606.
    Simmons: III.443.
    Warren Commission on serial number: WC Report, p. 81.
442 Serial number: XXV.808.
443 Latona: IV.24.
444 "FBI team": "Body of JFK Assassin Is Under Guard in FW," *The Fort Worth Press*, Nov. 25, 1963.
    Groody: author's interviews, 1979 and 1988.
    Harrison: Telephone interview with researcher Gary Mack, 1978.
    Wade: "Oswald's Prints Revealed On Rifle Killing Kennedy," *Dallas Times Herald*, Nov. 25, 1963.
    Drain: Hurt, p. 109.
445 Question over palm print: FBI memo, Rosen to Belmont, August 28, 1964 (FBI 105-82555-4814).
    Day: XXVI.829.
446 Wecht: HSCA VII.200.
    "no significant differences": Hurt, p. 80.
447 Hoover: HSCA I.558.
    Guinn: Hurt, p. 83.
    Western Cartridge: XXVI.62.
448 Bag touching blanket: Curry, pp. 88–89.
450 Connally's clothing: Penn Jones, Jr., *Forgive My Grief II* (Midlothian: The Midlothian Mirror, 1967), pp. 77–79.
451 Oswald to Fritz: WC Report, p. 608.
    Committee: HSCA II.358–359.
452 Hester: "Dallas Man Claims FBI Had Oswald Film," *Fort Worth Star-Telegram*, Sept. 20, 1978; author's interview with Patricia Hester, spring, 1986.
453 Pickard: Summers, p. 95.
    Thompson: Ibid., p. 96.
    White: author's interviews, 1978 and spring, 1988.
454 Blakey: HSCA II.319.
455 Breneman: author's interview, spring, 1978; "Surveyor: More Than 1 Man Shot Kennedy," *Fort Worth Star-Telegram*, April 14, 1978.
    West: author's interview, spring, 1978.

The Warren Commission

459 Hoover: Senate Intelligence Committee Report on the Kennedy Assassination, p. 33.
Media leaks: "FBI Data Seen Spiking Reports of Conspiracy," *Dallas Morning News,* Dec. 4, 1963.
Katzanbach memo: HSCA III.567.

461 Commission cut off inquiries: "President Names Board To Probe JFK's Slaying," *Dallas Morning News,* Nov. 30, 1963.
Gallup poll: "52% Believe 'Group' Tied to JFK Slaying," *Dallas Morning News,* Dec. 6, 1963.

462 Nixon badgered Eisenhower: Jack Harrison Pollack, *Earl Warren—The Judge Who Changed America,* p. 6.

463 Kennedy letter: Ibid., p. 220.

464 Warren: Ibid., p. 228.
"Johnson treatment": Ibid., pp. 228–229.
Eisenberg: Fensterwald, p. 73.

469 WC transcripts: Tad Szulc, "The Warren Commission In Its Own Words," *The New Republic,* Sept. 27, 1975.

470 "No more memorandums": Epstein, *Inquest—The Warren Commission and the Establishment of Truth,* p. 119.

479 Bowers: Lane, *Rush to Judgement* documentary.

480 Powell: Warren Commission Document 1542 in files of researcher J. Gary Shaw.
Holland: Thompson, *Six Seconds* (Berkley), p. 146; Holland's comment to Lane is from *Rush to Judgement* documentary.
Fischer: "Witnesses Overlooked In JFK Probe," *Dallas Morning News,* Dec. 19, 1978.
Belin changed testimony: Craig, p. 27.

481 Mercer: Shaw, p. 26; Garrison, *On the Trail of the Assassins,* p. 218.
Willis: "JFK Killing Witness Not Surprised Tests Indicate 2nd Gunman," *Fort Worth Star-Telegram,* Dec. 22, 1978.
Pipes: Ibid.
Breneman: author's interview, fall, 1978.

482 Yarborough: Shaw, p. 186; author's telephone interview, summer, 1986.

483 Hill: author's interviews, summer, 1986, and spring, 1988.

489 "reprehensible actions": Meagher (Vintage), p. xxiv.
Warren Report: Ibid., p. xxviii.

490 Questioning legitimate: Szulc, p. 9.
Senate Intelligence Committee: Report of Senate Select Committee to Study Government Operations with Respect to Intelligence Activities Report, 1976, pp. 6–7.

491 Schweiker: "Warren Report Held Unbelievable," *Fort Worth Star-Telegram,* June 24, 1976; NOTE: Senator Schweiker stated, "In short, the non-disclosures and investigative failures—intentional and otherwise (by the FBI and CIA)—documented in this (Senate Intelligence) report establish that the Warren Commission was deprived of such vital pieces

that there is no longer any reason to have faith in its picture of the
Kennedy assassination.''

The Garrison Investigation

495 Martin: Garrison, *On the Trail of the Assassins,* pp. 29–32.
Impressed with FBI: Ibid., p. 10.
Ferrie: Ibid., p. 6.

496 Ferrie released: Eric Norden interview, *Playboy,* October, 1967, p. 74.
''43 years old'': Garrison, *On the Trail of the Assassins,* p. 11.
Military engaged: Ibid., p. 12.

497 Lofty credentials: Ibid., pp. 14–15.
''Banister apparatus'': Ibid., p. 40.

498 Shaw background: *Who's Who in the South and Southwest,* 8th edition,
Chicago, Marquis—Who's Who, 1963 p. 755.
Permindex: Garrison, *On the Trail of the Assassins,* pp. 87–90;
Konstandinos Kalimtgis, David Goldman and Jeffery Steinberg, *Dope,
Inc.: Britain's Opium War Against the U.S.,* New York, The New
Benjamin Franklin House Publishing Co., 1978, pp. 301–320 and 321–329;
''Permindex: Britain's International Assassination Bureau,'' *Executive
Intelligence Review,* Nov. 14, 1981, pp. 5–23.

500 Shaw and CIA: Garrison, *On the Trail of the Assassins,* p. 90.

502 Operated secretly: Ibid., p. 130.
''I'm a dead man'': Ibid., p. 138.

505 Free press reappraised: Ibid., p. 161.
''Unusual steps'': Norden, p. 62.

506 Roselli meeting denied: Garrison letter to John Judge, Feb. 25, 1986;
Garrison reiterated this denial to author in fall, 1989.
CBS interview: Garrison, *On the Trail of the Assassins,* p. 172.

507 Propaganda blitzkrieg: Norden, p. 62.
Cardinal Cushing, Fensterwald, p. 461.
Hoffa: Ibid., p. 464.
Robert Kennedy: Arthur M. Schlesinger, Jr., *Robert Kennedy and His
Times,* New York, Ballantine Books, 1979, p. 665.

508 Novel note: Fensterwald, p. 456; Garrison, *On the Trail of the Assassins,*
p. 181.
Jurors agree on conspiracy: Garrison, *On the Trail of the Assassins,* p. 251.

510 ''dramatic finale'': ''Garrison Seeks High Court Help,'' *Fort Worth
Star-Telegram,* Feb. 20, 1969.
Garrison charges perjury: Garrison, pp. 252–253.

511 Federal judical system: Ibid., p. 253.
Shaw's death: Ibid., p. 274.

512 Garrison acquitted: ''Jury Acquits DA Garrison in Bribe Case,'' *Fort
Worth Star-Telegram,* Sept. 28, 1973. Upon his acquittal, Garrison commented, ''(The jury) recognized a government attempt to accomplish
retribution against an individual who has frequently criticized the federal
government.''

Garrison case "a fraud": Blakey and Billings, p. 46.
Blakey and agencies: Ibid., p. 401.
513 "extravagant charges": Schiem, p. 57.
Garrison's "purpose": Ibid., p. 59.
CIA disinformation: Garrison letter to researcher John P. Judge, Feb. 25, 1986.
514 "ambitious man": Norden, p. 68.
Garrison's outline of assassination: Norden, p. 74, 156–159.
515 Garrison on "right track": Blakey, p. 170.

The House Select Committee on Assassinations

518 Gonzalez: "Proceedings and Debates of the 94th Congress, First Session," *Congressional Record*, Vol. 121, No. 24 (Washington: 1975).
Criticism: Rep. Henry B. Gonzalez, "Assassinations and Lingering Doubts," *Witan*, Vol. 2, No. 8 (St. Mary's of Texas School of Law: 1975), pp. 7–8.
519 Downing: Remarks to U.S. House of Representatives, March 18, 1976.
520 Fensterwald: "Assassination Inquiry Stumbling—Is Fensterwald a CIA Plant?," *Washington Star*, Oct. 4, 1976.
521 Sprague and Specter: Groden and Livingston, p. 315.
Sprague and Gonzalez: Ibid., p. 317.
"strong investigation": Gaeton Fonzi, "Who Killed JFK?," *The Washingtonian*, November, 1980, 197.
Proposed budget: Ibid., p. 200.
Sprague: Ibid., p. 197.
522 Gonzalez: Ibid., p. 200.
Fonzi: Ibid.
523 "Gonzalez went beserk": Ibid.
Gonzalez: Ibid., p. 201.
524 Fonzi: Ibid., p. 203.
"no more news conferences": "JFK-King Panel Seeks Seclusion," *Fort Worth Star-Telegram*, June 21, 1977.
525 Blakey's contacts: Jerry Policoff and William Scott Malone, "A Great Show, A Lousy Investigation," *New Times*, Sept. 4, 1978, p. 6.
Secrecy agreement: author is grateful to researcher Richard E. Sprague for providing a copy of his secrecy agreement with the HSCA.
526 Blakey: "The Final Assassinations Report," p. xxxii.
527 Sprague: Policoff and Malone, p. 8.
Blakey: Jerry Policoff, "Investigations That Were Bound to Fail," *Gallery*, Special Report, July, 1979, p. 62–6.
528 Policoff and Malone, p. 12.
529 Blakey: "The Final Assasinations Report," pp. xxxvi–xxxvii.
AIB comment: "The JFK Hearings: A Preliminary Critique," *Clandestine America*, Newsletter of the Assassination Information Bureau, Vol. 2, No. 4, p. 1.

530 O'Reilly: Notes from interview with *Dallas Morning News* Reporter Earl Golz, January, 1982.
Fonzi: Ibid.
Fenton: Ibid.

531 Mack: "7 Shots Believed Fired at Kennedy," *Fort Worth Star-Telegram*, Sept. 1, 1977.

533 McLain: "Officer Says JFK Tape Not His," *Fort Worth Star-Telegram*, Jan. 5, 1979.

534 Ramsey: "Study To Belittle Assassination Data," *Dallas Morning News*, July 9, 1981.
HSCA reactions: "House Panel Claims Plots Likely in JFK, King Slayings," *Fort Worth Star-Telegram*, Dec. 31, 1978.

535 Groden: "JFK Panel Photo Expert Alleges Cover-Up," *Fort Worth Star-Telegram*, May 16, 1979.
Medical testimony: Harrison E. Livingstone, "Parkland Doctors' Testimony Shows Autopsy Photos Forged," *The Baltimore Chronicle*, July 30, 1979. (Reprinted in Penn Jones' *The Continuing Inquiry*, Oct. 22, 1980, pp. 5–6); "Dispute on JFK Assassination Evidence Persists," *Boston Sunday Globe*, June 21, 1981.

536 Groden: *Star-Telegram*, May 16, 1979, op. cit.
Kantor: author's interview, October, 1978.
Groden: author's interview, summer, 1986.
Blakey: "The Final Assassinations Report," p. XXXVIII.

537 Justice Dept. memo: "Papers Reveal Justice Ended Kennedy, King Death Probes," *Dallas Times Herald*, Sept. 4, 1988.

Was Oswald Really Oswald?

539 Passport Office message: HSCA III.573.
July 11, 1961, message: XVIII.374.

540 Deslatte: Summers, pp. 407–408.

541 Intelligence Committee: Fensterwald, pp. 404–405.
Dannelly: Fensterwald, pp. 393–394.
Hutchinson: WC Report, PP. 308–309.

542 Bogard: X.353.
WC conclusion: WC Report, p. 321.
Wilson: "Salesman Insists FBI Discounted Facts on Oswald," *Dallas Morning News*, May 8, 1977.

543 Hamblen: WC Report, pp. 309–310; Summers, p. 402; XI.312.
Fenley: XI.318.

544 Morgan's Gunshop: XXIV.704.
British reporter: Summers, pp. 403–404.
Ryder: WC Report, pp. 315–316; XXIV.328–329.

545 Sports Drome Rifle Range: WC Report, pp. 318–319.
WC conclusion: Ibid., p. 319.
Penn: Summers, pp. 405–406.

546 "no substantial basis": WC Report, p. 318.

547 Oswald's letter: XVI.33; (handwritten draft) XVI.443.
548 Norton: "Oswald Grave Now Battle Site," *Fort Worth Star-Telegram,* Oct. 19, 1979.
   Slawson: "Author Not the First to Ask Exhumation," *Fort Worth Star-Telegram,* Jan. 11, 1979.
   Groody: author's interview, November, 1988.
   Marguerite Oswald: "Oswald's Mother Asks Exhumation," *Fort Worth Star-Telegram,* Nov. 17, 1967.
549 Robert Oswald: I.330.
   Pic: XI.56.
551 Groody: author's interview, 1988.
552 "saw cut": Linda E. Norton, James A. Cottone, Irvin M. Sopher, and Vincent J. M. DiMaio, "The Exhumation and Identification of Lee Harvey Oswald," *Journal of Forensic Sciences,* Vol. 29, No. 1, January, 1984, p. 25.

Convenient Deaths

555 Whitaker: HSCA IV.464–465.
556 Hess: HSCA IV.467.
   CIA memo: CIA Memo to "Chiefs, Certain Stations and Bases" entitled, "Countering Criticism of the Warren Report, April 1, 1967," Document No. 1035-960.
557 Disguised murders: Philip H. Melanson, "High Tech Mysterious Deaths," *Critique,* Vol. IV, No. 3, 4, Fall/Winter 1984-85, p. 214.
   Beryllium: Ibid., p. 215.
564 Sullivan: Jeff Goldberg and Harvey Yazijian, "The Death of 'Crazy Billy' Sullivan," *New Times,* July 24, 1978, pp. 4–8.
   FBI deaths: "Ex-Agent 6th to Die in Six-month Span," *Fort Worth Star-Telegram,* Nov. 10, 1977.

Conclusions

576 Kearns: Jerry Policoff, "The Media and the Murder of John Kennedy," *New Times,* August 8, 1975, p. 31.
   "unaided assassin": "Ruby Murder Trial Postponed," *Dallas Times Herald,* Dec. 3, 1963.
577 "slanted propaganda": Policoff, p. 30.
   "biased offerings": Meagher, p. 459.
   Donovan: Policoff, pp. 35–36.
578 "mob of reporters": Robert Oswald, *Lee,* p. 23.
579 Press choices: Policoff, p. 36.
582 "No one has to direct an assassination": L. Fletcher Prouty, "An Introduction to the Assassination Business," *Gallery,* September, 1975, pp. 86–87.
589 RFK quote: Davis, *The Kennedys,* p. 603.

Selected Bibliography

Abel, Elie, *The Missiles of October*, London, MacGibbon & Kee, 1969. [QP]

Agee, Philip, *Inside the Company: CIA Diary*, New York, Bantam Books, 1976. [QP]

Alleged Assassination Plots Involving Foreign Leaders, Interim Report of the Select Committee to Study Governmental Operations, with Respect to Intelligence Activities, U.S. Senate, Washington, D.C., U.S. Government Printing Office, 1975. [QP]

Anson, Robert Sam, *They've Killed the President*, New York, Bantam Books, 1975. [QP]

Associated Press, Editors, *The Torch Is Passed: The Associated Press Story of the Death of a President*, New York, Associated Press, 1963. [QP]

Ayers, Bradley Earl, *The War That Never Was*, New York, Bobbs-Merrill, 1976. [QP]

Bain, Donald, *The Control of Candy Jones*, Chicago, Playboy Press, 1976. [QP]

Baker, Bobby, with Larry L. King, *Wheeling and Dealing: Confessions of a Capitol Hill Operator*, New York, W. W. Norton & Company, 1978. [QP]

Belin, David W., *November 22, 1963: You Are the Jury*, New York, Quadrangle Books, 1973. [QP]

Belli, Melvin, with Maurice Carroll, *Dallas Justice*, New York, David McKay, 1964. [QP]

Bishop, Jim, *The Day Kennedy Was Shot*, New York, Funk & Wagnalls, 1968. [QP]

Blair, John M., *The Control of Oil*, New York, Pantheon Books, 1976. [QP]

Blakey, G. Robert, and Richard N. Billings, *The Plot to Kill the President*, New York, New York Times Books, 1981. [QP]

Blumenthal, Sid, with Harvey Yazijian, *Government by Gunplay: Assassination Conspiracy Theories from Dallas to Today*, New York, Signet, 1976. [QP]

Bowart, Walter, *Operation Mind Control*, New York, Delacorte, 1977. [QP]

Brill, Steven, *The Teamsters*, New York, Simon and Schuster, 1978.

Bruno, Jerry and Jeff Greenfield, *The Advance Man*, New York, William Morrow and Company, 1971.

Buchanan, Thomas G., *Who Killed Kennedy?* New York, G. P. Putnam's Sons, 1964.

Canfield, Michael, with Alan J. Weberman, *Coup d'Etat in America: The CIA and the Assassination of John F. Kennedy*, New York, Third Press, 1975.

Curry, Jesse, *JFK Assassination File: Retired Dallas Police Chief Jesse Curry Reveals His Personal File*, American Poster and Publishing Co., 1969.

Cutler, Robert B., *The Flight of CE-399: Evidence of Conspiracy*, Beverly, Mass., Cutler Designs, 1970.

Davis, John H., *The Kennedys—Dynasty and Disaster 1848–1984*, New York, McGraw-Hill, 1984.

Demaris, Ovid, *The Last Mafioso: "Jimmy the Weasel" Fratianno*, New York, Bantam Books, 1981.

Denson, R. B., *Destiny in Dallas*, Dallas, Denco Corporation, 1964.

Dulles, Allen, *The Craft of Intelligence*, New York, Harper & Row, 1963.

Eddowes, Michael, *Khrushchev Killed Kennedy*, Dallas, self-published, 1975.

————, *The Oswald File*, New York, Clarkson N. Potter, 1977.

Eisenberg, Dennis, Uri Dan, and Eli Landau, *Meyer Lansky, Mogul of the Mob*, New York, Paddington Press, 1979.

Epstein, Edward J., *Counterplot*, New York, Viking Books, 1969.

————, *Inquest: The Warren Commission and the Establishment of Truth*, New York, Bantam Books, 1966.

————, *Legend: The Secret World of Lee Harvey Oswald*, New York, McGraw-Hill, 1978.

Exner, Judith, as told to Ovid Demaris, *My Story*, New York, Grove Press, 1977.

Fensterwald, Bernard Jr., with Michael Ewing. *Coincidence or Conspiracy?* (for the Committee to Investigate Assassinations), New York, Zebra Books, 1977.

Flammonde, Paris, *The Kennedy Conspiracy: an Uncommissioned Report on the Jim Garrison Investigation*, New York, Meridith, 1969.

Ford, Gerald R., with John R. Stiles, *Portrait of the Assassin*, New York, Simon & Schuster, 1965.

Fox, Sylvan, *The Unanswered Questions About President Kennedy's Assassination*, New York, Award Books, 1965 and 1975.

Gandolfo, Ted, *The House Select Committee on Assassinations Coverup*, Self-published by author, 1987.

Garrison, Jim, *A Heritage of Stone*, New York, G. P. Putnam's Sons, 1970; Berkeley, 1972.

————, *On the Trail of the Assassins*, New York, Sheridan Square Press, 1988.

Giancana, Antoinette, *Mafia Princess—Growing up in Sam Giancana's Family*, New York, William Morrow & Company, 1984.

Gosch, Martin A., and Richard Hammer, *The Last Testament of Lucky Luciano*, New York, Dell Publishing Co., 1976.

Groden, Robert J., and Harrison Edward Livingstone, *High Treason*, Baltimore, The Conservatory Press, 1989.

Hammer, Richard, *Playboy's Illustrated History of Organized Crime*, Chicago, Playboy Press, 1975.

Hanna, David, *The Lucky Luciano Inheritance*, New York, Belmont Tower Books, 1975.

Hepburn, James (pseud.), *Farewell America*, Liechtenstein, Frontiers Publishing Co., 1968.

Hoffa, James R., as told to Oscar Fraley, *Hoffa—The Real Story*, New York, Stein and Day, 1976.

Hougan, Jim, *Spooks*, New York, William Morrow & Company, 1978.

Hunter, Diana, with Alice Anderson, *Jack Ruby's Girls*, Atlanta, Hallux Inc., 1970.

Hurt, Henry, *Reasonable Doubt*, New York, Holt, Rinehart and Winston, 1985.

Investigation of the Assassination of President John F. Kennedy, Book V, Final Report of the Select Committee to Study Governmental Operations, with Respect to Intelligence Activities. U.S. Senate, 1976.

Joesten, Joachim, *Oswald, Assassin or Fall-guy?* New York, Marzani and Munsell, 1964.

Johnson, Haynes, *Bay of Pigs*, New York, Norton, 1964.

Johnson, Lyndon Baines, *The Vantage Point: Perspectives of the Presidency, 1963–1969*, New York, Holt, Rinehart & Winston, 1971.

Jones, Penn, *The Continuing Inquiry* and *Forgive My Grief* (Vols. I–IV), Midlothian, The Midlothian Press, 1978.

Kalimtgis, Konstandinos, David Goldman, and Jeffery Steinberg, *Dope, Inc.—Britain's Opium War Against the U.S.*, New York, New Benjamin Franklin House, 1978.

Kantor, Seth, *Who Was Jack Ruby?*, New York, Everest House, 1978.

Kennedy, Robert F., *The Enemy Within*, New York, Harper & Row, 1960.

Kirkpatrick, Lyman B., *The Real CIA*, New York, Macmillan, 1968.

Kirkwood, James, *American Grotesque: An Account of the Clay Shaw–Jim Garrison Affair in New Orleans*, New York, Simon & Schuster, 1970.

Kruger, Henrik, *The Great Heroin Coup: Drugs, Intelligence & International Fascism*, Boston, South End Press, 1980.

Kwitny, Jonathan, *Vicious Circles: The Mafia in The Marketplace*, New York, W. W. Norton & Company, 1979.

Lane, Mark, *Rush to Judgement*, New York, Holt, Rinehart & Winston, 1966.

————, *A Citizen's Dissent*, New York, Dell, 1975.

Lasky, Victor, *It Didn't Start with Watergate*, New York, Dell, 1978.

Lawrence, Lincoln (pseud.), *Were We Controlled?* New Hyde Park, New York, University Books, 1967.

Leek, Sybil, and Bert R. Sugar, *The Assassination Chain,* New York, Corwin Books, 1976.

Lifton, David S., *Best Evidence: Disguise and Deception in the Assassination of John F. Kennedy,* New York, Macmillan Publishing Co., 1980.

Lowenthal, Max, *The Federal Bureau of Investigation,* New York, William Sloan Associates, 1950.

McDonald, Hugh C., as told to Geoffrey Bocca, *Appointment in Dallas: The Final Solution to the Assassination of JFK,* New York, Zebra Books, 1975.

McDonald, Hugh, with Robin Moore, *L.B.J. and the J.F.K. Conspiracy,* Westport, Conn., Condor, 1978.

McKinley, James, *Assassination in America,* New York, Harper & Row, 1977.

McMillan, Priscilla Johnson, *Marina and Lee,* New York, Harper & Row, 1978.

Maas, Peter, *The Valachi Papers,* New York, Bantam Books, 1968.

Maclear, Michael, *The Ten Thousand Day War: Vietnam: 1945–1975,* New York, Avon Books, 1981.

Manchester, William, *The Death of a President: November 20–25, 1963,* New York, Harper & Row, 1967; Popular Library, 1968.

Marchetti, Victor, and John Marks, *The CIA and the Cult of Intelligence,* New York, Alfred A. Knopf, 1974; Dell, 1975.

Marks, John, *The Search for the "Manchurian Candidate": The CIA and Mind Control,* New York, New York Times Books, 1979.

Meager, Sylvia, *Accessories after the Fact: The Warren Commission, the Authorities, and the Report,* New York, Bobbs-Merrill, 1967; Vintage, 1976.

—————, *Subject Index to the Warren Report and Hearings and Exhibits,* New York, Scarecrow Press, 1966.

Melman, Seymour, *The Permanent War Economy,* New York, Simon and Schuster, 1974.

Messick, Hank, and Burt Goldblatt, *The Mobs and the Mafia,* New York, Ballantine, 1973.

Miller, Tom, *The Assassination Please Almanac,* Chicago, Henry Regnery Co., 1977.

Mills, James, *The Underground Empire: Where Crime and Governments Embrace,* New York, Dell Publishing Co., 1987.

Model, Peter, with Robert J. Groden, *JFK: The Case for Conspiracy,* New York, Manor Books, 1976.

Moldea, Dan E., *The Hoffa Wars,* New York and London, Paddington Press, 1978.

Mooney, Booth, *LBJ: An Irreverent Chronicle,* New York, Thomas Y. Crowell Company, 1976.

Morrow, Robert D., *Betrayal: A Reconstruction of Certain Clandestine Events from the Bay of Pigs to the Assassination of John F. Kennedy,* Chicago, Henry Regnery Co., 1976.

Mosley, Leonard, *Dulles: A Biography of Eleanor, Allen and John Foster Dulles and Their Family Network,* New York, The Dial Press, 1978.

Newlon, Clarke, *L.B.J.: The Man from Johnson City,* New York, Dodd, Mead & Company, 1964.

New York Times, The Pentagon Papers, June 13, 14, 15, & July 1, 1971.

Noyes, Peter, *Legacy of Doubt,* New York, Pinnacle Books, 1973.

O'Donnell, Kenneth P., David F. Powers, and Joe McCarthy, *"Johnny, We Hardly Knew Ye": Memories of John Fitzgerald Kennedy,* Boston, Little, Brown & Company, 1972.

Oglesby, Carl, *The Yankee and Cowboy War,* Mission, Kansas, Sheed, Andrews and McMeel, 1976.

Oswald, Robert L., with Myrick and Barbara Land, *Lee: A Portrait of Lee Harvey Oswald,* New York, Coward-McCann, 1967.

O'Toole, George, *The Assassination Tapes: An Electronic Probe into the Murder of John F. Kennedy and the Dallas Cover-up,* New York, Penthouse Press, 1975.

Phillips, David, *The Night Watch,* New York, Atheneum, 1977.

Pollack, Jack Harrison, *Earl Warren: The Judge Who Changed America,* Englewood Cliffs, N.J., Prentice-Hall, 1979.

Popkin, Richard H., *The Second Oswald*, New York, Avon Books, 1966.

Powers, Gary, with Curt Gentry, *Operation Overflight*, New York, Holt, Rinehart & Winston, 1970; London: Hodder & Stoughton, 1970.

Powers, Richard G., *Secrecy and Power: The Life of J. Edgar Hoover*, New York, Free Press, 1988.

Powers, Thomas, *The Man Who Kept the Secrets: Richard Helms and the CIA*, New York, Alfred A. Knopf, 1979.

Prouty, L. Fletcher, *The Secret Team*, Englewood Cliffs, New Jersey, Prentice-Hall, 1973.

Rather, Dan with Mickey Herskowitz, *The Camera Never Blinks: Adventures of a TV Journalist*, New York, William Morrow, 1977.

Reid, Ed, *The Grim Reapers*, Chicago, Henry Regnery Co., 1969; New York, Bantam, 1969.

Reid, Ed, and Ovid Demaris, *The Green Felt Jungle*, New York, Trident Press, 1963.

Report of the President's Commission on the Assassination of President John F. Kennedy, and twenty-six accompanying volumes of Hearings and Exhibits, 1964; published by U.S. Government Printing Office and also Doubleday, McGraw-Hill, Bantam, Popular Library, and Associated Press, 1964.

Report of the Select Committee on Assassinations, U.S. House of Representatives, and twelve accompanying volumes of Hearings and Appendices (on Kennedy case as opposed to Martin Luther King assassination), 1979, published by U.S. Government Printing Office; and *Report* (only) by Bantam, New York, 1979, under title *The Final Assassinations Report*.

Roffman, Howard, *Presumed Guilty*, Cranbury, N.J., Fairleigh Dickinson Press, 1975; London, Thomas Yoseloff, 1976; New York, A.S. Barnes & Co., 1976.

Sale, Kirkpatrick, *Power Shift: The Rise of the Southern Rim and Its Challenge to the Eastern Establishment*, New York, Random House, 1975.

Sampson, Anthony, *The Arms Bazaar: From Lebanon to Lockheed*, New York, Bantam Books, 1978.

Sauvage, Leo, *The Oswald Affair: An Examination of the Contradictions and Omissions of the Warren Report*, Cleveland, World Publishing, Co., 1966.

Scheim, David E., *Contract on America—The Mafia Murders of John and Robert Kennedy*, Silver Spring, MD, Argyle Press, 1983.

Schlesinger, Arthur, *A Thousand Days: John F. Kennedy in the White House*, Boston, Houghton Mifflin Co., 1965.

——————, *Robert Kennedy and His Times*, Boston, Houghton Mifflin Co., 1978.

Scott, Peter Dale, with Paul Hoch and Russell Stetler, *The Assassinations: Dallas and Beyond: A Guide to Cover-ups and Investigations*, New York, Random House, Vintage Press, 1976.

Scott, Peter Dale, *Crime and Cover-up: the CIA, the Mafia, and the Dallas-Watergate Connection*, Berkeley, Cal., Westworks, 1977.

Shaw, J. Gary, and Larry R. Harris, *Cover-up: The Governmental Conspiracy to Conceal the Facts about the Public Execution of John Kennedy*, Cleburne, Tex., 1976.

Sheridan, Walter, *The Fall and Rise of Jimmy Hoffa*, New York, Saturday Review Press, 1973.

Sorensen, Theodore, *The Kennedy Legacy*, New York, New American Library, 1970.

Sprague, Richard E., *The Taking of America 1-2-3*, Self-published by author, 1976.

Stafford, Jean, *A Mother in History: Mrs. Marguerite Oswald*, New York, Farrar, Straus & Giroux, 1966; Bantam, 1966.

Summers, Anthony, *Conspiracy*, McGraw-Hill Book Co., 1980.

Talese, Gay, *Honor Thy Father*, Cleveland and New York, World Publishing Co., 1971.

Teresa, Vincent, with Thomas C. Renner, *My Life in the Mafia*, London, Hart-Davis, McGibbon, 1973; Panther, 1974.

Texas Supplemental Report on the Assassination of President John F. Kennedy and the Serious Wounding of Governor John B. Connally, November 22, 1963, by Texas Attorney General Waggoner Carr, Austin, Tex., 1964.

Thompson, Josiah, *Six Seconds in Dallas: A Microstudy of the Kennedy Assassination*, New York, Bernard Geis Associates, 1967; (rev.) Berkeley, 1976.

Thornley, Kerry, *Oswald*, Chicago, New Classics House, 1965.

United Press International and *American Heritage* magazine, *Four Days*, New York, American Heritage Publishing Company, 1964.

Wallechinsky, David and Irving Wallace, *The People's Almanac*, Garden City, New York, Doubleday & Company, 1975.

——————, *The People's Almanac #2*, New York, Bantam Books, 1978.

——————, *The People's Almanac #3*, New York, Bantam Books, 1981.

Watters, Pat, and Stephen Gillers, eds., *Investigating the FBI*, Garden City, N.Y., Doubleday & Company, 1973.

Weisberg, Harold, *Oswald in New Orleans: Case for Conspiracy with the CIA*, New York, Canyon Books, 1967.

——————, *Post-Mortem*, Frederick, Maryland, 1975, self-published, available from author.

——————, *Whitewash* (Vols. I–IV), Hyattstown, Maryland, 1965, 1967, self-published; and (Vols. I & II) New York, Dell, 1966–67.

White, Theodore, *The Making of the President*, New York, Atheneum, 1965.

Whitehead, Don, *The FBI Story*, New York, Pocket Books—Cardinal Giant, 1958.

Wills, Gary, and Ovid Demaris, *Jack Ruby: The Man Who Killed the Man Who Killed Kennedy*, New York, New American Library, 1967; New American Library, 1968.

Wise, David, and Thomas B. Ross, *The Invisible Government*, New York, Random House, 1964.

——————, *The Espionage Establishment*, New York, Random House, 1967.

Wyden, Peter, *Bay of Pigs: The Untold Story*, New York, Simon and Schuster, 1979.

Zinn, Howard, *A People's History of the United States*, New York, Harper & Row, 1980.

Index

Accessories After the Fact (Meagher), 489–490

Adams, Victoria (witness), 44, 53, 325

Alpha 66 (anti-Castro Cubans), connection with Oswald, 149–154

Altgens, James (Associate Press photographer and witness), 33–34, 45–46, 55

Alyea, Tom, 437–438

Angleton, James Jesus (CIA chief of counterintelligence), and Nosenko (Soviet defector), 130–134

Anti-Castro movement. See Cuba

Arce, Danny G. (witness), 27

Arnold, Carolyn (witness), 49

Arnold, Gordon (witness), 78–79, 320

Assassination,
  aftermath in Dallas, 313–325
  evidence, 435–459

Assassination theories,
  French connection, 202–209
  Garrison investigation, 494–515
  "one gunman" or more, 530–538
  Russian link, 130–134
  single-bullet theory, 485–492
  Triple Underpass theory, 55–64
  of "umbrella man," 30–35

Atkins, Thomas (witness), 16–17

Austin, Emory (witness), 341

Autopsy of Kennedy, 368–373

"Babushka Lady," Beverly Oliver (witness), 36–39, 189

"Badge Man," evidence of uniformed officer, 79–81

Baker, Marrion L. (motorcycle policeman), 14, 50–51

Baker, Mrs. Donald (witness), 27

Baker, Mrs. Donald (witness). See also Rachley, Virgie

Banister, Guy (former FBI agent), 99–100, 235–237, 494, 499

Bay of Pigs Invasion, 5, 31, 138–147

Balknap, Jerry B. (seizure victim), 42–43

Belli, Melvin, *Dallas Justice,* 414

Bennett, Glen (Special Agent), 14

Best Evidence (Lifton), 373–378

Betrayal (Morrow), 201

Betzner, Hugh W., Jr. (witness), 23–24, 73

"Black Dog Man," 72–79

Blakey, G. Robert,
  as chief counsel and director for House Select Committee on Assassinations, 524–530
  The Plot to Kill the President, 335, 512

Bowers, Lee (witness), 75–78, 82, 332

Braden, Jim (Mafia courier), 337–340

Brading, Eugene Hale. See Braden, Jim

Brehm, Charles (witness), 34

Brennan, Howard Leslie (witness), 25–27, 319

Bronson, Charles L. (witness), 21–22

Browder, Edward (gun runner), 284

Brown, Earle (Dallas policeman), 59–60

Bucknell, David (Marine buddy of Oswald), 104

The Bureau (Sullivan), 217

Cabell, Mrs. Earle, testimony to Warren Commission, 16

Calloway, Ted (witness), 341

Calvery, Gloria (witness), 28, 46

The Camera Never Blinks (Rather), 68

Campbell, O.V. (Texas Book Depository Vice President), 27

Carr, Richard Randolph (witness), 21, 318–319

Castro, Fidel,
  anti-Castro movement in United States, 147–154
  Bay of Pigs Invasion, 138–147
  involvement in Kennedy assassination, 154

Castro, Fidel (continued)
    personal biography, 136–138
The Cellar (nightspot in Fort Worth), 15,
    246–251
Central Intelligence Agency. See CIA
Chaney, James (motorcycle officer), 14
Cheramie, Rose (Melba Christine
    Marcades), 401–402
Chism, John A. (witness), 29
CIA (Central Intelligence Agency),
    and anti-Castro Cubans, 149–154
    and the Bay of Pigs Invasion, 138–147
    CIA-backed Cuban Revolutionary
        Council, 235–240
    Document No. 632–796, 202–203
    history of, 181–184
    Item 450, 69
    and Mafia death plots, 187–188
    and mind control experiments, 184–187
    and Nosenko (Soviet defector), 130–134
    Oswald as agent, 104–105
    Zapruder film, 69
    ZR-RIFLE project, 205–207
Civil Air Patrol (CAP), and Oswald, 99
Clemmons, Acquila (witness), 319, 342
"Coke" issue, as anti-Oswald evidence,
    52
Connally, John (Governor), 6, 8
    at Parkland Hospital, 362–365
    in motorcade, 9
    testimony to Warren Commission, 12–13
Connally, Mrs., in motorcade, 11–13
Conservatives, in Dallas politics, 1
Conspiracy theories. See Assassination
    theories
Craig, Roger D. (deputy sheriff and
    witness), 20, 328–333
Cuba,
    anti-Castro movement in United States,
        147–154
    Banister and anti-Castro Cubans, 100
    Bay of Pigs, 138–147
    CIA-backed Cuban Revolutionary
        Council, 235–240
    and CIA-Mafia death plots, 187–188
    Fidel Castro, 136–138
    history of, 135
    and Jack Ruby, 391–401
    and organized crime, 168–171
    Shaw's "umbrella man" theory, 31
Curry, Jesse (Dallas Police Chief), 14, 47, 324
    after assassination, 361–362
    and man in doorway, 46
    in motorcade, 9

Cutler, Robert, "umbrella man" theory,
    30–31

Dallas,
    aftermath of assassination, 313–325
    Kennedy's trip, 6–8
    police radio recording, 530–537
    political climate, 1
Dallas Justice (Belli), 414
The Dallas Morning News,
    day of assassination, 7–8
    and Robert Groden, 22
Dallas Times Herald, day of assassination,
    7, 339
Davis, Barbara (witness), 346
Dealey Plaza, 10–11, 14–17
Decker, J.E. "Bill" (Dallas County
    Sheriff), in motorcade, 9, 14
Delgado, Nelson, 102, 109
DeMohrenschildt, George, 278–289
    relationship with CIA, 199–202
DeMohrenschildt, Jeanne, 122–123,
    278–289
The Depository. See Texas School Book
    Depository
Dillard, Tom, 53
Dodd, Richard C. (witness), 58–59
Dorman, Elsie, 44
Dougherty, Jack, 42
Downing, Thomas N. (Representative),
    and formation of House Select
    Committee on Assassinations,
    518–524
Duran, Silvia, arrest of, 193–195

Edward, Robert E., 23
The Enemy Within (Robert Kennedy), 383
Euins, Amos Lee (witness), 26

FBI. See Federal Bureau of Investigation
    (FBI)
Federal Bureau of Investigation (FBI),
    211–251
    Commission Document 1245, 24–43
    history of, 211–213
    and Julia Ann Mercer, 18–19
    manipulation of assassination investiga-
        tion, 238–240
    and Oswald, 226–235, 472–477
    search for Oswald in 1959, 123–124
    and Tague testimony, 62–63
    and witness Ed Hoffman, 81–86
Ferrie, David W., 99–100, 188–189, 338,
    494–496, 501–503

Firtz, Will (Dallas Police Captain),
    testimony to Warren Commission,
    314
Fischer, Ronald B., 23
Foster, J. W., and Triple Underpass,
    55–56
Frazier, Wesley, 40–42, 44–45
French connection, to Kennedy assassina-
    tion, 202–209

Garner, Dorothy Ann (witness), 44
Garrison, Earling Carothers (Jim) (New
    Orleans District Attorney), 494–498
    conspiracy theory of, 68
    A Heritage of Stone, 230–231
Garrison, Earling Carothers (Jim) (New
    Orleans District Attorney). See
    also Garrison investigation
Garrison investigation, 494–498
Giancana, Sam (Momo Salvatore
    Guingano), and organized crime,
    175–179
Gill, C. Wray, 100
Golovachev, Pavel (Oswald's friend in
    Russia), 122
Gonzalez, Henry (Congressman), formation
    of House Select Committee on
    Assassinations, 518–524
Grassy knoll, 18, 20–24, 31, 35, 56–64,
    435
    and Ed Hoffman, 81–86
    and Gordon Arnold, 78–79
    Holland's eyewitness report, 56–57
    and one-gunman theory, 202–203
Greer, William (Secret Service agent), in
    motorcade, 9, 12
Groden, Robert, on Bronson film, 22

Hardie, Julius (witness), 19
Hargis, Officer Bobby W., 73–74
    in motorcade, 15
Harkness, Officer D. V., 42, 320
Harrelson, Charles V. (convicted Texas
    hitman), 85, 333–337
Hartman, Wayne and Edna (witnesses),
    315–316
Hathaway, Phillip B. (witness), 17
Haygood, Clyde A., 60–61
Henderson, Ruby (witness), 21
A Heritage of Stone (Garrison), 230–231
Hickey, George W., Jr. (agent), 83
Hill, Clint (agent), 13, 15
Hill, Gerald (Dallas police sergeant), 342
Hill, Jean (witness), 37–39, 56, 322–324

Hoffa, Jimmy, and organized crime,
    171–175
The Hoffa Wars (Moldea), 169
Hoffman, Ed (witness), 81–86
Holland, Sam M. (witness), 56–59,
    320–321
Hollingsworth, Bob, of Times Herald, 10
Hoover, John Edgar,
    Masters of Deceit, 216
    role in FBI, 213–226
House Select Committee on Assassinations,
    on Altgens photo, 46
    on ammunition used at assassination,
        447–450
    Bronson film, 22–23
    conspiracy theory, 91
    on Edward Browder, 284
    and G. Robert Blakey (chief counsel and
        director), 524–530
    on gunman issue, 202–203, 530–538
    history of, 518–537
    and Kennedy's wounds, 24–25
    and Milteer's assassination plot, 46
    and Moorman photograph, 79–81
    on Oswald murder, 414–429
    on Soviet government and Kennedy's
        assassination, 133–134
    on Tippit murder, 349
    on "umbrella man," 31–33
HSCA. See House Select Committee on
    Assassinations
Hudson, Emmett J. (witness), 71–73
Hughes, Robert (witness), 21
Hutton, Bill (Deputy Constable), 74

Jacks, Hurchel (Texas state trooper), 9
Jackson, C.D., and Zapruder film, 66–67
Japanese Communists, and Oswald, 103
Jarman, James, 47–49
John Birch Society, 1
Johnson, Clemon E. (witness), 58
Johnson, Lyndon B.,
    knowledge of conspiracy, 289–298
    in motorcade, 9
Johnson, Priscilla, Marina and Lee, 120

Kantor, Seth,
    testimony to Warren Commission, 366–367
    Who Was Jack Ruby?, 206–207
Kellerman, Roy, testimony to Warren
    Commission, 12
Kennedy, Jacqueline,
    in motorcade, 11–14
    request for Agent Hill, 15

Kennedy, John F.,
  autopsy of, 368–373
  Bay of Pigs invasion, 5, 138–147
  and fatal shots, 15
  and military, 301–305
  1960 Presidential election, 3–5
  and oilmen, 276–278
  personal biography, 1–8
  Portrait of a President, 145
  Profiles in Courage, 3
  and right-wing extremists, 253–298
  and Vietnam, 306–311
  Why England Slept, 2
Kennedy, Joseph P., 2–3
Kennedy, Robert,
  The Enemy Within, 383
  and organized crime, 171–179
Kounas, Dolores (witness), 33
Ku Klux Klan, 1

Landis, Paul (agent), 14
Lansky, Meyer, and organized crime in
  Cuba, 168–171
The Last Two Days (Atkins), 17
Lawrence, Jack, 339–340
Lawrence, John (witness), 17–18
Lawson, Winston G. (Special Agent), 11,
  13–14
Legacy of Doubt (Noyes), 337–338
Liebeler, Wesley (Warren Commission
  attorney), 27–28
Lifton, David,
  Best Evidence, 373–378
  on Zapruder film, 69
Lovelady, Billy (witness), 45–46, 53
Luciano, Lucky, 161–164
Lumpkin, G. L. (Dallas Deputy Police
  Chief), in motorcade, 9

Mabra, W.W. (county bailiff), 19–20
McGann, George, 36
McKinnon, Cheryl (witness), 71
McMillan, Priscilla. See Johnson, Priscilla
Mcwillie, Lewis J., and organized crime,
  393–401
Mafia,
  and CIA-Mafia death plots, 187–188
  and Cuba, 168–171
  history of, 156–180
  and Jack Ruby, 387–401
  and Jim Braden, 337–340
  and Prohibition, 157–161
  Scheim and Mafia-did-it theory, 513
  See also Organized crime

Mannlicher-Carcano rifle claim, 41–42, 47,
  201, 439
  and incriminating palm print, 443–450
Marcades, Melba Christine. See Cheramie
  Rose
Marcello, Carlos, and organized crime,
  164–167
Marina and Lee (Johnson), 120
Marines, and Oswald, 101–111
Markham, Helen (witness), 340–342,
  345–346
Martin, Officer B. J., 15
Masters of Deceit (Hoover), 216
Matthews, Russell Douglas, 36–37, 335
Meagher, Sylvia, *Accessories After the
  Fact,* 489–490
Mercer, Julia Ann (witness), 18–19,
  324–325
Meyers, Lawrence (friend of Jack Ruby),
  338
Military, relations with Kennedy, 301–311
Miller, Austin, 59
Millican, A. J. (witness), 28
Milteer, Joseph A., and Kennedy
  assassination plot, 265–267
Mobsters. See Organized crime
Moldea, Dan, *The Hoffa Wars,* 169
Molina, Joe R., 54
Mooneyham, Lillian (clerk of 95th District
  Court), 52–53
Moorman, Mary (witness), 37–38
  photograph by, 79–82, 324
Morrow, Robert D., *Betrayal,* 201
Motorcade, 9–17
Muchmore, Maria (witness), 35
Murphy, Thomas J. (witness), 58–59

Newman, Bill and family (witnesses),
  38–39, 70
Newman, Jean (witness), 29
Nix, Orville (witness), 35
Nixon, Richard M., and Kennedy
  assassination, 267–274
Norman, Harold, 47–49
Nosenko, Yuri (Soviet defector), 130–134
Noyes, Peter, *Legacy of Doubt,* 337–338

O'Donnell, Kenneth (witness), 436
Oliver, Beverly ("The Babuska Lady"),
  35–39, 189
Operation Overflight (Powers), 115
Organized crime,
  and Carlos Marcello, 164–167
  and Cuba, 168–171

Organized crime *(continued)*
  and Hoffa, 171–175
  and Kennedy assassination, 156–180
  Lansky in Cuba, 168–171
  and Lewis McWillie, 393–401
  and Lucky Luciano, 161–164
  and Prohibition, 157–161
  and Ruby, 387–391
  and Sam Giancana, 175–179
Oswald, Lee Harvey,
  Alpha 66 (anti-Castro Cubans), 149–154
  arrest of, 350–358
  at Depository, 14, 40–42
  and Civil Air Patrol (CAP), 99
  and "coke" issue, 52
  evidence against, 435–457
  and FBI, 226–235, 472–477
  identity prior to assassination, 539–553
  and Japanese Communists, 103
  and Mannlicher-Carcano rifle, 443–450
  and Marina, 40–41, 124–134
  in Marines, 101–111
  in Mexico City, 193–196
  in New Orleans, 144–149
  personal biography, 90–112
  and Ruby, 402–414
  in Russia, 92–93, 118–130
  shooting of, 414–429
  as spy, 189–196
  U-2 program and, 114–116
Oswald, Marguerite, 91–99
Oswald, Marina, 40–41, 124–134
Oswald, Robert, 96–99
Owens, Ernest Jay (witness), 18

Paine, Ruth, 40–41
Permindex, 515
Pic, John (Oswald's brother), 97
The Plot to Kill the President (Blakey),
  335, 512
Poe, J. M. (policeman), 343
Portrait of a President (Kennedy), 145
Potter, Nolan H. (witness), 58
Powell, James (agent), 53
Power, Francis Gary (CIA pilot), 114–115
  Operation Overflight, 115
Powers, David (witness), 15–16, 436
Presidental election of 1960, 3–5
Price, Jesse C. (witness), 39
Profiles in Courage (Kennedy), 3, 145
Prohibition, and organized crime, 157–161

Rachley, Virgie (Mrs. Donald Baker)
  (witness), 277

Randle, Linnie Mae, 40–41
Rather, Dan,
  The Camera Never Blinks, 68
  on Zapruder film, 68
Reid, Mrs. Robert A. (witness), 27, 51–52
Reynolds, Warren (witness), 342
Right-wing extremists, enemies of
  Kennedy, 253–298
Rike, Aubrey, 42–43
Robert, Congressman Ray, 16
Rowland, Arnold (witness), 20, 50, 329
Ruby, Jack,
  at Parkland Hospital after assassination,
    365–373
  and Beverly Oliver, 36–37
  and The Cellar, 15
  and Cuba, 391–401
  in Dealey Plaza, 325, 327–328
  death of, 429–433
  as gangster, 387–391
  and Lawrence Meyers, 338
  link with Oswald, 402–414
  and Marguerite Oswald, 94
  and Mercer, 19
  personal biography, 380–387
Russia, 113–134
  history of Communism, 113–114
  and Nosenko (Soviet defector), 130–134
  Oswald in, 92–93, 114–130
  and Robert Webster, 116–121

Scheim, David E., Mafia theory, 513
Scoggins, William (witness), 341
Secret Service,
  history of, 240–246
  and Kennedy assassination, 211–226
  motorcade cars, 9
Senseney, Charles, 30
Shaw, Clay (New Orleans Trade Mart
  director), 68, 498–515
Shaw, Gary, 37, 449
  "umbrella man" theory, 31
Shelley, William (Texas School Book
  Depository Manager), 46, 49, 53
Similas, Norman (Canadian journalist and
  witness), 22–23
Simmons, James L., and the Triple
  Underpass, 58–59
Skelton, Royce G. (witness), 59
Smith, Joe M. (Dallas policeman and
  witness), 74–75, 319–320
Smith, L.C. (Deputy), 19
Somersett, William (Miami police
  informant), 265–267

Sorrels, Forrest V. (Dallas Secret Service), 14, 35, 321
Speaker, Sandy (witness), 26, 28–29
Stanton, Sarah (witness), 46
Stizman, Marilyn (witness), 65
Styles, Sandra (witness), 44
Sullivan, William C.,
  The Bureau, 217
  death of, 564

Tague, Jim (witness), 60–64, 485
Tannenbaum, Robert (HSCA attorney), 37
Tatum, Jack Ray (witness), 348
Terry, L. R. (witness), 26–27
Texas School Book Depository, 40–50, 435
Thornley, Kerry, 108–110
Tilson, Tom G. (Dallas policeman), 325–328
Tippit, Jefferson Davis (Dallas policeman), shooting of, 340–350
Towner, Jim (photographer), 31
Trafficante, Santos, 37
  and organized crime in Cuba, 168–171, 391, 395–401
Triple Underpass theory, 55–64
Truly, Roy (Depository superintendent), 14, 27, 41
  testimony to Warren commission, 51

U-2 program, 114–116
"Umbrella Man," theories of, 30–35
Union of Soviet Socialist Republics. See Russia

Veciana, Antonio (founder of Alpha 66), 149–154
Vietnam, and Kennedy administration, 306–311

Walker, Edwin A. (Maj. Gen.), 403
  assassination attempt on, 255–265
Wall Street, and Kennedy assassination, 274–276
Wallace, George (Governor), 8
Walter, Carolyn (witness), 20–21
Walthers, Eddy (Deputy Sheriff), 61, 313
Warren Commission,
  Bowers testimony, 75–78
  Document 205, 18
  formation of, 451–469
  Foster testimony, 55–56
  on General Walker's assailant, 255–265
  and Kantor testimony, 366–367
  on Oswald murder, 414–429
  on Oswald palm print on Mannlicher-Carcano rifle, 443–450
  on Oswald and Russian language, 105
  on Oswald/Ruby link, 402–414
  on Oswald's stay in Russia, 118–121
  on shell cases evidence, 343–345
  and single-bullet theory, 485–492
  testimony conflicts, 477–492
  Willis testimony, 25–26
Warren, Earl (Chief Justice), as Chairman of Warren Commission, 461–472
Webster, Robert E. (American defector to Russia), 116–121
Weigman, Dave (witness), 58
Weitzman, Seymour (witness), 74, 321
West, Robert H. (witness), 20
Westbrook, Karen (witness), 28
White, Jack, on Zapruder film, 69
White, Officer J. C., and Triple Underpass, 56
Whitmayer, Lt. Col. George, 9
Who Was Jack Ruby? (Kantor), 206–207
Why England Slept (Kennedy), 2
Williams, Bonnie Ray (witness), 47–49
Willis, Linda (witness), 25
Willis, Phillip (witness), 24–25, 73
Wilmon, Jim (witness), 23
Wilson, Steven F. (witness), 44
Winborn, Walter L. (witness), 58
Wise, Wes (witness), 325
Witnesses,
  along motorcade route, 17–29
  deaths of, 555–564
Witt, Louis Steven, "umbrella man," 32
Woodward, Mary E. (witness), 28

Yarborough, Senator Ralph, 6, 8, 16, 79
Youngblood, Rufus W., 9

Zapruder, Abraham. See Zapruder film
Zapruder film, 24, 26, 30, 64–72
ZR RIFLE project, 205–207

FINE WORKS OF NON-FICTION AVAILABLE IN QUALITY PAPERBACK EDITIONS FROM CARROLL & GRAF

☐ Anderson, Nancy/WORK WITH PASSION $8.95
☐ Cherry-Garrard/THE WORST JOURNEY IN THE
WORLD $13.95
☐ Conot, Robert/JUSTICE AT NUREMBURG $11.95
☐ De Jonge, Alex/THE LIFE AND TIMES OF GRIGORII
RASPUTIN $10.95
☐ Elkington, John/THE GENE FACTORY $8.95
☐ Freudenberger, Dr. Herbert/SITUATIONAL ANXIETY $9.95
☐ Garbus, Martin/TRAITORS AND HEROES $10.95
☐ Golenbock, Peter/HOW TO WIN AT ROTISSERIE
BASEBALL 1991 $8.95
☐ Harris, A./SEXUAL EXERCISES FOR WOMEN $8.95
☐ Hook, Sidney/OUT OF STEP $14.95
☐ Lewis, David/THE SECRET LANGUAGE OF SUCCESS $10.95
☐ Lifton, David S./BEST EVIDENCE $11.95
☐ Madden, David and Bach, Peggy/REDISCOVERIES II $9.95
☐ Marrs, Jim/CROSSFIRE $12.95
☐ McCarthy, Barry & Emily/COUPLE SEXUAL
AWARENESS $9.95
☐ McCarthy, Barry and Emily/FEMALE SEXUAL
AWARENESS $9.95
☐ McCarthy, Barry & Emily/SEXUAL AWARENESS $9.95
☐ Moorehead, Alan/THE RUSSIAN REVOLUTION $10.95
☐ Morris, Charles/IRON DESTINIES, LOST
OPPORTUNITIES: THE POST-WAR ARMS RACE $13.95
☐ Schul, Bill D./ANIMAL IMMORTALITY $9.95
☐ Stanway, Andrew/THE ART OF SENSUAL LOVING $15.95
☐ Stanway, Dr. Andrew/SECRET SEX $15.95
☐ Trench, Charles/THE ROAD TO KHARTOUM $10.95
☐ White, Jon Manchip/CORTES $10.95
☐ Wilson, Colin/BEYOND THE OCCULT $10.95
☐ Wilson, Colin/A CRIMINAL HISTORY OF
MANKIND $13.95